Our Southern Zion

Second Presbyterian Church, Charleston (photo by Wade Spees, courtesy of Patterson Smith, Charleston, S.C.)

OUR SOUTHERN ZION

A History of Calvinism
in the South Carolina Low Country,
1690–1990

Erskine Clarke

*To Gerry –
with best wishes –*
Erskine Clarke
2/3/96

The University of Alabama Press

Tuscaloosa and London

Publication of this book was made possible, in part, by a grant
from the Charleston-Atlantic Presbytery.

∞

The paper on which this book is printed meets the minimum
requirements of American National Standard for Information
Science-Permanence of Paper for Printed
Library Materials, ANSI Z39.48-1984.

Library of Congress Cataloging-in-Publication Data

Clarke, Erskine, 1941–

Our Southern Zion: A History of Calvinism in the South
Carolina Low Country,
1690–1990 / Erskine Clarke.
p.   cm.
Includes bibliographical references (p.   ) and index.
ISBN 0-8173-0757-5 (alk. paper)
1. Presbyterians—South Carolina—History. 2. South
Carolina—
Church history. I. Title.
BX8947.S6C57   1996
285′.17576—dc20
95-8150

British Library Cataloguing-in-Publication Data available

To
Elizabeth Duke Warren
and in Memory of
Dalton Townsend Warren, Sr.

Together they created a hospitable low country home.

Contents

Acknowledgments

IN 1987 Barry Van Deventer, executive presbyter of Charleston-Atlantic Presbytery, proposed that I write a history of the Reformed tradition in the South Carolina low country. The presbytery was planning a celebration of three hundred years of Presbyterianism in the region and wanted a history as a part of the celebration. When I accepted the commission, neither Dr. Van Deventer nor I anticipated the time that would be required before the publication of this book. I am grateful for his encouragement throughout this project and the leadership he provided in securing funds for it.

Columbia Theological Seminary generously granted me sabbatic leave for the 1988–89 academic year to spend in Charleston. President Douglas Oldenburg and Dean Oscar Hussell of Columbia supported me in my request for the sabbatical and in my work on the project. During my year in Charleston, many people assisted me with my research and helped me understand in greater depth the social and cultural history of the region. Ferdinand Pharr, stated clerk of Charleston-Atlantic Presbytery, provided minutes of the old Atlantic Presbytery, shared remembered traditions, and put me in touch with many members of the African American community. The staffs of the Charleston Library Society and the South Carolina Historical Society were most helpful as was the staff of the Presbyterian Historical Society, Montreat, North Carolina. Albert Keller and Faye Halfacre opened to me the archives of the Circular Congregational Church and assisted with the securing of pictures. Lois Averetta Simms and William Holmes were a great help in the development of social profiles within the African American Reformed community, especially in regard to family histories.

The following people gave their time to compile membership statistics for the post–World War II period: Mary Frances Parker, Bethel Presbyterian Church, Walterboro; Richard Cushman, Dorchester Presbyterian Church, Summerville; Bill Nisbet, First Presbyterian Church, Hilton Head Island; Coile Estes and Allyson Watkins, First (Scots) Presbyterian Church, Charleston; Karen F. Schweizer-Nagle, First Presbyterian Church, Orangeburg; Jervey Royall and Patricia S. Ayers, Mount Pleasant Presbyterian Church, Mount Pleasant; William Holmes, Saint Paul Presbyterian Church, Yonges Island; and Joe Johnson, Summerville Presbyterian Church, Summerville.

Professors Jane and Bill Pease not only opened to me their extensive files on antebellum Charleston but they also read early drafts of several chapters and made a number of suggestions, some of critical importance in the conceptualization of the project. Professor Edmund Drago discussed his study of the Avery Normal Institute and provided important insights into and contacts within Charleston's African American community. Professor Don Harrison Doyle of Vanderbilt graciously shared with me a manuscript copy of his *New Men, New Cities, New South: Atlanta, Nashville, Charleston, Mobile, 1860–1910* (Chapel Hill: University of North Carolina Press, 1990). Professor Robert Calhoon of the University of North Carolina at Greensboro was particularly encouraging during the final stages of my study.

One of the unexpected pleasures of this project has been my renewed contact with a friend of my youth, Joseph B. Martin III. This Charlotte, North Carolina, banker, with a Ph.D. from Duke in medieval English, not only read numerous drafts of this study but also contributed Appendix A, "Three Centuries of Reformed Congregations in the Carolina Low Country (1685–1985)." His "Guide to Presbyterian Ecclesiastical Names and Places in South Carolina, 1685–1985," published as a volume of the *South Historical Magazine,* has been a great help in sorting out ecclesiastical genealogies in the low country. I am deeply grateful for his careful reading of my manuscript, for his humor, and for his friendship.

Three of my colleagues at Columbia Theological Seminary read part or all of the manuscript and commented from the perspectives of their disciplines: George Stroup and Shirley Guthrie in Systematic Theology and Walter Brueggemann in Old Testament. The insights they brought as they crossed disciplinary lines were of great help, especially around the issues of ideology and utopia.

Lori Knight-Whitehouse served with special efficiency as an assistant in gathering statistics and reports. Elizabeth Clarke spent many hours (with few complaints!) in the tedious task of checking endnotes.

Malcolm MacDonald, director of The University of Alabama Press, gave wise advice and kind words when they were most welcomed. The University Press staff accomplished the publication process with unusual care. Beverly Denbow did the copy editing with an amazing concern for details. Where there was the possibility of a question, she asked it! Keeping track of three hundred years of low country names—with the decided low country tendency for first cousins to marry and make last names first—was a fine achievement.

During the sabbatic year, low country hospitality was extended by too many people to name them all, but gratitude demands acknowledgment of the hospitality of Jim and Martha Lowry, Priscilla and Grange Cuthbert, Bob and Connie Hawkins, Agnes Baldwin, Faye and Ben Morrison, Bob and Mary Lou Tapp, True Henderson, Tom and Lillian Duke, Legare and Sara Duke, and Roberta and Roy Winey. Jessie Mikell, Deborah White, and Patricia Ayers of the Mount Pleasant Presbyterian Church and Helen Petrill, Mary Lou Core, and Rita Dyer of the presbytery staff were especially kind and helpful.

As in the past, Betty Warren extended hospitality that was marked by grace and unsurpassed seafood dinners. This book is dedicated to her and in memory of Dalton Townsend Warren, Sr., in thanks for that hospitality and in gratitude for the loving home they created together.

Nancy Clarke took a year off from her own important work to be with me in the low country. She was a constant source of support and of delightful stories of her McClellanville childhood. Our daughters Legare and Elizabeth showed—to this parent largely bewildered by daughters—an amazing interest in the work of their father and the heritage of their mother.

Our Southern Zion

New Wappetaw Presbyterian Church, McClellanville (courtesy of
Charleston-Atlantic Presbytery)

Introduction

THE SOUTH CAROLINA low country has long been regarded—not only in popular imagination and paperback novels but also by respected scholars—as a region dominated by what earlier historians called "a Cavalier spirit" and by what later historians have simply described as "a whole-hearted devotion to amusement and the neglect of religion and intellectual pursuits."[1] With the elegant little city of Charleston at its center and with a hinterland of rice and cotton plantations—later, fashionable resorts—the Carolina low country has seemed to observers to be an intriguing region, a kind of counterpoint to the hustle and bustle of New York, to the seriousness of Philadelphia or Boston, or, with the rise of the New South, to Atlanta or Houston. Here beside dark flowing rivers and among great moss-laden oaks, down cobblestone streets and in the private gardens of handsome city houses, a way of life and a world view are said to have been nurtured that stand in contrast to dominant themes in the nation's history. Some have seen leisure in the low country and not restless energy, cultivated manners and not brash obtrusiveness, a "prebourgeois mentality" and not a business ethos. Extravagance and not frugality has been regarded as at the heart of this culture, while paternalism, racism, and hierarchical structures have been seen to rule the region, resisting the democratic impulses and business practices of the modern world.[2]

Such "Cavalier" images, of course, have been applied to the whites of the low country, but they also have had their parallel in images of low country African Americans who could sing "summertime and the living is easy" and "I got plenty o' nuttin' an' nuttin's plenty fo' me."[3] Low country African Americans, especially those with a Gullah dialect, have been regarded as culturally distinct and—depending on the perspective of the writer—needing to be made over in the image of "white America" or to be encouraged to retain their interesting "folk ways."[4]

Whatever ideological purposes may have been served by such images of the low country, the images themselves have been powerful interpreters of the region because they have had some foundation in social and cultural realities. This study asserts, however, that these images are significantly flawed and misleading because they are too monolithic, because they ignore powerful elements in low country society that stand in contrast to the "Cavalier" myth and its parallels for the African Americans of the region. Put most simply, it is a thesis of this study that there has been a strong Calvinist community in the Carolina low country since its establishment as a British colony and that this community (including in its membership both whites and after the 1740s significant numbers of African Americans) contradicts many of the images of the "received version" of the region. Moreover, this community's world view and ethos have not been peripheral in the region's life but have resonated deeply with main currents of its social and cultural history, particularly its "market-oriented" economy and the cultural climate in which such economic activity flourished. Rather than a devotion to amusement and a neglect of religion and intellectual interests, this community has been marked throughout most of its history by its disciplined religious life, its intellectual pursuits, and its work ethic. To note these characteristics is not to claim for the community some special brilliance or achievement—although it has had moments of brilliance and significant achievement—but rather to point to the existence of these characteristics as marks of an influential community within low country society.[5]

To be sure, the powerful contextual forces that gave rise to the Cavalier myth have been constantly at work on this Calvinist community, shaping it and giving it a distinct Carolina contour and accent. Among these forces were the Anglican establishment during the colonial period and the continuing strength and prestige of the Episcopal Church during the two hundred years that have followed. But above all, it was slavery and its legacies that influenced the particular developments within this Calvinist community and that brought to the fore certain characteristics inherent in Calvinism itself. The Calvinist community, in other words, while standing in contrast to the Cavalier myth, has been no more monolithic than the region of which it has been a part. The community has contained within itself complex and contradictory impulses: some encouraging and leading toward a "modern, market-oriented" world view and ethos, others echoing the particular anxieties and hierarchical assumptions of a society dominated by racial oppression and the needs for rigorous social control.

The complex character of this Calvinist community means that this study is necessarily and fundamentally an exploration of the ways a particular religious tradition and a distinct social context have interacted over a period of three hundred years. While the chapters that follow seek to define in some detail the character of both this religious tradition and this social context, brief preliminary definitions are perhaps helpful at this introductory point.

The term *Calvinism* has been used in the book's title and thus far to describe the community and its religious tradition because it is broadly and immediately recognized. I have chosen to use, however, the term *Reformed* in reference to the community and its tradition. There are several reasons for this choice. First, the term *Reformed,* which is widely used in Europe, indicates that the tradition's origins are broader than the work of one man, even one so influential on the community's life as John Calvin. Second, the use of *Reformed* makes it easier to avoid the almost immediate reactions modern people have to the term *Calvinist.* It makes it easier to divest the community and its tradition of both the hagiography and the demonology of Calvinist and anti-Calvinist. Third, and most important, *Reformed* points to the tradition's own understanding of its dynamic relationship with its surrounding social context. Springing from the theological conviction that only God is absolute, that all "truths" are as limited as the finite people who develop them, the Reformed tradition has insisted (even if it has sometimes forgotten this insistence) that Christian confessional statements are both directed to and limited by their particular time and place. This theological conviction has made those in the Reformed tradition, including those in the Carolina low country, concerned about *reform*—reform of the church and of the society, reform of culture, family, and politics.[6]

What is meant by the "Carolina low country" in this study is that region of South Carolina contained in the present counties of Charleston, Barnwell, Berkeley, Dorchester, Colleton, Beaufort, Jasper, Hampton, Allendale, Bamberg, and Orangeburg. It does not include the counties of Georgetown, Williamsburg, and Clarendon, which are usually included in any definition of the low country, because they had no significant Reformed presence (as in Georgetown) or because their Reformed communities were not generally linked in ecclesiastical structures with those in the designated counties above.[7] In other words, "Carolina low country" has been defined for purposes of this study by ecclesiastical as well as by the geographical and social boundaries outlined in chapter 2.

The study was begun with certain assumptions about the interaction between a religious tradition and its sociohistorical context. These assumptions need to be acknowledged to the reader from the first, for they have both guided the study and been tested by it.

The first assumption is that religion is not an autonomous cultural phenomenon but is rooted in a particular social reality. The religious life of a people reflects their historical setting no less than a people's art or science or technology reflects a particular historical and social setting.[8]

The second assumption is that religion, however clearly it is rooted in a particular social context, is not simply a projected image of humanity as Ludwig Feuerbach claimed, nor a secondary phenomenon dependent on socioeconomic circumstances—a kind of "spiritual aroma" arising from the social world—nor an "opium of the people" and a means of exploitation as Karl Marx asserted.[9] While religion undoubtedly reflects its social setting and serves to strengthen social solidarity, it also plays a role in helping to shape the social context itself.[10] Religion provides a powerful way of understanding the world, gives explanations of the incongruent and contradictory events of human life, offers emotional support and ways of comprehending human suffering, and provides to the believer ethical standards for living in such a world.[11] Because religion involves meaning, values, and norms, it establishes what Clifford Geertz has called "powerful, pervasive, and long-lasting moods and motivations" in people. It induces "a certain distinctive set of dispositions" and "a tendency to perform certain sorts of acts and experience certain sorts of feelings in certain sorts of circumstances." Religion, in other words, plays an important role in shaping the ways people interpret and respond to their social context and thereby helps to shape the context itself.[12]

Third, as implied in the second assumption, the social context is not a bare, uninterpreted reality but always includes an interpretative framework—as any history clearly reveals! The social context is symbolically mediated from the beginning. It is not a static "given" but a dynamic process that contains a "metaphoric quality." We only know a social reality within the multiplicity of ways that the reality is conceptualized.[13]

The fourth assumption, which emerges from the preceding three, is that a dynamic and reciprocal relationship exists between a religious tradition and its social context. The relationship is dialectical; it is a two-way street—the influences move both ways and not simply one way. Or, more precisely, religious symbols are both "a model *of* 'reality' and a model *for* 'reality.' " In Geertz's graphic phrase, religious symbols "both express the world's climate and shape it."[14] Important questions for this study will consequently be: How has the Reformed tradition as it has existed in the Carolina low country expressed the low country "climate," the social and culture history of the region? And, on the other hand, in what ways and to what *extent* has the low country's "climate," been shaped by the Reformed tradition?

Fifth, not only is religion in a dynamic and reciprocal relationship with its social context but it also serves ideological and utopian functions (again it is both a "model of" and a "model for" reality). Religion's ideological function is served (1) when it acts to *distort* or *hide* social realities,[15] as when it speaks of masters and slaves being "spiritual brothers" in ways that conceal the power of the masters, (2) when it acts to *legitimize* the power and wealth of dominant classes and the social order which keeps those classes powerful and wealthy,[16] and (3) when it acts positively as a means of *integration* and *social identity* for a community.[17]

But religion can also have a utopian function when it provides an alternative vision that challenges present social realities and the assumptions that support them.[18] Religion can call into question what presently exists by an imaginative exploration of alternative possibilities. When the sons and daughters prophesy, when the old men dream dreams and the young men see visions, the possibility emerges that what is distorted and hidden will be made clear, that the legitimacy of the present social order will be undermined, and that the authority which provides integration and identity to a community will be shattered— "Go down Moses," black slaves will sing, "tell ol' Pharoah to let my people go."

The tensions between these ideological and utopian functions of religion have been powerfully present in the Reformed tradition. Broadly speaking, the ideological function has been most clearly visible in the tradition's scholastic impulse that fears anarchy and seeks order, harmony, and the preservation of the existing order. The utopian function, on the other hand, has been most clearly seen in the tradition's radical impulse that seeks the transformation of society, that dreams of holy commonwealths and a new Zion. Which pole of this tension dominates at any moment has been largely shaped by specific social location and historical setting. The ideological function of distorting, legitimizing, and integrating, for example, can generally be seen in the religious life of white slave owners, while the utopian function of alternative imagining and shattering of present assumptions was often present among those African Americans who were a part of the Reformed community. But, as we shall see, the relationship between the two impulses and functions was not simple, and often both could be powerfully present within the same groups and even the same individuals.[19]

This study is not only an exploration of the reciprocal relationship between the Reformed tradition and the Carolina low country but is also about that relationship over a three-hundred-year period. The history and dynamics of social and cultural change are thus an important consideration in the study. More specifically, the study seeks to explore both the changes that came to the Reformed tradition when the low country's "climate" changed and the role—its nature and extent—that the Reformed tradition played in interpreting and shaping that changing climate. Because the low country has itself been a part of larger "climatic patterns" of North America and the Western world during a three-hundred-year period, those "patterns," while obviously not a primary focus, have of necessity been introduced, especially in chapters 1, 14, 16, and 17.

To speak of a "religious tradition" in such dynamic interaction with its sociohistorical context is to emphasize that a religious tradition is not a disembodied spirit but is, at least, a world view and an ethos embedded within a particular religious community. It is the interaction—and this is the critical point—between the religious tradition and the sociohistorical context that provides the *ethos* and the *world view* of that religious community. What is meant by "ethos" is the community's style of life, its tone and character, its moral and aesthetic spirit, its underlying attitude toward itself and its world. What is meant by "world view" is the community's picture of the "way things really are," its understanding of nature, of the self, and of society, and its most "comprehensive ideas of order."[20] The world view provides for individuals within the community answers to such basic questions as "Who am I? What is the reason I am in the world? What is really 'real'? What is time and what is space and how am I to be oriented toward them? Is there life after death?"[21] A world view not only tells a community what and how it is to think about life but also shapes the way the community feels about and reacts to life. This world view and the community's ethos come together, are fused, in *rituals* (sacred prescribed behavior), particularly public ones. Such prominent public rituals, for example, as Sunday worship services—together with the buildings in which they are performed—provide insights into the ethos and world view of the Reformed community in the low country and consequently about the interaction between the Reformed tradition and the low country context.

The Reformed tradition has been largely viewed by historians as essentially absent from the region. Indeed, the ethos of the region and its world view have often been contrasted with the Puritanism of New England.[22] While one of the surprising results of this study has been the uncovering of a remarkably strong and influential Reformed community in the low country, it is true that this community has always been a subgroup within the larger community—a "little world" within the "little world" of the low country. (It certainly never dominated the region in the way that Puritanism dominated so much of seventeenth-century New England.) The Reformed community's status as a subgroup has consequently been an important factor in shaping the nature and extent of the interaction between it and the low country "climate."

As a subgroup the Reformed community has had its own sense of identity, traditions, kinship ties, and rituals in addition to those that it has shared with the broader society. Again, a dynamic and complex interaction can be seen between the subgroup and its larger social context. The Reformed community has followed in part its own world view and lived out of its own ethos and has at the same time followed in part the spirit, identity, history, and culture that gave distinction to the Carolina low country as a region. This has meant that the boundaries that have marked the Reformed community have often been blurred, ambiguous, and difficult to identify because of the complex overlapping between this particular religious community and the broader society. These overlappings produce perhaps the greatest blurring of boundaries when it is remembered that the Reformed tradition has had a profound impact on other religious communities—especially the Anglican, Baptist, and Methodist—and that while they have their own theological and ecclesiastical traditions, they have also shared many of the characteristics of the more distinct Reformed community in the low country.[23]

To make the matter more complex, the Reformed community has itself been divided into what might be called sub-subgroups. There have been denominational divisions—primarily between Congregationalists and Presbyterians—and, much more important, divisions between whites and African Americans, between those who were slaveholders and those who were slaves, between an oppressor race and an oppressed race. Moreover, both whites and African Americans have been themselves part of racial subgroups that have their own separate but intertwined histories, traditions, social positions, economic functions, and self-interests. African Americans within the Reformed community have stood not only with that religious community, and not only within the broader community of the low country, but also within the community of African Americans. They have shared with other members of their race the powerful and bitter experience of slavery and racial oppression in the low country. Much of the story that follows is an exploration of the relationships between these various subgroups—and sub-subgroups—and their overlappings. Despite these overlappings and the difficulties of defining and identifying boundaries, a distinct Reformed community can be identified as existing in the Carolina low country for three centuries. During some periods its distinctiveness has been much more visible than at other times. Always, however, the community has reflected that complex interaction between a religious tradition and a sociohistorical context.

The approach of this study is historical, following a general chronological order. The first chapter, "The Tradition Established: A European Prologue," traces the rise and spread of Reformed communities in sixteenth- and seventeenth-century Europe and explores the theological foundations and ethos of the Reformed tradition as they have been classically described. A primary intent of the chapter is to provide the historical background to those Reformed communities who came to the Carolina low country and to arrive at some clarity about what is meant by the "Reformed tradition." Chapters 2–17 follow the general pattern of seeking first to give an analysis of the changing social context of the low country and then exploring the nature of the Reformed community in its relationship to that context. Questions in this exploration include: What ethos has been created and what world view can be discerned by the interaction between the Reformed tradition and this particular sociohistorical context? How extensive are such an ethos and world view (to whom do they extend?) and how pervasive are they—how deeply do they influence both the religious community and the individual members who make up that community?

These difficult and demanding questions are investigated by exploring three primary areas in the Reformed community's life. First, its intellectual life has been probed to discern the belief systems of the community—and their underlying assumptions—as they have been most clearly articulated in identifiable historical periods. What continuities and what changes are visible and how are they related to historical contexts? Second, social profiles of the community have been developed to discover what kind of people have been nurtured by or attracted to the Reformed community. Are there social characteristics that mark the Reformed community as a *community* and give it an identifiable *character* during a particular historical period? What continuities and what changes are visible over the years in this community and how are they related to changes and continuities in the larger social setting? Third, the history of institutional structures, the ways the community organized its life, has been analyzed to discern the outward contours of the community and the ways in which its ethos and world view have found expression in congregational life and benevolent societies, in presbyteries and associations, in schools and theological institutions. What were the purposes and roles of these institutions? What did their structures tell about the Reformed community? What did they do to and for the community, and in particular, what role did they play in character formation?

These three areas of the community's life—the intellectual, social, and institutional—have been intertwined and echo the dynamic and complex relationship of a religious tradition and its social context. The degree of consistency and harmony between the areas, or the inconsistency and disharmony, are important questions for the study. To what degree, for example, is the social profile of the community in harmony with the confessed beliefs and intellectual assertions of the community?

This study is presented primarily in a narrative style. A narrative not only provides what anthropologists like to call "rich empirical data" but also can provide the affective side of a community's ethos and world view. The study is not an uncritical narrative—as it is hoped the issues and questions raised in this introduction have made clear—but it is a narrative that is intended to communicate both information about the community and the "feel" of the community's life. As a genre, the narrative communicates the "story" of the Reformed tradition in the Carolina low country not simply as a historical artifact but as a living story of a continuing community, a community that in all the wonder and ambiguity of human existence is still seeking to live out its faith in its particular time and place.

1

The Tradition Established

A European Prologue

THE STORY OF the Reformed tradition in the South Carolina low country began not along its dark rivers or sandy shores but beside the Alpine Lake of Geneva. Here, long before the first permanent European settlers arrived in Carolina, a distinct religious tradition emerged in the midst of social and political transformations remaking Europe. This chapter introduces that religious tradition: its rise, its spread among the nations of Europe, its theological foundations and social characteristics. This "European Prologue" is intended to provide a brief historical overview of the rise of the European Reformed communities and some clarity about their nature and character—for it would be from among these communities that the Reformed tradition was transplanted to the low country of Carolina.

John Calvin

John Calvin's arrival in Geneva in the summer of 1536 as a young French refugee was a turning point for the Protestant Reformation.[1] Already his *Institutes of the Christian Religion,* published only a few months earlier in the neighboring Swiss city of Basel, was becoming a sensational best seller, destined to be one of those rare books that helps to shape the course of history.[2] Under Calvin's leadership a second phase of Protestant expansion—following the earlier Lutheran Reformation—was about to begin. This Reformed phase, riding waves of change that had long been building, would radiate from Geneva across Europe and in less than a hundred years across the North Atlantic.

Seismic disruptions had been shaking the old order of Western Europe for generations by the time Calvin arrived in Geneva. First in the city-states of Italy, then farther north, modern forms of commercial and industrial organizations had begun to emerge in the fourteenth and fifteenth centuries as a new and dynamic capitalist economy took shape. Cycles of economic crises, depressions, and social unrest were hastening the collapse of medieval ways and helping to usher in the modern world. Traditional society—in which hierarchy was the fundamental ordering principle, patriarchy and personal loyalty were primary forms of human relationships, and passivity was the normal political stance of common people—was giving way, leaving behind both an exhilarating new sense of freedom and mobility and a profound anxiety and fearfulness.[3] Both the freedom and the anxiety produced a restlessness, an unsettledness, that would long mark the Reformed communities and that would leave a deep and abiding mark on their character. This restlessness, unsettledness, can be seen in Calvin the refugee and exile and in antithetical impulses in his life and thought.[4]

On the one hand, Calvin responded to the turbulence of his age, to the "terror of the abyss," by seeking assurance in the order of nature and by following the lead of the medieval Scholastic tradition of Thomas Aquinas. This Scholastic Calvin sought order, harmony, and balance as a way of overcoming the chaos he saw all around in the collapse of the old medieval world. He called upon reason and fixed principles as a way of putting up boundaries, of providing intelligibility and certainty, in the face of what appeared to be the limitless disorders and uncertainties of his time. Calvin the Scholastic, the philosopher and rationalist, was a conservative seeking a way to control himself and his world.[5]

But there was another side to Calvin, a radical side, that recognized the powerlessness of human beings to control life, to construct boundaries, and to build perfect systems, that saw mystery in the universe, and that came face to face at some deep inner level with the ambiguities and paradoxes of the human condition. What filled this side of Calvin with anxiety was not the chaos of his time but the feeling of being trapped, of being constrained and boxed in by the rigid systems and enclosing boundaries of the old order. This was Calvin the humanist, more concerned with persuasion and its art—rhetoric—than with the neat systems and orderly arrangements of philosophy. Unlike the Scholastic Calvin who elevated reason above all other human faculties, the humanist Calvin dethroned reason and saw the human personality in more wholistic terms. For this Calvin the heart and the affections played as important a role as the mind and reason. This dethronement of reason, and with it a hierarchical understanding of the human personality, would help make manual labor for Calvin as noble a calling as scholarly endeavors and would raise troubling questions about all social hierarchies.[6]

These two tendencies lived side by side in Calvin and reflected the paradoxes and tensions of his age. Sometimes, as the Scholastic, he sought to reconcile these antithetical impulses, to systematize them and bring them into some order by saying that he stood in the middle, as a mean between extremes. At other times, Calvin the humanist would acknowledge that the tensions could not be reconciled or systematized but could only be recognized and lived with in a practical balance between competing tendencies. The consequences of this dual or composite quality in Calvin's life and thought had enormous implications for the far-flung children of Geneva. "Calvinism," William J. Bouwsma has written in his important study of Calvin, "could be made to sanction change while at the same time appealing to the most conservative of human instincts. Because it balanced, however precariously, the antithetical impulses of its age, it could attract the proponents of liberty and of order, and men and women of many nations and diverse social groups."[7]

These two tendencies would not be absent from the Reformed community in the Carolina low country. Indeed, competing elements within that Carolina context would nurture the tensions inherent within the Reformed tradition and encourage sometimes a Scholastic tendency and sometimes a humanist tendency. Broadly speaking, the Scholastic tendency with its fear of chaos, its hierarchical assumptions, and its quest for order, harmony, and balance would resonate most closely with a society dominated by race and the need for social control. The humanist impulse, on the other hand, with its fear of enclosing boundaries and constraining systems, would resonate more closely with those elements in low country society that were pushing toward the modern world: the region's early frontier character, its restlessness, its individualism, and its market-oriented economy. It was also, no doubt, this resistance to encircling boundaries and questioning of the authority of established systems that would offer some appeal to African Americans held in bondage. Whenever one tendency would dominate, however, the other was always there, looking over the shoulder, ready to step forward when the moment was right.

Despite the antithetical character of these competing tendencies and impulses, they have been held in tension in ways that give coherence to Reformed communities the world over. What provides the coherence and marks the communities as Reformed are certain theological affirmations and a discernible ethos that has existed in very different social contexts. Clarity about what is meant by "Reformed" and the "Reformed tradition" consequently calls for a plunge into theology and ethics, for it is in faith and practice that Reformed communities have found their own identity. Before that plunge is taken, however, a brief review of the spread of Reformed communities in Europe is necessary, for this familiar story of European developments provides an indispensable background to the Carolina story.

The Reformed Communities

Once Calvin was permanently established in Geneva, he helped to turn the city-state into a center of international Protestantism. Refugees, scholars, and reformers from all over Europe flocked to the city and to its great academy established by Calvin.[8]

Those who fled to Geneva for sanctuary were from time to time able to return to their homelands as tumultuous events opened the way for the spread

of the Reformed faith.[9] Some went to the other cities and cantons of Switzer-
land where they joined the work already begun by earlier reformers—Huldreich
Zwingli and Heinrich Bullenger in Zurich and John Oecolampadius in Basel—
so that by the time of Calvin's death in 1564 the Reformed faith was firmly
established among the Swiss as the church of their great cities: Zurich and
Basel, Bern and Geneva.[10] Other refugees returned to their homes in Holland,
Germany, Bohemia, and Hungary where they led in the establishment of
Reformed churches.[11] It would be, however, the Reformed communities in
France, Great Britain, and Ireland that would send their sons and daughters in
significant numbers to the far-off Carolina low country. For this reason special
attention needs to be focused on these communities, for their specific traditions
and memories would long play a part in the self-understanding of a Reformed
community in the Carolina low country.

French Huguenots

By 1562 there were perhaps 700 Reformed churches in France. Most of their
members were from the rising new middle class—merchants and skilled artisans—but they also included peasants and increasing numbers of politically
powerful nobles. Pastors who had received their theological training in Geneva
settled among the people as a French Reformed Church began to take institutional shape along presbyterian lines.

The social composition of the French Reformed Church meant that the
tensions and competing impulses of the Reformed faith would be clear in the
French church. The still-feudal nobility encouraged the Scholastic, medieval
side of Calvinism, as the church was integrated into an established system of
feudal connections and patronage. Local lords, for example, exercised great influence over consistories with the minister often a member of the lord's feudal
household. At the same time, the rising middle classes demanded legal control,
by means of church courts, over feudal households and patronage. "It was entirely possible," Michael Walzer has written of the French church, "for the two
different organizational systems—congregation, classis, and synod on the one
hand, feudal hierarchy and local connection on the other—simply to coexist,
although curious jurisdictional tangles might be the result."[12] These tensions,
as we shall see, would play their part in the response of French Protestants to
the social context of the Carolina low country.

The number of French Protestants, or Huguenots as they later were called,
grew in the face of the fiercest persecution.[13] At first hundreds and then thousands were martyred for their Reformed faith. In August 1572, approximately
70,000 Huguenots were butchered in the Saint Bartholomew's Day Massacre.
Intermittent wars between Catholics and Protestants followed until Henry IV

issued in 1598 the Edict of Nantes, which granted freedom of worship to Protestants in those areas—except Paris—where they had maintained churches the
previous year. The terms of the edict were, on the whole, kept until 1665. Under
Louis XIV, harassment and persecution began once again in earnest. In 1685
the Edict of Nantes was revoked and there began a mass exodus of French
Protestants, perhaps 200,000. Their exodus was a blow to France and its economy—although not the catastrophe once thought—for the Huguenots represented much of the nation's rising commercial and entrepreneurial classes.[14]
Many went to Switzerland and Germany; others went to Holland and England.
Some dared to cross the Atlantic and to settle in the British North American
colonies. Among these were some who settled in the young colony of Carolina.

Scottish and Scotch-Irish Presbyterians

While there was earlier dissatisfaction and protest in Scotland against corruption in the church, Protestantism as a movement came to the ancient kingdom of the Scots in 1526 with William Tyndale's English translation of the
New Testament. This revolutionary text, together with the "reek" of Protestant
martyrs burning at the stake, helped to prepare the way for John Knox. Thun-
dering from the pulpits of Scotland as the storm clouds of Reformation swept
across the land, Knox led the nation in its decisive break with Catholicism.[15] In
1560 the Scottish Parliament adopted the Scots Confession, largely written by
Knox and clearly Reformed. The pope's authority was repudiated and the *Book
of Common Order* and the *First Book of Discipline* were adopted for the Scottish
kirk. While the Reformed faith was thus established in Scotland, the shape of
the kirk was left an open question. Only after a long and bitter struggle, the
presbyterian nature of the Church of Scotland was finally settled in the Glorious Revolution of 1688.[16]

Across the Irish Sea from Scotland lay the counties of northern Ireland
and the ancient region of Ulster. At the beginning of the seventeenth century,
James I began the establishment of the Plantation of Ulster, encouraging Scottish settlers to come to this area that had been devastated by war. It was all a
part of the English attempt to "domesticate the wild Irish" and to provide a
place of settlement for increasingly restless lowland Scots. Those who came were
Presbyterians, and in their new Irish home the Presbyterianism of these Scotch-
Irish settlers became even more pronounced.[17]

The subsequent history of Scotch and Scotch-Irish Presbyterians revealed
how competing tendencies and paradoxical impulses within the Reformed tradition could live side by side: theologically, they tended to move toward a strong
Protestant Scholasticism; socially, they frequently exhibited the restlessness and
individualism of the modern world; and ecclesiastically, they became vigorous

supporters of the independence of the church and a Presbyterian court system. In the eighteenth century, economic and political difficulties set them moving again, with many finding their way to the South Carolina colony.[18]

English Puritans

Reformed influences came early to the English Reformation, especially by way of the Strasbourg reformer Martin Bucer who spent the last years of his life at Cambridge. When Archbishop Thomas Cranmer wrote the *Prayer Book* (1549, 1552), he reflected the significant influence of Reformed thought on the leaders of the English Reformation. The Thirty-Nine Articles, the doctrinal statement of the Church of England and of Anglican churches in other parts of the world, is sometimes listed as a Reformed confession primarily because it takes a Reformed position on predestination and the Lord's Supper.[19]

Whatever the Reformed influence on the Anglican establishment, it was not enough for increasing numbers of the English. They began to be called Puritans because of their desire to "purify" both the church and the society and reshape them along what they regarded as biblical lines. During the reign of Charles I (1625–49), their numbers grew as people reacted against Charles's claims of royal absolutism and the despotic activities of the archbishop of Canterbury, William Laud. As a result of the turmoil that followed, and especially the two disastrous Bishops Wars (1639 and 1640) against the Scottish Presbyterians, Charles found it necessary to call a parliament. It came to be called the "Long Parliament," for it stayed in session through years of tumultuous change. It was this Parliament that led the people through a civil war, destroyed royal absolutism in England, and called the meeting of the Westminster Assembly that would have—through its Westminster Confession of Faith and Catechisms—such a profound impact on the future of English-speaking Reformed communities.

While there were no clear class divisions between the two parties in the English Civil War, the Royalists represented the more conservative forces in the nation's life. Parliament, on the other hand, drew its support from those elements of British society that were closely aligned with the Reformed spirit, with commercial interests, and with democratic impulses. At its heart the war was between opposing political and religious passions represented by the popular images of the Cavalier and the Roundhead.

The Cavaliers, often romanticized by later generations in the American South who imagined themselves their descendants, were fiercely loyal to the Crown, to the social system it represented, and often to an Anglican establishment. The Roundheads, disdaining the long flowing curls of their opponents, wore their hair in simpler, shorter fashion. Many were Puritans, a term that now included Presbyterians, Independents, Baptists, and a growing host of smaller sectarian groups. What the Puritans had in common were a more or less close connection with mainstreams of Reformed thought, a strict morality, a hatred of ritualistic services, a distrust of bishops and all church hierarchies, and a growing conviction that they had a God-given duty to oppose all royal despotism. They stood as perhaps the clearest representative of the radical impulse within the Reformed tradition.[20]

The commonwealth and the protectorate under Oliver Cromwell that followed the Civil War, the Restoration under Charles II and James II, and the rule of William and Mary helped to draw the political, social, and cultural lines that would long be visible in the English-speaking world—including the young colony of South Carolina. Under Charles and James, Puritans became Dissenters. Under William, a Dutchman of the Reformed tradition, the Toleration Act of 1689 granted a measure of toleration to Dissenters from the Anglican establishment. As non-Anglican Protestants, they were allowed freedom of worship, but important civil liberties were denied them, including the right to attend the English universities and to hold public office. But most important, English, indeed British, civilization was left with the unmistakable mark of the Puritan spirit. "The growth, triumph and transformation of the Puritan spirit was the most fundamental movement of the seventeenth century," wrote R. H. Tawney of seventeenth-century England. "Puritanism," insisted Tawney, "not the Tudor secession from Rome, was the true English Reformation, and it is from its struggle against the old order that an England which is unmistakably modern emerges."[21] Sydney E. Ahlstrom, in his magisterial study of the religious history of the American people, reached similar conclusions about Puritanism's influence on the United States: "Puritanism, above all, would leave a legacy in America no less significant than the impact of Luther upon the German nation."[22] The low country of South Carolina would not be excluded from that legacy.

What marked all of these European Reformed communities as Reformed, and what would mark the Reformed community that grew on the dark soil of the Carolina low country, were certain theological affirmations and social characteristics. It is to these affirmations and to the ethos of the communities that claimed them that we now must turn.

Theological Affirmations

At the heart of the Reformed tradition lies a theological passion and piety that has marked Reformed communities wherever they live and whenever their faith has been vital. It is a frame of mind that acknowledges that always, in good or evil circumstances, one has to do with God—and not just any god, but the One God, "the high and lofty one who inhabits eternity, whose name is holy."[23] This Sovereign One is for the Reformed communities the life of the universe, the Transcendent Being who sustains from moment to moment all things in their being and guides all creation toward God's own holy and just purposes. The famous doctrine of predestination and election that has been so closely identified with the Reformed tradition is an attempt to express both the absolute miracle of salvation, that it comes as a free, undeserved gift, and the character of God as the Sovereign One.[24]

The passionate belief in such a sovereign God has been a fountainhead of contrasting elements of fundamental importance in the Reformed tradition and in Reformed communities the world over. Theological affirmations, in other words, no less than contextually induced anxieties, helped to shape the antithetical impulses of the tradition. On the one hand, the emphasis on the sovereignty of God has been the source of Reformed piety, the inspiration of the courage, self-sacrifice, and broad humanitarianism that has often marked the Children of Geneva. It has been this piety, and the passionate belief that God is working God's purposes out in human history, that has inspired in Reformed communities resistance to tyranny, that has sent their members out to do battle with evil, that has made them social reformers and in some places and circumstances revolutionaries.

Members of Reformed communities, believing their calling and election to be sure, have had a strong tendency not to be preoccupied with introspection, with worrying over the state of their soul—or much less "discovering their 'true self' "—but rather with action that will be to the glory of God. Freed from such preoccupation with personal moods and feelings, they have often given themselves to building a holy community and indeed a world that will reflect the will of God.[25]

On the other hand, the passionate belief in God's sovereignty has all too often encouraged a self-righteous, cold, and narrow sectarianism in Reformed communities—especially when they have forgotten their belief that election is a sign of grace and not of their own righteousness. The sovereignty of God has been used to justify not revolution but a vigorous defense of the status quo, emphasizing that every person has a God-given place in society with corresponding duties and privileges. With such a defense, there has often come an inward turn, a movement away from a concern for action—although action was rarely abandoned—to an increased introspection and a quest for self-understanding and spirituality.

Such contrasting elements and opposing impulses have not been neatly divided or clustered within Reformed communities—a point that must be emphasized—but have lived side by side in a greater or lesser tension. Sometimes one impulse dominates while its antithesis recedes; sometimes the opposite is the case. Always the social context and the place of the Reformed community in that context have been critical factors in shaping which elements of the tradition come to the fore and which elements remain in the background.

For the Reformed communities, the heart of sin is worshiping anything other than the sovereign God. Sin is making a god of that which is not God. Any attempt to control God, any endeavor to equate human understanding of God with God, must be rejected as idolatry. Of course, these communities have all too often done precisely that, especially when chaos threatens and there is a need for order and boundaries. Then they have substituted their theological statements, their convictions about God or God's causes, for God. But the Reformed tradition as a movement has insisted that the Transcendent One is both hidden and completely free and cannot be manipulated by even the most pious.[26]

The cool-eyed doctrine of total depravity, the insistence that the human heart is wonderfully deceptive, has meant that traditional Reformed communities are uneasy with any claims of pure motives. Reformed communities have consequently had a strong tendency to be realists in their politics: that is, they have been convinced both by Scripture and by what they see in the world around them that all have sinned and all are altogether sinful—all have fallen short of the glory of God, all follow the devices and desires of their own hearts. Such a conviction has made them suspicious of utopian dreams or claims of perfection and has led them to fear concentrations of power, of power that goes beyond its proper bounds, and to seek in their ecclesiastical polities and in the politics of nations ways of avoiding such concentrations.[27] At the same time, the sense of being numbered among God's elect has often pushed in the opposite direction—toward an arrogant confidence that they were on the side of right and that any who opposed their political visions were opposing God and God's coming Kingdom.[28]

For the Reformed communities, the transcendent, sovereign God, the hidden One, is revealed in Jesus Christ. And what is revealed in Christ is not only God's majesty and sovereignty but a majesty and sovereignty that expresses itself in mercy and forgiveness, gracious humility and compassion. Only the sovereign, elective grace of God, they believe, can free the human soul from its bondage and bring it to rest and peace in its Creator. Grace for those in the Reformed tradition is understood as a pure gift: it comes from above as a surprise, like rain to a dry and weary land, and is not the result of any human activity. The heart could and should be prepared through prayer, Bible study, worship, and a holy life for the coming of the Spirit, but the Spirit blows where it wills, and its coming is always a gracious gift from a sovereign God. Such grace is powerful and irresistible, pursuing and overwhelming the soul, cleansing it of its secret faults, and turning the heart to God.[29] But grace is not cheap—it cost the life of Christ on the cross—and it evokes a vigorous life of discipleship. So even the doctrine of grace could lead in a perverted way to the self-righteousness of the committed disciple, to the fanaticism of the holy warrior, and to the bigotry of those who are confident they are on God's side.

Reformed theology regarded such perversion as simply another sign of the total depravity of the human heart.[30]

For Calvin and his early followers, the emphasis on the sovereignty and providence of God was a source of comfort and strength.[31] But for later generations, it became increasingly a source of anxiety, encouraging the Scholastic side of the tradition. How could you know if you were among the elect or if you had experienced God's grace? It was a question of "assurance," and beginning in the seventeenth century, it became a deeply troubling question to many Reformed communities. While those included among the elect are always hidden in the mystery of God's grace, two signs, it began to be said, are present when a person experiences God's grace. First, a person can testify to an inward experience of being touched by the Spirit of God. Persons who have experienced God's grace know in their hearts that they have been seized by the Spirit and overwhelmed by the infinite. Second, they demonstrate by a morally upright life that God has granted them grace and touched their lives. If your heart has been changed, if you have had an experience of regeneration, then you will walk in the way of the Lord.[32]

Such an understanding of regeneration and assurance would, beginning in the seventeenth century, have an enormous influence on Reformed communities wherever they were found, including the Carolina low country. The church would be understood to be composed of the regenerate, of those who could testify to an inward experience and who walked a morally upright life. In North America, this ecclesiology would mean, as we shall see, that for generations more attended the churches than belonged to them or were communing members of them. Persons might believe and confess as true all the articles of the Apostles' Creed, might live morally respectable lives, might attend church regularly, might vote to call pastors, but if they could not testify to an inward experience of amazing, unmerited grace, then they could not come to the Lord's Table, they could not become communing members. At the same time, the emphasis on regeneration meant that church discipline would be taken very seriously. Discipline would be a means of acknowledging the glory and holiness of God, of seeking to keep scandal from falling over the church, and of helping the fallen back onto the path of righteousness. Until the closing decades of the nineteenth century, church sessions in the Carolina low country would be serious about such discipline and would enforce it vigorously.[33]

The Reformed Ethic

What a people believe is discovered not only in what they say but also in what they do—in the ways in which they order their lives, in the buildings they build, and in the songs they sing. Their theological convictions, in other words, find expression in their style of life. And conversely, their style of life, their ethos, helps to shape and inform their theological convictions. The kind of work they do, the homes they live in, the buildings they worship in, the organizational structures of which they are a part—all help to shape and give content to what they believe.

Reformed communities have been keenly aware of this relationship and have consequently sought to order both personal and social lives in such a way that will reflect theological convictions and at the same time strengthen them. "Blue laws," for example, that in the nineteenth century kept South Carolina stores closed on Sunday, expressed the conviction that the Sabbath is to be a day of rest. But these laws were also intended to encourage a belief that the Sabbath is a holy day by making sure that people experience it as a day of rest. Reformed communities have vigorously rejected any idea that religion is a purely "spiritual" matter (although some have argued vehemently for the "spirituality of the church") or that religion has to do only with the individual and not the society. Because in *all* of life one has to do with God, Reformed communities have sought to build their Holy Commonwealths, to reform societies of which they are a part, and to order their personal lives in such a way as to reflect their theological and ethical convictions.

Such an ordering of life and shaping of life-styles have not been for the Reformed communities—at least until the present generation—matters of personal inclinations, much less have they been the modern quest for self-fulfillment. Rather, the ordering of life and the shaping of a life-style have been understood as a disciplined journey, a pilgrim's progress toward the city of Zion. To guide the travelers on such a rigorous journey, the Reformed tradition has taught that there is a reliable guidebook—the Bible, the only infallible rule of faith and practice.[34] The sacred Scriptures tell the story of God's redemptive work in Jesus Christ, the pioneer and perfecter of the faith, who sets the travelers on the way and walks with them as their friend and guide. Yet in the law of the Lord, the Bible also gives explicit instructions for the trip. Reformed communities would thus be concerned with biblical law and (in contrast to Lutherans) would understand it as a positive gift of God, a help and a guide, always pointing to Christ and toward the goal of the journey, the coming Kingdom of God.[35]

This understanding of biblical law meant that the Old Testament would play a very important role in shaping the ways in which the Reformed communities sought to order human affairs. Most obviously, their affection for the Old Testament would be seen in their frequent naming of their children after Israel's heroes—Moses and Isaac, Jacob and David, Sarah and Rachel. More significantly, the communities would seek to make the law and the historical example of Israel an explicit basis for the ordering of human societies. Such a goal meant that their political visions were often marked by a powerful tension between a forward-looking, reformist spirit seeking the establishment of Holy Commonwealths and a backward-looking, conservative ethos guided by an already given historical model. This tension marked their work in Geneva and in the Netherlands, in Scotland and in New England. To an amazing extent, it also shaped those in South Carolina who sought to develop in the nineteenth century a vision of "our southern Zion," who sought a Christian social order in a slave society.

What guidance did the Reformed communities find in the law? First of all, they were convinced that "man's chief end is to glorify God and enjoy him forever" and that the "word of God which is contained in the Scriptures of the Old and New Testaments is the only rule to direct us how we may glorify and enjoy him."[36] The "most auspicious foundations upon which to establish one's life" were rooted in grateful response to God's grace.[37] When those in the Reformed communities turned to the Scriptures, they found that a spirit of thanksgiving and an ethic of grateful obedience were the sure foundations for a Christian life.

Second, they were convinced that the Bible gave detailed instructions about how to order the church. All areas of church life were to be governed by the Bible. Most, looking at the Bible, insisted on a presbyterian polity with a graded series of ruling bodies—session, presbytery, synod, general assembly—composed of ordained ministers and lay elders. Some found in the Bible a congregational polity where each local congregation was autonomous and an expression of the church universal. A few—the Reformed in Hungary and those Anglicans who were Calvinists—found an episcopal structure with diocesan bishops. All, however, insisted on justifying their polities on the basis of biblical law.[38]

But polity was not the only area of church life to be governed by the law. How churches were built, what was sung in church, the use of musical instruments, and what ministers wore were also to be regulated by biblical law. Could a man marry his first cousin? his dead wife's sister? the wife of his former brother-in-law? The answers were to be found by a careful examination of the Bible by a proper church authority. This insistence on following the law was behind the Presbyterian and Puritan controversy with the Anglicans and all who, in their eyes, went beyond what the Bible taught and used vestments and liturgies and had bishops and hierarchies. But those in the Reformed tradition could not always agree among themselves on what was lawful and what was not. Thus they fought over whether they could sing hymns or had to sing only Psalms, whether they could have an organ and a choir or simply had to "line out" a hymn, whether a presbytery could meet without lay elders or required them. So fierce would be the controversies and so innumerable the divisions that it is not surprising that Presbyterian governing bodies were known as church courts.[39]

Third, the Reformed tradition taught that the law provided instructions about personal behavior and holiness of life: what to do and not to do on the

Sabbath, how to run a business in an ethical manner, what was responsible behavior in regard to drinking and family life. Vain displays, intemperate use of drink or food, and idle recreations were to be rejected in favor of simplicity, moderation, frugality, and industry. Because personal holiness was believed to be a sign of election, Reformed communities often became moralistic and famous for their legalism and self-righteousness. Yet their ethic was not a gloomy, otherworldly ethic as it has sometimes been portrayed. Reformed communities have been convinced that the world God created is good, if fallen, and that history is moving, in spite of all the sins, trials, and tribulations of humanity, toward God's coming Kingdom. Personal holiness is consequently rooted in a *right attitude* toward the world and a *right use* of God's creation. Reformed communities have consequently sought to be in the world, but not of the world, to love the world with "weaned affections," to use the good things of the world "but not be wedded to them." Thus they could drink their ale and eat their cake, be diligent in their business affairs, enjoy the delights of the marriage bed, and be vigorous participants in civil society. But they were to do all these things knowing that the world, while good, was also fallen and passing; that true and lasting joy comes only from the inward experience of God's beauty and grace; and that sin is rooted in idolatry, in making a god of that which is temporal and not eternal, is created and not the Creator. The ethos of the Reformed communities was, in Max Weber's well-known phrase, a "this-worldly asceticism."[40]

Fourth, the law called for the disciplined use of the mind as a service to God. The first and great commandment taught, after all, not only that "you shall love the Lord your God with all your heart, and with all your soul" but also "with all your mind." Faith, for those in the Reformed communities, was both trust *and* understanding. But there were significant disagreements within the Reformed tradition about the relationship between the head and the heart, about the links between religious knowledge and holy affections. These disagreements were rooted in the tension seen between Calvin the Scholastic and Calvin the humanist. For Calvin the humanist, and for many of his early followers, religious experience came before understanding: it is necessary to believe, they said, in order to know the truth of the Christian faith.[41] But for Calvin the Scholastic and for many later followers it was necessary first to understand the true doctrines of the faith, and then this understanding would produce by grace a sense of awe and a love of God.[42] Whatever the uneasy tension between the head and the heart, the Reformed communities were never satisfied with an unthinking piety that glorified mere feelings. "The tongue without the mind," Calvin had taught, "must be highly displeasing to God."[43] Nor were they satisfied with a cold understanding of the faith that was not warmed by an experience of God's grace. It was true, they believed, that faith must be clearly and precisely articulated, doctrine supported by reason, and the heart guided by the mind. But the tradition also taught that the mind's understanding must be guided by the heart and that kindled affections must give life to Christian faith.[44] Sometimes in the Reformed communities the head would dominate; at other times, especially during periods of evangelical revival, the heart would seem primary. Almost always, however, there was an uneasy tension between the two competing impulses.

For these reasons, the Reformed tradition insisted that learning was a Christian duty and that logic, clarity, and mental discipline were to be highly valued. For ministers, who had the responsibility of guiding the communities in the ways of the Lord, learning was essential. In the same way the discipline of the mind in the service of God was also expected of laity, and the Reformed catechisms with their questions and answers were marvelously designed to provide the precise, carefully reasoned knowledge needed. On the other hand, as has been noted, membership in the church required a personal religious experience of God's grace as well as knowledge about correct doctrine.

Fifth, those in the Reformed tradition believed that simplicity was a major theme of the law. By simplicity they did not mean simple, unlearned, or crude, much less spontaneous, but rather they meant a style of life free of all ostentation, trivial externals, and love of art for art's sake. Simplicity was closely linked to sincerity and honesty.[45] It cut through all deceit and pretense and sought that which was clear and real. It was to shape the style of life needed for traveling the narrow way, the type of preaching necessary to inform the mind, and the kind of polity required for the ordering of church and society. The way those in the Reformed communities dressed, the manner in which they constructed and furnished their homes, the patterns of their towns and villages, their meetinghouses, their speech, their personal relationships, their business and civic affairs—all were to be guided by the quest for simplicity.[46] For the Reformed communities the motivation for such a quest was not a parsimonious or miserly spirit. Rather, it was a vision of the Divine simplicity, of the absolute integrity and unity of God in whom there is no deceit or pretense but only the great "I am." Yet this quest for simplicity and its accompanying frugality often led to a countervailing tendency—to the accumulation of wealth and with wealth a strong tendency to abandon the earlier ways for the more ostentatious and opulent.

Sixth, the law taught that all were to work in specific "callings" for the good of the community. Every Christian, wrote Cotton Mather, the New England theologian, has a "General Calling" that is "to serve the Lord Jesus Christ" and a "Personal Calling" by which "his Usefulness in his Neighborhood, is distinguished." This personal calling arises from the fact that "God made man a Sociable Creature. We expect Benefits from Humane Society. It is but equal, that Humane society should Receive Benefits from Us."[47] John Cotton, whose son John would be pastor of Charlestown's Independent Meeting House, saw three aspects to a person's "particular calling." First, it is one in which "we may not only aime at our own, but at the publike good." Second, God gives gifts and the necessary talents "fit for that place" to which God calls a person. And third, God opens a door for "entrance into" a particular calling through God's providence, "the counsell of friends, and encouragement of neighbors." While Reformed communities recognized that a particular calling might lead to riches, they saw personal wealth as incidental to work that benefits the public good. Moreover, those who prosper are not to lord it over their neighbors but in all things live in moderation. This the Christian has learned not to do, said John Cotton: "if God prosper him, he had learned not to be puffed up, and if he should be exposed to want, he could do it without murmuring. It is the same act of unbeliefe, that makes a man murmure in crosses, which puffes him up in prosperity."[48] People who have been raised on Reformed principles, according to the social historian Ernst Troeltsch, find "the lazy habit of living on an inherited income" a "downright sin." To live a life without a "definite end and which yields no material profit seems a foolish waste of time and energy" and "like indifference toward God." Laziness is thus a serious vice because it is both harmful to the individual soul and hurtful to the community.[49]

Such an understanding of "calling" and of the "sin of laziness" was not, as it might appear at first, antithetical to a slave society. While it might stand in contrast to the extravagances that sometimes mark such a society, it helped form a distinct personality type: one possessed of an intense consciousness of personal worth, a deep sense of Divine mission to the world, and a feeling of great privilege and immeasurable responsibility—characteristics well suited to paternalistic whites in a slave society. Moreover, the doctrine of "calling" could provide within a slave society two thrusts: one toward the mobility of the modern world—a man might leave the occupation of his father and become an exile and pilgrim as a part of his calling—and one toward a conservative, hierarchical emphasis on the status quo—you should stay in your place, in your "calling," and do your duty in the circumstances in which you had been placed by God.[50] This dual thrust would allow the Reformed community in the Carolina low country to live with the paradox of being intimately linked with the ethos of a modern economy while at the same time being strong supporters of a hierarchical world view in regard to African Americans.

For those in Reformed communities who came to Carolina, the theological and ethical convictions of their religious tradition would form a fundamental part of their world view. Such a world view would provide a symbolic system, a frame of reference and meaningfulness, within which they would both interpret and seek to shape their world. How those convictions, and the convictions of their descendants in the faith, interacted dialectically with the complex society of the Carolina low country is the focus of the story that follows.

2

The Context

The Colony of South Carolina

Historical Context: The Age of European Expansion

FORTY-FOUR YEARS before John Calvin arrived in Geneva, Columbus sailed out across the Western Sea, discovering what Amerigo Vespucci called "Mundus Novus," a New World, because, he said, "our ancestors had no knowledge of them." For the next four hundred years the dominant feature of world history would be the expansion of European civilization around the globe.[1]

The amazing Portuguese and Spanish led the way, taking their Roman Catholicism with them, as did later French explorers in their forest empire of New France. But by the seventeenth century, in northern Europe, rising new maritime nations—Holland and especially England—began to establish themselves as leading powers. Their Protestantism, deeply influenced by the Reformed tradition, would go with them in their remarkable empire building. Indeed, religious ideas and commitments would play no little part in providing the motivation and energy for Dutch and British expansion and colonization. In this way the spreading of the "Children of Geneva" to new lands across the oceans was both a part of a general European expansion and a reflection of their own restlessness and driving energy.[2]

Geographical Context: The Land

Along the southeast coast of North America stretched a section of land marked by marshes and sea islands, by tidal creeks and thick forests of ancient oaks and towering pines. In the north lay long white beaches, and in the center and southern end fine harbors formed at the confluence of slow-flowing rivers. This land, which in time would be called the coastal region of South Carolina, seemed to the first European explorers to offer rich opportunities for settlement. Yet for a variety of reasons, successful colonization was slow in coming and relatively late compared to many other coastal areas of the New World.

The sea islands, which dominated the southern two-thirds of the coast, were separated by tidal creeks and estuaries of surprising depth and width. Because these waterways offered apparently easy access into the interior and provided highways up and down the coast, their banks seemed attractive places for settlement. But such perceptions were deceptive. The tides that carried the explorers' ships with such ease rose and fell on an average more than seven feet and the currents they created were difficult if not treacherous for small boats. Thus the islands, once European settlements began, would remain relatively isolated and that their population would remain sparse until late in the colonial period.[3]

To the west of the islands, beyond waving marsh grasses, a coastal plain ran inland for approximately a hundred miles. For almost the first fifty of these miles a pine belt extended westward. Here the land was low enough to be flooded by rivers at high tide, and future settlers, using African slaves and African knowledge of rice production, would turn the region into a rice-producing area and make impressive fortunes for themselves.[4] An upper pine belt, covered by great stands of long-leaf pine interspersed with oak and hickory, was marked by rich bottomland that in time would bloom white with cotton.

Beyond the coastal plain, white sand hills, peppered with scrub oaks and pines, rolled largely barren across the land. These hills would become in the years ahead a boundary dividing the low country from the hardwood hills and valleys of the up-country, marking not only geographical differences but also distinct economies, political and social perspectives, and religious sensibilities.

The low country, however, is the setting of our study. Early European explorers often described it as a kind of tropical paradise, a latter-day Eden waiting for Europeans to subdue and have dominion over it. Jean Ribault, a Huguenot leader who sought long before the English to settle the area, wrote of Port Royal Sound that "nothing lacketh" in its waters or on its shores. It contained pepper trees and "the best watter of the worlde, and so many sortes of fishes that ye maye take them withowt nett or angle, as many as you will; also guinea foule and innumerable wildfoule."[5] Indeed, along the southern coast where the Gulf Stream flows close by and its influence is strongest, there is a nearly subtropical climate. But the climate was fickle throughout the low country and could vary greatly. The winters could be cold and the summers unbearably hot. To be sure, in the fall of the year the weather could be clear and balmy. And in the spring—even before the cultured azaleas, wisteria, and tea olives were introduced—the low country was beguiling. So charming was the springtime land that it seduced even the cool-eyed Scottish minister Alexander Hewat who, in the mid-eighteenth century, spoke of the land's "noble and striking appearance" and who in his history of the colony described in glowing detail the region's "natural beauties."[6]

For a people who lived close to nature as did the early European settlers of Carolina, to those whose lives were so intimately connected with the land, with its rivers and marshes, with the productivity of its soils, and with its sudden storms and beguiling springs, the environment was no incidental matter in the shaping of their values and culture, in the creating of what they came to call "our little world."

One thing, however, is clear. Whatever beauty the low country might have offered, whatever riches it might have promised, it was no Eden for the European settlers who came to its shores. Even less so was it an Eden to the Africans brought to clear its forests, to build the dikes for rice fields, and to harvest its indigo. The land did not give up its riches easily but only after the most unremitting toils, and even then it might—with a sudden freshet sweeping over dikes—take back what it had given. Moreover, the region was full of the "miasmas" of swamps and stagnant waters, the malignant vapors that the settlers thought caused the fevers and "agues" that struck almost all Europeans who sought to live in this land. Malaria and yellow fever were frequently deadly for newcomers. The "bloody flux," a virulent dysentery that killed children, left adults weak and shaky and susceptible to other diseases. A "Charnel House" was what some called the low country, and in faraway Germany a saying developed that warned that if you wanted to die quickly, then go to Carolina. White settlers soon learned to seek healthier places from spring through the first frosts of the fall. They sought out high grounds, bluffs and sandy hills where the tall pines grew, and established little communities for the sickly season. Later some would go to the beaches or to the up-country, while those who could afford it sometimes headed north to such resorts as Newport or Saratoga. The Africans, who possessed considerable natural immunity to the fevers because of their long exposure to them in their homelands, were more susceptible to lung and respiratory diseases. They, of course, could go nowhere for their health. Moreover, they were frequently overworked in the Carolina sun, and their unremitting toil took its bitter toll.[7]

The religious life of the people was not unaffected by this geographical context. Religion—no less than politics and economics—would not be immune to these low country "miasmas." Whites, in addition to their churches, would build chapels at their summer retreats that would over the years, on occasion at least, be converted into the primary places of worship. Blacks, left largely alone on the plantations for substantial periods of each year, would develop much of their religious life in isolation from the white community. Moreover, the ravages of disease, the constant threat of death, and the high infant mortality rates were all constant reminders of the fragile and transitory nature of human life. The early tombstones in the churchyards often provided in their art and messages visible acknowledgments of time slipping away, pictures of death's cold sting, and expressions of resurrection hope. Indeed, the tombstone art provides initial glimpses and hints into the ways a religious tradition and a specific context would interact in the shaping of a world view.

Such reminders of lurking death, difficult as their influences are to evaluate, would encourage in some a religious spirit that was decidedly otherworldly. Of

Tombstones from the Cemetery of the Independent Meeting House, Charleston (courtesy of Circular Congregational Church, Charleston, South Carolina)

course, they could also encourage just the opposite—a spirit of eat, drink, and be merry, for tomorrow you may die. Much clearer would be the influence of a plantation economy on the religious life of the region, in particular the influence of black slavery. But that is part of the story to come.

Social Context: The People

Whatever images European explorers promoted about this land, it was was not an empty Eden. Native Americans had "discovered" it long before the Europeans and were driven from it only by the fiery sword of European arms and diseases. Most devastating were the diseases—first smallpox, then measles and bubonic plague, diphtheria and typhus, cholera and scarlet fever. They spread like wildfire through a Native American population that was completely susceptible to their contagion. By the time the first permanent European settlements were established in South Carolina, the Native Americans had already experienced devastating pandemics from the introduction of these lethal pathogens against which they had little natural immunity.[8]

For John Archdale, Quaker governor of the young colony in 1695, "the hand of God was eminently seen in thinning the indians to make room for the english." It pleased "Almighty God," wrote Archdale, "to send unusual sicknesses amongst them, as the small-pox, &c. to lessen their numbers; so that the english, in comparison to the spaniards, have but little indian blood to answer for."[9] The land, appearing to the Europeans as largely vacant, seemed theirs for the taking.

As early as 1526 and again in 1561, the Spanish had attempted settlements on the Carolina coast, but shipwreck, fevers, and hurricanes turned these expeditions into disasters.[10] French Huguenots under Jean Ribault built in 1562 a small fort on what is today Parris Island, but it too soon ended in disaster.[11] Once again the Spanish returned, establishing a mission and small farming community on what they called Santa Elena on Port Royal Sound, only to abandon it when Sir Francis Drake sacked and burned Saint Augustine in 1586. More than eighty years passed before another European settlement was undertaken in the region. Then it was the English who came and stayed.

Like the Spanish and French before them, the first English settlers were drawn to Port Royal Sound. It seemed to have an almost magnetic attraction with its great harbor and fine vistas. But, as the Spanish and French had learned only too well, it had serious liabilities for a permanent settlement. The tides were treacherous, the ground was low lying, and the Indians around it were not always friendly. Moreover for the English, it was perilously close to the Spanish. Thus after a few months at Port Royal, the English moved north. They had found on the west side of the Ashley River, several miles from its mouth, some relatively high ground. Here they built a palisade at what would come to be called the "Old Town."

For ten years the settlers remained at Old Town, quarreling among themselves and trying to establish an economic base for their colony while keeping a sharp eye out for the Indians and the Spanish. But the river was relatively shallow at Old Town and vessels of large burden could not with convenience approach it, a decided disadvantage for the development of commerce. A much more attractive place appeared to be at Oyster Point at the confluence of the Ashley and Cooper Rivers. On this neck of land they laid out Charlestown with an orderly arrangement of streets running in straight lines and intersecting at right angles. Those streets going from east to west would in time extend from river to river and would provide, by means of subterranean drains, a means for "removing all nuisances, and keeping the town clean and healthy."[12] Moreover, sea breezes blew over the peninsula and would provide some relief from summer heat—especially after the people learned to build their houses with balconies and piazzas to catch the stirring air.

These early settlers were an aggressive, ambitious lot, often unscrupulous, certainly with only a minimum of concern for the common good of the colony. "Bold adventurers" is what Alexander Hewat, Presbyterian pastor and early historian of the colony, called them. They "improved," said Hewat, "every hour for advancing their interest, and could bear no restraints which had the least tendency to defeat their favorite views and designs." "The people here," said their Anglican minister, "generally speaking are the vilest race of men upon the earth." A recent historian said their leaders resembled pirates ashore.[13]

The proprietors, who had control of the colony during its early years, had, however, no desire for Carolina to be little more than a haven for pirates and ruthless adventurers. They consequently began a vigorous attempt to recruit sturdy settlers, particularly Huguenots, English Dissenters, and Scottish Covenanters.

The Children of Geneva

Huguenots

The persecution of French Huguenots, culminating in revocation of the Edict of Nantes in 1685, sent refugees streaming into the great Protestant cities of Europe—Geneva, Berlin, Amsterdam, and London. Here they created, as refugees of the twentieth century would create, large urban refugee communities. It was from among these communities that the proprietors hoped to draw settlers for their Carolina colony—settlers who would add a new element of industry, frugality, and enthusiasm for a home free from the fires of persecution.

The first Huguenots arrived in 1680 and settled on the banks of the Santee

River forty miles north of Charlestown. They built a small church overlooking the river, and later, in the first decade of the next century, they laid out a little village around the church and called it Jamestown.[14] Largely isolated, living on the edge of Hell Hole Swamp, they faced the hardships of life in a low country wilderness. Particularly devastating were the freshets, sudden risings of the Santee that caused it to spill over its banks and flood the low-lying land. But the flooding brought with it rich deposits of loam, and when the waters receded they left the land even more fertile. Such fertility, along with the labor of African slaves whom the Huguenots soon secured, provided the foundation for their rapidly increasing prosperity—once they learned to cope with the flooding and to cultivate rice and indigo. Among the Huguenot families who prospered in this region and who made a proud name for themselves in South Carolina were the Ravenels and Gaillards, the Horrys, the Porchers, the Mazycks, the Remberts, DuBoses, and Dupres.

Another Huguenot settlement was at Orange Quarter. It was reached by going up the Cooper River and following its east branch. Other Huguenots moved up the west branch of the Cooper to Saint John's Parish in Berkeley County where they developed great plantations: the Ravenels' Somerton, the Saint Juliens' Wantoot, Hanover, and Pooshee, the Gignilliats' and later Gaillards' Dawshee, and the Mazycks' Woodboo. Still another settlement was at Saint James Goose Creek, both a favorite residential resort for Charlestown people and an area destined to become one of the most affluent plantation regions in the North American colonies. The largest Huguenot settlement, however, was in Charlestown. Here, as might be expected, Huguenots were soon engaged in a variety of commercial activities. A number were in the cloth trades, others were merchants, a few were master silversmiths and goldsmiths, while others were blacksmiths, gunsmiths, shipwrights, and clock makers. Some offered their services as teachers; French was a popular subject but so were Latin, Greek, German, arithmetic, geometry, and history. Others offered medical services as doctors or as apothecaries who sold such cure-alls as a "Plaster for all sorts of Women's Hysteri[a] Vapours." But the lure of the land drew many away from their traditional occupations. Such vast tracts were available and the making of fortunes seemed to await the enterprising. Even among the many who remained in Charlestown, investments in lands and slaves were popular.[15]

Lord Cardross and the Scots at Port Royal

The years between 1680 and 1688 are known in Scotland as the "Killing Time," for during these bitter years many Scots met their death in defense of their kirk, and many a west country churchyard bears testimony to their courage. The "Killing Time" left an "indelible mark on the soul of Scotland," and we might add on many of her children abroad, as Charles II and then James II attempted to impose by brutal force an Episcopal establishment on the land of Knox and Melville. Only the overthrow of James II in the Glorious Revolution of 1688 ended the slaughter, and with the accession to the throne by William and Mary, the Church of Scotland was firmly established as Presbyterian.[16]

It was during the "Killing Time" that plans were laid for a Scottish colony in Carolina to which the persecuted Scots could flee. Under the leadership of Henry Erskine, Lord Cardross, a grant was received from the proprietors for a colony at Port Royal independent of the governor at Charlestown. In 1684 Cardross with 150 Scots sailed from Gourock Bay on the Clyde with the hope that 10,000 would follow. Many, including Cardross, had been imprisoned for their faith, and they now looked for a new start in Carolina. But it was not to be. Port Royal, as it had proved so often in the past, was not a hospitable place for a colony. Three years after their arrival, the Spanish attacked and the colony was dispersed. Cardross had already returned to Scotland and from there he had gone to Holland to participate with William of Orange in the bloodless revolution that overthrew James II. A little over a hundred years later, David Stewart Erskine, eleventh earl of Buchan and great-grandson of Cardross, sent to Charlestown the Cardross seal, the official seal of the Scots colony, as a reminder of the lost hopes for a great Scottish colony during the "Killing Time."[17] But there were other Scots who came to Carolina during these years, and they became part of a growing "Dissenter" group that played such an important part in the early history of the colony.

New England Puritans

Among those recruited for Carolina were New England Puritans. They had prospered, as Puritans were wont to do, since the great migration of the 1630s had brought over 20,000 to New England's rocky shores. Now they were ready to send colonies south to the new territory being opened by the proprietors of Carolina. In 1695 a company left New England bound for Charlestown. Shipwrecked at Cape Fear, they were rescued by Governor Archdale of Carolina and settled on the Wando River at Cainhoy, about twelve miles from Charlestown. Sometime before 1728 (the records are obscure about exactly when) they organized a Presbyterian church.[18] Another group of New Englanders settled up the coast from Charlestown, four miles from Sewee (Bull's) Bay, along the little road that ran north to the Santee. Here around 1700, or perhaps a few years before, they built the Wappetaw Independent Congregational Church.

At the same time that these settlements were taking place, a congregation of Puritans sailed south for Carolina. They came with their own pastor, and they understood their purpose to be the establishment of a missionary church on the Carolina frontier. They had received at their home in Massachusetts a letter from "sundry godly Christians" in the remote region that was Carolina.

The Carolinians longed "after the enjoyment of all the edifying ordinances of God" and for an ordained minister who might bring some gospel order to their land. In response Joseph Lord, a young graduate of Harvard who had been studying theology with his pastor, was ordained for the emigrant church. In December 1695 they sailed for Charlestown, and, after arriving safely through winter seas, they proceeded up the Ashley River to a place they named Dorchester, after their home in Massachusetts, which had itself been named after Dorchester in England. Shortly after their arrival, on February 2, 1696, they celebrated the sacrament of the Lord's Supper under the great spreading branches of an ancient oak and beside the dark waters of the Ashley.[19]

The Puritan community at Dorchester would play its part in the life of the Carolina low country in the coming years. More important, however, would be the influence of its daughter colony in Georgia. In 1752 the grandchildren of those who first settled in Dorchester secured a grant of 31,000 acres in Georgia and established themselves in what would become the rich rice-growing region of Liberty County. For a hundred years, until the Civil War shook the land, their Midway Congregational Church would be the most influential congregation in Georgia. During the hundred years it thrived, fifty of its sons would go into the Presbyterian ministry. Many of these would have, along with other children of Midway, a powerful influence on the Reformed communities of the Carolina low country.[20]

Other New Englanders settled in Charlestown where they soon became an important part of the little city's economic, social, and religious life. For almost a century and a half, a small if influential flow of New Englanders continued to trickle into the low country, until, with the Civil War, the trickle turned into a great flood of conquerors who came with the hope of remaking the region after the model of New England.

The Africans

By far the largest of all the immigrant groups to the low country were the Africans. They, of course, were not voluntary immigrants but came as slaves to be the "hewers of wood and drawers of water" for the European colonists. So important would be their influence in shaping the low country context—its economics and its politics, its religious life and cultural values—that a close investigation of their place in the region is necessary.

Throughout the seventeenth century, struggling Carolina had three Europeans for every African. Most of the Africans had come to the colony by way of the West Indies, and most were slaves of white colonists from Barbados.[21] But this racial balance soon changed, and with the change came social and cultural shifts of the most far-reaching consequences.

By 1720, when the colony became royal, 65 percent of the population in the Carolina low country was slave, 35 percent was free. By 1740 there were 20,000 whites throughout the whole colony, and the blacks—almost all of whom were in the low country—numbered approximately 40,000.[22] Some low country parishes were overwhelmingly black. Saint George, along the upper Ashley River and in the area around Dorchester where New Englanders had settled, had approximately 3,300 blacks and only 468 whites by 1741.[23] Between 1760 and 1774, nearly 42,000 more slaves were imported into the colony, and once again almost all of them were destined to labor in the low country. So numerous were they that the region seemed to an arriving Swiss immigrant "more like a negro country than like a country settled by white people."[24]

These Africans and African Americans were the indispensable, and perhaps primary, builders of the region's economic base and social fabric. They were the ones who cleared most of the land, who dug the muddy dikes and labored in flooded rice fields, who cut wood and kept fires going under indigo vats, and who, in innumerable other ways, made Carolina the wealthiest of all the mainland colonies of the British. They were also the ones whose presence in increasingly large numbers shaped much of white Carolina. Their unceasing labors, the constant threat they posed to white hegemony, the social and cultural traditions they brought from Africa, and the distinctive African American culture they built under the rule of slavery—all played fundamental parts in the creation of a low country society. Certainly the dynamic interaction between Europeans and Africans, each with their own cultural traditions, was an essential element in the shaping of colonial Carolina. Religion, no less than other sectors of the society, was influenced by this interaction.

African Background

Long before Europeans sailed south along the west coast of Africa or out across the Western Sea to the New World, great empires flourished in the African interior south of the Sahara—the empire of Ghana, its successor Mali, and its successor Songhai, an empire that centered around the rich lands along the Niger and on the walled cities of Gao, Timbuktu, and Jene. Largely Islamic, these empires carried on an extensive trade with the Moslem states across the Sahara. In woodlands west of the Niger delta the Oyo and the Benin empires were born and flourished from the fourteenth and fifteenth centuries until the nineteenth. Stretching inland along the Zaire River basin, the Kongo kingdom was a centralized state by the 1500s.[25]

Long before European slave ships arrived on the west coast of Africa, Moslem traders crossed the Sahara and entered into an extensive slave trade. Indeed, before they made such dangerous journeys, they were engaged in a sophisticated North African slave trade. Moslem states, from Spain to India, imported African slaves in total numbers that "may well have surpassed, over a period of twelve centuries, the African diaspora to the New World."[26] This Islamic trade helped to prepare the way for the immense transatlantic trade in human beings that began shortly after the European discoveries of the New World.

Between 1526 and 1870 approximately 10,000,000 men, women, and children were shipped across the Atlantic, including 1,552,000 to Spanish America, 3,647,000 to Brazil, 1,665,000 to the British Caribbean, 1,600,000 to the French Caribbean, and 500,000 to Dutch America. Approximately 400,000 went to British North America and the United States, and of these an estimated 40 percent arrived in Charlestown.[27]

Most of the slaves who came to South Carolina were from the west coast of Africa and from interior regions adjacent to it. Many were from the Gold Coast or from the Windward Coast, and among these were Ibo and Yoruba from present-day Nigeria and Ashanti and Fanti from present-day Ghana, sophisticated tribes with extensive agricultural experience. But the largest group was from the southwestern coast, from the Congo River southward, a great area loosely called Angola. From 1733 until 1807, almost 40 percent of those Africans imported into Carolina were from this vast region.[28]

By 1720, Africans who arrived in the low county found an already established African American community, many of whose members were born in Carolina. Unlike the Caribbean and large areas of South America, where the nature and conditions of slavery meant that the slave populations did not reproduce themselves,[29] in Carolina the black population had shown by 1720 a steady natural increase. While in the following decades the rate of increase probably slackened under the appalling conditions of rice cultivation, there nevertheless was in South Carolina a growing African American community.[30] This community, always in dynamic relationship with large numbers of recently arrived Africans, had by the end of the colonial period established the distinctive African American culture of the low country.

Slave Religion

The degradations, trauma, and physical horrors of the transatlantic passage meant death for great numbers of Africans. Among those who survived this descent into hell, the new world into which they were thrust was an alien and disorienting place. How much of their African culture, particularly their religious beliefs, survived such a trauma has been the subject of much scholarly debate. Some, following the lead of Melville J. Herskovits, have pointed to the continuities between African religions and the religious practices of African Americans. Others, following E. Franklin Frazier, have insisted that because the trauma of the midpassage was so great and the disorientation of the new world was so severe, there was little continuity with African religious beliefs.

The disruptions of kinship organizations, it is said, along with the removal from sacred places, meant religious myths and cults lost their religious significance.[31]

Most contemporary scholars have rejected both of these arguments. What they have pointed to are significant expressions of the African heritage informing a new African American Christianity that emerged out of the experience of black Americans. Professor Albert J. Raboteau in his study of slave religion concluded:

> It was not possible to maintain the rites of worship, the priesthood, or the "national" identities which were the vehicles and supports for African theology and cult organization. Nevertheless, even as the gods of Africa gave way to the God of Christianity, the African heritage of singing, dancing, spirit possession, and magic continued to influence Afro-American spirituals, ring shouts, and folk beliefs. That this was so is evidence of the slaves' ability not only to adapt to new contexts but to do so creatively.[32]

In the low country of South Carolina during the eighteenth century, however, the picture is more complex. First of all, outside of Charlestown, slaves were most often in areas where there were many blacks and few whites. As early as 1720, in seven of eleven parishes more than 60 percent of the population was black. Four of these seven parishes had populations that were at least 70 percent black.[33] In such circumstances blacks were largely isolated from the influences of European culture. Moreover, throughout the colonial period a substantial number of slaves were African born, in some decades as much as 50 percent. Because, as has been seen, most came from four major regions of Africa, many no doubt found themselves among their own tribespeople.

Such a situation of isolation from whites and proximity to those out of the same or similar tribal backgrounds provided a context for nurturing African cultural traditions, however battered such traditions may have been by the midpassage, by the harsh realities of slavery in the low country, and by the power of the often distant but still present white culture. Church records and missionary reports indicate that for at least the first seventy years of the colony, from 1670 to 1740, very few blacks formally adopted Christianity as their faith. This did not mean, of course, that significant elements of the Christian faith were not being slowly incorporated into the religious world view of slaves, but it did mean that important streams of African religious beliefs and practices flowed through the slave quarters and would continue to flow for generations to come.[34]

These streams of African American folk religion were a part of the secret world of the slaves, often hidden from the eyes of whites, surfacing in later generations in the stories, folkways, and art of the people. It would be out of this religious context, and not out of some religious or cultural vacuum, that

African American Christianity emerged, sometimes flowing with these ancient African streams, sometimes alongside them, and sometimes against them. The result was the shaping of a religious tradition that was African, American, and low country. For some of the sons and daughters of Africa, such a tradition would also be Reformed.

Economic and Political Contexts

While the details of the economic developments of the low country are far beyond the scope of this study, a brief sketch of these developments is necessary in the drawing of the contextual framework of colonial Carolina.

Fundamental to the history of the low country—including the history of those who stood in the Reformed tradition—was the region's rise from a struggling colony of half-starved settlers to a land of great wealth for its white inhabitants. By the end of the colonial period, the "white population of the low country was by far the richest single group in British North America." "Nowhere else in British North America," a distinguished economic historian has written, "or perhaps the world for that matter did so sizable a population live so well."[35] That wealth, of course, was based largely on the whites' expropriating the rice and indigo produced by black slaves.

Important and hotly debated issues surround the rise of this low country wealth, as well as the region's later stagnation and decline.[36] What were the forces at work in shaping the low country's economy? Peter A. Coclanis has argued that among the primary factors that largely determined the economic history of the region during the colonial period was "the *mentalité*," or world view and ethos, of the "whites of the low country and their British sources of capital."[37]

Coclanis's suggestion about the *mentalité* of the low country whites presents important and intriguing questions for this study. He argues that this *mentalité* was "informed from the start by a fierce adherence to the social ethos of the market." By the "social ethos of the market," Coclanis means that the whites of the region made rational decisions based on supply and demand and the requirements of an export economy. They were, in other words, market-oriented business people. While acknowledging that the "ethos of the market" did not penetrate all sectors of low country society, and that it was limited by its slave labor force, he nevertheless maintains that it dominated the region.[38] The low country, Coclanis argues, rather than being a "traditional" society based on a prebourgeois *mentalité* (what others have broadly called a "Cavalier" ethic), was in reality dominated by the rational world of the market. "For beneath the veneer of paternalism and the sheen of patriarchy in the low country were always the talons of the market, their hold sure, their mark deep."[39]

What makes such an argument important and intriguing for this study is that such a mentality has often been associated with the world view and ethos of those in the Reformed tradition. As we shall see in the next chapter, the discovery—in contrast to earlier pictures of the region—that in fact a substantial and influential Reformed community existed in the low country adds a degree of coherence to the social picture of the region.[40] There can be, of course, no suggestion here that the Reformed community was the cause of this "social ethos of the market" or that only those in the Reformed community shared a "modern" market-oriented mentality. Causation of a social ethos is too complex and pluralistic to be attributed to one factor.

What can be suggested is that both a social context in its complex totality and a particular religious tradition were in a dynamic and reciprocal relationship with one another. On the one hand, the "Scholastic" tendency of the Reformed community—with its fear of chaos, its hierarchical assumptions, and its quest for order, harmony, and balance—would provide powerful ideological support to that side of low country society that demanded the social control of African slaves and that sought the integration and preservation of the community through time by justifying the present system of authority. On the other hand, what has been broadly identified as "the humanist impulse" within the Reformed tradition—with its fear of enclosing boundaries—would resonate with the region's restlessness and its steady move toward the modern world. The Reformed community can consequently be seen as bringing with it and helping to create in the low country a complex mentality, a frame of reference that was both conservative and hierarchical *and* receptive to the development of a modern "market-oriented economy."

Coclanis saw these antithetical impulses in the low country with the eyes of an economic historian and noted their "oxymoronic nature" while at the same time insisting that it was the modern impulse that dominated the region.[41] From the perspective of the religious history of the low country, the contradictory impulses in the society—particularly in the economic sector—appear to stand in an antiphonal relationship with the powerful contradictions within the Reformed tradition itself. There is a reciprocal response, an echoing and reechoing, between the social context and this religious tradition. Put most simply and boldly, it was not a prebourgeois *mentalité* associated with a Cavalier ethic and the Anglican establishment that dominated the region. Rather, the low country was a much more complex picture—one that reflected in much of its life not only a Cavalier ethic but also a strong congruence with the ethos and world view of the Reformed tradition and its competing impulses. Socioeconomic contradictions and contradictions within the low country's Reformed community point to the region's transitional character: to its struggle as a slave society to maintain an older hierarchical and paternalistic world view while at the same time moving vigorously into an emerging modern world with its restlessness, its individualism, and its market-oriented economy.

With such a contextual framework in mind, we can now turn to a closer look at the Reformed community in the low country during the colonial period.

3

The Tradition Transplanted

The Reformed Communities

The society of [colonial] South Carolina was characterized by a whole-hearted
devotion to amusement and the neglect of religion and intellectual pursuits.
Economic affluence certainly contributed to the formation of such a society, but
an even more basic reason for the development of the Carolina society can be
found in the colony's religious tradition. The New England and middle colonies
had been founded by Calvinistic or pietistic religious dissenters, who took a stern
view of earthly pleasures but at the same time believed in the need for an
educated clergy and laity. By contrast, South Carolina at the
mid-[eighteenth]century was predominately Anglican, and the Church of
England made little effort either to regulate the lives of its communicants or to
promote intellectual pursuits. Consequently, while colonies like Massachusetts
and Pennsylvania had produced socially dull but mentally stimulating societies,
South Carolina had developed in just the opposite direction.

—M. Eugene Sirmans, *Colonial South Carolina: A Political History*

THESE CONCLUSIONS OF Eugene Sirmans reflect conventional wisdom in
regard to colonial South Carolina. Such conclusions, nurtured by the lingering myth of a "Cavalier" South, undoubtedly point to important aspects of
colonial society. Yet they also distort much of the picture, not only by ignoring
the high educational level of the Anglican clergy and many members of the
Anglican laity but also by ignoring the presence of a vigorous and lively Reformed community in the South Carolina low country.[1] This chapter focuses
on that community—its strength, its institutional structures, and its social
characteristics as they developed in relationship to a low country context.

Institutional Structures

Colonial Congregations

The center—the focal point and institutional expression—of the Reformed
communities that settled in the low country were the congregations they established. Here they organized their lives as religious communities, linked past

memories and loyalties with present needs, and sought to transplant their Reformed tradition into the rich dark soil of the low country. No less than other immigrant communities that would come to the shores of the New World, the congregation was at the vital center of much of the old communal life that these Carolina immigrants were seeking to transplant. The congregation provided a social center—perhaps especially in the scattered plantation regions, but also in the bustling little port of Charlestown—where old ways and values could be affirmed and ancient customs could be maintained. In the congregation the psyche, the folkways, the identity and self-understanding of the community could be nurtured, and a world view, a set of values, and an experiential link to the homeland could be shared. The religious traditions maintained in the congregation could provide meaning and order to the immigrant's internal world and a symbolic system, a frame of reference, for interpreting and acting in the strange and often hostile world of Carolina.[2]

Of course, not all immigrants belonged to a congregation, and the children born in the New World had not experienced the ways of the Old. So while the congregations were at the center of the Reformed communities in the low country, their strength should not be exaggerated nor should their function as conveyors of tradition be isolated from other functions. They were, after all, a place where past and present met, where acculturation to the new context was reflected in their own institutional structures and changing patterns of behavior. Nevertheless, there would have been no Reformed communities without the congregations—a theological affirmation of the communities themselves as well as a historical observation.

Huguenot Churches

The Huguenots established six churches in South Carolina that were Reformed in polity and doctrine: in Charlestown, at Jamestown on the Santee, at Saint John's Berkeley, at Orange Quarter, at Goose Creek, and later in the eighteenth century, at New Bordeaux far up the Savannah River.[3] All except New Bordeaux, which was established in 1763, were founded before 1706.

In 1706 the Huguenot churches outside Charlestown became Anglican. They continued as congregations around which the Huguenot communities gathered, but they did so as Anglicans and within several decades lost any distinctive French identity. This rapid acculturation had behind it the bitter political quarrels that divided the colony and led in 1706 to the Anglican Church becoming established by law, receiving the support of the government, while other churches were put at a decided disadvantage.

Given the history of the Huguenot resistance in France, on the surface it seems surprising that these churches so quickly gave up their French polity and identity. Such a move raises questions about the strength of the Reformed tradition in the low country and the role of the congregation among a pioneer people—and probably helps account for the endurance of the old Cavalier myth. More broadly, there is the question of why the Huguenots, in contrast to other minority immigrant groups in America, gave up so quickly their cultural identity and religious institutions. Some have argued that their quick assimilation is an indication of their cultural "sickness," of the weakness of their movement, and of the lack of depth of religious commitment by the laity, especially after years of religious disputes and persecution.[4] Others have argued that the speed of assimilation was a sign of cultural strength and not weakness. They have pointed out the international perspective of the Genevan theologians, who were always authorities within the Huguenot communities, and how these theologians had openly recommended conformity to the Church of England. The Huguenots' rapid movement into positions of economic, political, and cultural leadership, it is said, points to their self-confidence and strength.[5]

For those Huguenots who came to South Carolina, a variety of factors encouraged their movement into the Anglican establishment. A long-established policy by the Church of England had insisted on the reordination by Anglican bishops of French Protestant ministers who were refugees in England. Those who refused reordination were denied relief funds as were the laity who refused to take communion in an Anglican church. This pressure had been most successful among the small rural French congregations in England as similar pressures would be in South Carolina among the rural Huguenot churches. The urban congregation in Charlestown was in a better position to withstand such pressures. Thus it followed the pattern of those French congregations in London that remained independent of the Anglican establishment.[6] In addition to these coercive factors, however, there were positive reasons for Huguenots in South Carolina to join in the local Anglican establishment. The bitter divisions that had separated republicans and royalists in Britain were not part of their experience. When they looked at the Church of England, they saw, after all, a historic Protestant church whose classic documents reflected the influence of Geneva. And if they had reservations about the church hierarchy, about bishops and apostolic succession, those reservations seemed distant from the realities of church life on the Carolina frontier. Moreover, Anglican leaders had in 1688 successfully removed the Roman Catholic James II from the throne and placed upon it the Calvinist William of Orange.

Encouragement also came, no doubt, from the Anglican "Society for the Propagation of the Gospel in Foreign Parts" (SPG). Established in 1701, it had a strong ecumenical element with its "corresponding members" in other countries and would help supply badly needed ministers to those congregations that conformed. The French clergy in South Carolina were, in fact, generally strong advocates of conformity (sometimes against the strong opposition of the laity), and a number came to South Carolina already having Anglican ordination and under the auspices of the SPG. When all of these factors are added to the undeniable economic and political advantages of the establishment—which twentieth-century people are more likely to emphasize in any calculation of motivation—it is not surprising that most of the Huguenots and their churches became Anglican. Here they would find a home, and in the years ahead they would contribute dedicated clerical and lay leaders to this communion.

Still, not all followed this route. The Huguenot Church in Charlestown retained its independence, with the substantial help of a large endowment.[7] By the end of the colonial period, this congregation had set a pattern that it would follow for the next two centuries: the church would survive through the dedication of a few members, a substantial endowment, and the support of others of Huguenot descent. The congregation would be marked, however, not so much by the old theological vitality and passion of the French martyrs and exiles as by a memory of and genealogical pride in those who, as refugees to a new land, helped to shape a distinct colonial society.

Some Huguenots chose a third route and joined churches close to their own tradition—in particular the Presbyterian and Congregational churches that were being built in the Carolina low country. To these they added families distinguished both by their place in a young society and by their future service to the church. Prominent among these families would be the Legarés and Girardeaus, the DeSaussures, Bacots, LaMottes, DuBoses, and Nobles.

Congregational Churches

New England Congregationalists, with Presbyterians from Scotland and Ireland and with English Dissenters and a few Huguenots, organized in Charlestown, perhaps as early as 1681, the Independent Meeting House—later known as the Circular Congregational Church.[8] For two hundred years, until fire and the Civil War left it weak and in disarray, the congregation was one of the most important churches of the city, numbering among its membership many of the city's political, economic, and intellectual leaders.

Outside the city in the scattered plantation settlements, there were two Congregational churches, both established by New England Puritans: the White Meeting House at Dorchester and the Wappetaw Independent Congregational Church. Other congregations, especially in Beaufort and on James Island, had strong Congregationalist connections, but they were generally associated with the Presbyterians. In these connections they reflected the close relationship of Congregationalists and Presbyterians throughout the region.

Presbyterian Churches

The establishment of Presbyterian churches in the low country was closely linked to the life and labors of one indefatigable Scotsman—Archibald Stobo.

Stranded in Charlestown by a hurricane in September 1700, he was called to be pastor of the city's White Meeting House.[9] After serving this congregation for four years, he turned his attention to Protestant Dissenters in the countryside who were particularly strong in the region that streched southwest of the Stono River to the Combahee. For the next thirty-seven years he was a tireless pastor among these people, establishing churches at Wilton Bluff at Adam's Run on the lower Edisto River;[10] at Pon Pon further upriver;[11] at James Island;[12] and northwest of Charlestown, at Cainhoy among the New Englanders who settled there.[13] During this same period, if not earlier, Presbyterian churches were also established at Edisto Island[14] and Johns Island.[15] Back in Charlestown twelve Scottish families, no doubt with Stobo's encouragement, withdrew in 1731 from the Independent Meeting House and formed the First (Scots) Presbyterian Church.[16] In this way Presbyterian churches were slowly but surely established throughout the region. Always closely related to neighboring Congregational churches, and to the Huguenot Church in Charlestown, they set during the colonial period patterns that would long mark the life of Presbyterianism in the Carolina low country.

Numerical Strength

Among the white population, a substantial number from the earliest days of settlement were Dissenters. They identified themselves as "dissenting" from the established church, as "belonging" in some sense to a church other than the Anglican. Of these, most were "Presbyterian," a rather generic term that included not only those who were strictly Presbyterian after the Scottish model but also Congregationalists and those Huguenots who retained their Reformed tradition.[17] Their exact numbers are not easy to calculate—church records are limited and the meaning of "church membership" is not always clear.[18] But there are some church records and, more significantly, scattered references that together help paint a broad picture of the Presbyterian presence in low country during the colonial period.

In 1710 contemporaries estimated that 45 percent of the white population was Presbyterian, 42.5 percent Anglican, 10 percent Baptist, and 2.5 percent Quaker.[19] With a white population of a little over 6,000 in 1710,[20] these figures indicate that there were approximately 2,700 Presbyterians in the colony, making it at the time one of the strongest centers of Presbyterianism in the British North American colonies.[21] In 1750 Governor James Glen believed the percentages from 1710 were still accurate.[22] By the time of the American Revolution, William Tennent, pastor of the Independent Meeting House, could point out to the South Carolina Assembly that Dissenters had from the first made up more than half of the white population.[23]

In 1750, when Governor Glen made his estimate of Presbyterian strength, the low country had nine Presbyterian churches, three Congregational, and one French Huguenot. Twenty years later, on the eve of the Revolution, there were twelve Presbyterian churches, three Congregational with another one being planned for Charlestown, one French Huguenot, and one German Reformed. In addition, at least four churches also had chapels of ease located in a place central to part of the congregation: Wilton, Wappetaw, Dorchester (at Beech Hill), and Johns Island (on adjacent Wadmalaw Island). Anglicans, on the other hand, had seventeen churches and eleven chapels in this same region.[24]

The Anglicans thus had, by the end of the colonial period, the same number of churches and seven more chapels in the low country than did the Presbyterians and Congregationalists together with their close relatives in the German and French Reformed churches. If the strongly Calvinistic "Particular" Baptists are added, those churches in the Reformed tradition represent at the end of the colonial period, as they did at the beginning, a majority of the churches in the low country. Nevertheless the established church was clearly a powerful church in the region. Its power, however, should not be exaggerated, nor should the region be regarded as without a significant Reformed presence. The Anglicans had been able to build and sustain churches and chapels with public funds—£164,027 had gone from the public treasury to the support of the Anglican establishment in South Carolina in the decade 1765–75 alone.[25] In addition, the SPG had provided many of the ministers and supported them for long periods. The number of Anglican churches and chapels, in other words, does not clearly reflect the degree to which they had won the allegiance of the people in the region. Many of the rural churches and chapels reported only a few communicants and baptisms, although they claimed there were many in the parishes "who profess themselves of the Church of England."[26] Still, the established church had obviously shown sustained growth since the early years of the century and was the most powerful church in the region—not only in the number of churches and chapels, but also in political, economic, and social influence. Behind much of this influence stood a bitter political struggle at the beginning of the eighteenth century—a struggle the Anglicans had won.

The Struggle over Establishment

From the earliest years of the colony to the overthrow of the proprietary government in 1719, South Carolina was divided among several factions that included important religious dimensions. One faction supported the proprietors, another opposed them. One faction was composed of an ill-defined Dissenter group said to be closely tied to Presbyterian interests, while another faction was made up of an equally ill-defined Church Party linked to the Church of England. The religious factions overlapped the political and sometimes changed political allegiance, but generally the Dissenters were supporters of the proprietors, while the Church Party most often opposed them. The Dissenters were strongest in Colleton County and that area south and southwest of the Stono River, while the stronghold of the Church Party was among the Goose Creek men. Complicating matters further were ancient loyalties and animosities. The Goose Creek men were largely settlers from Barbados who brought with them the English scorn for the Scots and French. Many of the Dissenters, on the other hand, were Scots who had little love for the English. Other Dissenters were English Presbyterians or Congregationalists from England or New England with vivid memories of persecution by the Anglican establishment.

In 1704 Governor Nathaniel Johnson called a meeting of the Colonial Assembly. While it normally took several days to gather a quorum, Anglican members had apparently been notified earlier and gathered quickly. Before a number of Dissenter members arrived, the assembly passed by a vote of 12 to 11 an act excluding from the assembly all those who did not conform to the Church of England. With their position thus secured, the Church Party proceeded to establish the Anglican Church as the state-supported church of South Carolina. Seven parishes were designated, provisions were made for the use of public funds to build Anglican churches and pay their ministers, and Dissenting clergy were prohibited from performing legally recognized weddings. Rectors of Anglican parishes were to be elected by their Anglican parishioners with church commissioners retaining the right to suspend any clergyman.[27]

The Dissenters, led by the second Landgrave Thomas Smith, the second Landgrave Joseph Morton, by Landgrave Edmund Bellinger, and by John Ash, were outraged by this violation of their religious freedom and by the political maneuvering of the Church Party. Even the rector of Saint Philip's joined them in denouncing the act, but it did no good. The only course remaining appeared to be an appeal to the proprietors.

Pressing the Dissenters' case before the proprietors was Joseph Boone, a Charlestown merchant and wealthy planter. He found the proprietors divided on the issue. John Archdale, the mild-mannered Quaker who had once served successfully as governor of the colony, and Maurice Ashley, grandson of Anthony Ashley Cooper, supported the Dissenters. But Lord Granville, a High Church Tory who had the proxies of two absent proprietors as well as his own vote, won the day and the laws were ratified. Boone then appealed to the House of Lords, which was dominated by the Whigs, and enlisted the help of a fiery pamphleteer and leader among the English Dissenters, Daniel Defoe. In a few years Defoe would be writing *Robinson Crusoe* and *The Fortunes and Misfortunes of Moll Flanders*, but in 1705 he turned his attention to the little colony of Carolina and wrote two pamphlets defending the South Carolina Dissenters. With ridicule and sarcasm, he parodied the self-serving claims of the Anglican assembly, calling for a repeal of its establishment law.[28]

Meanwhile Boone gained the support of powerful London merchants, many of whom were Dissenters, and even got the SPG to oppose the bill because it gave the laity too much control over the Anglican clergy. Such political support, together with Defoe's pamphlets, had influence, and the appeal to the House of Lords was successful. The Lords asked the Crown to "deliver the said Province from the arbitrary Oppressions under which it now lies." The result was that the Privy Council directed the proprietors to overturn the legislation. When the news reached Charlestown, the assembly repealed the acts, then passed again an act of establishment minus the section that gave lay control to Anglican parishes. Dissenters were no longer excluded from the assembly, but they were never able to muster the numbers or the will to overturn the establishment bill until the Revolution. Two primary reasons appear to be behind this failure.

First, the political mood in England changed with the reign of Queen Anne (1702–14). A more conservative, High Church perspective increasingly dominated English life. At the same time the Church of England began to stir from its earlier doldrums and enter into vigorous missionary activity through the SPG. Under such conditions, appeals to English courts seemed unlikely to produce favorable results. Second, conditions in South Carolina began to raise more pressing issues. While some Dissenters elected to the Colonial Assembly refused to serve, in protest to the establishment act, others did. And some, such as Joseph Boone, became influential leaders. But they were faced with the growing crisis of security for the colony as the War of Spanish Succession (1701–13) raged and the French moved dangerously close from their stronghold in Mobile. Spanish settlements in Florida meanwhile remained an almost constant threat, while in South Carolina the number of black slaves ominously increased beyond the number of white colonists. Most immediately threatening, however, was the increasing tension with the Native Americans that soon broke out in the devastating Yemassee War.[29]

Thus the Dissenters gradually gave up their struggle against an Anglican establishment and turned their attention to other matters. The result was that for seventy years, until the American Revolution, the Anglican Church was the established church of South Carolina. Latitudinarian in its outlook, its relationship with Dissenter churches was generally relaxed. Some Dissenters served on local vestries, and prominent Anglicans were also pewholders in Dissenting churches. Nevertheless, the Anglican Church received hundreds of thousands of pounds from the public treasury and some of its commissaries used pressure tactics attempting to get non-Anglicans to join the Church of England.[30] As the established church, it moved into a position of political and social dominance in the low country.

Much of what was desired from such an establishment were social stability and order, a religious bond for colonial society, and an established means for promoting the public interests. Much of what was feared about the Dissenters were their "republican principles" and their raising of questions about *whose* interests were being promoted in the name of the public good. "How dare the ministers of Boston be such impudent dogs," cried Governor Francis Nicholson in 1720 to the newly arrived minister of the Independent Meeting House, "as to ordain you for and send you to a particular place in *my* Government." "I know," said Nicholson, "no Presbyterians here, nor will I know any, the laws are not for them but against them." They are, he said, of "factious and republican principles not worthy to be tolerated in his Majesty's dominions." When two Presbyterian ministers arrived a month later from Scotland, the governor wrote the SPG that these undesirables "Infuse Ante Monarchical Principles into the People and are Setting up for an Independt government both in Church and State."[31]

From the Presbyterian/Congregational perspective, Nicholson spoke the truth only too clearly. Those in the Reformed community were convinced that Anglicanism, centralized monarchical power, corruption, and tyranny marched together. An ideological and historical link existed, they believed, between religious and political authoritarianism. In contrast to Anglicanism, they saw themselves as standing for representative government, virtue, and freedom, for "civil liberty, equality, and independence."[32]

In spite of the opposition of Nicholson and the pressures to conform, the Presbyterians and other Dissenters did not quietly vanish from the low country scene as has so often been portrayed.[33] On the contrary, soon after the passage of the establishment act, the Presbyterians entered one of their most aggressive periods of church building. Moreover, they laid the foundation for the Carolina low country to become in the nineteenth century the single most influential region in the life of Southern Presbyterianism.

The Presbytery of Charlestown

Sometime before 1728—perhaps as early as 1722—the Presbyterian and Congregational ministers in the low country organized a presbytery.[34] It provided an institutional structure for bringing together the scattered Reformed communities, for expressing the unity they confessed, and for linking them into a single, if often stormy, Reformed community.

In the formation of the presbytery, the Carolina ministers had before them not only European examples but also the example of Presbyterian ministers in Maryland, Delaware, and Pennsylvania. The Northern ministers had formed in 1706, under the leadership of Francis Makemie, the Presbytery of Philadelphia. In 1717 the Synod of Philadelphia had been organized with four presbyteries— Long Island, Philadelphia, New Castle (Maryland and Delaware), and Snow Hill (eastern shore of Maryland). The synod became a rallying point for Presbyterians in the Middle Colonies and drew together ministers and congregations of mixed national backgrounds. Much the same pattern was true in the Charlestown Presbytery throughout the colonial period. The diversity added strength to scattered congregations, but it also became the source of major tensions that would long plague the presbytery and its successors.

Given its diversity, it is not surprising that among the earliest references to the Charlestown Presbytery are those that tell of controversy and divisions over subscription to the Westminster Confession. Adopted by the Church of Scotland and later by the Synod of Ulster in Northern Ireland, the Confession had become by the end of the seventeenth century both a standard to which ministers were required to subscribe and a source of great conflict in Ulster. Some Ulster Presbyterians favored requiring all ministers to accept every doctrine of the Confession as being agreeable to the Scriptures. Others rejected such strict subscription, insisting that a general acceptance of the substance of the Confession was all that was necessary. Still others objected to any test of divine truth other than the Scriptures themselves. Behind the bitter debate, stirring the Ulster blood, were the competing impulses within the Reformed tradition: the Scholastic need for order and fixed principles, the humanist fear of enclosing boundaries and restrictive systems. The conflict grew more intense until in 1726 the nonsubscribers were excluded from the synod.[35]

Such debates were not left behind in Ireland or Scotland but were part of the cultural baggage Reformed communities brought to the New World. The year after the Irish action, the controversy emerged in the British North American colonies. In the colonial disputes that followed, it soon became apparent that a compromise was needed, and at the Synod of 1729 the Adopting Act was passed. All ministers were required to declare their agreement that the Confession was "in all the essential and necessary articles, good forms of sound words and systems of Christian doctrine." The agreement was at best uneasy, and before too many years it was broken.[36]

The same year the Synod of Philadelphia was searching for a compromise with the Adopting Act, trouble began to brew in the Charlestown Presbytery. Josiah Smith, a Harvard graduate, feeling pushed by "the unbrotherly and unchristian manner" of the "Scotch brethren" who were urging a strict subscription to the Confession, entered the fray in 1729 by publishing a sermon entitled *Human Impositions proved unscriptural; or, the Divine Right of Private Judgment.* If, he asked, "Christians have not a Right to Examine all Doctrines by the Scriptures, . . . What use the Scriptures are to them?"[37] The "Scotch brethren" were, no doubt, led by Archibald Stobo, but their spokesman was, interestingly enough, the Reverend Hugh Fisher of Dorchester. A Scotsman and a minister of the Church of Scotland, he served the New England Congregationalists who had settled along the dark waters of the Ashley. When Smith published his sermon, Fisher responded with his own, *A Preservative against*

Dangerous Errors in the Unction of the Holy One, to which Smith responded with *No New Thing for Good Men to be Evil spoken of.*

Fortunately, the damage from such homiletical salvos fired between Cainhoy and Dorchester was not devastating. One significant consequence, however, did follow from the controversy. The pastor of the Independent Meeting House in Charlestown, the Reverend Nathan Bassett, sided with Smith and the non-subscriptionists. The Scots in the congregation, unhappy with such a position, withdrew in 1731 and organized the First (Scots) Presbyterian Church. Here they could maintain their strict subscriptionism, their "strong predilection for a strictly Presbyterian form of government, and the strong national partialities which they have ever manifested."[38]

The presbytery itself was formed after the model of the Church of Scotland and drew into its membership most of the ministers of the surrounding Congregational churches. It was organized, wrote Alexander Hewat,

> not only from a persuasion of its conformity to the primitive apostolic form, but also from a conviction of its being, of all others, the most favorable to civil liberty, equality, and independence. Sensible that not only natural endowments, but also a competent measure of learning and acquired knowledge were necessary to qualify men for the sacred function, and enable them to discharge the duties of it with honor and success, they associated on purpose to prevent deluded mechanics, and illiterate novices, from creeping into the pulpit, to the disgrace of the character, and the injury of religion.[39]

Thus the presbytery was regarded as a means of providing both freedom and order, both equality and standards for judging "a competent measure of learning and acquired knowledge." It was, Presbyterians thought, a middle way between the hierarchical structures of an episcopal establishment on the one side and anarchy on the other. It appeared to them the way "most favorable to civil liberty, equality, and independence." At the same time, the presbytery provided an institutional structure for holding in tension the competing impulses within the Reformed tradition itself. Without exaggerating their importance, it would be surprising if such ideas, institutionalized among a substantial part of a colonial society, did not have broader social consequences echoed in the events leading to 1776.

The Reformed community, with the establishment of the presbytery, transplanted a powerful institutional expression of its religious tradition. The presbytery was transplanted, however, into the soil of the low country, and that context profoundly shaped its life. Alexander Hewat, astute observer that he was, acknowledged that while the presbytery was modeled after the Church of Scotland, it was only modeled as closely as "local circumstances would admit."[40] The result of the interaction between the traditional polity from Scotland and the "local circumstances" was a distinct low country presbytery.

What were they, these "local circumstances," and how did they shape the transplanted polity? Certainly they included the distance of the low country from other centers of Reformed strength, making difficult any official connection with other presbyteries through a synod or General Assembly. Such isolation clearly marked the first hundred years of the presbytery's existence, as it remained independent until the 1820s. Yet even during the years that followed, when the presbytery provided both Southern and national leadership, there remained a certain isolation, an awareness that the low country was in some way a peculiar region, a little world to itself. Behind this peculiarity stood slavery and a black majority. This was the most fundamental of "local circumstances," the most critical factor in shaping the region and the various institutions that developed there. Slavery, the low country's black majority, and their legacies would shape the organization of the presbytery until late into the twentieth century. Certainly they would muffle for generations any role a Presbyterian polity might have in encouraging a belief in "civil liberty, equality, and independence" for all the people of the region.

The ways in which the Reformed communities in the low country organized their lives, both as congregations and as a presbytery, thus reflected a complex and dynamic interaction between a distinct religious tradition, with its own often contradictory impulses, and a particular social context. These institutional structures did not reflect—as on a clear, blank mirror—a religious tradition that had somehow fallen pure and unadorned from heaven or even from the cluttered minds of theologians. Nor were they simply a reflection—as on a clear, blank mirror—of the low country terrain, of its economic life and social systems. Rather they were part of a historic tradition reflected on the dark, cypress-stained waters of the low country. Both the tradition and the moving, rippling waters shaped the institutions' contours and gave them color and form. Both the tradition and the context, flowing together, provide the images that we see when we look at these colonial institutions.

A Social Profile

The Clergy

During the colonial period, approximately fifty-seven ministers in the Reformed tradition served in the low country of South Carolina.[41] Several biographical sketches together with a general social profile of the clergy give hints of the affective side of the community's life and help to clarify the character of the Reformed community during this period.

Benjamin Pierpoint (Harvard, M.A.) was the real founder of the Independent Church in Charlestown as a permanent organization. He came to Charlestown from Boston as a young man, worked hard at organizing the Independent Church, and was dead by the age of thirty, probably of the plague. He was followed by Hugh Adams, another Harvard graduate, who had a tendency to get himself in hot water over such questions as: should magistrates wear wigs? and should Sundays be called the Sabbath? When he arrived in Charlestown in 1698—the year Pierpoint died—the plague was still raging, and he found the "dead were carried in carts, being heaped one upon another. . . . Shops shut up for six weeks; nothing but carrying medicines, digging graves, carting the dead." He got sick himself of "a Putrid Feaver, and of the Tertian Ague and Feaver, the Dropsie, Scurvy, Pestilence, . . . and Gongra Gout." He also suffered, as well he might after such a siege, from "Hypocondriack Melancholy." Of necessity a resourceful person, there being no physician near, he studied "Physick and Chirurgey," began to practice on himself, and "with the Lord's blessing" recovered. After a year in Charlestown, he accepted a call from settlers along the Wando River and served two churches there, then a church on the Edisto, before returning to New England with an unpaid salary.[42] Such were the hazards of the Carolina low country at the beginning of the eighteenth century.

Among the most influential ministers at the Independent Church was Josiah Smith. A grandson of the Landgrave Thomas Smith, one of the colony's early governors, Josiah had graduated from Harvard College in 1725, been ordained in Boston by Cotton Mather, and had served as a minister for two years in Bermuda before returning to South Carolina as the pastor of the Cainhoy congregation on the Wando. In 1734 he began a long pastorate at the Independent Church in Charlestown. He kept his New England contacts and developed an extensive correspondence with English Dissenters, in particular the great hymn writer Isaac Watts.[43]

By the time of the Revolution, the pulpit of the Independent Church was occupied by William Tennent. A graduate of Princeton with an M.A. from Harvard, he came from a distinguished line of Presbyterian ministers in the Middle Colonies who had played leading roles in the Great Awakening and in the founding of Princeton. He played, as we shall see, an important role as a patriot in the Revolution.

The ministers at First (Scots) were, as might be expected, Scotsmen through and through. By far the most influential was Alexander Hewat, whose *History of the Provinces of South Carolina and Georgia* won him a Doctor of Divinity degree from the University of Edinburgh.

The country churches had their share of distinguished ministers, an indication of their growing affluence. The little New England settlement at Wappetaw on the headwaters of the Sewee River, prospering with the growth of rice and indigo plantations, numbered among its pastors John Joachim Zubly, a Swiss scholar, who later served in the Continental Congress from Georgia and made a name for himself first as a Patriot and then as a Tory. In 1774 Moses Allen came to Wappetaw recommended by the Presbytery of New Brunswick

(New Jersey) as an "ingenious, prudent, and pious man." A graduate of Princeton, Allen was a friend of James Madison and became a hero of the Revolution. At Dorchester there was the much esteemed John Osgood (Harvard, 1733). At Bethel Pon Pon, there was Philip Morrison (Saint Andrews, M.A.) and James Rymer (Saint Andrews, M.A.).[44]

And so it went from congregation to congregation, pastors drawn almost entirely from New England and Scotland, some dying quickly of the "strangers fever," others serving long and varied pastorates, but together forming an impressive group of clergymen whose social profile tells much about the communities they served.

The known salaries of these clergymen were equivalent to and at times exceeded those of the Anglican clergy whose salaries were supplied by the colonial government and the SPG. In the 1740s, the pastor of the Bethel Pon Pon received as much as £700 per year plus parsonage and glebe lands, while the salaries of rural Anglican clergy were apparently substantially less, even though there were "strong economic incentives for [Anglican] clergy to come to South Carolina."[45] In the 1760s and 1770s, the salary of the pastor of the Independent Meeting House in Charlestown was £1400 plus £500 for house rent, that of First (Scots) was £1455 plus a manse, while that of the ministers of Saint Philip's and Saint Michael's was £1450 each plus housing.[46] All received additional income from such sources as fees or honoraria for marriages and funerals and often the use of a domestic slave that together with the manse probably doubled the value of their salaries. Such income placed them among the more affluent of the white colonists—a small planter might clear £1400 currency a year by the end of the colonial period—but far from the fabled wealth of the great planters.

A few, however, became wealthy by that ancient route for Presbyterian ministers—they inherited their wealth or married it. Josiah Smith inherited a substantial fortune and his son, Josiah Smith, Jr., was among the most affluent men in Carolina at the time of the Revolution. Most distinguished among those who gained fortunes through marriage was William Hutson. He arrived in Charlestown poor but genteel, having studied law at that school for gentlemen lawyers, the Inns of Court, London. He married well—twice—and when he died in 1775 he left an estate that included over £75,000 in bonds alone. His sons became prominent members of the Carolina gentry and his daughters married into influential low country families.[47]

If few of the clergy had the economic success of Smith and Hutson, they nevertheless prospered and represented a well-educated and well-traveled group in colonial South Carolina.[48] The fifteen Presbyterian ministers who are identified as ministers of the Church of Scotland can be safely assumed to have degrees from one of the Scottish universities—a requirement for ordination—at a time when these universities were becoming among the most distinguished in Europe. Those whose degrees are known had them from Glasgow, Edinburgh, or Saint Andrews. Of the ten known ministers from New England, five are known to be graduates of Harvard and one of Yale. The three from England and Wales were graduates of Dissenting academies. Of the five from the Middle Colonies, one had degrees from both Harvard and Princeton, another was a graduate of Princeton, and one had studied in Virginia under Samuel Davies, an early president of Princeton. Both of the South Carolinians were graduates of Harvard.

The presence of these ministers in South Carolina undoubtedly strengthened the intellectual life of the colony, providing traditional elements of Reformed thought: clarity, discipline, and rigor. That the congregations were able to call them and that they were able to pay them—without the support of government funds or the benevolence of the SPG—at a level equal to and often exceeding that of the established Anglican ministers points toward a vigorous, disciplined, and affluent Reformed community in the low country.

The Laity

Who were the members of these churches, both in Charlestown and in the countryside, and what place did they have in colonial society? A social profile gradually emerges from a variety of sources that provides additional insight into the nature of the Reformed presence in the region.

For most of the early years of the colonial period, from 1670 to as late as the 1720s, the Dissenters represented, as we have seen, a substantial part of Carolina society. A number of early governors were Dissenters, as were many leaders of the Colonial Assembly. Included among the largest early colonial landholders were Landgrave Joseph Morton, Landgrave Edmund Bellinger, Landgrave Thomas Smith, John Barnwell, James Stanyarn, and Joseph Boone— all Dissenters. Prominent Dissenters were also active in the lucrative Indian trade during these years, including James Stanyarn, a wealthy planter who was a member of the Johns Island Church; John Bee, Sr., a member of the Independent Church and later First (Scots), and Samuel Eveleigh, "of South Carolina and Bristol, merchant," a member of the Independent Meeting House.[49]

When we turn to the later colonial period, from 1730 to 1776, the picture changes, but not as radically as often portrayed. The Dissenters were no longer the leading figures in colonial society, but they did play an active and surprisingly vigorous part, especially in Charlestown.

At the Independent Church, a strong and growing congregation included some of the city's wealthiest and most influential citizens. Perhaps first among these was Miles Brewton. His magnificent home at 27 King Street was a showplace of the city. But Brewton's home was not the only noteworthy one among the membership of the Independent Church—John Edwards's house at 15

Eighteenth-Century Homes of Members of Independent Meeting House, Charleston. *Clockwise from top left:* Miles Brewton House, 27 King Street; John Edwards House, 15 Meeting Street; Nathaniel Russell House, 51 Meeting Street; Josiah Smith House, 7 Meeting Street (photos by the author)

Meeting Street, George Mathews's at 37 Church Street, and David Ramsay's at 92 Broad were also marked by architectural distinction. After the Revolution Josiah Smith, son of the former pastor, built his stately home with its piazzas and cupola at 7 Meeting Street, and Nathaniel Russell oversaw the construction of his home at 51 Meeting Street, one of the most beautiful houses in the United States.[50]

Such homes reflected not a Reformed community that was somehow at the edges of low country society but rather one that was an integral part of the region's economic, political, and cultural life. This point becomes even clearer with an extended list of the wealthy merchants who belonged to the Independent Church. Among them were Daniel DeSaussure, William Cleland, Richard Hutson, Benjamin Savage, John Savage, Paul Jenys, James Fisher, John Ballentine, Hugh Swinton, Henry Perroneau, Solomon Legaré, Jr., and Daniel Legaré.[51] Together they formed tight business connections—Edwards, Fisher, and Company; Brewton and Smith; Smith, Brewton, and Smith; Savage and Legaré—and established close relationships with British merchants, especially those of Bristol. Certainly a powerful group of businessmen were associated with the Independent Meeting House. They constituted as a *group* perhaps the dominant segment of those in Charlestown whom Peter Coclanis has characterized as responding "to the stimuli and signals of the market in an economically rational way."[52] They certainly reflected the world view and social ethos of market-oriented merchants so often associated with the world view and ethos of those in the Reformed tradition.

The congregation at First (Scots) was, as the name implies, a center for the Scottish community in the city. Because it was the center of a sizable ethnic group, its social profile reveals a socially diverse congregation. Nevertheless, as Scots they had an identifiable character. The Scots, according to early historian David Ramsay, were together with the Germans the most useful immigrants to the colony. To the Scots, he said, "South Carolina is indebted for much of its early literature. A great proportion of its physicians, clergymen, lawyers, and schoolmasters, were from North-Britain." Nor did they lose in the Carolina low country their famous ways with money: they advanced themselves, said Ramsay, by marriage, and the "instances of their increasing the property thus acquired, are many—of their dissipating it very few."[53]

Among the most profitable activities of the merchants at the Independent Church and at First (Scots) was the slave trade. Between 1735 and 1740, when large numbers of slaves were being imported, three members of the Independent Meeting House alone imported 42 percent of all slave cargoes—Benjamin Savage, Paul Jenys, and William Cleland. From 1735 to 1775 at least fourteen members of the Independent Meeting House can be identified as importers of slave cargoes. Three of these, John Dart, Hugh Swinton, and Isaac Holmes, were only marginally involved, but among the rest were some of the largest importers—Miles Brewton, Paul Jenys, Benjamin Savage, William Cleland, and John Edwards. Between 1762 and 1772 Josiah Smith, Jr., son of the former pastor, would have investments in six cargoes. At First (Scots), George Inglis was a major importer of slaves, and five others can be identified who were involved to a lesser extent. This engagement in the slave trade was not some "dirty business" undertaken by disreputable merchants who were scorned by patrician planters.[54] The slave trade was rather at the heart of the low country's life and pointed toward the central place of a rational, market-oriented perspective in its economy.

In the countryside, the Presbyterians and Congregationalists were able to maintain relatively strong positions in those areas where the Dissenters had dominated. The Anglican minister of Saint Bartholomew's parish, Colleton County, wrote in 1734: "The Dissenters are superior to the Church Men, both in number and wealth; indeed the Church men are generally so poor that they can scarcely afford me a Convenient lodging till the parsonage house be built."[55]

The white membership of these rural churches represented a wide range in social status. There were small farmers and planters, but there were also a surprisingly large number of South Carolina's rising aristocracy. Stephen Bull, Jr., a member of one of the great planter families, was a member of Stoney Creek as was the wealthy planter Hugh Bryan. At Bethel Pon Pon there were Isaac Hayne of Hayne Hall and Robert Pringle, an affluent merchant with a plantation in the area. On Edisto Island there was Paul Hamilton with his great Brick House plantation. The Vanderhorsts, Legarés, and Capers were at Wappetaw; the Bees and Hamiltons at Wilton; the Legarés, Stanyarns, and Holmeses at Johns Island; the Cuthberts and Bowmans at Beaufort, and the Warings and Elliotts at Dorchester. Some leading merchants and lawyers in Charlestown also had plantations near these rural churches and their names appear in the church records; John Bee, Sr., of First (Scots) had a plantation near Bethel Pon Pon, John Rattray had plantations at Pon Pon and Stoney Creek, the Legarés moved between their plantations on Johns Island and their homes in the city, the De-Saussures moved between Charlestown and Beaufort, and the Vanderhorsts between Christ Church Parish (Wappetaw) and Charlestown.[56]

Within such a social context—congenial as it was in its early stages to the ethos of the Reformed tradition—members of the Reformed community prospered and made significant contributions to the political and intellectual life of the colony.

Political and Intellectual Life

With the establishment of the Anglican Church, members of that communion clearly moved into a dominant political position. Nevertheless, surprising numbers of Dissenters played important political roles in the colony. A brief listing of political leaders among the Dissenters throws light on their place in this sector of colonial life.

Among members of the commons house of the assembly identified as colonial leaders were Othniel Beale, John Dart, Paul Jenys, John Savage, and Thomas Lamboll of the Independent Church, Charlestown. Daniel Crawford and John Rattray from First (Scots) served and were leaders in the commons. George Murray of First (Scots) was deputy secretary of South Carolina (his wife, Lady Anne Murray, was the daughter of the the earl of Cromarty). James Johnson was attorney general. Edmond Atkins (Independent Church), Beale, and Crawford were also in the council, the prestigious upper chamber, and Beale served as its president in the 1760s. Atkins was selected by the British

Board of Trade as the first superintendent of Indian affairs in the South. By the time of the Revolution, other political leaders included William Tennent, John Edwards, John Mathews, and David Ramsay, all of the Independent Church. From the country churches came such political leaders as Stephen Bull of Stoney Creek and Thomas Bee of Wilton.[57]

Taken together these political leaders provide a picture of a Reformed community whose members—in contrast to the picture often painted of the low country—continued to be strong and vigorous participants in the political life of colonial society, in spite of the disadvantages they suffered as Dissenters. Beyond what other factors may have been involved in their political activism, it resonated with the traditional character of Reformed communities.

If members of the Reformed churches were not as politically dominant as members of the Anglican communion, they more than held their own with the Anglicans in the intellectual leadership they provided the colony. Particularly important in this regard was the Independent Meeting House. Here gathered a circle of intellectuals that was perhaps the most important in the city during the years immediately before the Revolution. At the center of this bright circle were the Princetonians David Ramsay, Richard Hutson, James Hampden Thomson, and William Tennent. Together they supported the development of a distinctly but not provincial American culture and intellectual life. Ramsay, the most illustrious of the group, will be considered in detail in a later chapter from the perspective of his lifelong work. Even as a young man in colonial Charlestown, he demonstrated the talents that would make him famous in the years following the war. No other Carolinian of his generation would have so many contacts among North American and European intellectuals, and the influence of his writings was unequaled by any other in the city.[58]

The Reformed community thus played a lively part in the region's political and intellectual life. It reflected in this role characteristics often associated with Reformed communities in other times and places and pointed toward important continuities in the tradition as it took root in the Carolina low country.

Slaves

Until the 1740s, when the revivals of the Great Awakening began to stir the churches, there is little indication that Africans or African Americans were a significant part of the Reformed congregations. Their early movement into the churches is therefore more appropriately a part of the Great Awakening, to which we will turn in the following chapter. From early in the eighteenth century, however, some blacks belonged to the churches in a distinctive way—they were owned by the churches, and their status as church property tells much about the social character of the congregations.

The labor of black slaves on glebe lands or in the rice fields of neighboring plantations provided income for the ministers and for the upkeep of the meetinghouses. At Bethel Pon Pon, for example, the congregation bought in the 1730s eight slaves to be employed in planting. Others were purchased in later years. These "hewers of wood and drawers of water" were usually hired out to one or two planters, often to members of the congregation, for one year or more at a time. In return the planters, after having put up a bond for the slaves, agreed to pay in barrels of rice for the use of the slaves and to provide them with "Good Cloaths, Shoes, Blankets and Tools." By 1748 the congregation's slaves included July, Phillis, Charity, Cyrus, Quarterman, Chloe, June, and Prime plus their six children. They were hired in that year for "40 Bbls. Merchantable Rice, 500 N^{ct} W^{it}, to be delivered at Pon Pon Bridge clear of all charges whatsoever, with the bbl. included." Earlier, the congregation had agreed to the Reverend Hugh Stewart's proposal that he receive the yearly income of the slaves' labors plus the income from a legacy rather than a salary.[59]

The danger to slaves of being "hired out" in such a way is clear in the Bethel session minutes. The person who hired the slaves in 1748 was Robert Oswald, a deacon of the church. In May 1750 the session refused him admission to the Lord's Supper because he had murdered one of his slaves during the preceding winter. He acknowledged the murder but did so with such indifference that the elders declared their "nonapprobation of so Superficial an acknowledgment of so heinous a Crime as that of Murder and declared it not Satisfactory to the Chh." Oswald "flew into a great rage" and said he would not bear with this "insinuation and that he had only set as an officer in the Chh. for the advancement of his Worldly Interest." After accusing the session of "Priestcraft," Oswald abruptly left, and the elders declared him no longer a member of the church. When in September 1751 the time came for Oswald to return the slaves of the church he had hired, he refused to do so. It was only after the church had established trustees the following year, with power to act on its behalf, that Oswald returned them. The slave Prime, however, was not listed among them, and it is possible that he was the one murdered. Oswald apparently continued a stormy relationship with the church, voting for but refusing "to sign with those who sign here" a call for a new minister in 1752.[60]

Oswald's story reveals much about the internal life of a colonial congregation and its relationship to its economic and social context. The story points to the tensions and accommodations between a religious tradition—that condemned "so heinous a Crime" as the murder of a slave—and the surrounding cultural ethos. The economic life of the congregation was directly dependent on slavery, and that reality, in interaction with the congregation's ethical tradition, shaped its response to the murder. The story also helps explain why so few slaves joined the churches and why they played a small role in the social profile of the Reformed community during the colonial period.

A Composite Picture

A social picture thus emerges of the Reformed community as a *community*. The community was, to be sure, at the same time a part of the larger community: a subgroup sharing many of the characteristics of the low country as a region. Its members were not only members of a religious community but were also part of complex economic and social circles and systems. Moreover, while some church members were deeply immersed in the ethos and world view of the Reformed community, others were only marginally associated with it. Yet in spite of the often blurred boundaries and the overlappings between this particular religious community and the broader society, the Reformed community possessed certain identifiable characteristics during the colonial period.

First, the community was served by a remarkably well-educated, well-traveled, and well-paid clergy. All but two came from outside the colony (a not surprising fact given the sickeningly high death rate for children in the low country). Many maintained, through correspondence and travel, broad contacts in Britain and the Northern colonies. Several played important roles in the intellectual life of the colony—particularly Josiah Smith, William Tennent, and Alexander Hewat.

Second, the Reformed community was much stronger and certainly much more influential than the picture given in traditional accounts of the low country. While it lost to the Anglicans significant numbers of its Huguenot constituency, it was able to maintain, even under the disadvantages imposed by the Anglican establishment, a sense of its own identity, traditions, and kinship ties. In Charlestown, the community included some of the city's wealthiest merchants. At First (Scots), with its ethnic character, there was a greater diversity of social and economic status than at the Independent Meeting House. The country and village congregations also included people of diverse economic status—small planters and shopkeepers as well as a substantial number of the colonial aristocracy, especially on the islands and in the area between the Stono and Combahee Rivers where much of the strength of the Presbyterians was concentrated. The Reformed community also provided leading players in the political and intellectual life of the region.

Third, the Reformed community was clearly a part of a slave society and reflected in its own institutional structures, ethos, and world view the influences of that society. Black slaves played little part in the community before 1740— and after then only a small part for several decades—except through their labors to provide much of the economic base for the community's life.

Anglican strength is not challenged by this picture of the Reformed presence in the low country. What is challenged are (1) the lingering images of a Cavalier low country "characterized by a whole-hearted devotion to amusement and the neglect of religion and intellectual pursuits" and (2) the picture of a weak and collapsing Presbyterian/Congregational life during the second half of the colonial period. Indeed, it can be argued that the Dissenters had a significant impact on the development of the Anglican Church in the low country—especially in the development of a strong, independent laity. The vestry, a colonial innovation, resembled nothing so much as the traditional Presbyterian session. At any rate, a highly educated and cosmopolitan clergy served Reformed congregations that were often vital and prosperous, especially, but by no means only, in Charlestown. This is not to say that the rural churches in particular were not vulnerable to the forces of dissolution when ministers were not available or that their members did not struggle to keep the churches viable. It is to say that to a far greater extent than has been recognized these Reformed churches were important institutions in the Carolina low country and played their own distinct role in developing the particular ethos of the region.

4

The Tradition Articulated

A Carolina Accent

THE CHARACTER AND values of a people are often most powerfully revealed not in the books a people write or even the deeds they do but in
the buildings they build. Of course, to understand a community we need to
listen to its words and see its deeds. But perhaps the most reliable door into a
community's world view and ethos is through its art and most particularly its
architecture. Through its visible language, the form of a building can reveal
the content of a culture, the values and the shared meanings of a people as well
as their technological development and economic condition. This is particularly
true when a building is designed for important public rituals, when the rituals
and architecture complement one another, and when together they present a
coherent picture of a people's understanding of the world. The meetinghouses,
the central public buildings of the Reformed community in the low country,
together with the rituals performed there thus act as messengers revealing the
spirit of the community, its imagination and world of thought. They provide
insights into the ways in which the Reformed tradition, with its contradictory
impulses, expressed itself in the low country context. The meetinghouses and
their rituals are consequently a good beginning point for exploring the intellectual life of the community during the colonial period.[1]

Meetinghouses with Slave Balconies

The only Presbyterian or Congregational church building from the colonial
period that is still standing in the low country is the Johns Island Presbyterian Church. This simple but elegant building, constructed in 1719, conveys the
spirit of Geneva as it took root in the black soil of Carolina. Here, behind later
additions, we see a meetinghouse similar to those that were built in New England in the seventeenth century: a wooden, square, two-story structure with a
distinctive dual row of windows and entrances on three sides. In 1823 a twenty-
foot addition changed it from square to oblong, a shape that had become popular in eighteenth-century meetinghouses.[2]

During the colonial period, similar meetinghouses were found wherever

Reformed communities gathered as congregations. At Dorchester the meeting-house was brick "and resembles very much in its form and arrangements the old Puritan structures of the seventeenth century." At Wilton a new meeting-house built in the 1760s followed the old style: forty feet square, three doors, sixteen windows, and "hipt roof." An old seal of Bethel Pon Pon reveals a modi-fied meetinghouse style. In Charlestown the Independent Meeting House was until 1730 a square brick building, forty feet on a side. When a new church was built in 1732, it was oblong. The meetinghouse was obviously an architectural style that the Reformed communities in the low country believed to be appro-priate as a "house of worship."[3] In such meetinghouses, as in other Reformed communities, a well-educated clergy led a people whose central public buildings emphasized the values they cherished.

To walk into the Johns Island church today provides a visual experience of the ethos and world view of the community that built it and a hint of what it felt like to worship in such a meetinghouse in the colonial period. A central pulpit, originally nine feet high, dominates the far wall and says clearly that this community's public ritual was highly verbal and disciplined, that the mind and will played more prominent parts than the emotions. High-boxed pews entered through wooden doors run in order across polished, heart-of-pine floors and, together with the balconies, speak of the social arrangements of the people. An eloquent simplicity and spaciousness—highlighted by the absence of any ornamentation and by the clear glass windows—indicate the social values of frugality and order and the psychological atmosphere of plainness that pervaded the worship. Here all is economical for all is eliminated that is not necessary in architectural structure, in furnishings, and in liturgy. Not aesthetics but theol-ogy dominates the meetinghouse, a theology rooted in the Old Testament. The intent is to remind the worshipers of the First Commandment: "I am the Lord thy God. Thou shalt have no other gods before me." And of the Second Com-mandment: "Thou shalt not make any graven image."

Those who built such a place believed that the God they worshiped was the "High and Holy One who inhabits eternity," in whose presence all pretense is cleared away, and before whom all are to stand in simplicity, even austerity, to hear God's word and to do God's will.[4] The high pulpit and the straight-back pews were for a disciplined congregation, a people committed to long sermons that were built upon expositions of biblical texts. The bare table before the pulpit was used only on Communion Sabbaths, no more than four times a year. There was no place in such a meetinghouse for the spectacular or for what Calvin called the "lifeless and theatrical trifles, which serve no other purpose than to deceive the sense of a people stupefied."[5] The rituals that found a home here were few in number, easy to observe, dignified in their simplicity, and clear in their meaning,[6] yet they were also subtle and often contradictory, obscur-ing with their simple rites powerful tensions within the low country meeting-

Low Country Meetinghouses
Clockwise, from top right: Bethel Pon Pon Presbyterian (courtesy of Bethel Presbyterian Church, Walterboro, S.C.); Dorchester Congregational (courtesy of Dorchester Presbyterian Church, Summerville, S.C.); Mount Pleasant Presbyterian, and Edisto Island Presbyterian Church (both photos by Jonathan T. Van Deventer, courtesy of Charleston-Atlantic Presbytery, Charleston, S.C.)

houses. In a similar manner, the mood was calm, orderly, and cerebral; but the clear windows and spacious atmosphere provided a contrasting sense of openness and freedom.

The surrounding sea island oaks that marked the approach to the Johns Island Meeting House, the building's heart-of-pine framing and cypress siding, and the hand-split black cypress shingles all made unmistakably clear that this was not a meetinghouse built anywhere, but one built on a Carolina sea island. The same was true inside. Here the simple and rational organization of the room—the high pulpit, the clear windows, the unadorned table, the wooden doors on high-boxed pews set within a spacious room, and above all the balconies with their long benches—stood out as messengers of a social system. They told of both a rational, orderly world and of black slaves. They spoke of freedom and openness and at the same time of being boxed in, constrained by rigid systems and enclosing boundaries.

In slowly increasing numbers after 1740, slaves sat at the edges of this eloquent simplicity and listened to the long, logical sermons of Presbyterian pastors, sang the Psalms and hymns, and on Communion Sabbaths sat down at the long tables across the front.[7] These "hewers of wood and drawers of water" and the social system of which they were a fundamental part had a powerful shaping influence, not only on the building itself with its balconies and benches, but also on the rituals that took place there and on the world view that informed those rituals. In such a setting, the music sung here on a Sabbath morning echoed with the antiphonal elements of the mood created by the building's arrangements and by the juxtaposition of white slave owners and black slaves.

Today a small choir loft is located behind the Johns Island pulpit, but it is a relatively recent addition. In colonial times the pulpit was against the wall, and the music was the music of the congregation. No organ or musical instrument led the singing, for such instruments would obscure, it was thought, the message of the words and would be an intrusion into the freedom of the congregation and into what was regarded as the highest form of human expression: the *vox humana* in praise of God.[8]

What the congregation sang were the Psalms together with hymns based on biblical texts. In 1796 Charleston Presbytery published *A Version of the Book of Psalms* bound with *A Collection of Hymns for Public and Private Worship, Approved of by the Presbytery of Charleston*. The book, filled with the music used throughout the colonial period, was a collection of Psalms that "poets had translated with success" and of hymns that drew on New Testament themes. In forming the collection, regard was paid "not only to poetical beauty, but also to simplicity of language, and to piety of sentiment."[9] The Psalms and hymns were arranged like a theological text; indeed they reflected much of the order of the Westminster Confession. Under "Part I: God" were hymns on "The Perfections of God," "The Unity of God," "The Spirituality of God,"

"The Eternity of God," "The Immutability of God," and so on, like some theological lesson outlined by a systematic professor. Some of the hymns of Isaac Watts and his freer translations of the Psalms were here as were those of "lesser poets" and some of the old "Scotch version."[10] Evangelical hymns that spoke of God's grace and Christ's redemption were included in the collection. And there were hymns with a moral, that taught the way a person ought to live, with titles such as "Prudence," "Gravity and Decency," and "Industry and Sloth Contrasted," intended to turn the Children of Geneva toward the narrow way.[11]

Such hymns, unhindered by musical instruments, echoed the Reformed tradition's impulse toward freedom and resistance to encroaching boundaries. Yet they also clearly and powerfully reproduced another impulse within the tradition that sought order and stability. Together the two competing impulses produced in the hymns—beneath their discontinuities—a tense harmony, a congruity and conceptual framework for white worshipers' understanding of the world. The hymns nurtured communal images and metaphors for the whites and reflected their "social construction of reality."[12]

The world that these whites constructed had room for their own quest for freedom but no room for such a quest by their slaves. The liturgy and hymns of the meetinghouse consequently served the social purpose of legitimizing the values of the white slave owners who structured the worship. Their monopoly of power and the social stability of the community were enhanced by the singing of these hymns that celebrated the world view and ethos of the whites. What was carefully kept out of the worship services (and they would be kept out of white-dominated services for two hundred years) were the spirituals beginning to emerge slowly out of the African American experience. These songs "from below," from the edges and backwaters of society, would present during the coming years powerful alternatives to the dominant ideology of the hymns. The spirituals through the power of their poetry would imagine an alternative reality to that constructed and celebrated by white slaveholders in their services and hymns. Away from the church and whites' monopoly of imagery and imagination, African American slaves would construct in their spirituals a world seen through a different set of memories and hopes: "Didn't my Lord deliver Daniel, then why not ev'ry man?"[13] Whites might remember Daniel and his deliverance, might link his story to their own quests for freedom, but what they could not do except on a "spiritual" level was include African Americans among "ev'ry man."

Among the hymns at worship services were those for "Before the Communion" and "Sacramental Hymns," and they, of course, pointed to the sacred ritual of the Lord's Supper.[14] The Communion service at the Johns Island church, as a reenactment of Christianity's founding event, acted out in a vivid fashion the complex interaction between a religious tradition and its social context heard in the hymns. Moreover, the Communion service itself revealed both the ideological and utopian character inherent in the Reformed tradition as it found expression in the Carolina low country. While the ideological character can be most clearly linked to white slave owners and the utopian to black slaves, such divisions were not neat and simple. The manner in which whites celebrated Communion not only served clear ideological purposes but also contained a powerful forward-looking and present-shattering utopian element. Similarly, African American participation in the Communion service had not only a utopian element but also served to help integrate them into the Reformed community and to provide them with a distinct social identity.

The table before the pulpit remained bare most of the year—without cloth or chalice or even the flowers that later, more sentimental generations would place there. But on four Sabbaths during the year the table was covered with a white cloth, hiding beneath it the Communion bread and wine until after the sermon, for not even the sight of the Communion elements was allowed to intrude into the hearing of the word. Hearing, it was insisted, must precede seeing "the outward and visible signs" of the sacrament. The eye looks out to its object, but hearing receives into the human heart God's word. Hearing, not seeing, was consequently the foundation of Reformed spirituality—for God speaks, and faith, it was said, consists of listening to the word of God. Moreover, for those in the Reformed tradition there was a conviction that when God is presented in an identifiable form, an image, the purpose is to control God, to domesticate and reduce God to the tool of those in power. Fixed religious images lead to consolidations of power and to social docility. So Scripture and sermon preceded and enlightened what followed in the visible sacraments.[15] The paradox, of course, was in white slaveholders' expressing such views, for they were anxious about *both* the dangers to their own liberty and the dangers of slaves breaking controlling images of hierarchy and submission.

On the Sabbath before the Communion, a service of preparation was held with often another on the Saturday immediately before the sacramental day. During the week the congregation would have been visited by the elders, and those who were found "walking in the ways of the Lord" were given a Communion token that would admit them to the table. Those who had been found wayward, who had been disciplined by the session, were "fenced off" from the table for a "season," the length determined by the severity of the sin.[16] When the time came to receive Communion, the white members who were to participate came forward, sat around the table, and gave their tokens to the elders who distributed the bread and wine. Then the blacks came down from the balcony to the same Lord's Table. There they handed over their tokens and received from the white minister and elders the bread and wine from the same silver trays and chalice that had served the whites.

This Lord's Supper in this well-lit, well-ordered meetinghouse was not thought of as a sacrifice, although it was a "sacrificial occasion." It was not "Christ offered up to his Father, nor any real sacrifice made at all for remission of sins of the quick or dead." Rather, it was regarded as "a commemoration of that once offering up" of Christ, "by himself, upon the cross, once for all, and a spiritual oblation of all possible praise unto God for the same."[17]

The Communion service thus enacted a coherent picture of a people's religious tradition—what they believed, the competing ideas that helped shape their understanding of the world, that offered emotional support in times of trouble, and that provided ethical standards for living in a world seen through such eyes of faith. But that was not all, for, as we have seen, the architectural arrangements of the meetinghouse and its rituals emerged not only out of the depths of the congregation's religious life but also from the geographical and social context in which the building was set. In the architecture and rituals of the meetinghouse there was a fusion of a world as understood by a religious tradition and a world as lived in a particular place and sociohistorical setting.[18]

The meetinghouse Communion service made explicit the social system of the low country reflected in the architecture and echoed in the hymns.[19] The celebration of the sacrament pointed to an emphasis on "order," to the relationships between whites, and to the "proper" relationship between white owners and black slaves. Moreover, the way the Lord's Supper was enacted served to nurture and transmit pictures of the world and the sentiments and values needed to maintain that world. For the white masters and mistresses, the ritual functioned to legitimize their power and social control over the African Americans while at the same time expressing a sense of social cohesion and solidarity among blacks and whites together.[20]

When the whites came forward to receive the Lord's Supper, they did not kneel before a priest or an Anglican rector who distributed the elements.[21] Rather they sat together, heard from the minister "the Words of the Institution," turned in their tokens, and received from the hands of elected lay elders the bread and the wine. The old hierarchical world was being replaced for *them* by a new world of collective discipline and purpose. A parity (at least for the men) and a plainness pointed toward an emerging new social order for whites. What was enacted when the whites sat at the table was an image of the equality of the "elect" set within an ordered system.

When the blacks came forward, they too sat together and received in the same manner the Communion elements. While they sat at the same table as the whites, they came only after the whites, a vivid reminder of their "place" in society. For them the old hierarchical order was still in place, a hierarchy based not only on birth and status but even more fundamentally on race. In this way the ritual served the ideological purpose of expressing a sense both of social cohesion and of social differences. It was a shared Communion, but it was a "Communion" that, while highlighting a "spiritual equality" among communicants gathered around the table, emphasized whites were first and blacks were second. Whites were clearly on top of a hierarchical structure and blacks were on bottom, but they were all seen as being a part of the same community of faith and social order.

The Communion service, by enacting a social drama of unity in spite of separation, helped to conceal the contradictions inherent in meetinghouses with slave balconies.[22] Whites could continue to confess that "in Christ there is neither slave nor free"[23] and insist on a parity among themselves while making clear at the Communion table that boundaries had to be maintained to keep chaos at bay and that there were most emphatically those who were white and those who were black, those who were slave and those who were free. Any mixture of the two would lead, whites were sure, to disorder, confusion, and impurity. Communion thus served (primarily for whites) an ideological function—it provided dramatic reassurance about the legitimacy of the slave system, helped to integrate the community and give it a sense of common identity, and all the while it concealed the inherent contradictions in a meetinghouse with slave balconies. Moreover, the Communion service itself, by its very nature, had as an essential element a powerful ideological thrust—it was a remembering of founding events, the Last Supper and the Crucifixion. "We do this in remembrance of Him," the minister declared. The holy meal thus supported the tradition, its authority, and those in authority.

But the Communion service had more than this conserving, integrating function. It also had a transforming, shattering thrust toward the future—it was to show the Lord's death "until he come." The meal was eschatological: it anticipated the Banquet of the Lord when people would come from the north and the south, from the east and west to sit together at the table. For the believers this was not merely a vision, but a vision that would be realized. Communion thus served (primarily for slaves) a utopian function—from such a place as the Final Banquet, the present order of masters and slaves did not appear eternal but passing and contingent. From such a place as the Final Banquet, it was possible to imagine an alternative to the present system of slavery and to construct an alternative reading of reality. The metaphor of hierarchy so powerfully present at the Communion service was challenged by a contrary metaphor of equality at the Lord's Table.[24]

Meetinghouses with their hymns, rituals, and slave balconies thus come across the years to speak of the ways the antithetical impulses and the competing ideas of the Reformed tradition (as a part of the larger Christian tradition) found expression in the specific context of the low country. The merging of two stories in the meetinghouse—the story of the tradition and the story of the social context—did much to shape the character and world view of those who worshiped there. These visual images of meetinghouses and their rituals, powerful as they may be, need, however, to be informed—checked, as it were—

by the articulated ideas of the community. This need is perhaps particularly true of a Reformed community that feared images and rituals and that claimed to put a high value on the carefully reasoned, articulated word. With this claim in mind, we turn to three leading clergymen. A brief review of their work can be a window into the intellectual life of the meetinghouses, providing a glimpse of at least important elements of the world as understood by the Reformed community during the colonial period.

Scholar Pastors

Josiah Smith

Josiah Smith, graduate of Harvard, pastor at the Presbyterian church at Cainhoy and then at the Independent Meeting House (Charlestown), had a number of his sermons published in Boston and Charlestown, in London, Edinburgh, and Glasgow. Together they provide insights into his world of thought and to the kind of messages delivered from meetinghouse pulpits in the low country. There were doctrinal and polemical sermons—*The Divine Right of Private Judgment Vindicated* (for whites, it is assumed) and *No New Thing to be Slander'd* (Boston, 1730). They showed him to be a nonsubscriptionist in the controversy regarding the Westminster Confession and helped to make him a well-known New Side preacher, but of a generally temperate and moderate sort.[25] But he was not just a polemicist; he was also a pastor, and a number of his pastoral sermons reflect a moderate spirit within the Reformed tradition. His *The Duty of Parents, to instruct their Children* . . . (Boston, 1730) emphasized the role of Christian nurture in the home. He saw, as a good Reformed theologian, the hand of God in the disasters of his time, yet he was generally cautious in drawing a direct line between catastrophes and sin. In *The Greatest Sufferers not always the Greatest Sinners. A Sermon* . . . *Occasioned by the Terrible Earthquake in New-England* (Boston, 1730), he defended suffering New England. Yet he took the occasion to issue a jeremiad, to warn his Carolina congregation, the children of New England immigrants, that their sins might very well evoke even greater wrath from the Lord. New England, he declared, in comparison to Carolina, was a paragon of virtue. Perhaps his congregation's ancestry and his social position as the grandson of a Carolina governor helped him get away with such a comparison. No doubt he thought the comparison was true. Ten years later, when Charlestown was devastated by a great fire, he preached on *The Burning of Sodom* . . . *Preach'd at Charlestown, South Carolina, after a most Terrible Fire* (Boston, 1741). He was not the last Harvard graduate to hint that Charlestown might be a Sodom, but he did not go so far as to say that the fire was the result of the city's sins.[26]

What Smith was struggling with in these last sermons was the problem that

had confronted Job in the Old Testament—the problem of theodicy, of vindi-
cating a good God in the face of physical and moral evil. However orderly the
meetinghouses in which Smith preached, however simple and rational their arrangements, they could not keep outside their doors the world's disorders and
incongruities, its sufferings and injustices. (Indeed, such incongruities and injustices within the meetinghouses were no doubt all too visible from a good
view in the balcony.) For the cosmic order reflected in the meetinghouses to
be believable, the disorders and imperfections of the world had to be addressed,
and Smith addressed them through the doctrine of providence. The "High and
Holy One who inhabits eternity" directs the affairs of human life and has ways
that are inaccessible to human understanding. Yet those ways are finally good
and just and call for obedience to God's laws. Here was a doctrine and a metaphor that later generations of low country preachers would use to justify slave
balconies in meetinghouses. Here was a way of constructing a world that served
to legitimize and preserve the present order.

Smith's most famous sermon, however, did not serve the present order but
was aimed at its breaking—at least for the whites. The sermon plunged Smith
into the midst of one of the most consequential events in American religious
history—the Great Awakening. In this shaking of the foundations, he sided
with the forces of the future, not with the older more familiar patterns of
religious life and the social structures that supported them. His sermon on *The
Character, Preaching, etc. Of the Reverend Mr. George Whitefield . . . Preach'd in
Charlestown . . . March 26th . . . 1740* helped to prepare the way for the great
Anglican evangelist.[27] It was printed in Boston, Philadelphia, and Glasgow and
forty-five years later was included as an introduction to *Fifteen Sermons Preached
on Various Important Subjects by George Whitefield*. In his vigorous support of
Whitefield and the Awakening, Smith helped to expand the tradition, to emphasize the piety and the affective side of religious life and the need for a conversion experience. Moreover, as we shall see in the following chapter, he helped
to imagine a different future, a millennial reign that appeared to be dawning
and that called into question the present order.

Alexander Hewat

Alexander Hewat, an antislavery Tory, came to First (Scots) as its minister
in 1763 and served until the rising passions of revolution sent him hurrying
back to Britain in 1777. Shortly after his arrival in Charlestown, he found that
there was no history of the colony, that no writer had "favoured the world"
with "any tolerable account" of Carolina or Georgia. For his own amusement
he began to gather old documents that told the story of the colony's life. Later,
as his pile of papers grew, he resolved to "arrange them, and form a kind of
historical account of the rise and progress of that settlement." The result was

An Historical Account of the Rise and Progress of the Colonies of South Carolina and Georgia (London, 1779). With its rambling style and long digressions it was no masterpiece, but it was the first genuine history of the state, and it did become an indispensable resource for future historians.[28] Hewat was modest about the work; he called it a rough draft and asked the public to be kind to a young author with his first publication. He knew its limitations. It was, he said, written when Charlestown was "agitated with popular tumults, military parade, and frequent alarms" that had left him in a situation "very unfavourable for calm study and recollection."[29]

Hewat's history not only provided much valuable information about the early years of the colony but also told much about the author himself, as any history does. It consequently helps us see the world as this Presbyterian pastor saw it, to understand the world as he understood it and put his own vision of order upon it.

Hewat was interested in the agriculture and commerce of the colony, its social conditions, its soil and climate. He gave an account of the colony's political history—he was biased against the Lords Proprietors, was for the royal government as a good Tory, and tried mightily to be fair to the Anglican establishment through the eyes of a Scots Presbyterian. He thought geography was important and noted that "when the extreme heat of summer is united with a low marshy soil, where the water stagnates, and the effluvia arising from it thicken and poison the air, it must prove the occasion of a numberless list of fatal distempers." He spoke about the beauty of the landscape and described the plants that thrive on low swampy ground and those that prefer the sand hills. The "rattle-snake" fascinated him. It was, he said, one of "the most formidable living creatures in the whole universe." And he noted—as anyone who has spent a summer in the low country could not avoid noticing—that during the summer millions of "pestiferous gnats, called Moschetoes, are hatched" and "swarm over the country in such numbers, that, during the day, it requires no small trouble for the inhabitants to defend themselves in every quarter against them; and, during the night, gause pavilions are necessarily used, to exclude them from their beds, without which it is impossible to enjoy undisturbed repose."[30] He obviously thought that the environment was an important factor in shaping the way a people live and in understanding their history.

Hewat's history is surprisingly free of those sacred myths that have so influenced the interpreters of American history—at least until the twentieth century. He had no illusions that South Carolina was part of God's New Israel, or that immigrants, fleeing a decadent Europe, were going on a New Exodus, or that America was the Promised Land with a special destiny. Unlike Cotton Mather's *Magnalia Christi Americana* (1702), which was written at the beginning of the eighteenth century to show "Christ's Great Deeds in America," or George Bancroft's *History of the United States* (1876), which sought toward the end of the nineteenth century "to follow the steps by which a favoring Providence, . . . has conducted the country to its present happiness and glory," Hewat took a more secular approach. He gave no hint that he believed the Almighty was at work in any special way in the "rise and progress" of South Carolina as did his fellow Charlestonian David Ramsay in his *The History of South Carolina* (1808). Perhaps this perspective was rooted in Hewat's British background. It would have been strange, after all, for a Tory to believe that God had selected America for some special destiny or to think that a favoring Providence was leading the South Carolinians in a great mission on behalf of the rest of the world. No doubt this Edinburgh graduate had been influenced by the ideals of the Scottish Enlightenment and by the great historian William Robertson, principal of the University of Edinburgh and pastor at Old Greyfriars. Such an influence would have moderated any tendency to see the Almighty guiding the history of a little corner of the British Empire. No doubt many of the Scottish community in Charlestown, which was largely Tory in its sympathies, shared this perspective. Most certainly, however, Hewat's understanding of the history of South Carolina was related to his own abhorrence of slavery and to his convictions about its influence on the life of the colony.

Hewat had no sooner begun his history than he launched into an attack on that "horrid and inhuman practice of dragging Africans into slavery." It is, he wrote, "a difficult matter to conceive a single argument in its defense. It is contrary to all laws of nature and nations to entice, inveigle and compel such multitudes of human creatures, who never injured us, from their native land, and dispose of them like flocks of sheep and cattle to the highest bidder; and, what completes the cruelty and injustice of the traffic, to consign them over to ignorance, barbarism, and perpetual slavery. After this, where will insatiable avarice stop?" Africans, he wrote, as a "free and independent people . . . had unquestionably an equal right to make slaves of the inhabitants of Europe. Nature has given the people of the one continent no superiority over those of the other; the advantages of Europeans were the effects only of art and improvement." Although policy might sanction such a trade, "yet every candid and impartial man must confess, that it is atrocious and unjustifiable in every light in which it can be viewed, and turns merchants into a band of robbers, and trade into atrocious acts of fraud and violence."[31] This was from a man who had been a popular pastor in Charlestown and who had among his congregation a number of merchants who dealt in the international slave trade.

Hewat had unavoidably close contact with slavery in Charlestown. During most of his years in the city the slave ships arrived regularly at Charlestown's wharves and nearly 40,000 African men, women, and children had been "unloaded" at Sullivan's Island for a short quarantine and then sold, often in front of the Exchange Building.[32] Perhaps it was his close contact with slavery, together with his later distance from it, that allowed Hewat to see so clearly its evils, to transcend the ideological forces that blinded others, and to become one of the early voices to speak out so passionately against it. He blasted all arguments in its defense. If, he said, "such a traffic be reasonable and just, there is no crime negroes can commit that may not be defended and justified upon the same principles. . . . Every argument that can be brought in support of the institution of slavery, tends to the subversion of justice and morality in the world."[33]

Hewat, this early champion of antislavery, was also, however, a conservative Tory who loved order, believed in a hierarchical structure for society, and abhorred any movement that might be socially subversive—a difficult position, to say the least, for an antislavery advocate in a slave society. Hewat was able to avoid the tensions in his own thought by leaving the low country and returning to Britain at the time of the Revolution. There, far removed from a social system based on African slavery, he was able to be an advocate of antislavery as well as the status quo. But for those who stayed in the low country and for those who followed in later generations, the tensions remained and grew more intense. Whites within the low country Reformed community would feel in themselves both the powerful pull of a democratic impulse and the stubborn resistance of a hierarchically ordered social system and its supportive world view. For whites in the Reformed tradition, the response would be an increasingly intentional—and often desperate—search for a middle way, a *via media*, between what they regarded as the extremes of one side or the other. This *via media*, holding together competing impulses, would provide a conceptual framework, a cultural imagination, that would long mark the Reformed community of the low country. Important elements of that middle way could be seen in the eighteenth century in William Tennent, Jr.

William Tennent, Jr.

In 1772 William Tennent, Jr., became pastor of the Independent Meeting House, Charlestown. A graduate of Princeton with a master's degree from Harvard, he was closely associated with David Ramsay and other members of his congregation in nurturing a lively intellectual life in Charlestown during the years immediately before the Revolution. Tennent's important role as a patriot in the Revolution, as a member of the provincial assembly and later the commons house of the assembly will be considered in a later chapter. Here it is enough to note the considerable intellectual powers he brought to bear on the political issues of his day. When he died suddenly in 1777, the Reverend Hugh Allison of the James Island Presbyterian Church preached a funeral oration. The sermon not only points to the character of Tennent but also reveals the erudition and values of Allison, a rural Presbyterian pastor:

> Few preachers . . . had a more majestic and venerable presence, or a more winning and oratorical address. Animated with a sacred regard for the honor of his divine Master, and the salvation of precious, immortal souls, he spake the

word with all boldness. A lively imagination, added to a careful study of the Scriptures, enabled him to bring forth out of his treasure things new and old; . . . Elegance of style, majesty of thought, and clearness of judgment, appeared in his discourses, and concurred to render them both pleasing and instructive. . . . His honest, disinterested, yet flaming zeal for the country's good demands from us a tribute of respect. Impressed with a sense of the justice, greatness, and vast importance of the American cause, he engaged in it with an ardor and resolution which would have done honor to an old Roman. . . . But Mr. Tennent's principal ornament was his unaffected and substantial piety. He was remarkably humane and benevolent in his disposition, and possessed every personal grace and qualification that could attract the esteem and reverence of his fellow creatures. . . . His appearance in company was manly and graceful; his behavior genteel, not ceremonious; grave, yet pleasant; and solid, but sprightly too. In a word, he was an open, conversable, and entertaining companion, a polite gentleman and devout Christian at once.[34]

With both Tennent and Allison we hear a disciplined eloquence marked by clarity and simplicity. There is with them, no less than with the meetinghouses in which they preached, an emphasis on authenticity and sincerity, an aversion to that which is ostentatious and pretentious, to any contrivance that obscures the real. Throughout Allison's description of Tennent runs an appreciation for a middle way and moderation that so clearly marked their successors in the nineteenth century: Tennent had a "lively imagination," but it was "added to a careful study of the Scriptures"; he was pious, but his piety was "unaffected"; he possessed a "flaming zeal for the country's good," but even his "flaming zeal" was "disinterested." An "unaffected and substantial piety" was what these pastors most valued. Yet both were not only pastors who stood in the Reformed tradition, they were also gentlemen: "manly and graceful;" "genteel, not ceremonious; grave, yet pleasant; and solid, but sprightly too." By the end of the colonial period, these were the ideals of the Presbyterian and Congregational clergy in the Carolina low country: "an open, conversable, and entertaining companion, a polite gentleman and devout Christian at once." A Reformed faith, a British moral tradition, and a social context were all at work in shaping them into "gentlemen theologians."[35]

Low country meetinghouses, the public rituals enacted within them, and the work of the Reformed pastors provide a coherent picture of the white Reformed community's world view and ethos during the colonial period. A transplanted religious tradition, with its own internal tensions, is revealed in a dialectical relationship with the social context of the low country. Contradictory elements and antithetical impulses are seen to be held together in a kind of complementarity in the community's collective depths, shaping the community's social and cultural imagination. That imagination did not emerge from some "nowhere," but from the interaction of a specific religious tradition with a specific sociohistorical context. How the Reformed community interpreted its world, how it reacted to it, and how it imagined the possibilities for the future were all mediated through a tension-filled but coherent frame of reference.

The tensions within the community's social and cultural imagination will be more clearly visible in a later chapter on the Revolution. Not least among the factors, however, that intensified the competing impulses and made more vivid the contradictions was a revival that broke out across the colonies and came to be known as the Great Awakening. How this great religious upheaval impacted the Reformed community in the low country is the subject of the following chapter.

5

The Tradition Expanded

The Great Awakening

Some great things seem to be upon the anvil, some big prophecy at the birth.

—Josiah Smith in George Howe, *History of the Presbyterian Church in South Carolina*

I N THE MIDDLE years of the eighteenth century, a powerful evangelical movement swept across western Europe, Britain, and the British North American colonies. On the European continent this movement took the form of Pietism, in Britain it centered around the Wesleys and their revivals, and in North America it was called the Great Awakening. In the Carolina low country, it would have an important influence in shaping the composition, world view, and intellectual life of the Reformed community for years to come.

What all these movements had in common was a new and intense piety. A restless longing of the human heart for a warm and personal relationship with God had, of course, deep roots in the Christian faith. But the new piety, expressed in distinct religious movements, emerged out of the tumultuous years of the late 1600s.[1] Many people yearned for a deeper religious life and reacted against the coldness and institutionalization that had captured much of Protestant orthodoxy. This new piety, while not indifferent to orthodoxy, was more interested in what a person felt than in what one believed, was more concerned with the living of a holy life than with the formalities of church organization. Theological orthodoxy, after all, had not prevented the terrors of the wars of religion; indeed, it had helped to intensify them. Rather than splitting theological hairs, or engaging in scholastic debates about theological points, the new piety wanted to encourage a warm, inward spirituality, a missionary zeal, and a concern for charitable activity. Those who were touched by this piety thought it was important for ministers to know theology but believed it was infinitely more important that they know God and that their ministries be shaped by a warm-hearted relationship to Christ. They insisted that the laity be more than observers of religion, that they be committed to the life of the spirit, and that their daily lives reflect the faith they professed. Thus they called for a strong discipline in the church's life and used, as a major strategy for the renewal of the church, small groups of devout people gathered for Bible study and prayer. Such groups were often viewed with great suspicion by church authorities, for they threatened to be disruptive of the regular life of the church and often called into question the legitimacy of "unconverted" church hierarchies. During the eighteenth century, this new piety stood in vigorous opposition to rationalisms of all sorts and what was regarded as the coldness and spiritual emptiness of the Enlightenment.[2]

In the British North American colonies, a series of local revivals in the 1730s prepared the way for a Great Awakening that reached from Georgia to New England.[3] What brought these local revivals together was the powerful preaching of the Anglican evangelist George Whitefield. The power of his preaching, the controversies that surrounded the Great Awakening, and the consequences that flowed from the revivals were nowhere more clearly visible than in colonial South Carolina.

George Whitefield arrived in Charlestown in January 1740, less than four months after the Stono slave rebellion had been crushed.[4] Fugitive rebels were still at large and another slave conspiracy, brewing in Berkeley County, would break out in a few months. Meanwhile a yellow fever epidemic had swept the colony the previous September and October. Before cool weather had finally arrived, the chief justice, the judge of the Vice-Admiralty Court, the surveyor of customs, the clerk of the assembly, and the clerk of the Court of Admiralty, along with scores of residents, had all died from what Lieutenant Governor William Bull called "the sickness with which it hath pleased God to visit this Province." During the following months, South Carolinians joined James Oglethorpe's Georgians in a disastrous attack on Saint Augustine. Then in November 1740, not long after the Carolina troops had straggled back to Charlestown, the most destructive fire of the colonial period swept the city. A strong wind pushed the fire from Broad and Church Streets toward the Cooper River. Before it was over, a third of the city was burned.[5]

In the midst of such tumultuous times, the fires of the Great Awakening swept across the low country. Some of the winds of change swirling through Carolina fanned the flames of the revival. Other winds arising out of the same turbulence stirred fears of social disorder, blew hard against the revival fires, and helped to limit their impact. Yet once the fires had been lit, they were hard to contain, especially once they were linked to those that soon began burning in the backcountry.

Whitefield had been in Charlestown once before, in 1738, when he was a young Anglican deacon only recently out of Oxford. Then he had been cordially received by the Anglican establishment and had been invited to preach at

Saint Philip's Church, which he did with great success. Whitefield noted "the neatness of the buildings and the largeness of the place." Alexander Garden, the bishop of London's commissary for the Carolinas, had been hospitable and Whitefield had called him a "good soldier of Jesus Christ."[6] But on his return to Charlestown in 1740, Whitefield had a quite different reception. The Anglican establishment in the city had not changed, but Whitefield had become a controversial evangelist. In England he had joined the Wesleys as itinerant ministers, disregarding the etiquette of parish bounds and "intruding" into the established territory of parish ministers. Moreover, he had raised questions about the piety of the Anglican clergy, charging them with slipping into Arminianism[7] and of emphasizing good works rather than justification by faith.[8] He had returned to the colonies in 1739 and made a triumphant campaign from Philadelphia to New York before turning south and arriving in Charlestown in January 1740.

Word of Whitefield's triumphs and his charges had reached Charlestown before he did, and he was not allowed to preach in Saint Philip's Church. Undeterred, he accepted an invitation from Josiah Smith of the Independent Meeting House and preached there on Sunday afternoon before a congregation that was "large, but very polite." Whitefield wondered in his journal "whether the court-end of London could exceed them in affected finery" and "gaiety of dress." He reminded them in his sermon of those "Divine judgments lately sent amongst them"—the Stono Rebellion and the epidemics of fever—and pointed out how their deportment was ill-becoming a people who had suffered so grievously for their sins. But, he noted, "I seemed to them as one who mocked."[9]

The next morning he preached in the French Huguenot Church before an even larger crowd, which flowed out of the building into the street. Many wept openly, and when the service was over the people left, not in a "light and unthinking manner" as they had done the day before, but with "a visible concern" on most of their faces. Whitefield was scheduled to leave for Savannah but was prevailed upon to preach again, which he did, before leaving the city for Georgia. In Savannah he was occupied for several months with his plans for building an orphanage for the homeless children that thronged the young colony. He took time, however, to write *A Letter to the Inhabitants of Maryland, Virginia, North and South Carolina*. In it he called for the evangelization of the slaves; show me, he said, a slave who has been "born again" and who has become a worse servant. He denounced the Anglican clergy in the South and the general state of religion in the Southern colonies. The recent disasters that had befallen South Carolina were clear signs of God's displeasure: "God first generally corrects us with Whips; if that will not do, he must chastise us with Scorpions."[10]

When Whitefield returned to Charlestown in March 1740, the battle lines were clearly drawn: on one side stood Alexander Garden, able spokesman for the establishment; on the other side stood Whitefield, unsurpassed as an orator, the prophet of a new way. Whitefield believed Garden to be not only "dry bones" but also unorthodox. Garden condemned the "crude Enthusiastick Notions" propagated by "Mr. Whitefield and his Brethren Methodists" and called for his Charlestown parishioners to turn from Whitefield, from the passions and prejudices of the Awakening, to the sound and reasonable position of the established church.[11] In the months that followed and for several years, letters and sermons were published attacking one side or the other, the local *Gazette* was full of the controversy, and the public was widely divided on the subject. Thirty years after Whitefield's first visit to Charlestown, local ministers were still debating the issues surrounding the Grand Itinerant.[12]

Whitefield preached when he was in Charlestown at the Independent Meeting House, at First (Scots), at the Huguenot Church, and at the Baptist Church. When he traveled into the countryside, he preached in Dorchester at the meetinghouse, at James Island and Johns Island at the Presbyterian churches there and at Bethel Pon Pon. When he traveled by land to Savannah, he stayed with Hugh Bryan and Stephen Bull, Jr., who, at least on one occasion, followed him to Savannah to hear him preach.[13] Many Presbyterians and Congregationalists—although not all by any means—were clearly receptive to Whitefield's message. There was no Old Side/New Side division among South Carolina Presbyterians and Congregationalists as there was in the Middle Colonies and New England, no formal split between those who supported the Awakening and those who opposed it.[14] But there were differences and they were reflected in the theological controversies that erupted between Garden and Whitefield. These controversies anticipated and illumined most of the issues that emerged from the Great Awakening to trouble the land. But they also pointed to the tensions within the Reformed tradition and the ways they emerged in the midst of a shifting social context.

First was the clash between the theology of the revival leaders and the "rational Christianity" of those who felt the pull of Sir Isaac Newton's harmonious universe. Unlike the Wesleys, who took an evangelical Arminian position, Whitefield and the colonial Awakening emphasized the old Reformed position of the sovereignty of God. Few would express this position more powerfully than John Newton, a young officer on a slave ship. On a visit to Charlestown, Newton heard Josiah Smith preach at the Independent Meeting House. Smith's words moved him, yet, wrote Newton later, they were "ineffectual" until they are "explained and applied by the Spirit of God, who alone can open the heart." The young seaman went to pray in the Carolina woods where he began to "taste the sweets of communion."[15] Later in England under the influence of Whitefield, Newton was converted, repented of his part in the international slave trade, and wrote the great hymn

Amazing grace—how sweet the sound—
  That saved a wretch like me!
I once was lost, but now am found,
  Was blind, but now I see.[16]

Garden, in contrast, insisted that humanity has an active role in the process of regeneration and is not simply the passive recipient of unmerited grace. Humanity, said Garden, "co-operates" with the Spirit as people throughout the whole course of their lives grow in grace.[17] Garden's associate at Saint Philip's, Samuel Quincy, went even further and declared that Christianity is a "Rational Religion." The "Doctrines of Christianity," he said, "are founded in Truth and Reason, and capable of being supported by clear and rational Arguments."[18] Those in the Reformed tradition agreed, of course, that reason is important, but they insisted that there are points beyond which reason cannot go. Moreover, most of those in the Reformed tradition also insisted that if the heart were not strangely warmed by the Spirit, then reason's best efforts were "ineffectual." The conflict between the Reformed view of fallen humanity and the Enlightenment's confident smile of reason was well under way. In the nineteenth century it would lead to a division within the Independent Meeting House and the formation of the Unitarian Church in Charleston.

A second issue focused on the nature of evangelical preaching that stirred the heart and aroused the "passions." The preaching of Whitefield and other leading evangelists of the Awakening was, it needs to be noted, far from the ecstatic outbursts of nineteenth-century revivalists. They were people of substantial intellectual attainments; one needs only think of Jonathan Edwards, who soared far above any other colonial thinker. Their preaching was disciplined but it did move the heart—and was intended to do so. Josiah Smith described the impact of Whitefield's preaching on Charlestown:

> *The Awe, the Silence, the Attention,* which sat upon the face of so great an audience, was an Argument how he could reign over all their powers. Many thought, *He spoke as never man spoke,* before him. So charmed were people with his manner of address, that they shut up their shops, forgot their secular business, and laid aside their schemes for the world; and the oftener he preached, the keener he seemed to put upon their desires of hearing him again! How awfully, with what thunder and sound did he discharge the artillery of Heaven upon us? And yet, how could he soften and melt even a soldier of Ulysses, with the love and mercy of God![19]

Rhetoric, the art of persuasion, was being used by Whitefield to touch the hearts of the people. In this bold use of rhetoric, Whitefield evoked one of the deep impulses of the Reformed tradition of which he was so much a part.[20] Language, for Whitefield, was power. It touched the whole person who was not merely an intellect, moved by rational conviction, but a passionate, active, and social being.

Garden, the English commissary, heard something quite different in Whitefield's preaching than did Smith, the Carolina-born grandson of a colonial governor. Garden was convinced that Whitefield was a mere demagogue whose mastery of dramatic rhetoric alone accounted for his success. It was "not the Matter but the Manner" of Whitefield's preaching, Garden told the Charlestonians, "not the Doctrines he delivered, but the Agreeableness of the Delivery," that had all the effect upon you."[21] But for the evangelist, what mattered was a person's heart. If the heart were not touched, if it did not *experience* the overwhelming regenerating power of God's grace, then it was lost. Critics could deplore preaching that "aroused the passions," but Whitefield and the revivalists that followed him insisted that their method of evangelical preaching was inseparably linked to their message. "With what a Flow of words, what a ready profusion of language, did he speak to us upon the great concerns of our souls," exclaimed Josiah Smith. "In what a flaming light did he set our eternity before us! How earnestly did he press Christ upon us! How did he move our passions, with the constraining love of such a Redeemer!"[22] Theirs was a revolution not only of rhetoric but also of logic, for what mattered most to them was not the internal logic of their doctrine but the doctrines' *effectiveness* in reaching and converting the human heart.[23]

With the human heart as the target of evangelical preaching, the experience of regeneration became a third subject of great debate. What did it mean to be "born again"? What was the nature of such an experience? How critical was it for the Christian life? Whitefield never explored these questions to great depth—that would be left to Jonathan Edwards's *The Distinguishing Marks of the Spirit of God* (1741) and his great *A Treatise Concerning Religious Affections* (1746). If Whitefield did not plunge with Edwards to these theological and philosophical depths, he obviously prayed and preached for conversions, for the miraculous touching of the heart by the Spirit.

For Garden, on the other hand, the "Work of *Regeneration* is not the Work of a *Moment,* a sudden *instantaneous* Work, like the *miraculous* Conversion of St. *Paul,* or the *Thief* on the Cross; but a *gradual* and *co-operative* Work of the *Holy Spirit,* joining in with our *Understandings,* and leading us on by *Reason* and *Persuasion,* from one Degree to another, of Faith, good Dispositions, Acts, and Habits of Piety."[24] An important shift was taking place here, whichever side of the debate one took. The older theological concern had centered around the will of God. Now the focus was shifting to the nature and experience of humanity. The human personality began to become the great object for analysis and in this focus the Awakening showed itself to be a harbinger of the modern world. It was for this reason that George Howe, writing in the nineteenth century his *History of the Presbyterian Church in South Carolina,* called Whitefield "that paragon of successful pulpit eloquence, . . . who, though disowned by his own church, had no small share in introducing that epoch which is the starting-point of our modern religious history."[25] Howe, a member of Charleston Presbytery, saw as he reviewed the region's history a turning point with the Awakening, for what followed Whitefield was "modern religious history," a period when religion would become increasingly a matter of feeling and experience.

Garden's antagonistic perspective toward the Awakening was shared by some of the Presbyterian ministers in the low country. Thirty years after Whitefield's first trip to Charlestown, Alexander Hewat of First (Scots) was still speaking "against Mr. Whitefield and ministers of his stamp." Hewat, under the influence of the Scottish Enlightenment and "Moderatism" in the Church of Scotland, was no friend of the Awakening and reflected that side of the Reformed tradition that championed order, harmony, and rationality. In his history of South Carolina, Hewat wrote that Whitefield, "this wanderer," "actuated by religious motives . . . several times passed the Atlantic to convert the Americans, whom he addressed in such a manner as if they had been all equal strangers to the privileges and benefits of religion with the original inhabitants of the forest." Alexander Garden, Hewat noted, "a man of some sense and erudition," in order to put the people of Carolina upon their guard, pointed out to them "the pernicious tendency" of Whitefield's "wild doctrines and irregular manner of life."[26]

But other Presbyterians and Congregationalists supported Whitefield. Josiah Smith, as has been seen, was an ardent supporter of Whitefield, and the Independent Meeting House, with all of its social, political, and economic influence, was a center of those who supported the Awakening.[27] In the decade before the Revolution, Archibald Simpson, pastor of Stoney Creek and founder of the Saltketcher Church, took issue with Hewat and those who spoke disparagingly of Whitefield. "I thought it my duty to speak freely," he wrote in his journal of a conversation with Hewat, "and stand up for the preaching warmly and zealously the doctrines of grace, the necessity of regeneration, the Catholic practice of preaching in all pulpits, employing pious ministers of every denomination, and holding occasional communion with all sound Protestants, with all Christians who held of the glorious Head, and both lay and ministerial communion."[28] Hewat and Simpson can consequently be seen as expressing, as the low country meetinghouses and their rituals expressed, the antithetical impulses within the Reformed tradition: rational conviction versus persuasion, hierarchies versus an egalitarian vision, boundaries and rigid systems versus freedom and openness.

Simpson's remarks provide a hint of a fourth issue that emerged from the Awakening and had important consequences—the Awakening's challenge to social stability and order. Whitefield intruded into Garden's territory, and Garden attempted to use his ecclesiastical authority to discipline him for his impertinences and the charges he had made against the Anglican clergy. The evangelist was called before an ecclesiastical court, tried by Garden, and after a two-year delay suspended from ministerial office within Garden's commissarial jurisdiction. Whitefield ignored the suspension and went on preaching. Garden was clearly no bishop, and what little authority he had could be disregarded. But the trial itself was not ignored. From New England came this warning:

> And thus Ends this famous & **FIRST** *Ecclesiastical* or rather *Clergical Court* in the British Colonies. . . . To begin with a *young Clergyman* of such extraordinary Sanctity of Manners, and of such flaming Zeal to promote the highest Degrees of Piety. . . . It cannot possibly recommend *these Courts* to the Esteem of the British Colonies; but rather to their universal and great Displeasure. For tho' the *common People* in *Europe* are generally so ignorant and weak as to hug the Chains of the Clergy, and keep them on as fast and long as possible—the **AMERICANS** live in a freer Air, more generally taste the Sweets of Liberty; and being nearer an Equality of Birth and Wealth, there being Land enough for every industrious Person; there are fewer among them in Dependence on others, they are generally more knowing than the *common People* in Europe, and are not likely for several Ages, or as long as this near Equality remains, to desire the Dominion of the Clergy over them.[29]

To the writer, Garden represented an old, decrepit Europe, a world of widespread ignorance and an authoritarian religion. But the **"AMERICANS,"** it was declared, living in a freer air, take a new way. Many feared the revivals precisely because of this new way, because the revivals threatened to introduce anarchy, to overthrow old established ways, and to make the individual's *experience* the measure of all things.

The Awakening encouraged a catholic spirit, a willingness to go beyond denominational rivalries and unite with other Christian brothers and sisters. The foundation was being laid for an evangelical consensus united for the cause of making America, and indeed the whole world, Christian on the basis of an evangelical vision. America would be seen as God's New Israel and the Awakening would be regarded as a sign of the approaching millennium. "What we now see in America," wrote Jonathan Edwards of the Awakening, "and especially in New England, may prove the dawn of that glorious day."[30] In South Carolina Josiah Smith declared: "It looks as if some happy period were opening, to bless the world with another reformation. Some great things seem to be upon the anvil, some big prophecy at the birth."[31] Here was a utopian vision full of dangers to the present social order, for it had the potential of providing a perspective from which to judge the arrangements of power in the low country and to challenge the dominant ways of imagining reality.

A Jubilee trumpet seemed to be sounding to awaken the people both to some great coming event and to their own power to decide for themselves and to act on behalf of their own welfare in light of their own experience. More than the anarchy let loose by the passions of the heart, more than the disorderly intrusion of itinerants into the territory of established parishes, this new sense of independence and this new confidence in the will of the people were threats to the establishment.

Whatever later historians might think, Alexander Hewat, looking back from the revolutionary years with the perspective of a Carolina Loyalist, saw a clear connection between the Revolution and the Awakening.[32] Whitefield's great ambition, wrote Hewat, "was to be the founder of a new sect, regulated entirely by popular fancy and caprice, depending on the gifts of nature, regardless of the improvements of education and all ecclesiastical laws and institutions." Following Whitefield was a "servile race of ignorant and despicable imitators" who sprung up and "wandered from place to place, spreading doctrines subversive of all public order and peace." Hewat acknowledged that Whitefield himself was a "friend to civil government," but his followers in America had been "distinguished for the contrary character, and have, for the most part, discovered an aversion to our [British] constitution both of church and state." No man, wrote the Tory pastor of First (Scots), "ought to claim any lordship over the conscience; but when the consciences of obstinate sectaries become civil nuisances, and destructive of public tranquillity, they ought to be restrained by legal authority."[33]

Those touched by the fires of the Awakening in the low country challenged Hewat's understanding of a hierarchical social order. What right did he have to call them "obstinate sectaries"?[34] With a new confidence in the authority of their own experience, they were unwilling to recognize the right of those "above" to make such distinctions or to decide what was in their best interest. Yet such radical propositions were dangerous in South Carolina, even for those who claimed them. A careful line had to be drawn in a slave society between black and white, and that line helped to limit, as we shall see, the impact of the Awakening's revolutionary message in the low country.

Church Growth

If the Awakening had an impact on the low country, some signs of church growth, some new indications of religious vitality, might be expected even in a region where the white population was small and had difficulty maintaining its numbers. Such signs would be needed to contradict the general image, rooted in the old "Cavalier myth," that there was no Awakening in the low country and that the stirrings connected with Whitefield had little impact on the region.

The signs of growth and religious vitality are visible and, though not written boldly across the sky, they do indicate a religious stirring following White-field's visits. The Baptists, weak and badly divided before 1740, entered a period of revivals that lasted throughout the remaining colonial years. Under the leadership of Oliver Hart, pastor of the First Baptist Church of Charlestown, the Charles Town Baptist Association was formed in 1751, the second Baptist association in America. They were "Particular Baptists"—that is, strongly Calvinistic—and adopted the "Philadelphia Confession," which was the Westminster Confession modified in regard to baptism.[35] By the time of the Revolution there were forty Baptist churches in South Carolina, and while most of these were in the up-country, their growth was substantial in the low country.[36]

Anglicans also felt the impact of the Awakening. While many supported Garden's moderate rationalism and feared the social disorders and implications of the Awakening, others were touched by the new evangelical zeal.[37] Slow but steady growth in the number of communicants can be seen in a number of the parishes. In 1751 the new parish of Saint Michael's was created in Charlestown, and while there were many factors at work in its creation, one was a certain religious vitality. If Anglicans enjoyed their liturgy and the restraints of "reasonable religion," many Anglicans also practiced a deep piety that was nurtured both by Anglican traditions and by the Awakening fires. Anglican vestries in the years following the Awakening moved toward an even greater independence from hierarchical authorities, approaching the position of many Dissenters. One disgruntled minister complained to the bishop of London that "the Principles of most of the colonists in America are independent in Matters of religion, as well as Republican in those of Government."[38]

Among the Presbyterians and Congregationalists throughout the low country, the most visible signs of the Awakening's influence were in their numerical growth and increased vitality between 1740 and 1770. The Stoney Creek and the Saltketcher churches were organized. New meetinghouses were built for the Bethel church and the Wilton congregation. In Charlestown the Independent Meeting House and First (Scots) found it necessary in the years before the Revolution to enlarge their church buildings. By the time of the Revolution, the Independent Meeting House was growing so rapidly that it was necessary to lay plans for a second building to house its expanding but still united congregation. These increases in church membership (most of which was white) and vitality took place at a time when the white population of the low country was not growing but rather struggling to maintain its numbers.[39] If the Awakening was not a great transforming fire sweeping the low country, it was nevertheless a fire that left an enduring mark on the religious life of the low country.

Clearly those within the Reformed tradition in the low country began to see the world in new if not radically altered ways after the Awakening. A new piety entered the region's meetinghouses, and if it did not disrupt their orderly ways, it did bring important shifts in the atmosphere and in the substance of the Reformed tradition. Feeling and experience, although always carefully balanced with reason, would come to play a more important part in the intellectual and religious life of the community. In no way, however, was the tradition expanded more visibly than in the increased numbers of African Americans who joined the churches. Within three generations the number of black members of the Johns Island Church, for example, would outnumber the whites ten to one. These African Americans brought with them their own history and traditions, their own way of viewing the world from "underneath," from "the bottom" of society, and the result was the emergence of a distinct African American Reformed tradition in the low country.

African Americans and the Awakening

Throughout Whitefield's low country travels and the controversies that followed him, a new interest in Christianity began to stir among black Carolinians. They were largely at the edges of the Awakening, peering in from the dark bondage of slavery at what was happening around the revival fires, wondering if here might be some genuine light and warmth and hope for them. Most rejected what they saw and found nothing appealing in the religious fervor of white oppressors. But some were drawn toward the Awakening fires, seeing in their dancing flames both images from their past and light for their future. In Charlestown, a few sought out Whitefield and talked to him. Others began, here and there, to be baptized and to join the churches. There was no rush to the churches, but a perceptible increase can be noticed in the years before the Revolution.[40] The ground was being prepared for a distinctive African-American Christianity to emerge from low country shadows.

One white who was moved by Whitefield's call to evangelize slaves was the wealthy planter Hugh Bryan. In him the tensions stirred by the Awakening came rushing to the surface in near schizophrenic behavior. A great admirer of Whitefield, Bryan had with his distinguished neighbor and brother-in-law Stephen Bull, Jr., followed the evangelist to Savannah to hear more of his sermons. Whitefield stayed with Bryan at his Granville County plantation when he passed through the region. On a visit to Charlestown when Whitefield was preaching, Bryan met William Hutson and invited him to return with him to his plantation and to become a teacher to his slaves. Hutson accepted the invitation, apparently serving in this capacity for several years before being ordained as the founding pastor of the Stoney Creek church with Bryan and his brother Jonathan as officers. Hutson, who had been trained for law at the Inns of Court, London, later became pastor of the Independent Meeting House, Charlestown. His registry shows that he baptized some slaves both at Stoney Creek and at the Independent Meeting House.[41]

More sensational than these educational efforts were Bryan's gathering in the woods, evidently in the neighborhood of his plantation, large numbers of whites and blacks together for revival services.[42] Some whites became alarmed, especially so soon after the Stono Rebellion, and a grand jury was called. It charged Bryan with uttering enthusiastic prophecies of the "destruction of Charles-Town, and of assembling great bodies of negroes under pretence of religious worship, contrary to law" and detrimental to the public peace. He was even said to have secured firearms in Charlestown for some dangerous purposes and to have assured slaves that they would one day be free. A warrant was issued for his arrest, but before it was delivered he saw the dangers of his "delusion." He became aware that the "invisible spirit" he had been listening to was none other than the "father of lies."

The spirit, Bryan believed, had commanded him to take a rod, like the great slave-liberator Moses, and with it divide the waters of the river (the Combahee?). When the waters refused to obey his command, Bryan plunged into them, wading deeper and deeper, striking with the rod, until his brother Jonathan, who was following him as fast as he could, reached him and saved him from drowning. The brother urged Bryan to go home, but the "invisible spirit" told him if he did he would die before morning. The cold weather and wet clothes prevailed, however, and when he found himself alive the next morning, he concluded that he had been listening all along to the "father of lies." Bryan must have realized then that he was no Moses and that he would be leading no slaves to freedom and the Promised Land. Whites in Carolina low country might imagine "some great things" to be "upon the anvil, some big prophecy at the birth," but those "great things" were not to be for slaves. The impulse that drove Bryan toward a radical utopian vision must be controlled, boundaries must be honored, and rigid systems maintained.

Immediately upon the discovery of his delusion, Bryan wrote on March 1, 1742, a letter to the commons house of the assembly, confessing his errors and asking pardon. "I find," he wrote, "that I have presumed, in my zeal for God's glory, beyond his will, and that he has suffered me to fall into a delusion of Satan." In a postscript, Bryan added: "May we all keep close to the law and to the testimony of our God, and hearken to no other revelation of divine truth, and watch and pray, that we enter not into temptation, is a further prayer of your most unworthy servant."[43] A clear line indeed had to be kept between blacks and whites. All needed to be "kept close to the law" and to the sure "testimony of our God." One was not to be presumptuous and go "beyond" God's will or one's allotted sphere and task. There was no place in South Carolina for a Moses to lead slaves out of the house of bondage, out of the land of Egypt—to think of such a utopian possibility was nothing less than "a delusion of Satan." Yet Bryan had stirred the waters even if he had not been able to divide them. Like his mentor Whitefield, he had challenged the social stability and order of the low country. Moreover he had helped to let loose among black slaves the great biblical image of Moses as liberator, an image blacks would appropriate in powerful ways as they shaped an African American religious tradition. And there were institutional results as well. The slave Andrew Bryan— he was owned by Hugh's brother Jonathan—touched by the revival stirrings that swirled around Stoney Creek, became the pastor of one of the earliest independent black churches in America (the First African Church of Savannah) and an important leader in early African-American Christianity.[44]

The radicalism of the Awakening and the image of Moses as liberator had to go underground for African American slaves, kept alive by oral tradition and the music of the spirituals. "Go down Moses," they would sing in the years ahead, "tell ole Pharoah to let my people go." Many white South Carolinians would also hear in the Awakening a liberation theme. But, like Hugh Bryan, they had to handle carefully any utopian vision, for they felt the power of countervailing impulses, believed that chaos and anarchy could erupt if not held in check, and knew that limits had to be imposed on themes of liberation and explorations of the possible. Whites might imagine an alternative future, but African Americans, it was believed, must be kept in their place, convinced that the present order was the unchanging, eternal order, the "way things are." The adrenaline that pushed whites toward revolution thus pushed them toward a defense of African-American slavery, for, as we shall see, they believed the two to be inseparable. Convinced that their own freedom was inseparably linked to the slavery of African Americans who surrounded them in the low country, whites in the Reformed community internalized powerful contradictions and brought them into a tense harmony.

These antithetical impulses and seemingly incompatible contradictions, these utopian visions and profoundly ideological reactions, were held together in the community's collective depths in a kind of complementarity—a single conceptual framework of a middle way, a *via media,* that increasingly marked the Reformed community. Such a framework was the lens through which the white Reformed community viewed the world—indeed it was the social imagination by which the white Reformed community helped to construct its own little world moving as it was toward 1776 and revolution.

6

Competing Impulses
Tories, Whigs, and the Revolution

IN THE American Revolution, South Carolinians fought a bloody civil war and not simply a war between opposing armies. "Savage" is the way many contemporaries described the often brutal fighting that raged across the state, especially after 1780. "The Whigs and Tories," wrote General Nathanael Greene, "pursue one another with the most relentless fury, killing and destroying each other wherever they meet."[1]

As many as one-fifth of South Carolina's whites may have taken the path of loyalty to Great Britain in 1775. After the fall of Charlestown to the British in 1780, another substantial group of white Carolinians, "protectionists," came forward and took an oath of allegiance to the king. Some of these protectionists were rebels at heart—some, including Rawlins Lowndes, Charles Pinckney, Daniel Horry, and Arthur Middleton, had even been leaders in the Revolution—but believed the British had all but won the war and that it was time to accept defeat. Others were Loyalists at heart but had accepted the earlier American victories and remained in the state under the revolutionary government. Thus a neat classification of people into either a Loyalist or a Patriot camp was not always easy to make, for as the fortunes of war ebbed and flowed for one side or the other, Carolinians were forced to decide their allegiance not one time but several. Of course there were also those who took their stand early and did not deviate. Some refused to abandon their allegiance to Britain and regarded those who did as lawbreakers and rebels. Others were uncompromising revolutionaries determined that the land be free of foreign control.[2]

Given such divisions, it is not surprising that those in the low country who stood in the Reformed tradition also divided and that their divisions were bitter and sometimes ambiguous. The Revolution brought forcefully into the open the tensions and antithetical impulses inherent in the Reformed tradition, illustrated the role of social context in shaping which impulse would dominate which part of the Reformed community in the low country, and pointed toward the ways the community would seek in the years ahead to find some *via media* between the competing tendencies of its tradition.

The divisions within the Reformed community were most clearly revealed in Charlestown in the differences between the strong Tory stance of First (Scots) and the Patriot leadership provided by the Independent Meeting House. The members of these two congregations, together with those in Presbyterian and Congregational churches in the countryside, were, of course, part of the broader community of the low country and belonged to other subgroups in addition to a distinct religious community. Overlapping boundaries linked the church members to several circles of influence that had their own economic functions, self-interests, and ideologies. Nevertheless, a picture emerges of Reformed congregations that reveals within them a general coherence in their response to the Revolution. This social and political unity suggests that the congregations functioned as powerful centers of cultural identity in the midst of the trauma and changing tides of war.

Low Country Tories

In the years leading to the Revolution and throughout the war, the Scottish community in Charlestown remembered a British home and remained faithful to a British king. Many in the Scottish community were recent immigrants. Most were merchants or artisan-shopkeepers. Others were printers, government officials, shipbuilders, and physicians. Many had business interests that helped to strengthen their attachments to Britain.

How many in the Scottish community were members of First (Scots) is not known (the records, taken to Columbia for safekeeping during the Civil War, were lost when that city was burned), but it can be safely assumed that most had some contact with the church, for they were a clannish bunch.[3] "*Scratch me, Countryman!—and I'll scratch thee*" was their prevailing attitude, complained the *South Carolina Gazette*.[4] Along with the Saint Andrews Society, the "Scotch" church provided a focal point in their community life and an important means of maintaining their national identity. When the Reverend Archibald Simpson returned to the city after the war, he noted in his journal that at the Scotch meetinghouse the congregation was "much broken up and scattered, the most of that congregation having joined the British and gone off with them when they evacuated this town." "The Scotch church," he wrote, "was a place for the Royalists from the country to live in."[5]

Among the ten trustees of First (Scots)—whose names are known—seven Tories can be positively identified.[6] Their experiences in the Revolution point to what must have been similar experiences of others in the congregation. Robert Rowand had come to Charlestown in 1756. He followed his brother-in-law, Robert Wells, who had come to the city earlier in the decade and established a successful printing and bookstore business. Wells's "Great Stationery and Book-Store on the Bay" was the largest bookstore south of Philadelphia, and his newspaper, the *South Carolina and American General Gazette*, was an important Tory voice in the city.[7] Rowand, following his brother-in-law, established himself as a merchant in the city. When war broke out, he refused to take the oath of allegiance to the state and was for a time confined in Charlestown and then at his plantation near Georgetown. When the opportunity presented itself, he chose to leave the state.[8]

Other Tory trustees of the congregation were James Johnson, William Ancrum, Robert Philp, Alexander Chisolm, William Glen, and Dr. Robert Wilson. Johnson was the attorney general of the royal government of South Carolina at the conclusion of the war. After helping to negotiate terms with state authorities, he returned with other royal officials to Britain. Ancrum and Philp had remained in the city after the beginning of the war as "reluctant rebels," but when the city was taken by the British in 1780, they came forward and took oaths of allegiance to the king. Philp served on two commissions set up by Lord Cornwallis that were charged with providing services to the city. He left when the British evacuated the city, joined the exile community in London, and evidently never returned to South Carolina. Ancrum, who had been in Charlestown at least since 1754 and had extensive business connections, had his property confiscated by the state government. Through his Camden associates Joseph and Eli Kershaw, he succeeded in having the confiscation repealed and instead was fined for having taken the protection of the British—a course followed by the state government with a number of Tories who did not vigorously support the British authorities.[9] Such was the case with Alexander Chisolm, another trustee of First (Scots). William Glen and Dr. Robert Wilson were "Petitioners to the British Commandant of Charles Town to be Amerced as Loyal Militia" and had "their Estates confiscated & their Persons to be Banished from the State."[10] Glen stayed in Britain, but Dr. Wilson evidently had his banishment lifted, as he was one of the elders when the church was reorganized in 1784. Among those banished was the Reverend Alexander Hewat. He too had his property confiscated for refusing to take an oath of allegiance to the new government at the beginning of the war. Included in his confiscated property was a thousand-acre plantation in Craven County that he had bought in 1772.[11] In such ways as these, the congregation of First (Scots) was "much broken up and scattered."

Among the Reformed clergy, most were vigorous supporters of the Revolution, but Alexander Hewat stands out as a Tory. Hewat, who was pastor of First (Scots) for fourteen years, returned to Britain in 1777 as revolutionary fervor struck Charlestown. An intimate friend of Lieutenant Governor—and sometimes Acting Governor—William Bull, Hewat moved in the highest circles of those loyal to the British Crown.[12] In his *An Historical Account of the Rise and Progress of the Colonies of South Carolina and Georgia,* he recounted the events leading to the Revolution. He wrote of the great benefits that flowed to the colonies from British trade and protection and intimated that the colonists were at heart simply British people living in a colonial context. But most of all he was incensed by the concessions of Parliament under William Pitt. What followed Pitt's return to Parliament, he wrote, "is disgraceful to Great Britain, being entirely composed of lenient concessions in favour of a rising usurpation, and of such shameful weakness and timidity in the ministry, as afterward rendered the authority of the British parliament in America feeble and contemptible." The repeal of the Stamp Act encouraged the "rising usurpation" and gave "such importance to the licentious party in America, and such superiority over the good and loyal subjects, as had a manifest tendency to throw the colonies into a state of anarchy and confusion."[13]

Hewat reveals the heart of the Tory argument: to challenge the legally established government was an irrational invitation to chaos and anarchy. The "licentious party" did not respect hierarchically established authority and depended upon their "private judgments." Hewat had disparaged George Whitefield and the Great Awakening for precisely the same reason: they encouraged people to walk by the light of their own experience, to reject authority from above, and to act on their own behalf. Now this same doctrine was at work in the political arena, and it was "subversive of all good government."[14]

What Hewat was reflecting in his argument was not only the Tory position but also the Reformed tradition's deep-seated fear of disorder, collapsing boundaries, and the "terror of the abyss." It was this fear within the Reformed tradition—and its corresponding impulse to seek order, harmony, and balance and to find in hierarchically structured systems the fundamental principle for ordering society—that marked the First (Scots) congregation as a congregation in its response to the Revolution. As we shall see, the social location of the membership was a critical factor in bringing this conservative side of the Reformed tradition to dominate the ethos and world view of the Scots congregation.

Patriots

Edward McCrady wrote in 1901: "We have pointed out the anomalous fact in the history of the Revolution in South Carolina that all of its leaders were churchmen [Anglicans], and that the dissenters took no conspicuous part in the movement. The leaders of the Revolution in South Carolina, with the exception of Gadsden, perhaps, were cavaliers in heart—they were devoted to the throne and to the church."[15]

Such was the power of the "Cavalier myth" in South Carolina that even so careful a historian as McCrady could express this view, which was echoed as well by later historians.[16] Without diminishing the important role of the Anglicans in the Revolution, it is also true that many of the leaders of the Revolution in the low country were Dissenters. Moreover, in their vigorous support of the Revolution they reflected a powerful impulse within the Reformed tradition and utilized its rhetoric to support the struggle against "British tyranny."

If First (Scots) was a center of Tory sentiment, the Independent Meeting House was a hotbed of revolutionary activity and reflected a competing impulse within the Reformed tradition—one that feared the enclosing bounds of the old order, that saw tyranny rooted in excess, and that believed a republic represented the best of all political systems.[17] The position of the congregation is indicated by its call to the Reverend William Tennent, Jr., to be its pastor in 1772. Tennent, as has been seen, was from a family famous in the Middle Colonies for its part in the Great Awakening and in the establishment of Princeton. Not long after the young pastor arrived in Charlestown (he was only thirty-two years old and held a degree from Princeton and a master's degree from Harvard), he began to address the great political issues before the community. He delivered *An Address, Occasioned by the Late Invasion of the Liberties of the American Colonies by the British Parliament.* "An unnatural Dispute," he declared, "hath arisen between *Britain* and the *American* Colonies, and the Question is of no less Magnitude than whether we . . . shall be reduced to a State of the most Abject Slavery." He was soon writing anonymous letters to the Charlestown papers on the actions of Parliament. In one he called on "the Ladies of South Carolina" to give up their tea as a way of resisting British tyranny. "Every ounce of tea you buy," he warned, "will, I fear, be paid for by the blood of your sons."[18]

Tennent was particularly outraged in 1774 by the action of the Episcopal clergy in Massachusetts in supporting the appointment of General Thomas Gage as governor of that colony. Behind his outrage was a long-smoldering controversy over church and state that now burst into flame and became one of the most heated issues of the revolutionary years. For decades Anglican leaders had been calling for the establishment of a colonial episcopacy. Bishops, it was said, would provide much needed leadership for the Anglican Church in the colonies, would end the need for Anglican colonials to travel to England for ordination, and would support the clergy in their struggles with the laity. With the appointment of bishops, the episcopal system would be in every way immeasurably strengthened.

Tennent shared the widespread belief that the attempt to secure colonial bishops was part of an ecclesiastical conspiracy. It was, he thought, an effort to impose episcopacy on the colonies and to strengthen British control over a free people. Bishops, after all, were members of Parliament who sat in the House of Lords. They identified with the nobility, had been vigorous ministers of the king in secular matters, and had been leaders in the oppression of Dissenters in England. Not only were past memories of episcopal tyranny revived, but the fears of an "Anglican plot" grew at the very time Parliament was attempting to assert its authority over the colonies. For Tennent, the two appeared to be linked, for bishops no less than taxes would be established on the basis of parliamentary authority. He joined the cry echoing through the colonies: "No Lords Spiritual or Temporal!"

In August 1774, Tennent wrote a letter to the *South Carolina Gazette; and Country Journal* in which he bitterly attacked the Anglican clergy of New England for supporting the appointment of General Gage as governor of Massachusetts. He began, shrewdly enough, by pointing to the contrasting development of the Church of England in the Southern colonies. In these colonies the Anglicans had adopted the position of the Dissenters: "The spirit of the Church of England in these Southern provinces shews that her members have as high a sense of the rights of mankind as any in the world. The Congregational discipline has been established in those colonies from their beginning. Their ancestors fled from the hand of Episcopal tyranny in the intemperate days of Laud. They brought with them, they have handed down, a spirit of independency and a resolution to think for themselves." If Tennent was exaggerating the flight of Southerners from "the hand of Episcopal tyranny in the intemperate days of Laud," he was not exaggerating the extent to which Southern Anglicans had adopted the "Congregational discipline" or a "spirit of independency"—the complaints of the Anglican clergy had made that all too clear.[19] Not an episcopal polity but a congregational polity had won the day, according to Tennent, in the low country.

Having identified the South Carolina Anglicans with the Dissenters and the spirit of independence, Tennent summarized the opposition to the appointment of colonial bishops by insisting that the "*design was too plainly to obtain bishops with civil powers.*" To the tyranny of the courts of admiralty would be added the tyranny of even more arbitrary spiritual courts. It was an insidious attempt to bring down on the colonies, without consulting them, "the tax of an enormous *hierarchy.*" The Anglican clergy's only hope of success in obtaining these "ecclesiastical principalities lies in the support of parliamentary power."[20]

A few months after he made this attack on the Anglican clergy of New England, Tennent was elected to the First Provincial Congress that met in January 1775. Here he sided with Christopher Gadsden and the more radical members who were already looking toward independence—the more conservative sought only the securing of American rights within the empire. In April 1775, Tennent was named to the Committee of Intelligence and was made, with William Henry Drayton, a commissioner of the Congress to the backcountry. Their task was to explain the causes of the disputes with the Mother Country and to enlist the support of the people in the American cause. By the time Tennent returned to Charlestown after almost six weeks of travel, he had not performed any miracles in the backcountry, but he had done the critical work of helping to prepare the way for a rising of revolutionary sentiment.[21] In less than two years he was dead of a fever.

Tennent was not the only member of the Provincial Congress connected with the Independent Meeting House. Miles Brewton played an important role in its deliberations and was a member of the important Council of Safety. Brewton represented the more conservative members of the Provincial Congress and the Council of Safety, but most of the other members of the Independent Meeting House sided with their pastor and took a more radical position.[22] Leaders among these members were John Mathews, Richard Hutson, John Edwards, David Ramsay, and Josiah Smith, Jr. Not only were they members of the Provincial Congress and later the assembly, but they were elected to the all important Privy Council that essentially ran the state government during much of the war. Their fellow church members Anthony Toomer, Isaac Holmes, and Daniel DeSaussure (also a member of the Privy Council) were members of the assembly and outspoken supporters of independence. In 1782 John Mathews was elected governor, Richard Hutson lieutenant governor, and David Ramsay won a seat in Congress—an impressive indication of the strength of the congregation in the Patriot cause. Ramsay would later serve as the presiding officer in Congress. Mathews had already served in the Continental Congress.[23]

The Independent Meeting House provided essential financial support as well as political leadership to the Patriot cause. John Edwards made the largest loans to the state government during the Revolution (£432,276.6.3) of any of the state's bondholders. Josiah Smith, Jr., was the second largest bondholder through his own personal funds and a number of others that he controlled. Edwards's business partners James Fisher and John Ballentine, also members of the Independent Meeting House, made substantial loans. Such financial support of the Revolution was critical for the Patriots' war efforts.[24]

When Charlestown fell to the British in May 1780, those who supported the Revolution and did not take "protection" were placed on parole, which restricted them to the city. The refusal to take protection was a bold act, and it served as an encouragement to the Patriots in the countryside who continued the resistance to British rule. Cornwallis, frustrated by the failure to gain control over the state, decided to send the paroled leaders into exile in order to diminish their influence. On Sunday morning, August 12, 1780, thirty-three citizens of Charlestown were seized by British soldiers and confined first to the Exchange and later to the ship *Sandwich*. In spite of their protests—no other American city suffered in this way—they were transported to Saint Augustine, where they remained until an exchange of prisoners allowed them to go to Philadelphia in 1781.

Among these Saint Augustine exiles were David Ramsay and Richard Hutson (two of the three Privy Councillors then in Charlestown), John Edwards, Josiah Smith, Jr., Anthony Toomer, and Isaac Holmes. But they were not the only members of the Independent Meeting House who were exiled: James Hampden Thomson, Daniel DeSaussure, and Edward Darrell were also sent by

Cornwallis to Saint Augustine. When they finally arrived in Philadelphia, they found another group of forced exiles including Thomas Legaré, Charles McDonald, Samuel Miller, Job Palmer, William Wilkie, H. W. DeSaussure, Thomas Hughes, Samuel Smith, James Fisher, and Samuel Baldwin—all members of the Independent Meeting House. With them was the Reverend James Edmonds, their former associate pastor who had provided occasional supply of the church's pulpit after Tennent's death.[25]

Even the Reverend Josiah Smith, Sr., was exiled as a part of his son's family. Now feeble and in his late seventies, the former pastor of the Independent Meeting House took ill and died far from home. He was buried in Philadelphia in the center aisle of the Arch Street Presbyterian Church. On one side of his grave was that of Gilbert Tennent, the great evangelist of the Awakening and uncle of Charlestown's William Tennent. On the other side was the grave of Samuel Finlay, another fiery leader of the Awakening and president of Princeton. Forty years earlier Smith had vigorously defended Whitefield and the Awakening and had noted that "Some great things seem to be upon the anvil, some big prophecy at the birth."[26]

The country churches stood firmly in the Patriot corner and furnished political leaders who played a conspicuous role in the Revolution.[27] Stephen Bull, Jr., of Stoney Creek was a member of the newly formed state legislature in 1776 and its legislative council. With him were Isaac Hayne of Bethel and Thomas Bee of Wilton. Bee had been in the thick of things from the first—a member of the Provincial Congress, the Council of Safety, the assembly and its legislative council. In 1779 he was elected lieutenant governor and the following year he was a member of the Continental Congress. In all of these positions he provided decisive and distinguished service for the American cause.[28] When the state assembly met at Jacksonborough, included in its members were Joseph and Thomas Bee from Wilton; Richard Singleton from Bethel; Joseph Legaré, Arnoldus Vanderhorst, and John Vanderhorst from Wappetaw.[29]

While most of those sent into exile were from Charlestown, a few were from country parishes. James Legaré and William Holmes were from the Johns Island church; Richard Waring and Thomas Waring were members of the Congregational church at Dorchester; Joseph Bee belonged to the Wilton congregation.[30] In addition the rural country churches furnished some of the Patriots' military leaders. Stephen Bull, Jr., was a colonel in the militia and later was raised to the rank of brigadier. Richard Singleton of Bethel served as a colonel in the militia; Colonel Arnoldus Vanderhorst and Major John Vanderhorst of Wappetaw rode as officers with Francis Marion.[31] But most famous of all was Colonel Isaac Hayne of Bethel, "the martyr to the cause of American liberty."

Hayne, who was married to the daughter of the Reverend William Hutson, was a member of the militia from his district. Captured by the British, he was taken to Charlestown and placed in the prison cellar of the Exchange. Without a trial, he was condemned to death by the military authorities on the charge of having broken his oath to the British government. His sister-in-law, Mrs. Henry Perroneau of Charlestown's Independent Meeting House, led a number of other ladies to plead for him. Later with Hayne's surviving children, she returned to Lord Rawdon, the senior British officer, and on their knees entreated Rawdon to spare Hayne's life. Even the royal Lieutenant Governor William Bull asked Rawdon for clemency for Hayne. It was all to no avail. On August 4, 1781, Hayne was led from the Exchange through streets crowded with thousands of spectators to a place somewhere near where Pitt and Vanderhorst Streets now intersect. There, after commending his children to the care of friends, he was executed.[32]

Hayne's execution caused not only great indignation and calls for revenge by Americans but an uproar in the British House of Lords. The issues were complex and involved questions about military authority and law, the nature of the oath Hayne had taken, whether he had broken it, and if so, the legal consequences of such a perjury. One thing, however, is clear: to the Americans, he became the "the martyr of the American Revolution," the "martyr to the cause of American liberty."[33]

Hayne, the most famous of all the low country Patriot martyrs, points with Tennent, Mathews, Hutson, and Ramsay, together with a host of other political and financial leaders, to the extensive engagement of the Reformed community in the Patriot cause. Rather than "taking no conspicuous part," as Edward McCrady and others have asserted, they participated at the center of the struggle in the low country for American independence. Furthermore, they were not "cavaliers at heart," nor were they missing "the same sense of connection with seventeenth-century revolutionary Calvinism as did, for example, their admired friend Samuel Adams, who saw himself as upholding the traditions and habits of his puritan ancestors."[34] On the contrary, they stood firmly within the Reformed community and called upon its rhetorical tradition to help justify revolution.

Revolutionary Ideology

Behind the revolutionary activity of these Patriots within the Reformed community were intellectual traditions and the experiences of a colonial people that shaped the ways they understood the Revolution and its causes. Reinforcing one another during the tumultuous years before the Revolution, these traditions and experiences changed the way the Patriots saw Great Britain.[35] They involved, however, not only a change in attitude toward Britain but also toward America and America's place in human history. Among low country Presbyterians and Congregationalists, an emerging revolutionary ideology was most clearly articulated by David Ramsay in his histories. Ramsay, the Patriot at the

Independent Meeting House, stands as a counterpoint to Hewat, the Tory at First (Scots).

One intellectual tradition was rooted in the political history of republican Rome. Educated Patriots found in the history of the ancient Romans the finest examples of the virtues needed for a republic and the dangers of concentrated power and corruption. Such a perspective had been nurtured and transmitted by the humanist impulse within the Reformed tradition that saw tyranny rooted in excesses.[36] When Patriots looked at the young American republic, they saw the ancient virtues of simplicity, sincerity, patriotism, and a love of justice and freedom. When they looked at Great Britain, they saw an empire corrupted by its growing wealth and moving steadily toward tyranny.[37] This is what Ramsay saw in the events leading toward the Revolution, and he wrote his histories of the state, of the Revolution, and of the Republic as some ancient Roman might write—or at least that is what many in the nineteenth century thought. Ramsay, exulted the future President James K. Polk, is "the Tacitus of this western hemisphere to transmit to posterity in the unpolished language of truth, the spirit of liberty which actuated the first founders of our republic."[38]

The Enlightenment provided a second intellectual tradition that helped to shape the way Patriots understood the Revolution. For Ramsay and other low country Presbyterians and Congregationalists, it was not the radical Enlightenment of Voltaire, Hume, and Holback that influenced their thinking but a moderate Enlightenment that was mediated through the Reformed tradition and came by way of Princeton and its Presbyterian president John Witherspoon.[39] A Scotsman, Witherspoon was a strong advocate of the Scottish Common Sense Philosophy. This philosophy, which would dominate much of nineteenth-century American thought and would have a profound impact on Presbyterianism in the United States, emphasized an acceptance of ordinary, common-sense perspectives on the nature of the world and God. Witherspoon taught his students at Princeton—including James Madison—that the moral law of God is the foundation of a just political system, that society is built on a civil contract that is based on the consent of the people and that guarantees certain "inalienable" natural rights of individuals, and that unjust rulers ought to be resisted—even with rebellion when necessary.[40] Such perspectives echoed through the histories of David Ramsay as he interpreted the causes of the American Revolution. Ramsay was Witherspoon's son-in-law and longtime friend, but perhaps even more important in nurturing such perspectives was Ramsay's mentor, Benjamin Rush, the great physician Patriot and Philadelphia's leading Calvinist.[41]

The Reformed tradition itself, with its political theories and memories of resistance and rebellion, operated as a third intellectual tradition that helped to shape interpretations of the Revolution. A body of Reformed thought, developed in the fires of persecution, was suspicious of all arbitrary human power. Moreover, vivid memories—told most dramatically in John Foxe's *Book of Martyrs*—encouraged resistance to political and religious tyranny. Of particular importance were memories of the English Civil War and the Glorious Revolution. "Every thing in South Carolina," wrote Ramsay, "contributed to nourish a spirit of liberty and independence. Its settlement was nearly coeval with the revolution in England; and many of its inhabitants had imbibed a large portion of that spirit, which brought one tyrant to the block and expelled another from his dominions."[42]

The intellectual tradition that flowed from this social and political thought emphasized individual rights and carried a profound suspicion of all governments as threats to human liberty and happiness. John Milton and Algernon Sidney were great spokesmen in the seventeenth century for this tradition. In the eighteenth century it was vigorously pushed by English Whigs and Dissenters. They opposed all establishments of religion and advocated natural rights, a social contract understanding of society, and a separation of power among several branches of government. When the "Country Whigs," as they were often called, looked at what was happening in British society, they were convinced they could see power and wealth corrupting Britain's civic virtues and threatening with tyranny the country's future. Such a perspective appeared to American Patriots to explain much of what was happening to them. The Stamp Act and the tea tax seemed nothing less than clear expressions of a growing tyranny encouraged by idleness and the love of extravagant luxuries. Liberty-loving people were to resist such decadence and its accompanying tyranny at all costs.

Ramsay made the point explicit in "An Oration on the Advantages of American Independence" delivered before the citizens of Charlestown on the second anniversary of the Declaration of Independence. The new Republic, he declared, was in every way to be preferred to the old royal government. Speaking as a Whig and one who stood firmly in the Reformed tradition, he insisted that the Republic "is much more favourable to purity of morals, and better calculated to promote all our important interests. Honesty, plain-dealing, and simple manners, were never made the patterns of courtly behaviour. Artificial manners always prevail in kingly governments; and royal courts are reservoirs, from whence insincerity, hypocrisy, dissimulation, pride, luxury, and extravagance, deluge and overwhelm the body of the people." Never were the Whig ideology and Reformed ethic expressed more sharply: "On the other hand, republicks are favourable to truth, sincerity, frugality, industry, and simplicity of manners. Equality, the life and soul of Commonwealth, cuts off all pretensions to preferment, but those which arise from extraordinary merit: Whereas in royal governments, he that can best please his superiors, by the low arts of fawn-

ing and adulation, is most likely to obtain favour." Ramsay then warned his
Charlestown audience of Britain's attempt to corrupt the colonists and under-
mine their virtues.

> It was the interest of Great-Britain to encourage our dissipation and extrava-
> gance, for the two-fold purpose of *increasing the sale of her manufactures,* and
> of *perpetuating our subordination.* In vain we sought to check the growth of
> luxury, by sumptuary laws; every wholesome restraint of this kind was sure
> to meet with the royal negative; While the whole force of example was em-
> ployed to induce us to copy the dissipated manners of the country from which
> we sprung. If therefore, we had continued dependent, our frugality, industry,
> and simplicity of manners, would have been lost in an imitation of British
> extravagance, idleness, and false refinements.[43]

Finally, the ideas and experiences connected with the Great Awakening had
their part to play in shaping the way Ramsay and other low country Presbyterians and Congregationalists understood the Revolution. The Awakening encouraged the awakened to trust their own experience, to walk in their own
light as God gave them light, without having to rely on the authority of those
"above" them. The Awakening played an important role in linking the colonies
and forging a sense of common identity as Americans—a fundamental concern
of Ramsay. It stirred millennial expectations, gave a special place to America as
God's New Israel, and encouraged a belief in a special destiny for the American
people. Perhaps, cried Ramsay to the citizens of Charlestown, "it is the will of
Heaven, that a new empire should be here formed, of the different nations of
the Old World, which will rise superior to all that have gone before it, and
extend human happiness to its utmost possible limits."[44]

Historians have largely ignored the influence of the Awakening on the low
country and Ramsay's connections with the evangelical stream that flowed
from the Awakening. Yet Ramsay was a leading layman in the Independent
Meeting House, the center of support for Whitefield and the Awakening in
Charlestown. When he first arrived in Charlestown, he immediately established
a close friendship with William Tennent, whose family had been so intimately
identified with the Awakening. His spiritual home was Princeton, an institution
whose founding and early history were inextricably linked with the Awakening
and its continuing influence. Many of his close friends and correspondents in
the North were closely identified with evangelical Christianity, including Benjamin Rush, Samuel Stanhope Smith of Princeton, and Jedidiah Morse, who
led the attack on Boston's Unitarians.[45] Ramsay was actively opposed to dueling
and drinking, and "his general distaste for social amusements," one historian
has noted with some surprise, made him "seem more like a nineteenth-century
evangelist than a radical revolutionary."[46] He made unmistakably clear, in his
concluding summary of the debate between Garden and Whitefield, his posi-

tive attitude toward the Awakening: "Both were good and useful men, but in different ways. The one [Garden] was devoted to forms, the other [Whitefield] soared above them. The piety of the one [Garden] ran in the channel of a particular sect of christians, but that of the other confined neither to sect nor party, flowd in the broad and wide-spreading stream of christianity."[47]

The different reactions to the Awakening in Charlestown's Reformed community throw light on the sharp contrast between the Independent Meeting House and First (Scots) in their attitudes toward the American cause and on the competing impulses within the Reformed tradition. Alexander Hewat was both a Tory and a vigorous opponent to the theological and political implications of the Awakening. The leadership of First (Scots) shared his Tory sympathies and his attitude toward the Awakening. Josiah Smith and William Tennent, on the other hand, along with the lay leadership of the Independent Meeting House, identified with both the cause of the Awakening and the cause of American independence. Such distinctions help to illumine differences within the Reformed community in the low country and within the tradition itself. But what brought one tendency within the tradition to a dominant position within one congregation and a competing tendency to a dominant position in another Reformed congregation only a few blocks away? Economics, the almost immediate response of twentieth-century people, does not seem an entirely adequate answer given the significant parallels that existed between the economic interests of the two congregations. Of greater importance was the level of identification with what might best be called "the American experience."

The membership of First (Scots) was composed largely of recent immigrants and those whose Scottish identity was still strong. They shared many of the intellectual traditions that encouraged others to move toward independence. But as a community, they had not drunk deeply at the well of American experience and it was this experience, more than any other single factor, that had brought together the various intellectual traditions and shaped them into an ideology of resistance and revolution. Ramsay explained the nature of this experience: "Every inhabitant was, or easily might be a freeholder. Settled on lands of his own, he was both farmer and landlord. Having no superiors to whom he was obliged to look up, and producing all the necessaries of life from his own grounds, he soon became independent."[48] At a gathering in Saint Michael's in 1794 to celebrate July Fourth, he declared: "From the first settlement of this country, everything concurred to inspire its inhabitants with the love of liberty. The facility of procuring landed property, gave every citizen an opportunity of becoming an independent freeholder. Remote from the influence of kings, bishops, and nobles, the equality of rights was inculcated by the experience of every day."[49]

It was this experience that was largely lacking at First (Scots) and that— together with ties to Great Britain—made the congregation a stronghold of

Tory sentiment. Ironically, it was also this "experience of every day" in a low country setting, with its peculiar pressures and distinct interests, that eventually led Ramsay to support the slavery of African Americans, while Hewat, removed from that experience, became an early antislavery advocate. For most whites in the Reformed tradition, the low country context thus encouraged a revolutionary impulse for themselves and, at the same time, a conservative, hierarchical ideology in regard to their African American slaves. These two polarities— the revolutionary impulse and the conservative ideology—located in the field of a low country context, were drawn toward one another into a quest for a *via media,* a middle way, that would provide the conceptual framework, the cultural imagination, through which the Reformed community would both express its present identity and shape its hopes for the future.

Freedom and Slavery

Throughout the war years, throughout the bitter struggles between Tories and Whigs, as questions of freedom were debated and fears of tyranny were raised, black slaves seemed to whites somehow beyond such issues, as if the question of freedom and the oppression of tyranny were of no concern to them. Yet they were there in the low country of South Carolina in greater numbers than Tories and Whigs combined. And no less than white South Carolinians, they suffered the ravages of the war. Some were killed in battles. Many more died of starvation and disease, especially those who flocked to crowded British encampments. Some who joined the British found the freedom they were seeking. Most who stayed with the British went to Jamaica still as slaves.[50]

The slaves themselves were not simply passive but often sought their own freedom by joining the British. Such a quest, no less than that of the whites, was sometimes bloody. At the Wappetaw church, where several prominent members were officers with Francis Marion, the pastor was murdered in the manse by his slaves. They were said to have been encouraged by the British and they very well may have seen their act as a means to their own freedom.[51] In the last year of the war, several black dragoons were organized by the British and their members were probably among those who gained their freedom with the evacuation of Charlestown. But whatever hopes the Revolution raised for the black slaves of South Carolina, it brought freedom to only a few. It would take another war, a much greater war, before slavery's chains would be broken.

To be sure, some whites saw the incongruity between the rhetoric of white revolutionaries and the realities of black slavery. "To speak as a Christian," Ramsay wrote shortly after his arrival in Charlestown, "I really fear some heavy judgement awaits us on that very score" (of slavery). Writing his mentor Benjamin Rush, a leading early abolitionist, Ramsay declared: "I think with you in respect of our enslaving the Africans and have a firm belief that there will not be a slave in these states fifty years hence." In 1779 he complained that "White Pride and Avarice are great obstacles in the way of Black liberty."[52] But life in Charlestown had a way of changing such perspectives. He was convinced that his defeat when he ran for the U.S. Congress in 1788 was directly linked to slavery: "I was a candidate and lost my election on two grounds. One was that I was a northward man and the other that I was represented as favoring the abolition of slavery." Yet even by that date his own views had changed. Writing to John Elliott, pastor of the New North Church in Boston, he said: "You speak feelingly for the poor negroes. I have long considered their situation but such is our hard case here to the Southward that we cannot do without them. Our lands cannot be cultivated by white men. The negroes are here & in a state of slavery. Experience proves that they who have been born & grown up in slavery are incapable of the blessings of freedom. Emancipation therefore would be ruinous both to masters & slaves."[53] Here was the startling contradiction being lodged deep within the collective psyche of the low country Reformed community: for whites in the low country to keep their freedom, they needed, they believed, to keep blacks in slavery. If blacks were not kept in their place, within carefully drawn boundaries, chaos would reign and white freedom would be swept away in the ensuing flood.

The influence of Southern society and Ramsay's metamorphosis set a pattern that would be followed, as we shall see, by well-meaning white Presbyterians and Congregationalists in the nineteenth century. They would seek a bitter "middle way" to resolve the tensions within the Reformed tradition between order and liberty and within Southern society between freedom and slavery.

The Revolution thus split the white Reformed community in the low country, revealing the deep tensions and complex impulses lodged in the community's collective depths. How different elements within the community viewed and acted in the world of 1776 was largely influenced by a complex interaction between its religious tradition—its world view and ethos—and the specific experience of living in the low country. For some, the "American experience" of independence with its egalitarian thrust brought to the fore the Reformed impulse that resisted tyrannies and any foreign restraints or enclosing boundaries. For others, especially Charlestown's Scottish community, in whom the "American experience" had not yet been deeply internalized, the Revolution seemed both an outbreak of anarchy and a threat to their identity as British citizens and members of the empire. For the Tories at First (Scots), the Reformed impulse that sought order and feared chaos was encouraged by their attachments to Britain and by their relatively recent arrival in the low country.

Whatever divisions marked the white Reformed community during the years of the Revolution, they would be overcome in the years that followed the end of war. A social and organizational unity would mark the community's "little world" and a tense harmony would once again be established between competing internal impulses. Encouraging that unity and harmony was the haunting presence of African Americans. As part of an economic and social system, as an embodiment of whites' racial assumptions and fears, African Americans would serve—in interaction with a theological tradition—as a magnetic center point, drawing together the antithetical impulses within the white Reformed community's life. Around such a center point, freedom for whites appeared to demand slavery for blacks, and the fear of enclosing boundaries needed to be balanced with the fear of any collapse of the boundaries between blacks and whites. The metaphor the community increasingly would use to express the unity of these contradictions was the "middle way," a *via media*. This metaphor, as we shall see, would provide the community in the years ahead a way of bridging the great rifts in its experience and of linking the competing impulses that rumbled in the collective depths of its life.

7

Institutional Developments

"Our Southern Zion"

WHEN THE LAST British troops sailed from Charlestown in 1782 and peace finally came to the South Carolina low country, a new period began in the region's history. It lasted for more than eighty years until another invading army, this one victorious, marched through the land. Between 1782 and 1865, the Carolina low country, with Charleston as its center, rose starlike to a position of preeminent social, intellectual, and political influence throughout a rapidly expanding South. Charleston (in 1783 the name of the city was officially changed from Charlestown to Charleston), it was claimed, was the "capital of the South." Yet during this same period, the low country began to lose much of its earlier economic vitality. By the time the guns fired on Fort Sumter, Charleston was no longer the South's largest city. It had moved from the nation's fourth-largest metropolis in 1782 to its twenty-second in 1860. At the heart of this decline were the weaknesses of its economic structures, dominated by the production of rice with a slave labor force and the geographical limitations of a low and swampy region. Moreover, the white inhabitants of the low country, struggling to maintain their social order, felt increasingly alienated from the Union that South Carolinians had helped to create. Many watched with alarm as threatening forces slowly began to arise in parts of the North. Humming industries and humanitarian impulses at first challenged and then succeeded in overwhelming what Carolinians sometimes called "our own little world."[1]

That "little world" was largely shaped by the presence of African American slaves. They provided, as they had during the colonial period, the foundation for the region's economic life. Outside Charleston, they continued to constitute the vast majority of the population.[2] This concentration of largely isolated slaves meant that the distinctive African American culture that had emerged during the colonial period would continue to develop in the low country.[3] It also meant that the culture of whites would be profoundly influenced by its interaction with the numerically dominant African American population of the region. The ways in which whites organized their lives, understood their economic interests, and interpreted their religious beliefs were all inescapably linked with the African Americans of the region and with the institution of human slavery. In a reciprocal way, from the oppressive underside of slavery, the developing African American culture reflected, even in its low country isolation, an inescapable link to the culture of whites and the institution of slavery.

This chapter focuses on the institutional developments of the whites in the Reformed tradition within this particular social and cultural context—how those in this tradition built new churches, organized presbyteries and associations, published newspapers, participated in benevolent societies, and helped to establish a theological institution. This chapter explores both the development of these institutions and the purposes they served. What did they do to or for the Reformed community and how did they relate to the larger social contexts of the low country and the nation? What if any correspondence can be discerned between the religious ideas of the Reformed tradition and the institutions developed by the Reformed community in the low country?[4]

The War's Aftermath and a New Awakening

The devastations of the Revolution brought with them a religious depression not only in the South Carolina low country but throughout the new nation. Congregational life was disrupted, schools were closed, and, much to the dismay of many church people, an aggressive cult of reason grew in popularity and prestige—encouraged both by the spreading influence of Enlightenment ideas and by the disorders of the time.[5] It was in such a context, as the American people sought to impose some order on their new nation and to gain a sense of national unity, that revival fires began to be stirred once again. They had never completely died out after the Great Awakening but had smoldered here and there, flaring up from time to time but never bursting into a great conflagration. By the beginning of the nineteenth century, however, they were once again burning bright and were soon racing across much of the young republic in a Second Great Awakening.[6]

The Second Great Awakening spread across the nation from several diverse points, but for the Carolina low country the primary links were with the revivals that spread up and down the eastern seaboard. Here the revival fires were more controlled and less boisterous than those that raced like wildfire across the West, but they were equally consequential. Of special significance was the revival that broke out at Yale under the fervent preaching of President Timothy Dwight. It was this eastern phase of the Great Awakening, and not the western, that would have such a profound impact on the Presbyterian and Congregational churches of the South Carolina low country.

From Yale, from Amherst and Brown, from Dartmouth, Williams, and Middlebury came pastors to fill the low country pulpits, to serve as missionaries in the city, or to be sent to "foreign shores" by low country churches. Many of the pastors were natives of the low country who had traveled north for their education. Others were New Englanders who came south. They were joined by those who had studied in the Middle States, at the University of Pennsylvania, at Dickinson, at Union College in New York, and, of course, at Princeton. After South Carolina Presbyterians established their theological seminary in Columbia, some began to receive their college degrees in the North and then to take their theological degrees at Columbia (see appendix C).[7] They all helped to strengthen the ties of low country churches to broad movements in American religious life and to stir the long-smoldering fires of religious commitment and moral earnestness within the low country Reformed community. From the devastations of war and the religious depression that followed, the Reformed community moved into one of its most vigorous periods as the Second Great Awakening swept over the low country, leaving behind new churches, significant increases in church members (especially among African Americans), and numerous benevolent societies committed to "doing good."

Rebuilding

The immediate tasks before the Reformed churches in the low country after the Revolution were the restoration of some order to their corporate lives and the creation of a new order to meet the challenges of American independence. With the end of the Anglican establishment in 1777, many of the Presbyterian and Congregational churches moved to incorporate—a decided advantage over the old system when only the Anglican churches could have the protection of law.[8] The new buildings they built functioned as centers of the Reformed community's life, as expressions of the world view and ethos of the community, and as indicators of the Reformed community's place within low country society.

In Charleston the Independent Congregational Church continued to play an impressive role in the life of the city. In order to meet the growing size of its congregation, a collegiate church had been begun on Archdale Street before the war and was completed in 1787. Two pastors—William Hollinshead and Isaac Stockton Keith—were jointly called to serve the two churches. By 1802 the congregations had grown to such an extent that all the pews in both churches had been sold and applicants were waiting for some accommodation. Under the leadership of David Ramsay, plans were made for a new church building on Meeting Street. Ramsay's wife, Martha Laurens, daughter of Henry Laurens, proposed a circular plan. Ramsay secured Robert Mills, the celebrated architect and devout Presbyterian from Columbia, to draw the design. The result was the beautiful Circular Congregational Church with its great domed ceiling over the sanctuary.[9]

Following the completion of the Circular Church, tensions began to build between the more orthodox members and those influenced more directly by eighteenth-century rationalism and an emphasis on the reasonableness of the faith. These tensions led to the Unitarian secession in 1817. By common agreement the congregation was divided—the orthodox remaining in the Circular Church while the much smaller group, which was moving toward a Unitarian position, organized in the Archdale Street church as the Second Independent Church of Charleston S.C. In 1839 they changed their name to the Unitarian Church in Charleston, S.C.[10]

During the years the Congregationalists were busy with the construction of their Circular Church, Presbyterians in the city were also feeling the need for a new church. In 1809 the Second Presbyterian Church was organized and construction was begun on Meeting Street of a great sanctuary, the cost of which exceeded even that of the Circular Church. A magnificent, white-columned building at the head of a park with a colonnade of trees, the sanctuary was so large that it would strain the voice of many a preacher for generations to come. Two years after the dedication of the Second Presbyterian Church, the congregation of First (Scots) began construction of a new building. Completed in 1814, it was marked by a Roman Doric style, by distinctive twin towers and cupolas, and by its large and handsome sanctuary.[11] The Third Presbyterian Church of Charleston was organized in 1823 on the corner of Archdale and West Streets. In 1850 the congregation erected at 273 Meeting Street a building modeled after the Church of the Madeleine in Paris. This architectural gem would be noted nationally as a particularly fine example of the Classic Revival.[12]

The French Reformed Church struggled through the years following the Revolution. Then, in the 1840s, a revival of interest in the congregation's Huguenot and Reformed tradition led to the construction of a new church, the earliest example of Gothic Revival in the city.[13]

During the 1840s the Second Presbyterian Church showed sustained growth. In response the Glebe Street Presbyterian Church was organized and its building completed in 1847.[14] In the same year a growing concern was expressed by the session and membership of the Second Presbyterian Church for the "religious instruction of slaves." In spite of much public opposition, a separate church for blacks was organized under the authority of the session of Second Church. In 1850 a handsome building was completed on Anson Street. "A neat Gothic structure," is the way the presbytery minutes described it, "capable of seating six hundred (600) blacks, after reserving one hundred seats for the whites."[15] This congregation became, under the leadership of John Lafayette Girardeau, the Zion Presbyterian Church. Girardeau's preaching attracted great numbers of blacks and the congregation soon outgrew the building on Anson Street. Through the contributions of several wealthy families in Second Church, the largest church building in the city was erected on the corner of Calhoun and Meeting Streets. Zion quickly became the most prominent gathering place for the African American community of the city.[16]

By 1860 a visitor riding down Meeting Street from the Battery would pass in order: First (Scots), Circular Congregational, Third Presbyterian, the Meeting Street side of Zion, and Second Presbyterian—all on a *one-mile* stretch of Charleston's central thoroughfare. Nothing portrayed the presence of the Reformed tradition in the city more clearly than these five congregations with their impressive buildings lined up so closely together on Meeting Street. The Reformed community was not marginal in Charleston. On the contrary, its powerful presence, so forcefully asserted on the city's primary thoroughfare, proclaimed the community's strength and vitality.[17]

The architecture of these Meeting Street churches pointed to the social locations of the congregations, to the ways in which the Reformed tradition was interacting with a specific social context, and to the changing ethos of the Reformed community in Charleston between the end of the Revolution and the beginning of the Civil War. Most notable was the replacement of the old meetinghouses by impressive church buildings of various architectural styles and considerable architectural distinction. Substantially larger than the colonial meetinghouses, the new buildings reflected the Reformed community's freedom, following the end of the Anglican establishment, to assert self-confidently its place in the low country. The affluence of the Reformed community, its own sense of identity, and its social and political leadership—all of which will be detailed in following chapters—was expressed by the imposing buildings erected along Meeting Street. At the same time, the new buildings revealed the tension between simplicity and the familiar demands of power and affluence to express themselves.

To be sure, the interior of the buildings revealed a continuity of long-established Reformed values. High, centrally located pulpits, bare Communion tables, clear windows, and little if any ornamentation spoke of a continuation of a spirit of simplicity and an emphasis on the discipline of the mind and will. The rituals conducted in the buildings continued old patterns: they were well ordered and highly verbal with an emphasis on the ear and not the eye; they expressed a rejection of the spectacular and disclosed inherent tensions between constraint and freedom. But in the new buildings everything was on a larger scale—grander and more elegant even in their simplicity. This was perhaps especially true of the slave balconies (in all except Zion, where the whites sat in the balconies and the slaves sat on the main floor). With the coming of the Second Great Awakening, slaves moved into the churches in increasing numbers and filled balconies that now stretched out far over the white congregations below. No less than in the colonial period, the architecture and rituals of the

Reformed Congregations on a One-Mile Stretch of Meeting Street, 1860
Clockwise, from top, left: First (Scots) Presbyterian (photo by Jonathan T. Van Deventer, courtesy of Charleston-Atlantic Presbytery, Charleston, S.C.); Circular Congregational (courtesy of Circular Congregational Church, Charleston, S.C.); Central Presbyterian (author's collection); Zion Presbyterian (courtesy of Charleston-Atlantic Presbytery, Charleston, S.C.); Second Presbyterian (author's collection)

churches illumined a world as understood by a religious tradition and a world as lived in a particular place and sociohistorical setting.

The congregations outside Charleston continued to worship in buildings largely in the old meetinghouse style. They did, however, exhibit the influence of climate and demographic shifts in shaping the institutional life of the Reformed community. During the years between the Revolution and the Civil War, four congregations—Wappetaw, Dorchester, Bethel Pon Pon, and Stoney Creek—saw their membership move gradually away from the old plantation areas into villages that originally served as more healthy summer residences. At Wappetaw the congregation prospered for some years, even after it began to cluster around two villages in the summer: Mount Pleasant and McClellanville. In 1827 those members of Wappetaw who summered for health purposes in Mount Pleasant built a chapel. Twenty years later they built a handsome meetinghouse that reflected the continuing values of their New England and Reformed heritage. After the Civil War, with Wappetaw in ruins, the Mount Pleasant congregation was officially organized as the Mount Pleasant Presbyterian Church. In 1872 the New Wappetaw Presbyterian Church was organized in McClellanville.[18]

The old Dorchester congregation reorganized and rebuilt its meetinghouse in the 1790s. Its members, however, slowly gravitated toward the higher, more healthy pine lands of Summerville, four miles away. In 1831 they built a chapel in the little village, and in 1859 the Summerville Presbyterian Church was officially organized.[19] The congregation at Bethel Pon Pon followed the same pattern, only earlier. In 1821 they built a chapel in Walterboro for summer residences and gradually it became the center of the church's life.[20]

Chapels were also built on the sea islands, but they never led to the abandonment of old places of worship. Johns Island had had a chapel on Wadmalaw Island since the early 1700s, and in the following century a summer chapel and manse were built at Legareville, closer to the ocean and its breezes. In the 1850s a handsome meetinghouse with a front portico and five large square columns was constructed at Rockville on Wadmalaw Island overlooking the Edisto River.[21]

The Edisto Island Presbyterian Church had a summer chapel and manse at Edingsville Beach. The congregation built in 1831 one of the most beautiful churches in the low country. Located at the site of the old meetinghouse in the center of the island, the new church kept many of the traditional features of the meetinghouse: a rectangular shape, the arrangement of the doors and windows, and a high central pulpit. But the large fluted columns of its portico, its arched ceiling, and its well-balanced steeple presented an elegance few churches could match.[22] Moreover, today with its island setting of palmettos and moss-draped oaks and with its ancient cemetery spreading out around it, the church at first appears to the imagination as the essence of the low country, as a symbol of romantic beauty that, together with the plantation houses of the island, might give shape to myths of the Old South—except that its meeting-house style, slipping through the romantic images, gives hints of a simplicity and rigor that make for a more complex picture of competing impulses and countervailing tendencies.[23]

Inland, Presbyterian churches began to be organized in the 1830s and 1840s as these areas became prosperous cotton regions. In Barnwell County, where the black population almost tripled between 1820 and 1860, a Presbyterian church was organized in the village of Barnwell and another in the neighboring hamlet of Boiling Springs. In Orangeburg, where there had been a German Reformed congregation from the period immediately after the Revolution, a Presbyterian church was organized in 1835.[24]

The institutional strength of the Reformed community, which had been firmly established in the low country during the colonial period, thus continued during the years between the Revolution and the Civil War. In Charleston the number of white members in the Presbyterian and Congregational churches exceeded, from the beginning of the century to the Civil War, the white membership in the Methodist and Baptist churches combined.[25] In Charleston and throughout the low country, the white membership of the Presbyterian and Congregational churches was greater than that of the Episcopal churches of the region.[26] In the countryside and villages of the low country, the whites in the Reformed community were widely scattered, as was the white population generally. The Reformed community maintained its numerical strength relative to whites in other denominations on the sea islands and in the areas close to the seaboard, but moving inland, the Baptists and Methodists increasingly outnumbered all other denominations.[27] Institutional unity as well as internal tensions were expressed within the Reformed community in the creation of the Charleston Union Presbytery.

Polity and Competing Impulses: Autonomy and Unity

The old Charlestown Presbytery had been dissolved during the Revolution by the death or removal of most of the ministers who constituted it.[28] It was only in 1790 that a new Presbytery of Charleston was incorporated, although it was probably organized ecclesiastically before that date. A weak organization, it never had the extensive jurisdiction of its predecessor.[29]

Throughout the low country a congregational polity permeated much of the church life. It had long been strong in Anglican churches where vestries were jealous of their prerogatives and suspicious of any attempts to interfere in the affairs of local congregations. Bishop Francis Asbury was deeply troubled by the independent ways of the Methodists in Charleston, and even the Roman Catholic hierarchy had a fight on its hands with the lay trustees of Saint Mary's

Catholic Church.[30] Many social factors were no doubt at work in the creation of such a congregational emphasis, perhaps especially the isolation of plantations and the fear that a slave society had any "outside interference." But the strong Dissenter tradition of colonial Carolina also had its part to play, and it helped to inform the ways people understood and interpreted church life. Certainly the Presbyterians, with their close connections with Congregational churches, had a strong tendency to push to the side the connectional nature of Presbyterianism and to emphasize the autonomy of local congregations.

The Presbytery of Charleston itself exhibited this desire for autonomy. Under the leadership of John Witherspoon of Princeton, a national church—the Presbyterian Church in the United States of America—had been organized in 1788. Following the model of the Church of Scotland, a General Assembly was established with four synods and sixteen presbyteries. The Presbytery of Charleston (1790–1819) never joined the Assembly. It tried, or at least it made inquiries, but it did not want to be connected with the Synod of the Carolinas. The synod protested. How could a presbytery be directly linked to the Assembly, the synod asked, without being in connection with a synod and under its review and control? But that was precisely what some low country ministers and churches did not want to be—under the review and control of anyone; thus for nearly thirty years there was an independent Presbytery of Charleston.[31] The synod, however, did not ignore the region, and when it organized Harmony Presbytery in 1809 it included in Harmony's bounds the territory of the Presbytery of Charleston. Significantly, the newly organized Second Presbyterian Church of Charleston—with its national outlook and connections—joined Harmony Presbytery and not the unaffiliated Presbytery of Charleston. Its pastor, Andrew Flinn, was elected moderator of the General Assembly in 1812.[32]

Behind the reluctance of some low country Presbyterians to join as a regular part of a national organization were the tensions within the Reformed tradition and a larger controversy in American society about the nature of governments and institutional life—about where power was to reside and what kind of unity could be maintained among a diverse people spread over an immense area.[33] Within the Reformed tradition were the tensions between order and freedom. The tensions between these two opposing impulses were particularly acute for whites in the low country. On the one hand was the need for control and systematic order in a slave society. On the other hand was the fear of any outside interference or control, of any authority that might limit the prerogatives of white slave owners. Whites felt the need both of rigid, authoritarian control in a slave society and of unlimited personal freedom. They would slowly and with difficulty move toward a unity and social solidarity that would provide, while limiting personal and congregational independence, a united front in the protection of their "little world."

Charleston Union Presbytery

In 1801 a number of the Reformed congregations in the low country joined together in the Congregational Association of South Carolina.[34] Thus by 1809 two presbyteries and one Congregational association were in the region. In an attempt to bring some order to these overlapping ecclesiastical organizations, the Congregational association made a proposal to Harmony Presbytery "of a corresponding Union of delegates." From this proposal emerged Charleston Union Presbytery, composed of both Presbyterian and Congregational churches in the area south of the Congaree and Santee Rivers and east of a line running roughly from Columbia to McCormick. Columbia, the new state capital with its College of South Carolina, was a part of the presbytery.[35]

For the next thirty years, the presbytery would have a stormy history, reflecting the tension between autonomy and unity. A bitter division would take place in 1839, with some even calling for a separate Southern Presbyterian Church, but the division would be short-lived as the threat and then the devastations of war would draw the Reformed community closer together than it had ever been before.[36] In the face of these dangers, the presbytery would function as a powerful institutional force for solidarity by linking congregations and providing a sense of identity for the Reformed community that would last well into the twentieth century.

Benevolent Societies

The Second Great Awakening not only brought a new religious vitality that led to the establishment of new churches, the enlargement of old ones, and the formation of Charleston Union Presbytery, it also encouraged the organization of interdenominational benevolent societies. Across the nation, people touched by the revival fires were filled with moral earnestness, reforming zeal, and millennial expectations. In response to the needs they saw about them, they organized tract and Bible societies, home and foreign mission societies, education and Sunday school societies, societies for the "recovery of fallen women," temperance societies, and societies for the support of orphans, for prison reform, for the colonization of black Americans in Africa, and for the abolition of slavery. Much of the organizing zeal for such societies came from New England, but they were much more broadly based than has often been assumed.[37]

In the Carolina low country, a number of such societies flourished—with certain important exceptions, most obviously those connected with the abolition of slavery. Nevertheless, Charleston, in contrast to its popular image as a city free from such benevolent impulses and reforming spirits, was at the center of the benevolence empire in the South. Among Southern cities, John W. Kuykendall has written in his careful study of native Southern support for benevolence, "Charleston was by far the most active" in organizing benevolent societies.[38] Together with the growth and vitality of its churches, this benevolent activity points to the significant extent to which "the capital of the South" experienced the religious revival of the Second Great Awakening.

Behind the benevolent societies was a shared evangelical faith mobilized for the conversion and reform of the nation and indeed of the whole world. "The spirit of the age," declared Thomas S. Grimké of the French Huguenot Church, "is beyond all parallel, the spirit of *SOCIAL ENTERPRISE,* abounding in energy and enthusiasm, in wisdom and benevolence. That spirit lives and moves everywhere; and with the aid of the Bible and the Tract, of the Missionary and the Sunday School, is traveling through the whole earth."[39] A spirit of active benevolence was understood to be the primary response of Christians to the grace of God. Benevolence, said the Honorable H. L. Pinckney of the Circular Congregational Church, is "the great principle that regulates the universe."[40] Such benevolence and the societies it spawned were filled with a buoyant optimism, a confidence that history was moving rapidly toward its glorious fulfillment and that America had a special role to play as God's New Israel in the coming of the millennium.

The times seemed to indicate that God was preparing the way for some great new thing. Even as the storm clouds of civil war gathered ominously on the horizon, Thomas Smyth declared in 1857 from the pulpit of the Second Presbyterian Church that all things were being made ready for the coming of the Kingdom.

> The world ere long will be traversed by line steamers, railroads, and telegraphs. Many will run to and from, and knowledge be increased. Notwithstanding all the evil reports of spies and traitors, of recreants and cowards, "the sacramental host of God's elect," will be gathered together for the combat. The order will be given to go forward. The pillar of cloud will precede them by day, and the pillar of fire by night. The Jordan will be crossed. Jericho will be surrounded, besieged, and fall. Every enemy will be encountered and overcome. The land will be given to the people of the saints of the Most High, and the kingdoms of this world will become the kingdoms of our Lord.

Smyth believed that his generation would not live to see the final victory of the Lord's hosts, but he was convinced that the time was drawing near: "Like Moses, God has called us up to Mount Nebo, and shown us, outstretched before us, in all its beauty and magnificence, the goodly land of promised inheritance. Like Moses, we can lie down in triumphant hope and joy, and with our last breath cry 'Victory!' and 'Onward!' "[41]

Here in the "capital of the South" was a utopian vision filled with millennial expectations and the imagery of both progress and conflict. Such a vision, however, was not so much a challenge to the present social order—though challenge was there—as it was a celebration of the present order; not so much a shattering through an imaginative exploration of alternative possibilities—though the Jordan must be crossed and Jericho must fall—as it was the confident march of a reforming social order into the future. The "goodly land of promised inheritance" will be given to "the people of the saints of the Most High." The utopian vision, emerging out of a dominant social stratum, was closely linked here with the ideological.[42] Moreover, the linkage of the utopian with the ideological would unite Smyth and his low country colleagues with powerful currents in the nation's life. (It is not by chance, as we shall see, that Smyth and his colleagues were Unionists up to the Civil War.) Those national currents would seek to find the way to the envisioned Promised Land by means of education, technological expansion (note Smyth's references to line steamers, railroads, and telegraphs), and the spread of evangelical Protestantism. For Smyth and the low country Reformed community, this way would be primarily a *via media*, for it is a middle way, they believed, that leads most directly and safely to the Promised Land.

The benevolent societies were primary tools (together with the churches themselves) for evangelical Christians to wage this great crusade for the Promised Land. In Charleston they organized the Charleston Bible Society (1810) and the Charleston Religious Tract Society (1815). The American Sunday school movement, in its early days dedicated to primary education for the poor, got its start in Charleston. (It received strong support in the 1820s from T. Charlton Henry, pastor of the Second Presbyterian Church, whose father Alexander Henry of Philadelphia was the first president of the American Sunday School Union.) The Ladies Benevolent Society was organized in 1813 to provide relief to the sick and the poor. The Charleston Orphanage was begun for the many children left without parents when deadly fevers swept the city. The South Carolina Education Society provided scholarships for college and seminary students. Women played a particularly conspicuous role in these societies. Martha Laurens Ramsay, daughter of Henry Laurens and wife of David Ramsay, was but one early example of a Charleston woman who found such societies an important means of expressing her piety and focusing her benevolent energy.[43]

Of all the benevolent societies in Charleston, none were more impressive than the mission societies. The Elliott Society (1819), named for the Puritan missionary John Elliott, was organized to sustain missions among the Indians. The Associate Reading Society met weekly to work for the Choctaw mission. The Charleston Juvenile Missionary Society was established in 1833 to raise money for the American Board of Commissioners for Foreign Missions.[44] Three societies were organized for work among the seamen of the city during Charleston's years as a bustling port: the Female Domestic Missionary Society (1818), the Charleston Port Society, and the Young Men's Missionary Society of South Carolina. They built a Seaman's Chapel and later named it Bethel, supported a marine hospital, and established a temperance boardinghouse. A host of missionaries were brought to the city, most from New England. From Yale and Andover came Zabdiel Rogers; from Williams and Andover came William Warner and Alfred Wright; from Middlebury and Andover came Joseph Brown, who worked for nine years with the seamen in Charleston before receiving a call in 1829 to the more abundant fields along New York's waterfront. Jonas King, ordained by the Congregational association, worked among the seamen, visited at the Alms House and at the orphanage, and sought to redeem the "fallen women" of antebellum Charleston.[45]

The Southern Board of Foreign Missions was organized largely under the leadership of Presbyterian and Congregational pastors in Charleston. A branch of the American Board of Commissioners for Foreign Missions, it sent out during the 1830s nine missionaries and their wives to foreign fields. George Boggs, educated at Hampden-Sydney, Amherst, and Princeton, ordained in the Circular Congregational Church, and commissioned at Second Presbyterian, went with his wife (she was a cousin of Margaret Adger Smyth) to India. John Fleetwood Lanneau, a Charleston graduate of Yale and Princeton and member of the Circular Church, went with his wife to Palestine. J. L. Merrick, a graduate of Amherst and Columbia Theological Seminary, sailed for Tabreez, Persia. John B. Adger, member of the Second Presbyterian Church and graduate of Union College and Princeton Theological Seminary, went to Armenia. John A. Mitchell, after serving in Charleston as a missionary among the seamen and hearing stories of distant lands, was commissioned in the Third Presbyterian Church as a missionary to China. He was joined there by T. L. McBryde, graduate of Franklin College (University of Georgia) and Columbia Theological Seminary, and by Dyer Ball and his wife, who went from the Circular Church to Singapore with a farewell sermon by Thomas Smyth ringing in their ears.[46] But the greatest of all these missionaries was John Leighton Wilson of the first graduating class of Columbia Theological Seminary. He freed his slaves, took them with him to Liberia, and helped them settle there. Wilson remained in Africa a number of years, wrote widely on West African culture, worked to stop the international slave trade, and on his return to the United States in 1854 became secretary of the Board of Foreign Missions of the Presbyterian Church, with offices in New York. When the Civil War broke out, he returned to South Carolina and did more than any other person for the establishment of foreign mission work by Southern Presbyterians.[47]

All of these benevolent societies, with their utopian visions, functioned to focus the energies released by the Awakening, to provide institutional expression to a world envisioned by the awakened, and, as we shall see more clearly, to serve the ideological purposes of those who gave themselves, often at great personal sacrifice, to the cause of benevolence.

Charlestonians were proud of these benevolent societies and the work that they did, but as in so many other matters, they felt they were not given proper credit, that somehow they were being overlooked so that it appeared only Northerners were interested in benevolence and Southerners were only interested in horse racing. Partly to correct this situation, the Presbyterian minister Benjamin Gildersleeve began his widely read *Charleston Observer* in 1827. "It is worthy of remark," he wrote in an opening editorial "that the efforts of the South, in the cause of benevolence are not appreciated, because they are not known." For Gildersleeve, the honor of the South, as well as the interest of religion, was "intimately connected with the establishment of every medium of religious intelligence that is calculated to give a true representation of our character."[48]

One way that Gildersleeve sought to give a "true representation of our character" was by publishing the activities of the various societies and by noting that support for these benevolent societies was widely based in Charleston among the various denominations.[49] Basil Manly, pastor of the First Baptist Church and later president of the University of Alabama, was a warm and thoughtful advocate. No one exceeded Thomas Grimké, a member of the French Huguenot Church and an Episcopal pew holder, in supporting the causes of benevolence. William Barnwell, pastor of Saint Peter's Episcopal Church, and John Bachman of Saint John's Lutheran were active members of many of the societies.[50] Nevertheless, in spite of this wide support, the Congregationalists and the Presbyterians were clearly the leaders. That was the way it was all over the country, and it was no different in Charleston.[51] Their Reformed tradition encouraged them to seek means of transforming society and to think of themselves as God's chosen instruments for bringing learning, culture, and religious sophistication to a waiting, if recalcitrant, world.

Many, however, were suspicious of these societies. Some feared the national organizations because they were dominated by Northerners.[52] Others, especially some Baptists and Methodists, were suspicious of them as instruments of Presbyterian or Congregational expansion.[53] But growing opposition to the societies existed even among the Presbyterians in the South. They insisted that the church, not interdenominational societies controlled by boards of directors, should be responsible for benevolence work. This was particularly true of mission societies.[54]

In the low country, however, there continued to be substantial support for the societies within the Presbyterian and Congregational churches long after enthusiasm for benevolence work had faded in other parts of the South. Thomas Smyth was a director in the 1840s and 1850s in the American Sunday School Union, the American Tract Society, and the American Bible Society. As late as 1861, Henry Van Dyke, pastor of the First Presbyterian Church of Brooklyn, was speaking at the Circular Church on behalf of the American Bible Society.[55] National benevolent societies, many believed, were not only great instruments for evangelization and for the transformation of society but were also part of the glue that held together a growing and diverse American population. As we shall see, the threats to their unity in the 1850s were regarded as ominous signs for the future of the country.

Columbia Theological Seminary

During the colonial period, many of the Congregational and Presbyterian clergy who served in the Carolina low country came from Great Britain and had been educated there, particularly in the Scottish universities. Following the Revolution, increasing numbers were educated in Northern colleges and, once they were established, in the seminaries of the North.[56] By the 1820s an increasing need was being felt for a Southern seminary. The challenge of an expanding Southern frontier called for a theological seminary in the South "to light up another sun which shall throw still farther west the light of the gospel, to shine upon the pathway of the benighted, and those who have long groped in the dim twilight of unenlightened reason."[57] It was, however, not only the challenge of the West but also an increasing Southern regionalism that called for a distinctly Southern theological seminary. The distance of Princeton from the region, declared the Presbyterian Synod of South Carolina and Georgia, and "the difference of habits and feelings on many subjects from those formed and entertained among ourselves and other circumstances that need not now be particularly detailed" justified and "to some degree" required the establishment of a Southern theological seminary.[58] Here at the beginning of the antebellum period, utopian and ideological elements were linked to one another as they were at the end of the antebellum period in Thomas Smyth's vision of "the goodly land of promised inheritance."

On the one hand, the establishment of the seminary reflected the utopianism and millennial expectations that so clearly marked the great benevolent societies and the influence of the Second Great Awakening. The seminary's constitution, issued in Charleston in 1826, declared: "in the economy of divine Providence, we are called, as it were, to prepare another wheel in that grand moral machinery, which centuries have been constructing; and which is destined, by the eternal decrees, to crush the powers of darkness, and usher in the brightness of millennial glory." The founders were confident that "the world is about to experience a wonderful moral change" that even "the most senseless must perceive." Already Andover and Princeton were "shooting into the darkest corners of the earth" rays of light, and Columbia would now do its part in bringing in "these days of the Prince of Peace, which we see, and which 'the prophets desired to see, but died with the sight.' "[59]

On the other hand, the seminary was to create (to take advantage of E. Brooks Holifield's phrase) a community of "gentlemen theologians." Their place in a hierarchical, paternalistic society was to be that of gentlemen who would be not Cavaliers but theologians.[60] Columbia had a primary ideological function to teach a body of gentlemen to be Reformed theologians who believed in order, propositional truth, and a social hierarchy dominated by white males.[61] Providing much of the emotional power to such ideas was an undergirding evangelical piety that had been forged in the revival fires of the Second Great Awakening. This linkage of the ideological with the utopian would mark much of the life and thought of those ministers who were associated with the seminary and who served in the low country throughout the antebellum period.

From the first, the low country Presbyterians and Congregationalists played a critical role in the establishment of the Columbia Theological Seminary. While the seminary would be located in Columbia, outside the low country, it was linked by ecclesiastical structure, financial support, and above all, family ties to the low country. For this reason, it must be included during the antebellum period as a part of the Reformed community in the low country.[62] This linkage was most visible in faculty and influential pastors who drew the seminary into the circle of low country influence and ethos and made the region the home of the most rigorous theological tradition in the antebellum South. Aaron Leland, Benjamin Morgan Palmer (the younger), Bazile Lanneau, and John Adger all came to the seminary faculty from the low country. Thomas Goulding and Charles C. Jones came from the Midway Congregational Church. James Henley Thornwell and George Howe were longtime members of Charleston Presbytery. Thornwell held a brief pastorate in Charleston and Howe was connected through marriage with extended low country families. Thomas Smyth, while refusing a position on the faculty, served on the board, left two generous bequests to the seminary, and saw his great library become the foundation of the seminary's library. John L. Girardeau, graduate of the seminary and after the Civil War a member of the seminary's faculty, led the attempt in Charleston to fulfill a paternalistic and hierarchical social vision articulated by Thornwell, Smyth, and their colleagues at Columbia.[63] These men were the primary players in shaping a distinctive Southern Presbyterian theological and ecclesiological tradition and social vision. Their thought, so closely identified with the ethos of affluent Presbyterian and Congregational churches in the low country, dominated for a hundred years the Southern Presbyterian Church and, through it, important aspects of the religious life of the South.

The institutional structures established or largely controlled by the whites of the low country Reformed community during the years between the Revolution and the Civil War provide important insights into the complex life of that community. They point to the community's strength within low country society and to the role of the Second Great Awakening in enlivening and strengthening the community. They reveal in their polity the competing impulses and internal tensions within the Reformed tradition. They all served to preserve, expand, and solidify the community.

At the same time, these institutional structures reflected, as did the rituals of the community, a fusion of the Reformed ethos and world view in a complex interaction with the social context of the low country. Institutions were part of a nexus of religious, economic, and ideological relationships linked to other nexuses in low country society. The institutions developed by the Reformed community, in other words, did not suddenly spring from fertile imaginations but emerged from a distinct religious tradition, located within and dynamically interacting with a particular historical and social setting, to serve perceived needs and social requirements.

To be sure, a utopian element also existed in these institutions. This utopianism and the powerful ideological functions of the institutions were drawn toward each other in a dialectical manner that provided a primary conceptual framework for the community—the quest for a middle way. In following chapters we shall explore that quest in detail. We must turn first, however, to the ways African Americans standing within the Reformed tradition developed their own institutional structures within an oppressive social context.

8

A Church Both African American and Reformed

O N THE AFTERNOON of May 30, 1822, a Charleston slave, after agonizing for days over rumors circulating on the docks and in the slave quarters, reported to his master what he had heard. Within two hours the plans for the largest slave revolt in U.S. history were revealed to city authorities. The leader of the revolt was Denmark Vesey, a member with his wife Susan of the Second Presbyterian Church. Born a slave in the West Indies, he had been brought to Charleston in 1783 as the personal servant of a Captain Vesey. In 1800 he won the handsome sum of $1,500 in the East Bay Street Lottery and was allowed by his owner to purchase his freedom for $600. Trained as a carpenter, he earned a living at his trade and built a reputation as a leader in the black community. In April 1817, he had joined the Second Presbyterian Church with two other "people of colour."[1]

Vesey hoped to bring together in one massive revolt the slaves of the city and those of the surrounding plantations. Acting in one coordinated assault on the whites, they hoped to seize the arsenals, set fire to the city, kill the whites as they rushed to fight the fire, and then sail to safety in Santo Domingo. They selected June as the month most likely for success, for many whites would be away from the city to escape the heat and the summer fevers.

When the plot was discovered, white military forces were organized under the command of Robert Young Hayne, and approximately 130 blacks were eventually arrested. George Warren Cross of the Huguenot Church represented Vesey and his chief lieutenant, Gullah Jack. Following secret trials, they were hanged with four others on July 2. A second trial followed with a court of six members including Hayne and Jacob Axson of the Circular Church and John Gordon of First (Scots). They condemned another 22 to be hanged.[2] John Adger, then a child, looked out of a third-floor window of his home and saw "a long gallows erected on 'The Lines,' and on it twenty-two negroes hanged at one time." The whole city, he later wrote, "turned out on this occasion, and this was certainly a sight calculated to strike terror into the heart of every slave."[3]

Utopian Visions: Revolutionary and Conservative

At Vesey's trial, a slave testified that "Vesey studies the Bible a great deal and tries to prove from it that slavery and bondage is against the Bible." Another testified that all Vesey's "general conversation was about religion which he would apply to slavery, as for instance, he would speak of the creation of the world, in which he would say all men had equal rights, blacks as well as whites, & all his religious remarks were mingled with slavery." Rolla Bennett, one of the leaders with Vesey, said in his confession that on the night during which the final plans for the rebellion were made, Vesey was "the first to rise up and speak, and he read to us from the Bible, how the Children of Israel were delivered out of Egypt from bondage."[4]

Whatever the sources of Vesey's religious beliefs—and they were no doubt multiple and complex—they both echoed and transformed powerful impulses within the Reformed community of which Vesey was a part. His use of religion functioned to create a utopian vision that challenged the picture of the world that whites had created—that said African Americans were to be slaves and whites were to be slave owners. Vesey's utopian vision was an imaginative construction of an alternative social reality. His was a vision that broke—for those who shared it—any fatalistic acceptance of the status quo, a vision that said things could be different and indeed were intended by God to be different.[5] Vesey's utopianism, emerging out of the experience of a bitterly oppressed people, grasped a powerful impulse that whites had claimed only for themselves and transformed it into a vision of liberation for African Americans. He took the freedom longings of African Americans that had been unfocused or that had been directed toward heaven and gave them a specific, historical goal: the burning of Charleston and the escape from the land of bondage. These longings now appeared to be realizable and consequently gave all who caught the vision a new courage and zeal that whites called fanatical.[6]

Vesey used the very biblical images that whites had used in their own struggles against hierarchies and oppressive systems. He used them to create his own utopian vision of liberated African Americans and to shatter those other biblical images whites had used to keep slaves "in their place." When Vesey was sentenced, the court acknowledged his use of the Bible while at the same time denouncing his "perversion" of it. "In addition to treason," the court declared, "you have committed the grossest impiety, in attempting to pervert the sacred words of God into a sanction for crimes of the blackest hue. It is evident, that you are totally insensible of the divine influence of that Gospel, 'all whose paths are peace.'" In contrast to Vesey's revolutionary utopianism, the court drew on an ideological interpretation of the Bible to legitimize the present social order and denounce any challenge to that order. "It was to reconcile us to our destinies on earth," declared the court, "and to enable us to discharge with fidelity, all the duties of life, that those holy precepts were imparted by Heaven to fallen man." The specific precepts the court cited as "imparted by Heaven" were, of course, Saint Paul's admonition, "Servants obey in all things your masters," and Saint Peter's charge, "Servants be subject to your masters with all fear, not only to the good and gentle, but also to the forward."[7]

With Vesey we thus see a utopian vision emerge out of an oppressed group. The vision contained no carefully designed social structure for the future, no blueprint for a new social order. Rather, the vision was a revolutionary, anarchic breaching of the present order, a shattering of the present image of the way things are and have to be for the future, the releasing of repressed energies, and a courageous calling to action. In response the court countered with a powerful ideology of a God-given place and responsibilities. The military power of the state and its authority rooted in such an ideology were finally too much for Vesey and his followers—at least for those followers of his generation. The consequences were of no little significance in the development of a distinct African American Reformed community in the low country.

Vesey's revolutionary utopianism not only provoked the ideological response of the court but also encouraged the development of a counterutopia, an alternative vision nurtured by whites in the low country's Reformed community.[8] This counterutopia was conservative and not revolutionary in nature. It envisioned an organic society where each person has duties and corresponding rights, where each person is linked to the whole society through complex mutual relationships, where whites would be kind, just, and paternalistic masters and African Americans would be dutiful, loyal, and obedient servants.[9]

Presbyterian and Congregational churches in the low country shared with other churches of the region a concern for the religious instruction of slaves and a growing zeal throughout the antebellum period for their evangelization. What was most distinctive about the white Presbyterian and Congregational approach to African Americans was the degree to which those whites in the Reformed tradition put into practice the paternalistic assumptions shared by all the churches. To be sure, the old tension in the Reformed tradition between freedom and order, between equality and hierarchy—or the tension between a conservative and liberal utopianism—was still there as we shall see in later chapters. But even as the white Reformed community sought a *via media* between these tensions, it began to articulate and to seek to embody a hierarchical and paternalistic society. Among the duties of whites, it began to be said over and over again after 1830, was the task of seeing that slaves receive "proper" religious instruction.[10] White Presbyterians and Congregationalists, struggling with their strong Reformed sense of duty and their concern for "right" thinking, consequently began to turn to this task with increasing vigor—especially as the attacks against slavery grew in intensity.

From the first reports of the Vesey revolt, rumors circulated that an independent African Church was involved. Emmanuel African Methodist Episcopal Church had been organized by the free black Morris Brown and had grown rapidly to the second largest A.M.E. church in the country (only Mother Bethel in Philadelphia was larger). Its size and strength, however, caused it to be a source of fear and growing anxiety to Charleston whites. African Americans meeting separately from whites, away from the observation and control of their masters, appeared to many whites to be a serious threat to the security of the city. While no link was ever established between the church leadership and the revolt (the accounts of the accused varied), the fears were enough to cause white authorities to close the church (the building had already been demolished) and exile Brown.[11]

One immediate result of the Vesey revolt was that whites in Charleston became convinced that no separate African American churches should be allowed in the city. Henceforth only one pattern for African American church membership would be allowed: if African Americans wished to worship or to belong to a church, they would have to go to a church clearly under the control of whites, with a white minister and white officers. Such was the context in which whites in the Reformed tradition began to articulate their conservative utopian vision. But it was also in this context, out of this travail, that African Americans, long members of the white-dominated churches, moved to institutionalize slowly developing practices and to create under the watchful eyes of whites "a church within a church." Here they would nurture a utopian vision that was, if not revolutionary on the model of Vesey's, subversive of both the ideological claims and the conservative utopianism of the whites.

The Emergence of a Distinct Community

Perhaps not surprisingly, given the increasing paternalism of the Reformed community, African Americans did not join the Presbyterian and Congregational churches in the low country in any great numbers. Certainly they never came close to the numbers that joined the Methodist or Baptist churches where African Americans had greater freedom to develop their religious life. Moreover, church membership rolls reveal that Charleston slaves, given the opportunity to choose their churches, joined in overwhelming numbers congregations other than those to which their owners belonged.[12] In 1815 there were 282 white Methodists in Charleston and 3,789 black Methodists. Forty years later, fewer than 700 whites and more than 5,000 blacks were associated with the three Methodist churches in the city. In 1845 the First Baptist Church of Charleston had 293 whites and 1,543 blacks.[13]

At the Presbyterian and Congregational churches the numbers were much more modest. In 1845, for example, the Second Presbyterian Church had 380 white members and 178 black members. Nevertheless, the Presbyterian and Congregational churches had an important place in the black community of the city. During the 1850s, Zion Presbyterian Church became a central gathering place for Charleston blacks with a membership of almost 500 African Americans and up to 2,000 blacks attending Sunday services. It became one of the most significant institutions in the city's black community, a role it would continue to play for several stormy decades.[14]

In the countryside the story was different—African Americans greatly outnumbered whites not only in the general population but also in the Presbyterian and Congregational churches. In 1845, reports were gathered on the "Religious Instruction of Slaves" that revealed the development of the African American church in the rural areas. From Walterboro, Edward Palmer wrote of his experience at Bethel and Stoney Creek: "During a ministry of 21 years, a part of every Sabbath has been *exclusively* devoted to the negroes. I have two appointments distant asunder 25 miles, which together, place under my spiritual charge some 600. I find a perfect willingness on the part of the several owners of these slaves to have them religiously instructed, and a constant and increasing attention on the part of the slaves themselves."[15] William States Lee, the longtime pastor of the Edisto Island Presbyterian Church, reported that 157 blacks were in communion with the church and that "from 250 to 300 attend our Sabbath services." In contrast to the churches in Charleston, Lee noted that "no persons of colour are authorized to teach in connection with our church."[16]

John Rivers, an Anglican layman on James Island, wrote that 300 blacks belonged to the Presbyterian church on the island. The church, said Rivers, has "several coloured class-leaders, who hold weekly or semi-monthly meetings, but it is thought they do little good: and there is a plan in contemplation by the Presbyterian Clergyman to go into effect the 1st of June, to supersede the necessity of them altogether." Rivers's comments reflect the whites' suspicion of black leaders. The plan of the "Presbyterian Clergyman" to assume more responsibility for the religious life of the slaves illustrates how a paternalistic concern often led to greater white control over the religious life of slaves. In spite of the effects of such paternalism, Rivers noted that there "are exemplary members on almost all the plantations, who hold the office of a kind of watchman." The blacks, he said, "attend public worship all the year, and after the morning services, on the Sabbath, there is a special service adapted to, and intended for, their use. They are then instructed in the catechism, the Lord's prayer, the Creed, and Commandments, all of which is explained."[17]

By 1860 at the Johns Island Presbyterian Church there were 60 white members and 510 African American members, making it the second-largest Presbyterian church in the South.[18] In that year, the membership of the rural and village churches was:

	BLACK	WHITE
JAMES ISLAND	188	23
ORANGEBURG	32	46
JOHNS ISLAND and		
WADMALAW	510	60
STONEY CREEK	132	35
WALTERBORO	155	51
SUMMERVILLE	31	8
WILTON	152	35

The black membership at Edisto Island Presbyterian Church, which was not reported to the presbytery, remained close to what Lee had given in 1845: around 150. The figures for the Wappetaw Congregational Church were probably close to that of Wilton. Everywhere, those who attended church exceeded the number of communicant members.[19]

Because rural churches were far apart, slaves could not move as easily between congregations as they did in Charleston. There are, for example, few records of transfers of slave membership in the rural and village churches. What is striking in their records is that slaves of one owner would often join a church together. Unlike the Charleston slaves, many joined the congregation where their owners worshiped. At the Stoney Creek church, for example, in November 1832, 13 slaves of Colonel James Cuthbert were baptized and were followed in the spring by another 9—all "Preparatory to Church membership." In 1860, 22 slaves of John Berkeley Grimball joined the Wilton congregation. Evidently, a religious revival occasionally swept a plantation and led a number of the slaves to join the church. On the other hand, between 1850 and 1861 more than 165 slaves joined the Johns Island Presbyterian Church, often in groups of 10 or more, but not representing one plantation or owner. Most were "servants of" white members of the congregation and none were received by "letters of transfer."[20]

It was in these low country communities, both urban and rural, that African Americans, working within the white-dominated structures of Presbyterian and Congregational churches, built their own church. While this African American church had colonial roots, institutional developments during the antebellum period laid the foundation for the Carolina low country to become one of the most important regions in the nation for a distinct African American Reformed community and tradition.[21]

Institutional Structures of the Community:
A Church within a Church

At the heart of this Reformed "church within a church" were the classes to which each black member was assigned.[22] In Charleston each class had a leader—a respected member of the black community but appointed by the white session or corporation. The classes, which met weekly for Bible study and informal worship conducted by their leaders, played an important role in the efforts of blacks to educate themselves. Their focus was on religious instruction, but such instruction, especially when away from the eyes and ears of whites, provided opportunities for blacks to interpret their experiences and to find strength and guidance for their lives under the harsh realities of slavery. Because many of the leaders could read and write (they had to prepare written reports for white sessions or committees), they could tell, no doubt circumspectly, of a broader world than Charleston and slavery.[23]

Because it was against the law in South Carolina for blacks to go under the designation of "preacher," careful rules were spelled out by the white Presbyterian and Congregational authorities about what the black leaders could do (the Baptists apparently ignored the legal restrictions on the use of "preacher" and had their black preachers).[24] At Second Presbyterian, the leaders could lead their classes with prayer and singing and could exhort "their brethren briefly and modestly when moved to do so," but they were "strictly prohibited all such utterances as by their length, or their formality and pretension may be likely to present them before the people in the attitude of Ministers of Jesus Christ." At Circular Congregational, the black leaders could not preach, but they could read the Scriptures, pray, lead singing, and exhort.[25]

These restrictions were intended to provide whites with a "monopoly of imagination."[26] The restrictions were to ensure that no revolutionary utopianism might be drawn from the Bible in the manner of a Denmark Vesey. By controlling the formal, official communication and interpretation of the Bible, whites hoped to ensure order, propriety, and the maintenance of the present system. Yet whatever restrictions might be placed on them, African American leaders could "deliver their message" and not be concerned about the difference between exhorting and preaching. Each Sunday at sunrise the leaders at Second Presbyterian, for example, held a worship service that was attended by 400 or 500 people. A second service was held "just before candle-light" and was attended by the same number.[27] To be sure, the leaders had to be discreet in what was said at such services. They had to avoid any "impropriety." Yet from the margins, away from the centers of official interpretation and communication, they were able to speak in ways that built up the community, encouraged a growing sense of identity, provided strength to face the daily oppression of slavery, and gave hope for the future.

One of the responsibilities of the black leaders was to visit as a pastor might in the homes of the black membership—a task that must have required remarkable tact not to offend white owners. If a member were found to be destitute, leaders could recommend that help be provided out of the congregation's "poor funds." Once such recommendations were approved by deacons or other white officers of the congregation, the leaders were given authority to deliver a small stipend and other aid to the one in need. At Circular Congregational an average of $375 a year was distributed to the needy members of the congregation throughout the antebellum period. Approximately half went to white members, distributed by the deacons, and half went to black members, distributed by the black leaders. "Fine warm clothing and nourishment" were also provided to those in need.[28] In a similar manner, burial funds were also collected to ensure that no one be denied a decent funeral. Such efforts on the part of the African American membership to look after one another's needs helped to build a sense of identity and solidarity as a distinct African American community.

African American church leaders also had oversight for the spiritual and moral life of the African American members of the congregation. As did the white church leaders, they encouraged those who were slack in their church attendance, counseled those facing particular difficulties, and, when they deemed it necessary, used the disciplinary power of white authorities. In such cases, the leaders acted as a kind of public prosecutor, presenting a case before the session or, at Circular Congregation, a committee of the white members. Most of the cases that came to trial involved sexual misconduct, although public drunkenness was also a common cause of discipline. If the accused were found guilty, the sentence might be six months' suspension from the communion of the church, if there were extenuating circumstances; one- to two-year suspensions, if the case were serious but the guilty party showed signs of genuine repentance; or excommunication, if there were no sign of repentance.

There is no evidence that the African Americans in the rural and small-town churches were able to organize extensive institutional structures within the confines of the white-dominated churches, as African Americans in Charleston were able to do. At the Johns Island Presbyterian Church, where there was a large black membership, blacks were frequently disciplined by the church session during the 1850s, but the session minutes provide no record of black leaders bringing charges or making presentations before the session.[29] While black leaders were selected for the James Island congregation, there was, as has been seen, opposition to them. Nevertheless, informal structures existed around persons of ability and piety—often called "watchmen," whose authority, if not institutionally formal, was real in the black community. Such was the case at James Island and at the Midway Congregational Church, and there is every reason to suppose the same was true of other rural churches in the low country.[30] One thing, however, is clear: whatever the paternalism of whites, whatever authority they exercised, a black church was being built up within these white-dominated congregations. African American churches were being formed with their own histories, their own traditions, and their own leaders. They would be ready when freedom came to move out on their own as clearly defined congregations.

These institutional structures were both a support to slavery and an important resource to African Americans in their resistance to slavery's oppression. The structures that were designed to provide aid to the needy, while ameliorative and consequently conservative in character, were also subversive of owners' authority, for they encouraged African Americans to develop systems of support outside the owners' control and challenged the dominant ideology that declared African Americans could not take care of themselves.[31]

In a similar manner, church discipline was both a support for slavery and a resource for resistance. It functioned as an important means of social control, helped to enforce through conscience and community pressure a sober and orderly life, and was intended by whites to have a "salutary effect" upon "slaves' labor and discipline."[32] For African Americans, however, the discipline of the "church within a church"—even through the use of the power of white church authorities—served other functions. It represented an important effort on the part of African Americans to bring some order to their community struggling in the midst of the chaos and disorder of slavery. By encouraging the development of a self-disciplined personal character, church discipline tended to subvert a powerful tool of oppression—one that declared African Americans to be undisciplined children (or sometimes beasts) needing the control of whites. And it helped to create a cohesive community with a self-imposed discipline and a clear identity that transcended the discipline of owners and the identity given by being owned.

This two-edged quality would long mark the community's relationship to white society. On the one hand, after the Civil War the African American Presbyterian and Congregationalist community in the low country would appear to be among the most acculturated of African American groups to the ways and values of white, bourgeois society—and among the most eager to be acculturated. On the other hand, this Reformed community would also possess important resources for resisting the degradations of racial oppression and would provide significant leadership in the long struggle against the forces of oppression.

The institutional structures described above were not peculiar to the African American Reformed community that developed in the Carolina low country. On the contrary, these structures were part of a much larger picture of the religious life of African Americans throughout the South. As such, they point to the ways in which the community's boundaries overlapped with other religious communities, particularly the Methodists, and with other regions of the country.[33] Nevertheless, distinctive characteristics marked this Reformed African American community in the low country. These distinctions were more of an emphasis and a nuance than something unique to the community, but they highlighted the dual roots of the community: African American and Reformed. To understand these nuanced distinctions, we turn to the ways in which a particular ethos and world view were developed and nurtured in the community.

The Character of the Community

The ethos and world view of the community emerged out of the complex and dynamic interaction between two cultural traditions in the Carolina low country. One was a cultural tradition rooted in Africa and developed over generations within a North American slave society. The other was the Reformed tradition rooted in Europe and also developed over generations in a North American slave society. The character of this African American Reformed community, its style of life, its moral and aesthetic spirit were all shaped by the dialectical interaction of these two traditions. In a similar manner, the community's picture of the world, its understanding of the "way things really are," and the ways it felt about and reacted to life were largely shaped by the dialectic of the two traditions within the specific social context of the Carolina low country. The result was a community that was both African American and Reformed, both Reformed African American and African American Reformed. Within this community two independent traditions became interdependent.[34]

Yet it was not simply the whole of each tradition that was in full interaction with the other tradition. Because both traditions were themselves complex, often reflecting within themselves competing tendencies and overlapping boundaries, those elements in each tradition that came to dominate the community were drawn to the fore by the community's social context during the antebellum period. The community's ethos and world view, forged in these complex interactions between traditions and social context, found expression in the processes by which persons entered the community and in the community's practices and rites.[35]

Preparations for Membership: Religious Instruction

Before an adult African American could become a full member of the Reformed "church within a church," a long period of religious instruction was necessary. This instruction was supervised by whites, although African American leaders or watchmen were often involved, especially in Charleston. The pedagogy was catechetical and oral, and after 1837 the content was a catechism prepared by Charles C. Jones while he was a professor at Columbia Theological Seminary. Jones, "the Apostle to the Negro Slaves," wrote the catechism specifically for slaves.[36] After its publication, it became the primary instrument used by the Reformed churches in the low country for the religious instruction of African Americans.[37] As such it reflected the conservative utopianism, as well as the ideological interests, of duty-driven whites in the Reformed community.

Jones's catechism had as its primary focus a Reformed and evangelical presentation of the faith: 150 pages present God as Creator, Lawgiver, and, through Jesus Christ, Savior to fallen humanity. "It does not matter," declared the catechism, "what country one comes from, whether we are from the East or from the West, the North or the South. It does not matter of what *colour* we are, whether of white, or brown, or black. It does not matter of what *condition* we are, whether rich or poor, old or young, male or female, bond or free. Jesus is able to save *all* who come unto him."[38] Set within this evangelical, orthodox presentation of the faith, however, was a social vision—a conservative utopianism—of the relationship of parents to children, of husbands to wives, and of masters to servants. Four pages of the catechism were given over specifically to the "duties of masters and servants."

Beginning with a presentation of God's omniscience, the catechism constructed a paternalistic order in which the slave's place and behavior were carefully defined and restricted.

Q. Is God present in every place?
A. Yes.
Q. What does he see and know?
A. All things.
Q. Who is in duty bound to have justice done Servants when they are wronged or abused or ill-treated by anyone?
A. The Master.
Q. Is it right for the Master to punish his servants cruelly?
A. No.

Masters, it was said, should not threaten their servants and should provide them with religious instruction. Slaves were told that there is one Master of all in heaven who does not show favor to earthly masters for they will have to "render an account for the manner in which they treat their Servants."

But if masters had their duties, slaves also had theirs.

Q. What command has God given to Servants, concerning obedience to their Masters?
A. "Servants obey in all things your Masters according to the flesh, not in eye-service as men-pleasers, but in singleness of heart, fearing God."
Q. What are Servants to count their Masters worthy of?
A. "All honor."
Q. How are they to do their service of their master?
A. "*With good will*, doing service unto the Lord and not unto men."
Q. How are they to try to please their Masters?

A. "Please them well in all things, not answering again."
Q. Is it right in a Servant when commanded to be sullen and slow, and answer his Master again?
A. "No."

Slaves were taught to be examples to one another in their love and obedience to their masters and in their patience in enduring unjust masters. Saint Paul's admonitions to the runaway slave Onesimus were recited to remind slaves that they should not run away or harbor runaways. If they were but faithful in the place in which God had placed them, if they did their duty as servants, then they would be respected by all and blessed and honored by God.[39]

Such was the content of Jones's catechism, and it was this content that was taught on Edisto Island and on Meeting Street, on James Island, at Bethel Pon Pon, and in the other Reformed congregations scattered throughout the low country. It presented a social vision of a harmonious, well-ordered, and tranquil society. Each person was said to have a place in such a paternalistic society; on Edisto, for example, the Seabrooks and the Townsends, the Whaleys, the Mikells, and the other white families were to be owners and masters. Cudjo and Judy, Mingo, Jack, Sue, and the other African Americans on the island were to be slaves and servants.

The religious instruction of slaves, rooted in the Reformed tradition, was thus a pedagogy of oppression. When African Americans accepted the dependence and submission taught in the catechism, when they believed that God had created a world of hierarchical social positions and that they were to "stay in their place," then their religious instruction functioned to reinforce the status quo.[40] In this way, religious instruction served ideological purposes for the whites. Yet it also reflected the conservative utopianism emerging among the whites within the Reformed community—a vision of moving toward a not yet orderly, organic community where everyone had certain rights, according to social place, and certain corresponding duties.

But such instruction also functioned for African Americans as a pedagogy of liberation. The long-term tendency of the instruction was to put limits to the power of owners, to set owners' power within the context of a larger disciplinary system, for owners were also under the discipline of the church, specifically in regard to their "servants." However poorly that discipline worked, however infrequently it was applied, it stood as a reminder that white owners would have to "render an account" to God "for the manner in which they treat their servants."[41] For African Americans to believe that the world was ordered in this way, that there was a system of divine law to which owners were accountable and that a day of judgment was coming, was a resource in their struggle for liberation. Linked with the traditional African religious belief that God is "the supreme Judge Who acts with impartiality," this world view, with its powerful utopian elements, was consequently subversive of the very hierarchical claims being taught by whites.[42]

If the catechetical teaching had an influence on the world view of the community, it also influenced its ethos. Together with the long, logical sermons African Americans heard every Sunday in Presbyterian and Congregational churches, the memorized questions and answers of the catechism helped to shape a distinct character structure: self-disciplined, preoccupied with order, and convinced of the importance of education. An African American Reformed community was emerging that would reflect, when freedom came, characteristics that marked other Reformed communities. African American Presbyterian and Congregational churches that emerged from "the church within a church" in the days following the Civil War would already be noted for their high regard for education, for their insistence on "doing things decently and in order," and for rigorous rejection of what W. E. B. Du Bois called the "frenzy" of much African American worship.[43]

Joining the Community

The character of African Americans who, after a period of religious instruction, joined a Presbyterian or Congregational church during the antebellum period is revealed in what were called "notes of permission" sent by owners to the churches. For slaves to join a Presbyterian or Congregational church, they were required to receive the permission of their owners. These notes of permission, together with notations in session records, indicate what was expected by the churches and patterns of character among those who joined the community. Typical in this regard, although more lavish in its praise, was the note of William Bell. His servant Boston, he said, had his permission to join the Third Presbyterian Church. "A better servant," Bell noted, "I do not know & his moral character, I believe to be unimpeachable."[44] Some of the notes indicate recent changes of behavior in the slaves: "it may be well to observe" wrote Mary Hughes, "that from an overbearing and almost ungovernable servant she is now humble, faithful and obedient." Other notes indicate hopes for such changes. Charles Maule wrote: "I am perfectly agreeable that my Servant Betsy should join your Church if it will make her do Better and she can get out every Sunday."[45]

Certain white assumptions about the general character of African Americans are revealed in many of the notes. "As far as our knowledge will allow," wrote William Maxwell, of one of his slaves, "we believe him to bear as fair a Character as most of his Colour." "I consider him," wrote Edward Horlbeck of his slave John, "as correct and prudent a Black man as I have known." On the other hand, the superintendent and several workers for the South Carolina Railroad recommended—in language they might have used for themselves—a slave owned by the company: "He is a very decent, steady, sober, industrious, faithful and trustworthy fellow, and we cheerfully recommend him to the Congregation of the Third Presbyterian Church." But they called him "the Boy Phillipp," a designation many used: "my boy Joshua," "my negro girl Judy."[46]

Most of the notes point to a character type closely associated with the Reformed ethic—temperate, disciplined, orderly, and industrious: "I have every reason to believe him perfectly Sober, Honest, and orderly"; "I have always found her honest & faithful and of good character"; "she has behaved remarkably well and I have every reason to believe that she is an honest and faithful slave."[47] The interest of the owners in having humble, faithful, honest, and obedient slaves and the hope of many owners that church membership would encourage such behavior clearly runs through the notes. What is important to note here, however, is not the familiar story of social control through religion but the emergence of a community marked by members who shared a particular character type. Even the discipline of the community, when members "stumbled and fell," helped to reinforce this character type and to shape the formation of personality. The community itself, in other words, both by its expectations for membership and by its internal life, would play an important role in the formation of a certain character and personality type.[48] The consequences will be clear in following chapters as social profiles of this African American Reformed community are developed.

Rites of the Community

Baptism

Increasing numbers during the antebellum period became part of the Reformed African American community not by joining as adults but by being baptized as infants or children. As the community grew in size and as the "church within a church" took on increasing institutional structure, the baptism of African American children became a more common practice. This rite both concealed and revealed profound contradictions within the community and pointed to the depth of courage and faith of African American parents.

Most African American children who were presented for baptism were brought by their parents. Standing before the white minister, the parents would be asked: "Do you acknowledge your child's need of the cleansing blood of Jesus Christ, and the renewing grace of the Holy Spirit?" "We do," they would reply. "Do you claim God's covenant promises in [his] behalf, and do you look in faith to the Lord Jesus Christ for [his] salvation as you do for your own?" "We do," they would reply. "Do you now unreservedly dedicate your child to God, and promise, in humble reliance upon divine grace, that you will endeavor to set before [him] a godly example, that you will pray with and for [him], that you will teach [him] the doctrines of our holy religion, and that you will strive, by all the means of God's appointment, to bring [him] up in the nurture and admonition of the Lord?" Once again they would respond, "We do." The minister, after asking the Christian name of the child, would, with cupped hand, pour water over the child's head while saying the ancient formula: "Child of the covenant, I baptize thee in the name of the Father, and of the Son, and of the Holy Ghost."[49]

Slave children, however, were not only regarded as the children of their parents but as the responsibility of their owners. The question was thus raised: "Should a master bring slave children to be baptized, since the master was head of his 'household'?" Given the paternalistic ideals by which Southern whites were defending slavery, did not those ideals impose on the white masters the responsibility for the baptism of slave children? Yes, declared the Synod of South Carolina in 1846. It is the duty, said the synod, "of believing masters to train up their servants, as well as their children, in the nurture and admonition of the Lord." The principles of "the Abrahamic covenant," said the synod, "as to the circumcision of servants, is still in force in reference to the infant offspring of those who stand to us in this relation; and that as baptism succeeds to circumcision, it is the duty of masters to dedicate such servants to God in the ordinance of baptism, and to do all in their power to train them up in a knowledge of the truth, and in the way of salvation through Christ."[50] While there is little indication that white masters made a regular practice of bringing slave children to baptism in the Presbyterian or the Congregational churches of the low country, either in the countryside or in the city, the synod's position was a logical expression of that conservative utopianism Reformed thought was articulating in the midst of a slave society.

These baptisms both concealed and revealed contradictions inherent within the African American Reformed community. The contradictions were between, on the one hand, the honor paid to family and to an organic, covenantal community and, on the other hand, the radical individualism of the slave society where individual slave masters possessed a fearsome power to destroy family and disperse community. The contradictions were concealed in the baptisms through the language of family and the images of stability, harmony, and covenantal community. But the contradictions were revealed in the discontinuity between the religious meaning of baptism and the social realities of the low country. Those to be baptized came as the owned, as property of whites. They came with the permission of owners and sometimes were specifically brought by the "head of the family," the white owner. Yet in the baptism itself they were named, were identified, as members of a larger family, the household of faith, in which all members stood equally helpless and in need before the throne of grace. Moreover, when parents took the baptismal vows, as was generally the case, they claimed that this was their child and they accepted the sacred responsibility of raising the child in "the nurture and admonition of the Lord." The rite thus functioned ideologically to legitimize the power of whites and to support the status quo, while at the same time it acted as a powerful subversive force in a slave society. Baptism provided a utopian vision, an alternative image of reality—one of fundamental equality—that contradicted the claims of a slave society that were said to be founded on eternal verities. A different way of imagining and construing the world and an alternative way of ordering experience could be heard in the vows and seen in the act of baptizing slave children.

Baptism consequently functioned as a symbol of an old world as lived by slaves and a new world as imagined by slaves. Baptism dramatized both evil and good: a world where one is treated and understood as chattel, as property, and a world where one is a child of God, where parents can in freedom and hope take vows for their children.

Marriage

The contradictions hidden and revealed in slave baptisms were even more acute in regard to marriage. Slave marriages were not recognized by the state. A slave's primary relationship was to a master or mistress and not to a husband or wife. For the state to recognize slave marriages would have left owners open to the charge that they were frequently putting asunder what God had joined together. Moreover, the official recognition of slave marriages would have had the potential of reducing the control owners had over their slave property. The slave system itself, as it had evolved in the South, depended on the owners' having complete authority to buy or sell slaves according to the owners' own economic interests. An all too frequent outcome was the selling of slaves and division of families no matter what baptismal or marriage vows had been taken.

In contrast to the state, the churches of all denominations insisted on the sanctity of slave marriages.[51] The tensions of attempting to uphold such an ideal within a system that worked directly against it can be seen in the church records. Over and over again, the church rolls note beside a black member's name "Removed" or "Sold away from the city."[52] But what of the marriage of one "sold away" so suddenly? How were the churches to regard the spouse left behind? As early as the 1820s, the session of the Second Presbyterian Church sought to answer this question. The session considered "whether a coloured member whose wife has been parted from him being sold & transferred to a distance, can marry again." It was "decided in the affirmative." But such questions were not easily settled, for they kept reappearing. Twenty years later the session again considered its policy and adopted as a bylaw:

Resolved, that this Session as a Court of Christ, know/ and ever have Known/ of no law of Marriage or divorce, except that laid down by Christ, for men of all classes, & all colours, and that as according to this law, "whom God hath joined together Man ought not to put asunder," the Separation of man & wife, when it is *voluntary* or *avoidable* on the part of any master is Sinful; and that this Session cannot sanction the remarriage of any parties so separated, unless when they have been so long and so irreparably apart, as to constitute in the eye of the law a practical demise of one or other of the parties.[53]

White members of the Second Presbyterian Church and the other Presbyterian and Congregational churches in the low country were disciplined for many things—going to balls or the theater, public drunkenness, improper business dealings—but there is no record of any white ever being disciplined for "putting asunder" what "God had joined together" in the marriage of blacks. The breakup of slave marriages was always, it is supposed, regarded as involuntary and unavoidable. Of course, if a white master had been brought to trial before a prominent church for breaking up a slave marriage, it would have been a crisis for the system of slavery and for the white community. The system itself, with owners' absolute control over their slaves, would have been challenged.

In spite of church pronouncements in regard to slave marriages, church courts never disciplined white members who sold a husband away from a wife, or a wife from a husband, and they did not even consider disciplining those who sold children away from parents or parents away from children, even those for whom baptismal vows had been taken.[54] As in other disciplinary matters, the power of whites would have been limited by setting it within a larger disciplinary system. Nevertheless, implicit in these church pronouncements were reminders that whites had a "master in heaven," before whom they stood in judgment. Such reminders pointed to the conservative utopian vision of a stable, orderly, and harmonious society.

If white church leaders failed to take action in regard to slave marriages, African Americans sought to uphold slave marriages and to find ways to strengthen slave families. Marriages were often festive occasions when slaves "dressed up" and feasts were prepared. While weddings were frequently encouraged by whites who recognized the importance of stable marriages for slave morale, there was also much criticism from whites about the "extravagance" of African American weddings. In 1859, after much public criticism of slave weddings at the Zion Presbyterian Church in Charleston, the white session ruled that there could be no more night weddings and that participants had to dress more modestly.[55] But for slaves, such occasions were opportunities to affirm the importance and dignity of marriage.[56]

African American leaders were the primary ones who brought before the churches cases of infidelity, insisting in their own community that marriage vows be honored. While fidelity in slave marriages reflected important traditions within the broader African American community and was much more widely practiced than white propaganda indicated, church structures and discipline became an organized means of strengthening impulses already present for honoring slave marriages.[57] Church discipline became a means of trying to bring some order to the lives of African Americans, constantly threatened as they were by the violence and disorder of the slavery system. In this way African American leaders, drawing on both African American and Reformed traditions, created a counterpolity to that of the state—a polity reflecting the vision, the alternative ordering of reality, seen in baptism. The state may have seen only property under the control of white owners. The state may have been blind to slave marriages and to the claims of slave parents for their children. But in the baptismal and marriage vows and in the discipline of the "church within a church," another way of understanding and ordering human life was claimed.

Funerals

The subversive and alternative ordering of reality seen in slave baptisms and marriages was also present in slave funerals. Here too the interaction between two traditions, set within a specific social context, are revealed. The importance of a proper funeral was widespread in the African American community and was rooted both in African funeral traditions and in African Americans' insistence that the slave was not a "nobody" but a "somebody," one whose body was important—even in death—and was to be treated with dignity and respect.[58] This tradition was reinforced by the Reformed tradition and was provided with a supportive institutional framework within the Reformed African American community.

When black members of a congregation died, their class leaders were responsible for many of the funeral arrangements. At the Third Presbyterian Church, for example, the charge for a funeral and burial in the church's "coloured members burial ground" was $5.00. Included for this charge was the use of the church's hearse and pall, a horse and driver, and grave digger. If an indigent member died without funds to pay, the charges were met out of a special burial fund.[59]

At Second Presbyterian, Thomas Smyth usually conducted the funeral service in the church sanctuary: a Scripture reading, a prayer, a hymn or two, and a brief meditation. Mention would be made of the person's life, and dying statements often would be noted. The dying, of whatever race, would have been asked: "Do you trust in Jesus?" and "Are you resting on the Everlasting arms?" At the funerals of the pious, black or white, it might be said of the departed one: "Died in confident hope," or "died trusting Jesus," or "died expressing trust in Christ and a readiness to depart this life."[60] After the service in the sanctuary, the class leaders assumed responsibility for the burial of their class members. The church's hearse carried the body to Rikerville where the congregation's "burying ground for our coloured people" was located. The sexton, Francis Dent, had the grave opened, and the leader conducted a simple service. As the coffin was lowered into the "house of silence," Maum Cinda, the assistant sexton, snatched "a fearful joy" from casting the first handful of dirt on the one who had passed over Jordan into the Promised Land. When Frederick Law Olmstead traveled through the South in the 1850s, he attended the burial of a black in Charleston. The service, he noted, was "simple and decorous" and was conducted by a "well-dressed and dignified elderly negro" who used the Presbyterian order. "The grave was filled by the negroes, before the crowd, which was quite large, dispersed. Beside myself, only one white man, probably a policeman, was in attendance."[61]

Such a funeral dramatizes the interaction between the two traditions in the shaping of a distinct African American Reformed community. Both traditions were present in the care given to the funeral of a member. The African American tradition can perhaps be seen most distinctly in Maum Cinda's "fearful joy" in casting the first handful of dirt into the open grave.[62] But the Reformed tradition's restraint can also be heard in the absence of the familiar shouts, chanting, and singing of most African American funerals and in the ordered service in the sanctuary. Furthermore, the community's own ordering of itself can be seen in the burial funds sometimes administered by African American leaders themselves.[63]

The funeral and the other rites of this "church within a church" functioned as a powerful instrument of social solidarity. They nurtured a distinct ethos and encouraged—amid countervailing tendencies—a utopian vision. This vision, if not revolutionary after the manner of Denmark Vesey, was nevertheless an alternative world view subversive of both the dominant ideology of slave owners and the conservative utopianism beginning to be forcefully articulated by whites in the Reformed community. In the process, an amazing, tightly knit little world was created that was both African American and Reformed. This little world—distinct and yet overlapping in so many ways the boundaries that marked it—was part of two worlds, one African American and one Reformed. By being fully a part of both worlds, it helped to demonstrate that neither world was monolithic, that both were complex, and that the complexity was rooted in a dialectical relationship between cultural traditions and a social context.

This community that was both African American and Reformed and that emerged during the antebellum period was disciplined, convinced of the importance of order and education, and had created institutional structures that would serve as the foundation of new churches once freedom came. To be sure, the community was inescapably and fundamentally set within a social context dominated by the harsh realities of slavery. That context was reflected in every aspect of the community life and set the limits and boundaries within which the community lived. Nevertheless, the community stood in contrast to those images of low country African Americans that paralleled the Cavalier myth among whites—that portrayed African Americans as lacking discipline, order, and a concern for education.[64] No less than the white Reformed community, this African American Reformed community would play a significant role—particularly in education and politics—in the years that followed the Civil War.

9

An Antebellum Social Profile in Black and White

"Our Kind of People"

T HE REFORMED COMMUNITY in the Carolina low country reflected certain social attributes that marked it as a community and gave it an identifiable character during the years between the Revolution and the Civil War. While it shared with other subgroups of the region many similarities and complex relationships, and while its boundaries as a community were often ambiguous and blurred, it nevertheless constituted a distinct community and its membership portrayed in broad strokes a dominance of certain social characteristics. Members of the community could increasingly speak of "our kind of people" and know that such language was not an illusion but was rooted in social and psychological realities.[1]

The social character of the community was both reflected in and shaped by the institutional structures and organizations described in the two preceding chapters. In a similar manner, the community's intellectual life, to be explored in a following chapter, was both a reflection of the community's social character and a force in shaping that character. The community's social character, in other words, was intimately related, in a dynamic and reciprocal fashion, to its institutional life and its intellectual traditions.

In this chapter we focus on the social character of the community itself during this period. What kind of people were "our kind"? What kind of people were nurtured by or attracted to the Reformed community with its colonial history and its particular social organization and intellectual traditions? What was the social location of "our kind of people" in the broader society and what distinctive social characteristics were connected to their various congregations and to the Reformed community as a whole? This chapter seeks to answer these questions first by establishing a social profile of the members and congregations and then by developing a composite picture of the community in black and white.

A Social Profile: The White Reformed Community

Max Weber, in his seminal and highly controversial work, *The Protestant Ethic and the Spirit of Capitalism,* argued that the Reformed emphasis on predestination and personal calling (vocation) provided a "psychological sanction" that unintentionally encouraged the accumulation of capital and the rise of a capitalistic economic system.[2] While this Weberian thesis has been the center of a heated debate that is too broad for the scope of this present study, the thesis—modestly presented—does provide a starting point for the exploration of the community's character during the years between the Revolution and the Civil War.[3] Was the Reformed community in the low country clearly marked by participation in a modern, market-oriented economy? Did the Reformed community nurture and attract a significant component of agricultural capitalists and urban bourgeoisie?[4] Such a starting point is particularly important given the traditional interpretation of the region as being dominated by a Cavalier ethic and a prebourgeois mentality.

A review of the membership of the Reformed churches in Charleston during the years between the Revolution and the Civil War presents a picture of whites who, rather than being peripheral, were at the heart of much of the economic activity of the low country.[5] Moreover, they were central players in a vigorous—if largely unsuccessful—attempt to increase the productivity of the region, to diversify the low country's economy, and to link Charleston with western trade.

Colonial patterns of the Reformed community's economic activity persisted and were expanded into more modern forms, such as involvement in the building of railroads. Familiar names from colonial days emerged as leaders in commercial life. By the beginning of the nineteenth century, they were being joined by others eager to follow their example and make a fortune and a name for themselves. A brief overview of the most prominent leaders helps to establish the character of the Reformed community and to evaluate its place in low country society.

Circular Congregational Church continued to be characterized by an exceptionally strong representation in the business and professional life of the city. Nathaniel Russell, Richard Hutson, Josiah Smith, the Perroneaus, the DeSaussures, the Bees, the Mathewses, the Vanderhorsts, and the Darrells represented those in the congregation who had roots in colonial society and who prospered after the Revolution as the city grew even more wealthy from the exports of low country rice and sea island cotton. Among the new business leaders associated with the congregation was Thomas Bennett, Sr., who built a fortune in the lumber business and with his famous rice mills. His son Thomas Bennett, Jr., expanded those businesses and was by the 1820s a powerful political figure in the state. Both father and son were active members of the Circular

Congregational Church, where the congregation, grateful for the leadership of the senior Bennett, erected a marble monument in his memory.[6] Throughout the antebellum period, the character of the congregation continued to be marked by such affluent business and professional leaders who composed a significant portion of the membership.[7]

At First (Scots) Langdon Cheves, James Lamb, Charles Edmonston, and Adam Tunno were the best known of a number of wealthy businessmen.[8] Cheves served as president of the United States Bank. Edmonston was one of the most economically powerful men in the city until the depression of 1837 sent him into bankruptcy. Tunno was one of the leading merchants of the city. But First (Scots), with its strong identification with Scotland, also attracted many small shopkeepers and "mechanics" of Scottish origin—leather workers and bakers, carpenters and grocers. Leslie O'Wen, for example, was in the dry goods business, practiced dentistry on the side, and lived over his place of business at 148 King Street. Perhaps more than any other church in Charleston, First (Scots) had great economic and social diversity among its white members.[9]

Second Presbyterian Church was well represented in the business community and as a congregation was notably affluent.[10] Business leaders included William Aiken, James Adger, and John Robinson. Adger is a particularly good example of a nineteenth-century immigrant success story that paralleled the successes of eighteenth-century immigrants such as Pierre Manigault. Adger arrived in Charleston as a young man from Belfast. Quickly prospering in the hardware business, he consolidated his enterprises on the Cooper River wharves that still bear his name. His commission and factorage business, along with his buying and selling as the agent for the banking giant of Brown and Company of Baltimore, led him to establish his own line of steamers—including the *James Adger*—that sailed to New York and other ports. By the 1830s Adger was reported by his son to rank fourth among the rich men of the country.[11] Together with his children and his son-in-law, Thomas Smyth, Adger was a leader among Presbyterians in the city.

The Third Presbyterian Church had an exceptionally high percentage of its membership from the Middle Atlantic and New England states. More people joined from New York than any other single place, followed by those from Connecticut and Massachusetts.[12] Many of these members were businessmen and among them were Thomas Napier and Thomas Fleming, whose names were closely associated with benevolent organizations of the city. The character of much of the congregation can be seen in the life of William H. Gilliland, a longtime elder of the church, who came to Charleston at a young age from County Antrim in Ireland. For over half a century he was engaged in the mercantile business, and by the time of the Civil War the wholesale establishment of Gilliland, Howell and Company "was known throughout the South, and was one of the most flourishing firms in the city." Gilliland, like Napier and Fleming, was active in the cause of benevolence and served for years on the board of the orphan house, a position that indicated his success in moving into socially elite circles. The first meeting of the Hibernian Society was held at his home about the year 1812, and at the time of his death he was serving as the society's president.[13]

At the French Huguenot Church a small group of socially elite families struggled to keep the character of their heritage of French Reformed. Among these church members, Elias Horry, Joseph Manigault, Daniel Ravenel, and George W. Cross were leaders in various business affairs of the city.[14]

One measure of the leadership provided by these congregations to the business community is the level of their participation in such joint efforts as the establishment of railroads linking Charleston to the interior and South Carolina to the West. Among the twelve men who memorialized the state legislature in 1827 for the construction of a railroad to Augusta were Charles Edmonston of First (Scots), John Robinson of Second Presbyterian, Thomas Fleming and Thomas Napier of Third Presbyterian, and George W. Cross of the French Huguenot Church. When the legislature appointed five commissioners for the proposed Western Railroad to link Charleston with Cincinnati, they included Robert Young Hayne of the Circular Congregational Church, Charles Edmonston of First (Scots), and Abraham Blanding, formerly of Circular and then a leading layman at First Presbyterian in Columbia (but later buried in the Circular churchyard). Five of the nine directors of the railroad were members of the Reformed community in Charleston: Hayne, Edmonston, and Blanding, Mitchell King of First (Scots), and Francis H. Elmore of Second Church. William Aiken of Second Church served as president of the newly established Charleston and Hamburg railroad and was followed by Elias Horry of the French Reformed Church. Robert Young Hayne served as president of the proposed Charleston to Cincinnati railroad, which he hoped would provide a "bond of political as well as economical union."[15]

Closely allied with the business community were a number of "Broad Street" lawyers, and the practice of law remained a popular profession among the white male members of the Reformed churches. Leading lawyers in the city during this period included John Geddes, Jr., Mitchell King, and A. G. Magrath of First (Scots); Robert Young Hayne, H. L. Pinckney, and Henry A. DeSaussure from Circular Congregational; R. B. Gilchrist from Second Presbyterian; and George Cross and Thomas Grimké from the French Huguenot Church. Chancellor Henry William DeSaussure was a child of the Circular Church and an elder in the First Presbyterian Church, Columbia. William L. Johnson, a graduate of Princeton and justice of the United States Supreme Court, was a member of Second Presbyterian.

To review the role of the Reformed community in the business establishment and its legal ally is, of course, not to claim that those who were a part of the Reformed community had some sort of monopoly on the business activity and practice of law in the low country. They obviously did not. The review does indicate, however, much about the social character of the Reformed community itself and points to the community's close identification with an influential sector of low country society and with that sector's world view and ethos.

Planters

However important Charleston's business and legal communities were for the economic activity of the region, planters represented the cultural ideal of the low country, a powerful image in the region's understanding of itself.[16] Planters were at the heart of the old Cavalier myth that pictured the low country as possessing a prebourgeois mentality and that imagined the region as being devoted to amusement and indifferent to religious and intellectual interests. For the Reformed community to have a significant representation among such a planter class would seem either to contradict the world view and ethos of the community as thus far developed in this study or to raise questions about the values and practices of the planters themselves. Once again the recent work of Peter Coclanis on the economic history of the region is helpful.

Coclanis has emphasized that the planters were agricultural capitalists who generally attempted to act in an economically rational manner. They were closely linked to the region's merchants, to market-oriented behavior and values, and to efforts at modernization and development.[17] Moreover, planters often had substantial holdings in stocks and bonds. Within such a context, it is not surprising that the strength of the Reformed community among the planter class during the colonial period continued during the years between the Revolution and the Civil War.

A review of the membership of the rural churches reveals that they included in their membership throughout this period a number of affluent low country planters. Wilton numbered among its membership such wealthy planters as Paul Hamilton, a church elder, and John Berkeley Grimball, chairman of the congregation's board of trustees. At Johns Island there were the Legarés, Townsends, Walpoles, Wilsons, and Fripps—all large planters of substantial means and many slaves. In a similar class were the Warings and Hutchensons at Dorchester and Summerville. The Vennings, the Toomers, the Morrisons, the Doars, and the Whildens helped to make the Wappetaw congregation economically secure with a substantial endowment. Stoney Creek attracted a number of wealthy planters in the area. Among its affluent pewholders were J. R. Pringle, William Heyward, Josias Heyward, and Edward Neufville. Thomas Heyward, a member of one of the wealthiest families in the low country, was married by the pastor, who also buried one of his children. Trustees at Stoney Creek included General John A. Cuthbert, A. F. Gregorie, and John McLeod, all wealthy planters.[18]

The white membership of the Presbyterian church on Edisto Island was composed of a small group of families that had gained great wealth by raising

Plantations and Manse in Presbyterian Community
Top, left: The Grove, Saint Paul's Parish, built ca. 1828, home of John Berkeley Grimball; *right:* William Seabrook House, Edisto Island, built ca. 1810, home of William Seabrook (both from *Plantations of the Low Country: South Carolina 1697–1865*, photos by N. Jane Isley). *Bottom, left:* Presbyterian Manse, Edisto Island, built 1838; *right:* Brick House, Edisto Island, built ca. 1725, home of Paul Hamilton (both courtesy of the Reverend Walk C. Jones IV, Edisto Island, S.C.)

sea island cotton. The Seabrooks were among the wealthiest planters in the South. As a capitalist, William Seabrook invested his earnings not only in slaves and acre upon acre but also in such industrial ventures as the Saluda Manufacturing Company. Other wealthy Presbyterian families included the Mikells, whose beautiful plantation home Point Saint Pierre was built in 1840 with a double piazza and a foundation of brick and tabby; the Townsends of Bleak Hall and Sunnyside; the Baynards of Prospect Hill; the Whaleys of Four Chimneys and Windsor; the Jamisons of Burwood; the Seabrooks of Seabrook House, Cassina Point, and Gun Point; the Murrays and the Clarks of Meggett's Point; and the Edings, who had the little village at the beach named after them—Edingsville. Even the Presbyterian manse was a home of some note with its three stories and shaded piazza overlooking the marsh. Some families also built fine homes in Charleston. Of these the best known is I. Jenkins Mikell's mansion at 94 Rutledge.[19]

In Charleston many members of the Reformed churches were not only engaged in business but were also planters. H. L. Pinckney of the Circular Church owned a plantation on the Cooper River; the Legarés of Circular Church moved back and forth between the city and their plantations on Johns Island; Hugh Wilson, Sr., of Second Church, who planted on Johns Island, was numbered among the South's great planters with more than 350 slaves in 1840. John Townsend planted on Edisto; Langdon Cheves of First (Scots) owned a plantation on the Savannah; the Manigaults, Mazycks, and Ravenels of the French Huguenot Church also were planters.[20] Planting, after all, was the occupation of gentlemen, and few could resist the temptation to invest in land and slaves.[21]

Both as an economic activity and as a social position and attitude, planting was not foreign to the Reformed community in the low country. On the contrary, some of the region's most affluent and influential planters were not only members of Reformed congregations but were closely connected—through family ties and personal involvement as lay leaders—to the community's life. The character of the Reformed community was consequently marked by the presence of a significant number of planters and their families. In a reciprocal manner, the character of the planter class in the low country was also marked by the presence of those in the Reformed community who, in varying degrees, reflected the world view and ethos of the Reformed tradition as it developed in the low country in interaction with its sociohistoric context. The consequences of this dialectical relationship were visible in the institutional structures described in the two preceding chapters and in the intellectual life of the community explored in a following chapter.

Political Leaders

The low country Reformed community contributed a distinguished group of political leaders to the state and nation throughout this period. As slavery became a subject of intense debate among white Americans, and as sectional tensions grew, politics came increasingly to dominate the thought and energies of many South Carolinians. In spite of the doctrine of the "spirituality of the church"—which was comprehensively developed by members of Charleston Presbytery and which insisted the church should not intrude into the political sphere—the Reformed tradition encouraged a vigorous and active participation in political affairs. Indeed, the political activity of members of the Reformed community provides, even in its diversity, important indicators about the community's strength and coherence.

In Charleston the congregation of the Circular Church represented a particularly powerful association of political leaders, especially in the critical decade of the 1830s. In the years after the Revolution, John Mathews, Richard Hutson, and David Ramsay continued to be active political leaders in the state. In 1802 Paul Hamilton, also of the Wilton congregation, was elected governor and from 1809 to 1813 served as secretary of the navy. Thomas Bennett, Jr., was elected governor in 1820 and Robert Young Hayne in 1832. Hayne, the great-grandson of the congregation's Rev. William Hutson and grandson of the martyr Isaac Hayne, was one of the most influential political leaders of his generation.[22] As United States senator, he was the defender of the South in the great Hayne-Webster debate in which he more than held his own—except, as his biographer points out, in the impossible task of defending slavery and justifying nullification.[23] With him at the Circular Church was his brother-in-law, H. L. Pinckney, longtime president of the congregation's corporation. A member of the U.S. House of Representatives, he lost his congressional seat in 1836 to Hugh Swinton Legaré, also of the Circular Church. Legaré, who had served as chargé d'affaires in Belgium, later served as the United States attorney general and briefly as secretary of state. Legaré was supported in his contest against Pinckney by Richard Yeadon of the Circular Church who was editor of the *Courier,* the primary paper in competition with Pinckney's *Mercury.* Legaré lost his congressional seat to Isaac "Ikey" Holmes, Legaré's boyhood friend who had grown up in the Circular Church. In local politics, both Pinckney and Hayne served as intendant (mayor) of Charleston, Pinckney defeating in his race fellow church member Henry A. DeSaussure.[24]

Langdon Cheves from First (Scots) served in the United States House of Representatives and was elected Speaker of the House. He later served as president of the United States Bank. General John Geddes, Jr., was elected governor in 1818 and A. G. Magrath in 1864 during the closing days of the Civil War. Mitchell King—a Scotsman who had made a fortune in Charleston—served as the highly respected mayor of the city as well as a judge.

Outside Charleston, Reformed churches were represented by numerous members of the state legislature and by Whitemarsh B. Seabrook of Edisto, who was elected governor in 1850, and General D. F. Jamison of Orangeburg, who was president of the session convention in 1860. Colonel John Taylor of Columbia, who was closely associated with low country Presbyterians, served in the U.S. House and Senate and was elected governor in 1826.[25]

Cheves, Hayne, Legaré, and to a lesser extent H. L. Pinckney were not only men of local fame but of national reputation. They represented the best of Charleston and the last generation of Charlestonians that would wield considerable national influence.

With the two major exceptions of Hayne and Pinckney, the political leaders in Charleston associated with Congregational and Presbyterian churches were Unionists. They continued much of the old Federalist tradition in Charleston and opposed nullification in the 1830s. Of the leading Nullifiers listed by David Duncan Wallace, only two were associated with these Charleston churches—Hayne and Pinckney. In contrast the Unionist list includes Thomas Bennett, Jr., Hugh S. Legaré, Henry A. DeSaussure, and Richard Yeadon of the Circular

Political and Intellectual Leaders
Top, left: David Ramsay, Circular Congregational; *right:* Robert Young Hayne, Circular Congregational (both from *The National Portrait Gallery of Distinguished Americans,* II and III [1837, 1836]). *Bottom, left:* Alexander Hewat, First (Scots) (courtesy of Cliffort L. Legerton, Summerville, S.C.); *right:* Langdon Cheves, First (Scots) (from *The Making of South Carolina* by Henry Alexander White [1906, 1914])

Church; Thomas Grimké of the French Huguenot Church; William Aiken and William Gilmore Simms of Second Presbyterian.[26] Other Unionists included Dr. F. Y. Porcher of Circular, Langdon Cheves and Mitchell King of First (Scots), and James Adger and John Johnson of Second Presbyterian. No doubt the strong connection of these churches with the business community encouraged Unionist sentiment among them, even though the division between Unionists and Nullifiers was not one simply between commercial and planting interests.

Education

Was the Reformed community in the low country marked by a concern for education during this period? The answer is mixed. Education, a traditional concern of Reformed communities, was not ignored by those in the low country.[27] However, in contrast to other Reformed communities, the low country had limited success in establishing educational institutions. Most low country Reformed leaders had received their education abroad or in the North during the colonial period, but by the outbreak of the Revolution they had begun to turn their attention to the establishment of a local academy of some note.

"If ever a Carolinian has reason to blush for his country," wrote Richard Hutson of Circular Church in 1784, "it must be, when he considers that it has advanced upwards of a century in age, before it has one academy of any reputation in it."[28] With the establishment of the College of South Carolina in 1804 the way was open for the development of a first-rate college in the state. Presbyterians and low country Congregationalists played an important role in the college's history throughout the years leading to the Civil War. In 1813, the college enrollment included 177 Presbyterian students, 31 Episcopalians, 20 Baptists, and a few Methodists.[29] Most influential of the Presbyterians who served on the faculty during the years before the Civil War was James Henley Thornwell.[30] A member of Charleston Presbytery, he came to the college in 1838 as professor of belles lettres and logic, soon switched to the chair of sacred literature and the evidences of Christianity, and in 1851 became president. He achieved, long before his presidency, "hegemony over the institution," and, in the words of the university's modern historian, was "perhaps the most important person connected with the institution during the twenty five years following his arrival."[31]

Thornwell also made significant contributions toward the establishment of a free public school system for all white children of the state and not just paupers. In 1853 he wrote an open letter to Governor J. L. Manning on "Public Instruction in South Carolina" in which he insisted that "Education is too complicated an interest, and touches the prosperity of the Commonwealth in too many points to be left, in reference to the most important class of its subjects, absolutely without responsibility to the Government."[32] It was, wrote Colyer

Meriwether, "the most important contribution to education ever written by an educator in the State on the institutions of the State."[33] Thornwell's challenge was taken up in Charleston and in 1856 a modern school system was adopted for the city. Among the three leaders most closely associated with this revolution in Charleston schools were W. J. Bennett of Circular Congregational and A. G. Magrath of First (Scots).[34]

Literary Efforts

Members of low country Congregational and Presbyterian churches played a prominent role in the literary life of the region. Hugh S. Legaré—the "Charleston Intellectual" is what Vernon Louis Parrington called him—made a name for himself as a literary man as well as a politician. He edited the *Southern Review* (1828-32)—perhaps the most influential literary journal that flourished and died in the Old South—and was widely acclaimed as a classical scholar. With Legaré in the establishment of the *Southern Review* was Robert Young Hayne, at whose home the plans were made for the journal in 1827.[35] Basil Gildersleeve, a child of the Presbyterian manse (his father, Benjamin, was editor of the *Charleston Observer*), became the leading classicist of his generation and, after the Civil War, established classical studies as a modern discipline at the newly organized Johns Hopkins University. William Gilmore Simms, a prolific writer of novels, short stories, and poetry, grew up in the Second Presbyterian Church and was a pewholder until he left the city in 1832. Paul Hamilton Hayne, one of the South's leading poets, was raised in the Circular Congregation Church where his wife was a pewholder, while another leading poet, James M. Legaré, grew up attending the Johns Island Presbyterian Church.[36] Richard Yeadon was longtime editor of the *Charleston Courier*, and H. L. Pinckney was influential in the affairs of the *Mercury*. James Henley Thornwell began editing in 1856 the *Southern Quarterly Review*, which for two decades had attempted to encourage a lively interest in Southern literature.

Women

The place of white women in low country society is indicated in part by their absence from these descriptions of the various sectors of low country society. Yet they were far from absent from the churches. Indeed, they represented substantial majorities in the membership of the churches, although they may not have attended more than the men. Between 1811 and 1839 at Second Presbyterian, for example, 78 white men and 258 white women became communicant members. Between 1840 and 1854, the ratios narrowed but the difference was still significant, with 210 women and 128 men becoming communicants.[37] Similar patterns prevailed in the other congregations.

With women outnumbering men by such substantial majorities, a "feminization" of the churches occurred during the years between the Revolution and the Civil War. This phenomenon was widespread among the evangelical churches of the country and was shared by the Presbyterian and Congregational churches of the low country with their middle- and upper-class communicants. Women of this class, especially in the city but also on the larger plantations, had been increasingly forced out of any economic sphere and into a distinctive role of domesticity. Their place was said to be in the home where they were to cultivate a sense of refinement, piety, and delicacy. From such a restricted sphere many women began to pour their energies into the churches and into the benevolent organizations associated with the evangelical empire of the nineteenth century. The result was that the churches took on many of the values of domesticity, became increasingly concerned with questions of nurture and propriety, and felt the powerful but indirect role of women who, as in the home, had to resort to subtle means of influence.[38]

Whatever informal influence women may have had in the churches, they held no church offices, were only occasionally owners of pews, and were generally without formal voice in church affairs. A revealing indication of their position in the churches is the way women were listed in the session records of the Third Presbyterian Church:

Caroline widow of Spears
Mary daughter of J. F. Grimké
Angelina daughter of J. F. Grimké
Ann wife of Joseph Wilkie
Clarissa Daughter of Thomas Walton
Caroline Daughter of Swinton

Such a listing paralleled the manner in which slaves were generally listed:

Sam	servant of	John Dawson
Stephen	" "	Mrs. Grimké
London	" "	Tho. Bennett [Jr.]
Judy	" "	Col. J. Bryan[39]

All were clearly part of a paternalistic, hierarchical society where their identification was determined by their relationship to a father or husband or, in the case of slaves, to an owner. White women and black slaves were, however, able to carve out places for themselves within the confines of such a social context. White women found an important place for themselves in the various benevolent organizations of the city, especially those associated with missions and education. Here they could express their benevolence, encourage a sense of independence, and nurture their own leaders. These benevolent societies prepared the way for the formal organization in the twentieth century of the

"Women of the Church," which in turn played an important role leading to the full participation of women in the life of the church.

The various ways in which antebellum women responded to such a social context can be seen in several outstanding examples. Angelina and Mary Grimké, daughters of a prominent judge of a distinguished Huguenot family, joined the Third Presbyterian Church at the same time. Angelina, increasingly distressed by the oppression of a slave society, left Charleston, became a Quaker, and joined the abolitionist movement.[40] With her other sister, Sarah, she toured the Northeast as an agent of the American Anti-Slavery Society and became a scandal to many, not only because of her call for the immediate abolition of slavery, but also because she had moved beyond what was regarded as the proper role for women and was speaking in public before audiences that included men.[41] Mary Grimké followed a more conventional route: she stayed in Charleston, was a faithful member of the Third Presbyterian Church all her life, and participated in a number of benevolent activities.

Somewhere between the paths of Angelina and Mary Grimké were those taken by Louisa Cheves McCord and Susan Petigru King. McCord, the daughter of Langdon Cheves, was a member of the First (Scots) Church and later an active participant in Columbia's circle of Presbyterian intellectuals. A poet and dramatist, she was accepted in the male intellectual world as a learned, incisive, and often engaging writer, but one who did not challenge the conventions of Southern society. Her best-known work, *Caius Gracchus,* had as its heroine Cornelia, whose sons were defenders of ancient Rome's independence and virtue. Woman's place, as Cornelia illustrated and Louisa McCord wrote in her essay "Woman and Her Needs," was to be "the conservative power" in the midst of a world in turmoil. While woman's role was not one of action in the world, she "may counsel, she may teach, she may uphold the weary arm of manhood—of the husband, the brother, or the son—and rouse him to the struggle for which nature never designed her."[42] Susan Petigru King, daughter of James L. Petigru, married Henry C. King, son of Mitchell King and a member of First (Scots). Her novels showed plantation life not as moonlight and magnolias but boring and intellectually deadening for women. In contrast, life in Charleston was glittering but finally little more than empty drawing-room chatter and flirtations.[43]

Another and more daring course was followed by Ada Agnes Jane McElhenney. The granddaughter of James McElhenney, a prominent Presbyterian pastor, she was raised after the death of her parents by her maternal grandfather Hugh Wilson, Sr., a member of both the Johns Island and Second Presbyterian churches. As a child, she later wrote, she had enjoyed "running, swimming, and climbing trees" and had resisted her "girl-slaughtering relatives" who tried to change her into "that devitalized and automatic thing, a perfect lady." After a disagreement with her grandfather Wilson, she ran away to New York, where she became a journalist, actress, and feminist and was known as "the Queen of Bohemia."[44]

These varying responses to their social context help to illumine both the place of women in a highly structured, hierarchical Southern society and the ways in which religion played a role (or failed to) in their lives. Angelina Grimké moved out of the conservative social world of Third Presbyterian—where she had first had a powerful religious conversion experience—and became a Quaker on her way to openly opposing the structures of a society that sought to "keep in their places" both blacks and white women. Her sister Mary sought to accommodate herself to Charleston society and evidently found in the church a place of nurture and some room for the expression of her benevolent impulses. Louisa McCord moved into the world dominated by men, particularly that world of Presbyterian intellectuals, by vigorously supporting its values and the place of women behind the scenes. Susan King saw the oppressive side of "woman's place" but was unable to move beyond a rather melancholy description of it. Ada McElhenney fled her "girl-slaughtering relatives" at Second Presbyterian who would make "a perfect lady" out of her. For her the church, no doubt, represented a powerful organ of social control and oppression.

The Clergy

The clergy who moved within this social context and served the low country churches or who were part of its presbytery or Congregational association were men of broad educational background and wide intellectual interests. Of all the Southern clergy, Elizabeth Fox-Genovese and Eugene D. Genovese have written, Presbyterian ministers "held pride of place as the best educated and most intellectually impressive of the denominational leaders. Their power and influence spread well beyond the number of their constituents in a society in which Presbyterians were heavily outnumbered by Methodists and Baptists."[45] Among these Presbyterian ministers, none did more to shape the life and thought of Southern society than those connected with Charleston Presbytery. During the generation preceding the Civil War, wrote Ernest Trice Thompson, the historian of Southern Presbyterianism, those connected with Charleston Presbytery were without question the most influential leaders of Southern Presbyterianism.[46] They included in their number several of the most disciplined intellectual leaders of the Old South, and one, James Henley Thornwell, ranked among the most important intellectuals of his generation.

Many served exceptionally long pastorates while others served equally as long as professors at Columbia Theological Seminary. If they survived yellow fever—"the strangers' fever," it was called, for many of its victims were strangers when they first arrived—they lived on and on, preaching thirty, forty, fifty years in the same pulpit, surely causing some of their parishioners to wonder if their ministers were not going to match the Old Testament patriarchs in longevity.[47] Such extended tenures provided much stability and continuity to church life during this period and meant that the number of pastors serving influential pulpits or as professors was relatively small. It also tended to encourage more conservative perspectives that would not jeopardize established ways or threaten comfortable positions.

Many of the ministers were related to one another and to influential members of the community in a bewildering web of connections. Benjamin Morgan Palmer, the younger, was the son of Edward Palmer of Bethel, and the nephew of Benjamin Morgan Palmer, the elder, of Circular Church. He married the stepdaughter of George Howe. Thomas Smyth was the brother-in-law of John Adger, the eldest son of James Adger. Smyth's son, Augustine, married the granddaughter of Langdon Cheves, the daughter of Louisa Cheves McCord. Such connections, and they were many, together with ecclesiastical ties, provided a close web of relationships.[48] Unlike the "Sacred Circle" of relationships that depended ultimately on friendships that Drew Gilpin Faust has described among some leading Southern intellectuals, this web was more tightly woven through the ties of family and church.[49] It consequently gave a familial and institutional framework that was both limiting and sustaining.

These pastors came to the Carolina low country and to Columbia from varied backgrounds and with degrees from leading colleges and theological institutions in the country.[50] Far from provincial, these ministers traveled widely and regularly entertained guests from other parts of the country and from Britain. They sent members of the presbytery each year to meetings of the General Assembly, which generally met in the North, and they received as visiting brothers pastors from the North who were spending their winters in the South.[51] With their wealthy parishioners, they vacationed—especially during the "sickly season"—at the Virginia springs, Newport, and Saratoga. They visited friends and sometimes family in New York and Philadelphia, in New Jersey and Boston. A number traveled abroad and some made several extended trips to Europe.[52]

Of course, not all the clergy took their vacations in the North or had the opportunity to travel to Europe. Some, especially in the newly established churches toward the interior, were glad to get paid regularly. At the little Summerville church, where the congregation moved from Dorchester to enjoy the healthy pine lands, the Reverend A. P. Smith was promised a salary in the church's call to him in 1859. This future pastor of the First Presbyterian Church in Dallas, Texas, wrote the Summerville session the next year that his salary had not been paid as promised and that he had to "go through the humiliating process" of begging his creditors for "a longer line of credit." Such things, he wrote, "do violence to all my ideas of right." You know me well enough, he told the session, to know "that I am not preaching for the money that is promised me. All that I have ever asked of you, is enough to enable me to live comfortably and decently, I as well as those who are dependent upon me cannot live alone upon either air or even promises. Flesh and blood require something more. . . . The great Head of the Church calls no man into the ministry that he may starve." The next month he announced that he was accepting a call to the Glebe Street church in Charleston.[53]

Pastors as well as professors were expected to be scholarly, and they were rewarded with a host of honorary degrees. George Buist and John Forrest received the honorary doctor of divinity degree from Edinburgh. The University of Pennsylvania gave an honorary degree to Isaac Keith, and Princeton College honored William Hollinshead and Thomas Smyth with divinity doctorates. Aaron Leland had honorary degrees from Brown and the College of South Carolina, Andrew Flinn and George Howe from the University of North Carolina, Daniel McCalla and Benjamin Morgan Palmer, Sr., from the College of South Carolina. Their scholarship was expected to be wide ranging, to include science as well as theology, history as well as biblical studies. Such expectations would of course change as the fields of study narrowed and experts moved toward knowing more and more about less and less. But as late as summer 1859, Thomas Smyth was reading Pascal's *Thoughts,* Buckland's *Elements of Geology* (in two volumes), Guyot's *Earth and Man,* a *Natural History of Trees* in two volumes and a *Natural History of Birds* in one volume, Macaulay's *History of the Reformation,* Goethe's *Poems,* Bunyan for devotional material, McCosh for philosophy, and a number of theological and exegetical works.[54]

They not only read, they wrote, a few of them prodigiously. In his quiet country parish at Wappetaw, Daniel McCalla found time to publish such pieces as "Remarks on the 'Age of Reason' by Thomas Paine" and "Remarks on Griesbach's Greek Testament" and to show his old revolutionary zeal and political colors with "Federal Sedition and Anti-Democracy" and "A Vindication of Mr. Jefferson." George Buist was a member of the Edinburgh Philological Society, wrote articles for the *Encyclopedia Britannica,* and prepared an abridgment of Hume's *History of England* that went through two editions for use in the schools of Scotland. William C. Dana wrote on church polity, John Forrest on the classics, and Hollinshead and Keith published collections of scholarly sermons.

No one, however, not even the professors in Columbia, matched Thomas Smyth in the volume or the range of his published works. From his pen poured forth learned treatises challenging the claims of the Oxford movement: *Lectures on the Apostolical Succession, Presbytery and Not Prelacy,* and *Ecclesiastical Republicanism.* He spent four years of unceasing labor on his *Unity of the Human Races* in which he defended the humanity of Africans against the deprecations of Harvard professor Louis Agassiz and his Southern supporters. He wrote some devotional discourses that were widely read: "Solace for Bereaved Parents," "Why Do I Live," and "Well in the Valley." Article after article appeared under his name supporting missions, Sunday schools, the American Tract Society, the Young Men's Christian Association, the Charleston Orphanage, and charitable work for the poor. He wrote articles on secession and the Civil War, a "Soldier's Prayer Book," and "Soldier's Hymnal." All in all his collected works totaled ten thick volumes plus his *Autobiographical Notes,* which is itself a large volume. His larger works were published in Great Britain and the United States and were reviewed on both sides of the Atlantic. Much to his delight, his *Unity of the Human Races* received favorable reviews in the *New York Journal of Medicine,* the *Southern Medical and Surgical Journal, Harper's New Monthly Magazine,* the *Scottish Guardian,* the *British Quarterly Review,* and a number of other journals.[55]

Periodicals also had their part to play in the literary and scholarly efforts of these pastors and professors. Benjamin Gildersleeve, father of Basil, began in 1827 the widely read *Charleston Observer,* the "most influential Presbyterian journal" throughout the South for almost twenty years.[56] In 1853 John Kirkpatrick moved the *Southern Presbyterian* to Charleston to begin a long and influential history as the leading Presbyterian newspaper of the Southeast for the next fifty years.[57]

The *Southern Presbyterian Review* was a quarterly of high distinction and one of the nation's leading theological journals. Managed by "an Association of Ministers" in South Carolina, its primary lights were all members of Charleston Presbytery: James Henley Thornwell, Thomas Smyth, George Howe, Benjamin Morgan Palmer, the younger, John Adger, and John L. Girardeau. Full of reviews on such scholarly works as John Daniel Morrell's *Historical and Critical View of the Speculative Philosophy of Europe in the Nineteenth Century,* it contained such learned articles as Joseph LeConte's "The Principles of A Liberal Education," Palmer's "Baconism and the Bible," Smyth's "The Province of Reason, Especially in Matters of Religion," and Thornwell's "The Philosophy of Religion." Nor did the authors avoid the great social and political issues of the day. Adger wrote heatedly against "The Revival of the Slave Trade" and more calmly on "The Christian Doctrine of Human Rights and Slavery." With secession and Civil War came Thornwell's "The State of the Country" and Smyth's "The Battle of Fort Sumter" and "The Victory of Manassas Plains"; and from New Orleans, where Palmer had recently moved, came his "Vindication of Secession and the South." With defeat, Palmer wrote defiantly "The Tribunal of History."[58]

The social character of the Reformed community during these years begins to emerge from this social profile of members, congregations, and clergy. As a coherent image begins to take shape and come into focus, it is important to remember, however, that what is missing from the picture so far drawn is the presence of African Americans. Not only were they a significant component of the total community, but they also stood as the inescapable background to any image of a white, low country Reformed community and of its place in low country society. Before attempting to draw a composite picture of the community, therefore, we must first seek to bring this background to the foreground.

A Social Profile: The African American Reformed Community

The presence, often in large numbers, of African Americans in the Reformed congregations of the low country presents a challenge to the thesis that the Reformed community reflected certain social attributes that marked it as a community and that gave it an identifiable character during the years between the Revolution and the Civil War. The challenge, put most simply, is this: did "our kind of people" include African Americans? The previous chapter identified a distinct ethos and world view emerging in the African American Reformed community during the antebellum period. Did these African Americans in the Reformed community portray any of the social characteristics and the social location broadly associated with the Reformed tradition—and more specifically, with the whites in the low country within that tradition? Such questions appear naive and incredible, given the bitter realities of slavery and the differences between the owned and the owners, between the oppressed and the oppressors. But within the harsh and narrow limits of slavery, are certain distinct social characteristics discernible among the African Americans who were members of Reformed congregations? If so, do these characteristics resonate—even through the distant and deep waters of slavery—with those social characteristics discernible among the whites in Reformed congregations?

It is highly probable that most of the slaves who joined a Presbyterian or Congregational church in Charleston were domestic "servants." A local census in 1848 reported that 70 percent of the adult slaves were "house servants" widely distributed throughout the white families of the city. There are indications, however, that those slaves who joined a Presbyterian or Congregational church represented an even higher percentage of domestics. In 1855, for example, of the sixty-eight slaves who joined the Zion church, ten had specific employment listed: three bricklayers, three carpenters, a painter, a porter, a barber, and a mill hand. If the rest, who were listed simply as "servant of," were domestics, then almost 93 percent were house "servants."[59] It is probable that among this 93 percent were some whose owners found it more profitable or convenient for them to earn wages, as hirelings engaged in a wide variety of tasks, rather than work as domestics.[60] One thing is certain, however. The great majority were not owned by whites who attended the congregation they joined, for the membership rolls of the churches reveal few slaves who attended the same churches as their owners.[61]

African American church members apparently selected churches that provided them some free space and distance from their owners. For Charleston domestics, who lived in much closer proximity to their owners than most rural slaves, such distance was no doubt eagerly sought. Slave quarters were intimately connected with white residences in Charleston with large brick walls often surrounding the yards and quarters forming with the white residences a compound for both privacy and confinement.[62] African American slaves, wrote John Adger, "are divided out among us and mingled up with us, and we with them in a thousand ways. They live with us, eating from the same store-houses, drinking from the same fountains, dwelling in the same enclosures, forming parts of the same families."[63] Whatever paternalistic images and conservative utopian visions Adger had of such "families," the great majority of the slaves of white Presbyterians and Congregationalists chose not to join their white "families" in church. Rather, they frequently joined another congregation within the Reformed community; slaves of white members of First (Scots), for example, often joined Second Presbyterian.

Given the ethos and world view emerging in the African American Reformed community, it is likely that substantial numbers of these domestics represented an elite place within the larger African American community. Such a social location was also indicated by the sizable percentage of free blacks who belonged to the Reformed congregations.[64]

Charleston's large free black population played a conspicuous role within the Reformed churches of the city and formed an important component of a social profile of their African American membership.[65] The free blacks who joined Third Presbyterian Church, for example, before 1840 constituted 39 percent of the African American membership. In contrast, free blacks constituted only 12 percent of the African American population of the city in 1830 and only 9.6 percent in 1840. Of the approximately 500 African Americans who joined Zion between 1856 and 1861, 134 (27 percent) were free.[66] Equally significant was their leadership in the churches. Among the nine official leaders at Second Presbyterian in the 1840s, six were free blacks.

These free blacks lived in a precarious twilight region between slavery and the freedom enjoyed by whites. Some belonged to an elite circle of generally light-skinned free blacks who owned substantial property and moved at the edges of white society. But most were laborers, "slaves without masters," who worked at various trades throughout the city or earned their bread through the most menial tasks. Whites had mixed feelings toward them: they feared their freedom and what it could teach slaves when they saw members of their own race living independently of white control. They consequently imposed severe restrictions on their freedom—making them pay heavy taxes, designating what they could wear in public, and prescribing how they were to act toward whites. But whites also knew that many free blacks were conservative supporters of the status quo, that some were slaveholders themselves, and that they played an important intermediate role in a slave society. In contrast to slaves, they could own property, engage in trades forbidden slaves, keep their earnings, and enter a legally recognized marriage.[67]

Prominent among the free blacks at Second Presbyterian were Robert Howard and John B. Matthews, both of whom were elected leaders by the white session. Howard, a mulatto, was in the wood-selling business and in the 1840s purchased two slaves to help him haul wood into the city. Later he bought four adult females who were probably hired out. As he prospered he began buying houses, and by 1860 he had an estate valued at $37,100, including a number of houses that he rented. Apparently committed to a slave system, he owned by the end of the war twelve slaves.[68]

Matthews was more typical of African American slaveholders. He owned three slaves, most likely family members he had purchased to free them from the dangers of being owned by someone else (there was little chance of securing from the legislature the right to free his family members even though he was their owner). When Matthews died in 1861, Girardeau wrote: "His end was peaceful and triumphant. He was one of the most pious men I ever knew. His love for Jesus was remarkable. He was not an ordinary man: courteous, tender-hearted, dignified, a noble specimen of a coloured Christian."[69]

With Matthews at Second Church during the 1840s were two free African Americans who decided to leave the city. Thomas Catto, one of the leaders, left to study at what Thomas Smyth called "our Seminary" and later became a pastor of an African-American congregation in Washington, D.C. Mom Sue, the nurse for the Smyth children, left with her husband, Joe Corker, and went to Liberia.[70]

A prominent free black at Third Presbyterian was the tailor James D. Johnson, who owned in 1860, in addition to rental housing, three slaves whom he employed as tailors. Thomas Smalls of the Circular Congregational Church reflected a perspective apparently held by a number of the free blacks of the city: he accepted slavery but sought to work within its system to alleviate some of the suffering of his race. Smalls, a carpenter, bought and sold several slaves whom he used in his carpentry business—a practice continued by his son Thomas Smalls, Jr. A man of dark complexion, he was one of the founders of the Society of Free Dark Men that stood in contrast to the Brown Fellowship Society, which was composed of only elite light-skinned "free persons of colour." Smalls was also responsible for helping to organize the Euphrat Society, which supervised the upkeep of the Circular Church's cemetery for African Americans and which provided help for the church's destitute African American members.[71]

Among the African American members of the Reformed churches, in the city and in the country, women outnumbered the men throughout the antebellum period, sometimes by substantial margins.[72] No women, however, were official leaders or watchmen in the churches. Whatever matriarchal influence they might have had within the African American community, it was not exercised through formal structures in the churches.

In the country churches, as might be expected, most African American members were plantation workers, although domestics were frequently among their numbers. Only a few free blacks lived in the countryside and small towns of the region and only an occasional free black belonged to one of the rural or small-town congregations.[73] In contrast to the urban congregations, African Americans who joined a rural Reformed church generally joined the congregations where their owners were members. Often a number of slaves from one plantation would present themselves at the same time for membership in a congregation, perhaps as some religious fervor swept through the quarters. Some who joined had been baptized in infancy, brought by slave parents or occasionally an owner. Others were baptized as adults. All had gone through the classes for the religious instruction of the slaves and were required to answer the questions that the white session members addressed to them about their religious beliefs and morals. They generally came, in other words, out of the little world of a single plantation and its close neighbors. They joined a congregation that was composed primarily of African Americans, together with a smaller number of whites, from those same neighboring plantations. Among these rural African American church members, the radical instability of slavery was not as clearly present as among the urban slaves, where "sold away" was a frequent notation on the church rolls.

From this tightly knit and relatively stable social context, the rural congregations began to take on a distinct character. That character bore the unmistakable marks of slavery, but it also gave hints—in its cohesiveness and in its emphasis on education and order—that it was being shaped by the Reformed tradition and its ethos. To be sure, the class and social location of these rural African Americans differed dramatically from that of the whites with whom they shared church membership. Yet, as we shall see, not only among the urban African Americans, but also among these rural church members, a community was beginning to take shape that would reflect, when freedom came, social characteristics that marked them and their community as both African American and Reformed.

A Composite Picture

In spite of the diversity within particular congregations and between congregations, a composite picture can now be drawn that gives in black and white a broad social profile of the low country Reformed community during the years between the Revolution and the Civil War.

The picture is clearest in regard to the whites. In Charleston the Reformed churches tended to nurture or attract those within the business community rather than planters—although there were important exceptions and although many of these business people also owned plantations. They included a concentration of some of Charleston's wealthiest citizens, who provided much of the leadership that struggled against the city's relative decline in wealth and influence. At First (Scots), where there was the greatest social and economic diversity, a number of shopkeepers and artisans, mostly recent arrivals from Scotland, also were members. Outside the city, Johns Island, Edisto, Stoney Creek, Wilton, and to a lesser extent Wappetaw congregations were composed almost exclusively of large planters, most of whom came from colonial families. The other churches tended to draw planters of more modest holdings and, in the villages, professionals and storekeepers.

The Reformed churches did not encourage a withdrawal from political activities but provided the region with some of its most influential political leaders. To a remarkable extent, Unionist political sentiment was present in the Reformed churches of Charleston. Even Robert Young Hayne, a leading spokesman for the right of secession, had strong nationalist sympathies, as his efforts to develop the Western Railroad connecting Cincinnati and Charleston indicate. Not surprisingly such political sympathies were generally linked to commercial interests and perspectives.

A well-educated, broadly traveled, often affluent clergy served the Reformed churches of the region throughout the entire period. They ministered to congregations composed primarily of male pewholders and entirely of male officeholders but with a sizable majority of female communicant members. These congregations held education in high regard and contributed significantly to the educational and literary efforts of the region.

The picture that thus emerges of the white, low country Reformed community during this period does not in broad outline present any startling divergence in social characteristics from the picture often drawn of Reformed communities in other times and places.[74] Yet it was a community clearly marked by its particular historical and social setting. The urban bourgeoisie and agricultural capitalists and their families who represented the dominant elements in the white component of the community were part of a slave society. Not only were their economic activities, their political perspectives, and their educational and artistic efforts largely shaped by the system of slavery, but also their religious life and the social character of their congregations emerged as a part of a slave system. Such a picture highlights both the power of a religious tradition and the dynamic ways in which it interacted with a specific social context.

For the African American membership of the Reformed churches, this much of a composite social profile can be reconstructed: Most were slaves, although in Charleston a significant percentage were free African Americans, including a number of elite African American slaveholders. In Charleston most members were domestics with strong links to elite circles. While members frequently came from Reformed "households," they consistently joined congregations other than those where their owners were members. In rural congregations, the great majority were agricultural laborers who came from the tight little world of neighboring plantations and, in contrast to Charleston, joined the churches where their owners were members.

In both the urban and the rural areas, women constituted between 55 and 66 percent of the African American membership. They did not share the limited formal opportunities for leadership that were available to African American males, although some women no doubt possessed significant informal authority within the African American Reformed community.

In Charleston the Reformed membership represented a small part of the African American population in the city. In the countryside the African American Reformed membership was also a small part of the total population. On Edisto and Johns and James Islands, however, and in Walterboro and vicinity, those who belonged to Presbyterian congregations represented a substantial part of the formal church membership among African Americans in those areas.

In summary, the African American membership in Charleston reflected from a distance some of the social characteristics and locations associated with the Reformed tradition. In the rural areas, only distant hints of such characteristics and locations can be discerned. Yet urban and rural church membership provided the foundation for influential African American congregations in the low country that would exhibit, when freedom came, not only their distinct African American traditions but also many of the values and much of the ethos associated with the Reformed tradition.

Two churches, one white and one African American, would go their separate ways after the Civil War. The differences of historical experience and social place and power that separated them would be clear. Yet both churches would be Reformed. They would share—within the limits of a racist society— theological commitments and social characteristics that would make their reunion a surprising discovery: "our kind of people" was broader than either had thought.

10

An Intellectual Tradition

The Quest for a Middle Way

IN 1851 Charleston Presbytery, meeting at the Second Presbyterian Church, assigned responsibilities for the examination of candidates for the ministry. George Howe and Benjamin Morgan Palmer, the younger, were to examine in "Ancient Languages, including Hebrew" (Howe was the one member of the presbytery who could converse fluently in Latin). James Dunwoody, graduate of Yale and Columbia Theological Seminary and pastor at Stoney Creek, was to examine in "Natural Sciences, including Mathematics" (and also including astronomy, geography, and botany). James Henley Thornwell and John L. Girardeau had responsibility for "Moral Sciences," which covered philosophy, rhetoric, and logic. Thomas Smyth, Edward Palmer, and Girardeau were given responsibility for "Natural Theology & Religion"; Aaron Leland, Palmer, and John Adger had "Evidences of Christianity"; "Christian Theology" was assigned to Leland and Thornwell; "The Sacraments" to Smyth and Howe; and "Church Government, History, & Pastoral Care" to Thornwell, Smyth, and Palmer. Before candidates reached such a formidable examination, they were to have presented—in addition to an exegesis of both an Old Testament Hebrew text and a New Testament Greek text—a paper in Latin on a theme such as "*An scriptura sit verbum Dei?*" and a theological paper on a subject such as "The nature and necessity of repentance." Finally the moderator was given responsibility to examine the candidates' "personal piety and reasons for seeking the ministry." Because presbytery meetings generally lasted three days, there was ample time for the papers to be read and the examinations given.[1]

Those who made it through such an examination—or even made it *to* such an examination—were representatives of an established order, expected to have a broadly based education, a thorough grounding in the traditional disciples of theology, and an evangelical piety and a moral rectitude. These cultured candidates for the ministry, bearers of civility and tradition, seemed far removed from the farmer preachers of the backwoods who plowed their farms during the week and sowed the Word on Sunday as the Spirit moved them, and far distant from the circuit riders who, with little formal education, were sweeping West across much of the nation. In contrast to the Charleston candidates, these popular preachers and other "religious insurgents" were speaking the language of the people, challenging old authorities, and organizing new religious movements.[2] They were part of a leveling and democratic spirit that had been reshaping much of the nation's religious life throughout the nineteenth century, inviting, in the words of Nathan O. Hatch, "even the most unlearned and inexperienced to respond to a call to preach."[3] At first glance—and even at a second—such a spirit appeared alien to this meeting in Charleston in 1851. Yet that spirit was there in the emphasis on religious experience, muted to be sure, but competing with an older, well-entrenched spirit of hierarchy and authority.

The ritual of the ordination examination, no less than the other rituals of the community, revealed tensions within the white Reformed community, the dialectical interaction of a religious tradition with a social context, and the resulting shifts taking place within the community over time. On the one hand, the examination ritual revealed a disciplined elite, carefully guarding the entrance into its membership—few, after all, had undergone the rigorous preparation required to pass such an examination.[4] The ritual served as a means by which the Reformed clergy, united in a community of interest and tradition, declared its self-understanding and asserted its legitimacy. The examination helped to transmit the tradition, to preserve the social identity of the clergy, and to integrate the Reformed community by justifying the present system of authority.[5] In this manner, this demanding ritual served an ideological function: it supported the tradition, its authority, and those in authority.

On the other hand, the examination with its emphasis on the personal experience of the candidates revealed a countervailing impulse within the Reformed tradition: one that feared enclosing boundaries and that resisted hierarchical structures. This impulse resonated deeply with the leveling and democratic spirit sweeping the country and with certain powerful elements within romanticism. What this impulse imagined was a personal religious experience, carrying its own authority, asserting its own right to be heard, declaring its own legitimacy. This impulse would later grow in strength within the low country Reformed community, insisting that a personal experience of a call to the ministry was what was fundamental, not a classical theological education. But in 1851 this democratic impulse was repressed, carefully kept in its place by the power and authority of a well-established tradition. The examination rite consequently revealed a grafting on to the world that the Reformed clergy knew, a world that they imagined.[6]

These two competing impulses were held together in tension through the quest for a middle way, a *via media* between extremes. The quest, as has been repeatedly emphasized, provided a conceptual framework—a social and cultural imagination—that reflected the world as formally conceived by the white Reformed community and that provided guidance for engaging that world. At the heart of this perceived world, encouraging the quest for a middle way, was the harmonious sphere of natural law.

Cordially yours

Rev. J. L. Girardeau.

Leading Members of Charleston Presbytery, 1851
Top, left: James Henly Thornwell (author's collection); *right:* Benjamin Morgan Palmer [the younger] (courtesy of Presbyterian Historical Society, Montreat, N.C.); *Bottom, left:* John B. Adger; *right:* John L. Girardeau (both from the author's collection)

Natural Law

The concept of natural law, which was so fundamental to the intellectual life of the low country Reformed community, had ancient origins. Rooted in classical philosophy, natural law had been a mainstay of medieval Christianity and had been vindicated by Newtonian science. English Puritans and American Patriots had used its doctrines to justify their revolutions. Theologians, lawyers, scientists, and politicians had all built their systems upon its principles. There are natural laws, it was claimed, that reflect the very essence of the universe and are an expression of the will of God operating with the mathematical certainty of Euclid's axioms.[7]

Thinking persons almost universally assumed throughout the antebellum period that a study of natural law reveals a moral order that is not a human creation. What is "good" or "beautiful" is not determined, they were convinced, by culture or economic interests, as so many twentieth-century people would come to believe. Rather, they believed that what is "good" or "beautiful," what is "just" or "right," are parts of a universal moral order created by God and expressed in the natural laws of the universe. This moral order served as the final guide for human behavior. Thus John C. Calhoun began his famous "Disquisition on Government" by declaring: "In order to have a clear and just conception of the nature and object of government, it is indispensable to understand correctly what the constitution or law of our nature is, in which government originates."[8]

Such an understanding of natural law could and did serve two masters within the Reformed community—the two competing impulses within the Reformed tradition. Natural law could serve, on the one hand, that impulse that emphasized the heart and affections, that sought truth in personal experience. Natural law, by challenging all "unnatural," "man-made" laws could serve a revolutionary function, questioning all laws, social systems, or intellectual traditions that appeared to box people in by rigid systems or enclosing boundaries. Carried to the extreme under the influence of the Enlightenment, natural law could assert humanity's ability to discover, on its own, religious truth and the requirements of moral rectitude and to reject the need for the Bible or any special revelation.[9]

But natural law could also serve another master—the impulse that feared anarchy, that sought order and balance, that used reason and fixed principles to put up rigid boundaries and keep at bay threatening chaos. It could serve those seeking to "uphold the natural order," who resisted any violent, "unnatural" rearranging of the spheres of a hierarchical social order, and who insisted that each person has, "as nature teaches," a specific place and function. Of course, such an impulse could also be carried to extremes—it could be used to support the old hierarchical systems of Europe and in the church the claims of episcopacy.[10] The task, those who gathered at Second Church in 1851 firmly believed, was to hold the two impulses in some tension, to find some middle way between the extremes.

The white Reformed community of the Carolina low country in the eighteenth century had known the tug of these competing impulses. Some in the community had leaned more in one direction than the other, but all had felt the tension between the two. Some had used natural law for their own revolutionary purposes while at the same time they used it to keep slaves "in their place." Josiah Smith, William Tennent, and David Ramsay at the Independent Meeting House were revolutionaries insisting on the natural rights of the people—that is, white men—to judge for themselves and to follow the lead of their own experience. Those who were not white men were to be left in their "natural place" of subordination. Alexander Hewat at First (Scots), on the other hand, was a Tory, railing against those opposed to the natural order of a hierarchical British government. But Hewat also railed against slavery, declaring it to be "contrary to all the laws of nature."[11]

The tension between the competing impulses was also felt in the nineteenth century. Those who gathered in the Second Church in 1851 believed themselves to be on the side of democracy and to share with other Americans the great forward thrust of history.[12] They were fond of denouncing tyrannies,[13] had attacked the hierarchical assumptions of episcopacy in favor of "ecclesiastical republicanism,"[14] and generally saw themselves as among the defenders of American democratic ideals. But they believed, as did their white parishioners, that what one found in natural law was social and moral order and not the chaos and anarchy of unbridled freedom and equality. This was one reason they examined candidates on "Natural Sciences" and on "Natural Theology"—because they believed that by understanding something of the moral order and its "eternal principles" they could understand something about both the Creator and the Creator's purposes for humanity.

Of course, being rooted in the Reformed tradition, these nineteenth-century ministers also believed that something more was needed for salvation and moral guidance than what the human mind can discover through the study of nature and nature's laws. Not only were they convinced that the mind of humanity is limited, but they also believed it to be fallen, corrupted by sin. Consequently what was needed for salvation and moral guidance was revelation, the Bible, a gift of God which told that which the natural mind could not grasp on its own and which provided guidance that amplified and clarified the laws of the moral order. Still, the natural law was fundamental. "God," insisted Thomas Smyth, "is a God of order not of confusion. . . . in the frame of the natural and moral world, 'order is heaven's first law,' and the bond and cement of the universe."[15]

Such an emphasis on law and order coupled with support of the status quo meant that these ministers sounded as if they were following closely that side of their tradition represented in the eighteenth century by Alexander Hewat. Yet the nineteenth-century ministers were also children of the Awakenings, for they insisted that the Christian life be informed not only by law but also by a love that strangely warms the heart.

A Faith: Both Warm and Reasonable

For those who listened to the music of the spheres and found in it the harmony of universal order, reason was clearly an important means to discovering Truth—especially reason that followed the inductive scientific methods of Sir Francis Bacon.[16] And what is Truth? For these pastors and professors, whatever else Truth might be, it certainly included correct doctrine, especially that taught by the Westminster Confession of Faith. They stood in the tradition of Protestant Scholasticism, were concerned with the relationship between reason and faith, and often emphasized the propositional statements of the faith. What you believed was vitally important: your eternal destiny was linked to, if not determined by, correct belief. And the correct thing to believe was not whatever warm feelings you might have in your heart, not whatever intuitive insights might spring from your soul, but carefully reasoned, logically stated, theological doctrines. You needed to know your catechism![17]

Religion, Thornwell declared in his inaugural address as a professor at Columbia Theological Seminary, "has no sanctity to protect it from the torch of a searching inquiry into principles."[18] "Where there is truth of doctrine," Smyth wrote, "there may we make a safe entrance on the way to heaven." Doctrines were the fundamental *truths* of Christianity: "Those truths on which Christianity rests, and by which it subsists, are fundamental, since without them the whole building and superstructure must fall." These truths "constitute its laws, its principles, its axioms, its data; the foundation on which rest its promises, its overtures, and all its blessings; and its essence, without which neither the form nor the substance of Christianity can remain."[19] Smyth could have been describing nature with its laws, its principles, its axioms, and its data. What he was doing was fitting doctrines into his world of natural law. The role of doctrines in relation to Christianity was made analogous to that of natural laws to nature: the eternal truths that constitute its essence.[20]

Strange as it may seem, this emphasis on doctrine did not lead these clergymen into a dead orthodoxy, for they felt a countervailing impulse and sought to unite their emphasis on reason and doctrine with a warm evangelical heart. Over and over again they insisted that right belief and correct doctrine, as important as they were, were not enough. The heart had to be united with the head, feeling and emotion had to give vitality to intellectual assent. This was a part of their personal experience, an essential milepost on the path to salvation.

Thus a young Thornwell, before his conversion, wrote in his journal: "My understanding assents [to the doctrines of Christianity], but my feelings are dead. My religion seems to be all in the head. Would to God it were otherwise."[21] "It is not enough," wrote Smyth, "to believe aright so far as mere words and doctrines can delineate the truth as it is in Jesus." Such a belief would be the faith of only a part of a person, "and that the least active, powerful, and controlling."[22] What was needed was the Spirit of Christ to breathe upon the dry bones of orthodoxy.

This union of correct doctrine with an evangelical fervor was the goal of the ministers who filled the low country Presbyterian and Congregational pulpits during the antebellum period. In contrast, however, to revivalism and the rising spirit of romanticism, they believed that genuine religious experiences flow from intellectual apprehensions of the truth. *You first understand* the correct doctrine, and that understanding produces genuine religious feelings. You first understand that Christ died for your sins, that forgiveness is a free and undeserved gift, and *then you feel* an overwhelming sense of gratitude and release. It was not the other way around: that you first have an emotional experience and then come to understand the doctrines of Christianity.[23] By emphasizing this sequenced order—first understanding, then genuine religious experience— the Reformed community sought to keep experience in check and to prevent personal experiences from overflowing their proper boundaries, flooding the land with the anarchy of unchecked beliefs and behaviors bubbling up from the chaotic depths of the human psyche. Clearly the Scholastic side of the tradition, with its concern for order, harmony, and balance, was dominant in the low country Reformed community.

The preaching of the low country pastors with their long and logical but intense sermons reflected their belief that understanding precedes genuine religious experience. Their preaching also distinguished them from much of the popular revivalism that was sweeping the country. The difference can be seen in the revivals that broke out under the preaching of Thomas Smyth and John L. Girardeau. In 1846 a revival began at the Second Presbyterian Church that soon brought in over a hundred new members to the congregation—a substantial number given the stable and conservative nature of Charleston. In 1858 another revival occurred at Second Church and an even larger one broke out under Girardeau's famous preaching at Zion.[24]

In these revivals all was orderly, nothing was indecorous: prayer and preaching, singing and reading were followed by private conversations with those who wished to talk with the pastors and elders and perhaps prepare to join the church. Even Girardeau—who more than any of his colleagues knew the power of rhetoric and who could sway the emotions and attract great crowds of blacks and whites—preached sermons fit for an orderly, rational world. He feared the danger of excitement replacing instruction, momentary impressions pushing aside permanent and abiding influences, and the awakening of the feelings supplanting the indoctrination of the understanding and the cultivation of the heart.[25]

In appealing to the troubled soul, Smyth pointed to power of the Sovereign God to rescue sinners: "In all of the Scriptures . . . there is not one hard word against a poor sinner, stripped of all self-righteousness, and who cast himself for life, light, and peace, on the Lord Jesus Christ." If you cannot make yourself believe, Smyth told his congregation, "you can remember that Christ 'is the author of faith.'" To you, he said, who feel no sense of pardon, "remember that Christ 'gives remission of sins,' and secures the favor of the Father." "Are you," he asked, "full of infirmities?" Christ "is not an high-priest who cannot be touched with them, but one who was at all points tried as we are." This same Christ "works in the heart to will and to do." "By grace, then," Smyth declared, "thou are saved through faith and that not of yourself, it is the gift of God."[26]

This was no altar call demanding that the sinner make a decision for Christ, but a call to trust in the mercy of the sovereign God. Echoing through the evangelicalism of these low country preachers and their colleagues at Princeton and in other parts of the country were the traditions of the Reformation and classical Protestantism. They had been vigorously upheld by Jonathan Edwards and other leaders of the First Great Awakening during the colonial period as they described the Awakening as "a marvelous work of God," a "shower of divine blessing," which, like a shower of rain in a parched land, came miraculously through the hand of divine Providence.[27]

In contrast to this traditional appeal to God's sovereignty, the revivalists followed the lead of their own experiences and, trusting the democratic impulses abroad in the land, called on people to take their religious destiny into their own hands—to make a decision for Christ. The creed of the new revivalism was carefully spelled out by the great evangelist Charles G. Finney:

> Whatever makes the impression on a sinner's mind that he is to be *passive in religion,* is calculated to give him false comfort. Give him the idea he has nothing to do but to wait God's time; tell him conversion is the work of God, and he ought to leave it to him; and that he must be careful, not to try to take the work out of God's hand; and he will infer . . . that he is not to blame, and will feel relieved. . . . But such instruction as this, is all wrong. If the sinner is thus to hold still and let God do it, he instantly infers that *he* is not to blame for not doing it himself. . . . The thing to be done is that which cannot be done for him. It is something which he *must do,* or it will never be done.[28]

This theological perspective was behind Finney's how-to-do-it instructions to ministers wanting to promote revivals and win souls. For Finney a revival was not the result of a miraculous outpouring of God's grace but was "a purely philosophical result of the constituted means." A revival for Finney and the host that followed him was simply the result of cause and effect in which the principal agent was the revival preacher: "The connection between the right use of means for a revival and a revival is as philosophically sure as between the right use of means to raise grain and a crop of wheat."[29] If a revival preacher plowed the ground carefully, sowed the seed expertly, nurtured the crop properly, then, according to Finney, the fruits of the harvest were sure to be his.

The evangelicalism of the low country Reformed community was consequently based on very different theological assumptions from that of the more popular evangelicalism associated with revivalism. The revivals in the low country Presbyterian and Congregational churches were orderly; the revivalism sweeping most of the country—including most of the South—was tumultuous. One emphasized God's grace, the other human freedom. Finney used new methods such as the anxious bench and extended meetings to get people into heaven; the low country preachers (with their Reformed colleagues in other parts of the country) awaited the natural course of God's providence. Finney's evangelicalism sprang from the pragmatism and piety of the new American; it was anthropocentric and individualistic and was associated with the rising Jacksonian democracy of the common person. The evangelicalism of Smyth, Thornwell, Palmer, Girardeau, and their colleagues was rooted in classical Protestantism; it emphasized God's elective grace and was associated with the conservative business elements in American life and the pursuit of a moderate, middle way.[30]

A Middle Way

The primary metaphor used by the white Reformed community in the low country for expressing its social and cultural imagination was the *via media,* the middle way.[31] This metaphor, as we have seen, had deep roots in the Reformed tradition and had clear expression in the low country Reformed community during the colonial period. The power and the centrality of the metaphor for the community's life, however, were not revealed until the antebellum period. Then the middle way blossomed as it appeared to be the way of natural law, the way to hold together the head and the heart, the way to understand the world and respond to it.

Through the use of this metaphor, the white Reformed community both expressed the reality of the world as the community experienced it and gave a distinct shape and contour to that world. When the metaphor expressed the reality of the world as the community experienced it, the middle way was acting as a mirror, reflecting the social location and self-interests of the community and its claims to legitimacy. The social profile of the white community, as developed in chapter 9, can be seen in the mirror of this metaphor. This world of moderation reflected the orderly, temperate world of urban bourgeoisie and agricultural capitalists. By mirroring the world as seen by white members of the community, by reflecting the social profile of the community and its ethos, the metaphor of the middle way served ideological purposes: it helped to distort and hide the harsh realities of a slave society; it acted to legitimize the power of whites; and it provided a means of integration and social identity for the community.

But the metaphor had not only this mirroring, reproductive function; it also had a productive function: it provided a way of conceiving of the world, of shaping and constructing it. For white members of the Reformed community, the middle way was not only an expression of their world but was an expression of the way they believed the world *ought* to be. The middle way was thus a guide, a path to follow, and consequently provided a conservative utopian vision: it challenged the present social order by envisioning a new order where extremes would be banished and moderation would rule. The middle way provided a single conceptual framework for linking the ideological and utopian elements in the community's thought.[32]

In a similar manner, the competing impulses within the Reformed tradition were held together and seen to have a coherence through the metaphor of the middle way. The middle way was the community's bridge over a great experiential and intellectual rift—a rift between an impulse that feared chaos and anarchy and sought order, harmony, and balance and an impulse that feared enclosing boundaries and restraining systems and sought freedom and openness. To be sure, the quest itself for a middle way indicated that the impulses in the antebellum period were not evenly balanced in strength, that the conservative, hierarchical, orderly impulse was the stronger of the two. Nevertheless, the metaphor of the middle way provided a conceptual framework for the community to bridge the rift in its world, to see the complementary nature of its competing impulses, and thereby to construct a harmonious world beyond the incongruities of the community's experiences and its intellectual systems.

The pastors and professors who gathered at the Second Presbyterian Church in 1851 were convinced that many of the troubles in society and church came when people went to extremes, when they wandered off the middle way or deliberately plunged off the *via media* into an extreme on the right or the left. The leaders in the Reformed community believed the need for a happy medium, a reasonable and golden mean, could be seen in three fundamental aspects of human life.

First, and in some ways most important, a golden mean needed to be followed in regard to the problem of knowledge. Rationalists went to one extreme, while romantics and many of the popular revivalists went to another. Rationalists such as eighteenth-century Deists or nineteenth-century Unitarians went beyond the limits of reason by trying to push reason into a sacred area, an area these Reformed scholars believed to be reserved for revelation alone. Thornwell, Smyth, and their colleagues began their thinking by insisting that the God revealed in the Bible is reasonable; therefore creation must be orderly. The discovery that creation is orderly simply confirms what is known of God from the Bible. Rationalists, on the other hand, started at the opposite end to arrive at a similar conclusion: nature is orderly; therefore God must be reasonable. By examining nature and learning its secrets, one learns something of its Creator. And by discovering that nature is not mysterious but reasonable, not unpredictable but orderly, it became clear to the rationalists that God too is reasonable and orderly, not mysterious and unpredictable.[33] By testing the Bible at the court of reason, it was said rationalists tried to make reason a judge and not a servant of revelation. By pushing reason beyond its proper place, rationalists were following all kinds of false paths, or so the Reformed claimed. It was, they insisted, simply human vanity to trust reason beyond its proper bounds.[34]

At the same time, romantics such as the transcendentalists were said to go to the opposite extreme. They wanted to forget that if reason had its limits, if it could not go alone into higher sacred areas, still it had its place and was able to confirm the truth of revelation. Romantics rejected any glorification of the intellect and scorned systematic thinking. They rather gloried in the supremacy of the heart, looked to instinct and imagination as the paths to Truth, and pointed to the inner, spiritual life of the individual as the measure of all things. "Trust thyself," declared Ralph Waldo Emerson, "every heart vibrates to that iron string." The world of the romantics such as Emerson stood in sharp contrast to the world of the Reformed scholars of the low country. The Reformed exalted the critical and analytic powers of the mind; the romantics exalted the power of the creative imagination and the role of feeling and intuition. The Reformed loved logic; the romantics loved art. The Reformed distrusted originality, believing an original mind was uneducated and undeveloped, and emphasized the corporate nature of knowledge; the romantics stressed the full and free development of the human personality, humanity's creative powers, and the wealth of possible human experience. The romantics, in other words, accentuated the originality of each person rather than what is common to all people.[35]

In a manner similar to romantics, religious insurgents, sectarian revivalists, and other popular preachers were insisting on the right and the need for common people to open the Bible and interpret it for themselves, unaided by tradition, the laws of logic, or the authority of educated elites. A populist hermeneutic, based on the ability and right of the individual conscience to search the Scriptures, needed no mastery of ancient languages, no familiarity with "natural" or "moral" sciences, no knowledge of the "Evidences of Christianity," no commitment to a religious tradition or community, but only the King James Bible open before the inquiring mind.[36]

The low country Reformed scholars insisted that a middle way be followed between the extremes of the rationalist on the one hand and the romantic and populist on the other. Both the head and the heart were required to find the Truth, both reason and religious feelings were needed, both tradition and freedom were necessary. The head and heart, tradition and freedom, needed one another. All had their limitations. For the Reformed, apprehension of the Truth followed a complex transmission of evidence through the senses to the common sense, to the judgment of reason, to the command of the will, and finally to the response of the passions. Their pursuit of this middle way relied on the inductive methods of Francis Bacon and on the insights of the Scottish philosophy of Common Sense. This philosophy emphasized the reliability of the common sense of the ordinary person, and had come to the United States primarily by way of the Reverend John Witherspoon, president of Princeton. It had its Carolina advocates too, including David Ramsay, Witherspoon's son-in-law. And there were others: George Buist, who came to Charleston with academic honors from the University of Edinburgh where the Scottish philosophy reigned supreme; and Robert Henry who, after studying with Buist, earned a master's degree from Edinburgh and taught his students at the College of South Carolina, including Thornwell, the Common Sense way of thinking.[37] But Common Sense needed tradition to help guide it, at least that was what the Reformed thought, and so they combined it with Protestant Scholasticism, and a theological tradition was established that had substantial appeal in the Old South and throughout the country in commercial and academic circles.

A middle way was needed not only in regard to the problem of knowledge but also in regard to ethics. Where did a person find guidance for ethical behavior? Were people to look within themselves or beyond themselves to discover the way they were to act? For the romantic the guide was to be the voice within. By looking within yourself, said the romantic, you will discover the Higher Law and God's Will, you will learn the proper course for ethical behavior.

Theodore Parker, the Boston transcendentalist, made clear the role of the inward voice, the human conscience, by explaining the "Function of Conscience in Relation to the Laws of Men." The law of God, said Parker, "has eminent domain everywhere. . . . My own consciousness is to declare that law to me, yours to you, and is before all private passions or public interests, the decision of majorities and a world full of precedents."[38]

Smyth, in contrast, declared in "The Living Christian Guided by the Law of Order" that

> God is a God of order. He is its origin and first exemplar. . . . As Divine law proceeds from the harmony of the divine attributes, and is based upon the order and propriety of duty, it follows that, both as a matter of acceptable service, and as a means of personal edification and delight, obedience must be rendered in accordance with that order. God being himself a God of order,

every thing that is must be established with certain relations, consequences, and if capable of them, rights and obligations. These are founded in nature and are necessary and inflexible. We are therefore required to observe this order, and to act in accordance with these relations, subject to inevitable retribution.[39]

The contrast is clear and striking, and what a difference it made between the Boston transcendentalists and the low country disciples of the middle way. Both thought they were following the law of God. The transcendentalists looked within and heard the law declare the natural rights of humanity; the Carolina ministers looked without and heard the law declare the order of the universe. For the transcendentalists, what was heard within was a Higher Law, higher than any human law, higher than any constitutions or extenuating circumstances. For the Carolina pastors, what was heard was a Harmonious Law, a law demanding obedience to the divine will. Following God's law then, like following reason, could lead different ways. It led some to challenge social structures and to abolitionism. It led others to seek to work within the structures of society and to attempt to improve the lot of the slave.

The Carolina ministers were convinced that theirs was the correct ethical decision because it was a middle way—it did not go to the extremes of individualism, but it did not ignore the individual and soar into the chaos of abstractions. In an orderly world persons must act according to the specific, concrete circumstances in which they are placed. The ethical problem, they thought, is not "what does my conscience demand?" or what are "the specific duties of all humanity?" but "what is my present allotted sphere and task?" God's will is indicated by God's providence as well as by God's law. "To act out of harmony with one, is as truly disobedient as to transgress the other; and conformity to one is necessary in order to conform to the other." For God has placed us in our particular circumstances. "Duty therefore requires us to accept God's arrangements, to acquiesce in them, to act in harmony with them, and not to fall behind or to go beyond them, until, in the use of proper means, God opens or shuts the door." To do otherwise, "to run ahead or forestall providence, is to imitate the prodigal, and involve ourselves in all the consequences of our self-will."[40]

For the Carolina ministers, there could be no inflexible conformity to a Higher Law. That would be making God's law into legalism, running ahead of providence, carrying matters to extremes. What is needed, they believed, are compromises. Because ethical duty is related to one's own situation, prudent compromises must be made in order to maintain the unity and harmony of God's law *and* providence. Through such compromises, reasonable people seek to do their duty, for this is the way of virtue, the way of moderation, the middle way.

If the way for an individual is the way of moderation, the Carolina ministers believed it is also the way for society. In a world of natural law, society too must attempt to conform to the harmony of the divine order, for harmony is not only the music of the spheres but also the melody of all peaceful and well-governed communities. They regarded society as an organism, an image that Southern scientists such as Joseph LeConte and Southern lawyers such as Hugh S. Legaré cherished as much as the clergymen.[41] Each part of the organism must do its duty or the whole body will become sick and be threatened with death.

Such an organic, corporate view of society went against the rising winds of radical individualism in American life. Two contrasting visions of society were coming into conflict with one another. Transcendentalists and revivalists regarded the individual as supreme. For the revivalist every person stood alone before God without the support of family or community. For the transcendentalist every heart must follow its own voice. For both the transcendentalists and the revivalists the emphasis was not on each person's fitting harmoniously into a social order but rather on the individual's freedom and responsibility.

The Carolina ministers, along with other conservatives, regarded this growing individualism as extreme, as a serious threat to social order, and as a fundamental misunderstanding of human nature. A man who lives to himself "is an anomaly in the universe," declared Smyth. "He is the only being and the only thing, in all the creation of God, that so exists." No lonely sojourn at Walden Pond for these ministers! For such radical individualism would "break up the human race into individuals, in violent opposition to every organic principle of human nature, and of the divine procedure in all departments of the natural world; and it would contradict that principle of representation where men are bound together under one law, one center of influence, one head or representative."[42]

To be sure, the Carolina ministers believed in the "sanctity of the individual." Smyth would remark that an emphasis on the individual was a primary difference between the New Testament and the Old. The Reformed community in the low country was, after all, Protestant and Reformed and it had as a powerful part of its tradition a conviction that the individual must make a confession of faith and must finally stand alone before God. The community never imagined during the antebellum period that its children would grow up never knowing a time when they were not Christian. No, independent of their families the children had to have an experience of regeneration, and the letters parents wrote their children were often filled with anxiety over this question.[43] Moreover, the social profile of the Reformed community, with its urban bourgeoisie and planter capitalists, encouraged an individualism that paradoxically marked whites of the region.[44] So a moderate, middle way was needed here as well—a middle way between an extreme individualism and an extreme organicism.

However much the Reformed scholars might have agreed that the individual is formed for a harmonious life in society, they also believed that human selfishness, pride, and ambition outweighed any altruism the individual might have. Because of this depravity, government is necessary for the peace and prosperity of society. The social contract theory of Hobbes, which said that humanity was originally in a state of war, joined with their Reformed tradition to emphasize the necessity of government to offer security to the individual.[45] Government, to secure this goal for which it was formed, must be in harmony with the natural order of the universe, must have at its foundation the natural laws that God has given to creation.

Lawyers and Theologians

The theological tradition of the Carolina clergy was closely allied to a legal mentality that exerted a powerful influence on the antebellum generation. The clergy marched beside a legal profession that sought to maintain a rational, moderate world in the midst of the romantic ebullience of revivalism and transcendentalism and the social dynamism of a young democracy.

With their busy offices on Broad Street, Charleston lawyers were among the esteemed leaders of the city. Those within the Reformed congregations—including the DeSaussures and the Grimkés, Langdon Cheves and Robert Young Hayne, William L. Johnson, Mitchell King, and Hugh Swinton Legaré—represented an impressive part of the intellectual leadership of the city. Blackstone was their bible—Blackstone who was a necessity for every Southern gentleman; Blackstone who declared that "All positive law is an endeavor to enact universal law." This was the creed of these Charleston lawyers—and their colleagues too in Philadelphia, New York, and Boston. They wanted to demonstrate that the truth revealed in the law was not an artificial invention of humanity, nor was it dependent upon the individual conscience, but belonged to the order of nature.[46]

This legal mentality was an important element in the background of the clergy as well. It indicates once again that their world of natural law was not alien to Charleston but was rather at the very foundation of the city's intellectual life. The lawyer like the theologian was concerned with maintaining reason as a bulwark against the irrational forces that seemed to be erupting everywhere in the modern world. Hugh Swinton Legaré, for example, no less than Smyth or Adger, was suspicious of the excesses of rationalism and enthusiasm. He distrusted the political philosophers and disdained the rowdy democrats. And against the fiat of individual statutes, he placed a rule of universality—the common law.[47]

It was, however, in regard to the Constitution that the world of the lawyer and the world of the theologian came closest to being one world. The lawyer loved the Constitution as the theologian loved the Bible. The lawyer looked to the Constitution as a bulwark against an explosive, dynamic democracy. In the midst of all of the irrational forces that threatened the country, the Constitution stood for moderation and reasonable compromises. The pastors and clergy professors shared the lawyer's enthusiasm for the Constitution. They cherished its republican nature and the Presbyterians among them were fond of pointing out what they regarded as its similarities with Scottish covenants and Presbyterian polity.[48] But their love for the Constitution went far deeper than any filial piety. It was rooted in the way they viewed the world and sought to understand it.

The clergy's approach to the Constitution reflected the Scholasticism that molded their theology. They saw the Constitution as a necessity because of the social nature of humanity. The compromises of the Constitution, its middle way between extremes of democracy and aristocracy, between the rights of majorities and the rights of minorities, were needed to maintain social harmony and political order. Reason must be used to interpret the Constitution as well as the Bible. Furthermore, the functions of the Constitution were much the same as those of the Bible: the legal document, no less than the sacred text, served as a final authority. It was the law of the land, but even more, it was a declaration of legal reason built upon natural law. Smyth believed the Constitution to be "an embodiment of wisdom, patriotism, sagacity and prudential foresight and moderation; of sterling good sense."[49] It was, in other words, the embodiment of natural law—at least it was as close as humanity had ever come to fulfilling such a goal.

In contrast to such an approach to the Bible and the Constitution, growing numbers in the North, who were rushing more rapidly toward the modern world, would accept no authority but the individual conscience. Did the Bible sanction slavery? Too bad for the Bible, declared Theodore Parker and other abolitionists. Did the Constitution make slavery the law of the land? It would be no law for them, for there was a Higher Law that spoke to their hearts and that they must follow. Boston transcendentalists like low country Reformed ministers would handle the Constitution as they handled the Bible. "Parker could take out those sermons and articles on religion and he wouldn't have to change a single idea. He could write 'State' where he had said 'Church,' change 'Bible' to 'Constitution,' and there you were."[50] The Carolina pastors and professors did the same thing—except that they wanted to guard against the very position Parker and his friends took. The Carolinians wanted to make sure neither the Bible nor the Constitution would be subject to the caprice of individual judgment. If abolitionists rejected the Bible and repudiated the Constitution, well too bad for them! The Carolina clergy would allow no individual judgment, no intuitive assurance of what was right, no self-asserting conscience to overrule the authority of the Bible or the Constitution; for such romantic individualism could only lead in the one case to heresy and in the other to anarchy.

The middle way was thus the way the white Reformed community sought to travel during the antebellum period. Following the narrow path between dangerous extremes, the community was guided by natural law, common sense, and Scholastic traditions. It used the metaphor of the middle way to bridge the rifts between the competing impulses within its life and the contradictions within its experience. This path was made up of the very ground over which the community walked, the social location and historical realities that marked it as a community. Yet the middle way was more. It was a conceptual map of the world, a guide to the future, a vision of what might lie ahead if the path were followed. By the late 1840s, the community found that this path, making its middle way across low country terrain, was leading it to a Charleston Zion and to an experiment in paternalism. What, however, the community could not see, or could see only dimly, was that this middle way was also leading the community toward its fears—toward 1861 and disillusionment, toward an abandonment of moderation and an embrace of extremes.

11

Slavery

"That Course Indicated by Stern Necessity"

A T THE TIME of the Denmark Vesey plot, Governor Thomas Bennett, Jr., of the Circular Congregational Church reached an unhappy conclusion: while slavery "abstractly considered would perhaps lead every mind" to wish for its end, "the period has long since passed when a correction might have been applied." For Bennett the "treasures of learning, the gifts of ingenuity and the stores of experience have been exhausted in the fruitless search for a practical remedy." Now, wrote Bennett, the institution is established, "the evil is entailed and we can do no more than steadily to pursue that course indicated by stern necessity."[1]

For some few low country whites, there would be a lingering hope that slavery might gradually die a natural death. Such hopes, however, had difficulty living in the low country world of the whites, for they increasingly seemed utopian in the pejorative sense—that is, impossible to realize. And of course such hopes were merely utopian from the perspectives of these low country whites, for to realize them would mean a radical new order—an overturning of the present social order—and that was a prospect the whites could only envision with horror.[2] From the whites' perspective, their world had no room, no possibility, for emancipation but only for "that course indicated by stern necessity."

For the low country Reformed community, the pursuit of "that course" meant following an increasingly lonely and isolated path. As the antebellum period moved toward its bitter conclusion, the community, as it sought to follow its middle way, found itself under growing attacks from the left, which began to insist that the only "stern necessity" was the liberation of the oppressed slave, and from the right, which began to call "stern necessity" a "positive good."[3] The attacks, especially from outside antislavery forces, encouraged the community to articulate its hopes and to move toward a conservative utopian vision of the good society. Drawing on impulses deep within its tradition and reacting to its social and historical context, the community began to envision a holy commonwealth in which a paternalistic social order would be balanced with social justice and the claims of society would be in harmony with the rights and dignity of the individual.[4] After the fall of Fort Sumter, the new Confederate States of America seemed to be emerging as just such a holy commonwealth—at least that was the way it would first appear to the embattled defenders of "our little world."

The Course Narrows

John Witherspoon, writing home to South Carolina during the old School–New School debate, had expressed reservations about slavery and the expectation that it would one day fade from the land. Others (their numbers were never great) clung to the hope that Robert Young Hayne had expressed in 1827—"that time would settle the matter, and that slave labor must give way and cease to be profitable when it came into competition with free labor."[5] Margaret Adger, soon to become Mrs. Thomas Smyth, wrote her brother John from Charleston in 1832: "You have seen the debate in the Virginia Legislature, the formation of a Colonization Society at Augusta, another at New Orleans—what do all these things betoken, surely that the day of their redemption from a cruel bondage draweth nigh."[6] Such sentiments, even when couched in the language of piety, became increasingly difficult to maintain in the low country. Pressures from all sides were building against them. The time was passing when Southerners could openly express, even in the most moderate terms, hopes for some future end to slavery. From one side came the pressure from the abolitionists for the immediate freeing of slaves and an end to the system of slavery. From the other side came the growing assertions by Southerners of the positive good of slavery. A decision was being called for: were you for the immediate abolition of slavery or did you see slavery as a positive good to be maintained at all cost? Those conservative Presbyterians and Congregationalists who saw the dangers in such extremes sought to continue their middle path. But even they discovered in the end that their middle way was dictated by what they regarded as "stern necessity." Thomas Smyth's ministry at Second Presbyterian throughout the whole of the antebellum period illustrates with particular clarity the difficulties of maintaining a moderate, middle-of-the-road position on the question of the South's "peculiar institution."

When Smyth arrived in Charleston in 1831, he came as one who, as a student in London, had been in the middle of British antislavery sentiment. Letters from classmates told of great rallies with William Wilberforce and other leaders of the British antislavery movement. A former professor wrote of being "engaged in a laborious correspondence on the Slavery question, previous to the approaching general election," and asking about conditions in Charleston.[7] Smyth shared the view that slavery was an evil that ought to be removed but not before God in His providence prepared the way for its removal. He found in the debates over Charleston Union Presbytery how difficult such a position was to maintain in Charleston. In 1844 he discovered how difficult they were to maintain outside the South, even in Presbyterian Scotland.

Many Protestants in the United States had been moved by what they regarded as the heroic stance of Scottish Presbyterians against the interference of the British government in the Church of Scotland's life. The right of congregations to call ministers of their choice had been rejected with contempt by the civil courts, a whole presbytery had been brought before a court and censured for ordaining a man in defiance of a court interdict, and the General Assembly had been prevented by a civil court from deposing seven ministers. Such interference in the Scotish kirk led 450 ministers in 1843 to walk out of the General Assembly meeting in Edinburgh and to constitute themselves the first General Assembly of the Church of Scotland Free. By this action they gave up their salaries, their manses, their parish churches, and their endowments. They were to start afresh with no material resources. Appeals for financial help to build new churches and schools and to pay ministers' salaries went out to evangelical Protestants in Britain and North America.[8] The appeal was heard in Charleston, and a public meeting was called to respond to the needs of the Free Church. Smyth addressed this large and influential gathering of the Reformed community on "the claims of the Church of Scotland to the sympathy and assistance of American Christians."

In his address, Smyth recounted the history of the struggles of Scottish Presbyterians against royal tyranny and told the story of the formation of the Free Church. Then turning to the Charleston audience, he declared: "This appeal addresses us, as Americans. To us as the friends of liberty and human rights, and the noble champions of civil and religious freedom, does the Free Church of Scotland look for sympathy, encouragement, and aid in this noble effort to better our example."[9] The Charleston audience responded generously, and over two thousand dollars was raised—a handsome amount, equaling Smyth's yearly salary and totaling twice that of Thornwell's at the South Carolina College. Smyth's address was soon published in Scotland with a preface by John Lorimer, minister of Free Saint David's Church in Glasgow.

That Smyth could make such a speech in Charleston where slaves were daily being sold and slavery defended reveals not only the endless power of self-deception but also the shape and contours of the world as whites in the low country Reformed community saw it: a world of two different levels, one white and one black, one free and democratic and the other slave and paternalistic.[10] Smyth's speech articulated the ideology of this world by attempting to hide both the astonishing paradoxes—vigorous defenders of liberty in the midst of a slave society—and the harsh realities of life in the low country. But such realities and the bitter irony of Smyth's speech were not hidden from the sharp eyes of abolitionists.

William Lloyd Garrison, the uncompromising Bostonian, saw the great gap, the yawning incongruities, between Smyth's claims for his Charleston audience—"the friends of liberty and human rights, and the noble champions of civil and religious freedom"—and the slave markets of Charleston. Garrison with considerable sarcasm, described what followed. "Charleston," Garrison snarled, "the cradle of lovers of freedom—in the abstract," had responded to the appeal of the Free Church. "The Rev. Thomas Smyth, D.D." had been asked to preach and "to pass the contribution box in his Presbyterian Church, which he did, with many touching references to tyranny and oppression, and many tropes in which Liberty cut a pretty figure." The Glasgow pastor of Free Saint David's, pleased with Smyth's sermon, reprinted "the Rev. D. Smyth's unmoral rhetoric." But a "well informed but irreverent Glasgow editor exposed the flashing, high-sounding, unmeaning words of the Charleston divine; and, hoping that the money had not yet arrived, looked to see the Free Church treasurer send it back by return of steamer, as blood-stained, together with a sermon suited to the circumstances of slaveholders, for the special benefit of the Rev. Dr. Smyth."[11]

The Glasgow editor had indeed been irreverent. He held up Smyth's speech as an incredible fabrication for someone living in the midst of slavery. "We announce," he said, "this one of the coolest of many cool productions of those in the Southern States, called ministers of Christ, who prate away, *ad nauseam,* on the unbounded freedom enjoyed under the American Constitution." These ministers had the audacity to carry on like this in the face of 2,500,000 slaves. "Ministers of Christ!!!" he exclaimed. "Servants, and willing ones too, of Satan, would be a more fitting designation." The editor then turned on Lorimer and denounced him for saying in his preface that such a work proclaims "the substantial unity of the Evangelical Church of Christ throughout the world." There could be no unity with slaveholders, nor could the Free Church accept "blood-stained money, wrung by the gory whip from poor, oppressed, down trodden slaves."[12]

But the money had already been accepted, and the cry went up to send the money back to Charleston. Frederick Douglass, the greatest of the black abolitionists, happened to be in Britain at the time, and he described what he found when he reached Edinburgh: " 'Send back the money!' in large capitals stared from every street corner: 'Send back the money!' was the chorus of the popular streetsongs; 'Send back the money!' was the heading of the leading editorials in the daily newspapers."[13] Lewis Tappan and other American antislavery leaders fired off letters to the Free Church demanding that the money be returned.[14] Smyth's name was painted on the walls and pavements of Glasgow and "Send back the money" was smeared in blood-red paint on Free Church buildings. Gradually the attack moved to the question of the Free Church's maintaining fellowship with churches that had slaveholders as members. But the blood-stained money was remembered, and two years later Henry Wright, an American abolitionist, wrote Garrison that "Send back the money" was painted in red over the door of the Free Church in Perth.[15]

In the midst of this uproar, Smyth sailed to Britain as part of an extended vacation. While he was surprised by the linking of his address to the slavery question, he received a warm reception from the leaders of the Free Church. They were grateful for his support and impressed by his recently published works on Presbyterianism and his challenge to the claims of the High Church Anglicans in the Oxford movement. In Edinburgh he was the frequent guest of Thomas Chalmers, the leader of the Free Church. Chalmers—a member of the Royal Society of Edinburgh and the Institute of France and a holder of a Doctor of Civil Law from Oxford—had been a leading reformer within Scottish society. Best known for his work in the slums of Glasgow, he had long been identified with the antislavery movement of British evangelicals that had pushed so hard and successfully for the abolition of slavery in the British colonies. But he was, like Smyth, a moderate, and he believed that reason must be followed and extremes avoided. Smyth requested of Chalmers an open letter stating his position. Chalmers agreed. "I do not need to assure you," he wrote Smyth, of how little "I sympathize with those who—because slavery happens to prevail in the Southern States of America—would un-Christianize the whole region; and who even carry their extravagance so far as to affirm that, so long as it subsists, no fellowship or interchange of good offices should take place with its churches, or its ministers." Chalmers noted that "As a friend to the universal virtue and liberty of mankind," he rejoiced in the "prospect of those days when slavery shall be banished from the face of the earth; but most assuredly the wholesome style of excommunication, contended by some, is not the way to hasten forward this blissful consummation." Few things, he wrote Smyth, "would afford me greater satisfaction than to hear of a commencement in your country, of that process by which the labor of free men might be substituted for that of slaves." "I feel," he said in conclusion, "it a great acquisition that I have made your acquaintance. We owe you much, and I trust the ministers of the Free Church of Scotland will ever entertain a grateful sense of your able and disinterested service."[16]

The letter, rather than quieting the cries of the abolitionists, only stirred them to greater fury. The Anti-Slavery Society of Edinburgh demanded that Chalmers repudiate the letter or give a fuller explanation of what he meant. Chalmers responded with a long letter to the *Edinburgh Witness* in which he declared that slavery, like war, is a great evil. But unless the slaveholder acted in an intemperate, licentious, or dishonest manner, the church should no more exclude the slaveholder than it should exclude the soldier. It is possible, said Chalmers, for Christians to be slaveholders just as it is possible for Christians to be soldiers. Abolitionism, he declared, is thus based on a false principle. It is, furthermore, "in itself a wrong procedure for hastening forward that object, for the accomplishment of which we are alike desirous with themselves; or in other words, it is not only wrong in principle, but hurtful in effect."[17] Such was the position of moderates in Scotland, but as in the American South, it was increasingly difficult to maintain.

Smyth returned to Britain in the summer of 1846 on another of his book-buying trips. When he arrived in Edinburgh he received from James Robertson, secretary of the Scottish Anti-Slavery Society, a challenge to a public debate with American abolitionists. Smyth refused, declaring that such a debate would only be in the interest of those who could "easily gratify the self-righteous spirit and self-glorying tendency of the national heart by the cheap and costless defamation of christian churches, ministers, and brethren in a distant land." But Smyth did not stop with such a dismissal, and for once abandoning the spirit of moderation that he loved so much, he added: "were it not objectionable on its own account I should feel called upon to decline holding it with men whose general character and reputation as religious men is such as is attributed, and I fear too justly, to the parties in question."[18]

The Scottish Anti-Slavery Society, outraged, published a letter in response. The American abolitionists were said to be known and well respected in Britain, but Smyth came from Charleston, South Carolina, and was the reputed defender and ally of man-stealers. "You are *accused*," they told Smyth

> of being the enemy of our race—of being identified with, if not yourself actually guilty of, crimes the most dreadful and heaven daring of which men on earth can be guilty . . . forget not that you come from Charleston, *South Carolina*—the land where men and women are degraded to the level of brutes—where the prerogative of God is invaded and where an interdict is put upon the Commission of the Saviour to preach the gospel to *every creature*—where the laws of the Eternal One are trampled openly under foot and where *might* and not *right* is the rule of actions for persons who claim to be the followers of Jesus Christ.[19]

There appeared to be little room for a moderate, middle-of-the-road course, but Smyth would try to make his position clear in London at the first meeting of the Evangelical Alliance.

Leaving Edinburgh with the denunciations of the abolitionists ringing in his ears, Smyth met in London his brother-in-law, John Adger, who was on his way home to Charleston from his mission work in Armenia. Together they attended the first meeting of the Evangelical Alliance. The alliance, a forerunner of the twentieth-century ecumenical movement, was a gathering of evangelical Christians from Britain, the Protestant countries of Europe, and from North America. Those from the United States read like a "who's who" of the country's Protestant establishment: Lyman Beecher, the patriarch of a tribe of Beechers (including his son Henry Ward, who was Adger's old classmate at

Union College, and his daughter Harriet Beecher Stowe); Robert Baird, author of *Religion in America;* Samuel Schmucker, a champion of evangelical unity and a professor at the Lutheran Seminary in Gettysburg; James Alexander of Princeton; and Samuel Cox, moderator of the New School General Assembly.[20]

On the ninth day of the meeting, Samuel Schmucker presented the report on the objectives of the Evangelical Alliance. The first section read: "That the Alliance shall consist of those persons, in all parts of the World, who shall concur in the Principles and Objectives adopted by the conference; it being understood, that such persons adhere as Christians in their individual capacity." When the report was introduced, Howard Hinton, an abolitionist from London, moved immediately to amend by inserting after the words "those persons" the phrase "not being slaveholders."[21] For the next five days, slavery and the meaning of evangelical unity were labored over by these earnest men. At the center of the discussion was slaveholding as a test of personal membership in the alliance. At stake was the nature of Christian unity. Not unlike the World Council of Churches in the 1970s debating South African apartheid, they had to decide if a great social evil excluded people from Christian fellowship.

Smyth made his position clear on the first day of the controversy. The question, Smyth argued, was not an abstract one as to the nature of slavery. They were all agreed on that point: "Slavery was an evil, and ought to be removed, as soon as God in His providence should open the way; and that every Christian man in America, as well as in Britain, as far as he was a Christian, would feel it his duty to aid in its removal." The real question was whether or not the alliance was called upon to "entertain the subject [of slavery] and to introduce it among those great, leading, prominent, principles upon which it was formed." As far as he was concerned, Smyth argued, such an introduction seemed unnecessary and inexpedient. To debate slavery would give the Evangelical Alliance a political bearing—and could anyone deny that slavery was founded on political legislation? That was slavery's source and only through the exercise of that political function could slavery be removed. "It was only by moral influence, brought to bear upon those who had the guidance of political affairs, that its removal could be secured."

If the alliance acted on this political problem, declared Smyth, it would introduce the question of church and state relations and give the Americans the chance to point the accusing finger at many of their European brethren in state churches. All that the Americans wanted, Smyth said, was the right to exercise their private judgment in attaining from the Bible "a knowledge of the will of the Lord, and of their own duty, in the trying circumstances in which they were placed." But he was sure of one thing: what was necessary was the creation of "a public sentiment which would ultimately overthrow the system of slavery." It had taken centuries to create such a sentiment in Europe through the work of "the Christian principle." If outsiders but left the Christian principle "to gain strength, and to act upon public sentiment, it would finally remove that evil not only from America, but from the World."[22]

In spite of his pleas, the members of the Evangelical Alliance voted to exclude slaveholders. But when the Americans reported the next day that such a position was impossible for them to support, the decision was reversed. It was decided that in reference to the various social evils that existed in different countries, the alliance would commend the amelioration of these evils to the district branches "trusting that they will study to promote the general purity and the Christian honor of this confederation by all proper means." The abolitionists were furious. Garrison began referring to the alliance as "The Evangelical Slaveholders Alliance," and for Frederick Douglass "the question of slavery was too large a question to be finally disposed of by the Evangelical Alliance, and from its judgement we appealed to the judgement of the people of Great Britain."[23]

Smyth and Adger hoped that such compromise would allow evangelicals to rise above the slavery questions, remain united, and work together for the causes of evangelism and benevolence. But that was not to be. Almost immediately the churches of Britain began to declare that they would no longer have Christian fellowship with slaveholders or their churches.[24] The Presbyterian and Congregational ministers in the low country who had long enjoyed broad international contacts began to feel the pressures of a growing isolation. Accused and scorned, they began increasingly to turn in on their own little world, to draw up their defenses, and to attempt to go their own way. To go their own way, however, called for a map and a vision, for some conceptualization of where they were headed and for some clarity about the good society they would seek.

Zion and the Good Society: A Conservative Utopian Vision

In 1847 John Adger, recently returned from the Evangelical Alliance and from his missionary work in Armenia, met with the session of the Second Presbyterian Church. He proposed a new mission effort among the African Americans of the city. He had made, he said, a study of Charleston's churches and he was convinced that they simply did not have enough seating space to accommodate the needs of blacks. Furthermore, he believed that the white-dominated churches were doing all too little to reach the blacks: the worship services were aimed primarily at the whites, and the African Americans seemed to be almost visitors listening in on what was an essentially white occasion.[25]

Adger's plan was for him to become a missionary to city blacks under the sponsorship of the Second Presbyterian Church. He would receive no financial support for his work—as the oldest son of James Adger he had no financial worries—but he would receive the endorsement and supervision of an affluent congregation of the city. Such endorsement and supervision, he hoped, would provide legitimacy to his work, would bring it within the established structures of the Presbyterian church, and would alleviate any anxieties the community might have about it. Not incidentally, it would help to answer the charges leveled against white Southerners that they were keeping the gospel from their slaves. The session gave its approval and recommended that the plan be presented to the congregation.[26]

In May 1847 a congregational meeting was called. Francis H. Elmore, soon to take Calhoun's place in the United States Senate, presided. Adger took for his text "The poor have the gospel preached unto them." And who, he asked, "are the poor of the city of Charleston?" They are, he said, easily distinguishable.

> They are a class separated from ourselves by their color, their position in society, their relation to our families, their national origin, and their moral, intellectual, and physical condition. Nowhere are the poor so closely and intimately connected with the higher classes as are our poor with us. They belong to us. We also belong to them. They are divided out among us and mingled up with us, and we with them, in a thousand ways. They live with us, eating from the same storehouse, drinking from the same fountains, dwelling in the same enclosures, forming parts of the same families. Our mothers confide us, when infants, to their arms, and sometimes to the very milk of their breasts. Their children are, to some extent, unavoidably the playmates of our childhood—grow up with us under the same roof—sometimes pass through all the changes of life with us, and then, either they stand weeping by our bedsides, or else we drop a tributary tear by theirs, when death comes to close the long connection and to separate the good master and his good servant.
>
> Such, my friends, are those whom we consider the poor of this city. There they are—behold them. See them all around you, in these streets, in all these dwellings; a race distinct from us, yet closely united to us, brought in God's mysterious providence from a foreign land, and placed under our care, and made members of our households. They fill the humblest places of our state of society; they serve us; they give us their strength, yet they are not more truly ours than we are truly theirs. They are our poor—our poor brethren; children of our God and Father; dear to our Savior; to the like of whom he preached; for the like of whom he died, and to the least of whom every act of Christian compassion and kindness which we show he will consider as shown also to himself.[27]

Adger's speech was a clear and eloquent expression of the paternalistic ideals that marked the Reformed community. The speech painted in memorable phrases and broad strokes a picture of the world as envisioned by whites in the community. It embodied the social and cultural imagination of that community and pointed toward a middle way as the path to the future. On the one hand, no question was raised about the system of slavery: it was accepted as a given, as a legitimate way of ordering human life and human relationships. On the other hand, whites had a special responsibility to "our poor brethren," the black slaves of the city, to whom they were to show the compassion and kindness they owed their Lord. Such a middle way called for an experiment in paternalism.

A similar movement was under way in the Episcopal Church under the leadership of Paul Trapier, the former minister at Saint Michael's. But while there was support in the city for such a movement, there was also opposition to the creation of separate churches for African Americans. Writing anonymously as "Many Citizens" in the Charleston *Mercury,* A. G. Magrath expressed grave concern over Adger's proposal. In a series of letters he noted that rather than gathering as they were accustomed to doing with whites, blacks would join together in an organized society with the right to consult, deliberate, and be heard in matters of church government. They would develop a spiritual allegiance to their church, learn that to suffer for the church is a proud distinction, and discover the lessons of zeal and the glory of martyrdom. "To minds thus matured," he asked, "what will be the language of the master or the owner?" For Magrath, a separate church for blacks would not be an opiate for the masses or a means of social control but an organization of revolutionary potential. Adger attempted to respond to the issues raised by Magrath, insisting that whites would be in control of the missionary efforts, and Thornwell, reviewing Adger's speech, dismissed Magrath's fears with scorn: "Very dreadful indeed!" was the theologian's sarcastic reply. "We fear that the nerves of 'Many Citizens' can hardly have recovered even after so long a time, from the severe shock which they must have received from the bare contemplation of all these horrors."[28] But fears were spreading nevertheless.

When the walls of the new Calvary Episcopal Church for African Americans began to rise, an angry mob gathered and threatened to pull them down. Only the intervention of several "influential citizens, jealous for the honor of their city," eased the tensions and dispersed the mob by promising a public meeting to discuss the whole matter.[29] A Committee of Fifty was appointed that, after considerable deliberation, presented a report favorable to the plans for a separate church for blacks under white control.

The report—echoing Thornwell's review of Adger's speech—declared that because religion is so fundamental a part of human nature, African Americans would have some type of religion. The question was: what type? Would it be a true and holy religion, or "an unholy and idolatrous religion; false and begotten; fraught with all the iniquities and horrid crimes, that ever mark superstitious zeal, and blind fanaticism; alike ruinous to its stolid subjects, and dangerous to the purity, peace and good order of society"? In order to avoid the latter, "to insure to the slave that appropriate Religious and moral Instruction, which will make him content with the station in which Providence has placed him, submissive to his superiors, and observant of the laws; . . . it is the duty of all and of the Churches especially, to be active in providing adequate means for his Religious Instruction, and to regard this provision as essential, not only to the welfare of the slave, but that of the State of which he is a humble but most useful component part."[30] On the basis of such reasoning, plans proceeded for the erection of both an Episcopal and a Presbyterian church designed specifically for African Americans but under white control.

In 1850 Calvary Episcopal Church and Anson Street Presbyterian Church were completed.[31] Thornwell, who was then serving as pastor of the Glebe Street Presbyterian Church in the city, was invited by Adger to preach the opening sermon for the Anson Street church. Given the sensitive nature of Thornwell's subject, only whites were allowed to attend.

Thornwell took for his text "Masters, give unto your servants that which is just and equal; knowing that you also have a master in heaven." What followed was a brilliant presentation of a social vision by the "Calhoun of the Church." His vision was of a paternalistic society, stable and orderly, where each person has certain rights and certain corresponding duties. The right of the master was to the labor of the slave. The right of the slave involved "all the essential rights of humanity" and included such temporal rights as the right to acquire knowledge—which though legally denied "is practically admitted" by Southerners—the right of the family, and the right to personal safety. Such rights were sacred and the state had a responsibility to protect them for the slave, to have the rights "defined by law and enforced by penalties." Included in the duties of masters was the solemn obligation to "give to the servants, to the utmost extent of their ability, free access to the instruction and institutions of the gospel." The Anson Street church, Thornwell declared, was proof that this duty had not been completely neglected.[32]

What Thornwell was seeking to present was a utopian vision of a proper social order. In the face of all the disintegrative forces of modern life, of an emerging industrial society, Thornwell sought to envision a paternalistic, class-stratified society. He set his vision within the broad context of the economic and political turmoil shaking the Western world. A student of the economists David Ricardo and Thomas Malthus, Thornwell believed that an industrializing economy was not leading to the amelioration of the conditions of labor but to a growing immiseration.[33] "The agitations which are convulsing the kingdoms of Europe [the revolutions of 1848–49], the mad speculations of philosophers, the excesses of unchecked democracy, are working out some of the most difficult problems of political and social science," he told his Charleston audience. The world, he said, is "now the theatre of an extraordinary conflict of great principles . . . the foundations of society are about to be explored to their depths, and the sources of social and political prosperity laid bare." The great question before them, he said, "is not the narrow question of Abolitionism or Slavery—not simply whether we shall emancipate our negroes or not; the real question is the relations of man to society, of states to the individual, and of the individual to States—a question as broad as the interests of the human race."[34]

Thornwell was convinced that the answer to this great question and the answer to the turmoils of the time was a humane, well-ordered, class-stratified society. Only such a social system could provide an order capable of withstanding the increasing anarchy of the modern world.[35]

Thornwell's utopian vision was a middle way between extremes, "resisting alike the social anarchy of communism and the political anarchy of licentiousness." It supported "representative, republican government against the despotism of masses on the one hand, and the supremacy of a single will on the other." The friends and enemies of slavery, he argued, "are equally tempted to run into extravagance and excess; the one party denying the inestimable value of freedom, the other exaggerating the nature and extent of human rights, and both overlooking the real scope and purpose of the Gospel, in its relation to the present interests of man."[36]

For Thornwell, such a middle way was seen in the "design of Christianity," which is to secure "the perfection of the race." When "that end shall have been consummated, Slavery must cease to exist." This affirmation "is only asserting there will be no bondage in heaven." But, said the Old School theologian, earth is not heaven—it is distorted, it is fallen. "If Adam had never sinned and brought death into the world, with all our woe, the bondage of man to man would never have been instituted; and when the effects of transgression shall have been purged from the earth, and the new heavens and the new earth wherein dwelleth righteousness given to the saints, all bondage shall be abolished." Slavery, a natural evil resulting from the Fall, is consequently "inconsistent with the spirit of the Gospel," because slavery "contemplates a state of things, an existing economy, which it is the design of the Gospel to remove." "Slavery," Thornwell declared to the white Charlestonians, "is a part of the curse which sin has introduced into the world, and stands in the same general relation to Christianity as poverty, sickness, disease or death. It springs, not from the nature of man as man, nor from the nature of society as such, but from the nature of man as sinful and the nature of society as disordered." In such a disordered world, the friends of slavery, "its most strenuous defenders," should not declare slavery a positive good or a blessing. So much for those Southern extremists! But antislavery extremists had their lessons to learn as well. The enemies of slavery should not forget that the "Gospel does not propose to make our present state a perfect one—to make our earth a heaven." No, what was needed was a middle way between such extremes, a course indicated by the stern necessity of a fallen, disordered world.[37]

That middle way was envisioned by Thornwell as leading to a society marked by what he called "regulated freedom" or "regulated liberty." In contrast to the abolitionists, who believed freedom was necessary for order, Thorn-well—ever the Old School theologian—insisted order was necessary for free-dom. Without order, freedom was an illusion and anarchy the result.[38] For Thornwell the fundamental building block for a well-ordered society was the family. He was envisioning, of course, not only a nuclear family but an extended family, a family that reached out to include not only networks of white families but also black slaves. It was no mere sentimentality for Thornwell to consider slaves a "part of our family"; it was fundamental to his social vision. Through the family each person was united in an organic relationship to the other mem-bers of the society. Within the family there could be "regulated liberty" un-der the authority of white males.[39] Such a paternalistic society with "regulated liberty" did not, of course, exist in the low country. The church records them-selves made that only too clear with their notations of "sold away." The gap between the reality and the vision made Thornwell's well-ordered society truly utopian.

Thornwell's conservative mentality—and that of the white low country Reformed community—was not ordinarily given to utopian speculation.[40] A certain comfortableness, a sense of being in harmony with its environment, characterized the community. But the attacks from others and the general dis-orders of the age broke through the community's sense of comfort and caused it to question its own presuppositions. "The slave-holding States," Thornwell acknowledged before his Charleston audience, "have been placed under the ban of the public opinion of the civilized world. We have been denounced, with every epithet of vituperation and abuse, as conspirators against the dignity of man, traitors to our race, and rebels against God."[41] In the face of such at-tacks—and Smyth and Adger had felt them all too sharply in Britain—Thorn-well's vision emerged as a counterutopia.[42] It stood over against both the radical utopianism of Denmark Vesey and, more immediately, the liberal utopianism of antislavery forces. To be sure, Thornwell and others in the audience—in-cluding Adger and Smyth—shared elements of a liberal utopianism. They were, after all, nineteenth-century Americans. They saw a great future for the Re-public and could speak of growth and progress and the power of education—key themes in liberal utopianism.[43] But they saw dangers in its extremism, and these dangers were motivational sources for the conservative vision that Thorn-well articulated for the community.

The well-ordered society of "regulated liberty" envisioned by Thornwell had little room for abstractions, especially abstract notions about humanity or about human rights in the abstract. Rather, his utopian society was rooted in the concrete, in the particularities of the present social order. So Thornwell talked about the duties and rights of masters as masters and the duties and rights of slaves as slaves, each in their own concrete place, each according to their God-given responsibilities.[44] With the roots of such a vision so deeply embedded in the particular social realities of the low country, growth of the vision could not be hastened, patience must be practiced, time was needed for change. This call for patience, for the working out of divine providence in history, had been Smyth's plea at the Evangelical Alliance meeting in London, was Adger's plea at Anson Street, and it would long be the plea of well-meaning whites in regard to African Americans.[45]

Thornwell's conservative vision obviously reflected the self-interest of whites in the low country Reformed community. It helped to legitimize the present order—with whites in control—even as it called for a new order. It provided a sense of identity, and it stood as a preserving counter-vision to the challenges of revolution, antislavery, and the disintegrative forces of the modern world. Thornwell's vision, in other words, was not only utopian, it was also profoundly ideological. Both the utopian and the ideological elements were held together in a single conceptual framework. That framework—a fusion of the world view and the ethos of the low country Reformed community—with its primary metaphor the middle way, led to the Anson Street church and to the experiment in paternalism that followed.

The Anson Street Church was a neat Gothic structure that would seat six hundred blacks after reserving one hundred seats for whites. Adger served as its pastor for only two years until his failing eyesight forced him to resign. The church under Adger's leadership had shown little prospect of attracting many African Americans. The same was true of Calvary Episcopal Church where Paul Trapier was struggling to gather a congregation. Neither Adger, the Old School Presbyterian, nor Trapier, the High Church Episcopalian, seemed particularly well suited for the work. While Calvary would continue to languish, Anson Street experienced explosive growth under Adger's successor, John Girardeau. A child of the sea islands, Girardeau was at home with the Gullah dialect and the African Americans of the city. A powerful preacher, a master of classical rhetoric and the techniques of folk preaching, he could deeply move a congregation of blacks or whites.[46] Under his leadership the Anson Street church was soon overflowing and, in conversation with Smyth and the session of Second Church, it was decided that a new building and a new organization were needed. It would be an important step, they believed, toward the embodiment of the utopian vision Thornwell had articulated at the opening of Anson Street.[47]

On the motion of Smyth, the presbytery made the church independent of the Second Church, and soon more than $25,000 had been raised for a new building (with the Adgers suppling most of the money). The African Americans named it Zion and watched with pride at the largest church in Charleston was raised on the corner of Calhoun and Meeting Streets. A small core of whites belonged and served as officers. All the elders came from Second Presbyterian: Robert Adger, who assumed in 1858 oversight of his father James's extensive business operation and who had been moved by the call of his brother

John for special work among the African Americans of the city; Edward C. Jones, friend of the Adgers and a successful businessman who had been one of two whites to go with John Adger from Second Church to the Anson Street work; Archibald Campbell, who had come to the city from Scotland in 1817 and was in 1858 city treasurer; J. A. Enslow, a prominent commission merchant and advocate for modern business practices; and Dr. F. M. Robertson, whose family had long been a part of Second Church. Many of the white members also came on the transfer of their membership from Second Church—especially from the growing Adger clan—but others came from First (Scots), from Central, from Circular Congregational, and from the newly established Glebe Street church. Most, however, came "on examination," primarily young adults from different churches around the city, moved by the preaching of Girardeau to make a "profession of faith" for the first time.[48]

Zion was intended to be different, and the whites who joined found their places in the balcony while the African Americans took seats on the main floor. This symbolic reversal of place was part of the Zion experiment. "We enter this church," declared the white members in their covenant, "as white members of the same, with the fullest understanding that its primary design and chief purpose is to benefit the coloured and especially the slave population of this city, and that the white membership is a feature added to the original organization for the purpose of better securing the ends of that organization."[49]

What they had in mind for the African Americans was Thornwell's "regulated liberty." The whites provided the official leadership to the congregation and vigorous oversight of its activities—they would do the "regulating," even if they sat in the balcony. But there was also a significant expansion of the freedom for African Americans, and an African American controlled structure was put into place with black leaders and teachers. The African American congregation was divided into classes with their own leaders who met with their classes weekly, visited their members, looked after the sick and poor, examined applicants for marriage, conducted funerals, and reported cases requiring discipline. Under these familiar arrangements—other churches had long had similar ones—Girardeau sought both to extend the work of the African American leaders, providing space for more initiative on their part, and to move toward the vision of a well-ordered, class-stratified society.

The most important symbol of that move could be found in the roll book of the Zion congregation. Across the South, whites had refused to recognize that African Americans had surnames—blacks were simply Sam and Toney, Rose and Mingo, Tissey and Joe, with no surnames acknowledged—except that when needed, the name of the owner could be used. Such a practice was a powerful symbol, declaring that African Americans, within the world view of the whites, had no lasting family connections of their own; they were rather the property of whites and belonged to their owners. Such a symbol allowed African Americans to be sold and to be separated from parents and children, from husbands and wives, without the appearance of any separation but only as a transfer of property. In the low country and elsewhere, such a world view and its accompanying ethos and social system were legitimated in the roll books of the churches. When a slave joined a church, only the Christian name was listed, followed by "servant of" or occasionally "slave of": "London, servant of Tho. Bennett," "Judy, servant of Col. I. Bryan."[50]

At Zion, however, African Americans were able to publicly claim their surnames. The white clerk of the session at Zion recorded not only the owners of hundreds of slaves who joined Zion but also the surnames of the slaves. By the late 1850s, more than 92 percent of the slaves who joined Zion gave as their own surnames names that were different from those of their owners. Moreover, in addition to claiming the name of their families of origin, wives gave the surnames of their husbands, affirming their slave marriages. Such a practice was not confined to the roll book, for the session of Zion also came to know and to refer to the family names of African American slaves.[51]

This practice functioned as a powerful countersymbol to the no-name symbol long utilized by whites. It provided an alternative way of perceiving the world and the place of African Americans in it. As such it was both a bold act on the part of African Americans who publicly rejected the pretensions of their owners and an important indication of the middle way and utopian vision that guided the whites in the Zion experiment. Slave owners were acknowledged in the Zion roll book, and consequently the slave system with its hierarchical structures was acknowledged. But slave families and marriages were also sanctioned and given public recognition. This balancing of the two was the kind of "regulated liberty" Thornwell had envisioned. It imagined the family—the African American family as a distinct unit and the extended "family" under the control of white males—to be the basic building block for a good society, one united in an organic relationship.

The gap between the utopian vision that informed the Zion experiment and the realities of the low country could be found in the records of Zion itself. Not only did the records have the family names of African Americans and the names of owners but they also had beside the names of some members the notation "sold away": "Martha Foster, servant of John Otten, sold away from the city. Did not apply for a certificate; probably had not the opportunity to do so. She gave evidence of being a humble Christian." The session found itself forced in 1859 to give Girardeau the unusual power of granting letters of dismissal to African Americans who were suddenly "sold away" with no opportunity to apply to the session for an orderly transfer of membership.[52]

The distance between the utopian vision and the realities of the low country could be seen even more clearly in regard to the marriages of African Americans. A paternalistic social order with the family as the foundational element needed stable marriages. But the state did not recognize the marriage of slaves. Church records reveal the resulting gap. Perry Peak, a member of Zion, had left his wife in Alabama when his master had brought him to Charleston. Could he, he asked the session, marry again? Or Dolly Fraser? Thirty years earlier, her mother had joined Second Church and the young Dolly had grown up hearing Smyth preach, reciting Charles C. Jones's catechism, and going to class meetings. In 1858 she married without the permission of her owners. She had become pregnant, but now the owner of her "proposed husband" would not allow an official marriage. What action was the Zion session to take? Similar cases filled the records of the Charleston churches.[53]

An incongruence between social realities and a utopian vision is, of course, to be expected if the vision is indeed utopian—otherwise the vision would simply be ideological.[54] But the incongruence at Zion pointed to a radical flaw in the vision. Behind the organic community of whites and African Americans envisioned by Thornwell and his colleagues lay force and coercion. They had envisioned a community where people were not only linked through the structures of society but through a sense of belonging, even of affection, where family was fundamental.[55] What they failed to take into full account was the degree to which slavery was a system of coercion and not of organic, affectional links.[56] Moreover, and this was a critical flaw, their utopian vision of a paternalistic society failed to take into account that the society which they defended was *already* and had long been a capitalistic society of urban bourgeoisie and planter capitalists. However much they claimed a paternalistic, class-stratified society as a defense against the modern world, that modern world was already a part of the low country and intruded into the records of the Zion experiment. A modern, capitalist individualism—with so many intimate connections with the Reformed tradition in which Zion so firmly stood—was clearly at work in the low country. Individual slave masters, acting on the basis of their own economic interests, bought and sold slaves and divided slave families. They made decisions that were governed by market forces, however tempered they may have been by a sense of paternalistic duty.

Perhaps the greatest irony of this experiment in paternalism—and a revealing indicator of its fatal flaws—was found in the white leadership of Zion. They did not represent a prebourgeois mentality. They were rather representatives of Charleston's commercial and business interests. The Adgers in particular, who provided the funds for the building and much of the vision and leadership for Zion, certainly were among the most affluent and aggressive practitioners of capitalism in the city. Together with their cousins the Smyths they would provide significant leadership after the Civil War in the development of South Carolina's textile industry.

Zion nevertheless represented for these whites a moderate, middle way along that "course indicated by stern necessity" and between the competing impulses of their Reformed tradition. They saw in it a model for the future, and when war came they were ready to envision a holy commonwealth, a new confederacy of "regulated liberty." Because that vision hid and distorted the realities of life as already lived in the low country, and indeed throughout the South, this utopian vision of a paternalistic social order was finally little more than ideological, little more than an attempt to legitimize the power and authority of whites over African American slaves.[57]

12

Secession and Civil War

The End of Moderation

As THE STORM tides of civil war began to stir during the 1850s, the Reformed clergy in the low country called for reason and moderation in the hope that they would stem the tide and preserve the Union. But when they saw Abraham Lincoln elected and the war break over Fort Sumter, they abandoned moderation and took their stand with Southern extremists whom they had long opposed. This chapter explores first the clergy's struggle to follow their middle way up until 1861 and, second, their attempt to envision the new Confederacy as a Holy Commonwealth, preserver of the sacred traditions of the American republic, with a social order marked by "regulated liberty."

The Union: "Commissioned from the Skies"

The Unionist spirit continued to dominate the political and social perspectives of low country Presbyterian and Congregational leaders during the decade leading to the Civil War, even as the low country itself became a hotbed for secession. The reunion in 1852 of those who had been separated by the 1839 division of the old Charleston Union Presbytery strengthened this Unionist spirit and brought a new social solidarity to the low country Reformed community under the banner of Old School Presbyterianism.[1] Seeking to walk an increasingly narrow middle way, Old School Presbyterians across the nation—unlike the Methodists and Baptists who divided along North–South lines in 1844/45—remained united until after the shots were fired on Fort Sumter and great battles were being fought between Northern and Southern armies.

Throughout the 1850s an ardent love for the Union and its Constitution was expressed by Presbyterian and Congregational church leaders in the low country. In January 1851, shortly before he began his pastorate at Glebe Street in Charleston, Thornwell wrote on the sacred character of the Union. "The finger of God," he said, could be traced "in every stage of its history. We have looked upon it as destined to be a blessing to mankind." The geography of the United States—between Europe and Asia, "in the very center of the earth"—and its history seemed to Thornwell "to be commissioned from the skies as the apostle of civilization, liberty, and Christianity to all the races of man." Thornwell was convinced that "We cannot relinquish the idea of this lofty mission: WE HAVE BEEN CALLED to it; and if in our folly and wickedness we refuse to walk worthily of it, we may righteously expect, in addition to the ordinary disasters of revolution, the extraordinary retributions of God." Thornwell the Unionist could not "sympathize with the light and flippant tone in which the question of the value of the Union is too often approached. . . . As long as our voice can be heard we shall endeavor to avert [this] calamity."[2]

Thornwell's voice was that of a Southern Unionist and it reflected the sentiments of church leaders at a time when the foundations of the Union were threatened in the debates that surrounded the Compromise of 1850. His, however, was not an isolated voice, even in such a hotbed for secession as South Carolina.[3] John Adger and Thomas Smyth were well known for their support of the Union. Reuben Post at Circular Congregation had close ties with the North, and his successor in 1860, Thomas Rice of Massachusetts, represented conservative New England interests.[4] William C. Dana at Central (Third) Presbyterian, in spite of his earlier call for a Southern Presbyterian Church at the time of the Old School–New School controversy, had a congregation with a substantial Northern element and Unionist sympathies, which he shared.[5] George Howe was an ardent Unionist, and even Benjamin Morgan Palmer, child of Walterboro who would later become famous as a Confederate zealot, did not hesitate to express his love for the Union during the 1850s.[6]

Such Unionist sentiment, however, was soon to fade and be replaced by bitterness and blood. These developments in the low country Reformed community can best be seen in the struggles of moderates to pursue their middle way and keep the South from being cut off from, or cutting itself off from, the great benevolence societies that united evangelical Protestants across the country.

No Middle Ground

Struggles within the American Sunday School Union and the American Tract Society were minor skirmishes on the road to full-scale war. Yet these struggles were classic examples of the ways reasonable and moderate church leaders hoped to deal with the question of slavery and to maintain unity in both the church and the nation. Their struggles were a part of their little war of words and logic in which they hoped the power of reason would hold back the storm tides and save the country from a real war.[7]

Both the American Tract Society and the American Sunday School Union had to face the question of what references to slavery would be allowed in their literature. For the Sunday school union the question was seriously raised in 1847. The organization for a number of years had attempted to avoid any controversy over slavery by ignoring it. Its catalog, however, did contain a little book, *Jacob and His Sons* (1829), that referred to slaves as poor creatures sold like beasts, who could be cruelly treated, beaten, starved, and killed because they had no one to help them. During the same summer in which questions were being raised about Adger's plans for a separate work among African Americans in the city, a correspondent in the Charleston *Mercury* indignantly called attention to the book and recommended the withdrawal of Southern subscribers from the Sunday school union.[8]

Thomas Smyth was an active supporter of the Sunday school union and had delivered in 1846 an address to its annual meeting in Philadelphia.[9] He had called for cooperation and charity among evangelicals so that united they could advance the crusade that was building God's Kingdom on earth. In early August 1847, he had sent to the *Mercury* a letter from an officer of the union, emphasizing the society's desire to publish only what was acceptable to all sections of the country. This letter had perhaps been the stimulus for the protest letter that followed. At any rate, Smyth immediately sent a copy of the *Mercury* to Fred Packard, secretary of the union. In his reply, which Smyth made sure was printed, Packard stated that *Jacob and His Sons* had been out of print for fifteen years and would be dropped from the catalog. He then stated the reasonable position that the Unionists sought to maintain: The Sunday school union's position, Packard wrote, "is one of entire *neutrality* on the subject of which you speak. Our Society does not and will not take any men, views or principles in a sectional or party light." As a national society, Packard insisted, the Sunday school union was bound "to respect alike the interests and regulations of all parts of the country, and we would not knowingly do anything which would impair our legitimate influence as the Am. S. S. Union in any State or County of the country."[10]

The American Tract Society took the same position of official neutrality. But it did not have such an easy time remaining neutral. The constitution of the society had certain provisions that were supposed to make it catholic by making it dead center. If a member of the publishing committee—a conglomerate of evangelicals from across the country—objected to a tract, it could not be published. Such provisions were intended to ensure national support from many denominations. They worked until 1856.[11]

In that year the Congregational Association of New York asked the society to begin issuing antislavery tracts. In an attempt to find an acceptable compromise, the society declared that if there were tracts on "duties and evils" connected with the subject of slavery "in which evangelical Christians north and south would agree," they knew no reason why they should not be approved and published.[12] Such a decision appeared to be a reasonable compromise, but it almost wrecked the tract society. The problem was that evangelical Christians could not agree about the duties and evils connected with slavery.

Shortly after the society's decision, it was called upon to publish none other than Thornwell's sermon, "Duties of Masters," which he had preached at the opening of the Anson Street church. Immediate objections came from the South, and many in the North found it acceptable only as the first of a series that would ultimately condemn slavery. Because of the opposition, the publishing committee decided to discontinue any further consideration of the sermon. That decision only added fuel to the fire. In order to attempt to still the controversy, a Special Committee of Fifteen was appointed "to investigate and review the proceedings" of the publishing committee. The special committee was composed of some of the most distinguished Protestant leaders in the country, including a number of college presidents: Theodore Frelinghuysen of Rutgers, Martin Anderson of Colgate, Mark Hopkins of Williams, and Francis Wayland of Brown.[13]

As the committee was beginning its investigation, Wayland surprised them all by publishing in the *New York Observer* a strong attack on the tract society's position. Long known for his antislavery position, Wayland now wrote that as tracts on "dancing, theatrical amusements, intemperance, lying and perjury" would not receive the approbation of church members who erred in these matters, so tracts on slavery were not welcome to those who sinned in that way, but they were nonetheless to be published. If the usefulness of the tract society in the South were impaired by such publications, then, he said, "the South if it please will form a society of its own for the teachings of which we are not responsible."[14] Here was the old cry Smyth and Adger had heard at the Evangelical Alliance meeting in London: "No union with slaveholders!"

As it turned out, some in South Carolina were thinking about doing just what Wayland suggested. The South Carolina Branch of the American Tract Society, headed by the Episcopalian C. C. Pinckney, Jr., wrote the Committee of Fifteen protesting against any publication on the subject of slavery. It would be, the South Carolinians insisted, a violation of the society's constitution to issue tracts the South would not tolerate. If the society issued such tracts, the South Carolina branch declared it would withdraw from the parent society.[15] For moderates, it seemed clear that extremists on both sides were making demands that threatened the unity of the society and endangered a great cause.

In the midst of this turmoil, Smyth began to work desperately to heal the divisions and reach a reasonable compromise. Long letters were exchanged with William Hallock, secretary of the society.[16] In a flurry of work he published five articles in an attempt to bring people to their senses and persuade them to be reasonable and moderate. Three articles were published in the *Southern Episcopalian*. "Why do I love the American Tract Society?" he asked his Southern readers. Because it is American, he replied, not Northern, nor Southern, Eastern, or Western. It unites evangelical Christians all over the country in order to carry on its "blessed work of reclaiming . . . lost and perishing sinners," binding

its supporters together by the catholic character of its constitution. There was
no reason Southern evangelicals could not continue to support the tract society.
It had done nothing but reaffirm its old position of neutrality on the question
of slavery. If Southerners withdrew from the society, said Smyth, they would
only be playing into the abolitionists' hands. The result would be that Southerners would be cut off from evangelical Christians in other parts of the country—exactly what the abolitionists had been attempting to accomplish. The
only proper course was for Southerners to trust the provisions of the society's
constitution and stand firmly by the principles on which the society was
founded. Such a course would defeat the abolitionists and allow the society to
continue in its great evangelical work.[17]

Smyth also attacked what he regarded as the extremism of Wayland's position. Writing in the *New York Observer,* he attempted to refute Wayland's arguments and tried to establish a basis of cooperation between the antislavery
evangelicals and evangelicals of the South. Wayland had demanded that the
tract society publish "the whole will of God" on the subject of slavery. Whatever the results, this was the society's clear duty, he had declared. For Wayland,
intentions were what counted, not consequences. Duty and conscience were the
only guide for ethics, never prudence or moderation, or a consideration of a
God's providence in a person's "present alotted sphere and task."[18] Smyth, of
course, disagreed. As far as the tract society was concerned, he wrote, the whole
will of God was "to some extent a matter of dispute among evangelical Christians." Evangelicals, for example, held different views on baptism, communion,
and church government, and it had been agreed that the society would not
publish tracts on these subjects. The society was able, however, to publish on
subjects that met general approval. It was, said Smyth, the same with slavery.

> Dr. W. like many sound orthodox evangelical Christians, is *opposed to Slavery,*
> and anxious to see it, and all the evils they believe to be inseparable from it,
> removed. Be it so. Evangelical christians at the South can love and honor
> them, as they do Dr. Wayland, none the less on this account. They would not
> restrain or hinder their opinions or philanthropic Christian exertions. But as
> they cannot unite with them on this subject, they would unite heart and hand
> in promoting the interests of all that is dear to them in common as evangelical
> christians—and such is our union in this Society.

Southerners do not want to withdraw from the society, Smyth told his Northern readers. All they want is for the society to be and do "*what it has been, and
has done, from the beginning.* They neither wish the Society to know slavery or
anti-slavery, to be pro-slavery, or abolition, but just to keep to its constitution
and sole purpose."[19]

Smyth's plea—and it was the plea of other middle-of-the-road moderates—
was that slavery not be allowed to divide evangelical Christians or divert them

from their great mission. Slavery, it was hoped, was not a question that demanded a total commitment either for it or against it. Like baptism, slavery was said to be a debatable subject, one on which reasonable people could reach a compromise and agree to disagree. Such a compromise would grow out of mutual respect. It would be based on recognition of the right to hold differing opinions on the subject and would be guaranteed by compacts mutually accepted. This was the hope of Presbyterian and Congregational leaders in the low country. If people would only accept one another in spite of their differences over slavery, if they would but recognize the limitations and guarantees imposed by laws and constitutions, then the extremists could be defeated, the Union could be preserved, and the great hopes of the nation advanced.

Whatever the hopes of moderates, events were rapidly moving the nation toward a great civil war. By 1860 the divisions between North and South were clear and apparently inescapable. Following the Democratic convention in Charleston (Smyth's opening prayer at one of its sessions was a fervent plea for unity) that party was left divided and in disarray.[20] Lincoln was elected president in November, South Carolina seceded in December, and war followed in April.[21]

These events and the bloody battles that followed illumined the fatal flaw of the Reformed community's middle way: the community did not fully grasp the growing chasm between extremes nor adequately comprehend that its middle way could not bridge the distance between those extremes. The metaphor of the middle way assumed a common language and world view shared by North and South. The success of that middle way through three decades of controversy was a confirmation of that shared language. But each side began, as it were, to ex-communicate the other, to speak increasingly in ways the other did not understand. When war came, it came not only as the result of conflicting social and economic forces but also as a consequence of this ex-communication, of this disruption of communication between North and South. The ex-communication was not simply a matter of the peculiarities of accents in Boston and Charleston, though that was perhaps involved as each side felt the other to be increasingly strange and peculiar. More fundamental than accents, style, and lexicon in the ex-communication were the differences in the ways North and South saw the world, the differences between the symbolic systems through which they looked at one another.[22] Nowhere were these differences more sharply focused than around the word *liberty*.

When Thornwell spoke of "regulated liberty" at the opening of the Anson Street church, he meant a liberty that stood between the extremes of tyranny on the one hand and anarchy on the other. Such an understanding of liberty was shared with many in the North, not least of whom was Lincoln, who treasured "ordered liberty" and saw the South's secession as the outbreak of a lawless anarchy.[23] Lincoln and the leaders in the low country Reformed community had conservative Whig roots and saw dangers to liberty in extremes.[24] But the meaning of liberty was different for each, and it was this difference that revealed the chasm between them that a middle way could not bridge. Lincoln saw the chasm. "The world has never had a good definition of the word liberty, and the American people, just now, are much in want of one," he said. "We all declare for liberty; but in using the same *word* we do not all mean the same *thing*. With some the word liberty may mean for each man to do as he pleases with himself, and the product of his labor; while with others the same may mean for some men to do as they please with other men, and the product of other men's labor." Here, declared Lincoln, "are two, not only different, but incompatible things, called by the same name—liberty."[25]

For the low country Reformed community, "regulated liberty" meant a liberty whose character was determined by one's place in society. In Southern society, whites had one place and blacks another, and whites were determined both to resist outside interference in their own liberty and to "regulate" the liberty of African American slaves. Such an understanding of liberty had allowed Smyth in the 1840s, in his speech on behalf of the Free Church of Scotland, to refer to his Charleston audience "as the friends of liberty and human rights." In 1860 and 1861, such an understanding allowed him to insist that the South was defending its liberty against the tyranny of the North.[26] For Lincoln and increasing numbers in the North, however, such language sounded like what William Lloyd Garrison called it in the 1840s—an "unmoral rhetoric." For them African Americans were included when the Declaration of Independence declared "all men are created equal," and such an inclusion meant a very different liberty than that of which Smyth and others in the low country spoke.[27] The incompatibility of these two understandings was the chasm that moderation and a middle way could not cross. In January 1861 Thornwell would acknowledge this incompatibility and conclude that "two Governments upon this continent may work out the problem of human liberty more successfully than one."[28]

In a similar manner, the distance that separated North and South was revealed in the meanings each attached to the words *tyranny* and *anarchy*. As with liberty, both sides used these same words but did not mean the same thing. For the low country conservatives, Lincoln was a tyrant who sought to impose the will of the North on the South through the power of a "consolidated despotism" and one who was unleashing anarchy and revolution precisely because of his understanding of liberty. For Lincoln and growing numbers in the North, on the other hand, the South was both the home of tyrannical slave owners and the hotbed of anarchy.[29]

The fatal flaw of the middle way was that this metaphor could not draw within its circle of conversation and interpretation these incompatible and conflicting meanings. Smyth, Thornwell, Adger, and their low country colleagues wanted compromises; they wanted to agree to disagree about slavery. But such reasonable agreements were impossible when each side increasingly used a different language and thereby ex-communicated the other. The distance between the sides was not a simple misunderstanding that could be overcome by well-meaning moderates seeking understanding. Two symbolic systems, rooted in and dialectically linked to their own social and economic contexts, had no middle place between them on which to stand. One had to be on one side or the other; one had to mean one thing or the other; one eventually had to make a decision for or against slavery and stand with either the North or the South. When the time came for such a decision, there was no question where the low country Reformed community stood.

The Confederacy: A Holy Commonwealth

When Lincoln was elected, Governor William H. Gist of South Carolina called for a day of humiliation and prayer, a time "to implore the direction and blessing of Almighty God in this hour of difficulty, and to give us *one heart and one mind,* to oppose, by all just and proper means, every encroachment upon our rights." "The curse of God," cried Smyth in his Fast Day sermon, "is poured out upon us." America, said the old Unionist, "that bright hope of the world, has fallen. That sun of liberty whose rays shone so brightly over every land and sea . . . has gone down while it is yet day." What, he asked, has brought this curse? Do not blame a political party, do not look to the recent triumph of sectional pride, or accuse a traitorous disloyalty to the Constitution, he replied. They are but the "results,—the consummation of a tragedy which has been long progressing to its last act,—when the curtain fell upon the dismembered body of the Union." The true cause of this curse of God can be laid on the heads of "atheists, infidels, communists, free-lovers, rationalists, bible haters, anti-christian levellers, and anarchists," he said. They have perverted, said Smyth, "the great doctrines of personal responsibility, *liberty* of conscience, *liberty* of thought, *liberty* of opinion and *liberty* of action," by making their own conscience, rather than the Bible, the infallible standard of right and wrong."[30] With the North ex-communicated—given over to "atheists," "infidels," and "anarchists"—the South was ready to establish a new Confederacy, a Holy Commonwealth, ready to shed its blood to "defend the cause of God and religion."

"We have crossed swords with the North over the Bible," Smyth told his congregation after the battle of Fort Sumter. "We have met each other face to face at the same altar, invoked fire from heaven on each other, and appealed to the God of Battles . . . to avenge us against our adversaries." The Confederacy was the faithful remnant in the Promised Land of America. The South was on an exodus from a now-corrupt nation as the Confederacy attempted to establish a new republic on the firm foundation of the Bible and the "immutable laws of God." "God spoke as with a voice from heaven," thundered Smyth, "saying 'come out of the Union, My People.' Then came up from the millions of hearts the shout, 'Go forward! for God is with us.' "[31] The South as a Holy Commonwealth—the South as the faithful remnant of God's Chosen People, leaving behind the once chosen but now unfaithful and excommunicated Union—became the central image the leaders of the low country Reformed community used for the Confederacy. Around this image their conservative utopian vision now found its focus. For a few fleeting, bloody years they hoped that their vision might finally be realized in the Confederacy.

Thornwell preached his Fast Day sermon on "National Sins." In it, he articulated once again the utopian vision that had moved him at the opening of the Anson Street church. But this time he saw more clearly the power and dangers of the social system developing in the North and soon to be at war with the South. Capital and labor were divided in the North. As capital accumulates, looking only to its own interests and not the interests of labor, and as the number of laborers increase, a revolution of the masses, he said, is sure to result. The only way to avoid such a revolution is for the government to provide the masses the necessities of life. "But," asked Thornwell, "shall it support them in idleness? Will the poor, who have to work for their living, consent to see others, as stout and able as themselves, clothed like the lilies of the field while they toil not, neither do they spin?" Will this not, he asked like some twentieth-century critic of social welfare, "give a premium to idleness?" The government then, Thornwell said, "must find them employment; but how shall this be done? On what principle shall labour be organized so as to make it certain that the labourer shall never be without employment, and employment adequate for his support?" The only way, Thornwell insisted, "which it can be done, as a permanent arrangement, is by converting the labourer into capital; that is, by giving the employer a right of property in the labour employed; in other words, by Slavery." Thornwell thus concluded that "non-slaveholding States will eventually have to organize labour, and introduce something so like to Slavery that it will be impossible to discriminate between them, or else to suffer from the most violent and disastrous insurrections against the system which creates and perpetuates their misery, seems to be as certain as the tendencies in the laws of capital and population to produce extremes of poverty and wealth."[32]

Against this social order that they saw rising in the North, Thornwell and his colleagues envisioned the Confederacy as an alternative class-stratified society that would stand against the increasing anarchy of the modern world. What they envisioned was not a feudal Confederacy. Their vision did not emerge out of a prebourgeois mentality. Rather, they saw in the Confederacy the opportunity to establish a commonwealth that was *both* capitalistic and hierarchical. Such a commonwealth would not be a society of democratic capitalism committed to an equality of opportunity, but a commonwealth whose capitalism would be controlled by a commitment to "regulated liberty."[33]

The society envisioned by these Southerners would be, in Smyth's words, based on the firm foundation of the Bible and the "immutable laws of God." What this vision meant was spelled out by Thornwell in a remarkable document presented to the first General Assembly of the Presbyterian Church in the Confederate States of America. Entitled "Relation of the State to Christ," it was intended as a petition of the Presbyterian General Assembly to the Congress of the Confederacy, but because the rushed circumstances of the General Assembly "did not permit a full discussion of the subject" he withdrew it from consideration. In the paper, Thornwell argued that the Constitution of the United States, for all its greatness, was flawed because it rested on a partial truth—"that popular governments are offspring of popular will; and that rulers, as the servants and not the masters of their subjects, are properly responsible to them." For Thornwell what the Constitution failed to acknowledge was "that all just government is the ordinance of God, and that magistrates are His ministers who must answer to Him for the execution of their trust." The consequence of this failure was to make the people "a law unto themselves; there was nothing beyond them to check or control their caprices or their pleasure." A foundation was thus laid "for the worst of all possible forms of government—a democratic absolutism" in which the "will of majorities must become the supreme law, if the voice of the people is to be regarded as the voice of God."[34]

What was being envisioned for the Confederacy was not a union of church and state but of "religion and State." The individual's freedom of conscience would be preserved, for, wrote Thornwell, "We utterly abhor the doctrine that the civil magistrate has any jurisdiction in the domain of religion, in its relations to the conscience or conduct of others, and we cordially approve the clause in our Confederate Constitution which guarantees the amplest liberty on this subject." But the state itself may believe the Scriptures "to be true, and regulate its own conduct and legislation in conformity with their teachings." What the state does, and "what it enjoins upon others to do, are very different things. It has an organic life apart from the aggregate life of the individuals who compose it; and in that organic life, it is under the authority of Jesus Christ and the restraints of His holy Word." Only on this basis, on Smyth's "firm foundation of the Bible," could the dangers of democratic absolutism be avoided and the will of the people held accountable to the will of God revealed in Jesus Christ. "We long to see, what the world has never yet beheld, a truly Christian Republic, and we humbly hope that God has reserved it for the people of these Confederate States to realize the grand and glorious idea."[35]

The utopian vision was thus complete: the Confederacy would be a Holy Commonwealth, a class-stratified society of "regulated liberty." An organic state, it would acknowledge the freedom of the individual conscience, but, Thornwell proposed, it would also declare in its Constitution: "we, the people of these Confederate States, distinctly acknowledge our responsibility to God, and the supremacy of His Son, Jesus Christ, as King of kings and Lord of lords; and hereby ordain that no law shall be passed by the Congress of these Confederate States inconsistent with the will of God, as revealed in the Holy Scriptures."[36]

Secession and the formation of the Confederacy provided a critical moment for the creation of a new order. What was envisioned in that moment by Thornwell and his colleagues, not suddenly but after a generation of struggle and thought, was a conservative counterutopia. The new Confederacy would stand against the liberal utopian vision of Lincoln and the "Second American Revolution," against what this Reformed community saw as the anarchy and the disintegrative power of the modern world. That this vision for the Confederacy was profoundly ideological, that it served to legitimize the power and authority of whites, that it sought to create a world reflective of their own domestic arrangements, is all too clear. That it was also utopian, however, was proved not only by its vision of what the Confederacy might become but also by the productivity of Northern factories, the strength of Northern armies, and the power of Lincoln's vision "of a new birth of freedom."

These antithetical utopian visions point once again to the chasm separating the two sides and to the fatal flaw of moderation. Each side represented a conflicting symbolic system—that is, each side represented a culture that was incompatible with the other. The metaphor of a middle way could not encompass both. Unable to build bridges cross-culturally, unable to find some transcendence beyond their mutual ex-communication, both sides were left with only one common language—the language of violence. Whose vision of the future, whose understanding of liberty, whose domestic arrangements would prevail would be determined on bloody battlefields. It was in this context of ex-communication and counterutopian visions that the Old School Presbyterian Church, long a bastion of Unionism, divided, and a Presbyterian Church in the Confederate States of America was organized. Its primary leadership came from Charleston Presbytery and out of the Reformed community of the low country.[37]

The Presbyterian Church in the Confederate States of America

In December 1860, at the height of the excitement over secession, the Synod of South Carolina met in Charleston. Those who had worked for a separate Southern Presbyterian Church twenty years earlier once again came forward with calls for a division of the church. William Yates, who had stood with other separatists in 1840, moved that "fidelity to the South requires us to dissolve all connection with the Northern position of the Presbyterian Church" and to form a separate Southern Presbyterian Church. The Old School leaders, however, were not ready for such a division, even if the nation was dividing. John Adger moved and the synod passed a substitute motion that a committee be appointed to prepare a report on the views of the synod "in relation to the duty of our churches and people in the present condition of the country." When the committee reported, it declared that Southerners had received nothing but justice and courtesy at the General Assemblies and that the General Assembly of 1845 had declared almost unanimously that it had no authority to make any laws on the subject of slavery. All of this history had resulted in a harmony of the whole church over the question of slavery "unbroken in the least degree to the present time." Consequently there was no need to rush. "It is not for us," said the committee, "to inaugurate as a Synod any movement towards a separation from the Northern branch of our church. . . . such a movement would be in advance of the action of the State."[38]

Only after the battle at Fort Sumter did the ties that had kept Old School Presbyterians together begin to break. That battle, Smyth told his congregation, had providentially "opened the eyes of the South, to see that the soul of the Northern confederacy was consolidated despotism" and to see that "conservative and Christian men in the North, if not in heart and in unison with it, were impotent against it."[39]

One month after Sumter, the General Assembly met in Philadelphia. Conservative men who had long supported a neutral, moderate course, one that it was thought reasonable people in both the North and the South could follow, now gathered as North and South prepared for war. Gardiner Spring of the Brick Church in New York, who only two years earlier had nominated Benjamin Morgan Palmer for a professorship at Princeton, introduced a resolution calling on the church to "promote and perpetuate, so far as in us lies, the integrity of these United States, and to strengthen, uphold, and encourage, the Federal Government in the exercise of all its functions under our noble constitution: and to this constitution in all its provisions, requirements, and principles, we profess our unabated loyalty." Charles Hodge of Princeton protested. The General Assembly, he declared, was neither Northern or Southern and was the last evangelical body uniting the two sections. To adopt Spring's resolution, Hodge argued, would be a novel introduction of political questions into the church and would mean its sure division. Gardiner Spring did not think it novel and later wrote that Southerners had been introducing politics all along: Palmer and Thornwell, Leland, Adger, and Smyth, "men of distinguished abilities," men who could sway the popular will, had not only justified and counseled the rebellion but had "instigated and urged it with all the enthusiasm and vehemence of the pulpit, and all the weight of their personal and official character."[40]

The passage of the Gardiner Spring Resolution meant that division of the church could no longer be avoided. For Smyth, the General Assembly had "willingly, wilfully and wickedly" severed the last link that held North and South together. By its action it had vindicated the North in "waging the most unchristian, wicked and atrociously despotic war ever waged by a civilized not to say Christian country." The resolution was nothing less than treason against the church, against the gospel, against Christ, against the Constitution, which is ignored and set aside, and against "all the rights and liberties of freemen."[41] North and South, moderation had clearly been thrown to the winds of war.

In December 1861, twelve months after South Carolina had seceded, the Presbyterian Church in the Confederate States of America was organized in Augusta, Georgia. Palmer was elected moderator, but it was Thornwell who dominated the General Assembly. It was at this General Assembly that he presented his "Relation of the State to Christ." More significantly, he was given the responsibility for writing "An Address to All the Churches of Jesus Christ Throughout the Earth." This address, perhaps the most important single document in the history of the Southern Presbyterian Church, announced to the churches of the world the formation of a new and independent church. A separate and distinct identity was articulated for both a Southern church and for Southern society.

Thornwell gave two reasons for the creation of the new church. First, the General Assembly of the old, still united, church had abandoned the doctrine of the "Spirituality of the Church." The Gardiner Spring resolution, wrote Thornwell, "conclusively shows that if we should remain together, the political questions which divide us as citizens, will be obtruded on our Church Courts, and be discussed . . . with all the acrimony, bitterness and rancor with which such questions are usually discussed by men of the world. . . . commissioners from the Northern would meet with Commissioners from the Southern Confederacy, to wrangle over the questions which have split them into two Confederacies, and involved them in furious and bloody war." In his paper, "Relation of the State to Christ," Thornwell had argued for a union of religion and the state, for a "truly Christian Republic," and had insisted that this was a different matter than a union of church and state or the overlapping of the spheres of church and state. Now in the "Address to All the Churches," he proceeded to develop in the most careful and logical manner the doctrine of the "spirituality of the church": that the "provinces of Church and State are perfectly distinct, and the one has no right to usurp the jurisdiction of the other." The state, he said, is "designed to realize the idea of justice. It is the society of rights." The church, on the other hand, is "designed to realize the idea of grace. It is the society of the redeemed." Church and state "are as planets moving in different orbits, and unless each is confined to its own track, the consequences may be as disastrous in the moral world, as the collision of different spheres in the world of matter."[42]

This doctrine of the "Spirituality of the Church" had been carefully developed throughout the antebellum period. It was a fundamental position of the Old School in its debates with the New School in the 1830s; Smyth used it effectively not only at the General Assembly but also in the controversies of Charleston Union Presbytery. Thornwell had articulated it time and again: in the 1840s for the General Assembly in response to British churches on the slavery question, in his Anson Street sermon, and in his Fast Day sermon, "National Sins." The doctrine was fundamental for his ecclesiastical polity and shaped his response to a wide range of issues, from boards and agencies for the church to support of benevolent societies and to slavery.[43] Adger, Girardeau, and Palmer all shared a deep commitment to the doctrine and used it frequently to explain their ecclesiology.[44] But they all agreed that the "spirituality of the church" was a different matter from Christianity's influence in society. They saw Christianity at the heart of Southern *culture*. If church and state as institutions (or societies) had distinct spheres, whose overlap would bring chaos, that did not mean that religion was not at the heart of a culture, shaping its values, its shared meanings, and its identity and providing the foundation for the state. It was this distinction between the church as an institution on the one hand and the cultural role of religion on the other that allowed Thornwell to present at the same General Assembly both his "Relation of the State to Christ" and his doctrine of the "Spirituality of the Church."[45] As forcefully articulated in the 1861 "Address to All the Churches," the "Spirituality of the Church" became "the distinctive doctrine of the Southern Presbyterian Church" until at least the 1930s.[46]

The distinction between the church's relationship to the state and Christianity's relationship to culture permitted Thornwell in the 1861 address to churches to move from the "Spirituality of the Church" to the maintenance of a distinctive Southern society. Thornwell identified national distinctions in the address as a second reason for the creation of a separate church. In Protestant churches, said Thornwell, church organizations follow national lines. After pointing to obvious examples of national churches and to the benefits that flow from them, he insisted that it was altogether proper that there be a separate church for the new nation of the Confederacy. The presbyteries of the Confederate States, Thornwell wrote, "have not ceased to love the church of their fathers" or "abjured its ancient principles." Rather, they have sought "to give these same principles a richer, freer, fuller development among ourselves than they possibly could receive under *foreign culture*." In subjection to "a *foreign power*, we could no more accomplish [this development] than the Church in the United States could have been developed in dependence upon the Presbyterian Church of Scotland." The difficulty was not so much geographical distance but cultural distance: "the difference in the manners, habits, customs and ways of thinking, the social, civil and political institutions of the people." These same cultural difficulties "exist in relation to the Confederate and United States, and render it eminently proper that the Church in each should be as separate and independent as the Governments."[47]

Thornwell, the old Unionist, thus insisted that the Confederate States had a separate culture from that of the Northern states.[48] There were differences "in the manners, habits, customs and ways of thinking" and in "the social, civil and political institutions of the people." Here was the source of the ex-communication and of the inability to build bridges from one side to the other. Despite the cosmopolitan background and interests of church leaders, despite their Unionist sentiments and years of struggle to follow what they regarded as a reasonable middle course, they now asserted that a separate culture existed for the Southern states. Here they finally—and bitterly—acknowledged, as battles raged between competing armies, that their middle way lacked what it most needed: a common culture, a shared language and set of assumptions, across which a middle way could traverse.

Thornwell did not hesitate to push ahead with his argument and to name slavery as that which "so radically and fundamentally distinguishes" the North and the South. What followed was a brilliant summary of the classic proslavery argument as it had been developed in the Southern church.[49] Thornwell and his clergy colleagues thus championed a view of the South as a distinct culture, one based on a hierarchical understanding of society and on pervasive racial assumptions. This was the homeland they were defending, one in which whites would have their place and blacks would have theirs.

So these Old School Presbyterians turned their former Unionist position on its head in 1861 and argued for the South as a separate culture. But they knew that the war which raged was a civil war, that it involved two sides that shared not only much history but also many values and common commitments. That confession, after all, had been the strength of their middle way, however profound its flaws. As developments following Appomattox would show, the Civil War was more a war between subcultures than a war between completely alien cultures. That each subculture ex-communicated the other and poured out its blood in fierce fighting was an indication of the intensity of the struggle within American society about competing visions. The victory of Northern armies meant that the Northern vision, so powerfully articulated by Lincoln, would be perceived as the mainstream of American life.

It would not be, however, the only stream, for another with origins deep in Southern history would continue to flow. This Southern stream, shed of its burden of slavery but carrying with it hierarchical and racial assumptions, would reemerge with surprising strength.[50] Flowing far beyond Dixie, joining similar streams from other sections of the country, it would slowly merge following Reconstruction with the mainstream of American life and become a powerful current within it. Flowing within this conservative current would be reminders here and there of the dark soil of the Carolina low country and the religious and cultural perspectives articulated by Reformed theologians in defense of that little world.

13

The Challenge of an Almost New Order

"Hold Your Ground, Sir!"

WHEN PEACE CAME in 1865 the low country was a defeated and devastated land. Only eighty-two years earlier, an invading army and a bloody civil war between Whigs and Tories had left the region wasted. Now, in 1865, smoke from the fires of war once again hung over the land. Only this time the invading army was victorious and what followed the fighting was not a new prosperity for the low country but a grinding poverty. A region that had been famous for its wealth now became marked by its poverty.[1]

Much of Charleston was in ruins. In addition to the bombardment of the city by Federal forces, the city's defenders had done their own damage: great mounds of earthwork defenses and deep holes for artillery spread poxlike along White Point Garden and up adjacent streets, while fires and exploding ammunition, ignited by hastily retreating Confederates, had burned large areas of the upper peninsula. More devastating than these wounds of war, however, had been the great fire of December 1861. Beginning in a kitchen on Hasell Street, the flames had spread westward over the peninsula. Roaring uncontrolled, they destroyed a third of the city before finally dying on the banks of the Cooper. Among the many public buildings burned was the Circular Congregational Church. With its interior gutted, its domed ceiling collapsed, its massive steeple tottering, and the columns of its once elegant portico standing unattached, it seemed in 1865 a symbol of "A city of ruins, of desolation, of vacant houses, of widowed women, of rotting wharves, of deserted warehouses, of weed-wild gardens, of miles of grass-grown streets, of acres of pitiful and voiceful barrenness." A *New York Times* correspondent wrote that the city "is an indescribable scene of desolation and ruin . . . silent to all sounds of business, and voiceless only to the woe-begone, poverty-stricken, haggard people, who wander up and down amid the ruins, looking to a jubilant past, a disappointed present, and a hopeless future."[2]

The destruction in the countryside matched, or perhaps even surpassed, that in the city. Most of the sea islands, easy prey for Federal naval forces, had fallen early in the war. Raiding parties had made their way up the Edisto, the

Ashepoo, and the Combahee. They burned plantations, carried off booty, and returned to their bases accompanied by large numbers of escaped slaves. With Sherman's army came more raids, more burning, more destruction of rail lines until the region was securely in Federal hands and peace finally came.[3]

Many of the country churches had been damaged and most had their members widely scattered. The movement of white congregations into village chapels, under way for a generation, was largely finished through the ravages of war. The congregation of Stoney Creek, its old country church burned by a raiding party, completed the move to its summer chapel in McPhersonville. Dorchester's congregation, with roots in the seventeenth century, was gone to Summerville. Left behind to crumble and decay near the Ashley's dark waters was its White Meeting House. Ancient Wappetaw lay desolate—its pews and woodwork burned by Union troops for firewood, its once substantial endowment of $28,000 reduced to a meager $600, and its congregation of Legarés, Vennings and Morrisons, of Jerveys, Whildens, and Vanderhorsts gone to Mc-Clellanville or Mount Pleasant. Wilton was left a struggling remnant of its former prosperous self, its white congregation sliding slowly toward extinction.[4]

The fire in Charleston and the devastation in the countryside, together with developments during closing years of the antebellum period, meant the effective end of white Congregationalism in the low country—at least as a lively and indigenous denomination. Country churches that had been Congregational completed the move to Presbyterianism that had begun with their return to Charleston Presbytery in 1852.[5] In Charleston the great Circular Congregational Church became only a shadow of what it once was. To be sure, a handsome but smaller building was built—with the help of Northern funds—where the old one had stood. But the congregation itself never recovered its earlier strength, as families that had been associated with it since early colonial days drifted off to other churches. The destruction of the great sanctuary and the time that elapsed before its more modest replacement, together with conflict within the congregation, left the church greatly weakened.[6] But perhaps most important for Circular's decline was Congregationalism's identification with New England, with "Yankee imperialism," and the attempt following the war to impose an "alien culture" on the South. At any rate, Circular Congregational moved from a central place in Charleston's economic, political, and cultural life to the edges. As the impoverished region, struggling with its own self-understanding following the war, expanded the "Cavalier myth," Circular's earlier place in the city's life was marginalized if not completely forgotten.[7] The primary signs of Congregationalism's life in the low country would be through the work of Northern missionaries among African Americans, especially in the establishment of Avery Normal Institute.[8] Avery—together with Plymouth Congregational Church, which was composed primarily of African Americans who had been formerly members of Circular—would represent until the 1950s the most important remnant of Congregationalism's once impressive place in the low country.

More devastating than the fires and the destruction of property had been the loss of life within the low country Reformed community. The low country, the birthplace of the Confederacy, had sent the fathers and sons of its white families into the terrors of modern warfare. Old Wappetaw lost both Gabriel Jervey, over sixty years old, and John Whilden, boy-major who fell at the first battle of Manassas. Six more from the little congregation were killed in battle: Colonel Thomas Wagner at Fort Moultrie in 1861; William Jervey at Petersburg and John Jervey at Seven Pines; Lieutenant James Anderson and Colonel Robert Jeffords at Cold Harbor; and Captain L. A. Whilden at Drewrys Bluff. Others from the congregation were badly wounded. Young Bacheldor Anderson died of disease contracted in a wretched army camp. Such was the story across the churches of the low country, as bitter lamentation rose from the land.[9] From Second Presbyterian twenty-two fell in battle—young Edward Fogartie and his friend Fleetwood Lanneau, Jr., Frank Hughes and William Hughes, Arthur Robinson and Samuel Robinson, the joy and bright hopes of their families. They all died, declared the defiant but revealing memorial erected by the congregation at the entrance to the sanctuary, "FOR THEIR COUNTRY, WHILE IN THE SERVICE OF THE CONFEDERATE STATES. 1860–1865."

Free at Last

The Civil War, of course, meant not defeat but freedom for the majority of those who lived in the low country. For African American slaves, the war's end meant that "Slavery's chains done broke at last, broke at last, broke at last," although they too knew the war's destruction and pillage.[10] With Northern armies tramping out the bitter vintage of slavery, African Americans began to reorder their lives and explore the meaning of their new freedom, often to the surprise and consternation of Southern whites.[11]

In the years ahead, African Americans would have to struggle against their vulnerability to white prejudice and power, shape new assumptions about their place in society, and join in political alliances. In all of these things, many would draw on the faith that had sustained them through the deep waters of slavery and would find in the black church a center for their life as a people.

African Americans greeted the end of the war by joining in great celebrations of a Jubilee and by interpreting the victory of Federal forces in deeply religious terms. "Us looked for the Yankees on dat place," a former South Carolina slave recalled, "like us look now for de Savior and de host of angels at de second comin'." For the elderly in particular, who had spent almost a lifetime waiting for deliverance, the hand of God seemed to be moving in their midst.

Yankee liberators were clothed in biblical images—they were "Jesus's Aids," General William T. Sherman was no one less than Moses who had led the Children of Israel out of the house of bondage, and Lincoln, the Great Emancipator, was held in awe by some as the Messiah.[12]

Soon after the Federal troops marched into Charleston, black leaders at Zion together with leaders from Bethel Methodist organized a huge parade to celebrate the Union victory, the end of slavery, and their day of Jubilee. Beginning across the street from Zion at Citadel Square, the parade made its way down Meeting Street between cheering crowds, circled the battery, and came back up Meeting Street. Leading the parade were two mounted black marshals wearing red and blue rosettes and blue sashes. They were followed by the black troops who had taken the fallen city and by the band of the Twenty-first U.S. Colored Infantry. On a mule-drawn cart, two black women with their children sat next to a mock slave auctioneer shouting, "How much am I offered?" Behind the cart came sixty men tied together as a slave gang. They in turn were followed by a cart containing a black-draped coffin with the sign: "Slavery is Dead." Prominent among the marchers were the "Zion Bible Society of Zion Church" and the "Preachers, Elders, and Sunday School Teachers of the several colored congregations of Charleston, each bearing a bible and Hymn Book."[13]

In Charleston the Zion church became the meeting place and rallying point for the African Americans of the city and for their Northern liberators. The sanctuary, with a seating capacity of two thousand, was filled to overflowing time and again for mass meetings celebrating the death of slavery, Northern victories, and the end of the Confederacy. On April 5, 1865, a huge crowd at Zion passed resolutions thanking the liberation army. Eight days later, Henry Ward Beecher—brother of Harriet Beecher Stowe and provider of rifles ("Beecher's Bibles") that had made Kansas bleed before the war—preached from Girardeau's old pulpit. His packed congregation included leading abolitionists and prominent members of Charleston's black community.[14] The next week, Chief Justice Salmon Chase spoke from the pulpit to cheering crowds, assuring them that suffrage would come to the freedmen "sometime; perhaps very soon; perhaps a good while hence." In November, after white South Carolinians had attempted to reimpose a code to regulate blacks in the state, the African American community of Charleston met in Zion to denounce the code and to ask Congress for relief from such oppressive measures. For years to come Zion would continue to be the gathering place for the city's black community.[15]

Despite the victories of Northern armies and the celebrations in the Zion church, the whites remained largely committed to the old patterns and, if not to slavery itself, at least to white power and paternalism. Henry Ward Beecher, speaking to the American Home Missionary Society (Congregational) a few weeks after he had preached in Zion, declared: "The great trees of rebellion have been cut down by the sword of war. The stumps of treason still remain rooted in the hearts of the people. And these must be taken away before we shall obtain the fruits of a permanent peace." A new battle, Beecher warned, was about to begin: a "battle of thoughts, ideas, of truth against falsehood, of civilization against barbarism. Lee has capitulated; but the devil has not." The old ideas of the South, he said, have powerful champions: "There will be Lees, and Johnstons, and Jacksons, in the Southern pulpits. And we must send there Grants and Shermans, and Sheridans to wield our sword of God's truth. For the Southern clergy are neither conquered nor converted. . . . The work of the army is over. The work of the churches just begins. . . . The nation has conquered. The churches must redeem."[16]

The transformation of the South was thus to be accomplished not only through legislative Reconstruction but also through the work of Northern missionaries and teachers. They would establish in the South, in the midst of the ruin and apostasy of the Southern churches, Northern churches that would teach love of country and liberty and that would instill in the Southern people, black and white, the New England virtues of industry, sobriety, self-control, and godliness.[17] But as Beecher knew only too well, such a transformation of the Confederacy into a New England would be no easy task. Many powerful champions of the Old South would resist mightily—and for generations—what they regarded as the cultural imperialism of such an arrogant agenda.

"We Must Cling to Our Identity as a People!"

On Confederate Memorial Day in 1871, as the Carolina dead from Gettysburg were reinterred in Charleston's Magnolia Cemetery, John L. Girardeau spoke to six thousand gathered in the devastated old city. Had those who died, he asked, died in vain? Was their sacrifice a useless one? There are two senses, Girardeau said, "in which it must be admitted that they lost their cause—they failed to establish a Confederacy as an independent country, and they failed to preserve the relation of slavery."[18]

But Girardeau, the Confederate army chaplain and preacher to the African Americans at Zion, could not admit that the sons of the South had died in vain, that the suffering, terror, and blood had been for a lost cause. There were, he insisted, "fundamental principles of government, of social order, of civil and religious liberty, which underlay and pervaded that complex whole which we denominate our Cause. And the question whether those who fell in its support died in vain, *as to those principles,* must depend for its answer upon the course which will be pursued by the people of the South." Only one reply "deserves to be returned to these inquiries—our brethren will not have died in vain, if we cherish in our hearts, and, as far as in us lies, practically maintain, the principles for which they gave their lives."[19] Here was the challenge for Southern whites—at least from the perspective of those who wanted to take their stand with the old order against an emerging liberal society of the modern world.

Girardeau insisted, as Thornwell, Smyth, and others had before him, that what the white South had been fighting against and against which it must now contend was "radicalism" and all the disintegrative forces of modern life. Radicalism was a "ruthless, leveling Spirit" waging war against the Family, the State, and the Church. It was rooted in what Girardeau called "democratic license," where everyone followed the devices and desires of their own consciences. Radicalism worshiped a "Higher Law"—higher than the Constitution and the Bible, higher than the ordained order of family and social relationships. It let loose lawlessness and, if unchecked, would plunge people into the vortex of anarchy. The miseries that would follow, warned Girardeau, would send people for refuge to autocratic despotism. This in turn would be united with the habits of "democratic license" and the final result would be a union of despotisms.[20]

What Girardeau feared was the decadence of a people who surrendered their liberty to an autocratic central government in order to pursue their own desires. The virtues of the early American republic, pleaded the low country Reformed theologian, must be maintained in the face of the growing luxuries, excesses, and enticements of a gilded age. The South must resist "that corruption of manners which is incompatible with the simplicity of free institutions, and the purity and integrity of moral character." (How much he sounded in this address like David Ramsay of Circular Church after the Revolution!) Girardeau was holding before those gathered at the graves of the Gettysburg dead the old image of an organic society, of what he called "regulated government and constitutional liberty," that was built upon the republican virtues of frugality and simplicity of manners. Girardeau's vision, however, was not simply of a republic but of a class-stratified society of "regulated liberty" where each person had a place and responsibilities and where it was clear that blacks should stay in their place.[21]

To meet the challenge of radicalism, Girardeau called on the white South to retain its cultural independence—to resist being overwhelmed by the egalitarian and anarchic forces of the modern world. "We must cling to our identity as a people!" he cried. "The danger is upon us of losing it—of its being absorbed and swallowed up in that of a people which having despoiled us of the rights of freemen assumes to do our thinking, our legislating and our ruling for us. Influences are operating on us with every breath we draw which, if we be not vigilant, will sooner or later wipe out every distinctive characteristic which has hitherto marked us."[22]

But the danger could be met through maintaining the heart of a culture—what Girardeau called "the inalienable, indestructible powers of thought and language—the faculty by which we form our opinions, and that by which we express them." The preservation of a Southern culture could be accomplished, he said, by "scrupulously adhering to the phraseology of the past—for making it the vehicle for transmitting to our posterity ideas which once true are true forever. . . . We may do it by the education we impart to the young; by making our nurseries, schools and colleges channels for conveying from generation to generation our own type of thought, sentiment and opinion, by instamping on the minds of our children principles hallowed by the blood of patriots."[23]

In the midst of the dislocations following the war, Girardeau spoke to the great fears of any people—the fear of losing their identity; the fear of no longer having any center, any cultural glue, to hold their little world together; the fear of being absorbed, in the vulnerability of crisis and confusion, by an alien culture. In brilliant fashion, Girardeau proposed a maintenance of the language and ideology of the past as primary defenses against such a loss. In the face of a cultural imperialism from the North, the "phraseology of the past" could become the bearer of an ideology that could integrate and consolidate the culture and identity of the white South. The "phraseology of the past," as a coherent body of shared images and ideas, could provide both a sense of identity and a guide to the future; it could provide a unity to the white South not only in space, as a distinct geographical region, but also in time, linking the South's past to the present critical moment and to the shape of the region's future.[24] If the South could only keep its language, its symbolic system and way of seeing the world, then its Cause would not be lost. Girardeau's strategy for resistance was, like Robert E. Lee's before Richmond, brilliant, but it was also marked by an important ambiguity.

Significantly, the first reason Girardeau gave for the maintenance of this distinct Southern identity was for the good of the whole nation. If the South failed to maintain its culture, the result would be "that the only remaining representatives on this continent of free republican principles—especially in their federative form—will have ceased to exist, and the faintest, the last hope of a return to the noble, the glorious estate inherited from our patriotic ancestors will have gone out in the blackness of darkness." What Girardeau thought Confederate armies had been defending when they defended their Southern home was nothing less than their American home. He along with Adger and Smyth and the old Unionists—whose values were so closely aligned with conservatives in the North—believed that the true heart of the Republic, the genius that had led to its founding, was in the South.[25] They believed it had been to protect the original purity of the republic that the South had seceded in the first place. For them, to be true Americans was to take the side of the South, to defend those values of the republic that the Confederacy had sought to uphold against the assaults of radicalism that had overthrown regulated government and constitutional liberty. Their Southern nationalism was thus at its heart an American nationalism. This ambiguity not only marked their attitude toward the Confederacy but would also haunt their children as they struggled with the question of "our identity as a people" and the calls to build a New South.[26]

In the same way, Girardeau, Smyth, Palmer, and Adger with a host of other religious leaders believed that the true religion of the republic was most safely kept and was most purely practiced in the Protestant South. To defend the purity of religion in the South was at the same time to defend the purity of religion of the republic.[27] They saw no more contradiction in this claim than New Englanders saw in identifying New England values with those of the nation.

But what specifically did Girardeau have in mind when he spoke of the "ideas which once true are true forever" and the "principles hallowed by the blood of patriots"? They included states' rights and the "Spirituality of the Church," but they had to do above all with keeping the South white. "There is a race," cried Girardeau, "which, coming down through the centuries enveloped with antagonistic influences and hostile nationalities, has stood out in perpetual protest against amalgamation with other peoples."[28] What he had in mind was clear to any Southerner, black or white.

The victory of Northern armies and the power of Lincoln's understanding of liberty had been a breach, as it were, in the ideology of the Old South. This breech gave African American resistance to white authority, suppressed in the low country since the Denmark Vesey insurrection, an opening for expression. The result had been, from white Southerners' perspective, a great wave of disorder and anarchy rushing through the breach and across the land. For African Americans to assert themselves, for them to reject the assumptions and world view that had played such a powerful role in keeping them in their place, and for them to move beyond their allotted sphere was for white Southerners the essence of anarchy. To fill the breach and stop the anarchy called for a solid white South, united around a clearly articulated and deeply felt ideology—what Girardeau called those "fundamental principles of government, of social order, of civil and religious liberty, which underlay and pervaded that complex whole which we denominate our Cause." The very occasion on which Girardeau spoke—Confederate Memorial Day—would become a powerful ritual of remembrance, reinforcing the ideology and serving to legitimize and preserve the power and authority of whites.[29]

Girardeau's call at the graveside of the Gettysburg dead was thus no call for accommodation to "Yankee ways" but for a sustained resistance to the social anarchy and despotism he believed was inescapably linked to those ways. The spirit of that resistance he summarized with the words of the dying Stonewall Jackson at Chancellorsville: "Hold your ground, Sir!" "The bleeding form of Liberty," cried Girardeau, "rises from the earth before us and utters the same command. We must, by God's help, hold our ground, or consent to be traitors to our ancestry, our dead, our trusts for posterity, to our firesides, our social order, and our civil and religious liberty."[30]

Once again it was around the idea of liberty that the lines were drawn. The liberty for African Americans that had been unleashed by Northern armies was for Girardeau only anarchy. The liberty the white South stood for, the liberty whose "bleeding form . . . rises from the earth before us," was the liberty rooted in freedom from outside interference. This liberty was not simply a Southern ideology but was, white Southerners believed, at the heart of the American experiment. It had as its chief contemporary philosopher John Stuart Mill, who defined liberty as "protection against the tyranny of the political rulers" and as involving the limitation "of the power which can be legitimately exercised by society over the individual."[31] For the white South, such liberty would mean for generations to come freedom from "outside agitators" and from the interference in the "Southern way of life" by the federal government. Against Lincoln's revolutionary idea of liberty—which included African Americans in its benefits and which had a positive role for the federal government in securing that liberty—the white South would conduct a successful counterrevolution at the end of Reconstruction based on its own understanding of liberty. In cooperation with powerful conservative forces in the North, this counterrevolution would dominate Southern society for the next eighty years, even as the South moved deeper into the modern world.[32]

The Southern Presbyterian Church

Holding their ground, Southern Presbyterians refused reunion with Northern Presbyterians after the war—and until the 1980s—primarily over questions surrounding a separate Southern identity and the doctrine of the "Spirituality of the Church."[33] This doctrine, developed most forcefully by Thornwell and other leaders connected with Charleston Presbytery, was forged as a critical weapon for the struggle over slavery. It was for this reason that Thornwell was known as "the Calhoun of the Church."[34] Like Calhoun, he forged a powerful weapon to keep the South white. Calhoun developed the states' rights doctrine to ensure that there would be no interference in the South's peculiar institution. Thornwell developed the "Spirituality of the Church" doctrine to keep the church silent on slavery, to be sure that there was no interference on the part of the church with slavery. States' rights and the "Spirituality of the Church" thus functioned in the South as parallel doctrines serving the same purpose. In the years after Reconstruction, states' rights would be used to maintain the South's distinct culture, to ensure that the South remained white, while the "Spirituality of the Church" would make the white churches of the South strong if silent props to such a social order.[35]

In this way the question of a Southern identity—of a Southern culture that was regarded as the last representative of the old republican virtues that had once made America great—and the struggle against the modern world were intertwined around the issue of race and, to a lesser extent, gender. Once again, what was being advocated was an organic understanding of society. Such a social system seemed to these church leaders the only bulwark against the chaos and anarchy of "democratic license" and autocratic despotism. The dominant image of such a social system was the family, with the South itself understood in an almost mythical sense as a "family," a people, a folk. And of course, those who were to stand at the head of this family, with authority over it, giving it direction and paternal care, were the white males of the South. Once again, relational images and the language of affection largely hid the coercive power needed for such a system.

Southern whites' determination to hold their ground and to maintain control of the region was clearly revealed in the dramatic events at the old Edisto Island Presbyterian Church. In the years before the war, the congregation had been overwhelmingly black but under the complete control of a few affluent white slaveowners. The whites had fled to the mainland early in the war.[36] After the island fell to Federal forces the black majority of the congregation continued to worship in their old church under their own leaders.

In 1866, I. Jenkins Mikell, a white elder of the church and one of the island's wealthiest planters before the war, sought and received restoration papers from the Andrew Johnson administration in Washington. Mikell, together with several family members, four white neighbors, and the longtime pastor, William States Lee, came to the church on a Sunday in late May 1866. A service was under way and the sanctuary was overflowing with black worshipers who thronged around the front door. The little group of whites went to a side door, by the rear of the building, that stood open near the pulpit. A hymn was being sung and was followed quickly by another, and then another. Lee led the whites inside as the third hymn began. Peter P. Hedges, the black preacher, raised his hands for silence. "What means this unseemly disturbance of public worship of Almighty God?" he asked. Lee, holding the Bible in one hand and the restoration papers in another, declared from the foot of his old pulpit: "In the name of God, and by the authority of the United States Government, I demand possession of this building." Hedges took the papers, read them, and replied, "Your titles, sir, are clear so far as might and power can make them so. We will vacate." The black worshipers went out singing a hymn but not before Lee "extended a cordial invitation" for the "former" black members to stay and continue worshiping. No doubt it was the expectation that the black majority would take their old place in the balconies. Lee then preached to the white remnant of the congregation—seemingly unaware of the self-deception involved—on the text "I determined not to know anything among you save Jesus Christ and Him crucified."[37] In such a way, the white minority of the congregation gained control of the building to which they had title and which had been built by the wealth drawn from the labors of the black majority.

A similar story unfolded in Charleston at the Zion Presbyterian Church, only in less dramatic fashion. When Girardeau returned to Charleston after having served as a chaplain in the Confederate army, he found his old pulpit occupied by Jonathan C. Gibbs, a black missionary under the auspices of the Northern General Assembly. A bitter debate followed in which Gibbs sought under the Civil Rights Act to secure the building for the black members; the white trustees appealed to General Rufus Saxton of the Freedmen's Bureau for the return of the building; and John Adger appealed to the Northern General Assembly to oppose Gibb's action. The military authorities finally acted, returning the building to the white trustees with the stipulation that a school for blacks operated by the Northern Assembly be allowed to continue on the ground floor of the building. Girardeau, who had been preaching to the white congregation at Glebe Street, returned to the pulpit at Zion in January 1867, while continuing to be the pastor of the white Glebe Street congregation.[38]

Soon a substantial congregation of blacks once again gathered at Zion under Girardeau's preaching. They came from churches all over the city: from First (Scots) and Second Presbyterian, from Methodist churches and Baptist churches, and from First Colored Presbyterian (the congregation of Gibbs). They came from country churches too: from Johns Island and Edisto, James Island and Wadmalaw. A few came from other parts of the state: from Sumter and Columbia and Spartanburg. Most, however, came not by transfer from another church but on examination, joining a congregation for the first time. They were all a people on the move, working out the meaning of their new freedom. Within two years, four hundred blacks had joined Zion, and many more were worshiping there every Sunday.[39]

Zion became one congregation: the whites meeting at Glebe Street, the blacks meeting at Zion on Calhoun Street, both under the authority of a white session. Robert Adger, who had largely assumed his father James's business interests in Charleston and who had his brother John's concern for the religious instruction of blacks, was the most influential member of the session.[40] The old paternalism was once more at work, only under different circumstances.

Girardeau tried mightily to envision how a new order might be worked out, how the paternalistic ideals that had guided him before the war and his vision of an organic society could be institutionalized after the war. He presented a paper to the Southern General Assembly (now the Presbyterian Church of the United States) in which he sought to mix the new social realities with the old paternalistic assumptions and produce an institutional structure. Such a structure needed to acknowledge and take seriously not only the new civil status of blacks and their demands for an equal place in the church but also white Southerners' insistence that blacks be kept in "their place" within the

Southern "family." Yet African Americans, it was insisted, left on their own, without white guidance and a trained African American leadership, would surely descend into "a baptized heathenism." Girardeau succinctly summarized the dilemma of well-meaning whites. They acknowledge, he said, "the natural unity of the races; . . . the spiritual oneness of believers in Christ; . . . [and] the civil equality of colored people with the whites." Yet "we have difficulties arising from social differences which invincibly oppose the realization of this spiritual unity and civil equality in an outward and formal ecclesiastical shape." Here was the burden of paternalistic whites: whatever natural and spiritual unity they might confess, whatever civil equality they might acknowledge, they were unwilling for such ideals to be put into practice, to take institutional shape. They were left "looking with an eye of kindness and Christian love upon the freed people" and asking "What is the policy which ought to be adopted by us?"[41]

This dilemma of well-meaning, paternalistic whites meant that their vision for the future was blurred, that it had little focus or power. A utopian element was included in this postbellum vision in only the most marginal way—as a quest for a different social arrangement—because its primary thrust was backward and not forward. The consequence was that the vision was soon obsolete because it could not cope with the present realities or future possibilities— it could only remember an increasingly mythic past that offered no guide for the future. The best that Girardeau could propose was a modification of Adger's plan presented to Second Presbyterian Church in 1848: branch congregations for blacks with their own elders and deacons but united with adjacent white churches under a common pastorate. The Presbyterian General Assembly adopted the proposal, although apparently without much enthusiasm, and it was soon repealed. The result, as might be expected from such a debate and the persistence of old assumptions, was that by 1876 only a few blacks were connected with the Southern Presbyterian Church.[42]

As for Zion, after the General Assembly's action in 1874 Girardeau convened the congregation, "explained the situation to them, and gave them the liberty, *if they pleased,* to set up for themselves." Most of the old people, Girardeau later wrote, "strenuously opposed the separation, but Young Africa was in favor of it. The *majority* favored the separation. . . . That was how the breach occurred. The colored people voted for it, and I gave them the road."[43] Four years later Zion joined the Northern General Assembly and called its first black pastor, the Reverend William C. Smith.

These developments at Zion point to a broader redrawing of boundary lines within the Reformed community, the low country itself, and indeed throughout most of the South. For generations the boundaries of the Reformed community as a distinct subgroup within the low country had included, not only at an institutional level but also at conceptual and experiential levels, whites and African Americans. Whites had their place and blacks theirs, but both were included within the boundaries of the community. To be sure, whites and African Americans in the Reformed community were also part of racial subgroups, but despite their fundamental differences and the tensions that separated them, they were united in significant ways. What the divisions at Zion indicated was that the old unity no longer held in what was becoming a segregated South.[44]

For whites the idea of worshiping with African Americans would become both an increasingly distant memory and an idea to be violently resisted. The paternalistic images that John Adger had so powerfully painted in 1847 became largely repugnant to whites in a segregated South.[45] At the same time, African Americans were no longer willing to accept the old dependencies. They knew that behind the paternalism—however well-intentioned and kind—lay both racist assumptions and coercive power. No longer forced to accept such paternalism as the basis for community, they moved to establish their own independent churches.[46] As a consequence, the Reformed community in the low country divided into two clear sub-subgroups—one African American and one white. These sub-subgroups would now have their own distinct boundaries, and within these boundaries two Reformed traditions and communities would develop in the low country. Each would have their institutional structures, each would have their distinct ethos and boundaries, and each would see the world from different perspectives.

14

The African American
Reformed Community

Between Two Worlds

A DISTINCT African American Reformed community, with roots in the colonial period, had evolved in the Carolina low country during the antebellum period. More than the aggregate of individual members of Reformed
churches, the community had taken institutional shape as a "church within a
church" and had developed its own tradition that was both African American
and Reformed. This community emerged at the end of the Civil War to form
the basis for the new, yet old, black Presbyterian and Congregational churches
in the low country.

The traditions of the community, its world view and ethos, marked it as it
sought to respond to its new social context following emancipation. The freed
men and women of the South found themselves in 1865 in a situation others
around the world would increasingly face: how were they to respond to the
modern world, and, in particular, how were they to respond to the aggressive
expansion of Western civilization with its raw power supported by a complex
array of cultural skills? Non-Western peoples, living in cultures that had evolved
in response to unique circumstances, would face the "World Revolution of Westernization" as a powerful cultural imperialism.[1] How were they to live in the
modern world if they did not abandon their cultures and adopt that of the
West? Was it possible to have a modern society without adopting the culture of
the West on which modernity was based?[2]

For the freed men and women of the South, this momentous question for
the twentieth century would have its own distinct shape: how were they to respond, and what resources did they bring in response, to this "World Revolution of Westernization" that had come to them from the outside as a liberator?
Put most simply, were the freed African Americans to join the "mainstream"
of American life that had overwhelmed the white South and freed the slaves?
Were African Americans, as they faced the continuing power of racism, to internalize the values and world view of their liberators—in particular, the ascetic
self-discipline and sense of civic responsibility and cooperation that marked the

Yankee?[3] Were the African Americans, after generations of bitter oppression, to internalize such values and become acculturated—or reculturated, to use an ugly but perhaps more accurate term—to the ways of modern America?[4] Or were they to try to maintain their traditional culture—with its distinct African American language, mythopoetic world view, sense of time, and experience of suffering and oppression—for an alternative, but marginal, place in the midst of modern society?

The African American Reformed community in the low country came to this question in 1865 already well on the road to reculturation. It was not, of course, the only segment of the larger African American community in the low country that shared this position, for, as it has been emphasized through this study, the African American Reformed community's boundaries overlapped with other subgroups and were often blurred and ambiguous.[5] Nevertheless, this distinct community brought from its history during the antebellum period a commitment to self-discipline and education, a preoccupation with order, and a rejection of religious "frenzy" in worship.[6] To be sure, the harsh realities of slavery and white racism had acted, and would continue to act, as powerful limits to such reculturation, and the internalization of modern values was certainly more complete in 1865 in Charleston than in the isolated countryside. But the community was Reformed: it shared in greater and lesser degrees those Protestant values emanating from Geneva that were so intimately associated with the rise of the modern world. To be Reformed, of course, was not the same as being modern—the Reformed tradition, as we have seen over and over again, had its own internal tensions that increasingly centered around questions of modernity. Nevertheless, a powerful impulse within the tradition pushed toward the modern world, and it was this impulse that produced the primary tension for the African American Reformed community. In an ironic way, the community found itself in an ambiguous situation similar to that of the white Reformed community in the low country.

For the whites, with their Reformed ethos and world view and their market-oriented economic activity, the values of self-discipline and a sense of spontaneous civic responsibility were fundamental. Indeed, paternalistic whites in the Reformed community had taught the catechism and administered discipline in the churches during the antebellum period precisely to encourage those values among African Americans. A primary argument for the "religious instruction of slaves" had been that such instruction would be a means of slaves' internalization of self-discipline and order. But for the white Reformed community, their defense of a class-stratified society and their racism hid from them how much they were already a part of the modern world, how much they were indeed agents of that world. Their fear of certain emerging aspects of that world—its radical egalitarianism and anarchy—did not keep them from being a part of it. As we shall see in a following chapter, the white Reformed community moved deeper into the modern world during the decades following

Reconstruction while trying at the same time to affirm its own cultural identity and hold in check modernity's egalitarian and anarchic impulses.

For the African American Reformed community, the tension with the modern world was not with its egalitarianism but with its cultural imperialism that discounted and marginalized much of the African American experience. The community consequently found itself in the years following the Civil War in the position of those who were both champions of reculturation and champions of a proud African American heritage. With elites in non-Western cultures, the community was caught between two worlds in an invidious comparison. The community believed that the way to the future demanded accommodation, skills that produced power, and the internalization of critical attitudes and values.[7] At the same time, however, it heard in its collective depths the voice of ancestors, of those who had gone before through the deep waters of slavery, whose courage, resourcefulness, and spirituality came across the years as a great cultural legacy and alternative. From such a middle place, with the burden of white racism always over it, the community would struggle with questions of identity and purpose and would forge its own utopian vision to lead it toward a new future.

That vision, rooted in an experience that was both African American and Reformed, would seek to subvert claims that a community could not be both truly African American and truly Reformed, resisting claims that the two traditions were each monolithic and incompatible. In this way, it faced as a religious community—in its own little world of the Carolina low country—the larger, encompassing question of two worlds, one Western and one traditional, that would dominate so much of the twentieth century. The question the community faced, as a religious community, was thus a part and an echo of a question non-Western peoples were facing everywhere: is it possible for a people to be rooted firmly in two cultural traditions with each tradition a complex universe, each hiding much of its shaping power in the vast recesses of the subconscious?[8] Or were those in such middle places condemned to be in a constant search for roots and identity? What follows in this chapter and the next is an exploration of this religious community's life from 1865 to 1941 as it struggled between two worlds and as it sought to express its own utopian vision of a coherent community with roots in two cultural traditions. Before turning to the details of the community's life, however, the specific changing social context of the low country—in particular demographic shifts—must be drawn into the picture.

Demographic Shifts

Of no little consequence for the churches of the region was the steady increase of both the white and the black populations during the decades following the Civil War. From 1870 to 1900 the population of the low country grew from slightly more than 200,000 to almost 340,000. Much of this growth was in the African American population.[9]

Beginning in the 1880s, however, African Americans began moving out of the region and indeed out of the whole state. At first it was only a small stream of emigrants heading for New York, Philadelphia, Washington, and the other beckoning cities of the Promised Land in the North. But by the time of the First World War the small stream had turned to a great flood. During the 1920s more than 200,000 left the state. By 1930 the census was reporting that almost one-quarter of all native South Carolinians were living outside the state and that 87 percent of the former Carolinians were African Americans.[10]

These black Carolina emigrants were set in motion by the heavy burden of racial oppression and by the stark poverty of the region. But the emigrants were also drawn to the magnetic North by its economic opportunities and its promises of greater political and social equality. No less than other Americans, black Carolinians were not inclined to stay on the farm once they had glimpsed city lights. The result was a negative growth rate for the African American population of the low country during the first three decades of the twentieth century. By 1923 the population of white Carolina had surpassed that of black Carolina for the first time since the early eighteenth century—although in the low country blacks continued to outnumber whites by substantial if declining majorities.[11]

The African American Presbyterian and Congregational churches and their members knew these winds of change that were blowing across the low country from the sea islands and coastal marshes to the inland piny woods and cotton fields. In some ways they felt these changes more sharply than white Presbyterians, for their poverty made them more vulnerable, more exposed to the winds that uprooted many and sent them streaming, often eagerly, northward. In other ways their poverty kept them low, away from the winds' intensity and from the full brunt of the rushing modern world. Whatever their exposure to the changes sweeping the land, these churches and their members interpreted and responded to them as people and congregations who also stood in a distinct religious tradition—a tradition that struggled to live between two worlds, between the broad religious heritage of African Americans and a Reformed tradition that was also a part of their history and their religious heritage.

The Establishment of Independent
Reformed African American Congregations

A brief review of the Reformed African American churches established in the years immediately following the Civil War illustrates the extent to which they represented congregations with their own histories and traditions. As we shall see, the possession of such histories and traditions would be critical for the survival of congregations seeking to be both Reformed and African American.

In 1860 more than five hundred blacks had belonged to the Johns Island and Wadmalaw Presbyterian Churches. Both islands had been hard hit by the war and many of their inhabitants, white and black, had been scattered. By 1867, however, a "Colored Presbyterian Church, Johns Island" had organized with 530 communicants and a building valued at $800 on land donated by "a ruling elder of the Southern Presbyterian Church." Within five years the membership was divided among at least four churches—Bethel, Hebron, Zion, and Salem. The first three were strategically located, all within three or four miles from the old Johns Island church, and Salem was well placed on Wadmalaw. A fifth church, Saint Andrews (it had gone under the name of Buleau), was located across the Stono on the mainland next to Bear Swamp, an area that was regarded as a part of Johns Island. It is probable that most of its membership was also drawn from the old Johns Island and Wadmalaw churches. The five churches together numbered 430 members in 1873, 80 less than belonged to the Johns Island and Wadmalaw churches in 1860. The numbers reflect both the continuity of membership that reached back to antebellum years and the movement of blacks out of the area as they sought new opportunities away from their old places of bondage.[12]

At James Island, where there had been more than 200 African American members in 1860, a strong black congregation—James Island, later Saint James—was organized as soon as the fighting was over. By 1867 it numbered 270 members. It grew rapidly and after 1876 became the largest Presbyterian church in the low country, black or white, a position it held for a number of decades.[13]

When the whites took possession of the old church on Edisto Island, the African American members went a short distance down the road and established their own church, at first meeting in nothing more than a bush arbor. Later they were able to obtain from the whites the little chapel at Edingsville Beach. They took it down board by board, floated it up one of the many creeks, hauled it to the site where they had been meeting, and reconstructed it as their new church. They even kept the old name—Edisto Presbyterian Church—dropping only "Island" to distinguish it from the whites' Edisto Island Presbyterian Church. By 1873 they had organized on Little Edisto the small congregation of Calvary Presbyterian.[14]

Not far from the Wilton church, where 158 African Americans had been communicant members in 1860, the blacks built at Adam's Run the Saint Paul's Presbyterian Church. By 1870 it had 139 members. Further inland, African Americans had been members of Bethel Pon Pon for at least 120 years by the time the guns were fired on Fort Sumter. In addition to the 155 black members of Bethel reported in 1860, Edward Palmer had served for a number of years two preaching stations that he estimated reached another 600 blacks. After the war, black Presbyterians in Walterboro organized two congregations: Young Bethel and Hopewell. These congregations soon came together in the one congregation of Hopewell, which stood two blocks from Bethel where they had formerly worshiped. Out in the country, other African American Presbyterians organized Aimwell on the road that ran from Bethel Pon Pon to Walterboro, near one of the old preaching stations where blacks had long gathered.[15]

Perhaps the oldest of all the African American churches in the low country was linked to the Stoney Creek church. Legal papers in the Beaufort County Court House indicate that at least as early as 1828 Salem Colored Presbyterian Church stood near the Stoney Creek church. The congregation may have had its roots in the work of George Whitefield and the Bryans at the time of the Great Awakening. Here, no doubt, the 132 black members of the Stoney Creek church worshiped in 1860. After the war, they continued to use their former building, kept the name Salem, and remained a part of the Stoney Creek church until 1870, when a separate congregation was formally organized.[16]

African American Presbyterians in Charleston came together from a number of churches in the city to form what was at first called the Charleston Mission under the leadership of the New School black pastor Ennals Adams. They met first at Zion and then at Thornwell's old church on Glebe Street before securing their own building on George Street. Three elders were elected. All were former leaders or watchmen at Second Presbyterian and a part of the old free black elite—Robert Howard (one of the wealthiest free blacks in the city before the war), William Ford, and Robert Morrison. By 1870 it listed 500 members.[17] Meanwhile the Wallingford Presbyterian Church was organized in 1867 in association with its academy; Zion continued to function as an important institution in the African American community, first under Girardeau and then as a separate African American congregation that became a part of the Northern General Assembly in 1879; and a number of mission posts were scattered around the city. By 1877 the number given with the Charleston Mission had declined to 250. Many of those listed under the mission apparently became affiliated with Wallingford, Zion, and then after 1878 with the Olivet Presbyterian Church. Nevertheless, by 1880 it was clear that a substantial number of African Americans had been lost to the Presbyterian churches in the low country—approximately 18 to 20 percent between 1860 and 1880.[18]

Almost all of this loss occurred after 1871 and most of it was in Charleston itself. Critical factors included the decline of Zion's membership after Girardeau's leaving and the inability of the Charleston Mission to establish itself as a self-sustaining independent church. The ambiguous relationship of the Charleston congregation to white authorities no doubt had an important part, perhaps the most important part, to play in their decline.[19] They bore the burden of appearing not only under the control of whites—at the very time African Americans were asserting their independence in almost every area of their lives—but also of being too "white," of having acculturated too quickly to the ways and values of the whites. James T. Ford, the white pastor of Plymouth Congregational, saw the problem of white leadership for these churches. When the dedication of the Plymouth church was being planned, Ford urged that a black Congregational minister speak. A black minister, he said, "would have great influence for good" because he "would help remove the thought too common among colored men here that our church brings them under white domination."[20]

In contrast, the country churches demonstrated considerable vitality. Their independence was more clearly established than at Zion or the Charleston Mission, and their leadership was more firmly in the hands of African Americans; in contrast to all the Charleston churches except Zion and Plymouth, they had a clearer congregational identity that reached back at least into the antebellum period. They were able to maintain their membership and in some cases add to it significantly. This stability was true even though much of the rural population was on the move during this period and was often in much turmoil.[21]

These churches were congregations whose lives were deeply rooted in low country history. They did not suddenly appear but were a continuation, in new and liberated forms, of congregations that had long existed within white-dominated churches of the region.[22] Even in Charleston this continuity was true, especially with Zion and Plymouth but also with Wallingford and the Charleston Mission, which were largely formed out of the membership of several antebellum churches. All of these old but new African American congregations took with them into the postwar period histories and traditions, leaders and a sense of identity that had been nurtured and kept alive during the difficult days of slavery. They indicated that African Americans, no less than whites, had a sense of loyalty to congregations and theological traditions. With the end of the war, they faced the challenge of drawing their congregations together once again, of forging new traditions and institutions as freed people, and of walking together along the difficult road between two worlds. That road, they believed, for all its ambiguity and difficulty, was the only road that led toward a still distant freedom and justice.

Critical for the community's institutional solidarity and for the nurture of a coherent culture caught between two worlds was the organization of an African American presbytery. In October 1866 Catawba Presbytery was organized, under the Northern Old School General Assembly, for African American churches in North and South Carolina.[23] In 1868 Catawba was divided and Atlantic Presbytery was formed for those churches in the South Carolina low country.[24]

With the formation of Atlantic Presbytery, African American Presbyterians in the low country, with close links to their Congregationalist neighbors, had an institution that could provide solidarity among their congregations and nur-

ture their vision of a community that was both African American and Reformed. The tensions between these two traditions—and the larger, encompassing tension between an indigenous culture and the modern world—could
be seen in almost every aspect of the community's life.

The Road to the Future

The impulse toward reculturation, already strong in the community's life
at the end of the Civil War, was strengthened by its vision of the future. This
vision saw a road leading out of the degradations of slavery and into a bright
future by way of reculturation. Formal education in the knowledge and skills
of Western civilization, it was believed, was essential for traveling such a road.
In order to escape the oppression and humiliations of the past and present,
African Americans had to acquire the cultural skills that were fundamental to
white power. They had to internalize, as quickly as possible, those values and
skills that had been developed in whites over many generations and under specific historical circumstances. Among the most vigorous advocates in the low
country of such reculturation were the ministers of the African American Presbyterian and Congregational churches.

During the years between the end of the war and 1890, twenty-five Presbyterian and Congregational ministers can be identified as pastors of African
American congregations in the low country. Of these, twelve were white, twelve
were black, and one's race is unknown. Ten of the whites (five served Plymouth
Congregational) and six of the blacks were from the North.[25] These Northern ministers represented a powerful force for reculturation as they were determined that Northern values be inculcated into the hearts and minds of the
newly freed African Americans of the low country. They were, of course, part
of that larger force of Northern missionaries who came South, and their story
is part of the familiar story of attempts to make over the region after the image
of New England.[26] The Presbyterian and Congregational ministers, however,
came to a Reformed community in the low country that was particularly well
prepared and receptive to their message. This community would prove to be a
critical testing ground for the missionaries and their messages.

The best-known and probably the most influential of all the ministers
who came to the low country was Francis L. Cardozo. His coming, however,
was a return. He had been born in Charleston in 1837: his mother was a free
black woman and his father was—at least he was reputed to be—the Jewish
economist, J. N. Cardozo, an ardent Unionist and a person who moved among
Charleston's intellectual elite. Young Francis attended for eight years a school
for free blacks in the city and worked five years as a carpenter's apprentice and
four as a journeyman. A member of the Second Presbyterian Church, his "conversion and Calvinistic experience," wrote Thomas Smyth, "were very clear,

thorough and remarkable." When he was twenty-one, he sailed for Glasgow with a thousand dollars in his pocket that he had saved from his earnings. He attended the University of Glasgow and won honors in Latin and Greek and a scholarship to study theology, first in Edinburgh and then in London. Returning to the United States, he served as pastor of the Temple Street Congregational Church in New Haven, Connecticut. Within weeks of the occupation of Charleston by Union forces, he was back in his home city.[27]

Cardozo came as a missionary for the American Missionary Association (AMA). It had been established by Congregationalists and New School Presbyterians in 1846 on both evangelical and abolitionist principles and, with the war's end, had become the major educational agency at work in the defeated South. While its missionaries were as a group far more sensitive to African American needs and culture than was the country at large, its tone and paternalistic assumptions were indicated by its charge to its missionaries. They were to take the freedmen and freedwomen "by the hand, to guide, counsel and instruct them in their new life, protect them from the abuses of the wicked, and direct their energies so as to make them useful to themselves, their families and their country."[28] Given their assumptions about the need for radical reculturation, it is not surprising that such a paternalistic tone marked their work.

Cardozo returned to Charleston as a minister and an educator, convinced that the moral education of the freed people was a high and noble calling. "If I can influence and shape the future life of a great number," he wrote in 1865, "if I can cause them to love and serve Christ, I could not aspire to a nobler work." There are, he said, "so many of these boys and girls that are just at that age when their whole future may be determined." For this reason, he left "all the superior advantages and privileges of the North and came South," and it was for this reason, he declared, he was willing "to *remain* here and make this place my home." In Charleston he played an important part in the organization of Plymouth Congregational Church and in the establishment first of the Saxton School and then of Avery Normal Institute.[29]

Close to Cardozo in commitments and organizational skills was Jonathan C. Gibbs. A graduate of Dartmouth, he had attended Princeton Theological Seminary before becoming pastor of Philadelphia's First African Presbyterian Church in 1860. Shortly after Union troops entered Charleston, Gibbs arrived in the city and received permission from the military authorities to organize a school and begin religious services in the Zion church. When he left Charleston in 1868 for a distinguished career in Florida, he left behind a flourishing school that became Wallingford Academy.[30]

Ennals Adams was another college-trained minister who arrived in Charleston shortly after its fall. A black New School pastor working under the sponsorship of the AMA, he had served churches in Pennsylvania and New York during the 1850s, had gone as a missionary with the AMA to the Mendi Mission in Sierra

Leone during most of the war, and in 1865 had been sent to Beaufort where he preached to the freed people. Arriving in Charleston in summer 1865, he soon organized the Charleston Mission meeting on George Street and watched it grow to 500 members as most African Americans left their old white-dominated churches. His most important work, however, was as the longtime principal of Shaw Memorial School. A firm believer in reculturation, he insisted that blacks provide their own leadership and subvert the myth of white superiority. The establishment of black leadership, he was convinced, could be accomplished by reculturated blacks showing the freed people that "they can teach them as much as they can learn from the whites."[31]

Out on James Island, another African American preacher from the North took up the cause of reculturation. Hezekiah Hampleton Hunter left Brooklyn to work among the freed people because he realized that the future of the Southern blacks was his future too. They would, he said, "rise or fall" together. When he first arrived on James Island, he reflected the patronizing attitude of many of the Northern missionaries. He was, he said, undertaking the "Great Work of Bringing these people to the standard of Man and Woman Hood," for there are "many on the plantations, [and] They are but a step above the *Brute Creation.* Only I know God is able for all States—conditions of mankind [otherwise] I would say none are able for the work." Whatever his early sentiments, Hunter was "able for the work" and became a popular and longtime pastor and teacher among the island people.[32]

Working with these African American pastors was a small group of white ministers who came to the South as missionaries during Reconstruction.[33] Particularly noteworthy were the white Congregational ministers associated with the Plymouth Congregational Church (its name "Plymouth" told volumes about the New England expectations of launching a new errand into the wilderness, this time a Southern wilderness). Benjamin F. Jackson, pastor of the congregation in 1868, articulated the New England agenda of reculturation with particular clarity. The African Americans' *"gross errors* and superstitions" must be eradicated, he declared. "Their ideas that dreams, visions, voices, spasms &c are necessary to or parts of conversion. Their vague conception of the connection of relig^n with morality and the duties of life. All those things must be corrected if this part of the U.S. is ever to advance to a high state of civilization." Despite the "gross errors and superstitions" that Jackson regarded as so rampant throughout the low country, he was pleased about the extent that the Plymouth congregation had already internalized the "values of New England." The congregation had, he reported, requested him shortly after his arrival to preach a series of doctrinal sermons on a broad range of theological issues. He did not acknowledge that such preaching was precisely what they had heard for generations at Circular Congregational.[34]

Because these African American ministers, together with their white allies, had already internalized the values and mastered the skills needed for power in the modern world, they quickly became political leaders representing the interests of the newly freed African Americans. Cardozo, the most influential of them all, served as secretary of state for South Carolina and as state treasurer, positions he used to push for reforms, to advocate public education, and to fight corruption in the state government.[35] Jonathan C. Gibbs, after leaving Charleston in 1867, became secretary of state and superintendent of public instruction in Florida.[36] Ennals Adams was a political activist, was elected to the Charleston city council in 1868, and later became a judge.[37] H. H. Hunter served in the state legislature, representing the district that included James Island.[38] Benjamin F. Jackson was elected to the state legislature, where he soon became chair of the important house labor committee.[39]

The leadership these men provided in both education and politics was a powerful illustration of the need for reculturation. For the African American Reformed community to live in the modern world, it needed to claim and nurture that impulse within its tradition that encouraged the internalization of Western values. Without such an internalization, the community would lack the cultural skills needed to break the very oppression long imposed by the power of Southern white representatives of Western civilization. Moreover, reculturation served to help shatter the ideology of whites—South and North—that insisted African Americans were backward, that they were undisciplined children needing the control and guidance of civilized, mature whites.

The community thus shared with non-Western peoples around the world a tragic dilemma: it could only move toward equality with whites if it adopted the terms imposed by whites, most particularly an ascetic rationalism, highly developed organizational skills, and an aggressive competitiveness curiously linked to a spontaneous civic cooperation.[40] These terms undercut and discredited the traditional culture of African Americans, yet such terms appeared the way to escape white oppression and to move toward an improved material well-being. The old structures of African American society and the invisible substructures in the collective depths of the African American psyche that had been shaped during generations of bondage now seemed inadequate for the new situation in which the community found itself following the Civil War. Indeed, those structures and cultural assumptions had appeared inadequate to many in the African American Reformed community long before freedom came.

Remembering the Past

The Reformed community that traveled this road to the future did not travel it, however, as a community without a past. Whatever the compelling reasons for reculturation, the community traveled the road as a part of a larger

African American community that brought with it the collective memory of generations as well as the present realities of racial oppression. That memory and the experience of those present realities not only rumbled in the subconscious depths of the Reformed African American community's cultural life, emerging in "embarrassing lapses" from "white standards," they also emerged to challenge the ideological assumptions of Western cultural superiority. A different reading of history was available to the community as African Americans challenged the received interpretation that whites gave to the past.[41] Had it not been precisely aggressive bearers of Western civilization who had enslaved millions and whose ways had brought unprecedented violence, misery, and cultural chaos to the non-European continents? And did not the African American experience itself, in all of its diversity, have a spiritual depth—welling up from years of pain and struggle—that was more profound than anything Western culture could offer with its ascetic rationalism? Was there not a spiritual nobility in traditional African American culture that revealed itself supremely in slave songs and spirituals?[42]

Such arguments for the depths of African American spirituality would grow in intensity as the community advanced deep into the twentieth century and became increasingly reculturated. The deeper this Reformed community moved into the modern world—the greater the distance it moved from slavery—the more it began to articulate appreciation for traditional African American culture and its values.[43] In this process the community was, once again ironically, in a situation similar to that of the white Reformed community. When John L. Girardeau and those who followed him called for the maintenance of a Southern culture against the cultural imperialism of the North, and when they spoke of the white South as the defender of all true religion, they were using—even as representatives of Western civilization—a similar tactic against the assaults of modernity. Indeed, claims of spiritual superiority by traditional cultures would be a defense used wherever peoples felt their cultures giving way before the rush of modernity. The claims of romanticism—glorifying and idealizing indigenous roots, insisting on their greater spirituality in contrast to a decadent West (or for Girardeau and his followers a decadent North)—was a widespread and appealing if largely ineffective strategy for resisting the forces of reculturation.[44]

Beyond such defensive strategies, the retention of elements of traditional African American culture was encouraged by the isolation of much of the population, especially on the sea islands; by limitations imposed by white racism; and by the ability of this traditional culture to satisfy many of the deepest needs of the Reformed African American community. The community was able to find in this side of its cultural heritage resources for understanding the world and for facing its hardships and incongruities. The extent to which the traditional African American culture was able to provide such resources pointed not only to the ways familiar patterns were able to communicate with the subconscious but also to the continuity between the antebellum situation of the community and its situation following the war. The community was still faced, in other words, with the realities of isolation, poverty, and white oppression, and elements of traditional African American culture provided resources to help it understand and deal with those realities.[45]

Among important bearers of African American traditions were the old leaders or watchmen from the antebellum days. They were made "catechists"— an office revived as "peculiarly meeting the present condition and necessities" of the "Southern field." They were given responsibility for assisting the ministers in visiting the people, gathering the congregations for worship, and leading public worship when ministers were not present. Perhaps most important, the catechists were the superintendents of the Sabbath schools. In all of these tasks, they, together with the lay elders, helped to keep alive (often to the frustration of those who sought the people's "advancement") the traditions of congregations that reached back many generations.[46]

In addition to these older leaders, there were the new pastors who came out of slavery and were bearers of an African American cultural tradition. While Cardozo, Gibbs, Adams, and Hunter represented the college-educated African American pastors who arrived from the North on the wings of the army, Ishmael Moultrie was an outstanding representative of African American pastors who emerged from the ranks of the freed people to serve them as ministers.[47] Moultrie had been a slave on Edisto Island who was taken by his owner to the interior of the state shortly after the war began. Seizing an opportunity to escape, he had led a band of slaves on a 150-mile trek back to their island home. A "jetblack, full-blooded Negro, broad shouldered, and heavyset," he spoke what was described as "a jargon that was hard to understand."[48] His language—a Gullah dialect—was a symbolic system for conveying an African American cultural tradition. Gullah communicated, through an unconscious process of assimilation, the collective, largely subconscious memory of the people. It conveyed to rising generations the survival skills that low country African Americans had forged under the isolated and bitter conditions of slavery. To the extent that those conditions continued as present realities to the community, the Gullah of Moultrie would speak out of and to the deepest levels of the community's life.

But Moultrie was not only a Gullah-speaking bearer of an African American tradition; he was also an agent of reculturation. Unlike the catechists, or those who as pastors remained licentiates, he received enough private instruction in theological disciplines to satisfactorily pass the ordination requirements for Atlantic Presbytery. He helped to bring into the organizational structures of the presbytery—with all of its operational assumptions about order and ascetic discipline—the congregations at Edisto, Saint Paul, Salem, and Saint Andrews.[49] Together with Peter Hedges, an ordained freedman who had come to Edisto from North Carolina, he organized the Hope School (later Larimer), which served as a major force for reculturation of the African Americans of Edisto for ninety years.[50]

The community's tradition, its world view and ethos, was thus forged in a dialectical interaction between two worlds—one African American, the other Reformed—set within a particular social and historical context in the low country.[51] This Reformed African American tradition both reflected *and* shaped the character of these newly emerged congregations. Their style of life, their moral and aesthetic spirit, their picture of the world and of the way "things really are" all overlapped with other African American groups *and* with other Reformed groups. The dialectical interaction between the two worlds and the community's social and historical context following the Civil War made the community what it was. The interaction between the two worlds and the resulting coherent character of the community can be seen in the schools and the "little world" of the community.

15

The African American
Reformed Community

"Two Warring Ideals in One Dark Body"

THE AFRICAN AMERICAN Reformed community, in spite of its tensions, possessed an inner coherence that gave it a distinct character. In addition to its congregations, the community developed, with the help and sometimes the initiative of Northern philanthropy, an extensive school system throughout the low country. These schools helped to link congregations and families in an extended web of connections and played a central role in consolidating and shaping the character of the community. Beginning on the sea islands before the end of the Civil War, the system reached its high point during the first three decades of the twentieth century only to almost disappear during the Great Depression. Part of an extensive system throughout the state (there were by 1917 forty-seven Presbyterian schools alone in South Carolina), most of the schools were day schools that ran through the elementary levels, but they also included a number of academies and institutes that took their students through the higher levels and provided college preparation. In addition, for a few years there were two junior colleges sponsored by the Presbyterians.[1]

One of the first schools organized for blacks in Charleston after the war was the Saxton School, established in 1865 by Thomas Cardozo, brother of Francis L. Cardozo, under AMA sponsorship. By 1868 it had 541 pupils—almost equally divided between males and females—enrolled during at least part of the year. Francis Cardozo, who followed his brother, was superintendent with eight white teachers.[2] In 1867 Francis Cardozo organized for Saxton's most promising students the Avery Normal Institute. With the support of the AMA and the federal government's Freedmen's Bureau, Avery was designed as a normal (or teachers') school. It soon gained the reputation of providing the highest quality education in the state for African Americans. Intimately linked to the Plymouth Congregational Church, Avery's roots reached deep into the history of the black membership of the Circular Congregational Church. These Congregationalists brought with them into freedom their old church's long-standing commitment to the life of the mind. Avery would maintain over the years the traditions of rigorous academic work established by Francis Cardozo, and as late as 1940 it would still be supplying most of the African American public school teachers for the region.[3]

Even before Thomas Cardozo had established the Saxton School, Jonathan C. Gibbs had organized the Zion School. Located on the ground floor of the Zion Presbyterian Church on Calhoun Street, the school numbered 525 students by spring 1868 with nine black teachers, including the principal Martin Van Horne, a Presbyterian minister. The following year, the school was moved to a new facility on Meeting Street (which the Freedmen's Bureau had helped to purchase) and its name was changed to Wallingford after a Pittsburgh donor. The new school was housed in a two-story, frame building, forty by eighty feet. Four classrooms on the first floor were divided by a central hall. At the rear was a recitation room, with a vestibule and portico on the street front. The second floor was "fitted up" and occupied by the Wallingford Presbyterian Church. A Teacher's Home fronted on the opposite street. With the move to the new facility came a new white superintendent, J. H. Bates, and white teachers who largely replaced the African Americans for the remaining years of Reconstruction. The curriculum included—in addition to basic courses in reading, writing, and arithmetic—classes in English literature, history, natural philosophy, physiology, and algebra. During the next decade the school had an annual enrollment of approximately 260 students, but by the 1880s the enrollment had climbed to over 600. While it never matched Avery in providing black teachers or as a cultural center for elite African Americans, Wallingford would play for more than sixty years an important role in the education of Charleston's black community.[4]

A "Presbyterian School" was operated for several years on George Street between King and Saint Philips Streets. Sponsored by the Home Mission Committee of the New School General Assembly, it was linked to the work of Ennals Adams and the Charleston Mission. In 1870 it had four teachers, all of whom were black, and 160 students.[5] More significant was the Shaw School, which operated under the auspices of the New England Freedmen's Aid Commission. Located on Mary Street, it had close ties to the Plymouth Congregational Church and to the Charleston Mission. The Presbyterian minister Ennals Adams served as its principal for a number of years, even after it later became a public school under the Charleston school board. In 1870, before Adams became principal, Shaw had 366 students and ten white teachers. Adams, always sensitive to the influence of teachers as role models for their students, later insisted on the need for African American teachers who would prove the lie of black inferiority.[6]

Out in the countryside, a number of schools were established in connection with Presbyterian churches. On James Island, the Reverend H. H. Hunter organized a school in 1867 that operated for several years with him as the sole teacher.[7] The school evidently continued for forty years out of sight of official

African American Schools and Educators
Clockwise, from top left: Zion School; Avery Institute, Class of 1924; Francis L. Cardozo (all courtesy of Avery Research Center for African-American History and Culture, College of Charleston, Charleston, S.C.); Thomas E. Miller (courtesy of Saint Luke Presbyterian Church, Orangeburg, S.C.)

denominational records until, in 1926, it was taken under the care of the Northern Presbyterian board as the Saint James Parochial School. The next year the school reported 400 pupils, half of whom met in a two-room schoolhouse and half of whom met in the church. With the board's help, a four-room schoolhouse was soon built.[8]

The church on isolated Edisto Island had established a school before the war's end. By 1866 it had 110 pupils taught by Jacob Charles Moultrie and under the care of the General Assembly's Committee on Freedmen. Named Hope School by the Gullah-speaking African Americans of the island, it reached in 1870 a high point in enrollment for the Reconstruction years with 200 students and two white teachers. By 1877, when the island no longer attracted strong outside support, E. B. Moultrie, wife of Ishmael Moultrie, kept the school open, teaching by herself 40 to 60 students. The school was given a new lease on life as the Larimer High School, first through the efforts of the Presbyterian minister J. W. Mahoney, who secured a much needed new building in 1912, and then through his successor, William Lee Metz, who with his wife Eola taught in the school during his long pastorate from 1916 to 1946. In 1929 Larimer had 120 students with three teachers.[9] As Larimer High School, it became "the community center for all progressive activities on the island."[10]

A school was started at Bluffton in Beaufort County under New School Presbyterian auspices after the war. Formally established as an academy in 1882, it had 560 pupils, eight teachers, and a newly constructed boys' dorm in 1893. It flourished for several decades and then, after a slow decline, it was gone even before the impact of the Great Depression. A freedmen's school, typical of the common schools established by the AMA throughout the South, was also located in Beaufort.[11]

Important schools flourished during the first three decades of the twentieth century in Allendale, Bamberg, and Blackville. The Harden Academy in Allendale had been founded by W. H. Mitchell in 1895. Mitchell, a Presbyterian minister, began the school in his home, requested aid from the Northern Presbyterian Committee of Missions For Freedmen, and with the funds received built a schoolhouse on the edge of the little town. When the schoolhouse burned in the 1920s, a new five-room building was constructed, largely with funds from the Northern church. In 1929 it had 148 pupils after having reached a peak enrollment of 272 in 1918. A similar pattern was followed at the Frasier Excelsior School in Bamberg. In Blackville the Emmerson Industrial Institute had a 108-acre farm connected with it and in 1929 had 225 students. Small Presbyterian churches were established in connection with each of these schools.[12]

Other schools, built beside a Presbyterian church usually under the instigation and supervision of a black Presbyterian pastor, were scattered throughout the low country—at Hardeeville and Ravenel, on Wadmalaw at Martins Point, in Orangeburg and in Walterboro, out in the country at the Aimwell Church, and the Mary A. Steele Memorial School on Johns Island. They were all small. Most had only one teacher and no more than forty or fifty students who, if they were lucky and worked hard, made it through the eighth grade. A few bright ones, whose families could scrape together enough cash or goods to barter, were able to go on to one of the Presbyterian boarding schools—to Immanuel Institute in Aiken or to Brainerd Institute in Chester, or to one of the two jewels in the crown of Presbyterian academies: Coulter Memorial in Cheraw or Harbinson in Irmo. From among the graduates of these schools, a few were able to go to Charlotte and Johnson C. Smith University.[13]

All of the schools were vulnerable to changing economic conditions. This was especially true of those that were not firmly connected to a well-established African American congregation. In addition, the slow development of black public schools made the denominational schools seem less necessary, although the denominational schools supplied in the low country most of the teachers for the public schools.[14] Furthermore, in 1928 the U.S. Bureau of Education was critical of what it called "the long-distance administration" of the denominational schools. The charge ignored the advantages for African Americans of such "long-distance"—it provided them, after all, much independence—but the charge was nevertheless convincing to many in the North. Thus when the Great Depression swept over the land, the schools were particularly vulnerable and all were carried away by its devastation except Avery, Saint James Parochial, and Larimer. By the early 1950s these too had either been closed or turned over to an expanding public school system for African Americans.[15]

While the schools thrived, they embodied the competing impulses between reculturation and the preservation of a distinct African American identity. The schools' role as agents of reculturation was present from the day the first doors were opened during the Civil War until their last doors were closed in the 1950s.[16] "Slavery," remarked Francis Cardozo after he had returned to his hometown of Charleston, "has produced such corrupting and degrading influences, that it requires a generation to remedy, and the whole of the social organization must be remodelled."[17] The schools were consequently regarded not simply as tools for the education of individuals but as powerful instruments for the reculturation—for the "remodeling"—of the African American population of the low country. Central in this task were the efforts of the teachers, most of whom were women.[18] They sought to reshape the world of their students by insisting that they leave behind their African American dialect and adopt "standard" English. Such a move carried with it—through grammatical structure, syntax, and vocabulary—new ways of understanding the world and was an essential instrument for the internalization of Western values.[19]

Intimately connected with the teaching of "standard" English was the insistence on a strict discipline, the renunciation of impulses, and the development of a new sense of propriety and civic responsibility. It was all intended to instill—down into the psychic depths of the students—the virtues of modesty, industry, sobriety, self-control, and godliness. Only by a process of such reculturation, again largely done by women, could the students learn the skills needed in the new world that was breaking over them.[20]

Yet these schools, no more than the churches, did not drop suddenly from the sky on a people who previously had no interest in education. While the need for reculturation played a central part in the establishment and support of the schools, that reculturation had been going on for at least several generations. The African American Presbyterians and Congregationalists had been nurtured in a tradition that had emphasized the importance of education even while largely denying any formal education to them. Beyond whatever formal education an elite free black such as Francis Cardozo was able to attain as a youth in Charleston, the Reformed community had heard for generations the scholarly sermons of low country white preachers, had memorized with whites the questions and answers of catechisms, and had worshiped in churches that affirmed order, reasonableness, and simplicity and that deprecated emotionalism and disorder. They had had, in other words, adequate time over several generations and the needed context to have already internalized to a significant extent a Reformed tradition, its world view, and its ethos. Their African American tradition included the values the schools were seeking to inculcate.

The schools also served, however, a countervailing impulse—the preservation of an African American identity and the consolidation of a distinct African American Reformed community. What we see in this extensive network of schools is a utopian vision that pointed to a new and better life for the people. Here, through education and reculturation, was the way out of the poverty and oppression that rested so heavily on the people's backs. But that vision, that exploration of the possible, had to confront the community's own ideological needs for identity.[21] What the community might become had to confront what the community was—an African American community in the Carolina low country, a community that had lodged within its psychic depths the experience of a people in bondage and the memory of a long struggle against oppression and slavery. This was the shared heritage of African Americans, the deep river they had crossed together to Jordan's stormy shore. The schools consequently became places where African American history was taught and a pride in racial identity was encouraged.[22] More important perhaps than such formal instruction in preserving a distinct identity was the socialization role the schools played in nurturing a tightly knit community. The schools, with the churches, became central institutions around which the community's life was built.

The governance of most of the schools encouraged a sense of local ownership and strengthened community solidarity and identity. The Presbyterian schools of the low country after Reconstruction, in contrast to those schools sponsored by the Congregationalist AMA, were operated by local African American pastors and teachers.[23] The schools did receive critical financial support from Northern Presbyterians and made reports to them, but most of the schools were first established by a local pastor, who then requested aid from the North. The request, however, had to be approved by their own Atlantic Presbytery, requiring the presbytery to make decisions about the best use of the limited resources available from the North.[24] Far from being institutions from

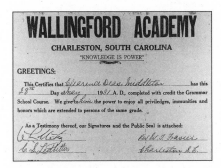

African American Schools
Left: Certificate from Wallingford Academy, 1931 (courtesy of Charleston Atlantic Presbytery, Charleston, S.C.). *Right:* Avery Institute, early twentieth century (courtesy of Avery Research Center for African-American History and Culture, College of Charleston, Charleston, S.C.)

the outside, imposing an alien culture on their students, the schools emerged from the community's life as it sought to draw on its traditions to meet the demands of its present.

The schools consequently reflected a continuity with the community's history, even as they sought to meet the challenges of reculturation while preserving a distinct identity. Two worlds—one African American, the other Reformed—had come together in a complex interaction during the antebellum period to form an African American Reformed community. That dialectical interaction, set within a new historical and social context, echoed in the schoolrooms of the low country the interaction between two larger worlds, between traditional cultures and Western culture. Such an interaction continued to be the creative force in the community's life, linking it to struggles far beyond the low country while at the same time producing clearer boundaries around its "own little world."

Their "Own Little World"

The pattern of Presbyterian families, so easy to trace in the white churches, also appears in the African American churches, although it is more difficult to trace specific black families back through the deep and murky waters of slavery. Nevertheless, it is clear, as has been seen, that long-established African American congregations with their own tradition emerged from the white-dominated churches after the Civil War. Their membership, no less than that of whites, was composed of great networks of families closely connected to the Presbyterian churches and to Plymouth Congregational. The Mitchells and Browns, Washingtons and Rivers, Whaleys and Bligens, Campbells and Jenkins, together with a host of other families too numerous to name, filled the rolls of the

Presbyterian churches, went to school together, and married the sons and daughters of their Presbyterian neighbors. Jenkins from Edisto married Jenkins of Wadmalaw (just as white Presbyterian Jenkins of Edisto married white Presbyterian Jenkins of Wadmalaw) and had Jenkins relatives at Saint Paul and Saint Andrews. The Capers family of Charleston's Zion were cousins to the Capers family at Hebron; the Charleston Smalls family at Plymouth and Zion were relatives of the Edisto and Beaufort Smalls families; the Pearsons of Olivet were related by marriage to the Browns of Zion, and so it went. Such close family connections served to heighten the churches' sense of self-identity and social cohesion and helped to cultivate the distinct African American Reformed tradition of the Carolina low country.[25]

From among these families came some of the outstanding lay leaders of the African American community of the low country—leaders who exhibited a firm commitment to the Reformed ethic in which they had been nurtured. The little Berean congregation in Beaufort, for example, had a cluster of leaders whose contributions to the black community and the state far transcended their numbers. At their center was S. J. Bampfield, clerk of court for Beaufort County, elder of the church, and a Republican leader of such integrity that even the Democratic Governor Wade Hampton referred to him as "an excellent official." Bampfield was the son-in-law of Robert Smalls (the black hero of the Civil War who led a group of black sailors to take over the Confederate steamer *Planter* and to sail to Beaufort and freedom) and was editor of the Beaufort *New South*. With Bampfield as editor of the *New South* was G. W. Anderson, a Presbyterian teacher at the Beaufort Normal and Industrial Academy. They used the newspaper to speak forcefully for the civil rights of African Americans.[26]

More influential than Bampfield or Anderson, and perhaps the most influential African American leader in the state for a generation, was their fellow member at Berean, Thomas Ezekiel Miller. Born a free black in Charleston, Miller grew up in the city's Presbyterian circles and, when the war was over, went off to the Presbyterian Lincoln University in Pennsylvania. Returning to South Carolina, he moved to Beaufort in 1874 and was elected first to the lower house of the state legislature and then in 1880 to the state senate. He became state chairman of the Republican Party in 1882 and was elected to the U.S. Congress in 1888 and 1890. When the state organized its new college for African Americans in Orangeburg in 1896, Miller was selected to be its president, a position he kept for fifteen years until ousted by the racist policies of Governor Cole Blease. When Miller arrived in Orangeburg in 1896, one of the first things he did was to organize Saint Luke Presbyterian Church, where he served as a founding elder and leading layman in Atlantic Presbytery.[27]

Miller was a constant champion for the cause of the civil, economic, and educational rights of African Americans. As a state senator he was a vigorous opponent of the literacy tests for voting, calling them a sham whose true purpose was not to secure a literate electorate but to keep "the middle classes and the poor whites, together with the negroes, from having anything to do with the elections." He spoke out frequently about the abuses connected with share-cropping and denounced the injustices African Americans suffered in the court system. Miller was, however, no radical calling for sweeping changes in the social system. He spoke as one who wanted for blacks admission to the system, rather than one who wanted a fundamental overhaul of the system. Thus he reflected the reformist position that had long dominated the low country Reformed community in its quest for a middle way.[28]

Speaking during the "Negro Day" exercises at the South Carolina and West Indian Exposition in Charleston in 1902, Miller declared that "There is no such thing as social equality anywhere in the world." No sane "white man or negro," he insisted, "should pay any attention to the clatter about social equality, for it is all bosh to talk about it. No sensible negro aims at it or expects it. But we do aim at, and expect to achieve, all the enjoyment of domestic happiness that belongs to a free and untrammeled citizenship." Miller, while a champion for the civil rights for African Americans, insisted that they must "pull themselves up by their own bootstraps," that they must rely on themselves for their "advancement." Miller's solution for the problems faced by his people was a vigorous adoption of the now transformed Reformed ethic that emphasized economic success as a sign of human achievement and that called for an increased commitment to bourgeois individualism. "The foundation of all racial virtues has been, is now and ever will be frugality," Miller declared. "Show me a people that is frugal and I will show you a people that is strong, virtuous, wealthy and happy."[29] Whatever else might have influenced such a position, he was standing in the traditions of the Reformed community of which he was so much a part. Certainly he was an advocate of reculturation, insisting on the internalization of a Reformed ethic because "our advancement must come from within our beings."

Miller's dilemma paralleled in important ways that of well-meaning white reformists during the antebellum period. John Adger and Thomas Smyth, J. H. Thornwell and John L. Girardeau, speaking as members of the oppressing race and class, had sought to work within the system of slavery to make it more humane. Miller, as a privileged member of an oppressed people, sought in his generation to work within a segregated society to make it more just. Miller knew even more forcefully than the antebellum reformers the restraints of Carolina society. Given the power and violence of whites, it is unlikely he could have stayed in South Carolina and, from a position of leadership, worked for the "advancement of his people" if he had taken a more radical position.

Other African Americans, standing in different circumstances and at some distance from the oppressive realities of the low country, would take a much more radical position than Miller in regard to social equality for African Americans. One was the Charleston Presbyterian Francis Grimké, son of a slave mother and a white owner. From his Presbyterian pulpit in Washington, D.C., Grimké insisted that no compromise could be tolerated with the system of segregation. In this stance he followed the path taken by his white aunts Sarah and Angelina, who had left Charleston years earlier and had become leading abolitionists in the North.[30] Geography, where one lived, obviously helped to shape what one saw. For Miller and Grimké, geography also helped to determine which of the competing impulses within the Reformed tradition would dominate their perspectives.

Miller's way, however—as might be expected—was the way the Reformed African American community in the low country traveled. Its members, after all, had little opportunity to consider Grimké's uncompromising position as a real option, and Miller's way offered sacrifices enough. On Edisto Island, for example, where the African Americans were desperately poor and their isolation had left them far removed from the dominant white society, any move toward accommodation with white culture demanded great discipline and perseverance, whatever judgments later generations—wanting to maintain the purity of Gullah culture—might make about such accommodations. At the end of Reconstruction, most of the African American Presbyterians on the island had been small farmers or laborers. Slowly as the years passed, their congregation nurtured through its school a number of its children who went on to become teachers and ministers who, in their turn, taught the next generation a Reformed faith and ethic. They built a gin and then a bakery next to the church, developed agricultural projects, emphasized over and over again the need to master "standard English" while at the same time emphasizing, long before it was popular, African American history. Perhaps most important, the congregation and its ministers encouraged their young people to go to college.[31] Again, what the community was reflecting was the dialectic between two worlds, between reculturation and the preservation of an African American identity, between a utopian vision and the ideological drive for identity. Forged in this dialectic interaction was not only an ethos and social profile but also a conceptual framework, a social and cultural imagination, that both reflected the world as seen from Edisto Island and provided guidance for engaging that world. Such a social and cultural imagination led the community to seek to be transformers of their island culture, not radical opponents of the dominant white society.[32]

The interaction between two worlds was perhaps most clearly present in the African American ministers who came out of the community. They were a part of the African American world—they shared its history, its memories, and its cultural legacy—and part of a distinct subgroup within that world, members of their own little African American Reformed community. This little world swirled around networks of family connections and churches and was given an additional social and cultural coherence by the schools attached to the various congregations—especially Avery and Wallingford in Charleston, Hope (Larimer) on Edisto, and Saint James on James Island. By the late nineteenth century, increasing numbers of ministers were being educated at these schools and then at Biddle University (later Johnson C. Smith) or Lincoln University in Pennsylvania.[33]

Typical was Jacob Moultrie. Born in Beaufort, he went to the Presbyterian academy there and then North to Lincoln where he received his bachelor's degree in 1886 and his theological degree in 1889. He returned to Beaufort, taught in the academy, and was pastor at Beaufort Salem, Saint Paul, and Saint Andrews. Moultrie was followed at Saint Paul and Saint Andrews by Joseph Pearson, who was born in Walterboro and studied in the little school run by the wife of the local Presbyterian minister. He went off to high school, college, and seminary at Biddle, returned to the low country, served the Saint Andrews, Saint Paul, and Faith congregations for three years, and then went to Olivet in Charleston where he was pastor from 1906 to 1943.[34]

These ministers, like their congregations, lived in a world that was low country and African American, a world both restricted by poverty and racism and marked by a rich cultural tradition. Yet they also lived in another world, not only through the reculturation going on in their community but also through the connectional links of the Presbyterian system, or for the Congregationalists, through the American Home Missionary Association. African American Presbyterian pastors from the low country attended the annual meetings of the Northern Presbyterian General Assembly. These meetings, held in the great cities of the North and the West, provided regular opportunities for the pastors to see beyond low country horizons. Each year a minister, with a lay elder, traveled to Minneapolis or Philadelphia, to Cleveland or Portland or Pittsburgh, to Syracuse or Denver or Chicago. There they met with Presbyterian pastors and elders from around the country, heard reports and debates, and saw the sights of the cities.

In 1893, for example, Adam Frayer, pastor of the Hopewell church in Walterboro and the rural Aimwell, traveled to Washington, D.C., for the meeting of the General Assembly. He had been born near McClellanville among the Gullah-speaking blacks of the Santee and had received both his bachelor's degree and his theological education at Biddle where he had been a part of those closely connected circles of low country Presbyterians. With him at the General Assembly in Washington was J. J. Lesesne, an elder from the Zion church. Together they heard reports from all over the country and participated in the great heresy trial of Charles A. Briggs, professor of Old Testament theology at Union Theological Seminary in New York. They heard Professor Briggs defend the "findings of modern biblical scholarship" and vigorously condemn "the inerrancy dogma" of Protestant orthodoxy, and they had to decide if his position meant he should be suspended from the Presbyterian ministry.[35] Such experiences year after year for pastors and elders, reported to the presbytery meetings that followed, provided windows to a world that stretched far beyond the sandy roads and familiar ways of the low country and gave indications of the great social and intellectual challenges of the modern world.

The pull of two different worlds was also visible in the presbytery, which provided institutional unity to the community. In their presbytery meetings, these African American Presbyterians showed themselves, like other Children of Geneva, committed to doing things decently and in order. The minutes of their Atlantic Presbytery read like those of the white Charleston Presbytery: carefully structured meetings used the formal language inherited from earlier generations of Presbyterians and followed the prescribed ways of the "Form of Government," a polity whose roots reached back to the Scottish Second Book of Discipline (1581). Such procedures were part of that complex cultural heritage of the West—with its ascetic self-discipline and sense of civic responsibility and cooperation—that needed to be internalized for reculturation. At the same time, the more immediate influence of the modern world became visible as, over the years, presbytery meetings grew shorter, became more highly organized, and the role of committees increased as theological discussion decreased. Requirements for ministerial candidates also reflected similar changes: the Latin thesis was dropped and college degrees were substituted for examinations in the liberal arts.

There was, however, the continuing influence of an African American world. Unlike the white Charleston Presbytery, which began in the 1880s to move disciplinary cases into the quiet and discrete chambers of committees influenced by a growing therapeutic ethos, the black presbytery continued the ancient practice of bringing disciplinary cases before the presbytery. The old linkage of discipline to the welfare of the community and to legal rights was maintained. African American Presbyterians, for example, were more likely to bring a minister to formal trial before the presbytery for some accusation of misconduct than to see that misconduct in psychological terms.[36] Accusations of misconduct were, in other words, more likely to be placed in a community context with a carefully framed legal process than to be understood in individualistic terms that called for a therapeutic response. The reasons for this difference in approach were most likely found in African Americans' being less exposed to the winds of cultural change and, at the same time, in need of strong community solidarity in the midst of an oppressive society. The ways they organized their presbytery and conducted its business was consequently shaped not only by their Reformed tradition and the pull of the modern world but also by their identity and social location as African Americans.

Their Own Kind of People

While Presbyterianism and Congregationalism did not have a broad appeal in the black community, vigorous efforts were made to build new churches and establish new congregations. Nine new churches were established between 1900 and 1930, even as the black population experienced a rapid decline throughout the region. Black Congregationalism, moving from its base in the low country, grew to ten churches statewide by 1916 in addition to Plymouth in Charleston. All of these churches, both Presbyterian and Congregationalist, established during the first four decades of the twentieth century, were gone by 1940. Most collapsed during the 1930s.[37] Their rise and fall was largely linked to the rise of neighboring schools and the schools' fall under the impact of the Great Depression.

By 1940 the African American Reformed community in the low country was reduced to the churches whose roots reached deep into the history of the region. All of the surviving congregations could trace their histories to the long if often hidden traditions of the "church within a church," the slave congregations that had existed for generations within the confines of the white-dominated churches. Among these old congregations, however, there were significant signs of strength in 1940. Even with the loss of churches and the general decline of the black population in the region, the presbytery had shown a slight gain in membership between 1920 and 1940. Saint James, under the vigorous leadership of its pastor Marion Sanders, had almost doubled the size of its membership and was in 1940 the largest Presbyterian congregation in the low country, black or white, while Plymouth Congregational was at the high point in its membership in the twentieth century.[38] Moreover, through the schools they had supported and the leaders they had produced, these congregations had made significant contributions to the larger African American community, even as they remained a small part of that community.

But for all their accomplishments, the point remains that the community was unable to expand beyond those congregations that had deep roots in the antebellum period. The reasons for this limitation were no doubt complex, including the important identification of the congregations with Northern white money, interests, and control. What seems clear, however, and of importance to this study, was the critical need for time for individual congregations to synthesize the competing impulses of two traditions. A congregation's internalization of a world view and ethos that was both African American and Reformed apparently required several generations and a supportive context. Congregations could not quickly internalize at a sustaining depth the distinct culture of the African American Reformed tradition.[39]

The African American Reformed community thus reflected in the varied elements of its life the dialectical relationship between two worlds. These two worlds—one African American, the other Reformed—were each complex. Each had its own internal tensions, and each was a part of a larger world. Even the tension itself was part of a larger tension felt by elites the world over as their traditional cultures came under the assault of a relentless Western imperialism, or more neutrally stated, of a relentless modernity. In the United States, no one articulated the tension for African American elites more forcefully or with greater power than W. E. B. Du Bois. This brilliant "Westernized non-Western" intellectual, whose thought would be of such influence at Avery, saw the ways the cultural imperialism of whites—modernity itself—imposed a standard to which African Americans had to submit, however reluctantly. "It is a peculiar sensation," Du Bois wrote, "this double-consciousness, this sense of always looking at one's self through the eyes of others, of measuring one's soul by the tape of a world that looks on in amused contempt and pity. One ever feels his two-ness,—An American, a Negro; two souls, two thoughts, two unreconciled strivings; two warring ideals in one dark body, whose dogged strength alone keeps it from being torn asunder." Du Bois felt the longing that would mark so many in his circumstances—"to attain self-conscious manhood, to merge his double self into a better and truer self." Such a "merging" required not only reculturation, the internalization of cultural values and skills that meant power in the modern world, but also the maintenance of identity as an African American. The African American "would not bleach his Negro soul in a flood of white Americanism, for he knows that Negro blood has a message for the world. He simply wishes to make it possible for a man to be both a Negro and an American, without being cursed and spit upon by his fellows, without having the doors of Opportunity closed roughly in his face."[40]

For the Reformed African American community, this "two-ness" and the dialectic between these "two warring ideals" focused most directly on religious traditions—African American and Reformed. During the antebellum period, the community's own little world had been given birth through the dialectical interaction of these traditions. That little world as it developed during the years following emancipation knew within the depths of its cultural life the competing gravitational pull of the worlds that had given it birth. Yet it did not simply gravitate between these two competing worlds—it sought to follow a utopian vision that affirmed its own integrity, that provided it with its own sense of identity, and that saw its double self merging "into a better and truer self." Such a vision shattered any ideological assertion that the community could not be both truly African American and truly Reformed. That it was a "little world," that it was linked to boundaries largely drawn during the antebellum period, revealed not only the community's weaknesses but also the creative force that gave it birth, that sustained it over the generations, and that enabled it to make a contribution to its low country home far beyond its little size.

16

The White Reformed Community, 1876–1941

A "Little World" in Travail and Transition

LESS THAN A hundred years before the Civil War, the South Carolina low country was a region of extraordinary wealth. "By many standards of measurement," an economic historian recently concluded, the low country was "the wealthiest area in British North America, if not the entire world."[1] Of course the wealth was in the hands of whites, and African Americans constituted in their own bodies a substantial portion of the region's affluence. Yet even including the slave population in the calculation of per capita wealth, the low country remained fabulously affluent. By the beginning of the Civil War, its wealth had declined relative to other parts of the country, but it had managed to keep its premiere position.[2]

The years following the Civil War saw a stunning reversal in the low country's economic status. Rather than the land of fabled wealth, it became the land of grinding poverty, one of the poorest of the poor regions of the country. This poverty, so all-encompassing and pervasive, so stark in its contrast to remembered white wealth, would mark the low country for more than a hundred years.[3]

Accompanying the economic demise of the low country was its loss of political power. Once the proud region that produced national political leaders, the low country lost even its old domination of state politics. Indeed, it became the "whipping boy" of rising new political forces in the state, especially those represented by "Pitchfork" Ben Tillman. Sectional and class jealousies were turned against the low country and were used in shaping a powerful populist movement. Perhaps most revealing, no one from Charleston was elected governor between the end of the Civil War and 1938. This loss of political power was rooted in the economic decline of the region, in the abolition of slavery, and in political and social developments during and immediately following Reconstruction. Constitutional conventions during Reconstruction broadened the electorate, abolished property qualifications for office holding, apportioned legislative representation to the advantage of the up-country, and made provisions for a system of universal education. Added to these reforms were the up-country's resentment of low country "aristocracy" and fears of its black majority.[4]

While emigrants—mostly black—were leaving South Carolina, few immigrants were arriving.[5] Until the 1960s, the low country remained remarkably homogeneous, bound together in both the white and the black communities by ties to family and place. Such homogeneity was clearly visible in the churches where clusters of family names on church rolls pointed to continuity with the past and an intense social and cultural solidarity that was rooted in antebellum communities.

Still, it should not be imagined that the white community—any more than the African American community—was somehow isolated from the assaults of the modern world. Indeed, it was that world that had largely shaped the low country with its market-oriented economy and that in a Yankee form had marched into the region. If the tensions between two worlds—one traditional and one modern—were less visible among the whites of the low country than among the African Americans, the tensions were nevertheless there, slowly remaking the character of the region as it struggled to regain some measure of prosperity. As we shall see, these same tensions were also at work reshaping the "little world" of the white Reformed community.

A Social Profile: "Presbyterian Families"

The church rolls of the years between the end of Reconstruction and the beginning of the Second World War reveal an amazing continuity of families connected with the Reformed churches of the region. Within the white community, as in the African American, there were Presbyterian families whose denominational roots reached back for generations, some into early colonial days. At First (Scots) there were the Porchers and Bees, the Townsends and the Jenkinses, the Chisolms and the Trenholms. At Second Church, there were the Legarés and DeSaussures, Grimké's and Lanneaus, the Robertsons, Kings, Roses, and Rowands. At once proud but still beautiful Edisto the church roll continued to be dominated by Mikells, Seabrooks, and Whaleys, by Baynards, Murrays, and Edings. At Johns Island the Fripps, Walpoles, Stanyarns, Legarés, Townsends, Wilsons, and Jenkinses still filled the old pews, as had their colonial ancestors.[6]

As might be expected, the Charleston churches had on their rolls many whose roots were in the countryside and country churches—Whildens and Royalls from Wappetaw; DuPonts, Swintons, and Bryans from Wilton; Oswalds from Walterboro and Dorchester; Seabrooks and Baynards from Edisto; Glovers from Orangeburg; and Hutsons from Stoney Creek. But the flow was not one way, for Charleston families also moved out to the little towns growing in the city's hinterland and the membership of new village churches echoed with family names long connected with Presbyterianism in the low country. At the same time a few names became increasingly prominent during these years, especially in the small towns: Wymans were officers in Denmark, Estill, Bamberg, Barnwell, and Crockettville; Hays were elders in Allendale, Barnwell, Boiling Springs, and Johns Island; Hills were scattered through the rolls at Summerville and McClellanville, Orangeburg and Johns Island. Not surprisingly there was much intermarriage among these Presbyterian families that produced a bewildering array of names—Townsend Mikell and Mikell Townsend, Leland Morrison and Morrison Leland and such combinations as Hugh Swinton Legaré Chisolm and Louisa Cheves Smythe Stoney. And so it went from church to church across the low country, names too numerous to mention but long associated with the Reformed tradition and Presbyterian churches.[7]

It all pointed to what low country people had called since colonial days "our little world," a world that was increasingly isolated as its fortunes plummeted. While it should not be exaggerated—people after all were linked in many other ways than in the churches—a clear subculture or sub-subculture of white Presbyterian families existed within this little world of the low country. In earlier years, national and even international connections had worked against provincialism among the affluent white members of the Reformed churches. Such connections, with some notable exceptions, no longer loomed large in the lives of the people nor assumed the role they once had in the churches. The result was that the white low country churches became more intensely parochial, more narrowly focused in their interests and activities, and a kind of "backwater" in American religious life rather than the influential force they had been during earlier days. Yet, these white Presbyterian families also felt the transforming winds of modernity blowing across the low country.

A Social Profile: Women

Women continued throughout this period to constitute a majority of the congregations.[8] Not only were these women the majority in the churches, they also stood at the heart of the Presbyterian families and the network of relations that played such an important role in the churches. A mother's love was said to pervade a Christian home, and to the mother was given responsibility for cultivating the family's sensibilities, moral values, and piety.[9] Most particularly, the mother had the task of nurturing children, now regarded as malleable and carefree, destined for heaven if only properly cared for and guided.[10]

In earlier generations, white women had played, in the midst of a hierarchical and paternalistic society, a more direct role in the family's economy— many a farm wife or plantation mistress had had a vital part in the overseeing of various aspects of the family's economic activity. But as those responsibilities

Women Leaders

Top, left: Margaret Adger Smyth, Advocate of Benevolence (from *Letters and Reflections* by Thomas Smyth [1914]); *right:* Louisa Cheves Smythe Stoney, Historian for the Women of the Church (from *Presbyterian Women of South Carolina* [1929]). *Bottom, right:* Annabelle (Mrs. Marion A.) Sanders, Teacher at St. James School (courtesy of Charleston-Atlantic Presbytery); *left:* Ida Wells, First Woman Pastor in Atlantic Presbytery (courtesy of the Reverend Ida Wells) decreased and women became even more economically dependent on men toward the late nineteenth century, it appeared that the Bible and the very foundations of the universe decreed that women should be confined to the tasks of nurturing children and being makers of the home—at least that white women should.[11]

Many white women soon felt the need to move out of the home and to work to make the society a more wholesome place in which to send their sons and daughters. For many Presbyterian women, the route to such work was through the church and its women's organizations. In 1921, for example, their state women's synodical called "our beloved commonwealth" to repentance for "her general lawlessness, bloodshed and varied crimes." The synodical called on ministers to "preach at an early date upon the sacredness of human life from God's standpoint and upon the certainty of punishment for breaking down and disregarding God's standards," while the synodical itself formed committees on "race relations" and "children's welfare."[12] The place of white women in society and in the churches was thus expanding during these years, even in the midst of the narrowing of the low country world and its increased parochialism. Clearly women were organizing and speaking out in ways that few of their grandmothers had dreamed of or dared.

A Social Profile: Ministers

The narrowing of the low country world for whites was seen in its ministers—in where they came from, in where they went to school, in where they received their theological education, and in the role they played in the larger church. In contrast to their predecessors, they were, in significantly increased numbers, from the South.[13] Many were part of those complex family networks that marked the Presbyterian churches of the region, so that only a committed and long-suffering low country genealogist could chart the family relationships between the Presbyterian clergy of the region.[14]

Not only were most of the ministers now from the South, but most now went to Southern schools.[15] In contrast to their predecessors, most of whom went to Ivy League or Scottish universities, the great majority now went to Davidson or Washington and Lee, to Hampden Sydney or Presbyterian, or to the state university at Charlottesville or Chapel Hill or Columbia. Not only did they no longer have the money to go outside the South as their predecessors had, but they wanted to go to schools with Southern accents, to schools that reflected their way of thinking, their values, and their Southern way of life. They wanted what Girardeau had so forcefully urged—to keep their Southern identity, to scrupulously adhere "to the phraseology of the past," to attend colleges that were channels "for conveying from generation to generation our own type of thought, sentiment and opinion" by "instamping" on the mind "principles hallowed by the blood of patriots."[16]

More striking than the colleges they attended was the narrowing of their theological education. During the earlier period between the Revolution and the Civil War, the ministers in the low country had been almost evenly divided in their theological education between the seminaries at Princeton, Columbia, Andover, Edinburgh, and private instruction. Between the Civil War and the Second World War, however, nearly two-thirds of the number attended Columbia alone.[17] They entered a theological institution whose economic foundations had been shattered by the Civil War and whose intellectual life was dominated by the thought of Thornwell, Adger, and Girardeau. If that thought had been vigorous and powerful in the decades before the Civil War, it had become largely isolated from the main currents of contemporary thought by the end of the nineteenth century.[18]

These ministers thus reflected the increasingly parochial world of the Carolina low country. Yet however parochial their world, they represented, as their predecessors had, a well-educated and articulate group within their particular social context. If they were more limited—as indeed their whole world was— they nevertheless attempted within that world to pursue the old value of a disciplined use of the mind. Davidson may not have been Princeton, but those who went there liked to think of it as the Princeton of the South. A few went beyond the familiar schools of the South—to the new university at Johns Hopkins, or to the expanding Princeton, or to the prestigious Columbia University, or occasionally into the dangerous world of a German university. But these ministers were the exception, and most followed more modest paths and more constricted ways and sought in such circumstances to be faithful to their traditions.

A Social Profile: Business Leaders

Whatever general loss of prosperity and influence came to the white Presbyterians of the low country, and whatever narrowing of interests and focus occurred in their churches, there remained nevertheless a strong, if significantly transformed, expression of the old Reformed ethic among the people and a vigorous spirit of entrepreneurial enterprise. Indeed, leaders emerged from low country Presbyterian families who played important roles in the transformation of the old plantation economy and in the rise of new industries in South Carolina. The economic decline of the region, however, was real and its severity showed itself in the difficulties faced by those with even the most entrepreneurial of spirits.

Factors, who bought rice and cotton from planters and supplied them with provisions, had been at the center of the commercial life of the low country since the eighteenth century. Following the Civil War the economic foundations of their business activities began to crumble, but they continued as important elements in the Charleston business community. In the years immediately after the Civil War, Presbyterians constituted a powerful element in this sector of the business community.

At First (Scots) Robert D. Mure, and then his son Robert D. Mure, Jr., with their partner William Middleton, headed R. D. Mure and Company, one of the leading cotton factors in the city. John Fraser, of John L. Fraser and Company, oversaw one of the largest cotton factorages in the entire South. William Ravenel, longtime member at First (Scots), recovered some of his losses during the war by having a New York partner join his influential factorage business of Ravenel and Company, formerly Ravenel and Huger. All of these firms, however, suffered severe losses within two decades after the war.[19]

More successful in meeting the demands of a changing economy was a remarkable group of businessmen at Second Presbyterian and, by way of Zion's white membership, at Westminster Presbyterian. Preeminent among these were members of the Adger and Smyth families. Their business activities reveal the extent to which they followed the traditions that had marked their families throughout the earlier part of the nineteenth century.

Robert Adger had largely assumed the supervision of his father James's business interests in 1858. His broad investments and connections with British and Northern firms allowed him to emerge from the Civil War in a strong financial position and he soon expanded his cotton brokerage and hardware business. When the value of rich phosphate beds in the low country was discovered, he moved quickly to invest in their mining, becoming the principal owner of the Coosaw Mining Company, the leading river mining company and "the most prosperous example of Charleston's postwar enterprise." Under Robert Adger's leadership, Coosaw's production was so high that its royalties paid to the state during the phosphate boom of 1880–96 exceeded that of all other river mining companies combined. Adger also invested heavily in the developing fertilizer business and became one of the primary owners of the Etiwan Fertilizer Works, the largest in the 1880s of the locally owned fertilizer companies. In the meantime, James Adger and Company continued as a prosperous cotton factorage and as the agent for a New York steamship line.[20]

Ellison Smyth, Robert Adger's nephew, went to work in his uncle's hardware business after the war. He moved to the up-country in 1881 and plunged into the textile business as president and primary owner of the Pelzer and then the Belton mills. He returned to Charleston in 1887 and with his family joined once again the Second Presbyterian Church. Smyth's Pelzer mill was by far the most prosperous in the state and by 1908 the value of its yearly product exceeded by almost half that of its nearest rival. He was, according to a historian of the textile industry, "the single most important up-country industrialist" between 1880 and 1920. Smyth's daughter, Margaret Adger, married Anthony McKissick in 1891. Six years later McKissick was president of the newly organized Grendel Mills in Greenwood and then in 1902 of the Ninety Six Cotton Mills in Ninety Six, South Carolina.[21]

With the Smyths and Adgers thus playing leading roles in the textile and phosphate industries in the state during the last two decades of the nineteenth century, they were clearly examples of considerable business enterprise, as their father and grandfather had been during the first half of the century. But these families were not the only ones associated with Second Presbyterian and Westminster who were vigorous participants in an attempt to build a new economic base for the region and the state. At Westminster with Adger was John A. Enslow—he had been one of the white elders at Zion—a prominent "commission merchant" and a leading advocate in the city for developing modern business practices and centralizing transportation facilities. F. S. Rodgers, also at Westminster, was a partner in the firm of Pelzer, Rodgers, and Company, "one of the strongest houses in the South," which organized the Atlantic Phosphate Company in Charleston and textile mills in the up-country. At Second Presbyterian there was James Gibbes, one of Charleston's most influential businessmen after the war: president of the People's National Bank, vice-president of the Home Insurance Company, and a director of the South Carolina Railroad and the Gas and Light Company. George H. Cornelson of Second Presbyterian moved to Orangeburg and developed a large cotton mill, "an extensive warehouse of many departments," and promoted "enterprises at other cities in the South."[22]

Leaders connected with the low country Presbyterian churches not only pursued their own business interests but also were involved in a wide range of activities aimed at the general economic welfare of the low country.[23] Perhaps most prominent was J. Adger Smyth, mayor of Charleston from 1895 to 1903 and influential cotton factor and former president of the chamber of commerce. During his tenure as mayor, he was a key figure in two major efforts to revive the city's prosperity: the securing of the Charleston Naval Yard and the celebration of the South Carolina and West Indian Exposition. When the Spanish American War broke out, Smyth urged the use of Charleston as a rendezvous for the invasion of Cuba. He then oversaw the completion of the jetties that allowed the harbor to receive the largest of ships, and he was largely responsible for the establishment of the naval yard that would have such a profound influence on the future economy and culture of the region. At the same time he was an enthusiastic champion of the South Carolina and West Indies Exposition of 1903. The exposition was first suggested in 1899 by Colonel John H. Averill of Westminster Church. Averill, a railroad executive, had a vision of a new commercial empire for Charleston in the Caribbean. When the exposition opened in 1901 Mayor Smyth declared: "This day marks the beginning of the new era for this staid old city." His friend John Averill served as the exposition's secretary and director general.[24]

The impulse within the Reformed tradition that had long encouraged vigorous business activity and capitalist endeavors was clearly visible in these Presbyterian businessmen and pointed to significant cultural continuity within the Reformed community in the low country.[25] These businessmen were not simply individuals but were part of a community possessed of a world view and ethos. As members of such a community—and most had been members since their childhood—they had internalized in varying degrees a conceptual framework in which their world was experienced and interpreted. Moreover, such a conceptual framework significantly shaped their response to a world so experienced and interpreted. Members of the Reformed community were not, of course, the only ones in the low country who showed considerable business enterprise.[26] Nor was it simply a matter of their Reformed ethic producing a capitalist spirit. Rather, a complex interaction between two contexts—one social, the other interpretative—resulted in a Reformed community in the low country that was marked by considerable business enterprise of an increasingly modern nature.

At the same time, it needs to be emphasized once again that the Reformed ethic was itself not a static or abstract ideal but was undergoing important changes as the nineteenth century drew to a close. The Reformed tradition had long taught that work was a calling and a moral duty and that thrift and a simple life-style were signs of a sanctified life. The rewards of work were to be understood as gifts of God's grace and were to be used for the purpose of creating a holy commonwealth. The Adgers, Smyths, and other affluent families connected with the work at Zion during the 1850s reflected perhaps most clearly such an ethic. Profits, a sign of Divine blessing, were not to be used for purely personal interests but for the good of the community, especially through the means of church benevolence. It was, however, this sense of grace together with an organic understanding of community that appear to have weakened by the end of the nineteenth century as secular perspectives increasingly dominated the emerging modern world. After all, Adam Smith's laissez-faire economics had long insisted that if governments did not meddle with the market mechanism then the wealth and welfare of the nations had a much greater chance of increasing; and, by the closing decades of the nineteenth century, social Darwinism was announcing the "survival of the fittest." Such ideologies encouraged a belief that economic success was a sign of human achievement and nurtured an increased commitment to bourgeois individualism.[27] Being left behind was the old organic understanding of society that had dominated the thought of James H. Thornwell and Thomas Smyth, David Ramsay and Alexander Hewat.

Still the old ideal of an organic society did not suddenly vanish. Most particularly, it could still be seen in Ellison Smyth's attempt to create a model factory town at Pelzer. More than any other industrialist in the state, Ellison Smyth mastered the rhetoric of paternalism and attempted to develop in Pelzer a well-regulated and orderly community.[28] It is not surprising that one who grew up in the Smyth and Adger households, where the Zion experiment played such an important part in their lives, should adopt much of the language and assumptions of paternalism. But there were differences between the paternalism of the Zion experiment and that of Ellison Smyth's cotton mill town. Those differences, and the weakening of important elements in the old Reformed ethic, can be seen in cultural shifts that were slowly but surely reshaping much of the life of the Reformed churches in the low country.

The Modern Way

The Reformed churches of the Carolina low country, no less than others throughout the United States, were deeply influenced by the rising tide of Victorian culture. Named for Britain's eminently pious and respectable queen, Victorianism reached its high point as a cultural epoch in the decades that followed the Civil War and—in the low country, at least—only slowly faded during the early decades of the twentieth century. Essentially Protestant and middle class, Victorianism gloried in respectability, morality, and sentimentality. It blended elements of the old Reformed ethic with the demands of an increasingly modern, industrial society: people were to work hard, stay sober, repress themselves sexually, improve themselves, and postpone gratification. At the same time there were growing temptations to indulge themselves in the stuffy comforts of a Victorian parlor and the delights of consumer goods that were pouring forth in ever greater volumes from American industries.[29]

Closely connected with this Victorianism was a quest for order and efficiency, for planning and control, that would bring some direction and stability to an emerging modern world that often appeared to be in danger of being overwhelmed by change. The values of a rising bureaucratic-minded middle class were making themselves felt in the Reformed churches of the low country no less, if sometimes a little slower, than in other areas of American life.[30]

Most obvious were changes in the ways the white churches began to understand themselves. In previous generations, church sessions had been concerned primarily with discipline as a way of protecting the Lord's Supper from profanation. While such discipline frequently led to legalism and sometimes to a stern self-righteousness, it was rooted in a sense of the holy and in reverence for the sacrament as the meeting of Christ and his people, and of the people as one body in Christ. By 1890, however, the days were gone when white sessions called before them members who had strayed from the straight and narrow and whose behavior threatened to bring scandal upon the church. No more were the adulterer and the liar disciplined, or the indiscreet warned, or the theatergoers admonished. Church discipline, which had sought to draw a line between the worldly and the redeemed, faded into the gentle light of respectability. Now the person troubled with some sin of the flesh was quietly invited into the pastor's study for counseling or was referred to a growing host of trained professionals schooled in the new sciences of psychology and sociology.[31]

At the same time church membership, which in previous generations had been reserved to those who could testify to an experience of regeneration, now became open to all who were respectable members of the community: to "Christian gentlemen" of good reputation and "Christian ladies" of good character who were carefully guided in their behavior by the requirements of proper etiquette. Those who had been only pewholders—and not communicants—in earlier years now left behind them any reservations about their place in the "household of God" and were welcomed into full membership of the churches. The ancient practice of renting pews—with its assumption that many would be attending church who were not communing members—was given up and the new practice of stewardship was adopted following the most modern of principles and methods.[32]

As the meaning of church membership shifted and church discipline essentially vanished, the white churches became more highly organized. Sessions began to have standing committees organized around specific programs. The old three-day meetings of Charleston Presbytery were slowly abandoned in favor of shorter meetings and greater efficiency. Examination of candidates still took much of the presbytery's time, but after 1914 the Latin thesis was no longer required and a college degree was accepted in lieu of the examination on academic subjects. More and more it was church business and committee reports that dominated the meetings.[33]

Changes in church buildings reflected these cultural shifts. Before the Civil War, congregations frequently had "lecture-rooms" where the pastors delivered long and scholarly discourses on a variety of theological or ecclesiastical subjects. In Second Presbyterian's lecture-room, a "beautiful and creditable edifice" on Black Bird's alley, Thomas Smyth had lectured to crowded audiences on "Apostolic Succession" and "Presbytery and Prelacy." By the early 1880s such buildings were outdated and a need was felt for a more modern approach to Christian education. The result at Second Presbyterian was the construction of a "new and more convenient" Sunday school building and "the concentration of the whole strength of the Church" in Sunday school work. Soon the new building became a center of social activity and not only a place for education and worship. Women came to its comfortable parlor for their meetings, young people assembled in its rooms for their youth league, and the whole congregation gathered in its hall for concerts. The school was said to owe its success "largely to the service of song," accompanied by an orchestra conducted by an accomplished musician. The leader in this effort was the superintendent of the Sunday school, Augustine Thomas Smythe (he added the *e* that had long been dropped from his family's name). A leading lawyer in the city, he brought "his practical wisdom and administrative ability" to the reorganization and management of the school, causing it—like his family's successful textile endeavors—to more than double in size in a short time.[34]

Not everyone approved of these changes, especially the use of instrumental music and the employment of professional musicians. Such developments would lead, some feared, to ritualism and would turn the churches away from the old simplicity of worship that had long marked the Reformed tradition. Girardeau, ever the guardian of the old ways, was the leader of the opposition in the Southern Presbyterian Church. Before the war he had quietly quarreled with Thomas Smyth about the subject, objecting to Fleetwood Lanneau, Sr., playing the violin from the back balcony of Second Church and disapproving the organ that had long been a part of worship at First (Scots) and Circular Congregational. Unimpressed by these affluent city churches' ways, he had allowed at Zion and Glebe Street no "display of music; not even an organ or a set choir," but only "the simple, old-time Presbyterian worship. . . consisting of solemn, earnest prayers led by the minister, plain congregational singing, the impressive reading of the Scripture, and the zealous, faithful exposition and application of the Word, followed by an offering for the service of the Lord."[35]

In 1888, as the white churches moved steadily away from the old ways, Girardeau published *Instrumental Music in the Public Worship of the Church.* The heart of the matter, he said, was that whatever is not *commanded* by God as a part of worship is forbidden. There had been, he admitted, instruments of music used in the Old Testament temple. Psalm 150, after all, called on the people to praise God with "the sound of the trumpet," with "the timbrel and dance," with "stringed instruments and organs." But it was all part of the Old Testament dispensation, said Girardeau. The temple worship pointed toward Christ and ended with his advent. Now there was no place for trumpet and timbrel, stringed instruments and organs, or—heaven forbid!—dance in worship. But it was a losing fight. The old quest for simplicity in worship was passing slowing away as organs and choirs, creeds and recited prayers were eased into the patterns of worship not only at First (Scots) and Second but at many of the other low country Presbyterian churches as well.[36]

Not to be outdone in adopting modern practices that emphasized efficiency were the women of the church. Indeed, their changing role in the churches and the growing sophistication of their organizational structures reflected the shifting of values taking place in the churches. Louisa Smythe Stoney traced in the 1920s the evolution of "women's work." She noted the changing place of women in Southern society since the Civil War and the ways in which "women's work" had become increasingly organized to meet the demands of the modern world. Central to this effort had been the creation of a denomination-wide women's auxiliary.[37] "Women have learned," wrote Myrta J. Hutson of Second Church in the 1920s, "that efficiency and concentrated effort, marshalling the combined force for *all* the women for *all* the causes of the church, can be most successfully employed through the agency of this *one* twentieth century society." The auxiliary, wrote the historian of the little Bamberg congregation, was organized "on a modern basis."[38] Certainly that "modern basis" emphasized efficiency and "concentrated effort" and pointed to the shifting values in the churches.

Fueling these cultural shifts were economic forces that were reshaping all of American life. The importance of planning and control and the emphasis on efficiency and concentrated effort, so crucial for the rise of a modern society, were not lost in the mists of low country nostalgia. To be sure, there were those who opposed the shifts, who saw in them an end to a "South worth living for and worth dying for."[39] But the shifts came and by the 1920s they were, as we have seen, clearly reflected in the Reformed churches of the low country.

In many ways the move toward an emphasis on efficiency, planning, and control was not alien to the old Reformed impulse that sought order and feared chaos. Presbyterians, after all, had long been noted for their preoccupation with "decency and order," and the rationalism of their theology had certainly encouraged a highly structured, tightly controlled, and orderly way of looking at the world. Moreover, the new economic system that had emerged in the United States since the Civil War and that created a highly interdependent social order did not seem so far removed from the old Reformed concept of an organic society. These similarities simply help to emphasize the congruence of important impulses within the Reformed tradition with fundamental elements of modern Western society. But there were important differences, and the cultural shifts described above were significant.

The ancient organic understanding of society that had so profoundly shaped the thinking of the low country Reformed community had been based on the conviction that every person has a God-given place in society. Social order was said to reflect the "order of creation," with each person having duties and privileges that correspond to his or her place in society. But the interdependence of the new social system was based not on such organic metaphors but on the demands of efficiency. Ellison Smyth's ideal of the perfect workman in his textile towns was of a workman who possessed "a hightoned moral life, loyalty to his friends and to his employer, honesty in fulfilling his contracts and in giving full return for value received." Here the emphasis was not on an organic social order but on the demands of efficiency with its calls for standardization, cooperation, and concentrated effort. The quest for order in Ellison Smyth's mill town in 1900 might serve the same purposes as it had for his father Thomas Smyth and his uncle John Adger in the 1840s—social control and stability, the keeping at bay of chaos and anarchy.[40] But the order that was sought in 1900 was rooted in efficiency and not in natural law or a vision of an organic, God-given, hierarchical structure. Increasingly in the churches, values of good management, of know-how and administrative skills, would replace the older values of theological acumen and rectitude and the older ideals of an organic society. Moreover, the ideological function of theology was being replaced by a market ideology. No longer was there the same need for a Thomas Smyth to articulate a theology with a powerful ideological function. For his son Ellison, the market itself provided its own legitimation of power. It also provided its own utopian vision—not of a holy commonwealth, but of a society marked by unlimited growth and consumption.[41]

Closely linked to these changes was the growth of a new type of individualism suited for a consumer society. Thornwell, Smyth, Girardeau, and Adger had all fought vigorously against the rising tide of individualism that had threatened to undercut their organic understanding of society. This individualism had seemed to them both a serious threat to social order and a fundamental distortion of human nature. By the 1920s, however, there were clear signs that the low country, like the rest of the nation, was moving headlong toward an individualism whose primary values were the quest for self-fulfillment and self-expression.[42] The 1920s were, after all, not only the age of the businessman but also the jazz age with the Charleston as its dance. The efficiency of the nation's booming economic system was creating a growing demand for consumers of goods and good times. Together with the popularization of Freudian insights, a therapeutic quest for instant gratification, self-fulfillment, and unrestrained self-expression was coming into vogue. These new values were subversive of the old Reformed ethic of delayed gratification, frugality, and suppression of instinct.[43]

What these changes meant was that the white churches were slowly adopting new values and new ways to help guide them through the following decades of the twentieth century. Both the values of management and the values of therapy would play increasingly important roles in the lives of the churches.[44]

From Pastor-Theologians to Pastor-Administrators and Therapists

As might be expected in such a social/cultural context, the role of theology in the church's life was largely transformed. In earlier periods, theology—understood as a rigorous intellectual discipline and faith commitment—had been central to the church's life. Moreover, theology was called upon to serve clear ideological purposes, to legitimate the present social order and to help preserve a social identity. Such an understanding of theology's role did not suddenly disappear from the churches of the low country. On the contrary, it continued to be affirmed. But the practices of the churches suggested that theology as a rigorous intellectual discipline was moving to the edges of the church's life and that its social role was significantly weakening.

This movement could be seen most clearly in the shift of the ministers from being pastor-theologians to being pastor-administrators and pastor-therapists. Except for Girardeau and Adger (both of whom lived to the 1890s but represented an earlier generation), the ministers of Charleston Presbytery between 1876 and 1940 produced no scholarly books or articles.[45] Most striking was the contrast between the pastors of the leading churches in Charleston and their predecessors. At First (Scots), at Second, and at Westminster there were ministers between 1876 and 1940 who were highly esteemed and whose ministries saw their churches grow in numbers and activities. All were thoughtful and serious pastors, but they published nothing except an occasional devotional pamphlet or a guidebook.[46] Whatever one might think about the importance and implications of publishing scholarly works, the contrast between these pastors and the voluminous scholarly publications of their predecessors such as Alexander Hewat and Thomas Smyth is clear. Ministers were turning their energies away from scholarly pursuits and toward the administrative and therapeutic tasks needed for successful pastorates in the twentieth century.

Not writing scholarly theological works did not mean, of course, that they did not have pronounced theological perspectives or interests. On the contrary, they continued in the theological traditions of Thornwell, Adger, Smyth, and Girardeau—but they continued as those for whom it was increasingly a distant tradition, one whose lifeblood was slowly draining away. Still, they nurtured the tradition along, and it was enough to keep them somewhere in the theological middle of American Protestantism. There was little hint that they were attracted to Fundamentalism—although as Old School Presbyterians they could have easily turned in that direction. Neither, of course, did they flirt with theological liberalism. They had little confidence in the inevitability of progress or the innate goodness of the human heart. Bostonians or scholars at the University of Chicago might be able to believe such, but not pastors walking the streets of Charleston or traveling past the once prosperous fields of the low country. Their history was too different; they knew only too well the smell of defeat and the burdens of guilt that lay so deep in the psyche of Southern whites. No, the old *via media* was their way, as it had been Thornwell's and Smyth's. They did not go to what they regarded as the extremes of either Fundamentalism or liberalism, but they sought to follow the genteel path of Old School orthodoxy even as they lost interest in the particulars of its winding ways and its growing obscurity.[47] Their world view and ethos, the symbolic structure within which they understood and interpreted their world, continued to bear the marks of their Reformed tradition, but that tradition itself would be increasingly interpreted in terms of the rising bureaucratic and therapeutic culture making its way across the low country.

The white Presbyterian churches of the low country thus reflected in important ways the social and cultural history of the region during its long struggle to regain some measure of its once fabled prosperity. Their narrowed world, their changing institutional structures and organization, their often hesitant but steady move toward modern ways, their faltering interest in theology as a rigorous intellectual discipline, and their rising interest in administrative and therapeutic tasks were all part of broader movements that were slowly remaking the low country after the emerging image of the New South. Yet the churches did not simply reflect the social and cultural developments of their world. They also sought to maintain a distinct religious tradition, even as it evolved in interaction with its context. Their Reformed tradition, its world view and ethos, helped to shape the ways they understood their changing world and their reactions to it; their tradition was both a "model of" and a "model for" their little world. In such a dynamic and complex manner, their religious tradition interacted with powerful social and cultural forces that would dominate much of the New South.

17

From "Our Little World" to the Sun Belt

I F THE Civil War marked a great turning point for the low country, the Second World War also marked a great shift in its fortunes. It brought the region out of the depression and set it on the road to fundamental economic and social change. During the years that followed the Second World War, the low country's "little world" lost much of its old social coherence. The remnants of that little world—its architectural artifacts, family connections, and "quaint low country ways"—would be increasingly regarded as museum pieces and curiosities for the newcomers who came to the region in growing numbers. By 1980 the Carolina low country was becoming a part of the rising new Sun Belt, an amorphous region marked by economic growth and a population expansion that stretched from the southeastern states across the Southwest to southern California.[1]

What the Carolina low country shared with the prospering parts of the Sun Belt were great outlays of federal dollars, an attractive quality of life, a vigorous recreation and tourist industry, and popular retirement centers. Culturally, the Sun Belt was marked by a decided tendency toward hedonism and the pursuit of the "good life."[2] Not all of the low country was a part of this new Sun Belt—the interior counties continued to remain largely a part of the old rural Black Belt—but all felt the Sun Belt's rising influence.[3]

Most obvious were increases in population in the metropolitan Charleston area and in Beaufort County and changes in black-white and rural-urban ratios. Between 1940 and 1980, the population of Charleston County more than doubled, Beaufort County and Dorchester County almost tripled, and Berkeley County more than tripled. The interior rural counties showed only slight growth reflecting the continuing emigration of African Americans from the region.[4]

The African American population, which had constituted approximately 70 percent of the total population of the low country in 1880, continued its decline relative to the white population. By 1980 blacks represented only 33 percent of the combined populations of Charleston, Berkeley, and Dorchester Counties. In Beaufort County, where a hundred years earlier there had been eight blacks to every two whites, there were two whites for every black in 1980. Even in the stable interior counties, where African American populations generally continued to outnumber whites, they did so with significantly decreased percentages.[5]

This decline in the proportion of African Americans in the population both reflected and encouraged profound cultural shifts remaking the Carolina low country. Old ways—the manners and customs, the values and shared meanings that whites had nurtured for generations as means of "keeping in their place" the great black majorities that surrounded them—began to lose some of their former power and vitality. Long-standing white fears began to be eased and the way was paved for slowly improving race relations. At the same time, African Americans were able to gain some substantial advances in their civil rights while losing much of their old cultural power and demographic domination.

Ironically for the region that had long feared the power of the national government, federal dollars fueled much of the economic growth that came to the area—especially through the expansion of military bases and the interstate highway system. By 1988 the Charleston Naval Base and the Charleston Air Force Base employed more than 47,000 military and civilian personnel.[6] These bases—together with those in Beaufort—brought people from all over the country to flow in a steady and ever changing stream through the low country, helping to reshape much of the region's social landscape.[7] Perhaps of even greater significance were the bureaucracies and their values that accompanied such large-scale organizations and that inevitably penetrated and transformed much of the ethos of region.

By 1990, metropolitan Charleston stretched out approximately thirty-odd miles from the old parent city.[8] Within these larger metropolitan boundaries were towns made into suburbs, island resorts, inner city public housing projects, huge military complexes, plantation tourist attractions, and national forests. All were connected in a web of social networks—in commuters pouring down I-26 or slowly making their way across the river bridges, in telephone calls, in the links between work, play, and school, and in the other innumerable exchanges of life in a modern metropolitan area.

The old city of Charleston, with its historic areas, retained much of its former distinctiveness, but in many more ways it had become a very ordinary place, not unlike other metropolitan areas its size. What was perhaps most noticeable about Charleston was the incongruous blending of competing elements: great military complexes existed alongside a tourist industry that promoted sentimental images of the Old South; submarines loaded with nuclear missiles quietly passed in and out of the harbor, while on the beaches and in low country gardens young adults and retirees pressed their restless probe of nature for some emotional sustenance; and within the old city, "below Broad Street," a respect for the past was encouraged while the old residential area of the city increasingly took on a museumlike quality for the benefit of tourists.

In such a context the Reformed churches of the region grew substantially, changing in the process much of their character as closely knit enclaves of "old Presbyterian families" and increasingly reflecting the managerial ways and therapeutic values of the Sun Belt. Yet even as the churches reflected their changing social context, they continued to remain a part of a distinct religious tradition as it had developed in the low country. The ways in which the Reformed communities—black and white—responded to the changes sweeping over the region was informed by their religious commitments and by their memories of long-cherished values and long-established patterns of behavior. Once again, while these communities were sub-subgroups within the larger context of low country society, and while their members were influenced by the values and practices of other overlapping groups, as communities they had their own sense of identity and their own distinct traditions. An evolving Reformed world view and ethos provided a symbolic structure within which these communities interpreted and reacted to the rising tides of modernity.

The White Reformed Community

Between 1940 and 1980 the number of white Presbyterians in the low country grew at a substantially greater rate than the population as a whole. While the total population of the low country almost doubled during this period, membership in white Presbyterian churches more than tripled.[9] The patterns of this growth reflected the changing social landscape of the region, most particularly the social characteristics of many of the white newcomers.

Among white Presbyterians, most of the growth was in what came to be called the Charleston Trident Area (the tricountry area of Charleston, Berkeley, and Dorchester) and in the Beaufort-Hilton Head region. Between 1940 and 1980 nine new white Presbyterian churches were successfully established in the Trident metropolitan area, while on Hilton Head the First Presbyterian Church was well on its way to becoming the largest in the presbytery. Between 1980 and 1988 four additional new churches were organized in centers of population expansion—two in Beaufort County, one in Mount Pleasant, and one in the retirement community of Santee in Orangeburg County.[10]

This pattern of growth stood in contrast to what happened in most of the inland counties where small churches had largely clustered around a few families. In Hampton County, for example, the ancient Stoney Creek congregation, whose members had welcomed George Whitefield in the 1740s, was finally laid to rest. Its handsome church building became museumlike, a carefully maintained reminder of earlier days. In such old plantation areas, a number of congregations were quietly dissolved. There were fewer whites and few among them fit the social profile of those who found Presbyterian ways and Presbyterian theology attractive.[11]

The End of a Little World

Polls indicated that Presbyterians nationally composed by 1984 a largely affluent, well-educated, and aging church.[12] Many of those flocking to the Sun Belt region of the low country fit these social characteristics. They provided a growing pool of prospective church members whose social circumstances encouraged membership in one of the socially respectable, increasingly affluent, Presbyterian congregations of the region.[13] At the same time, young professionals also found in the low country an ethos that encouraged church membership and made the Presbyterian churches attractive to them. Unlike regions of the country where secularism had made heavy inroads among young professionals, the social conservatism of the low country limited such trends and large numbers of this social class joined certain strategically located congregations.[14]

A careful review of the session records and church rolls of eight white congregations between 1945 and 1988 provides substantial statistical information about the composition of the Presbyterian churches in the low country.[15] Approximately 10,000 adults joined these congregations during this period by transfer from another congregation. What emerges from a review of these transfers is a picture of Presbyterianism in the low country undergoing significant demographic changes. New members coming from outside South Carolina constituted 54 percent of the total, with 25 percent coming from outside the Southeast. The majority of these new members came from Presbyterian churches (69 percent), but 14 percent were Methodists, 9 percent were Baptists, 3 percent were Episcopalians, and 3 percent were Congregationalists. Clearly the "little world" of tightly knit white Presbyterian families was no longer as tightly knit as it had been for generations.[16]

That loosening of ties can also be seen in the records of the 7,350 members dismissed from these same congregations or removed from the active rolls. Almost half (49 percent) of all losses to these congregations were dismissed to churches outside South Carolina, pointing to the growing mobility of the people. The majority (52 percent) of all members lost went to other Presbyterian churches; another 15 percent went to other denominations. Most striking of all, one-third of the losses came from members placed on the inactive roll, an indication that they had stopped participating in the life of the congregations. Whatever else such an inactive status meant, it indicated that the social role of the churches had weakened as a source of identity and community. It also, no doubt, reflected the nationwide pattern of Presbyterians losing members to a growing secularism, even within the conservative cultural ethos of the low country.[17]

Women continued to constitute the majority of church members throughout the presbytery, but that majority was substantially reduced from what it had been in earlier years. From antebellum days to the 1920s, women had represented 60 to 65 percent of the church members. By the mid-1980s they constituted only 52 to 53 percent of the total membership of the churches.[18] The feminization of the church that had been such a prominent aspect of the low country since the American Revolution had significantly weakened as men constituted an increasingly large percentage of church membership. At the same time, women moved into leadership positions as their place in the church, as in society generally, underwent radical transformations.[19]

The most obvious change for women in the churches was their movement into formal leadership positions. Casting aside ancient prohibitions and the hierarchical assumptions that had informed them, the Southern Presbyterian Church in 1964 approved the ordination of women to both the ministry and the lay eldership. While elections of women to these positions came slowly at first to the low country churches, they did come. By 1980, the number of women elders (37) represented only 12 percent of the elders in the presbytery and there were no women ministers in the presbytery. By 1988, however, the number of women elders (110) had risen to 28 percent of the elders in the white churches and there were 5 white women ministers. For the churches, these developments not only meant new positions of leadership for women but also reflected and shaped, as we shall see, changes in the world view and ethos of local congregations.[20]

Two congregations are particularly revealing of the changes taking place. The Mount Pleasant Presbyterian Church—with roots that went back to the seventeenth century and the old Wappetaw congregation—had 66 members in 1945. They included among others ten members of the Seabrook family, six Royalls, clusters of Colemans and Framptons, a Lucas, and the McIver family. All of these families had long been associated with Presbyterianism in the low country and with the little village of Mount Pleasant. Many, along with other longtime members of the congregation, were "kissing-cousins"—if not to one another, then to one of the other neighboring "Presbyterian clans." By 1988 the congregation had grown to 1,090 with most of the new members coming from outside the state. The church session still included a Seabrook and a Royall, but most of the congregation's leadership was composed of those who had moved more recently to the fast-growing and prospering Mount Pleasant. Many of these newcomers were well educated and increasingly affluent and the results could be seen in the growth of professionals in the congregation from 6 percent of the membership in 1945 to 38 percent in 1985.[21]

The congregation in 1988, to be sure, retained significant continuities with its past—continuities seen most clearly in its beautiful old meetinghouse and in the number of "old families" who continued to provide important leadership in the congregation's life. But the church had moved out of the "little world" that was still lingering around the quiet streets of Mount Pleasant in 1945. The old village, with its moss-hung and history-heavy oaks, had become prime Sun Belt real estate.

If Mount Pleasant represented the social transformations overtaking a congregation with deep roots in the low country, the First Presbyterian Church of Hilton Head represented the most dramatic success story of the new Presbyterian congregations growing under the warm light of the rising Sun Belt. After the Civil War, Hilton Head Island had entered a period of isolation that eclipsed even its lonely antebellum days. The island population, almost entirely Gullah-speaking African Americans, constituted one of the most distinct and isolated subcultures in the United States until the 1950s.[22] By the end of the 1950s, however, Hilton Head was well on its way to new status as a fashionable resort and retirement community. Under the leadership of two Presbyterian families with roots deep in low country history—the Frasers and Hacks—the island was carefully but vigorously transformed from a home for poor, Gullah-speaking blacks to a home for affluent, largely Yankee-accented whites.[23] The First Presbyterian Church was the first white congregation to be established in this new context.

With its prominent association with the island developers, the First Presbyterian Church became the most influential congregation on the island for several decades. By 1980 it had a membership of 931 out of a resident population of less than 10,000. During the next eight years the island resident population doubled while the church's membership grew to 1,698 and a new Presbyterian church (Providence) quickly reached a membership of 304.[24] Clearly First Presbyterian Church, the largest and wealthiest Presbyterian congregation in the region, was a very long way from the tightly knit circles of families that had long dominated the Presbyterian churches in the low country.

The social profile of this congregation reflected both the characteristics of a Sun Belt resort/retirement community and the startling changes overtaking the region. The members carried a low country post office address, but "in terms of a religious subculture," noted a congregational consultant, the church "resembles churches located in Ohio, Pennsylvania, New York, and New Jersey more than it does the churches located on the mainland of South Carolina or Georgia." And these Presbyterians were affluent, many of the men having retired from corporate executive positions. (The newly established Providence congregation had an annual giving of almost $700,000 for a congregation of 304 members in 1988.)[25] The genteel poverty that had marked low country Presbyterians for a hundred years seemed as far away as the kissing cousins of an earlier day. Without doubt, the Sun Belt was shining in all its glory on Hilton Head.

In contrast to the shifting profile of the membership, the clergy who served the churches between 1945 and 1990, for five years or longer, continued to reflect many of the earlier patterns. While the membership of the churches was increasingly from outside the South, the clergy was increasingly Southern. Eighty-four percent of the pastors during this period came from the Southeast, a higher percentage than any previous period. Only 14 percent of the clergy received their baccalaureate degrees outside the South, much less than any previous period. Sixty-four percent graduated from one of the colleges associated with the Southern Presbyterian Church, with 45 percent graduating from one of only two colleges: Presbyterian or Davidson. Their theological education was even more restricted: 88 percent went to either Columbia (which had moved in the late 1920s to Atlanta) or to Union in Richmond.[26]

With their more indigenous backgrounds, ministers bore increased responsibility for the transmission of a religious tradition, not only because of their clerical office but also because of their own personal memories and experiences. Powerful forces were at work, however, undercutting both the coherence of that tradition and the pastors' sense of responsibility for its transmission. These forces can be seen most clearly in the shifting of values that was remaking much of congregational life.

New Pathways: The Manager and Therapist

The breakup of the "little world" of white Presbyterians in the low country was accompanied by profound shifts in the values and the ethos of the churches. Cultural changes—changes in the norms, standards, beliefs, and ideas underlying behavior—were going hand in hand with changes in the economic and social patterns of the region.

As the economic activity of the region changed, the role of large bureaucratic organizations in the communities of the low country increased. The organization of thousands of military and civilian employees called for professional managers and the creation of an environment that encouraged the smooth running of bureaucracies. Primary values required in such organizations are know-how, efficiency, and effectiveness. The managers' tasks are to persuade and inspire—and often manipulate and intimidate—those who are managed in order to ensure that the organization is run efficiently and can grow.[27]

The churches of the low country were not immune to the creation of these bureaucratic organizations and their managerial values. Together with an increased programmatic emphasis, managerial values penetrated the churches and challenged older values that were built around networks of families and friends and that were more interested in questions of "know why" than "know how."

The changes could be seen in the creation and growth of presbytery staff and the creation of increasingly complex functions and responsibilities for the presbytery. Charleston Presbytery had existed for more than two hundred years before it was felt necessary to establish a presbytery staff. In 1962, as the population and number of churches grew, the presbytery created the position of executive presbyter with a primary responsibility for "new church development" or "growth." In the next twenty-eight years the number of staff members grew, until in 1990 Charleston-Atlantic Presbytery's staff was composed of eleven paid employees.[28] They were busy with a wide range of programs that often involved numerous committees composed of approximately fifty ministers and a hundred laity. For such an organization to function smoothly, the values and practices of management were of increasing importance—goals and priorities had to be set, meetings had to be run efficiently, people had to be persuaded and inspired and programs evaluated in order for the presbytery and its functions to grow. A similar phenomenon occurred in the larger congregations where staff, programs, administrative responsibilities of pastors, and managerial values all grew in importance.

If the values of a managerial society moved forcefully into the churches and other public areas of the low country, they did so in tandem with other values that were coming to dominate much of the private areas of life and that were also rooted in a consumer-oriented technological society. A therapeutic culture, long on the horizon, was arising in the low country, no less than elsewhere in the United States. It emphasized a radical individualism and the importance of feelings, using the language of therapy to express its primary values—"health," "wholeness," "self-fulfillment," "self-expression," and "personal growth." The ancient confession "I believe" was being replaced with "I feel."[29]

This spreading culture's influence on the churches was visible, in its early stages, in the disappearance of discipline. As we have seen, congregations no longer made moral demands on their members or called—except in the most perfunctory manner—for renunciations of wayward ways. Indeed, in the years after the Second World War the perception that any way might be "wayward" began to be called into question—if not openly, at least in the actions of the churches that refused to discipline any members. In the place of such discipline came pastoral counseling and referral to the therapist, who like the manager is primarily concerned with the effectiveness of means, not ends. Commitments in marriage and in work, church, and community were becoming not so much *moral* imperatives as they had been for earlier generations but opportunities for self-fulfillment.[30]

By the 1970s the traditional language of the faith—which had informed the ways in which generations within the low country Reformed community had perceived the world and themselves in it—was under great pressure and was in danger of giving way to a new therapeutic language. Fewer and fewer members of the congregations could speak knowingly of such traditional terms as "justification" or "sanctification," nor did they often hear their ministers expound on the *doctrines* of the faith. Rather a "Christianizing" of popular psychological language was under way. The "righteous person" (so highly regarded by earlier generations but highly suspect by those of the twentieth century) was largely replaced by the "healthy personality" while the term "sinful" was giving way to "unhealthy." Behind much of this shift in language was a changing perception of truth. No longer was truth universally regarded by the ministers as propositional, as Buist, Thornwell, Smyth, and Adger had taught, but it was now increasingly viewed in relational terms. Earlier generations had been convinced that what you *believe* is important, that it shapes what you feel and how you live. If such a conviction did not disappear, it was largely overshadowed by the conviction that what is really important are your "own true feelings" and that what was essential was to "get in touch" with those feelings. Even the earlier relational emphasis on "getting right with God" began to be identified with "being your own person." Both came to be regarded as the same act of self-reliance.[31]

The practice of ministry had been significantly transformed by the impact of the changing social context of the low country and the accompanying shifts in values. Administrative and managerial skills had become requirements for success. Institutional maintenance, often on a complex and demanding level, had come to demand more and more of the minister's time. Those ministers who had administrative skills, who knew the language and shared the values of the manager, generally received the rewards of successful advancement. In both the local congregation and in the larger church, statistical and programmatic successes were generally more highly regarded than the concern of earlier generations for theological acumen.[32]

At the same time, there had been a growing emphasis on the pastoral functions of the ministry. Pastors found themselves helping individuals cope with personal difficulties of a wide variety. For resources, they turned increasingly to the skills, language, and values of the therapeutic culture—much of which was taught in their theological education.[33] What was different from the pastoral care that had long been practiced in the churches was that pastoral care in the 1970s and 1980s, informed as it was by the therapeutic value of neutrality, often lacked the intention of redirecting life, of seeking the renewal of life in the image of Christ.[34]

By the 1980s Presbyterian ministers were thus spending much more of their time administering programs and counseling people than in the work their predecessors had thought central to ministry—the transmission of ideas and articulation of theological truth.

Assertion of the Tradition

Ironically, the breakup of the local "little world" of the low country and particularly of low country Presbyterians did not lead to a larger sense of community but to *many* "little worlds." To be sure, low country society was vastly more integrated economically, technically, and functionally with the larger world. But a sense of social and cultural coherence that had long marked it as the low country seemed to be slipping away. The culture of the manager and of the therapist pointed the individual not toward some larger context of shared meanings but toward everyone's making their own little worlds, at the office and at home. In the many little worlds, increasingly little was left that was common, that allowed persons to understand themselves and their work as related in some morally comprehensible manner or that provided some shared home for those who now lived in the low country.[35]

In the midst of this changing context and its influence on the churches, the religious tradition that marked the Reformed community as Reformed did not disappear into the dark reflective waters of the contemporary low country context. On the contrary, a sustained effort by church leaders—always in a dynamic interaction with the surrounding society—asserted the theology and ethic of the Reformed tradition and sought to sustain a cohesive world view.

The traditioning of the faith, its conveyance from one generation to the next and its nurture in the life of the congregation, had meant for the Reformed community a strong emphasis on education. That emphasis grew in importance as the churches in the low country found themselves in an increasingly secular and pluralistic society. Indeed, and perhaps ironically, much of the programmatic development of the churches and the presbytery focused on education as the "little world" of low country Presbyterianism—with all of its familial props to the faith—faded. On the presbytery level, a vigorous educational program, led by an expanding staff, grew in intensity as the Sun Belt began to spread over the region. Between 1975 and 1990 an array of retreats, workshops, and "professional development events" provided courses intended to transmit the tradition. Distinguished faculty, brought from around the country, led courses for clergy and laity in the areas of biblical study, theology, ethics, and church history.[36] The well-known composer and theologian, Brian Wren of Essex, England, taught a course for clergy, music directors, and choirs on "Hymns for Worship and Theological Empowerment." Similar serious efforts were under way in local congregations—Mount Pleasant was an outstanding example under the leadership of its scholarly pastor, James Lowry.[37] In addition, some pastors gave considerable attention to an analysis and critique of the dominant culture in light of the Reformed tradition. At Westminster, for example, the senior pastor, Robert Dunham, completed a graduate degree at Yale with a thesis on "The Self and Its Potential: Theological Considerations" in which he sought to analyze and challenge many of the assumptions of the therapeutic culture.[38] To be sure, such efforts were confronted by the massive influence of the surrounding culture whose values had been absorbed in varying degrees by the churches. Nevertheless, within the churches there could be discerned a concerted struggle to articulate and live out—in contrast to the values of the Sun Belt—an alternative vision of life.

Those congregations with a clear sense of identity, that nurtured in their members a memory and a commitment to a distinct religious tradition and that used those resources to both critique and be at ministry in the dominant culture, were largely the congregations that showed steady growth and significant intellectual leadership in the presbytery. Together with vigorous leadership from the presbytery staff, they largely accounted for the presbytery's being the second fastest growing in the nation in the late 1980s.[39]

The African American Churches

While African Americans lost their commanding position as a major percentage of the low country's general population during these years, they nevertheless showed some substantial population gains, especially in Charleston and Beaufort Counties.[40] The number of African American Presbyterians also grew between 1940 and 1980 but slowly, showing only a 10 percent growth, a rate far below that of the African American population. Five churches were closed during this period, but more revealing was the absence of any new congregations in the midst of the region's growing African American population and rising black middle class. The pattern that had appeared clear in 1940 was even clearer in 1990: only those African American Presbyterian congregations with roots deep in antebellum, and even colonial, history were able to thrive in the low country. All of the congregations by 1990 represented long-established African American communities that had origins in the slave congregations, the "church within a church," that had existed for generations within the white-dominated churches.[41] The continuities within these congregations, their social coherence, and their role in the larger community can be seen in a social profile of their members.

The "little world" of Presbyterian families that was breaking up in the white Presbyterian churches continued to dominate the African American Presbyterian congregations of the region. Most obvious were the networks of closely connected families that continued to provide much of the membership of the churches. Often these families extended beyond one congregation with branches providing leadership in neighboring Presbyterian churches. On Edisto, for example, there were Campbells, Bligens, and Johnsons on the session in 1970 as there had been Campbells, Bligens, and Johnsons in 1906. With them in 1970 were a Washington, a Whaley, a Wood, a Gadsden, and a Spears, family names long prominent in the congregation and in other Presbyterian churches of the low country.[42] At Saint James Presbyterian, the Richardsons were related by marriages between 1940 and 1970 to the Chisolm, Watson, Smalls, Whaley, Brown, Middleton, and Chavis families, all of whom were members of the same

Saint James congregation.[43] Similar networks were evident in the other churches, emphasizing their social cohesion and their continuity with earlier patterns.

In contrast to the increasing percentage of male members in the white congregations, men continued in the African American churches to be a significant minority. In 1988, men represented only 35 percent of the African American Presbyterians in the low country. Because the African American congregations had been a part of the "Northern" Presbyterian Church, African American Presbyterian women had the right of ordination as elders and the opportunity for official leadership in their churches for thirty years before their Southern white sisters. By 1988, African American women represented 57 percent of the African American elders in the low country. In two of the small congregations they were the only elders, and in Saint James, by far the largest of the congregations, women constituted 70 percent of the elders.[44]

The continued numerical dominance of women in these congregations, together with the growing numbers of women elders, inevitably contributed to the character of the congregations. The experience and concerns of black women—more specifically, African American Presbyterian women in the low country—found strong expression in congregational life. Their experience was part of the long history of African Americans in a racist and oppressive society that had done much to break down African American families and that had long tried to make "boys" of black males and matriarchs of black women. The maintenance of close family ties and networks, the nurture of the young, and the support of strong male leadership—in particular strong male pastors—consequently continued as important characteristics of these congregations.[45]

The membership of the African American congregations during this period also reflected the characteristics associated with the Reformed tradition as a social and religious phenomenon. Indeed, the social profile of the members indicated the ways in which the values and ethos of an African American Reformed tradition—faithfully nurtured for generations—helped to shape the nature of a distinct, socially cohesive community in the low country. A careful investigation of the members of the Zion-Olivet congregation points to the power of a religious tradition, in interaction with a particular sociohistorical context, to create a social identity and perhaps even a destiny.

In 1978, college graduates composed 21 percent of the adult active membership of Zion-Olivet. This number placed them below the national percentage for Presbyterians (25 percent) but above the national percentage for Methodists (12 percent), Lutherans (12 percent), Catholics (12 percent), and white Southern Baptists (6 percent). Among African American Protestants, they were also substantially above other groups.[46] Reflecting the long-standing Presbyterian emphasis on education, there were thirty-one teachers, five principals, two librarians, one school counselor, and two teachers' aides among approximately 190 active adult members of Zion-Olivet. Physicians, nurses, funeral directors, postal workers, and a wide variety of local business people were well represented in the congregation, as were a number of skilled laborers.[47]

Similar educational and occupational patterns, with local variations, were evident in the other low country Presbyterian churches and at Charleston's Plymouth Congregational.[48] Saint Luke in Orangeburg, for example, was well known in the African American community of Orangeburg as a congregation that drew much of its membership from faculty and staff of the South Carolina State College.[49] Even rural congregations, whose histories were largely isolated from the influences of strong educational institutions, reflected the power of a religious tradition to influence educational and occupational patterns. Saint Paul on Yonges Island, for example, a rural African American congregation in the midst of the old Gullah region, was solidly middle class in its social profile.[50]

These African American congregations continued to draw many of their ministers from the Presbyterian families of the region, including the Presbyterian enclave around Sumter. Familiar names point to the continuities, but what was most striking was the length of many of their pastorates—in contrast to the growing mobility and short pastorates of white ministers in the region.[51] William L. Metz completed in 1949 a thirty-three-year ministry on Edisto. His son, Perry Metz, retired in 1983 after a thirty-nine-year pastorate at Olivet and then Zion-Olivet. The pastorates of these and other long-serving ministers, together with the family connections that many of them had in the region, encouraged a conservative and stable congregational life among their churches.[52]

These pastors developed—to a remarkable extent, given the small size of their Presbyterian constituencies—significant leadership roles in the larger African American communities. Ferdinand Pharr was president of the Charleston branch of the National Association for the Advancement of Colored People during the "Charleston movement" of 1963.[53] On Edisto Island, the newly arrived pastor McKinley Washington organized in 1964 a branch of the NAACP and was soon leading a successful voter registration drive. Others played similar roles as the civil rights movement broke over the low country.[54]

With the Civil Rights Act of 1964 and the Voting Rights Act of 1965, African Americans were able to register to vote in large numbers, and they sent Robert Woods, pastor of Wallingford, to the state legislature where he served for fourteen years. McKinley Washington was elected in 1974 to the legislature for the house district covering Johns, Wadmalaw, and Edisto Islands. In 1990 Washington was elected to the state senate.

The social profile that thus emerges during this period reveals striking continuities with earlier profiles of African American Presbyterians and Congregationalists in the low country. They composed a tightly knit community, a "little world" of friends and family that had not experienced the breakup and expansion that had largely remade white Presbyterianism in the region. They continued their leadership roles in their communities to a disproportionate degree given their small numbers, providing particularly strong educational and political leaders. With an impressive educational level, they reflected the successes of the school systems established by the Presbyterians and Congregationalists after the Civil War and the continuing emphasis on education that had been nurtured in their churches.

Despite the social position of the African American Presbyterian churches, they had not been able by 1990 to attract many new African Americans moving into the professions and the middle class. Familiar and comfortable patterns of organization and informal authority structures appeared well established and were apparently hard to break. A general reluctance to reach beyond "Presbyterian families" was indicated by the absence of any significant growth since 1945.[55]

These African American churches, with their strong sense of identity, their educational standards, and leadership positions in their communities, were, however, ready to meet the challenges of uniting in the 1980s with the white Presbyterians of the region. The challenges included questions of power, wealth, racial bias, and profoundly different historical experiences and perspectives. But what was to be surprising to blacks and whites alike was how much they shared in common after 120 years of separation.

Reunion

The move toward the union of the white Charleston Presbytery and the black Atlantic Presbytery came as the result of the union of the "Northern" United Presbyterian Church and the "Southern" Presbyterian Church in the United States and larger social changes. The years that followed 1945 had seen the slow crumbling of the old system of segregation in the South. These events were greeted by low country whites with anger and determined opposition if eventual acceptance.[56] A similar pattern was evident in the white Presbyterian churches.

When the U.S. Supreme Court ruled in 1954 that "in the field of public education the doctrine of 'separate but equal' has no place," the General Assembly of the Southern Presbyterian Church, meeting ten days later, commended the principle of the Supreme Court's decision and urged its members to aid those charged with its implementation.[57] The reaction in the white churches of the low country was decidedly different. The Johns Island session postponed the construction of a new educational building "while it further studies the possible effects of the Assembly's action on segregation."[58] The Westminster session protested "that it is not our responsibility to undo that which God hath done, by amalgamating the races as non-segregation would lead to.[59]

In its resolution against a "non-segregated church," the Westminster session also went on record opposing union with "Northern" Presbyterians. The General Assembly that had commended the principle of the Supreme Court's decision also had voted for union with "Northern Presbyterians." In the minds of many white Presbyterians in the South, the "race issue" and the "union issue" became inextricably bound up with one another. When the "Plan of Union" was sent to the presbyteries the next year for their consent, it was defeated. Charleston Presbytery voted overwhelmingly against the union. Almost thirty years later, when a vote for union came before the presbyteries once again, Charleston Presbytery, through the leadership of pastors such as J. Phillips Noble of First (Scots), voted for union. The difference between those two votes reflected the breakup of the "little world" that had so long marked white Presbyterians in the region.[60] Perhaps most remarkably, in contrast to other parts of the South, no congregation within Charleston Presbytery withdrew from the denomination as a result of the reunion.[61]

For its part, the black Atlantic Presbytery also voted in favor of the union, although it did so with some genuine reservations. African American Presbyterians of the low country had their own keen sense of identity and experience of independence, and they had no interest in being treated in a paternalistic fashion by the wealthier and more numerous whites. What they wanted were guarantees that their traditions, experiences, and voices would be well represented and respected. To ensure representation, they secured, working with other African American Presbyterians in the South, "minority" provisions in the Plan of Union. Among these provisions were guarantees in regard to representation in the presbytery, its committees, and its commissions. Once union was accomplished, the new Presbytery of Charleston-Atlantic was organized in ways that sought to ensure a genuine mutuality and power sharing between blacks and whites.[62]

The Presbyterians of the low country who came together in the 1980s to work out the agreements of their reunion discovered that although they did not know much about one another, they had much in common. In spite of their clear differences, in spite of the fact that one had been an oppressor race and the other a part of an oppressed people, they shared an elusive style and a commitment to doing things decently and in order. Moreover, they shared a polity that had largely shaped their institutional lives, a religious tradition (however much it was buffeted by winds of change), and an ethic that helped to create important similarities in their social profiles. Issues of power and race remained. White congregations remained white, and African American congregations remained black, with only a few individuals crossing these lines.[63] Racism and racial tensions did not go away, only now it was not so much a low country accent that marked them as it was a national language and mood.

Perhaps the greatest surprise came to those white Presbyterians who represented important remnants of a little low country world, who remembered

Leaders at the time of the 1983 Reunion
Clockwise, from below, left: McKinley Washington, Jr., Pastor, Edisto Presbyterian Church; Barry D. Van Deventer, Executive Presbyter, Charleston Presbytery; Ferdinand O. Pharr, Executive Presbyter, Atlantic Presbytery (all courtesy of Charleston-Atlantic Presbytery, Charleston, S.C.); J. Phillips Noble, Pastor First (Scots) Presbyterian Church (courtesy of J. Phillips Noble)

when most white Presbyterian congregations were made up of tight networks of families and shared values. What these white Presbyterians found were African Americans who knew that world, who still maintained in their own congregations a life that, while being in many ways fundamentally different from the fading "little world" of whites, was also surprisingly similar. To be sure, this world of African American Presbyterians reflected the deep waters of the African American experience and the long struggle against white oppression. But it also echoed with many of the ways once cherished by whites of the low country before the dawning of the Sun Belt—the family ties, the sense of identity that comes from being a part of a congregation, and the memory of place and of a people. Perhaps it was this echo—this shared history and memory in the midst of the social changes that had swept over the low country—together with shared religious commitments that helped blacks and whites of goodwill struggle to seek a more just basis for their new life together.

Imagining a New World

By 1990 reunion and a transformed social context had brought into sharp focus the fundamental questions of this study—the Reformed community's complex relationship to its context and its place in low country society. What social and cultural imagination would mark the community as it entered the twenty-first century? What symbolic system, frame of reference and meaningfulness, would shape its interpretation and reaction to the transformed low country world of which it was so much a part?

Certainly that world in 1990 was more pluralistic and secular than anything the community had known before in its history. In earlier times, when there had been for whites the possibility of imagining a low country world as "our Southern Zion," as a part of a holy commonwealth, as reflecting an organic society hierarchically structured, the white Reformed community had served in its life and thought important ideological functions. Through its paternalistic language and behavior it had acted to distort and hide the harsh realities of low country life and to legitimize the power and authority of whites. Moreover, it had been an important means of integration and social identity within its own "little world." These ideological functions, while not absent in 1990, had been largely taken over by secular forces. The question was consequently being forced upon the community more sharply than ever before in its history—what vision of the future informed and shaped the community's social and cultural imagination? As the community's ideological role diminished, as the community's responsibility to justify the existing system of power in the low country faded, it appeared to have greater freedom to imagine alternatives, greater freedom for its sons and daughters to prophesy, for its old to dream dreams, and for its young to see visions.

The growing pluralism and secularization of society had, in other words, provided the community an opportunity to imagine a new world. That its imagining would be projections from within its own concrete sociocultural reality was all too clear from its history. But such imaginings would not have to be simply "models of" society—they could also be "models for" society, conceptions of the way things ought to be. Drawing on rich theological and cultural traditions—and perhaps especially an African American Reformed tradition that was forged between two worlds—a coherent vision could provide the community a new identity and new pathways to the future. Certainly the community's own shared tradition confessed "*Ecclesia Reformata, Sed Semper Reformanda*"—"The Church Reformed, but always being reformed."

Sunbelt Churches
Above: Sunrise Presbyterian Church, Sullivan's Island (courtesy of Sunrise Presbyterian Church, Sullivan's Island, S.C.). *Below*: First Presbyterian Church, Hilton Head Island (courtesy of First Presbyterian Church, Hilton Head Island, S.C.)

APPENDIX A

Three Centuries of Reformed Congregations and Institutions in the Carolina Low Country (1685–1985)

Compiled by Joseph B. Martin III

HISTORICAL INFORMATION FOR the churches and other institutions listed here may be found in "A Guide to Presbyterian Ecclesiastical Names and Places in South Carolina, 1685–1985," *South Carolina Historical Magazine* 90, nos. 1–2 (January–April 1989): 4–212, and in additions and corrections scheduled for publication in the same magazine in 1993–94.

In general, the dates indicated for each church begin with the date of organization and affiliation with a presbyterial association. In some cases, a Reformed congregation's existence predates any such affiliation, and the founding date recognized by the congregation is the date accepted here. Reference to "present" indicates that the organization was still active as of 1985. Presbyterial affiliation is generally straightforward but is sometimes hybrid, sporadic, or unclear. More detailed information about dates and affiliations may be found in the "Guide" (cited above) along with principal historical sources for each church.

Changes in county lines and actual moves of churches have resulted in certain churches being resident over time in multiple counties; churches are listed here by their location in a county defined by 1988 boundaries. The counties included are those that constituted Charleston-Atlantic Presbytery at its organization in 1988.

Congregations and Schools

Allendale County

ALLENDALE PRESBYTERIAN CHURCH, ALLENDALE (1878–present). Charleston and Charleston-Atlantic Presbyteries.
HARDEN ACADEMY, ALLENDALE (1898–1933). Atlantic and McClelland Presbyteries.

SECOND PRESBYTERIAN CHURCH, ALLENDALE (1905–31). Atlantic and Mc-Clelland Presbyteries.

Bamberg County

BAMBERG PRESBYTERIAN CHURCH, BAMBERG (1895–present). Charleston and Charleston-Atlantic Presbyteries.

DENMARK PRESBYTERIAN CHURCH, DENMARK (1894–present). Charleston and Charleston-Atlantic Presbyteries.

FRASIER EXCELSIOR SCHOOL, BAMBERG (1916–c.1930). Atlantic Presbytery.

ZION'S HILL PRESBYTERIAN CHURCH, BAMBERG (1923–39). Atlantic Presbytery.

Barnwell County

BARNWELL PRESBYTERIAN CHURCH, BARNWELL (1840–present; perhaps founded as early as 1832—certainly a preaching point from that time). Charleston and Charleston-Atlantic Presbyteries (and perhaps Charleston Union 1840–1852).

BOILING SPRINGS PRESBYTERIAN CHURCH, BARNWELL (1842–present; a preaching point from 1820; combined with Barnwell Presbyterian Church about 1851; reorganized as a separate church in 1896). Sometimes known as Second Presbyterian of Boiling Springs after the 1896 reorganization. Charleston and Charleston-Atlantic Presbyteries.

BRIGGS MEMORIAL PRESBYTERIAN CHURCH, BLACKVILLE (1893–1968). Known before c.1940 as Blackville Presbyterian Church. Charleston Presbytery.

EMMERSON INDUSTRIAL INSTITUTE, BLACKVILLE (c.1885–1933). Atlantic and McClelland Presbyteries.

EMMERSON PRESBYTERIAN CHURCH, BLACKVILLE (c.1915–40). Atlantic and McClelland Presbyteries.

SAINT BARTHOLOMEWS CHURCH, BARNWELL (or Colleton?) COUNTY (c.1790s). German Reformed and Lutheran congregation on the Salkehatchie River.

WILLISTON PRESBYTERIAN CHURCH, WILLISTON (1920–present). Charleston and Charleston-Atlantic Presbyteries.

Beaufort County

BEAUFORT ACADEMY, BEAUFORT (1882–c.1925). Atlantic Presbytery.

BEAUFORT SALEM PRESBYTERIAN CHURCH, YEMASSEE (1870–present). Successor to Salem Colored Presbyterian Church, a chapel of Stoney Creek Church (in Hampton County) as early as 1828. Charleston, Atlantic, and Charleston-Atlantic Presbyteries.

BEREAN PRESBYTERIAN CHURCH, BEAUFORT (1884–1931). Atlantic Presbytery.

BLUFFTON INSTITUTE, BLUFFTON (1877–79; possibly established along with a mission c.1868 by the New School's South Carolina Presbytery). Atlantic Presbytery.

FIRST PRESBYTERIAN CHURCH, BEAUFORT (before 1756–present; inactive after the Revolution, independent 1803–83, dissolved 1908, and reorganized 1912). Also known as Beaufort Independent and as Beaufort Presbyterian. Congregational Association of South Carolina; Charleston, Charleston Union, and Charleston-Atlantic Presbyteries.

FIRST PRESBYTERIAN CHURCH, BEAUFORT (1886–88). Atlantic Presbytery.

FIRST PRESBYTERIAN CHURCH, HILTON HEAD (1957–present). Charleston and Charleston-Atlantic Presbyteries.

HILTON HEAD PRESBYTERIAN CHURCH, HILTON HEAD (1982–present). Calvary and Palmetto Presbyteries.

LINDEN PRESBYTERIAN CHURCH, BLUFFTON (1870s). Listed 1870 in South Carolina (New School) Presbytery as a mission (and also in 1869 by location only). Listed 1880 in Atlantic Presbytery as College Presbyterian Church.

PORT ROYAL CONGREGATIONS. French Protestant Huguenot settlement (1562–65); Church of Scotland (as Stuart-Town, 1683–86); subsequent congregation reported to Synod of New York and Philadelphia as vacant in 1767.

PORT ROYAL PRESBYTERIAN CHURCH, PORT ROYAL (1881–1908). Charleston Presbytery.

PROVIDENCE PRESBYTERIAN CHURCH, HILTON HEAD (1986–present). Charleston and Charleston-Atlantic Presbyteries.

TRINITY PRESBYTERIAN CHURCH, BEAUFORT COUNTY (c.1909–13). Atlantic Presbytery.

Berkeley County

BELLE ISLE PRESBYTERIAN CHURCH, PINEVILLE (1981–present; a Sunday school mission from 1951). Harmony and New Harmony Presbyteries.

CAINHOY PRESBYTERIAN CHURCH, BERKELEY COUNTY (before 1728–c.1810). Also known as the Saint Thomas congregation and as "the Old Ruins." Congregational Association of South Carolina and Charleston Presbytery.

FIRST PRESBYTERIAN CHURCH, MONCKS CORNER (1944–present). Also known as Moncks Corner Presbyterian Church. Charleston and Charleston-Atlantic Presbyteries.

FRENCH PROTESTANT HUGUENOT CHURCH OF ORANGE QUARTER (c.1686–1706). Affiliated with Church of England (as Saint Denis Church) in 1706, independent c.1718–c.1726.

FRENCH PROTESTANT HUGUENOT CHURCH OF SAINT JOHNS BERKELEY (c.1700–1706). Affiliated with Church of England in 1706, with sporadic presbyterial affiliations until the Revolution.

PEACE PRESBYTERIAN CHURCH, GOOSE CREEK (1962–present). Founded as Goose Creek Presbyterian Church; name changed 1986. Charleston and Charleston-Atlantic Presbyteries.

SAINT STEPHEN PRESBYTERIAN CHURCH, SAINT STEPHEN (1950–present; a preaching point from 1920). Harmony and New Harmony Presbyteries.

YEAMANS PARK PRESBYTERIAN CHURCH, HANAHAN (1955–present). Charleston and Charleston-Atlantic Presbyteries.

Calhoun County

FORT MOTTE PRESBYTERIAN CHURCH, FORT MOTTE (1888–1900, 1916–39).
Charleston and Congaree Presbyteries.

MOUNT NEBO PRESBYTERIAN CHURCH, LONE STAR (1897–1950). Also known
as Nebo Presbyterian Church. Atlantic Presbytery.

SAINT MATTHEWS PRESBYTERIAN CHURCH, SAINT MATTHEWS (1906–
present). Charleston, Congaree, Calvary, and Palmetto Presbyteries.

Charleston County

ANSON STREET PRESBYTERIAN CHURCH, CHARLESTON (1854–58; a chapel
of Second Presbyterian Church from 1850). Succeeded by Zion Church. Charleston
Presbytery.

ARCHDALE STREET CHURCH, CHARLESTON (1773–1817). A collegiate church
of the Circular Church, Archdale Street became a separate church in 1817, subsequently Unitarian. Harmony Presbytery (1815–17 only).

BETHEL PRESBYTERIAN CHURCH, JOHNS ISLAND (c.1875–present). Atlantic
and Charleston-Atlantic Presbyteries.

CENTRAL PRESBYTERIAN CHURCH, CHARLESTON (1823–82). Founded as
Third Presbyterian Church; name changed 1852. Merged 1882 with Zion-Glebe
Street to form Westminster Presbyterian Church. Charleston Union and Charleston
Presbyteries.

CHARLESTON MISSION, CHARLESTON (c.1866–77). Founded as First African or
First Colored Church. South Carolina (New School) and Atlantic Presbyteries.

CHURCH CREEK REFORMED PRESBYTERIAN CHURCH, CHARLESTON
(1972–present). Founded as Charleston Reformed Presbyterian Church; name
changed 1978. Southeast, Calvary, and Palmetto Presbyteries.

CIRCULAR CONGREGATIONAL CHURCH, CHARLESTON (1681–present).
Also known as the Independent Church of Charleston, the White Meeting
and (very early in its history) the Presbyterian Church of Charleston. Congrega-
tional Association of South Carolina; Charleston Union, Charleston, Atlantic, and
Charleston-Atlantic Presbyteries (the last two as a Union church with the United
Church of Christ).

COMMUNITY PRESBYTERIAN CHURCH, CHARLESTON (1921–26). Charleston Presbytery.

COVENANT PRESBYTERIAN CHURCH, CHARLESTON (1964–70). Merged into Westminster Presbyterian Church in 1970. Charleston Presbytery.

EDISTO ISLAND PRESBYTERIAN CHURCH, EDISTO ISLAND (c.1690–present). Charleston, Charleston Union, and Charleston-Atlantic Presbyteries.

EDISTO PRESBYTERIAN CHURCH, EDISTO ISLAND (1865–present). Also
known as Edisto Island Presbyterian and as First Colored Presbyterian. Atlantic
and Charleston-Atlantic Presbyteries.

FELLOWSHIP PRESBYTERIAN CHURCH, CHARLESTON HEIGHTS (1952–
present). Charleston and Charleston-Atlantic Presbyteries.

FIRST (SCOTS) PRESBYTERIAN CHURCH, CHARLESTON (1731–present).
Also known as Scotch Presbyterian Church or Scots Kirk. Edinburgh, Charleston,
Charleston Union, and Charleston-Atlantic Presbyteries.

FOURTH PRESBYTERIAN CHURCH, CHARLESTON (1876–1903). Founded as Ebenezer Presbyterian Church; name changed 1899. Charleston Presbytery.

FRENCH PROTESTANT HUGUENOT CHURCH, CHARLESTON (1687–present). An independent church, although several of its ministers were affiliated with Charleston Presbytery.

FRENCH PROTESTANT HUGUENOT CHURCH OF GOOSE CREEK (c.1680–c.1706). Members affiliated with Church of England after 1706.

FRENCH PROTESTANT HUGUENOT CHURCH OF SANTEE, JAMESTOWN (1686–1706). Affiliated with Church of England in 1706. Also known as Santee Church.

GLEBE STREET PRESBYTERIAN CHURCH, CHARLESTON (1847–c.1870). Merged c.1870 with Zion Presbyterian Church, Charleston, to form Zion-Glebe Street Presbyterian Church. Charleston Presbytery.

HARBOR VIEW PRESBYTERIAN CHURCH, CHARLESTON (1968–present). Charleston and Charleston-Atlantic Presbyteries.

HEBRON PRESBYTERIAN CHURCH, JOHNS ISLAND (c.1875–present). Atlantic and Charleston-Atlantic Presbyteries.

HERITAGE PRESBYTERIAN CHURCH, MOUNT PLEASANT (1984–present). Charleston and Charleston-Atlantic Presbyteries.

ISLE OF PALMS PRESBYTERIAN CHURCH, ISLE OF PALMS (1959–62). Charleston Presbytery.

JAMES ISLAND PRESBYTERIAN CHURCH, JAMES ISLAND (1706–present). Also known as the Independent Church on James Island. Congregational Association of South Carolina; Charleston and Charleston-Atlantic Presbyteries (also South Carolina, Second South Carolina, Harmony, and Charleston Union Presbyteries through its ministers).

JEREMY CREEK REFORMED PRESBYTERIAN CHURCH, McCLELLAN-VILLE (1979–83). Southeast and Calvary Presbyteries.

JOHNS ISLAND PRESBYTERIAN CHURCH, JOHNS ISLAND (1710–present). Also known as the Independent Church of Johns Island and as the Presbyterian Church of Johns Island and Wadmalaw. Congregational Association of South Carolina; Charleston, South Carolina, Second South Carolina, Harmony, Charleston Union, and Charleston-Atlantic Presbyteries.

KNOX PRESBYTERIAN CHURCH, CHARLESTON (1914–25). Merged into Westminster Presbyterian Church in 1925. Charleston Presbytery.

LARIMER HIGH SCHOOL, EDISTO ISLAND (c.1865–1955). Originally called Hope School. Atlantic Presbytery.

MARINER'S CHAPEL (OR CHURCH), CHARLESTON (1884–98; reported sporadically from about 1822, often as Seaman's Chapel or Bethel Union or the Port Society—possibly different sites or missions). Charleston Presbytery.

MARY A. STEELE MEMORIAL SCHOOL, JOHNS ISLAND (1917–33). Atlantic Presbytery.

MOUNT PLEASANT PRESBYTERIAN CHURCH, MOUNT PLEASANT (1870–present; before 1870 a chapel of Wappetaw Church, through which it traces its history to 1697). Charleston and Charleston-Atlantic Presbyteries. (Also see Zion Presbyterian Church, Mount Pleasant.)

NEW WAPPETAW PRESBYTERIAN CHURCH, McCLELLANVILLE (1872–present; from 1869, a preaching point and successor to Wappetaw Independent Congregational Church, through which it traces its history to 1697). Also known as McClellanville Presbyterian. Charleston and Charleston-Atlantic Presbyteries.

NORTH CHARLESTON PRESBYTERIAN CHURCH, NORTH CHARLESTON (1921–25). Charleston Presbytery.

OLIVET PRESBYTERIAN CHURCH, CHARLESTON (1879–1959; a chapel of Wallingford Presbyterian Church before 1879). Merged 1959 with Zion Presbyterian Church to form Zion-Olivet. Atlantic Presbytery.

PARK CIRCLE PRESBYTERIAN CHURCH, NORTH CHARLESTON (1941–present). Founded as Cosgrove Avenue Presbyterian Church; name changed 1948. Charleston and Charleston-Atlantic Presbyteries.

RIVERS CHAPEL PRESBYTERIAN CHURCH, EDISTO ISLAND (1880–1963). Founded as Deem Presbyterian Church; name changed 1883. Atlantic Presbytery.

ROCKVILLE PRESBYTERIAN CHURCH, ROCKVILLE (1909–present; a chapel of Johns Island Presbyterian Church from about 1710). (See Wadmalaw Island Presbyterian Church.) Charleston and Charleston-Atlantic Presbyteries.

SAINT ANDREWS PRESBYTERIAN CHURCH, CHARLESTON (flourished about 1814 with dissident members of First [Scots] Church). Charleston Presbytery (?).

SAINT ANDREWS PRESBYTERIAN CHURCH, CHARLESTON (1944–present). Charleston and Charleston-Atlantic Presbyteries.

SAINT ANDREWS PRESBYTERIAN CHURCH, JOHNS ISLAND (c.1870–present). Buleau was a variant name. Atlantic and Charleston-Atlantic Presbyteries.

SAINT JAMES PAROCHIAL SCHOOL, JAMES ISLAND (c.1926–61; perhaps operated as early as 1865). Atlantic Presbytery.

SAINT JAMES PRESBYTERIAN CHURCH, JAMES ISLAND (c.1870–present). Founded as James Island Presbyterian Church; name changed c.1920. Atlantic and Charleston-Atlantic Presbyteries.

SAINT PAUL PRESBYTERIAN CHURCH, YONGES ISLAND (c.1870–present). Atlantic and Charleston-Atlantic Presbyteries.

SALEM PRESBYTERIAN CHURCH, WADMALAW ISLAND (c.1870–present). Charleston, Atlantic, and Charleston-Atlantic Presbyteries.

SECOND PRESBYTERIAN CHURCH, CHARLESTON (1809–present). Harmony, Charleston Union, Charleston, and Charleston-Atlantic Presbyteries.

SHAW SCHOOL, CHARLESTON (1870s). Sponsored by the New England Freedmen's Aid Commission and affiliated with Charleston Mission.

SUNRISE PRESBYTERIAN CHURCH, SULLIVAN'S ISLAND (1953–present). Founded as Sullivan's Island Presbyterian; name changed 1976. Charleston and Charleston-Atlantic Presbyteries.

WADMALAW ISLAND PRESBYTERIAN CHURCH, WADMALAW ISLAND (c.1793). Sometimes recorded as a separate church, but considered by George Howe in his *History of the Presbyterian Church in South Carolina*, vol. 1 (Columbia: W. J. Duffie, 1883) as a single church by 1810 with Johns Island (or as a chapel of Johns Island): "The Presbyterian Church of Johns Island and Wadmalaw Island." Whether Wadmalaw Island was a separate church or branch of Johns Island before that time is unclear. Predecessor of Rockville Presbyterian Church.

WALLINGFORD ACADEMY, CHARLESTON (c.1868–1933). Atlantic Presbytery.

WALLINGFORD PRESBYTERIAN CHURCH, CHARLESTON (1867–present; before 1867 a Sunday school mission of Zion Presbyterian Church, Charleston). Founded as Siloam Presbyterian Church; name changed 1870. Atlantic and Charleston-Atlantic Presbyteries.

WANDO ASSOCIATE REFORMED PRESBYTERIAN CHURCH, MOUNT PLEASANT (1978–83). Founded as Mount Pleasant Associate Reformed Presbyterian Church, a mission of Catawba Presbytery; name changed 1980. Dissolved as a mission 1983.

WAPPETAW INDEPENDENT CONGREGATIONAL CHURCH, McCLELLANVILLE (c.1700–c.1865). Also known as Christ Church congregation and Wappetaw Independent Presbyterian Church. Succeeded by Mount Pleasant Presbyterian Church (1870) and New Wappetaw Presbyterian Church (1872). Congregational Association of South Carolina; Charleston, Charleston Union, and Harmony Presbyteries.

WESTMINSTER PRESBYTERIAN CHURCH, CHARLESTON (1823–present). Founded as Third Presbyterian Church; subsequently known as Central Presbyterian Church (from c.1850), United Zion and Central Churches (1882); renamed Westminster in 1983. Charleston Union, Charleston, and Charleston-Atlantic Presbyteries.

WHALEY MEMORIAL PRESBYTERIAN CHURCH, EDISTO ISLAND (1908–32). Atlantic Presbytery.

ZION–GLEBE STREET PRESBYTERIAN CHURCH, CHARLESTON (c.1869–82). Formed as merger between Zion Presbyterian Church (founded 1858) and Glebe Street Presbyterian Church (founded 1847) and known as Zion Church on Glebe Street; merged 1882 with Central Presbyterian Church to form Westminster Presbyterian Church. Charleston Presbytery.

ZION-OLIVET PRESBYTERIAN CHURCH, CHARLESTON (1959–present). Founded in merger of Zion Presbyterian Church (founded 1858) and Olivet Presbyterian Church (founded 1879). Atlantic and Charleston-Atlantic Presbyteries.

ZION PRESBYTERIAN CHURCH, CHARLESTON (1858–1959). Successor to Anson Street Presbyterian Church. Also known as Zion–Calhoun Street. White members merged about 1869 with Glebe Street Presbyterian Church to form Zion–Glebe Street. Black members merged 1959 with Olivet Presbyterian Church to form Zion-Olivet. Charleston and Atlantic Presbyteries.

ZION PRESBYTERIAN CHURCH, JOHNS ISLAND (c.1870–present). Atlantic and Charleston-Atlantic Presbyteries.

ZION PRESBYTERIAN CHURCH, MOUNT PLEASANT (c.1878–1950). Founded as Mount Pleasant Presbyterian Church; name changed 1908. Atlantic Presbytery.

(Also see Calvary and Faith Presbyterian Churches listed in Colleton County.)

Colleton County

AIMWELL PRESBYTERIAN CHURCH, WALTERBORO (1870–present). Founded with a second site, Young Bethel Church at Glover. Charleston, Atlantic, and Charleston-Atlantic Presbyteries.

BETHEL PRESBYTERIAN CHURCH, WALTERBORO (1728–present). Founded as Bethel Presbyterian Church on Pon Pon in Saint Bartholomew's Parish. Established summer chapel in 1921 at Walterboro, which became its principal place of worship by 1832. Name changed c.1835 to Walterboro Presbyterian Church and again in 1926 to Bethel Presbyterian Church, Walterboro. Also known as Bethel Pon Pon, Jacksonborough congregation, and Saint Bartholomew's congregation. Edinburgh, Charleston, and Charleston-Atlantic Presbyteries.

CALVARY PRESBYTERIAN CHURCH, ADAM'S RUN (c.1875–c.1922). Atlantic Presbytery. (Possibly in Charleston County.)

CORINTH PRESBYTERIAN CHURCH, WALTERBORO (1891–1966). Charleston Presbytery.

FAITH PRESBYTERIAN CHURCH, ADAM'S RUN (1894–1969). Atlantic Presbytery. (Possibly in Charleston County.)

HOPEWELL PRESBYTERIAN CHURCH, WALTERBORO (1871–present). Charleston, Atlantic, and Charleston-Atlantic Presbyteries.

NEW CALVARY PRESBYTERIAN CHURCH, WHITEHALL (1945–76). Atlantic Presbytery.

SAINT MICHAELS PRESBYTERIAN CHURCH, ROUND O (c.1880–1935). Atlantic Presbytery.

SALKEHATCHIE PRESBYTERIAN CHURCH, YEMASSEE (1766–1845). Also known as Saltketcher or Salt Catcher and incorporated in 1808 as Saltkehatchee Independent Presbyterian Church. Charleston and Harmony Presbyteries.

WALTERBORO ACADEMY, WALTERBORO (c.1835–40). Conducted by the minister of the Salkehatchie Presbyterian Church.

WILTON PRESBYTERIAN CHURCH, ADAM'S RUN (1727–1928). Also known as Willtown Church. Congregational Association of South Carolina; Charleston and Charleston Union Presbyteries.

YOUNG BETHEL CHURCH (see Aimwell Presbyterian Church, Walterboro).

Dorchester County

DORCHESTER PRESBYTERIAN CHURCH, SUMMERVILLE (1976–present). Charleston and Charleston-Atlantic Presbyteries.

GERMAN PROTESTANT CHURCH OF SAINT GEORGE, INDIANFIELD CREEK (flourished c.1790). *Corpus Evangelicum.* Possibly Methodist after c.1800.

GROVER PRESBYTERIAN CHURCH, GROVER (1897–1904). Fairfield Presbytery.

JEDBURG PRESBYTERIAN CHURCH, JEDBURG (c.1905–c.1945 as a chapel or preaching point served by ministers of Summerville Presbyterian). Charleston Presbytery.

OAKBROOK MISSION, SUMMERVILLE (c.1985–present). Palmetto Presbytery.

SUMMERVILLE PRESBYTERIAN CHURCH, SUMMERVILLE (1696–present). Founded as United Independent Church of Dorchester and Beech Hill; established summer chapel at Summerville in 1831; name changed to Summerville Presbyterian Church in 1859 and congregation consolidated to that facility. (The Old White Meeting House near Dorchester and Bacon's Bridge may have remained a preaching point until 1886.) Congregational Association of South Carolina; Charleston, Charleston Union, and Charleston-Atlantic Presbyteries.

SUMMERVILLE PRESBYTERIAN CHURCH, SUMMERVILLE (c.1870–1950). South Carolina (New School) and Atlantic Presbyteries.

SUMMERVILLE PRESBYTERIAN HOME, SUMMERVILLE (1958–present). Sponsored by the Synod of South Carolina, Presbyterian Church in the United States.

Hampton County

ESTILL PRESBYTERIAN CHURCH, ESTILL (1898–present). Charleston and Charleston-Atlantic Presbyteries.

HAMPTON PRESBYTERIAN CHURCH, HAMPTON (1953–present). Charleston and Charleston-Atlantic Presbyteries.

HARMONY PRESBYTERIAN CHURCH, CROCKETTVILLE (1870–present). Charleston and Charleston-Atlantic Presbyteries.

STONEY CREEK INDEPENDENT PRESBYTERIAN CHURCH, YEMASSEE (1743–1967). Also known as the Independent Church of Indian Land. Congregational Association of South Carolina; Charleston and Charleston Union Presbyteries.

VARNVILLE PRESBYTERIAN CHURCH, VARNVILLE (1917–19). Charleston Presbytery.

Jasper County

BLACK SWAMP PRESBYTERIAN CHURCH, ROBERTVILLE (c.1902). Possibly predecessor of First Presbyterian Church, Hardeeville.

BROWN'S CHAPEL, COOSAW (1886–93). A Sunday school mission of Charleston Presbytery.

COOSAW PRESBYTERIAN CHURCH, COOSAW (1883). Probably only a mission chapel, perhaps predecessor of Brown's Chapel. Charleston Presbytery (listed 1883 only).

FIRST PRESBYTERIAN CHURCH, HARDEEVILLE (1903–24). Founded as Little Zoar Presbyterian Church; name changed c.1915. Atlantic Presbytery. (Also see Black Swamp Presbyterian Church.)

MOUNT ZION PRESBYTERIAN CHURCH, HARDEEVILLE (c.1900–1967). Atlantic Presbytery.

NEW LIFE PRESBYTERIAN CHURCH, ASSOCIATE REFORMED SYNOD, HARDEEVILLE (1982–present). Catawba Presbytery.

PURRYSBURG CHURCH (1790?). The so-called French Protestant (Huguenot) Church at Purrysburg was affiliated with the Church of England, not an organized Huguenot church or a Reformed congregation. It is possible that a successor congregation with Reformed connections existed briefly c.1790.

RIDGELAND PRESBYTERIAN CHAPEL, RIDGELAND (1959–64). A mission of Charleston Presbytery.

Orangeburg County

ANTIOCH PRESBYTERIAN CHURCH, ORANGEBURG (c.1912–20). Atlantic Presbytery.

BRANCHVILLE PRESBYTERIAN CHURCH, BRANCHVILLE (1926–61). Charleston Presbytery.

EUTAWVILLE PRESBYTERIAN CHURCH, EUTAWVILLE (c.1878–c.1910). Atlantic Presbytery.

FIRST PRESBYTERIAN CHURCH, ORANGEBURG (1835–present). Charleston Union, Charleston, and Charleston-Atlantic Presbyteries.

FREDERICIAN CHURCH, CATTLE CREEK (c.1780–c.1800; perhaps with antecedents to c.1735). Charleston Presbytery (?) and *Corpus Evangelicum*. Probably Methodist by c.1800.

GERMAN CALVINISTIC CHURCH OF SAINT JOHN ON THE FOUR-HOLE, ORANGEBURG (c.1788–c.1800). *Corpus Evangelicum*. Probably Methodist by c.1800.

GERMAN LUTHERAN CHURCH OF SAINT MATTHEW, CAMERON (c.1735–1824). Founded as Amelia Township Church; name changed c.1760. *Corpus Evangelicum*. From about 1760 to 1824, affiliated variously with Episcopalians and Lutherans; Lutheran after 1824.

GRACE PRESBYTERIAN CHURCH, ORANGEBURG (1882–97). Succeeded by Railroad Avenue Church (see Saint Luke Presbyterian Church). Atlantic Presbytery.

ORANGEBURG FEMALE ACADEMY (1850s). Charleston Presbytery.

SAINT LUKE PRESBYTERIAN CHURCH, ORANGEBURG (1897–present). Founded as Railroad Avenue Presbyterian; name changed c.1900. Atlantic and Charleston-Atlantic Presbyteries.

SANTEE PRESBYTERIAN CHURCH, SANTEE (1988–present; from 1985, a chapel). Charleston-Atlantic Presbytery.

TURKEYHILL CHURCH (c.1795). Possibly Swiss Reformed (or French Huguenot) congregation on Turkey Hill Creek.

Presbyteries and Associations

Through a complex history of shifting boundaries and affiliations, most presbyteries have represented a variety of counties and churches over time. The presbyteries listed here have included at least some counties and churches in the low country at one time or another. Detailed information about presbytery records and boundaries and about synod and General Assembly affiliations may be found in the "Guide" cited at the beginning of this appendix.

ATLANTIC PRESBYTERY (1868–1988). Affiliated with the Synod of the South (and its predecessors, Atlantic and South Carolina–Georgia) of the United Presbyterian Church in the United States of America. With formation of the Presbyterian Church (U.S.A.) in 1983, Atlantic Presbytery was succeeded (1988) by Charleston-Atlantic Presbytery and New Harmony Presbytery.

CALVARY PRESBYTERY (1973–present). Affiliated with the Presbyterian Church in America (formed as the National Presbyterian Church in 1973; name changed in 1974). In 1984, churches and counties in the low country were transferred to Palmetto Presbytery.

CATAWBA PRESBYTERY (1919–present). Affiliated with the General Synod of the Associate Reformed Presbyterian Church, including all counties east of the Broad River.

CHARLESTON-ATLANTIC PRESBYTERY (1988–present). Affiliated with South

Atlantic Synod of the Presbyterian Church (U.S.A.). Includes churches formerly in Atlantic and Charleston Presbyteries in Allendale, Bamberg, Barnwell, Beaufort, Berkeley (except certain churches assigned to New Harmony Presbytery), Calhoun, Charleston, Colleton, Dorchester, Hampton, Jasper, and Orangeburg Counties.

CHARLESTON PRESBYTERY (1722–c.1780, 1790–c.1819, 1823–1988). Known as Charleston Union Presbytery 1823–39. Independent prior to 1823, then affiliated with the Presbyterian Church in the United States and its predecessor General Assembly. Variant names: South Carolina or Old South Carolina (1722), Scotch (1722), Presbytery of the Province (1722), Old Charleston (1790), Charleston Union (1823–39). After formation of the Presbyterian Church (U.S.A.) in 1983, Charleston Presbytery was merged (1988) with portions of Atlantic Presbytery to form Charleston-Atlantic Presbytery. (See Charleston Union Presbytery.)

CHARLESTON UNION PRESBYTERY (1823–52). Affiliated with the Presbyterian Church in the United States of America. Formed by Harmony Presbytery in 1823 after merger with the Congregational Association of South Carolina and renamed Charleston Presbytery in 1839. Charleston Union Presbytery was maintained as an independent presbytery after 1839 by some of its former members and was reunited with Charleston Presbytery in 1852.

CHARLESTON UNION PRESBYTERY (1869–82). A small and independent presbytery of four members, including the pastors of First (Scots) and Central Churches in Charleston.

CONGREGATIONAL ASSOCIATION OF SOUTH CAROLINA (1801–22). Merged with Harmony Presbytery in 1822, its churches primarily assigned to Charleston Presbytery in 1823.

CORPUS EVANGELICUM (1788–c.1800). An association of German and Swiss Reformed and Lutheran churches (nine predominantly Lutheran and six predominantly Reformed, but with mixed congregations and sometimes with shared ministers).

EDINBURGH PRESBYTERY. A presbytery of the Church of Scotland, with which some colonial churches affiliated, especially before the organization of presbyteries in South Carolina.

FAIRFIELD PRESBYTERY (1870–1959). Affiliated with the Presbyterian Church in the United States of America, primarily serving north-central South Carolina but with one church (Grover) in Dorchester County (1897–1904). Merged into Fairfield-McClelland Presbytery in 1959, without churches or counties in the low country.

FRENCH PROTESTANT (HUGUENOT) CHURCH. Huguenots established five churches in the low country from 1680 to 1700, of which the church at Charleston is the sole survivor. There was also a colony at Port Royal in the sixteenth century.

GERMAN REFORMED CHURCHES (see *Corpus Evangelicum*).

HARMONY PRESBYTERY (1809–1988). Affiliated with the Presbyterian Church in the United States and its predecessor and successor assemblies. From 1809, Harmony included counties that were located northeast of the Congaree and Santee Rivers. In 1810, counties southwest of these rivers and below an unspecified line running roughly from Columbia to McCormick (and extending into Georgia) were transferred to Harmony from Second South Carolina Presbytery. Charleston Union Presbytery was formed from a portion of Harmony in 1823; Pee Dee Presbytery was formed from a part of Harmony in 1889. With formation of the Presbyterian

Church (U.S.A.) in 1983, Harmony was merged into New Harmony Presbytery in 1988.

McCLELLAND PRESBYTERY (1885–1959). Affiliated with the Presbyterian Church in the United States of America. Organized with churches formerly in Fairfield Presbytery located west of the Broad River and north of Barnwell and Orangeburg; included Barnwell and Allendale Counties from 1921. Merged 1959 into Fairfield-McClelland Presbytery, without churches or counties in the low country.

NEW HARMONY PRESBYTERY (1988–present). Affiliated with the Presbyterian Church (U.S.A.). Organized from portions of Atlantic, Harmony, and other presbyteries, including certain churches in the northern part of Berkeley County.

OLD CHARLESTON PRESBYTERY (see Charleston Presbytery, 1790).

OLD SOUTH CAROLINA PRESBYTERY (see Charleston Presbytery, 1722).

PALMETTO PRESBYTERY (1984–present). Affiliated with the Presbyterian Church in America. Formed from the eastern portion of Calvary Presbytery and including all the counties in the low country.

PROVINCE, PRESBYTERY OF THE (see Charleston Presbytery, 1722).

SCOTCH PRESBYTERY (see Charleston Presbytery, 1722).

SOUTH CAROLINA (NEW SCHOOL) PRESBYTERY (1868–70). Organized 1868 by the Northern (New School) General Assembly of the Presbyterian Church in the United States of America for African-American congregations established in South Carolina by the Freedmen's Department of the assembly. Surviving low country congregations were merged into Atlantic and Fairfield Presbyteries by 1871. Statistical reports are recorded in the New School Assembly Minutes for 1868–69 and in the reunited assembly for 1870.

SOUTH CAROLINA PRESBYTERY (1784–1988). Affiliated with the Presbyterian Church in the United States and its predecessor and successor assemblies. Divided in 1800 into First and Second South Carolina Presbyteries. First South Carolina was succeeded by Harmony Presbytery in 1809. Second South Carolina was renamed South Carolina Presbytery in 1810 and included no counties in the low country. (Note that Charleston Presbytery of 1722 was sometimes called South Carolina or Old South Carolina Presbytery.)

SOUTH CAROLINA PRESBYTERY (see Charleston Presbytery, 1722).

SOUTHEAST PRESBYTERY (1961–82). Affiliated with the Evangelical Presbyterian Church (formerly the Bible Presbyterian Church), which became the Reformed Presbyterian Church, Evangelical Synod, in 1966 and merged into the Presbyterian Church in America in 1982. Southeast Presbytery was succeeded by Calvary Presbytery in 1982.

APPENDIX B

Known Pastors in Colonial Presbyterian and Congregational Churches

Name	Place of Birth	Education	Church
Adams, Hugh	Massachusetts	Harvard	Independent (Charlestown)
Alison, John	Ireland		Wilton
Allen, Moses	Massachusetts	Princeton	Wappetaw
Allison, Hugh	Pennsylvania	Princeton	James Island
Anderson, George	Scotland	Edinburgh (?)	Wilton
Atkins, ?			Wappetaw
Bassett, Nathan	Massachusetts	Harvard	Independent (Charlestown)
Baxter, John	New England (?)		Cainhoy
Bell, Thomas			James Island
Bennett, Andrew	England	Private	Independent (Charlestown)
Cotton, John	Massachusetts	Harvard	Independent (Charlestown)
Edmonds, James	England		Independent (Charlestown)
Fisher, Hugh	Scotland	Edinburgh (?)	Dorchester
Gordon, Charles	Scotland		Bethel Pon Pon
Gourlay, James	Scotland	Edinburgh (?)	Stoney Creek
Grant, Thomas	Scotland	Scottish University	First (Scots)
Henderson, Thomas	Scotland	Scottish University	Edisto
Hewat, Alexander	Scotland	Edinburgh	First (Scots)
Hutson, William	England	Inns of Court, London	Stoney Creek; Independent (Charlestown)
Kier, Patrick			James Island
Latta, James	"from the North"	Yale (?)	Johns Island
Livingston, William	Ireland (?)		James Island
Lord, Joseph	Massachusetts (?)	Harvard	Dorchester
Lorimore, Charles	Scotland	Scottish University	First (Scots); Johns Island
McLeod, John	Scotland	Scottish University	Edisto
Maltby, John	Connecticut	Yale; Princeton	Wilton
Martin, John	Virginia (?)	Private (with Samuel Davies)	Wappetaw; Wilton
Moore, Hugh	Scotland (?)		Edisto
Morrison, Philip	Scotland	Saint Andrews M.A.	First (Scots)
Osgood, John	South Carolina	Harvard	Independent (Dorchester)
Parker, James	England	London	Independent (Charlestown)

Name	Place of Birth	Education	Church
Pierpont, Benjamin	Massachusetts	Harvard	Independent (Charlestown); Wappetaw; Wilton (?)
Porter, Jonathan S.			
Porter, William	New England		Wappetaw
Ross, Thomas			Wilton
Rymer, James	Scotland	Saint Andrews	Bethel Pon Pon
Simpson, Archibald	Scotland	Glasgow	Stoney Creek
Smith, Josiah	South Carolina	Harvard	Independent (Charlestown)
Stewart, John	Scotland	Edinburgh (?)	First (Scots); Bethel Pon Pon; Wilton
Stobo, Archibald	Scotland	Glasgow	Independent (Charlestown); Cainhoy; Wilton; Bethel Pon Pon
Tennent, William	Pennsylvania	Princeton; Harvard	Independent (Charlestown)
Thomas, John	Wales	Dissenting	Independent (Charlestown)
Trainable, John			Johns Island
Witherspoon, John	Scotland		James Island
Zubly, John Joachim	Switzerland		Wappetaw; Cainhoy

APPENDIX C

Presbyterian and Congregational Ministers, 1783–1861

Name	Home State/Country	College	Theological Education	Church/Institution
Adams, Robert M.	Scotland	Edinburgh	Edinburgh	Stoney Creek
Adger, John B.	South Carolina	Union (N.Y.)	Columbia	Anson Street; CTS*
Buist, Arthur	South Carolina	South Carolina	Edinburgh	First (Scots)
Buist, George	Scotland	Edinburgh	Edinburgh	First (Scots)
Dana, William	Massachusetts	Dartmouth	Andover; Columbia	Third
Douglass, John	South Carolina	South Carolina	Columbia	Johns Island and Wadmalaw
Dunwoody, James	Georgia	Yale	Columbia	Stoney Creek; Walterboro
Flinn, Andrew	North Carolina	North Carolina; North Carolina, D.D.	Private	Second, Charleston
Forrest, John	Scotland	Edinburgh	Edinburgh	First (Scots)
Girardeau, John L.	South Carolina	Charleston	Columbia	Wilton; Zion; CTS*
Gourlay, James	Scotland	Edinburgh	Edinburgh	Stoney Creek
Henry, T. Charlton	Pennsylvania	Middlebury	Princeton	First, Columbia; Second, Charleston
Hollinshead, William	Pennsylvania	Pennsylvania; Princeton, D.D.	Private	Circular
Howe, George	Massachusetts	Middlebury	Andover	CTS*
Keith, Isaac	Pennsylvania	Pennsylvania	Princeton	Circular
Lanneau, Fleetwood, Sr.	South Carolina	Yale	Princeton	Missionary, Syria
Lee, William States	South Carolina	Princeton	Private	Edisto Island
Legaré, I. S. K.	South Carolina	Yale	Private	Orangeburg
Leland, Aaron W.	Massachusetts	Williams; Brown, M.A.; South Carolina, D.D.	Private	First (Scots); CTS*
McCalla, Daniel	Pennsylvania	Princeton	Private	Wappetaw
Palmer, B. M. (the elder)	South Carolina	Princeton; South Carolina, D.D.	Private	Circular
Palmer, B. M. (the younger)	South Carolina	Franklin	Columbia	First, Columbia; CTS* Walterboro
Palmer, Edward	South Carolina			

Name	Home State/Country	College	Theological Education	Church/Institutuion
Post, Reuben	Vermont	Middlebury	Princeton	Circular
Rogers, Zabdiel	Connecticut	Yale	Andover	Wilton
Smyth, Thomas	Ireland	Highburg (London)	Princeton	Second, Charleston
Thornwell, James Henley	South Carolina	South Carolina	Andover; Harvard	College of South Carolina; CTS*
White, Elipha	Massachusetts	Brown	Andover	Johns Island

*Columbia Theological Seminary

APPENDIX D

Pastors of Black Presbyterian and Congregational Churches and Principals of Black Institutions

1865–1889

Name	Home State	College*	Theological Education*	Church Institutuion	Race
Adams, Ennals	New Jersey	"college trained"		Charleston Mission	B
Bates, J. H.	Vermont	Vermont	Presbyterian Seminary of the Northwest	Wallingford; Johns Island	W
Campbell, Smart	South Carolina		Private	Johns Island	B
Cardozo, Francis L.	South Carolina	Glasgow	Edinburgh; London	Plymouth	B
Chavis, Jared M.				Hopewell; Aimwell; Beaufort Salem; Saint Michaels	B
Coles, S. C.	(North)			Plymouth	W
Deckert, H. P.				Missionary; Edisto	?
Ford, James T.	(North?)			Plymouth	W
Garden, Elias	South Carolina	(Wallingford)	Private	Summerville; Wallingford; Hebron; Bethel; Zion (Johns Island)	B
Gibbs, Jonathan C.	Pennsylvania	Dartmouth	Princeton	Zion	B
Girardeau, John L.	South Carolina	Charleston	Columbia	Zion	W
Hedges, Peter P.	North Carolina			Edisto	B
Hunter, H. H.	New York			James Island	B
Jackson, Benjamin F.	(North?)			Plymouth	W
Logan, Robert	(North)			Charleston Mission	W
Mack, J. B.	New York	Jackson (Tenn.)	Columbia	Zion	W
Marts, W. G.	Pennsylvania			Plymouth	W
Merritt, ?	(North?)			Plymouth	B
Morris, W. H.	(South)			Charleston Mission	B
Moultrie, Ishmael	South Carolina		Private	Edisto; Salem; Saint Paul; Saint Andrews; Calvary	B
Patton, William	Pennsylvania	Hanover, B. A., M. A.		Wallingford	W
Pease, Giles	(North?)			Plymouth	W

Name	Home State	College*	Theological Education*	Church Institutuion	Race
Robinson, Douglas	(North)			Bluffton; Principal, Bluffton Institute	W
Smith, William C.	Pennsylvania		Presbyterian Seminary of the Northwest	First Colored; Zion	W
Van Horne, Martin	(North)			Charleston Mission	B

1890–1900

Name	Home State	College*	Theological Education*	Church Institutuion	Race
Brooks, William F.				Beaufort Salem; Berean	B
Brown, David	North Carolina	Biddle	Biddle	Olivet; Mount Pleasant; Principal, Wallingford Academy	B
Ellerson, L. B.	South Carolina	Biddle; Lincoln, D. D.	Princeton	Berean	B
Elliott, George M.	Virginia	Geneva	Reformed (Pa.)	Berean	B
Frayer, Adam	South Carolina	Biddle	Biddle	Hopewell; Aimwell; Saint Michaels	B
Garden, Elias	South Carolina	(Wallingford)	Private	Wallingford; Summerville; Zion (Johns Island); Hebron; Bethel	B
Grove, Thomas	Pennsylvania	Muskingum	Western	Olivet; Mount Pleasant	B
Holman, Robert W.	South Carolina	(Wallingford)	Private	Zion	B
Hunter, H. H.	New York			Saint James	B
Johnson, William L.	New York	Lincoln	Lincoln	Grace (Orangeburg)	B
Middleton, W. Blake	South Carolina	Biddle	Biddle	Wallingford Academy	B
Moultrie, Ishmael	South Carolina		Private	Edisto; Salem; Saint Paul; Saint Andrews; Calvary; Rivers Chapel	B
Moultrie, Jacob	South Carolina	Lincoln	Lincoln	Beaufort Salem; Saint Paul; Saint Andrews; Faith; Rivers Chapel; Calvary	B
Rollins, Joseph A.				Hopewell; Aimwell; Saint Andrews	B
Rowe, George C.	Connecticut			Plymouth	B

*I have been unable to identify the college or theological seminary for many of these pastors. Their ordination by a Presbyterian or Congregational church would ordinarily require both a college and a theological education.

APPENDIX E

Leading White Presbyterian and Congregational Ministers or Those with Five or More Years in the Low Country

1876–1900

Name	Home State/ Country	College	Theological Education	Church/Institution
Adams, William H.	Massachusetts	Harvard	Columbia	Circular
Adger, John	South Carolina	Union (N.Y.)	Columbia	Columbia Theological Seminary
Boggs, W. E.	India	South Carolina	Columbia	Columbia Theological Seminary; Chancellor, University of Georgia
Brackett, G. B.	Massachusetts	Amherst; Davidson, D. D.	Columbia	Second, Charleston
Brown, J. D. A.	New York	Oglethorpe	Columbia	Orangeburg
Chichester, C. E.	Pennsylvania	South Carolina	Columbia	Mariner's Chapel
Dow, John	Scotland			Evangelist
Dunwoody, James	Georgia	Yale	Columbia	Stoney Creek
Fogartie, James E.	South Carolina	Davidson; North Carolina, M.A., Ph.D.	Columbia	Edisto
Girardeau, John L.	South Carolina	Charleston	Columbia	Zion; Columbia Theological Seminary
Hay, Thomas P.	South Carolina	Hampden Sydney	Columbia	Edisto
Junkin, William F.	Pennsylvania	Washington and Lee	Princeton	Westminster
Mack, J. B.	New York	Jackson (Tenn.)	Columbia	Zion; Columbia/Davidson financial agent
Missildine, A. H.	Missouri			Circular
Murchison, H. R.	South Carolina	Davidson	Columbia	Bamberg; Denmark; Edisto
Murray, E. Clark	South Carolina	Union (N.Y.)	Columbia	Summerville
Patterson, A. L.	Tennessee	King (Tenn.)	Columbia	Walterboro
Stevens, Joseph L.	South Carolina	Virginia	Columbia	Johns Island and Wadmalaw
Thompson, W. T.	Virginia	Virginia	Columbia	First (Scots)
Vardell, William G.	South Carolina		Private	Johns Island; New Wappetaw
Vedder, C. S.	New York	Union (N.Y.); New York, D. D.	Columbia	Huguenot
Wardlaw, A. G.	Georgia	Emory	Princeton	Westminster

1900–1940

Name	Home State/ Country	College	Theological Education	Church/Institution
Beckett, T. A.	South Carolina	Davidson	Columbia	Johns Island; Rockville; James Island

Name	Home State/ Country	College	Theological Education	Church/Institution
Brown, Paul F.	Indiana	Hampden Sydney	Union (Va.)	Estill
Caldwell, S. C.	Georgia	Princeton, M.A.; Columbia, Ph.D.		Walterboro; Stoney Creek; Edisto
Clark, Melton	South Carolina	South Carolina	Columbia	Second, Charleston; Columbia Theological Seminary
DuBose, Palmer C.	China (South Carolina)	Davidson	Columbia	Missionary, China
Edwards, George N.				Circular
Erve, J. van de	Netherlands	Hope; Rush Medical College, M.D.; Chicago	Princeton	Summerville; Huguenot
Fraser, John K.	Canada	Dalhousie	Union (N.Y.)	Second, Charleston
Harvin, S. T.	South Carolina	South Carolina	Columbia	Williston; Summerville
Hickman, J. W.	Tennessee	Austin	Union (Va.)	Second, Charleston
Jenkins, C. Rees	South Carolina	Davidson; Johns Hopkins	Columbia	Missionary, Japan
Junkin, Daniel P.	Virginia	Washington and Lee	Union (Va.)	New Wappetaw; Mount Pleasant
Kirkpatrick, M. R.	Alabama	Davidson	New Brunswick Theological Seminary	Johns Island; Rockville
McLees, J. L.	South Carolina	Adger	Columbia	Orangeburg
Mayes, Francis B.	South Carolina	Presbyterian	Columbia	Beaufort; Harmony
Nickles, G. A.	South Carolina	Presbyterian	Columbia	Westminster
Paddock, George E.	South Crolina			Circular
Parker, H. M.	South Carolina	Private (Paris, Brussels, and England)	Alexandria (Episcopal)	Johns Island; James Island
Rankin, Henry	Pennsylvania	Reformed Episcopal	Reformed Episcopal	Walterboro; Stoney Creek
Robertson, C. E.	Alabama	Alabama Polytechnical Institute	Columbia	Edisto; Walterboro
Sadler, W. Weston	South Carolina	Erskine	Columbia	New Wappetaw
Smyth, L. C. M.	South Carolina	Virginia, M.A.; Heidelberg; Marburg	Princeton	Missionary, Japan
Sprunt, Alexander	Scotland	Davidson	Union (Va.)	First (Scots)
Thomas, John N.	Virginia	Washington and Lee; Edinburgh, Ph.D.	Union (Va.)	Second, Charleston
White, Henry Alexander	West Virginia	Washington and Lee, Ph.D.	Princeton	Columbia Theological Seminary

Abbreviations

CAPO	Charleston-Atlantic Presbytery Office, archives
CLS	Charleston Library Society
COF	Committee on Freedmen, Presbyterian Church, U.S.A. (located in PHSP)
COMFF	Committee of Missions for Freedmen, Presbyterian Church, U.S.A., Old School (located in PHSP)
FBR	Freedmen's Bureau Records (located in National Archives, Washington, D.C.)
MGAPCCSA	*Minutes of the General Assembly, Presbyterian Church in the Confederate States of America*
MGAPCUS	*Minutes of the General Assembly, Presbyterian Church in the United States*
MGAPCUSA	*Minutes of the General Assembly, Presbyterian Church in the U.S.A.*
MGAPCUSA(NS)	*Minutes of the General Assembly, Presbyterian Church in the U.S.A. (New School)*
MGAPCUSA(OS)	*Minutes of the General Assembly, Presbyterian Church in the U.S.A. (Old School)*
MGAPC(USA)	*Minutes of the General Assembly, Presbyterian Church (USA)*
MGAUPCUSA	*Minutes of the General Assembly, United Presbyterian Church in the U.S.A.*
PHSM	Presbyterian Historical Society, Montreat, North Carolina
PHSP	Presbyterian Historical Society, Philadelphia
SCHS	South Carolina Historical Society, Charleston
SCHGM	*South Carolina Historical and Genealogical Magazine*
SCHM	*South Carolina Historical Magazine*
SPR	*Southern Presbyterian Review*

Notes

Introduction

1. M. Eugene Sirmans, *Colonial South Carolina: A Political History, 1663–1763* (Chapel Hill: University of North Carolina Press, 1966), 232. For the enduring strength of such a perspective on the Carolina low country, see, from the first decade of the twentieth century, Edward McCrady, *The History of South Carolina in the Revolution, 1775–1780* (New York: Macmillan, 1901), 205–06. Almost ninety years later similar perspectives are echoed by Walter J. Fraser, Jr., in *Charleston! Charleston! The History of a Southern City* (Columbia: University of South Carolina Press, 1989). Fraser writes: "The climate, the evolving agricultural society, the institution of slavery, and Anglicanism were shaping in the hearts and minds of Charlestonians a world view different from that of Bostonians, New Yorkers, and Philadelphians. White Charlestonians hungered after pleasure, profits, property, and status" (45). See also Pauline Maier, "Early Revolutionary Leaders in the South and the Problem of Southern Distinctiveness," in Jeffrey J. Crow and Larry E. Tise, eds., *The Southern Experience in the American Revolution* (Chapel Hill: University of North Carolina Press, 1978), 14.

2. See, in addition to n. 1 above, Don Harrison Doyle, "Urbanization and Southern Culture: Economic Elites in Four New South Cities (Atlanta, Nashville, Charleston, Mobile): c. 1865–1910," in Orville V. Burton and Robert C. McMath, Jr., eds., *Toward a New South? Studies in Post–Civil War Southern Communities* (Westport, Conn.: Greenwood Press, 1982), 23, 31; Frederic C. Jaher, "Antebellum Charleston: Anatomy of an Economic Failure," in Orville V. Burton and Robert C. McMath, Jr., eds., *Class, Conflict, and Consensus: Antebellum Southern Community Studies* (Westport, Conn.: Greenwood Press, 1982), 207–31; Frederic C. Jaher, *The Urban Establishment: Upper Strata in Boston, New York, Charleston, Chicago, and Los Angeles* (Urbana: University of Illinois Press, 1982); John P. Radford, "Social Structure and Urban Form: Charleston, 1860–1880," in Walter J. Fraser, Jr., and Winfred B. Moore, Jr., eds., *From the Old South to the New: Essays on the Transitional South* (Westport, Conn.: Greenwood Press, 1981), 81–91; and Don Harrison Doyle, "Leadership and Decline in Postwar Charleston, 1865–1910," in Fraser and Moore, 93–106.

3. The songs, of course, are from the opera *Porgy and Bess* by DuBose Heyward and George Gershwin.

4. Many of the issues surrounding images of low country African Americans in the years following the Civil War and their "accommodation" to white culture are discussed with insight in Edmund L. Drago, *Initiative, Paternalism, & Race Relations: Charleston's Avery Normal Institute* (Athens: University of Georgia Press, 1990).

5. See Peter A. Coclanis, *The Shadow of a Dream: Economic Life and Death in the South Carolina Low Country, 1670–1920* (New York: Oxford University Press, 1989). In this brilliant new economic history of the low country, Coclanis provides an important context for understanding the place of a Calvinist community in the economic and social fabric of the region. This is especially true when Coclanis speaks of a "considerable enterprise" marking the leadership of the region "rather than entrepreneurial lethargy." See esp. 49–51, 139, 157.

6. See John Leith, *Introduction to the Reformed Tradition: A Way of Being the Christian*

Community (Atlanta: John Knox Press, 1977); William J. Bouwsma, *John Calvin: A Sixteenth Century Portrait* (New York: Oxford University Press, 1988), 160; and Michael Walzer, *The Revolution of the Saints: A Study in the Origins of Radical Politics* (Cambridge: Harvard University Press, 1965), 10–11.

7. Coclanis, 268, n. 5.

8. The model, as developed by Ludwig Feuerbach, of religion as a reflection of a social context presents religion as an inverted reflection of reality. For Feuerbach, religion is precisely a reversal of subject and predicate—humanity is the creator of God and not God of humanity. A particular people's understanding of God is consequently a reflection of their social reality. See Ludwig Feuerbach, *The Essence of Christianity*, trans. George Eliot (1841; reprint, New York: Harper, 1957).

9. See ibid.; Karl Marx, *Critique of Hegel's "Philosophy of Right,"* ed. Joseph O'Malley (Cambridge: Cambridge University Press, 1970), esp. 131; and Karl Marx and Friedrich Engels, *On Religion* (Moscow: Progress, 1957), 37–38. See also Maurice Bloch, *Marxism and Anthropology* (Oxford: Oxford University Press, 1983), esp. 17–18.

10. Emile Durkheim is most closely associated with sociological explanations of religion. "God," he wrote, "is only a figurative expression of the society." Religious rituals are consequently to be understood as a primary means by which a group expresses and reinforces its sentiments and solidarity. See Emile Durkheim, *The Elementary Forms of the Religious Life* (1915; reprint, London: Allen and Unwin, 1964), esp. 226, 387.

11. Classical works that help shape such an understanding of religion include Edward B. Tylor, *Primitive Culture* (London: Murray, 1913); Max Weber, *The Sociology of Religion*, trans. E. Fishoff, ed. Talcott Parsons (London: Methuen, 1965); and Bronislaw Malinowski, *Magic, Science and Religion, and Other Essays* (1925; reprint, London: Souvenir Press, 1974).

12. "Religion as a Cultural System," in Clifford Geertz, *The Interpretation of Cultures: Selected Essays* (New York: Basic Books, 1973), 123–24. Even the orthodox Marxist Louis Althusser came to acknowledge that the superstructure has the capacity to react back on the infrastructure and that the superstructure (including religion) has a relative autonomy. See Louis Althusser, *For Marx*, trans. Ben Brewster (New York: Vintage Books, 1970), esp. 113–16. More positively, and in sympathy with Geertz, Paul Ricoeur has argued that it is meaningless to insist that something economic acts on ideas in a causal manner. For Ricoeur, the effects of economic forces on ideas need to be understood within a *motivational* framework. See Paul Ricoeur, *Lectures on Ideology and Utopia*, ed. George H. Taylor (New York: Columbia University Press, 1986), 183–97.

13. Ricoeur has most powerfully shown this "metaphoric quality" by emphasizing the role of social imagination as constitutive of social reality. See this role most succinctly stated in Ricoeur, *Lectures*, 3, 10, and 254–66.

14. Geertz, 95. Michael Walzer has clearly shown the dynamic and reciprocal relationship between the English Puritans and their social context. Speaking of the "crisis of modernization," Walzer wrote: "In a sense, the saint [the Puritan] is the cause rather than the product of that crisis; it occurs, in different countries at different times, whenever a group of men, hardened and disciplined by an ideology, decisively challenge the old order, offering their own vision as an alternative to traditionalism and their own persons as alternatives to the traditional rulers. But in another, equally important, sense, the saint is a product of his times: for men are open to ideological discipline only at certain moments in history. Most often, they are immune, safe from whatever it is that inspires self-discipline and activism, disdainful of all enthusiasm" Walzer, *Revolution of the Saints*, 19.

15. Marx enlarged Feuerbach's model by extending the reversal to the whole realm of ideas and not simply to religion. For Marx this reversal constitutes ideology, a distortion of

reality (praxis) by means of a reversal. A people's daily life—their work, their praxis—is real reality. This reality, according to Marx, is represented in the shadow world of ideas. But the representation is false because this shadow world presents itself as autonomous, as having an existence independent from the social reality that gave it birth. For Marx, "man makes religion; religion does not make man." The *making* of religion means that religion is not simply a representation, as with Feuerbach, but a production, and that production serves the interests of those doing the making. It is consequently ideological. See Marx, esp. 131.

16. See esp. Max Weber, *Economy and Society,* ed. Guenther Roth and Claus Wittich, 2 vols. (1968; reprint, Berkeley and Los Angeles: University of California Press, 1978). The third chapter, "The Types of Legitimate Domination," provides Weber's important typology of claims to legitimacy.

17. For the integrative function of ideology that provides social identity, see Geertz, 193–223, "Ideology as a Cultural System"; and Ricoeur, *Lectures,* 3, 185, 254–66.

18. See Ricoeur, *Lectures,* xvi, xxi–xxiii, 15–17, 269–314; and Karl Mannheim, *Ideology and Utopia,* trans. Louis Wirth and Edward Shils (New York: Harcourt, Brace, and World, 1936). See also Paul Ricoeur, "Ideology, Utopia, and Faith," *Center for Hermeneutical Studies* 17 (1976): 9–28. Marxism sees little distinction between ideologies and utopias, as both are regarded as the efflux of a certain social stratum and a disguise of interest. See Friedrich Engels, "Socialism: Utopian and Scientific," in Karl Marx and Friedrich Engels, *Basic Writing on Politics and Philosophy,* ed. Lewis S. Feuer (Garden City, N.Y.: Doubleday, 1959), 68–111. Mannheim and Ricoeur, in contrast, emphasize that utopia, rather than legitimating the present social order, shatters it.

19. Mannheim sees ideology as being linked primarily to dominant groups. Utopias, on the other hand, are more closely related to ascending groups and consequently are more generally supported by the lower stratum of society. See Mannheim, esp. chapter "The Utopian Mentality" and particularly p. 208. For the difficulties of making this linking too tight, see Ricoeur, *Lectures,* 274, 285–314. In this present study, ideology is seen most powerfully in dominant groups—most particularly white slaveholders. But whites also had their conservative utopias that challenged (1) "outside" groups that sought domination and (2) the utopian vision of black revolutionaries such as Denmark Vesey. See chaps. 8 and 11.

20. See Geertz, 127, "Ethos, World View and the Analysis of Sacred Symbols."

21. See Louis J. Luzbetak, *The Church and Cultures: New Perspectives in Missiological Anthropology* (Maryknoll, N.Y.: Orbis Books, 1988), 249–55.

22. See nn. 1 and 2 above and see, for example, Maier, 14. For the ignoring of the Reformed African American presence and influence on the sea islands, see Margaret W. Creel, *"A Peculiar People": Slave Religion and Community-Culture among the Gullahs* (New York: New York University Press, 1988). Creel makes no mention, for example, of the large and influential African American Presbyterian church on James Island with its school or the critical role the Larimer School played on Edisto Island in the acculturation ("reculturation") of the island's Gullah-speaking population.

23. The influence of the Reformed tradition on the Anglican, Baptist, and Methodist Churches has been described by a number of writers. See, for example, Ernst Troeltsch, *The Social Teaching of the Christian Churches,* trans. Olive Wyon, 2 vols. (New York: Harper Torchbooks, 1960), 2:688–91, 706–08, 721–24; and Sydney E. Ahlstrom, *A Religious History of the American People* (New Haven: Yale University Press, 1972), 94, 97–98, 132–34, 170–76, 324–29. It is also true, of course, that these churches have influenced those more closely connected to the Reformed tradition, such as the Congregationalist and Presbyterian Churches but perhaps especially the Baptist Church with its sectarian social ideal of a free church.

1. The Tradition Established: A European Prologue

1. The story of Calvin's arrival in Geneva is told in John T. McNeill, *The History and Character of Calvinism* (1954; reprint, London: Oxford University Press, 1967), 129–44. See also William Monter, *Calvin's Geneva* (New York: Wiley, 1967), and Jeannine E. Olson, *Calvin and Social Welfare: Deacons and the Bourse Française* (Selinsgrove, Pa.: Susquehanna University Press, 1989).

2. Calvin revised and greatly expanded the *Institutes* over the course of the next twenty years. The final Latin edition was published in Geneva in 1559. See John Calvin, *Institutes of the Christian Religion*, ed. John T. McNeill, vols. XX and XXI of *Library of Christian Classics* (Philadelphia: Westminster Press, 1960).

3. For the social transformations remaking Europe and their implications for the Reformed tradition, see Michael Walzer, *The Revolution of the Saints: A Study in the Origins of Radical Politics* (Cambridge: Harvard University Press, 1965), 1–21, 300–20; Reijer Hooykaas, *Religion and the Rise of Modern Science* (Edinburgh: Scottish Academic Press, 1972); and Hugh R. Trevor-Roper, *Religion, the Reformation, and Social Change*, 3d. ed. (London: Secker and Warburg, 1984).

4. William J. Bouwsma has developed most clearly and convincingly the portrait of Calvin as a prominent example of the deeply divided mind of the Christian West. My indebtedness to Bouwsma's *John Calvin: A Sixteenth Century Portrait* (New York: Oxford University Press, 1988) is obvious throughout this study.

5. For the Scholastic Calvin, see ibid., chaps. 4, 5, and 6. For the development of Protestant Scholasticism in France see Brian Armstrong, *Calvinism and the Amyraut Heresy: Protestant Scholasticism and Humanism in Seventeenth-Century France* (Madison: University of Wisconsin Press, 1969).

6. For Calvin the humanist, see Bouwsma, chaps. 7–11 and "Calvinism as Renaissance Artifact," in Timothy George, ed., *John Calvin & the Church* (Louisville: Westminster/John Knox Press, 1990). See also André Biéler, *The Social Humanism of Calvin* (Richmond: John Knox Press, 1964), and Quirinus Breen, *John Calvin: A Study in French Humanism* (Chicago: University of Chicago Press, 1931).

7. Bouwsma, 233.

8. McNeill, 178–79.

9. A helpful map and description of the spread of Calvinism can be found in Geoffrey Barraclough, ed., *The Times Atlas of World History* (London: Times Books, 1979), 182–83. See also Menna Prestwich, ed., *International Calvinism, 1541–1715* (Oxford: Clarendon Press, 1985).

10. For the influence of Zwingli and Bullenger on the Reformed tradition, see G. W. Bromiley, ed., *Zwingli and Bullenger*, vol. 24 of *Library of Christian Classics* (Philadelphia: Westminster Press, 1953).

11. McNeill, 255–89; Barraclough, 182–83; and Gordon A. Craig, *The Germans* (New York: Meridian, 1983), 89–90.

12. Walzer, *Revolution of the Saints*, 70.

13. The origin of the name "Huguenot" is obscure. Some scholars believe that it comes from the Swiss Eidgenossen, "of confederates."

14. For a helpful bibliography on the Huguenots as refugees, see the extensive notes in Jon Butler, *The Huguenots in America: A Refugee People in New World Society* (Cambridge: Harvard University Press, 1983).

15. J. H. S. Burleigh, *A Church History of Scotland* (London: Oxford University Press, 1960), 122. This is the best survey of Scottish church history.

16. Ibid., 281–85.

17. The most comprehensive treatment of the Scotch-Irish remains James G. Leyburn, *The Scotch-Irish: A Social History* (Chapel Hill: University of North Carolina Press, 1962).

18. On the Scottish and Scotch-Irish movement to North America, see Bernard Bailyn, *Voyagers to the West: A Passage in the Peopling of America on the Eve of the Revolution* (New York: Vintage Books, 1988).

19. See Philip Schaff, *The Creeds of Christendom, with a History and Critical Notes,* 6th ed., 3 vols. (Grand Rapids: Baker House, 1967), 1:620–21, 3:486–516.

20. There is an enormous body of literature on Puritanism, the English Civil War, and the Glorious Revolution. A convenient bibliography that emphasizes the American connections can be found in Sydney E. Ahlstrom, *A Religious History of the American People* (New Haven: Yale University Press, 1972), 1102–03. Indispensable is Walzer, *Revolution of the Saints;* see also R. T. Kendal, *Calvin and English Calvinism to 1649* (Oxford: Oxford University Press, 1980). For Cromwell, see Christopher Hill, *God's Englishman: Oliver Cromwell and the English Revolution* (New York: Dial Press, 1970), and Antonia Frazer, *Cromwell: Our Chief of Men* (London: Weidenfeld and Nicolson, 1973).

21. R. H. Tawney, *Religion and the Rise of Capitalism* (1926; reprint, New York: New American Library, 1947), 165.

22. Ahlstrom, *Religious History,* 98.

23. Isa. 57:15.

24. This theological starting point for the Reformed tradition can be seen in the various creeds of Reformed churches, written in different historical periods, in different regions of the world, and under different social circumstances. See Heidelberg Catechism, question 1; and Westminster Confession of Faith, chaps. II and III. A collection of twentieth-century Reformed confessions from around the world is in Lukas Vischer, *Reformed Witness Today: A Collection of Confessions and Statements of Faith Issued by Reformed Churches* (Bern: Evangelische Arbeitsstelle Oekumene Schweiz, 1982).

25. For the use of political discipline to calm inner anxieties, see Walzer, *Revolution of the Saints,* 30–65.

26. See Heidelberg Catechism, pt. I, questions 3–11; Scots Confession, chap. III; Westminster Confession of Faith, chap. VI; and Declaration of Faith, chap. II:6.

27. Calvin was well known for fearing concentrations of political power. He shared with other humanists revulsion to the Roman Empire's subversion of the Roman republic. See his *Commentary on Daniel,* 2:39, and *Institutes,* IV, xx, 8. See also Quentin Skinner, *The Foundations of Modern Political Thought,* 2 vols. (Cambridge: Cambridge University Press, 1978), 2:189–358.

28. The Puritan sense of fighting the Lord's battles is explored with insight in Walzer, *Revolution of the Saints,* 268–99.

29. See *Institutes,* III, i, 3. See also Scots Confession, chap. XII; and Westminster Shorter Catechism, 33.

30. "Arrogance arises from a foolish persuasion of our own righteousness," wrote Calvin, "when man thinks that he has something meritorious to commend him before God" (*Institutes,* III, xii, 8). For the fear of Christian freedom, given by grace, being abused, see ibid., III, ix, 4–13. For the tendency of Reformed communities to move toward self-righteous moralism, see John Leith, *Introduction to the Reformed Tradition: A Way of Being the Christian Community* (Atlanta: John Knox Press, 1977), 76–77.

31. See Bouwsma, 171–72.

32. Ahlstrom, *Religious History,* 130–32, 145–46, 158–60.

33. See Scots Confession, chap. XVIII.

34. See Larger Catechism, 5; *Institutes,* I, vi, 4; and Declaration of Faith, chap. VI:3.

35. See *Institutes,* II, vii, 9–12. This third and principal use of the law as a teacher, guide,

and encouragement would have a profound influence on Reformed communities. See Ronald S. Wallace, *Calvin's Doctrine of the Christian Life* (Edinburgh: Oliver and Boyd, 1959), and John Leith, *John Calvin's Doctrine of the Christian Life* (Louisville: Westminster/John Knox Press, 1989).

36. Shorter Catechism, 1, 2. See also Geneva Catechism, 1.

37. *Institutes,* III, vi, 3.

38. See *Institutes,* IV. For particular polities, see James K. Cameron, ed., *First Book of Discipline: With Introduction and Commentary* (Edinburgh: Saint Andrew's Press, 1972); *The Confession of Faith, the Larger Catechism, the Directory for Public Worship, the Form of Presbyterial Church Government* (Edinburgh: William Blackwood and Sons, 1959). See also Robert M. Kingdon, *Geneva and the Consolidation of the French Protestant Movement, 1564–1572* (Madison: University of Wisconsin Press, 1967); Williston Walker, *The Creeds and Platforms of Congregationalism* (Boston: Pilgrim Press, 1960); and Leith, *Reformed Tradition.*

39. Burleigh uses a chart, "The Divisions and Reunions of the Scottish Church, 1690–1929," that provides an all too clear image of the controversies that have wracked one Reformed community.

40. See Max Weber, *The Protestant Ethic and the Spirit of Capitalism,* trans. Talcott Parsons (1930; reprint, New York: Scribner, 1958). See also Perry Miller, *The New England Mind: The Seventeenth Century* (New York: Macmillan, 1939). In a famous passage, Calvin wrote of the good gifts God gives humanity to be enjoyed. See *Institutes,* III, x, 2. For indications of Calvin's attitude toward sculpture and paintings, eating, drinking, and sexuality, see ibid., I, xi, 12; III, x, 2; II, ii, 4; and II, vii, 43.

41. See *Institutes,* III, vi, 4.

42. See ibid., III, ii, 2. In the nineteenth century, Charles Hodge of Princeton insisted that religious experience flows from a proper understanding of correct doctrine. See his "Inspiration," *Princeton Review* 29 (October 1857): 692, and his *Systematic Theology,* 3 vols. (New York: Charles Scribner's Sons, 1893).

43. *Institutes,* III, xx, 33.

44. Ibid., III, ii, 8.

45. Leith, *Reformed Tradition,* 82–83. Leith's chapter on "The Reformed Ethos" provides an exceptionally clear and helpful summary of the characteristics discussed here. For the role of self-examination as an antidote to hypocrisy, see Bouwsma, 179–82.

46. For the expression of this simplicity in the meetinghouse architectural style, see Edmund W. Sinnott, *Meeting House and Church in Early New England* (New York: McGraw-Hill, 1963).

47. Moses Rischin, ed., *The American Gospel of Success* (Chicago: Quadrangle Books, 1965), 23.

48. Perry Miller and Thomas H. Johnson, eds., *The Puritans: A Source Book of Their Writings,* rev. ed., 2 vols. (New York: Harper Torchbooks, 1963), 1:320, 324. See also Bouwsma, 195–96.

49. Ernst Troeltsch, *The Social Teaching of the Christian Churches,* trans. Olive Wyon, 2 vols. (New York: Harper Torchbooks, 1960), 2:611.

50. Max Weber, whose seminal work, *Protestant Ethic,* sparked much of the debate surrounding the questions of Calvinism's relationship to capitalism, insisted that there was, at least, a congruence between the Calvinist ethos and the spirit of capitalism. For Weber, there was a psychological sanction inherent in the Reformed emphasis on predestination and personal calling that encouraged the unintentional result of capital accumulation and the rise of a capitalistic economic system. "Perhaps no work within the social science tradition," a recent scholar has written, "has generated as much discussion and controversy" as Weber's thesis

(Brian Morris, *Anthropological Studies of Religion: An Introductory Text* [Cambridge: Cambridge University Press, 1987], 66).

The unresolved controversies surrounding the Weberian thesis are too broad for the scope of this study. The following chapters explore these questions in light of the antithetical impulses of the tradition as they are expressed within a particular Reformed community, in a specific geographical location, over a three-hundred-year period. My general inclination, however, is clear, as I lean toward a modest interpretation of Weber's thesis—not claiming a direct *causal* link between a Reformed ethos and a modern, market-oriented economy but seeing a mutually supportive congruence between the two. "To ask," Paul Ricoeur has written, "whether the ethics produced the capitalist mind or vice versa is to remain in an inappropriate framework. Instead, I would rather say that the ethics provide the symbolic structure within which some economic forces work. It is more an issue of the relation between a framework of reference and a system of forces." Paul Ricoeur, *Lectures on Ideology and Utopia,* ed. George H. Taylor (New York: Columbia University Press, 1986), 213. See also Frank Parkin, *Max Weber* (London: Tavistock, 1981), 43.

For discussions of Weber's thesis, see Troeltsch, 576–660; B. Morris, 61–67; Robert W. Green, ed., *Protestantism and Capitalism: The Weber Thesis and Critics* (Boston: D. C. Heath, 1959); Reinhard Bendix, *Max Weber: An Intellectual Portrait* (London: Methuen, 1959); Samuel N. Eisenstadt, *The Protestant Ethic and Modernization: A Comparative View* (New York: Basic Books, 1968); Benjamin Nelson, "Weber's Protestant Ethic: Its Origins, Wanderings and the Foreseeable Future," in C. Y. Glock and P. E. Hammond, eds., *Beyond the Classics? Essays in the Scientific Study of Religion* (New York: Harper and Row, 1973), 71–130; Gianfranco Poggi, *Calvinism and the Capitalist Spirit* (London: Macmillan, 1983); and Gordon Marshall, *Presbyteries and Profits: Calvinism and the Development of Capitalism in Scotland* (Oxford: Oxford University Press, 1980), esp. the conclusion on p. 138. Walzer sees the "saint" of radical politics as corresponding "in a rough way" to "Weber's economic entrepreneur" (*Revolution of the Saints,* 17), but see his treatment of Weber, 300–20.

2. The Context: The Colony of South Carolina

1. For atlases that provide helpful overviews of European expansion, and in North America in particular, see Geoffrey Barraclough, ed., *The Times Atlas of World History* (London: Times Books, 1979); and Lester J. Cappon, et al., *Atlas of Early American History: The Revolutionary Era, 1760–1790* (Princeton: Princeton University Press, 1976).

2. See Nicholas P. Canny, "The Ideology of English Colonization: From Ireland to America," *William and Mary Quarterly* 30 (1973): 575–98. See also chap. 1, n. 50, above.

3. Robert M. Weir, *Colonial South Carolina: A History* (Millwood, N.Y.: KTO Press, 1983), 37.

4. See Peter H. Wood, *Black Majority: Negroes in Colonial South Carolina from 1670 through the Stono Rebellion* (New York: W. W. Norton, 1974), 84, 89; and Alexander Hewat, *An Historical Account of the Rise and Progress of the Colonies of South Carolina and Georgia,* 2 vols. in 1 (London, 1779), reprinted in R. B. Carroll, comp., *Historical Collections of South Carolina,* 2 vols. (New York: Harper and Brothers, 1836), 1:110.

5. See Jean Ribault, *The Whole and True Discoverye of Terra Florida: A Facsimile Reprint of the London Edition of 1563 together with a Transcript of the English Version in the British Museum* (Deland: Florida State Historical Society, 1927). See also Charles F. Kovacik and Lawrence S. Rowland, "Images of Colonial Port Royal, South Carolina," *Annals of the Association of American Geographers* 63 (September 1973): 331–40.

6. Hewat, 1:77–78. See also John M. Barry, *Natural Vegetation of South Carolina* (Columbia: University of South Carolina Press, 1980).

7. See David Ramsay, *The History of South Carolina, From its First Settlement in 1670 to the Year 1808*, 2 vols. in 1 (Charleston: David Longworth, 1809), 2:49–120. For modern perspectives, see Joseph I. Waring, *History of Medicine in South Carolina, 1670–1825* (Columbia: South Carolina Medical Association, 1964); Harry Roy Merrens and George D. Terry, "Dying in Paradise: Malaria, Mortality, and the Perceptual Environment in Colonial South Carolina," *Journal of Southern History* 50 (November 1984): 533–50.

8. Gene Waddell, *Indians of the South Carolina Lowcountry: 1562–1751* (Spartanburg, S.C.: Reprint Co., 1980); Henry F. Dobyns, *Their Number Become Thinned: Native American Population Dynamics in Eastern North America* (Knoxville: University of Tennessee Press, 1983), 8–45. See also Alfred W. Crosby, *The Columbia Exchange: Biological and Cultural Consequences of 1492* (New York: Cambridge University Press, 1986).

9. Ramsay, 2:34–35.

10. Paul E. Hoffman, "Legend, Religious Idealism, and Colonies: The Point of Santa Elena in History, 1552–1566," *SCHM* 84 (1983): 59–71.

11. Paul Quattlebaum, *The Land Called Chicora: The Carolinas under Spanish Rule with French Intrusions, 1520–1670* (Gainesville: University of Florida Press, 1956).

12. Hewat, 1:501.

13. Weir, 61; and see Richard S. Dunn, "The English Sugar Islands and the Founding of South Carolina," *SCHM* 72 (1971): 81–93.

14. Arthur Henry Hirsch, *The Huguenots of Colonial South Carolina* (London: Archon Books, 1962), 15–20.

15. Jon Butler, *The Huguenots in America: A Refugee People in New World Society* (Cambridge: Harvard University Press, 1983), 95, 96, 131.

16. J. H. S. Burleigh, *A Church History of Scotland* (London: Oxford University Press, 1960), 238–58.

17. George Pratt and J. G. Gunlop, "Arrival of the Cardross Settlers: *The Carolina Merchant;* Advice of Arrival," *SCHGM* 30 (1929): 69–79, and Mabel L. Webber, ed., "Spanish Depredations, 1686," *SCHGM* 30 (1929): 81–89.

18. George Howe, *History of the Presbyterian Church in South Carolina*, vol. 1 (Columbia: Duffie and Chapman, 1870), 185.

19. Ibid., 120–22.

20. Robert Manson Myers, ed., *The Children of Pride: A True Story of Georgia and the Civil War* (New Haven: Yale University Press, 1972), 8–9; Erskine Clarke, *Wrestlin' Jacob: A Portrait of Religion in the Old South* (Atlanta: John Knox Press, 1979), 4–6.

21. P. Wood, 131.

22. Ibid., 131, 146, 147, 149, 152.

23. These figures were the calculation of the Reverend Stephen Roe of Saint George parish for the year 1741. See Frank J. Klingberg, *An Appraisal of the Negro in Colonial South Carolina: A Study in Americanization* (Philadelphia: Porcupine Press, 1975), 87.

24. R. W. Kelsey, "Swiss Settlers in South Carolina," *SCHGM,* 23 (1922): 22.

25. For these African empires and states see Barraclough, 136–37.

26. David Brion Davis, *Slavery and Human Progress* (New York: Oxford University Press, 1984), 46.

27. Barraclough, 166; P. Wood, xiv.

28. See Bureau of the Census, *Historical Statistics of the United States: Colonial Times to 1970*, 2 vols. (Washington, D.C.: U.S. Government Printing Office, 1975), 2:1155, 1174; W. Robert Higgins, "The Geographical Origins of Negro Slaves in Colonial South Carolina," *South Atlantic Quarterly* 70 (Winter 1971): 34–47; Weir, 179; Daniel C. Littlefield, *Rice and*

Slaves: Ethnicity and the Slave Trade in Colonial South Carolina (Baton Rouge: Louisiana State University Press, 1981), 8–32.

29. Philip D. Curtin, *The Atlantic Slave Trade: A Census* (Madison: University of Wisconsin Press, 1969), chap. 3.

30. P. Wood, 95, 96; Weir, 187, 188.

31. Melville J. Herskovits, *The Myth of the Negro Past* (Gloucester, Mass.: P. Smith, 1924); E. Franklin Frazier, *The Negro in the United States* (Chicago: University of Chicago Press, 1940), chap. 1.

32. Albert J. Raboteau, *Slave Religion: The "Invisible Institution" in the Antebellum South* (New York: Oxford University Press, 1978), 92. Other important treatments of slave religion can be found in Eugene D. Genovese, *Roll, Jordan, Roll: The World the Slaves Made* (New York: Pantheon Books, 1974); John Boles, *Black Southerners: 1619–1869* (Lexington: University Press of Kentucky, 1983); Mechal Sobel, *Trabelin' On: The Slave Journey to an Afro-Baptist Faith* (Westport, Conn.: Greenwood Press, 1979); and John Boles, ed., *Masters and Slaves in the House of the Lord: Race and Religion in the American South, 1740–1870* (Lexington: University Press of Kentucky, 1988).

33. P. Wood, 147.

34. For an insightful and vivid account of nineteenth-century African American folk religion in the low country, see Charles Joyner, *Down by the Riverside: A South Carolina Slave Community* (Urbana: University of Illinois Press, 1984), 141–71. Joyner's endnotes for this chapter are an extensive bibliography in African American folk religion.

35. Peter A. Coclanis, *The Shadow of a Dream: Economic Life and Death in the South Carolina Low Country, 1670–1920* (New York: Oxford University Press, 1989), 7, 90–91. See also Alice Hanson Jones, *Wealth of a Nation To Be: The American Colonies on the Eve of the Revolution* (New York: Columbia University Press, 1980), 357.

36. See Coclanis, passim, and Converse D. Clowse, *Economic Beginnings in Colonial South Carolina, 1670–1730* (Columbia: University of South Carolina Press, 1971).

37. Coclanis, 50.

38. Ibid., 51.

39. Ibid., 50, 51, 49. See also Jeanne A. Calhoun, Martha A. Zierden, and Elizabeth A. Paysinger, "The Geographic Spread of Charleston's Mercantile Community, 1732–1767," *SCHM* 86 (1985): 182–220.

40. It is important to note that Coclanis—in contrast to the assumptions in this study about the relationship between religion and its sociohistorical context—takes a materialist position that sees economic activity as the basis for the social and cultural life of the region. "Seventeenth-century Charleston was in the last analysis a function of South Carolina's seventeenth-century economy" (Coclanis, 5).

41. Ibid., 26.

3. The Tradition Transplanted: The Reformed Communities

1. For the number of Society for the Propagation of the Gospel in Foreign Parts missionaries in South Carolina who had master's degrees, mostly from Oxford, see Frank J. Klingberg, *An Appraisal of the Negro in Colonial South Carolina: A Study in Americanization* (Philadelphia: Porcupine Press, 1975), 140–42 and passim. For an appreciative but generally balanced summary of the important role of the Anglican Church in South Carolina, see S. Charles Bolton, *Southern Anglicanism: The Church of England in Colonial South Carolina* (Westport, Conn.: Greenwood Press, 1982), 154–63. The ignoring of a vigorous Reformed tradition in the South Carolina low country can be seen, for example, not only in M. Eugene

Sirmans, *Colonial South Carolina: A Political History, 1663–1763* (Chapel Hill: University of North Carolina Press, 1966), and earlier studies but in so careful a recent study as Robert M. Calhoon, *Evangelicals and Conservatives in the Early South, 1740–1861* (Columbia: University of South Carolina Press, 1988). "Until [Samuel] Davies and other Pennsylvania Presbyterians came to Hanover County, Virginia [in 1747]," Calhoon wrote, "the only Presbyterians in the southern colonies were among pockets of Scottish and Scots Irish settlement in the Valley of Virginia and on its eastern shore, the Cape Fear valley in North Carolina, and among French, Swiss, and German Calvinists in South Carolina and Georgia" (16). As will be seen, the Presbyterians had long constituted the largest portion of the white population's church membership in the South Carolina low country by the time Samuel Davies came to Virginia. These Presbyterians included French Huguenots and a few Swiss and German Calvinists, but most were of British origin.

2. A helpful introduction to the themes and issues connected with the role of religion and the immigrant experience can be found in Randall M. Miller and Thomas D. Marzik, eds., *Immigrants and Religion in Urban America* (Philadelphia: Temple University Press, 1977), xi–xxii.

3. Arthur Henry Hirsch, *The Huguenots of Colonial South Carolina* (London: Archon Books, 1962), 47. The French-Swiss settlement at Purrysburg, between Savannah and Augusta but on the South Carolina side of the Savannah River, evidently had both an Anglican and a Presbyterian congregation. See ibid., 81–84; George Howe, *History of the Presbyterian Church in South Carolina*, vol. 1 (Columbia: Duffie and Chapman, 1870), 479, 578.

4. This perspective is presented by Jon Butler, *The Huguenots in America: A Refugee People in New World Society* (Cambridge: Harvard University Press, 1983), following the lead of Emile Leonard, *A History of Protestantism* (London: Nelson, 1967).

5. See Henri Dubief's article in *Theologische Realenzyklopaedie*, vol. 15 (1986), 624–25. Dubief notes that in contrast to the work of Leonard, contemporary scholarship has pointed to the strength and unity of French Protestantism.

6. See Butler, *Huguenots in America*, 32–40.

7. For questions concerning the founding of this church and its early history, see ibid., 136–37, 142–43; Hirsch, 50–60; and Howe, *History of the Presbyterian Church*, 1:100–11. The *Transactions of the Huguenot Society of South Carolina* has had, throughout a substantial part of the twentieth century, articles too numerous to list related to the Charleston congregation. See Carl Bridenbaugh, *Myths and Realities: Societies of the Colonial South* (Baton Rouge: Louisiana State University Press, 1952), 120.

8. For discussion of its date of organization, see Howe, *History of the Presbyterian Church*, 1:122–25, and 70, 77, 86, 122, and George N. Edwards, *A History of the Independent or Congregational Church of Charleston South Carolina* (Boston: Pilgrim Press, 1947), 1–8.

9. Howe, *History of the Presbyterian Church*, 1:137–45.

10. For the founding of the Wilton Presbyterian Church, see ibid., 145–46, 187–96. See also Slann L. C. Simmons, ed., "Records of the Willtown Presbyterian Church 1738–1841," *SCHM* 62 (1961): 33–50, 107–63, 172–81, 219–24.

11. The Pon Pon church was established as the Bethel Presbyterian Church on Pon Pon (a variant for the Edisto River). For its founding, see Howe, *History of the Presbyterian Church*, 1:187, 203, and E. T. H. Shaffer, *History of Bethel Presbyterian Church: From the Founding in 1728 Down to the Present Time—1928* (Walterboro, S.C.: Press and Standard, [1928]), 1–8. There are extensive colonial records of this congregation at the PHSM.

12. See Howe, *History of the Presbyterian Church*, 1:170, 187, 204–05.

13. See ibid., 185, 204–05. The PHSM has historical notes on Cainhoy collected by the Huguenot Society of South Carolina.

14. For the founding and early history of the Edisto Island church see, in addition to

ibid., 170, 202, 252–53, the manuscript history of the church by S. C. Caldwell, "Early History of Edisto Island Presbyterian Church, 1700–1860," at the PHSM, and S. C. Caldwell et al., *The Presbyterian Church of Edisto Island* (1933; reprint, 1963).

15. Howe, *History of the Presbyterian Church*, 1:191, 207–08. See also Isabel H. Hills, "Historical Sketch of the Johns Island Presbyterian Church, 1710–1937" (1937), at PHSM.

16. See G. Edwards, 18–20; Howe, *History of the Presbyterian Church*, 1:201–02, 251–52; Edward G. Lilly, *Beyond the Burning Bush: First (Scots) Presbyterian Church, Charleston, S.C.* (Charleston: Garnier, 1971), esp. 52–57, the extract from Aaron Leland's sermon at the dedication of the building in 1814; and see the Lilly papers at SCHS.

17. In addition there were several German Reformed churches in the low country at the end of the colonial period. See G. D. Bernheim, *History of the German Settlements and of the Lutheran Church in North and South Carolina* (Philadelphia: Lutheran Bookstore, 1872).

18. For complexities of church membership, see chap. 1 above and see, for example, Bethel Pon Pon Presbyterian Church, Session Minutes, 1736–76, PHSM.

19. Robert M. Weir, *Colonial South Carolina: A History* (Millwood, N.Y.: KTO Press, 1983), 210.

20. See ibid., 207; Bureau of the Census, *Historical Statistics of the United States: Colonial Times to 1970* (Washington, D.C.: U.S. Government Printing Office, 1975), 2:1168–71; Klingberg, 28; Weir, 209; and Peter H. Wood, *Black Majority: Negroes in Colonial South Carolina from 1670 through the Stono Rebellion* (New York: W. W. Norton, 1974), 146, 147, 152.

21. In 1710 there were five Presbyterian churches in Pennsylvania, four in Maryland, two in the Jerseys, and one in Virginia. See *Records of the Presbyterian Church in the United States of America* (Philadelphia: Presbyterian Board of Publication, 1841), 18.

22. Weir, 210. In 1760 the Anglican minister of Saint Bartholomew's reported 1,280 white inhabitants of whom 460 were Dissenters. The remainder were said to be "those who profess themselves of the Church of England," but only thirty-three communicants of the Church of England were reported. Evidently, those who did not declare themselves Dissenters were designated Church of England. See Florence Gambill Geiger, "St. Bartholomew's Parish As Seen By Its Rectors, 1713–1761," *SCHGM* 50 (1949): 175 f. In 1767 a missionary from the Synod of New York and Philadelphia, writing to Ezra Stiles, future president of Yale, estimated that there were fifty Presbyterian families in the church at Wilton, fifty families at Bethel Pon Pon, fifty at Stoney Creek, thirty at James Island, sixty at Wappetaw, and "near Savannah" (Beaufort? Port Royal? Purrysburg?), thirty families. See Howe, *History of the Presbyterian Church*, 1:363.

23. See Howe, *History of the Presbyterian Church*, 1:370–71, and Newton B. Jones, ed., "Writings of the Reverend William Tennent, 1740–1777," *SCHM* 61 (1960): 196–209.

24. The Presbyterian churches were First (Scots), James Island, Johns Island, Edisto Island, Wilton, Bethel (Pon Pon), Stoney Creek, Cainhoy, Saltketcher, Beaufort, Port Royal, and Purrysburg. The Congregational churches were the Independent Meeting House (Charlestown), Dorchester, and Wappetaw. The French Huguenot church was the French Reformed Church in Charlestown, and the German Reformed church was located at Indian Field Swamp. Whether a church was Presbyterian or Congregational was not always clear. In 1775 there were forty-five Presbyterian churches, three Congregational, two French Reformed, and four German Reformed throughout the state with most congregations in the up-country. Those that were Presbyterian, even without the others in the Reformed tradition, represented the largest denomination in South Carolina. See Lester J. Cappon et al., *Atlas of Early American History: The Revolutionary Era, 1760–1790* (Princeton: Princeton University Press, 1976), 39.

25. This amount is given by Tennent in his address to the assembly. See Howe, *History of the Presbyterian Church*, 1:371.

26. The reports of the Anglican missionaries point to the ambiguities. See Bolton, 89, and Klingberg, 63, 65, 87. See also the laments of Commissary Gideon Johnston in 1713 in Amy Friedlander, ed., "Commissary Johnston's Report, 1713," *SCHM* 83 (1982): 259–71.

27. For details of the establishment of the Anglican Church, see Bolton, 16–36; Howe, *History of the Presbyterian Church,* 1:155–63; Weir, 75–80; Sirmans, 86–88; and Alexander Moore, ed., " 'A Narrative . . . Of An Assembly . . . January the 2d, 1705/6': New Light on Early South Carolina Politics," *SCHM* 85 (1984): 181–86.

28. Weir, 77. For more background on the activity of Defoe in behalf of South Carolina Dissenters, see Richard Beale Davis, *Intellectual Life in the Colonial South, 1585–1763* (Knoxville: University of Tennessee Press, 1978), 45, 53, 783.

29. A classic account of the Yemassee War can be found in Verner W. Crane, *The Southern Frontier, 1670–1732* (Ann Arbor: University of Michigan Press, 1929), 162–86.

30. Bolton, 155–56.

31. Ibid., 41.

32. Alexander Hewat, *An Historical Account of the Rise and Progress of the Colonies of South Carolina and Georgia,* 2 vols. in 1 (London, 1779), 316.

33. See, for example, Ernest Trice Thompson, *Presbyterians in the South,* 3 vols. (Richmond: John Knox Press, 1963, 1973), 1:29–40; and David Duncan Wallace, *The History of South Carolina,* 3 vols. (New York: American Historical Society, 1934), 1:419.

34. For the date of the presbytery's organization see Howe, *History of the Presbyterian Church,* 1:190, and Thompson, *Presbyterians in the South,* 1:33. Variant names for this presbytery were South Carolina Presbytery, Old South Carolina Presbytery, Scotch Presbytery, and Presbytery of the Province.

35. John M. Barkley, *A Short History of the Presbyterian Church in Ireland* (Belfast: Publications Board, Presbyterian Church in Ireland, 1959).

36. For the Adopting Act, see Leonard J. Trinterud, *The Forming of an American Tradition: A Re-Examination of Colonial Presbyterianism* (Philadelphia: Westminster Press, 1949).

37. R. Davis, 765.

38. Howe, *History of the Presbyterian Church,* 1:210.

39. Hewat, 1:316.

40. Ibid.

41. For low country colonial pastors in the Reformed tradition, see app. B. In contrast to these approximately 57 Reformed ministers in the low country, during the same period there were 124 Anglican ministers throughout the *whole* colony, but most were located in the low country. The SPG alone supported 53 clergymen in South Carolina between the society's formation in 1701 and 1776. The superior ability of the established church to supply ministers was clear. See Bolton, 97, 166–74.

42. G. Edwards, 8–9.

43. Ibid., 21–22. See also John Cotton in ibid., 12.

44. Howe, *History of the Presbyterian Church.* For quote on Allen, see 1:376.

45. Bolton, 98. Bethel Pon Pon, Session Minutes, 1736–76. See also Howe, *History of the Presbyterian Church,* 1:253, 256, 257. For exchange rates of currency with sterling, see Hewat, 1:320, and Sirmans, 206, 317. After 1756, the salaries of rural Anglican ministers were apparently substantially increased.

46. G. Edwards, 31; Lilly, *Beyond the Burning Bush,* 54; Bolton, 100. The amounts are given in currency at an exchange rate with sterling of 7 to 1.

47. Howe, *History of the Presbyterian Church,* 1:248, 310–12.

48. But see ibid., 252, and Mary A. Tennent, *Light in Darkness: The Story of William Tennent, Sr. and The Log College* (Greensboro, N.C.: Greensboro Printing Co., 1971), 211.

49. Crane, 108–36.

50. For the homes listed, see Samuel Gaillard Stoney, *This Is Charleston: A Survey of the Architectural Heritage of a Unique American City* (Charleston: Carolina Art Association, 1944); and Henry F. Cauthen, Jr., *Charleston Interiors* (Charleston: Preservation Society of Charleston, 1979).

51. G. Edwards, 2, 44. See also Mabel L. Webber, "Register of the Independent or Congregational (Circular) Church," *SCHGM* 18 (1917): 27–37, 53–59, 135–40. See also Jeanne A. Calhoun, Martha A. Zierden, and Elizabeth A. Paysinger, "The Geographic Spread of Charleston's Mercantile Community, 1732–1767," *SCHM* 86 (1985): 182–220. Along with such leading Anglican merchants as Henry Laurens and Peter Manigault, many of the merchants at the Independent Church carried on extensive international trade and moved in the elite circles.

52. Peter A. Coclanis, *The Shadow of a Dream: Economic Life and Death in the South Carolina Low Country, 1670–1920* (New York: Oxford University Press, 1989), 50.

53. Hewat, 1:475. At First (Scots)—where the records are much less complete—leading merchants included John Bee, Sr., and Daniel Crawford. John Rattray was one of the most prominent lawyers in the city and had plantations at Pon Pon and Indian Land. Among those Huguenots who continued to maintain their loyalty to the French Reformed Church in the city was the wealthy merchant Isaac Mazyck.

54. For importers between 1735 and 1740, see P. Wood, 334–39. For importers between 1735 and 1775, see W. Robert Higgins, "Charles Town Merchants and Factors Dealing in the External Negro Trade: 1735–1775," *SCGHM* 65 (1964): 205–17. Prominent Anglicans are also listed.

55. Geiger, 175 f.

56. See Simmons, 148–62, 219–24; E. Shaffer, passim; Stoney Creek Independent Presbyterian Church, Covenant and Register, 1743–60, PHSM; Bethel Pon Pon, Session Minutes, 1750; Caldwell, passim; Caldwell et al., passim; Hills, passim; Petrona Royall McIver, "Wappetaw Congregational Church," *SCHM* 58 (1957): 84; Howe, *History of the Presbyterian Church,* 1:passim.

57. Sirmans, 247, 314, and passim.

58. See Arthur H. Shaffer, "David Ramsay and the Limits of Revolutionary Nationalism," in Michael O'Brien and David Moltke-Hansen, eds., *Intellectual Life in Antebellum Charleston* (Knoxville: University of Tennessee Press, 1986), 52. For libraries of those in the Reformed tradition, see names in R. Davis, 573–74; Walter B. Edgar, "Notable Libraries of Colonial South Carolina," *SCHM* 72 (1971): 107; and Edgar L. Pennington, "Original Rules and Members of the Charlestown Library Society," *SCHGM* 23 (1922): 169–70.

59. Bethel Pon Pon, Session Minutes, 1746–48.

60. Ibid., 1750–52. Other congregations also had slaves—including Stoney Creek, which bought slaves in the 1770s and hired them out to local planters, and the Presbyterian congregation on Edisto Island, which received as a gift "certain negro slaves" to be employed on lands owned by the congregation. Howe, *History of the Presbyterian Church,* 1:202.

4. The Tradition Articulated: A Carolina Accent

1. "If I had to say," Sir Kenneth Clark once declared, "which was telling the truth about society, a speech by a Minister of Housing or the actual buildings put up in his time, I should believe the buildings." Kenneth Clark, *Civilization: A Personal View* (New York: Harper and Row, 1969), 1. See also Rhys Isaac's discussion of the architecture of Anglican churches in Virginia in *The Transformation of Virginia, 1740–1790* (Chapel Hill: University

of North Carolina Press, 1982), 61–64. Isaac notes that the "architectural plan maximized the visibility to the assembled community of a numerous emulative gentry."

2. For the development of the New England meetinghouse style, see Edmund W. Sinnott, *Meeting House and Church in Early New England* (New York: McGraw-Hill, 1963). For Johns Island Presbyterian Church, see Edward G. Lilly, ed., *Historic Churches of Charleston* (Charleston: John Huguley, 1966), 108–09.

3. For Dorchester, see George Howe, *History of the Presbyterian Church in South Carolina,* vol. 1 (Columbia: Duffie and Chapman, 1870), 567; for Midway, see James Stacy, *Published Records of Midway Church* (Newnan, Ga.: S. W. Murray, 1894), 51, and idem, *History of the Midway Congregational Church, Liberty County, Georgia,* rev. ed. (Newnan, Ga.: S. W. Murray, 1903), 1–20; for Wilton, see Slann L. C. Simmons, ed., "Records of the Willtown Presbyterian Church, 1738–1841," *SCHM* 62 (1961): 45; for Bethel, see title page of E. T. H. Shaffer, *History of Bethel Presbyterian Church: From the Founding in 1728 Down to the Present Time—1928* (Walterboro, S.C.: Press and Standard, [1928]).

4. See John Leith, *Introduction to the Reformed Tradition: A Way of Being the Christian Community* (Atlanta: John Knox Press, 1977), 165–86.

5. John Calvin, *Institutes of the Christian Religion,* ed. John T. McNeill, vols. XX and XXI of *Library of Christian Classics* (Philadelphia: Westminster Press, 1960), XXI:1421 (IV, xvii, 43).

6. Ibid., XXI:1193 (IV, x, 14).

7. For the slowly increasing numbers of slaves in the churches see William Hutson, "Account of Marriages, Baptisms, and Burials &c.," PHSM; Stoney Creek Independent Presbyterian Church, Covenant and Register, 1743–60, PHSM; Bethel Pon Pon Presbyterian Church, Session Minutes, 1740–70, PHSM; Howe, *History of the Presbyterian Church,* 1:389; and Frank J. Klingberg, *An Appraisal of the Negro in Colonial South Carolina: A Study in Americanization* (Philadelphia: Porcupine Press, 1975), 96–98, 103. See also Mechal Sobel, *The World They Made Together* (Princeton: Princeton University Press, 1987), 178–203; John Boles, ed., *Masters and Slaves in the House of the Lord: Race and Religion in the American South, 1740–1870* (Lexington: University Press of Kentucky, 1988).

8. As late as the 1880s this argument was still being made by John L. Girardeau, who grew up on neighboring James Island and served churches throughout the low country. See John L. Girardeau, *Instrumental Music in the Public Worship of the Church* (Richmond: Whittet and Shepperson, 1888).

9. *A Version of the Book of Psalms Selected from the Most Approved Version Now Used by Different Denominations of Christians, Approved of by the Presbytery of Charleston* (Charleston: J. MacIver, 1796), vii.

10. *A Collection of Hymns for Public and Private Worship, Approved of by the Presbytery of Charleston* (Charleston: J. MacIver, 1796).

11. Ibid., 134–36.

12. See Peter L. Berger and Thomas Luckmann, *The Social Construction of Reality* (Garden City, N.Y.: Doubleday, 1966). And see "Monopoloy and Marginality in Imagination," in Walter Brueggemann, *Interpretation and Obedience: From Faithful Reading to Faithful Living* (Minneapolis: Fortress Press, 1991), 184–204.

13. On the comparable social role of lament psalms, see Brueggemann, 194–200.

14. *Collection of Hymns,* 196–97.

15. See *The Westminster Directory for Worship,* chap. 9. For the Reformed emphasis on hearing, not seeing, in worship, see James Hastings Nichols, *Corporate Worship in the Reformed Tradition* (Philadelphia: Westminster Press, 1968), esp. 29–33; and see Michael Mullett, *Radical Religious Movements in Early Modern Europe* (London: Allen and Unwin, 1980), 25–28.

16. Early examples of discipline can be found in the records of Stoney Creek, where

members were disciplined for fornication, drunkenness, and fighting. See Stoney Creek, Covenant and Register, 1743/44. At Bethel a deacon was suspended from church membership and the Lord's Table for the murder of a slave. See Bethel Pon Pon, Session Minutes, 1750. For discipline at Wilton, see Howe, *History of the Presbyterian Church,* 1:276.

17. Westminster Confession of Faith, XXXI:2.

18. See "Religion as a Cultural System," in Clifford Geertz, *The Interpretation of Cultures: Selected Essays* (New York: Basic Books, 1973), esp. 112–23.

19. "Ritual makes explicit," Edmund Leach has written, "the social structure. . . . The structure which is symbolized in ritual is the system of socially approved 'proper' relations between individuals and groups" (*Culture and Communication: The Logic by Which Symbols are Connected* [Cambridge: Cambridge University Press, 1976], 14–15). Leach understands rituals, "the structure of ideas," and social structures, "the structures of society," as elements within a "single interacting whole."

20. "Rites," Emile Durkheim wrote, "are a means by which the social group re-affirms itself periodically. Men who feel themselves united . . . by a community of interest and tradition, assemble and become conscious of their moral unity" (*The Elementary Forms of the Religious Life* [1915; reprint, London: Allen and Unwin, 1964], 387).

21. Rhys Isaac noted of Anglican churches in colonial Virginia that their seating plans, "accentuated by the manner of entry and exit—exhibited the community to itself in ranked order. The form and tone of the liturgy reinforced the demonstration inherent in the physical setting. The services of the book of Common Prayer had been given their vernacular shape in the sixteenth century and expressed strongly an ethos of English Christian gentility. The appointed set of words, read in the midst of a community ranged in order of precedence, continuously evoked postures of deference and submission. Liturgy and church plan thus readily combined to offer a powerful representation of a structured, hierarchical community" (Isaac, *Transformation of Virginia,* 64). See also his treatment of Baptist and Methodist buildings, 315–16.

22. For the concept of social drama as a means through which conflicts within a community are resolved, see Victor Turner, *Schism and Continuity in an African Society* (Manchester: Manchester University Press, 1957). See also his *The Ritual Process* (Chicago: Aldine, 1969).

23. Gal. 3:28.

24. See Max Weber, *The Sociology of Religion,* trans. E. Fishoff, ed. Talcott Parsons (London: Methuen, 1965). Weber insisted that "classes with high social and economic privilege" will "assign to religion the primary function of legitimizing their own life pattern and situation in the world" (107). Mannheim makes a similar point by stressing that ideology is linked primarily to dominant groups while utopias are supported primarily by ascending groups. See "The Utopian Mentality," in Karl Mannheim, *Ideology and Utopia,* trans. Louis Wirth and Edward Shils (New York: Harcourt, Brace, and World, 1936), esp. 208. See also Paul Ricoeur's reservations about too close an identification of either ideology or utopia with a particular stratum of society in his *Lectures on Ideology and Utopia,* ed. George H. Taylor (New York: Columbia University Press, 1986), 274, 285–314.

25. In all of his sermons Smith showed himself to be a moderate within the Reformed tradition, reflecting "gentlemanly" virtues his Charlestown congregation desired when they sought to call an associate for his fast-growing congregation. See George N. Edwards, *A History of the Independent or Congregational Church of Charleston South Carolina* (Boston: Pilgrim Press, 1947), 22.

26. Nor was Josiah Smith the last low country preacher to warn against the dangers of drink, which he did with his sermon *Solomon's Caution against the Cup . . . Delivered at Cainhoy* (Boston, 1730).

27. See Alan E. Heimert and Perry Miller, *The Great Awakening: Documents Illustrating the Crisis and Its Consequences* (Indianapolis: Bobbs-Merrill, 1967), 62–89.

28. Early historical accounts include Governor John Archdale's *New Description of That Fertile and Pleasant Province of Carolina* (1707) and Governor James Glen's *Description of South Carolina* (1761).

29. Alexander Hewat, *An Historical Account of the Rise and Progress of the Colonies of South Carolina and Georgia,* 2 vols. in 1 (London, 1779), reprinted in R. B. Carroll, comp., *Historical Collections of South Carolina,* 2 vols. (New York: Harper and Brothers, 1836), 1:lxxii.

30. Ibid., 75, 81–82.

31. Ibid., 28–29.

32. For the number of slaves imported during this period and for the listing of the merchants engaged in the trade, see W. Robert Higgins, "Charles Town Merchants and Factors Dealing in the External Negro Trade, 1735–1775," *SCHGM* 65 (1964): 205–17; and Robert M. Weir, *Colonial South Carolina: A History* (Millwood, N.Y.: KTO Press, 1983), 178.

33. Hewat, 1:355.

34. Howe, *History of the Presbyterian Church,* 1:372–73.

35. For a discussion of "gentlemen theologians" in the nineteenth century, see E. Brooks Holifield, *The Gentlemen Theologians: American Theology in Southern Culture, 1795–1860* (Durham: Duke University Press, 1978), 36–49. It needs to be noted that the ideals of gentility and rationality were well established among the Presbyterian and Congregational ministers of the Carolina low country by the end of the colonial period.

5. The Tradition Expanded: The Great Awakening

1. This piety was especially present in Germany, where the population had been decimated by the thirty-year wars of religion (35 percent of the population was lost). See Gordon A. Craig, *The Germans* (New York: Meridian, 1983), 18–21, 86–88.

2. For the rise of Pietism and its characteristics, see F. Ernest Stoeffler, *Continental Pietism and Early American Christianity* (Grand Rapids: Eerdmans, 1976).

3. An important introductory analysis of these developments, along with a now dated but still useful bibliography of the Awakening, can be found in Sydney E. Ahlstrom, *A Religious History of the American People* (New Haven: Yale University Press, 1972). Standard monographs on the Awakening are Edwin S. Gaustad, *The Great Awakening in New England* (New York: Harper and Row, 1957); C. C. Goen, *Revivalism and Separatism in New England* (New Haven: Yale University Press, 1962); and Alan E. Heimert, *Religion and the American Mind from the Great Awakening to the Revolution* (Cambridge: Harvard University Press, 1966). For more recent debates over the nature and extent of the Awakening, see Jon Butler, "Enthusiasm Described and Decried: The Great Awakening as Interpretive Fiction," *Journal of American History* 69 (1982): 305–25; Susan O'Brien, "A Transatlantic Community of Saints: The Great Awakening and the First Evangelical Network, 1735–1755," *American Historical Review* 91 (1986): 811–32; and Jon Butler, *Awash in a Sea of Faith: Christianizing the American People* (Cambridge: Harvard University Press, 1990), esp. 164–224.

4. On Sunday morning September 9, 1739, Archibald Stobo was preaching at the Wilton Presbyterian Church when a Mr. Golightly came riding at a gallop to the church with the news that a slave rebellion had broken out. The men, who by law were required to carry their arms to church, immediately formed themselves into a militia under the leadership of Captain John Bee, Jr., a member of the congregation. Leaving the women "in church trembling with fear," they marched off to meet a rapidly growing rebel force, which they surprised and defeated near the Jacksonborough ferry. For this Stono Rebellion, see George Howe,

History of the Presbyterian Church in South Carolina, vol. 1 (Columbia: Duffie and Chapman, 1870), 202, 227–28; Robert M. Weir, *Colonial South Carolina: A History* (Millwood, N.Y.: KTO Press, 1983), 193–94; Alexander Hewat, *An Historical Account of the Rise and Progress of the Colonies of South Carolina and Georgia,* 2 vols. in 1 (London, 1779), reprinted in R. B. Carroll, comp., *Historical Collections of South Carolina,* 2 vols. (New York: Harper and Brothers, 1836), 1:332–33; Peter H. Wood, *Black Majority: Negroes in Colonial South Carolina from 1670 through the Stono Rebellion* (New York: W. W. Norton, 1974), 308–26.

5. M. Eugene Sirmans, *Colonial South Carolina: A Political History, 1663–1763* (Chapel Hill: University of North Carolina Press, 1966), 209–10; Walter J. Fraser, Jr., *Charleston! Charleston! The History of a Southern City* (Columbia: University of South Carolina Press, 1989), 78–80.

6. For the details of Whitefield's relationship with Garden, see William Howland Kenny III, "Alexander Garden and George Whitefield: The Significance of Revivalism in South Carolina, 1738–1741," *SCHM* 71 (1970): 1–16. A standard biography of Whitefield is Stuart C. Henry, *George Whitefield: Wayfaring Witness* (New York: Abingdon Press, 1957).

7. Arminianism was split into two camps—an evangelical, with Methodism as its most prominent advocate, and a rationalistic, which tended later toward Unitarianism. The rationalistic camp, in an early and relatively mild form, was best represented in Charlestown by Garden's associate, Samuel Quincy. "Rationalistic Arminianism" gradually lost its force within Anglicanism.

8. See Kenny, 2.

9. George Whitefield, *Journals* (London: Banner of Truth Trust, 1965), 384.

10. See S. Charles Bolton, *Southern Anglicanism: The Church of England in Colonial South Carolina* (Westport, Conn.: Greenwood Press, 1982), 51.

11. Alexander Garden, *Regeneration, and the Testimony of the Spirit. Being the Substance of Two Sermons . . . Occasioned by some erroneous Notions of certain Men who call themselves Methodists,* in Alan Heimert and Perry Miller, *The Great Awakening: Documents Illustrating the Crisis and Its Consequences* (Indianapolis: Bobbs-Merril, 1967), 47.

12. Archibald Simpson Journal, January 6, 1768, CLS.

13. Howe, *History of the Presbyterian Church,* 1:235–41.

14. Ibid., 227–50.

15. Ibid., 260.

16. Another great hymn that would express the Reformed position—"Rock of Ages"— was written by an Anglican minister, Augustus M. Toplady, in 1776.

17. Garden, 56.

18. Samuel Quincy, "Christianity a Rational Religion," in H. Shelton Smith, Robert T. Handy, and Lefferts A. Loetscher, *American Christianity: An Historical Interpretation with Representative Documents,* 2 vols. (New York: Charles Scribner's Sons, 1960), 1:407–11.

19. Josiah Smith, "A Sermon, on the Character, preaching, &c. of the Rev. Mr. Whitefield," in Howe, *History of the Presbyterian Church,* 1:233–34, and in Heimert and Miller, 62–69.

20. See William J. Bouwsma, *John Calvin: A Sixteenth Century Portrait* (New York: Oxford University Press, 1988), 231–32.

21. Garden, 47.

22. Smith, in Howe, *History of the Presbyterian Church,* 1:233.

23. See Heimert and Miller, xxvi–xxvii.

24. Garden, 56.

25. Howe, *History of the Presbyterian Church,* 1:233.

26. Simpson Journal, January 6, 1768; Hewat, 1:405–06.

27. As will be seen in chap. 7, the evangelical element at the Independent Meeting

House was far stronger in numbers and in social, economic, and especially political influence than the Unitarian element that broke off in 1817.

28. Simpson Journal, January 6, 1768.

29. Kenny, 12–13.

30. "Thoughts on the Revival," in Jonathan Edwards, *The Works of President Edwards,* ed. Sereno E. Dwight, 10 vols. (New York: S. Converse, 1829–30), 3:316.

31. Smith, in Howe, *History of the Presbyterian Church,* 1:234, and in Heimert and Miller, 69.

32. See Butler, "Enthusiasm Described and Decried," 305–25; and idem, *Awash,* 194–224. Butler sees the Revolution "at its heart" a "profoundly secular event" (*Awash,* 195). If some historians have overemphasized the role of religion in the Revolution, making religion the almost single factor in its origins, Butler surely underestimates religion's influence and earlier historians' identification of that influence. David Ramsay—whom Butler claimed saw the Revolution as "a thoroughly secular event"—was deeply influenced by the Reformed tradition and the Great Awakening and was intimately connected with those most prominently associated with the Awakening. Ramsay's providential and millennial interpretations are discussed later in chap. 6. In addition to Hewat and Ramsay, Charles Woodmason, Anglican missionary to the backcountry, noted in the 1760s the links between religious commitments and revolutionary sentiments: "Not less than 20 Itinerant Presbyterian, Baptist and Independant Preachers are maintain'd by the Synod of Pennsylvania and New England to traverse this Country Poisoni[n]g the Minds of the People—Instilling Democratical and Common Wealth Principles into their Minds—Embittering them against the very Name of Bishops, and all Episcopal government and laying deep their fatal Republican Notions and Principles—Especially—That they owe no Subjection to Great Britain—That they are a free People—That they are to pay allegiance to King George as their Sovereign—but as to Great Britain or the Parliament, or any there, that they have no more to think of or about them than the Turk or Pope—Thus do these Itinerant Preachers sent from the Northern colonies pervert the Mind of the Vulgar." Charles Woodmason, *The Carolina Backcountry on the Eve of the Revolution: The Journal and Other Writings of Charles Woodmason, Anglican Itinerant,* ed. Richard J. Hooker (Chapel Hill: University of North Carolina Press, 1953), 240–41.

33. Hewat, 1:410–11.

34. William Tennent's speech before the South Carolina Assembly in behalf of religious freedom is a clear expression of these sentiments. See Howe, *History of the Presbyterian Church,* 1:370–71, for important excerpts. For the evangelical challenge to the Anglican social order in Virginia, see Rhys Isaac, *The Transformation of Virginia, 1740–1790* (Chapel Hill: University of North Carolina Press, 1982); idem, "Evangelical Revolt: The Nature of the Baptists' Challenge to the Traditional Order in Virginia, 1765–1775," *William and Mary Quarterly* 31 (1974): 345–68; and see Patricia U. Bonomi, *Under the Cope of Heaven: Religion, Society and Politics in Colonial America* (New York: Oxford University Press, 1986).

35. See A. H. Newman, *A History of the Baptist Churches in the United States,* vol. 2 of *American Church History Series,* ed. Philip Schaff et al., 13 vols. (New York: Christian Literature Co., 1894), 311, 256–59, 308–12.

36. See ibid., 312–15; Henry Allen Tupper, *Two Centuries of the First Baptist Church of South Carolina* (Baltimore: R. H. Woodward, 1889); Leah Townsend, *South Carolina Baptists, 1670–1805* (Florence, S.C., 1935), 115.

37. Bolton, 116–19.

38. Ibid., 53–56, 74; Frank J. Klingberg, *An Appraisal of the Negro in Colonial South Carolina: A Study in Americanization* (Philadelphia: Porcupine Press, 1975), 96–103; Kenny, 15.

39. For a discussion of the low country population between 1740 and 1770, see Peter A.

Coclanis, *The Shadow of a Dream: Economic Life and Death in the South Carolina Low Country, 1670–1920* (New York: Oxford University Press, 1989), 63–68. Whatever growth came in the low country, the great growth of Presbyterianism was in the up-country. Here Scotch-Irish immigrants, pouring in from Pennsylvania, began to be touched by the Awakening just as its fires began to flicker on the seaboard. Through these frontier fires and those that followed in the next century, a vast region—the American South—would be significantly shaped and tempered by an emergent evangelical Protestantism. The low country would feel, long after its own Awakening had cooled, the consequences of these revivals burning so fiercely among the pioneers of the Piedmont.

40. See Klingberg, 96–98, 103; William Hutson, "Account of Marriages, Baptisms, and Burials &c.," PHSM; Stoney Creek Independent Presbyterian Church, Covenant and Register, 1743–60, PHSM; Bethel Pon Pon Presbyterian Church, Session Minutes, 1740–70, PHSM; Howe, *History of the Presbyterian Church*, 1:389; Whitefield, *Journals*, 444; Allan Gallay, *The Formation of a Planter Elite: Jonathan Bryan and the Southern Colonial Frontier* (Athens: University of Georgia Press, 1989), esp. 30–54. For Whitefield's call for the evangelization of slaves, see his "An Open Letter to the Inhabitants of Maryland, Virginia, North and South Carolina concerning the treatment of their Negroes," in George Whitefield, *The Works of the Reverend George Whitefield*, 6 vols. (London: Edward and Charles Dilly, 1772), 4:35–41.

41. See Hutson; Stoney Creek, Covenant and Register.

42. Whites were apparently also part of the gatherings inasmuch as reports said that Bryan was "gathering multitudes of people around him, especially negroes." See Howe, *History of the Presbyterian Church*, 1:244.

43. Ibid., 244–45; Weir, 186–87. There is a growing scholarly interest in Bryan. See Harvey H. Jackson, "Hugh Bryan and the Evangelical Movement in Colonial South Carolina," *William and Mary Quarterly* 43 (1986): 594–614; Leigh Eric Schmidt, " 'The Grand Prophet,' Hugh Bryan: Early Evangelicalism's Challenge to the Establishment and Slavery in the Colonial South," *SCHM* 87 (1986): 238–50; Alan Gallay, "The Origins of Slaveholders' Paternalism: George Whitefield, the Bryan Family, and the Great Awakening," *Journal of Southern History* 53 (August 1987): 369–94; and idem, *Formation of a Planter Elite.*

44. Gallay, *Formation of a Planter Elite*, 52–54. Jonathan Bryan was equally involved in the evangelization of African Americans. "The introduction of evangelism to slaves on the Bryans' plantations," Gallay wrote, "was a seminal moment in the spread of Christianity among Afro-Americans. Jonathan Bryan not only sought the conversion of slaves but also was one of the first southern planters to promote their evangelization by black preachers" (52). Bryan's wealthy neighbor, John Lambert, touched by the revival fires, became committed to the evangelization of slaves. His plantation in Liberty County, Georgia, became the center of religious activity among slaves. Lambert left this plantation and its slaves in a charitable trust, administered by the Midway Congregational Church. Slaves from the plantation long served as preachers in the community, and the plantation itself was a center of African American life. See James Stacy, *History of the Midway Congregational Church, Liberty County, Georgia*, rev. ed. (Newnan, Ga.: S. W. Murray, 1903), 164–68, 189–93; and Midway Congregational Church, Minutes of the Session, May 20, 1837, PHSM.

6. Competing Impulses: Tories, Whigs, and the Revolution

1. Robert Stansbury Lambert, *South Carolina Loyalists in the American Revolution* (Columbia: University of South Carolina Press, 1987), 198.

2. Ibid., 186, 306–07.

3. The congregation of First (Scots) was large and prosperous. As has been seen, the

building had been enlarged in 1763 and the pastor's salary exceeded that of the ministers of Saint Philip's and Saint Michael's. Certainly most of its members were Scots.

4. Robert M. Weir, *Colonial South Carolina: A History* (Millwood, N.Y.: KTO Press, 1983), 286.

5. Archibald Simpson Journal, September 1783, CLS.

6. The names of the trustees are found in Aaron Leland's sermon preached at the dedication of the new building of First (Scots) in 1814, printed in Edward G. Lilly, *Beyond The Burning Bush: First (Scots) Presbyterian Church, Charleston, S.C.* (Charleston: Garnier, 1971), 54.

7. Weir, 287.

8. Lambert, 6, 60, 63, 64.

9. Ibid., 251, 252, 180, 296, 280, 298.

10. Mabel L. Webber, ed., "Josiah Smith's Diary, 1780–1781," *SCHGM* 34 (1933): 196.

11. Lilly, *Beyond the Burning Bush*, 55. See also Lorenzo Sabine, *Loyalists of the American Revolution*, 2 vols. (Boston, 1864), 1:475; 2:471, 566, 597.

12. The best account of Hewat's life and work is Geraldine M. Meroney, "Alexander Hewat's Historical Account," in Lawrence H. Leder, ed., *The Colonial Legacy*, 3 vols. (New York: Harper and Row, 1971), 1:135–63.

13. Alexander Hewat, *An Historical Account of the Rise and Progress of the Colonies of South Carolina and Georgia*, 2 vols. in 1 (London, 1779), 528–31.

14. Ibid.

15. Edward McCrady, *The History of South Carolina in the Revolution, 1775–1780* (New York: Macmillan, 1901), 205–06.

16. The conspicuous part played by low country Dissenters in the Revolution has evaded more contemporary historians as well as McCrady. Pauline Maier in her study of early revolutionary leaders in the South—including the Carolina low country—has written: "A majority of southerners might have belonged to Calvinist denominations, but the revolutionary leaders considered here were Anglican or Catholic. Nor did southern revolutionaries have the same sense of connection with seventeenth-century revolutionary Calvinism as did, for example, their admired friend Samuel Adams, who saw himself as upholding the traditions and habits of his Puritan ancestors." Pauline Maier, "Early Revolutionary Leaders in the South and the Problem of Southern Distinctiveness," in Jeffrey J. Crow and Larry E. Tise, eds., *The Southern Experience in the American Revolution* (Chapel Hill: University of North Carolina Press, 1978), 14.

17. For Calvin's preference for republican government over monarchical, see John Calvin, *Institutes of the Christian Religion*, ed. John T. McNeill, vols. XX and XXI of *Library of Christian Classics* (Philadelphia: Westminster Press, 1960), XXI:1493–94 (IV, xx, 8). See also William J. Bouwsma, *John Calvin: A Sixteenth Century Portrait* (New York: Oxford University Press, 1988), 208–10. In contrast to McCrady's position, probably no congregation in the city was as united in its support of the Revolution as was the Independent Meeting House. The Anglican congregations were often bitterly divided between Tories and Whigs.

18. Newton B. Jones, ed., "Writings of the Reverend William Tennent, 1740–1777," *SCHM* 61 (1960): 130, 138–39.

19. See S. Charles Bolton, *Southern Anglicanism: The Church of England in Colonial South Carolina* (Westport, Conn.: Greenwood Press, 1982).

20. N. Jones, 140–42. For the widespread suspicion of Anglican bishops in the colonies, see Carl Bridenbaugh, *Mitre and Scepter: Transatlantic Faiths, Ideas, Personalities, and Politics, 1689–1775* (New York: Oxford University Press, 1962), esp. 233, for remarks of John Adams.

21. For an evaluation of Tennent's efforts in the backcountry, see John Richard Alden, *The South in the Revolution, 1763–1789*, vol. 3 of *A History of the South*, ed., Wendell H.

Stephenson and E. Merton Coulter (Baton Rouge: Louisiana State University Press, 1957), 200, and McCrady, *South Carolina in the Revolution, 1775–1780,* 41–44.

22. McCrady, *South Carolina in the Revolution, 1775–1780,* 5, 7, 20, 30, 31, 183–84.

23. Ibid., 362, 465; Edward McCrady, *The History of South Carolina in the Revolution, 1780–1785* (New York: MacMillan, 1902), 572, 685; Webber, "Smith's Diary" (1933): 200–205. Mathews and Ramsay are buried in the Independent Church's cemetery.

24. Robert W. Higgins, "The South Carolina Revolutionary Debt and Its Holders, 1776–1780," *SCHM* 72 (1971): 15–29.

25. Mabel L. Webber, ed., "Josiah Smith's Diary, 1780–1781," *SCHGM* 33 (1932): 3–4, 6–7, 282–84, and (1933): 78–83. Wives and children were also exiled. Shortly after her arrival in Philadelphia Mrs. Palmer gave birth to a son, Benjamin Morgan Palmer, who became in 1814 pastor of the Independent Meeting House in Charleston. Ibid. (1933): 78–83; George Howe, *History of the Presbyterian Church in South Carolina,* vol. 1 (Columbia: Duffie and Chapman, 1870), 455–56; McCrady, *South Carolina in the Revolution, 1780–1783,* 378.

26. Webber, "Smith's Diary" (1933): 209–10; McCrady, *South Carolina in the Revolution, 1775–1780,* 717, 724; McCrady, *South Carolina in the Revolution, 1780–1783,* 358–59.

27. Only two Tories stand out as exceptions to the rule of the country churches' membership being firmly on the Patriot side—Paul Hamilton, a wealthy planter and member of the Presbyterian church on Edisto Island, and Paul Capers of the Wappetaw church. Hamilton's father, Paul Hamilton, Sr., had been a leader in the Wilton church, and his cousin, also Paul Hamilton, was a leading Patriot and governor of the state in 1802–04. The governor was an officer in the Wilton church. See Lambert, 65, 87, 280; and Slann L. C. Simmons, ed., "Records of the Willtown Presbyterian Church, 1747–1841," *SCHM* 62 (1961): 109. For Capers, see Lambert, 254, 251, 266; and Petrona Royall McIver, "Wappetaw Congregational Church," *SCHM* 58 (1957): 84.

28. McCrady, *South Carolina in the Revolution, 1775–1780,* 5, 73, 110, 115, 212, 281, 465. Bee's family provided many of the leaders in the Wilton church. He spent much of his life in Charleston. See Simmons, 47.

29. Webber, "Smith's Diary" (1933): 200–205.

30. Howe, *History of the Presbyterian Church,* 1:455; Webber, "Smith's Diary" (1932): 282–84.

31. McCrady, *South Carolina in the Revolution, 1775–1780,* 12, 14, 331, 354, 577, 651.

32. See David K. Bowden, *The Execution of Isaac Hayne* (Lexington, S.C.: Sandlapper Press, 1977); and McCrady, *South Carolina in the Revolution, 1780–1783,* 130–33, 318–21, 382–98.

33. For the reasons, amid all of the ambiguity of his situation, Hayne was viewed as a martyr, see McCrady, *South Carolina in the Revolution, 1780–1783,* 402, 412. For the implications of Hayne's execution, see also Bowden, 47–66.

34. Maier, 14.

35. See John Adams's "Letter to Hezekiah Niles" (1818), quoted in Sydney E. Ahlstrom, *A Religious History of the American People* (New Haven: Yale University Press, 1972), 262.

36. See Bouwsma, 206–10.

37. See *Institutes,* XXI:1108–11 (IV, vi, 8–9).

38. Arthur H. Shaffer, "David Ramsay and the Limits of Revolutionary Nationalism," in Michael O'Brien and David Moltke-Hansen, eds., *Intellectual Life in Antebellum Charleston* (Knoxville: University of Tennessee Press, 1986), 48. See also Bernard Bailyn's masterful *Ideological Origins of the American Revolution* (Cambridge: Harvard University Press, 1967).

39. For an indication of the influence of the College of New Jersey (Princeton) on low country Presbyterians and Congregationalists, see Howe, *History of the Presbyterian Church,* 1:378, and note the number of Princeton graduates serving as ministers in the low country.

40. For the role of Witherspoon and the influence of Scottish Common Sense Philoso-

phy in American life, see Donald H. Meyer, *The Instructed Conscience* (Philadelphia: University of Pennsylvania Press, 1972), and Henry F. May, *The Enlightenment in America* (New York: Oxford University Press, 1976).

41. For Ramsay's connections with Princeton as his "spiritual home," see Shaffer, "Revolutionary Nationalism," 51–53.

42. David Ramsay, *The History of South Carolina, From its First Settlement in 1670 to the Year 1808,* 2 vols. in 1 (Charleston: David Longworth, 1809), 2:221–22. Ramsay's remarks here have been largely ignored by historians; see Maier, 14, and Jon Butler, *Awash in a Sea of Faith: Christianizing the American People* (Cambridge: Harvard University Press, 1990), 195. Ramsay's remarks, together with the evidence presented here of extensive involvement of Dissenters in the Revolution, call for a careful reevaluation of important issues in the study of the South and the Revolution. Among these issues are the role of the Reformed political traditions and ethic on Southern revolutionary leaders and the personality types of those leaders. See Edmund S. Morgan, "The Puritan Ethic and the American Revolution," *William and Mary Quarterly* 24 (1967): 3–43; C. Vann Woodward, "The Southern Ethic in a Puritan World," ibid., 25 (1968): 343–70; and Michael Walzer, *The Revolution of the Saints: A Study in the Origins of Radical Politics* (Cambridge: Harvard University Press, 1965).

43. David Ramsay, "An Oration on the Advantages of American Independence," in Robert L. Brunhouse, ed., *David Ramsay, 1749–1815: Selections From His Writings* (Philadelphia: American Philosophical Society, 1965), 183. Once again, this study points in a different direction from Maier, who asked "How, then, did the creed of sacrifice, austerity, and industriousness appear in the South? Not, it seems, through Calvinist tradition" (Maier, 14). If one sees a strong Dissenter tradition in the low country that provided significant leadership to the Revolution, then the "creed of sacrifice, austerity, and industriousness" that Ramsay advocated does not seem so perplexing.

44. Ramsay, "An Oration," 188.

45. See letters between Ramsay and Rush, Smith, and Morse in Brunhouse.

46. Shaffer, "Revolutionary Nationalism," 67. The reluctance of some historians to see any influence of the Awakening on Ramsay may be rooted in a confusion of the Awakening with later nineteenth-century revivalism and twentieth-century Fundamentalism. This seems particularly true of Brunhouse.

47. Ramsay, *History of South Carolina,* 2:15–16. Ramsay's point about Whitefield and "the broad and wide-spreading stream of christianity" helps to illustrate the influence of the Awakening in creating a Protestant consensus in American religious life. Differences that had long divided Protestants did not seem so important in light of the common experience of revival. See Ahlstrom, *Religious History,* 293–94. This aspect of the Awakening's influence no doubt played as important a role in Ramsay's own tolerant attitude toward other Christians as did the influence of Enlightenment ideas.

48. Ramsay, *History of South Carolina,* 1:222.

49. Ramsay, "An Oration," 191.

50. The best general study that treats slaves and the Revolution continues to be Benjamin Quarles, *The Negro in the American Revolution* (Chapel Hill: University of North Carolina Press, 1961). See also Sidney Kaplan, *The Black Presence in the Era of the American Revolution* (1973; reprint, Amherst: University of Massachusetts Press, 1988); Ira Berlin and Ronald Hoffman, eds., *Slavery and Freedom in the Age of the American Revolution* (Charlottesville: University of Virginia Press, 1983); Duncan J. MacLeod, *Slavery, Race and the American Revolution* (London: Cambridge University Press, 1974); Donald L. Robinson, *Slavery in the Structure of American Politics, 1765–1820* (New York: Harcourt Brace Jovanovich, 1971).

51. Howe, *History of the Presbyterian Church,* 1:461. See also Peter Wood, " 'Taking Care of Business' in Revolutionary South Carolina: Republicanism and the Slave Society," in Crow

and Tise, 268–93; and M. Foster Farley, "The South Carolina Negro in the American Revolution, 1775–1783," *SCHM* 79 (1978): 75–86.

52. Shaffer, "Revolutionary Nationalism," 73, 74.

53. Ramsay to John Elliott, November 26, 1788, in Brunhouse, 123. For a more extensive discussion of Ramsay and slavery, see Arthur H. Shaffer, "Between Two Worlds: David Ramsay and the Politics of Slavery," *Journal of Southern History* 50 (April 1984): 175–96.

7. Institutional Developments: "Our Southern Zion"

1. See Peter A. Coclanis, *The Shadow of a Dream: Economic Life and Death in the South Carolina Low Country, 1670–1920* (New York: Oxford University Press, 1989), 111–58; Richard C. Wade, *Slavery in the Cities: the South 1820–1860* (New York: Oxford University Press, 1964), 10–12; Alfred Glaze Smith, Jr., *Economic Readjustment of an Old Cotton State: South Carolina, 1820–1860* (Columbia: University of South Carolina Press, 1958), 1–18; and George C. Rogers, Jr., *Charleston in the Age of the Pinckneys* (Norman: University of Oklahoma Press, 1969), 3–25.

2. The census of 1850 provides a picture in black and white of the region: 58,339 whites; 5,148 free blacks; 137,818 slaves. See J. D. B. DeBow, *Statistical View of the United States* (Washington, D.C.: A. O. P. Nicholson, 1854), 302–03. Rural Charleston County, for example, was composed of 4,996 whites, 420 free blacks, and 35,243 slaves. See ibid. The low country had more large slave owners than any other region of the country in 1850. See ibid., 302, 96; Wade, 326.

3. See, for example, the networks of slave families, in Herbert G. Gutman, *The Black Family in Slavery and Freedom, 1750–1925* (New York: Pantheon Books, 1976).

4. The functionalist emphasis on the role of institutions in a society, while exaggerating consistency and purposefulness, nevertheless provides important questions to ask about the functions of Reformed institutions within low country society. See especially Emile Durkheim, *The Elementary Forms of the Religious Life* (1915; reprint, London: Allen and Unwin, 1964); A. R. Radcliffe-Brown, *Structure and Function in Primitive Society* (London: Cohen and West, 1952); and Talcott Parsons, *The Social System* (Glencoe, Ill.: Free Press, 1951).

5. For the disorders of the time in the low country, and especially the disruptions of church life, see Archibald Simpson Journal, 1783, CLS; George N. Edwards, *A History of the Independent or Congregational Church of Charleston South Carolina* (Boston: Pilgrim Press, 1947), 39–48; George Howe, *History of the Presbyterian Church in South Carolina*, vol. 1 (Columbia: Duffie and Chapman, 1870), 461–73.

6. There is a vast literature on the Second Great Awakening and its impact on American religious life. Among the most important studies are Whitney R. Cross, *The Burned-Over District: The Social and Intellectual History of Enthusiastic Religion in Western New York, 1800–1850* (Ithaca: Cornell University Press, 1950); George M. Marsden, *The Evangelical Mind and the New School Presbyterian Experience* (New Haven: Yale University Press, 1970); Donald G. Mathews, *Religion in the Old South* (Chicago: University of Chicago Press, 1977); John Boles, *The Great Revival, 1787–1805: The Origins of the Southern Evangelical Mind* (Lexington: University Press of Kentucky, 1972); and Anne C. Loveland, *Southern Evangelicals and the Social Order, 1800–1860* (Baton Rouge: Louisiana State University Press, 1980), see esp. chap. 6, "Benevolence and Reform." Loveland has a particularly helpful bibliography related to the South. Nathan O. Hatch's important book, *The Democratization of American Christianity* (New Haven: Yale University Press, 1989), emphasizes that the Second Great Awakening needs to be interpreted primarily as a "populist upsurge" of society's outsiders. According to Hatch, rather than bringing unity and coherence, the Awakening "splintered

American Christianity and magnified the diversity of institutions claiming to be the church" (226). Behind the Awakening was a crisis in authority in popular American culture that challenged and soon overwhelmed the authority of educated elites. While the Second Awakening had an important enlivening influence on the low country, there is little evidence of such a populist impulse among the whites in the region. As this chapter shows, the Reformed churches continued through the Civil War to outnumber in white membership the more populist Baptists and Methodists. On the other hand, the African American "church within a church"—and the "African Church" closed by white authorities—reflected much of the populist impulse described by Hatch. See chap. 8. Hatch notes that only in the South did the conservative theological spirit of Calvinism hold sway (201).

7. Louis C. LaMotte, *Colored Light: The Story of the Influence of Columbia Theological Seminary, 1828–1936* (Richmond: Presbyterian Committee of Publication, 1937), 298–308.

8. In order to protect their property under colonial law, non-Anglican churches were forced to vest their property in trustees, a far from satisfactory arrangement. For William Tennent's role in disestablishment, see Howe, *History of the Presbyterian Church,* 1:370–71.

9. Rhodri W. Liscombe, *The Church Architecture of Robert Mills* (Easley, S.C.: Southern Historical Press, 1985), 5–7.

10. The Charleston Unitarians represented an important link with the commercial society of maritime New England.

11. During the ten years that important new buildings were being constructed by First (Scots), the Circular Church, and Second Presbyterian, only one new Episcopal church was built—Saint Paul's. Dr. William Percy, who organized the congregation out of a group that withdrew from Saint Philip's, was "in his religious opinions" a Calvinist. "He believed the Church [Anglican/Episcopal] to be Calvinistic in its Articles." Frederick Dalcho, *An Historical Account of the Protestant Episcopal Church in South Carolina* (Charleston: E. Thayer, 1820), 240. Without making too much of his Calvinism, the strength of the Reformed tradition in the city is given additional support by the Reformed influence in the only Episcopal church built in the city during the first decades of the nineteenth century.

12. Third Presbyterian Church, Session Minutes, 1824–61, PHSM.

13. Howe, *History of the Presbyterian Church,* 1:325, 452. For the French Reformed Book of Liturgies and the French Reformed Confession of 1559, which began to be used again by the Huguenot Church in Charleston, see John T. McNeill, *The History and Character of Calvinism* (1954; reprint, London: Oxford University Press, 1967), 246–47.

14. The building has been for a number of years the Mount Zion African Methodist Episcopal Church at 5 Glebe Street.

15. Charleston Presbytery, Minutes, 1851, PHSM.

16. See Erskine Clarke, *Wrestlin' Jacob: A Portrait of Religion in the Old South* (Atlanta: John Knox Press, 1979), 140–58.

17. In addition to the five churches of the Reformed tradition on Meeting Street, there were Saint Michael's Episcopal and, after 1856, the Citadel Square Baptist Church.

18. Petrona Royall McIver, "Wappetaw Congregational Church," *SCHM* 58 (1957): 85–93.

19. The congregation continued to worship at Dorchester at least on occasion during the winters. See Howe, *History of the Presbyterian Church,* 1:566–69, 588–89; idem, *History of the Presbyterian Church in South Carolina,* vol. 2 (Columbia: W. J. Duffie, 1883), 213; Dorchester Independent Church, Records, 1794–1854, PHSM; and Summerville Presbyterian Church, Minutes of the Session, 1859–1905, and Miscellaneous Records, 1859–61, PHSM.

20. Bethel Pon Pon Presbyterian Church, Session Minutes, 1783–1861, and Trustee Minutes, 1783–1861, PHSM. For similar developments at Stoney Creek, see Stoney Creek Inde-

pendent Presbyterian Church, Session Minutes, 1855–61, Minutes and Accounts, 1773–1860, Book of the Congregation, 1823–61, and Financial Records, 1823–61, PHSM.

21. Annie Jenkins Batson, *Rockville Presbyterian Church, Wadmalaw Island, South Carolina* (Charleston: Walker, Evans and Cogswell, 1976).

22. In 1836 William Seabrook left a $5,000 legacy to the church. This money was used to add the fluted columns and the arched ceiling.

23. For strength of some of the other Presbyterian congregations not mentioned, see *MGAPCUSA(OS)*, 1840–60, PHSM; and esp. James Island Presbyterian Church, Records, 1833–61, PHSM; Wilton Presbyterian Church, Records, 1850–61, PHSM; and Howe, *History of the Presbyterian Church*, 1:474, 2:50.

24. Howe, *History of the Presbyterian Church*, 2:passim.

25. In 1851, for example, the white membership of the Charleston Methodist churches was Trinity, 302; Cumberland, 75; and Bethel, 155. (The number of white Methodists in the city had grown slowly since the early days in the century.) The following year the white membership of the Baptist churches of the city was First Baptist, 293; Wentworth Street, 178; and Morris Street, 33. The combined white membership of both denominations was less than 1,100. The white Congregational and Presbyterian membership in these years was conservatively between 1,100 and 1,200: First (Scots), 350; Circular Congregational, 325; Glebe Street, 100; Third [Central], 120; and Second, 300. In addition there was the small congregation of the French Huguenot Church. See Minutes of the Charleston Baptist Association, 1840–61, SCHS; Reports of State Conventions of Baptist Churches in South Carolina, 1821–60, Furman University Archives, Greenville, S.C.; First Baptist Church, Minutes of the Board of Deacons, First Baptist Church, Charleston, S.C., 1847–70, First Baptist Church archives, Charleston; Henry Allen Tupper, *Two Centuries of the First Baptist Church of South Carolina* (Baltimore: R. H. Woodward, 1889); Minutes of the Annual Conference of the Methodist Episcopal Church in South Carolina, 1831–60, Wofford College Archives, Spartanburg, S.C.; F. A. Mood, *Methodism in Charleston: A Narrative* (Nashville: E. Stevenson and J. E. Evans, 1856), esp. 87, 184–85; *MGAPCUSA(OS)*, 1850–60, PHSM; Charleston Presbytery, Minutes, 1850–60, PHSM; Third Presbyterian Church, Register, 1827–81, PHSM; Second Presbyterian Church, Minutes of the Session, 1840–60, PHSM; First (Scots) Presbyterian Church, antebellum membership list, First (Scots) archives; Circular Congregational Church, Record Book, 1850–60, Circular Congregational archives; Zion Presbyterian Church, Communicants Roll Book (white membership), 1855, PHSM.

26. In 1814, for example, the white membership of the Episcopal churches of the city was: Saint Michael's, "about 240"; Saint Philip's, "about 240"; and Third [Saint Paul's], "from 40 to 50," for a total white membership of approximately 530. See Dalcho, 539. That same year, Circular Congregational had 340 white members; First (Scots) had approximately 250; and Second Presbyterian approximately 140. In addition there was the small congregation of the French Huguenot Church. In the countryside the white membership in Episcopal churches was less than 175 in 1814: Saint Helena's, Beaufort, 40 out of total white and black communicants of 58 (estimates of whites are based—and probably exaggerated—on comparison to city churches in Charleston); Saint John's Berkeley, 19; Saint Thomas and Saint Dennis, 1; Saint Andrew's, 5? out of total black and white communicants of 7; Edisto, 18; Saint Helena Island, 7? out of total of 9 black and white communicants; Hilton Head, 3? out of total of 3 black and white communicants; Saint Bartholomew's, 20? out of total of 30 white and black communicants (see report of 1815, in Dalcho, 517); Saint Paul's, Stono, 6? out of total of 8 black and white communicants; Christ Church, 7? out of total of 9 black and white communicants; Lower Clarendon, 4; Saint James, Santee, "4 or 5"; Saint James Goose Creek, 18? out of total of 20 black and white communicants. Dalcho, 539, 547. Esti-

mates for the following congregations, not given for 1814, are drawn from reports in 1815: Saint Helena Island; Saint Paul's, Stono; Christ Church; and Lower Clarendon. Saint James Goose Creek is from report of 1817. See Dalcho, 547, 557.

A conservative estimate of white membership during the same period in the Presbyterian and Congregational churches outside Charleston in the low country is 251: James Island, 20; Johns Island, 40; Edisto, 16; Wilton, 40; Stoney Creek, 15; Bethel Pon Pon, 25; Dorchester, 15; Wappetaw, 40; Beaufort, 15; and Salkehatchie, 25 out of a total of 30 black and white communicants. See Howe, *History of the Presbyterian Church*, 2:194–96, 213–16, 229–33, 319–21, and 330–37; Stoney Creek, Minutes and Accounts, 1773–1860; Bethel Pon Pon, Session Minutes, 1783–1861, and Trustee Minutes, 1783–1861; Dorchester Independent Church, Records, 1794–1854.

Many of these churches, both Episcopal and Presbyterian, showed relatively substantial growth by 1820, indicating the influence of the Second Great Awakening. See especially Dalcho, 542–73, and *Journal of the Proceedings of the Protestant Episcopal Church in the Diocese of South Carolina, 1825–1860*, SCHS.

27. See Bureau of the Census, *Statistical View of the United States . . . A Compendium of the Seventh Census* (Washington, D.C.: A. O. P. Nicholson, 1854), 136–37.

28. David Ramsay, *The History of South Carolina, From its First Settlement in 1670 to the Year 1809*, 2 vols. in 1 (Charleston: David Longworth, 1809), 1:26.

29. Ramsay provides a list of churches belonging to the new presbytery of Charleston as well as those in the old presbytery. See ibid., 25; see also Howe, *History of the Presbyterian Church*, 1:674.

30. Francis Asbury, *The Journal and Letters of Francis Asbury*, ed. Elmer T. Clark, 3 vols. (Nashville: Abingdon Press, 1958), 2:passim; Mood; and James Hennesey, *American Catholics: A History of the Roman Catholic Community in the United States* (New York: Oxford University Press, 1981), 91.

31. See Howe, *History of the Presbyterian Church*, 1:675–76; 2:167–71, 219. But compare n. 29 above.

32. Ibid., 1:164.

33. For the debate over the nature of governments, see Bernard Bailyn, *The Ideological Origins of the American Revolution* (Cambridge: Harvard University Press, 1967), 230–319.

34. Ramsay, 2:28–30. Some churches were associated with both the Congregational association and a presbytery at the same time.

35. In addition to those churches in the mainstream of the Reformed tradition in the low country, there were also German Reformed congregations that were organized in the years around the Revolution. These congregations tended either to move toward a Lutheran connection or, under the influence of Methodist circuit riders, to become Methodists. See the South Carolina Synod of the Lutheran Church in America, *A History of the Lutheran Church in South Carolina* (Columbia: R. L. Bryan, 1971), 106 ff.

36. The details of the 1839 division can be found in Erskine Clarke, "The Strange Case of Charleston Union Presbytery," *Affirmation* (Fall 1993): 41–58.

37. See John W. Kuykendall, *Southern Enterprise: The Work of National Evangelical Societies in the Antebellum South* (Westport, Conn.: Greenwood Press, 1982); and Lois W. Banner, "Religious Benevolence as Social Control: A Critique of an Interpretation," *Journal of American History* 60 (1973): 25. For an analysis that sees social control by a narrow group as a primary element in the benevolent societies, see Clifford S. Griffin, *Their Brothers' Keepers: Moral Stewardship in the United States, 1800–1965* (New Brunswick: Rutgers University Press, 1960).

38. Kuykendall, 47.

39. Thomas S. Grimké, *Address at the celebration of the Sunday School Jubilee, or, the fiftieth*

year from the institution, in the hall of the Sunday School Depository, on Wednesday evening, 14th of September, 1831 (Philadelphia: American Sunday School Union, 1832), 9.

40. H. L. Pinckney, *An address delivered before the Methodist Benevolent Society, at their anniversary meeting, in the Methodist Protestant Church, in Wentworth Street, on the 1st Monday in July 1835* (Charleston: E. J. Van Brunt, 1835), 4.

41. Thomas Smyth, "Faith, the Principle of Missions" (1857), in *The Collected Works of the Rev. Thomas Smyth, D.D.*, ed. J. W. Flinn, 10 vols. (Columbia: R. L. Bryan, 1908), 7:28–29.

42. See Karl Mannheim's description of conservative utopianism in Karl Mannheim, *Ideology and Utopia*, trans. Louis Wirth and Edward Shils (New York: Harcourt, Brace, and World, 1936), 229–39. Smyth and his colleagues in the low country Reformed community did not simply reflect, however, this conservative type of utopianism but, as the above quote makes clear, there was also an important element of what Mannheim calls liberal utopianism (219–29). This type of utopianism emphasizes growth, maturity, and education. The Unionism of Smyth, Adger, and other leaders in the low country Reformed community carried with it elements of this nineteenth-century liberal utopianism, although it was in tension with their conservatism.

43. See Kuykendall, 46–48.

44. The constitution of the Charleston Juvenile Missionary Society can be found in Louisa Cheves Stoney, ed., *Autobiographical Notes, Letters and Reflections by Thomas Smyth, D. D.* (Charleston: Walker, Evans and Cogswell, 1914), 139–41.

45. Howe, *History of the Presbyterian Church*, 2:336, 402–03. For the Southern Board of Foreign Missions, see Ernest Trice Thompson, *Presbyterians in the South*, 3 vols. (Richmond: John Knox Press, 1963, 1973), 1:296–97.

46. Howe, *History of the Presbyterian Church*, 2:558–61; Henry Alexander White, *Southern Presbyterian Leaders* (New York: Neale, 1911), 144.

47. White, 394–409.

48. *Charleston Observer*, January 6, 1827.

49. Ibid., October 1, 1836; July 21, 1839; September 21, 1839; August 5, 1837.

50. See Raymond Morris Bost, *The Reverend John Bachman and the Development of Southern Lutheranism* (Ph.D. diss., Yale University, 1963; Ann Arbor, Mich.: University Microfilms, 1963), 390–403.

51. Kuykendall, 3–22, 88. For the influence of Congregationalists and Presbyterians nationally in the benevolent organizations, see Griffin; Sydney E. Ahlstrom, *A Religious History of the American People* (New Haven: Yale University Press, 1972), 637–47; and Timothy L. Smith, *Revivalism and Social Reform in Mid-Nineteenth-Century America* (New York: Abingdon Press, 1957).

52. *Charleston Observer*, May 8, 1830.

53. Kuykendall, 38–53.

54. This issue came to a head in the Old School–New School division.

55. L. Stoney, 596–98.

56. This educational pattern was a part of the "Americanization" of Carolina society. See David Moltke-Hansen, "The Expansion of Intellectual Life: A Prospectus," in Michael O'Brien and David Moltke-Hansen, eds., *Intellectual Life in Antebellum Charleston* (Knoxville: University of Tennessee Press, 1986), 3–44.

57. George Howe, "History of Columbia Theological Seminary," in *Memorial Volume of the Semi-Centennial of the Theological Seminary at Columbia, South Carolina* (Columbia: Presbyterian Publishing House, 1884), 140.

58. William Childs Robinson, *Columbia Theological Seminary and the Southern Presbyterian Church* (Decatur, Ga.: 1931), 14, 27–29.

59. Howe, "History of Columbia Theological Seminary," 139.

60. See E. Brooks Holifield, *The Gentlemen Theologians: American Theology in Southern Culture, 1795–1860* (Durham: Duke University Press, 1978). For the image of the "godly gentleman" in Puritan and Huguenot thought, see Michael Walzer, *The Revolution of the Saints: A Study in the Origins of Radical Politics* (Cambridge: Harvard University Press, 1965), 20–21, 232–67. For Presbyterian concern for a cultured and respectable ministry at the time of the Second Great Awakening, see Hatch, 17–46.

61. The neighboring College of South Carolina had as a primary function teaching students how to be "Southern gentlemen." See Daniel W. Hollis, *The University of South Carolina*, 2 vols. (Columbia: University of South Carolina Press, 1951).

62. Howe, "History of Columbia Theological Seminary," 139–40; W. Robinson, 14–23. Not surprisingly, Columbia's board of directors was dominated by the low country. Most of the early financial support for the seminary came from low country wealth. William Seabrook of Edisto Island made the largest contribution in the seminary's early history. Many of the students also came from the low country, particularly from Circular and Second in Charleston and Midway Congregational.

63. In his published Harvard dissertation, William Childs Robinson ignored the social, economic, and cultural links to the low country. Moreover, in pointing to Leland and Palmer as examples of New England influence, he exaggerated. Leland had lived most of his life in the low country, had married into an important low country family, and had served for years as a low country pastor before coming to Columbia. Palmer grew up in Charleston. See W. Robinson, 16–21.

8. A Church Both African American and Reformed

1. Second Presbyterian Church, Minutes of the Session, April 1817, PHSM. The two other "people of colour" who joined with Vesey were baptized at the time they joined, while Vesey was not, indicating that he had been previously baptized and that he probably belonged to another church before transferring to Second. Several blacks with the name of Vesey were members of Second Church throughout the antebellum period, including Susan Vesey and Robert Vesey, who became a leader at Zion Presbyterian. Robert Vesey, a son of Denmark and a carpenter of some note, was the architect for the great Emmanuel A.M.E. Church when it was rebuilt after the Civil War. Denmark Vesey has generally been identified with the A.M.E. church of Morris Brown that was closed following the attempted insurrection. While his name does not appear on any of the early Methodist records in the city, there is no conclusive evidence that he was not associated in some way with the A.M.E. church. What is clear is that he was a member of Second Presbyterian for five years before the attempted insurrection and that the Vesey family continued its connection with that congregation and then Zion Presbyterian until the Civil War. See Record of the Colored Members in the Methodist Church, Charleston, S.C., 1821–80, Trinity Methodist Church archives, Charleston. In 1850, "A Colored American," probably a free black from Charleston, published in New York a pamphlet that included a personal reminiscence of the Vesey insurrection. Vesey was described as "the philanthropic and patriotic Denmark Vesey, well known for his industrious habits as a carpenter, and moral pursuit in life as a Christian, in full communion in one of the Established churches in Charleston." See A Colored American, *The Late Contemplated Insurrection in Charleston, S.C. . . .* (New York: Printed for the Author, 1850), 4–5. Two other leaders of the insurrection associated with Second Presbyterian were John Enslow and Bacchus Hammett, both of whose owners were members of that congregation.

2. Details of the Vesey conspiracy, along with excerpts of the official report of the trials, can be found in Robert S. Starobin, ed., *Denmark Vesey: The Slave Conspiracy of 1822*

(Englewood Cliffs, N.J.: Prentice-Hall, 1970). See also John Lofton, *Insurrection in South Carolina: The Turbulent World of Denmark Vesey* (Yellow Springs, Ohio: Antioch Press, 1964), and Richard C. Wade, *Slavery in the Cities: the South 1820–1860* (New York: Oxford University Press, 1964). Wade's view that a serious insurrection was never planned has not been widely accepted by historians. See, for example, Starobin. For the official report itself, see Lionel H. Kennedy and Thomas Parker, *An Official Report of the Trials of Sundry Negroes, Charged with an Attempt to Raise an Insurrection in the State of South Carolina* (Charleston: James R. Schenck, 1822).

3. John B. Adger, *My Life and Times* (Richmond: Presbyterian Committee of Publication, 1899), 52–53.

4. Starobin, 31, 33, 21.

5. While Vesey used biblical imagery and religious insights to construe his utopian vision, his utopianism does not appear to have contained an apocalyptic note or to represent a chiliastic movement. I have been unable to find any evidence that Vesey believed his movement would be the spark for a millennial kingdom coming from heaven. While Vesey's vision gives hints of a transcendent point of departure for a social revolution (his references to creation and the Children of Israel being delivered out of Egypt), his religious insights and motives led him to a revolutionary utopianism more closely aligned with twentieth-century liberationist themes than with the chiliasm of the sixteenth-century revolutionary Thomas Munzer. Nevertheless, there were important parallels between Munzer's utopianism and that of Vesey. For the character of Munzer's chiliastic utopianism, see Karl Mannheim, *Ideology and Utopia,* trans. Louis Wirth and Edward Shils (New York: Harcourt, Brace, and World, 1936), 211–19.

6. See Mannheim's treatment of Munzer in ibid., 212–13.

7. Starobin, 34–35.

8. For counterutopias, see Mannheim, 212–13, and Paul Ricoeur, *Lectures on Ideology and Utopia,* ed. George H. Taylor (New York: Columbia University Press, 1986), 275, 289.

9. See chap. 11 below.

10. See, for example, Charles C. Jones, *Annual Report of the Missionary to the Negroes, in Liberty County, (Ga.) Presented to the Association, November 1833* (Charleston: Observer Office Press, 1934), and the regular reports that Jones presented in following years. For Calvin's and later Calvinists' insistence that the nobility "spread the true religion among its dependents," see Michael Walzer, *The Revolution of the Saints: A Study in the Origins of Radical Politics* (Cambridge: Harvard University Press, 1965), 51.

11. The history of the Emmanuel A.M.E. Church adds to the ambiguity surrounding the church's relationship to the Vesey insurrection. In order to avoid increasing harassment, the church had presented to the legislature in 1820 a petition to recognize its right to worship. When the petition was rejected, the church building was demolished by Charleston authorities. By 1821, approximately 3,000 African Americans, including most of the class leaders, had returned to the white-dominated Methodist congregations. Morris Brown and the others who had gone to Philadelphia did not, however, return, and the remnant of Emmanuel evidently went underground. The continuation of the "African Church" was an important source of anxiety for whites. None of the recognized Emmanuel leaders—those who appeared in the official church records—were accused, however, in 1822 of participating in the Vesey plot. The congregation nevertheless was frequently mentioned in the trial record, and some of those executed were said to be associated with the church. See F. A. Mood, *Methodism in Charleston: A Narrative* (Nashville: E. Stevenson and J. E. Evans, 1856), 130–33; Daniel A. Payne, *History of the African Methodist Episcopal Church* (New York: Arno Press, 1969), 13–30; and Trinity Methodist, Record of the Colored Members.

12. At Third Presbyterian, for example, a comparison of the white membership roll with

the list of owners in the black membership roll reveals that of the ninety-eight slaves who joined between 1823 and 1856, only four can be positively identified as belonging to white members of the congregation. See Third Presbyterian Church, Register of the Coloured Members of the 3rd. Presbyterian Church, 1826–60, and Roll Book and Letters of Transfer, PHSM; and Second Presbyterian, Minutes of the Session, 1840–49.

13. Mood, passim; and Henry Allen Tupper, *Two Centuries of the First Baptist Church of South Carolina* (Baltimore: R. H. Woodward, 1889); Thomas Leonard Williams, "The Methodist Mission to the Slaves" (Ph.D. diss., Yale University, 1943), 32–57; and *Minutes of the Annual Conference of the Methodist Episcopal Church in South Carolina*, 1856, SCHS; Minutes of the Charleston Baptist Association, 1845, SCHS.

14. *Minutes of the Synod of the Presbyterian Church in South Carolina*, 1845–60, PHSM; *MGAPCUSA(OS)*, 1845–60, PHSM.

15. *Proceedings of the Meeting in Charleston, S.C., May 13–15, 1845, on the Religious Instruction of the Negroes, Together with the Report of the Committee, and the Address to the Public* (Charleston: B. Jenkins, 1845), 47.

16. Ibid., 45–46.

17. Ibid., 46–47.

18. *MGAPCUSA(OS)*, 1860, 230. During the pastorate of William States Lee at Edisto Island Presbyterian Church, 89 whites and 338 blacks joined the church between 1821 and 1858. See George Howe, *History of the Presbyterian Church in South Carolina*, vol. 2 (Columbia: W. J. Duffie, 1883), 618.

19. *MGAPCUSA(OS)*, 1860, 230–31.

20. Stoney Creek Independent Presbyterian Church, Register, 1832–33, PHSM; Wilton Presbyterian Church, Register of Communicants, 1860, PHSM; Johns Island Presbyterian Church, Minutes of the Session, 1850–61, PHSM.

21. By the late twentieth century, no presbyteries in the country would have a larger portion of their constituency African American than did those which covered the low country. The African American Congregational community would be centered for almost a hundred years around Plymouth Congregational Church and Avery Normal Institute. See *MGAPC(USA)*, 1990, PHSM; and Edmund L. Drago, *Initiative, Paternalism, & Race Relations: Charleston's Avery Normal Institute* (Athens: University of Georgia Press, 1990).

22. The classes were also at the heart of the much larger Methodist African American community in the low country. Indeed, the class system had been developed by early Methodist leaders and reflected Methodism's relationship to Pietism with its emphasis on small groups within a congregation's life. See Trinity Methodist, Record of the Colored Members.

23. For the requirement that black leaders give written reports to church authorities, see, for example, Circular Congregational Church, Record Book, June 24, 1844, Circular Congregational Church archives.

24. At the First Baptist Church in 1851, Jacob Legaré, Ned Laurens, and Thomas Bell were listed as "coloured preachers of the congregation." First Baptist Church, Minutes of the Board of Deacons, First Baptist Church, Charleston, S.C., September 8, 1851, First Baptist Church archives.

25. Second Presbyterian, Minutes of the Session, September 1850; Circular Congregational, Record Book, July 1848.

26. For the use of the term "monopoly of imagination," see Robert K. Merton, *Social Theology and Social Structure* (Glencoe, Ill.: Free Press, 1957), 157, and "Monopoly and Marginality in Imagination," in Walter Brueggemann, *Interpretation and Obedience: From Faithful Reading to Faithful Living* (Minneapolis: Fortress Press, 1991), 184–204.

27. *Proceedings of the Meeting in Charleston*, 39. For general discussions of African American preachers during this period, see Eugene D. Genovese, *Roll, Jordan, Roll: The World*

the Slaves Made (New York: Pantheon Books, 1974), 255–79; Charles Joyner, *Down By the Riverside: A Carolina Slave Community* (Urbana: University of Illinois Press, 1984), 169–71; Albert J. Raboteau, *Slave Religion: The "Invisible Institution" in the Antebellum South* (New York: Oxford University Press, 1978); Henry H. Mitchell, *Black Preaching* (Philadelphia: Westminster Press, 1970); and John Blassingame, "Status and Social Structure in the Slave Community," in Randall M. Miller, ed., *The Afro-American Slaves: Community or Chaos* (Malabar, Fla.: R. E. Krieger, 1981), 114, 120–21.

28. Circular Congregational, Record Book, February 18, 1856.

29. Johns Island, Minutes of the Session, 1850–60.

30. See Erskine Clarke, *Wrestlin' Jacob: A Portrait of Religion in the Old South* (Atlanta: John Knox Press, 1979), 52–54.

31. Daniel Payne, the African Methodist Episcopal bishop, emphasized the importance of African Americans' taking control of their own institutions as a way of counteracting the slander that claimed they were incapable of taking care of themselves. See Payne, *African Methodist Episcopal Church.*

32. See *Proceedings of the Meeting in Charleston,* 9–11.

33. John Boles has emphasized in his study of slave religion the importance of slave participation in the worship of white or mixed churches in contrast to the "underground church." Boles is convinced that "in no other aspect of black cultural life than religion had the values and practices of whites so deeply penetrated." Boles sees in the style of preaching and the emotionalism of the African American church parallels with white Baptists and Methodists. John Blassingame makes a similar point: "the church was the single most important institution for the 'Americanization' of the bondsman." See John Boles, *Black Southerners, 1619–1869* (Lexington: University Press of Kentucky, 1983), 153–86, and John Blassingame, *The Slave Community: Plantation Life in the Antebellum South,* rev. ed. (New York: Oxford University Press, 1979), 98. The point here, of course, was not the "emotionalism" or the style of preaching of Baptists and Methodists but the world view and ethos of the Reformed tradition that marked the African American Reformed community in the low country.

34. I have consequently written sometimes of the African American Reformed community and at other times of the Reformed African American community to indicate the interdependence of the two traditions in the one community.

35. While he insists on the dominance of the African religious tradition, Sterling Stuckey offers some suggestions on the interaction between Christianity and African influences in shaping African American religion. See Sterling Stuckey, *Slave Culture in America: Nationalist Theory and the Foundations of Black America* (New York: Oxford University Press, 1987), 35–36. A more dialectical relationship than Stuckey presents is seen between traditions in the Reformed African American community of the low country. Moreover, it is not so much African as African American traditions that are clearly visible and at work in the community by the antebellum period. Charles Joyner has written of slave religion along the Waccamaw River in South Carolina: "The originality of slave religion on the plantation streets and in the plantation chapels resides neither in its specifically African features nor in its specifically Christian features, but in its unique and creative synthesis in response to the reality of slavery." Joyner, 154; see also 141–43.

36. See Robert Manson Myers, ed., *The Children of Pride: A True Story of Georgia and the Civil War* (New Haven: Yale University Press, 1972), 7–31.

37. *Proceedings of the Meeting in Charleston,* 47–48.

38. Charles C. Jones, *A Catechism of Scripture, Doctrine and Practice: for Families and Sabbath Schools, Designed also for the Oral Instruction of Colored Persons,* 3d. ed. (Savannah: T. Purse, and New York: Leavitt, Trow, 1845), 69.

39. Ibid., 129–31.

40. The catechetical pedagogy itself reflects what Paulo Freire has labeled "the banking" concept of education (the depositing of information into empty minds), which can function as a powerful tool of oppression. The epistemological assumptions inherent in such a pedagogy portray the student as "a spectator, not re-creator." A person is "not a conscious being (*corpo consciente*); [but] is rather the possessor of a consciousness: an empty 'mind' passively open to the reception of deposits of reality from the world outside." Paulo Freire, *Pedagogy of the Oppressed,* trans. Myrna Bergman Ramos (New York: Herder and Herder, 1970), 62. Obviously white slave owners were greatly concerned that "sound deposits" be made in the minds of slaves.

41. See Bethel Pon Pon Presbyterian Church, Session Minutes, 1739–43, PHSM, for example of church discipline of a white in regard to treatment of slaves in the eighteenth century. For an important case involving the grandfather of John L. Girardeau, see Slann L. C. Simmons, ed., "Records of the Willtown Presbyterian Church, 1738–1841," *SCHM* 62 (1961): 177.

42. John S. Mbiti, *African Religions and Philosophy* (Garden City, N.Y.: Anchor Books, 1970), 60. See also J. Omosade Awolalu and P. Adelumo Dopamu, *West African Traditional Religion* (Ibadan, Nigeria: Onibonoje Press, 1979), 16, 272–73. Michael Walzer has noted the role of church discipline among Puritans and Huguenots in limiting the "extent of paternal power," with the consequent political implications. See Walzer, *Revolution of the Saints,* 50, 57–61.

43. See Genovese, *Roll, Jordan, Roll,* 238.

44. Central [Third] Presbyterian Church, Letters of Transfer and Materials Relating to "Colored People": 1822–74, PHSM.

45. Ibid.

46. Ibid.

47. Ibid. Some owners went beyond morals and character and called attention to the need for the church to decide questions of religious convictions and experience: "Mr. McDowell," wrote the mother of Angelina and Mary Grimké, "no doubt will examine her [the slave Bess] before he admits her to Membership, & therefore it must depend on his judgement alone, whether she is prepared to enter into so solemn a covenant" (Ibid).

48. Psychological anthropology points to the role organizations play in personality formation. For helpful overviews, see Erika Bourguignon, "Psychological Anthropology," in John J. Honigmann, ed., *Handbook of Social and Cultural Anthropology* (Chicago: Rand McNally, 1973), 1073–118; and George Devos, "Psychological Anthropology: Humans As Learners of Culture," in Ino Rossi, ed., *People in Culture: A Survey of Cultural Anthropology* (New York: Praeger, 1980), 170–204.

49. "Of the Admission of Baptism: The Baptism of Infants," *Westminster Directory for Worship,* chap. IX.

50. *Minutes of the Synod of South Carolina,* 1846, 21.

51. The struggle over slave marriages can also be seen in other denominations. For the Protestant Episcopal, see *Report of the Special Committee Appointed by the Protestant Episcopal Convention, at its Session in 1858, to Report on the Duty of Clergymen in Relation to the Marriage of Slaves* (Charleston: Walter, Evans, 1859), 1, 5–6. For the Methodist, see Trinity Methodist Church, Minutes of Quarterly Conference Meetings of Cumberland Church and Trinity Church, 1845–91, Trinity Methodist Church archives, Charleston.

52. Zion Presbyterian Church, Communicants Roll Book (black membership), 1856–61, PHSM.

53. Second Presbyterian, Minutes of the Session, April 16, 1825; November 1846.

54. For an introduction to extensive historical studies of the slave family, see Herbert G. Gutman, *The Black Family in Slavery and Freedom, 1750–1925* (New York: Pantheon Books,

1976). Gutman argues, from extensive research, that blacks were able to establish surprisingly strong family ties given the disruptive forces of slavery. For another perspective, see J. Deotis Roberts, *Roots of a Black Future: Family and Church* (Philadelphia: Westminster Press, 1980); E. Franklin Frazier, *The Negro Family in the United States* (Chicago: University of Chicago Press, 1968); and Stanley M. Elkins, *Slavery: A Problem in American Institutional and Intellectual Life* (Chicago: University of Chicago Press, 1959). Roberts, Frazier, and Elkins insist that slavery destroyed the black family.

55. Zion Presbyterian Church, Minutes of the Session, 1859, PHSM.

56. For a treatment of slave marriages, see Genovese, *Roll, Jordan, Roll,* 458–81.

57. See ibid., 459, and Gutman, *Black Family.*

58. See Mbiti, 195–210, 329; Awolalu and Dopamu, 253–78; Genovese, *Roll, Jordan, Roll,* 194–202; Joyner, 138, 140; Wade, 169–70; and Roger Bastide, *African Civilization in the New World* (New York: Harper and Row, 1971), 57–58, 79–82, 103–04.

59. Third Presbyterian Church, Rules for the Burial Ground Held by the Third Presbyterian or Central Church, Charleston, for the Use of its Colored Members, PHSM.

60. Thomas Smyth, *An Order for Funeral Services* (Boston: S. N. Dickinson, 1843); Second Presbyterian, "Bye Laws for Manual of Burying Ground for Our Coloured People," in Minutes of the Session, May 1850.

61. L. Stoney, 200; Wade, 169–70.

62. For throwing dirt in the grave, see Genovese, *Roll, Jordan, Roll,* 200.

63. See Circular Congregational, Record Book, June 24, 1844.

64. These characteristics (discipline, order, and concern for education) can be put in the context of a larger debate about the work of slaves and the efficiency of slave labor. See Kenneth Stammp, *The Peculiar Institution: Slavery in the Ante-Bellum South* (New York: Knopf, 1956), 141–91; Robert W. Fogel and Stanley L. Engerman, *Time on the Cross: The Economics of American Negro Slavery* (Boston: Little, Brown, 1974); Herbert G. Gutman, *Slavery and the Numbers Game: A Critique of "Time on the Cross"* (Urbana: University of Illinois Press, 1975); and Herbert G. Gutman and Richard Sutch, "Sambo Makes Good, or Were Slaves Imbued with the Protestant Work Ethic?" in Paul A. David et al., *Reckoning with Slavery: A Critical Study in the Quantitative History of American Negro Slavery* (New York: Oxford University Press, 1976), 55–93.

9. An Antebellum Social Profile in Black and White: "Our Kind of People"

1. The concept of different sociocultural contexts developing different personality types has been explored by anthropologists and cross-cultural psychologists. The general assumption is that members of any given culture share many common early experiences that result in their having many elements of personality in common. Because the Reformed community in the low country was clearly a subgroup within the broader sociocultural context, any social characteristics and personality type that marked that community obviously did not emerge simply out of this specific community in isolation. Once again, while affirming a coherence for the community, its boundaries need to be understood as blurred and ambiguous. Important studies on the relationship between personality and culture include Abraham Kardiner, *The Psychological Frontiers of Society* (New York: Columbia University Press, 1945); Ralph Linton, *The Cultural Background of Personality* (New York: Appleton-Century-Croft, 1945); M. E. Spiro, "Social Systems, Personality, and Functional Analysis," in Bert Kaplan, *Studying Personality Cross-Culturally* (Evanston: Row, Peterson, 1961), 93–127; and Marshall H. Segall et al., *Human Behavior in Global Perspective* (New York: Pergamon Press, 1990). A. F. C. Wallace has criticized, in a way helpful to this study, any tendency to think of societies

as culturally homogeneous with individuals within them sharing a uniform nuclear character. Rather, he has emphasized the diversity with cultures. See his *Culture and Personality*
(New York: Random House, 1961). See also Erika Bourguignon, "Psychological Anthropology," in John J. Honigmann, ed., *Handbook of Social and Cultural Anthropology* (Chicago:
Rand McNally, 1973), 1073–118; and George Devos, "Psychological Anthropology: Humans
As Learners of Culture," in Ino Rossi, ed., *People in Culture: A Survey of Cultural Anthropology* (New York: Praeger, 1980), 170–204.

2. See chap. 1, n. 50, for discussion of Weber's thesis.

3. See Frank Parkin, *Max Weber* (London: Tavistock, 1981), esp. 43; and Gordon Marshall, *In Search for the Spirit of Capitalism* (London: Hutchinson, 1982), 83–88, 97–131.

4. See Peter A. Coclanis, *The Shadow of a Dream: Economic Life and Death in the South
Carolina Low Country, 1670–1920* (New York: Oxford University Press, 1989), 137.

5. In their careful study of Charleston between the years 1828 and 1843, William H.
Pease and Jane H. Pease found that the Congregational and Presbyterian churches they in-
vestigated had approximately 64 percent of their white membership—with any visible
influence in the city—in categories they classified as "High Farming" (plantation owners),
"High Professional," and "High Commercial." The Peases had access primarily to the records
of the Circular Congregational Church, Second Presbyterian, and to a limited extent, First
(Scots). They have kindly allowed me access to their extensive files and computer printouts.
Their materials were checked against my computer list of membership in Reformed congregations. See the Peases' important study, *The Web of Progress: Private Values and Public Styles
in Boston and Charleston, 1824–1843* (New York: Oxford University Press, 1985). My own
study of the Reformed congregations in the city throughout the years between 1782 and 1861
confirms the general image conveyed by their statistics.

6. See Circular Congregational Church, Independent C. Church Register, 1796–1824,
Book of Church Records, 1825–50, and the 1818 Statement of Faith and Constitution with
list of signatures, Circular Congregational Church archives.

7. The Peases calculated that 26 percent of Circular Congregational's "elite" belonged
in "High Professional"—the highest of any denominational group—and approximately 23
percent in "High Commercial."

8. Other business leaders at First (Scots) included William Birnie, William Davidson,
John Gordon, John C. Kerr, Andrew McDowall, and John White. See First (Scots) Presbyterian Church, Membership List, First (Scots) Presbyterian Church archives.

9. The Peases were able to identify, out of fifty names they had for First (Scots), a
number of shopkeepers and mechanics. At the same time, with my larger list of members, I
have identified eighteen members of First (Scots) whom the Peases classified as the "Super
Elite" because of their power and influence. The "Super Elite" included William Birnie, Lang-
don Cheves, George Chisolm, George Chisolm, Jr., William Davidson, Charles Edmonston,
John Gordon, John C. Kerr, Mitchell King, James Lamb, Andrew McDowall, A. G. Magrath,
James O'Hear, J. R. Pringle, Charles E. Rowand, Thomas Y. Simons, Adam Tunno, and John
White.

10. The Peases identified 108 members of Second Presbyterian who belonged to the
Peases' "Elite" classification. Most received this classification because of their economic power
and wealth. Those who were classified as "Super Elite" included James Adger, William Aiken,
William Bell, John Bryan, John Johnson, William L. Johnson, Thomas M. Mathews, and
Hugh Wilson, Sr.

11. John B. Adger, *My Life and Times* (Richmond: Presbyterian Committee of Publication, 1899), 34–37.

12. Third Presbyterian Church, Session Minutes, 1824–26, and Register, 1827–81,
PHSM.

13. Newspaper clippings, Third Presbyterian Church file, PHSM.

14. Horry, Manigault, and Cross were classified by the Peases as "Super Elite."

15. Theodore D. Jervey, *Robert Y. Hayne and His Times* (New York: Macmillan, 1909), 391–92, 409, 419. David Duncan Wallace, *South Carolina: A Short History* (Columbia: University of South Carolina Press, 1961), 449.

16. See Pease and Pease, 18.

17. Coclanis, 296–97, n. 123.

18. Slann L. C. Simmons, ed., "Records of the Willtown Presbyterian Church, 1738–1841," *SCHM* 62 (1961): 172–81; George Howe, *History of the Presbyterian Church in South Carolina*, vol. 2 (Columbia: W. J. Duffie, 1883), 624; Johns Island Presbyterian Church, Minutes of the Session, PHSM; Dorchester Independent Church, Records, PHSM; Summerville Presbyterian Church, Minutes of the Session, PHSM; Wappetaw Independent Presbyterian Church, Congregational Record Book and Treasurer's Record Book, PHSM; Stoney Creek Independent Presbyterian Church, Minutes and Accounts and Book of the Congregation, PHSM.

19. Edisto Island Presbyterian Church, Session Records, PHSM. Comparable wealth of the Johns Island Presbyterian Church can be seen in the number of white male members who were classified by the Peases as "Super Elite"—eight of seventeen. The "Super Elites" include Charles Fripp, James Legaré, Sr., Thomas Legaré, Sr., Solomon Legaré, Sr., Horace Walpole, J. C. W. Legaré, Hugh Wilson, Sr., and Hugh Wilson, Jr. The other nine were related to the "Super Elite."

20. Others with substantial planting interests included Robert Young Hayne, Charles Fripp, John Berkley Grimball, Isaac Holmes, Mary Inglis, Daniel Legaré, James Legaré, Sr., J. C. W. Legaré, Solomon Legaré, Thomas Legaré, James E. McPherson, John R. Mathews, Thomas Mathews, Mrs. E. C. Mikell, James O'Hear, F. Y. Porcher, John Ramsay, James Rose, Charles E. Rowand, Thomas Y. Simons, Anthony Toomer, Horace Walpole, Morton Waring, and Edward Whaley.

21. See also Coclanis, 296–97, n. 123, and Simmons, 179.

22. See, for example, Jervey, 151.

23. Ibid., 240.

24. These political developments can be followed in ibid. and in Linda Rhea, *Hugh Swinton Legaré: A Charleston Intellectual* (Chapel Hill: University of North Carolina Press, 1934).

25. Taylor also served on the board of trustees for Columbia Theological Seminary and had a close relationship with its faculty.

26. Wallace, *South Carolina*, 397.

27. For the concern for education in Reformed communities, see, for example, Donald G. Tewksbury, *The Founding of American Colleges and Universities Before the Civil War* (New York: Bureau of Publications, Columbia University, 1932), 90; and William J. Bouwsma, *John Calvin: A Sixteenth Century Portrait* (New York: Oxford University Press, 1988), 14–15, 90–92.

28. Wallace, *South Carolina*, 458. Hutson was speaking on behalf of the Mount Zion Institute in Winnsboro. For widespread support of such academies by low country Presbyterians and Congregationalists, see George Howe, *History of the Presbyterian Church in South Carolina*, vol. 1 (Columbia: Duffie and Chapman, 1870), 504–07, 598. The most famous of these academies was established by Moses Waddel at Willington in present-day McCormick County. Waddel served on two different occasions the churches at James Island, Johns Island, and Wadmalaw. Waddel, the brother-in-law of his student John C. Calhoun, also taught at his little academy U.S. Senators William H. Crawford and George McDuffie; Hugh Swinton Legaré; and James L. Petigru.

29. Wallace, *South Carolina*, 465.

30. An influential low country professor was Robert Henry, who was ordained by Charleston Presbytery in 1817. See James O. Farmer, *The Metaphysical Confederacy: James Henley Thornwell and the Synthesis of Southern Values* (Macon: Mercer University Press, 1986), 139.

31. Daniel W. Hollis, *The University of South Carolina*, 2 vols. (Columbia: University of South Carolina Press, 1951), 1:161–62. See also idem, "James Henley Thornwell and the South Carolina College," *Proceedings of the South Carolina Historical Association* (1953): 17–36. Elizabeth Fox-Genovese and Eugene D. Genovese have written that "Presbyterian ministers wielded great influence over the educational system, from the old field schools through the academies or high schools right up to the colleges and universities. They exercised, for example, the single most powerful influence upon the state-supported College of South Carolina, the strongest and most prestigious institution of higher education in the Lower South [during the antebellum period]." Elizabeth Fox-Genovese and Eugene D. Genovese, "The Divine Sanction of Social Order: Religious Foundations of the Southern Slaveholders' World View," *Journal of the American Academy of Religion* 55 (Summer 1987): 227. Thornwell, while from the South Carolina up-country, is necessarily included here and elsewhere in the study because he was a longtime member of Charleston Presbytery, served briefly a church in Charleston, and was intimately associated with the Reformed community in the low country. To omit him from the study of the antebellum low country Reformed community would be to omit a person whose life, ecclesiastical membership, and thought were intimately linked to that community.

32. James Henley Thornwell, "Public Instruction in South Carolina," *SPR* 8 (January 1854): 435–40.

33. Colyer Meriwether, *History of Higher Education in South Carolina* (1889; reprint, Spartanburg, S.C.: Reprint Co., 1972), 198.

34. Wallace, *South Carolina*, 464–65.

35. Rhea, 95.

36. James M. Legaré became an Episcopalian. It is interesting to note that while many of these writers did not remain in the churches of their youth, all grew up in homes deeply influenced by Reformed thought and piety. The Reformed tradition, however, at least the Carolina variety, had little place for the romanticism that came to dominate many of the writers of the period. Their movement away from the Reformed churches is consequently not surprising. Simms, interestingly, became involved in Spiritualism, as did many of the New England romantics, and consulted in 1856 a medium in New York. For Simms, see Drew Gilpin Faust, *A Sacred Circle: The Dilemma of the Intellectual in the Old South, 1840–1860* (Baltimore: Johns Hopkins University Press, 1977), 67.

37. Second Presbyterian Church, Minutes of the Session, 1840–54, PHSM.

38. See Samuel Miller, *Letters on Clerical Manners and Habits* (New York: G. and C. Carvill, 1827), 339. See also Richard D. Shiels, "The Feminization of American Congregationalism, 1730–1835," *American Quarterly* 33 (1981): 46–62; Ann Douglas, *The Feminization of American Culture* (New York: Alfred A. Knopf, 1977); and Fox-Genovese and Genovese, 226–27.

39. Third Presbyterian, Session Minutes, March 25, 1824, and Register of the Coloured Members of the 3rd. Presbyterian Church, 1826, 1827, PHSM.

40. Third Presbyterian, Session Minutes, March 25, 1824. For two treatments of Angelina Grimké's relationship to Third Presbyterian Church and its pastor, William A. McDowell, see Gerda Lerner, *The Grimké Sisters from South Carolina: Rebels against Slavery* (Boston: Houghton Mifflin, 1967), 68–85, and Katherine Du Pre Lumpkin, *The Emancipation of Angelina Grimké* (Chapel Hill: University of North Carolina Press, 1974), 24–53.

41. Catherine H. Birney, *The Grimké Sisters: Sarah and Angelina Grimké* (Westport, Conn.: Greenwood Press, 1964), 204.

42. Louisa McCord, "Woman and Her Needs," *DeBow's Review* (1852): 289–90. For analysis of Louisa McCord, see Margaret F. Thorp, *Female Persuasion: Six Strong-Minded Women* (New Haven: Yale University Press, 1949), and Richard Lounsbury, "*Ludibria Rerum Mortalium:* Charlestonian Intellectuals and Their Classics," in Michael O'Brien and David Moltke-Hansen, eds., *Intellectual Life in Antebellum Charleston* (Knoxville: University of Tennessee Press, 1986).

43. See J. R. Scafidel, "Susan Petigru King: An Early South Carolina Realist," in James B. Meriwether, ed., *South Carolina Women Writers* (Spartanburg, S.C.: Reprint Co., 1979), 101–15.

44. See Gloria Goldbatt, "The Queen of Bohemia Grew Up in Charleston," in the South Carolina Historical Society's *Carologue* (Autumn 1988): 10–11.

45. Fox-Genovese and Genovese, 227.

46. Ernest Trice Thompson, *Presbyterians in the South,* 3 vols. (Richmond: John Knox Press, 1963, 1973), 1:453.

47. See app. C.

48. See Robert Manson Myers, ed., *The Children of Pride: A True Story of Georgia and the Civil War* (New Haven: Yale University Press, 1972), 1449–738.

49. Faust, *Sacred Circle,* 1–6.

50. See app. C.

51. Charleston Union Presbytery, Minutes, 1822–40; and Charleston Presbytery, Minutes, 1850–60, PHSM.

52. Those known to have traveled abroad include Buist—father and son—Adams, Forrest, Howe, Lanneau, Smyth, Thornwell, Leland, and Adger.

53. Summerville Presbyterian Church, Minutes of the Session, 1859.

54. Others with honorary degrees included Reuben Post, William McDowell, Daniel Dana, I. S. K. Axson, B. M. Palmer, Jr., T. Charlton Henry, and Edward Palmer. See Howe, *History of the Presbyterian Church,* 2:passim. For Smyth's summer reading, see Louisa Cheves Stoney, ed., *Autobiographical Notes, Letters and Reflections by Thomas Smyth, D. D.* (Charleston: Walker, Evans and Cogswell, 1914), 520–21.

55. See Thomas Smyth, *The Collected Works of the Rev. Thomas Smyth, D. D.,* ed. J. W. Flinn, 10 vols. (Columbia: R. L. Bryan, 1908). For the reviews see 7:18–30.

56. Thompson, *Presbyterians in the South,* 1:291.

57. See the *Presbyterian Outlook* (January 2, 1979): 1.

58. *SPR,* 1848–66, passim.

59. Zion Presbyterian Church, Communicants Roll Book (black membership), 1855, PHSM.

60. For the place and role of domestics or "house servants" in the antebellum South, see Genovese, *Roll, Jordan, Roll,* 327–65; John Blassingame, "Status and Social Structure in the Slave Community: Evidence from New Sources," in Harry P. Owens and Carl N. Degler, eds., *Perspectives and Irony in American Slavery* (Jackson: University Press of Mississippi, 1976), 137–51; John Blassingame, *The Slave Community: Plantation Life in the Antebellum South,* rev. ed. (New York: Oxford University Press, 1979), 311–13.

61. At Third Presbyterian, for example, of the ninety-eight slaves who joined between 1823 and 1856, only four can be positively identified as belonging to white members of the congregation. At Second Presbyterian no more than 10 percent of the blacks who joined during the 1840s were slaves of white members of the congregation. See Third Presbyterian, Register of the Coloured Members, and Roll Book and Letters of Transfer, PHSM; Second Presbyterian, Minutes of the Session, 1840–49.

62. In 1848, while most white families in Charleston lived in "single family units," approximately 23 percent of these units included at least ten slaves. For a computation of these

figures and for a description of housing in Charleston, see Richard C. Wade, *Slavery in the Cities: the South 1820–1860* (New York: Oxford University Press, 1964), 55–59.

63. Adger, *My Life*, 166.

64. Robert L. Harris, "Charleston's Free Afro-American Elite: The Brown Fellowship Society and the Humane Brotherhood," *SCHM* 82 (1981): 289–310. For emergence of the world view and ethos in the African American community, see chap. 7 above.

65. For an indication of free black numbers in relationship to the rest of the population, see Wade, 236. See also Harris, 299.

66. Third Presbyterian, Register of the Coloured Members; Zion Presbyterian, Roll Book (black). In 1860, approximately 18.8 percent of the blacks in Charleston were free.

67. See Ira Berlin, *Slaves Without Masters: The Free Negro in the Antebellum South* (New York: Random House, Pantheon Books, 1974); Marina Wilkramanayake, *A World in Shadow: The Free Black in Antebellum South Carolina* (Columbia: University of South Carolina Press, 1973); Larry Koger, *Black Slaveowners: Free Black Slave Masters in South Carolina, 1790–1860* (Jefferson, N.C.: McFarland, 1985); Michael P. Johnson and James L. Roark, *No Chariot Let Down: Charleston's Free People of Color on the Eve of the Civil War* (Chapel Hill: University of North Carolina Press, 1984).

68. Koger, 157, 197.

69. Ibid., 202, 204. Second Presbyterian Church, Manual of the Roll of The Colored Communicants of the Second Presbyterian Church, PHSM; Zion Presbyterian, Roll Book (black).

70. L. Stoney, 205, 393, 394.

71. Third Presbyterian, Register of the Coloured Members; Circular Congregational Church, Record Book, February 18, 1856, Circular Congregational Church archives; Koger, 141–43. See also Harris, 289–310.

72. Of the African Americans who joined the Third Presbyterian Church between 1823 and 1856, 66 percent were women. In the 1850s the percentages of women among blacks who joined were: Second Presbyterian Church, 55 percent; Zion, 62 percent; Johns Island, 63 percent.

73. See Bureau of the Census, *Statistical View of the United States . . . A Compendium of the Seventh Census* (Washington, D.C.: A. O. P. Nicholson, 1854), 302.

74. See Ernst Troeltsch, *The Social Teaching of the Christian Churches*, trans. Olive Wyon, 2 vols. (New York: Harper Torchbooks, 1960), 2:579–691.

10. An Intellectual Tradition: The Quest for a Middle Way

1. Charleston Presbytery, Minutes, 1851, PHSM.

2. See Nathan O. Hatch, *The Democratization of American Christianity* (New Haven: Yale University Press, 1989), esp. 49–66. See also Richard Carwardine, *Trans-Atlantic Revivalism: Popular Evangelicalism in Britain and America, 1790–1865* (Westport, Conn.: Greenwood Press, 1978).

3. Hatch, 57.

4. For the social significance of the control of entrance into a religious group, see "Monopoly and Marginality in Imagination," in Walter Brueggemann, *Interpretation and Obedience: From Faithful Reading to Faithful Living* (Minneapolis: Fortress Press, 1991), 184–204; Fernando Belo, *A Materialist Reading of the Gospel of Mark* (Maryknoll, N.Y.: Orbis Books, 1981), pt. 2; and Paul Hanson, *The Dawn of Apocalyptic* (Philadelphia: Fortress Press, 1975), esp. chap. 3.

5. For this social function of the examination rite, see Emile Durkheim, *The Elemen-*

tary Forms of the Religious Life (1915; reprint, London: Allen and Unwin, 1964), 387. "An orderly social life," A. R. Radcliffe-Brown has written, "amongst human beings depends upon the presence in the minds of members of a society of certain sentiments, which control the behaviour of the individual in relation to others. Rites can therefore be shown to have a specific social function when . . . they have for their effect to regulate, maintain and transmit from one generation to another sentiments on which the constitution of the society depends." A. R. Radcliffe-Brown, *Structure and Function in Primitive Society* (London: Cohen and West, 1952), 157.

6. See "Religion as a Cultural System," in Clifford Geertz, *The Interpretation of Cultures: Selected Essays* (New York: Basic Books, 1973). "In a ritual," Geertz writes, "the world as lived and the world as imagined, fused under the agency of a single set of symbolic forms, turn out to be the same world" (112–13).

7. For introductions to the massive literature on natural law, see Benjamin Flecher Wright, *American Interpretations of Natural Law* (1931; reprint, Russell and Russell, 1962), 11–12; Richard Tuck, *Natural Rights Theories: Their Origin and Development* (Cambridge: Cambridge University Press, 1979); Michael Bertram, *The Changing Profile of the Natural Law* (The Hague: Nijhoff, 1977); Anthony Battaglia, *Toward a Reformulation of Natural Law* (New York: Seabury Press, 1981); and J. M. Finnis, *Natural Law and Natural Rights* (Oxford: Clarendon Press, 1980).

8. Ralph Gabriel, *The Course of American Democratic Thought* (New York: Ronald Press, 1940), 14–19.

9. Natural law thus served eighteenth-century revolutionaries like Thomas Jefferson and James Mason and nineteenth-century liberal revolutionaries like William Lloyd Garrison and Theodore Parker.

10. See Thomas Smyth, *Lectures on the Apostolical Succession* (1844), vol. 1 in *The Collected Works of the Rev. Thomas Smyth, D.D.*, ed. J. W. Flinn, 10 vols. (Columbia: R. L. Bryan, 1908).

11. Alexander Hewat, *An Historical Account of the Rise and Progress of the Colonies of South Carolina and Georgia*, 2 vols. in 1 (London, 1779), 29.

12. See Smyth, "Faith, the Principle of Missions" (1857), in *Works*, 7:28–29; Louisa Cheves Stoney, ed., *Autobiographical Notes, Letters and Reflections by Thomas Smyth, D. D.* (Charleston: Walker, Evans and Cogswell, 1914), 554–57; John B. Adger, *My Life and Times, 1810–1899* (Richmond: Presbyterian Committee of Publication, 1899), 82, 160–62, 201–02; idem, "Christian Doctrine of Human Rights and Slavery," *SPR* 3 (March 1849): 582–83; James Henley Thornwell, "Critical Notice," *SPR* 5 (January 1851): 110–15; Benjamin Morgan Palmer [the younger], ed., *The Life and Letters of James Henley Thornwell* (Richmond: Whittet and Shepperson, 1875), 468–71, 477, 478, 482–83; George Howe, "The General Assembly of 1859," *SPR* 12 (October 1859): 276–81; and Benjamin Morgan Palmer's speech before the Presbyterian General Assembly, reported in ibid., 278. Thornwell wrote of America's role in the divine plan that we "stand, indeed, in reference to free institutions and the progress of civilization, in the momentous capacity of the federal representatives of the human race." James Henly Thornwell, *Thoughts Suited to the Present Crisis; A Sermon on the Occasion of the Death of the Hon. John C. Calhoun . . . April 21, 1850* (Columbia, 1850), 4–5.

13. A good example of denunciations of tyranny is Smyth, "The Claims of the Free Church of Scotland," in *Works*, 3:505–06.

14. See Smyth, *Ecclesiastical Republicanism* (1843), in ibid.; and Ernest Trice Thompson, *Presbyterians in the South*, 3 vols. (Richmond: John Know Press, 1963, 1973), 1:510–29.

15. Thomas Smyth, *Presbytery and Not Prelacy* (1844), in *Works*, 2:52.

16. The *Southern Presbyterian Review* (*SPR*) is a fruitful field for those wishing to explore the influence of Francis Bacon on Southern religious thought. See, for example, Benjamin

Morgan Palmer [the younger], "Baconianism and the Bible," *SPR* 6 (October 1852): 226–53. For studies of the subject, see esp. Theodore Dwight Bozeman, *Protestants in an Age of Science: The Baconian Ideal and Antebellum Religious Thought* (Chapel Hill: University of North Carolina Press, 1977); E. Brooks Holifield, *The Gentlemen Theologians: American Theology in Southern Culture, 1795–1860* (Durham: Duke University Press, 1978); for Thornwell in particular, see James O. Farmer, *The Metaphysical Confederacy: James Henley Thornwell and the Synthesis of Southern Values* (Macon: Mercer University Press, 1986), 138–52; and nationally, see Herbert Hovenkamp, *Science and Religion in America, 1800–1860* (Philadelphia: University of Pennsylvania Press, 1978).

17. See, for example, Smyth, "The Province of Reason, Especially in Matters of Religion" (1855), in *Works*, 9:19–35; James Henley Thornwell, "The Office of Reason in Regard to Revelation," in John B. Adger and John L. Girardeau, eds., *The Collected Writings of James Henley Thornwell*, vols. 3 and 4 (Richmond: Presbyterian Committee of Publication, 1873), 3:183–220.

18. John B. Adger, ed., *The Collected Writings of James Henley Thornwell*, vols. 1 and 2 (Richmond: Presbyterian Committee of Publication, 1871), 1:579.

19. Smyth, *Lectures on Apostolic Succession*, 533.

20. Charles Hodge of Princeton, friend and professor to many of the Reformed clergy in the low country, began his *Systematic Theology* by insisting: "We find in nature the facts which the chemist or the mechanical philosopher has to examine, and from them to ascertain the laws by which they are determined. So the Bible contains the truths which the theologian has to collect, authenticate, arrange, and exhibit in their internal relation to each other." Charles Hodge, *Systematic Theology*, 3 vols. (New York: Charles Scribner's Sons, 1893), 1:1.

21. Palmer, *Life and Letters of Thornwell*, 142. For examples of the agony of conversion experiences among conservative Reformed scholars such as Thornwell, see L. Stoney, 18; Adger, *My Life*, 62–67; Thomas Cary Johnson, *The Life and Letters of Benjamin Morgan Palmer* (Richmond: Presbyterian Committee of Publication, 1906), 54–57; and James W. Alexander, *The Life of Archibald Alexander* (New York: Charles Scribner, 1854), 70.

22. Smyth, "The True Basis of Charity and United Christian Effort," in *Works*, 5:592–93.

23. A clear expression of this Old School Presbyterian perspective can be see in Charles Hodge, "Inspiration," *Princeton Review* 29 (October 1857): 692. The assertion that true religious experience flows from a proper understanding of correct doctrine reflects the Scholasticism of Old School Presbyterians. Calvin, in contrast, had emphasized that religious experience came before understanding. See James Henley Thornwell, "Religion Psychologically Considered," in Adger and Girardeau, 3:78–152.

24. The 1858 revivals were part of a large revival that swept many of the cities across the country. See Timothy L. Smith, *Revivalism and Social Reform: American Protestantism on the Eve of the Civil War* (New York: Abingdon Press, 1965); and William G. McLoughlin, *Revivals, Awakenings, and Reform: An Essay on Religion and Social Change in America* (Chicago: University of Chicago Press, 1978).

25. For a description of Girardeau's preaching techniques with his black congregation, see George A. Blackburn, ed., *The Life Work of John L. Girardeau, D. D., LL.D., Late Professor in the Presbyterian Theological Seminary, Columbia, S.C.* (Columbia: State Co., 1916), 70–72.

26. Smyth, "The Duty and Privilege of Belief and Confession," in *Works*, 6:42.

27. See Jonathan Edwards, *The Works of President Edwards*, ed. Sereno E. Dwight, 10 vols. (New York: S. Converse, 1829–30), 4:27, 80, 120–21.

28. Charles G. Finney, *Lectures on Revivals of Religion*, ed. William G. McLaughlin (Cambridge: Harvard University Press, 1960), 341–42.

29. Ibid., xi.

30. For the Old School critique of Finney, see Keith J. Hardman, *Charles Grandison Finney, 1792–1875: Revivalist and Reformer* (Syracuse: Syracuse University Press, 1987), 286–92. See also Hatch, 196–201.

31. See, for example, Smyth, "The Call to the Ministry" (1848), in *Works*, 6:579; and Thornwell, "Office of Reason," 183–84. For B. M. Palmer, see T. Johnson, 145.

32. See Geertz, 118; Paul Ricoeur, *Lectures on Ideology and Utopia*, ed. George H. Taylor (New York: Columbia University Press, 1986), 1, 2, 182, 265.

33. See Carl Becker, *The Heavenly City of the Eighteenth-Century Philosophers* (New Haven: Yale University Press, 1932), esp. 54–63; Ernst Cassirer, *The Philosophy of the Enlightenment* (Princeton: Princeton University Press, 1951); and Sydney E. Ahlstrom, *A Religious History of the American People* (New Haven: Yale University Press, 1972), 343–59.

34. See James Henley Thornwell, "An External Standard Vindicated," in Adger and Girardeau, 3:9–77; and "Religion and Revelation," 3:153–82, "Office of Reason," 3:183–220, and "Miracles," 3:221–76, in ibid.; Smyth, "Province of Reason"; and "Unitarianism Another Gospel" (1852), in *Works*, vol. 9, and "The Bible, and Not Reason, the Only Authoritative Source and Standard of Our Knowledge of the Nature of God—What it Teaches Concerning the Unity of God" (1856), in *Works*, vol. 9; George Howe, "The Genuineness of the Pentateuch," *SPR* 4 (October 1850): 365–73; "Renan's Origins of Christianity," *SPR* 17 (January 1866): 301–30.

35. For an introduction to romanticism see Frederick Copleston, *A History of Philosophy*, 10 vols. (Garden City, N.Y.: Image Books, 1965), 7:29–38.

36. See Hatch, 179–89.

37. Introductions to Scottish Common Sense Philosophy can be found in Bozeman; Farmer, *Metaphysical Confederacy*; and Holifield, *Gentlemen Theologians*. See also Sydney E. Ahlstrom, "The Scottish Philosophy and American Theology," *Church History* 24 (September 1955): 257–72.

38. Henry Steele Commanger, *Theodore Parker* (Boston: Little, Brown, 1936), 206–07. "Religious insurgents"—popular preacher of a religious egalitarianism—also insisted that one look within for guidance on ethical behavior. Many, however, also insisted that the inward look be done before an open Bible. See Hatch, 162–89.

39. Smyth, "Why Do I Live," in *Works*, 7:718.

40. Ibid., 719. See also James Henley Thornwell, "The Rights and Duties of Masters," in Adger and Girardeau, 4:422–27.

41. Farmer, *Metaphysical Confederacy*, 106–10, 158–59. See Smyth, *The Unity of the Human Races*, in *Works*, vol. 8; George Howe, "Unity of the Race," *SPR* 3 (July 1849): 124–66; "The Unity of the Human Race," *SPR* 5 (April 1852): 572–601; Thornwell, "The Christian Doctrine of Slavery," in Adger and Girardeau, 4:398–436, esp. 428; Adger, *My Life*, 167; see also Elizabeth Fox-Genovese and Eugene D. Genovese, "The Divine Sanction of Social Order: Religious Foundations of the Southern Slaveholders' World View," *Journal of the American Academy of Religion* 55 (Summer 1987): 211–29.

42. Smyth, "The Conversion of the World," in *Works*, 7:54. For this organic view of society, see John C. Calhoun, "Disquisition on Government," in the *Works of John C. Calhoun*, ed. Richard K. Cralle, 4 vols. (New York: D. Appleton, 1854), 1:1–2.

43. See, for example, Palmer, *Life and Letters of Thornwell*, 294–95, 350–51; L. Stoney, 196–97, 335–36; and Robert Manson Myers, ed., *Children of Pride: A True Story of Georgia and the Civil War* (New Haven: Yale University Press, 1972).

44. For the individualism and love of liberty in white Southerners—in the midst of a slave society—see Edmund S. Morgan, *American Slavery, American Freedom* (New York: W. W. Norton, 1975); William J. Cooper, *Liberty and Slavery* (New York: Knopf, 1983); and

Kenneth S. Greenberg, *Masters and Statesmen: The Political Culture of American Slavery* (Baltimore: Johns Hopkins University Press, 1985).

45. See Smyth, "The Relation of Christianity to War," in *Works,* 5:359–60; and Farmer, *Metaphysical Confederacy,* 155.

46. Perry Miller, *The Life of the Mind in America from the Revolution to the Civil War* (New York: Harcourt, Brace and World, 1965), 164, 117–55.

47. Ibid., 133. See also Vernon Louis Parrington, *Main Currents in American Thought,* vol. 2, *The Romantic Revolution in America, 1800–1860* (New York: Harcourt, Brace, 1927), 114–24, and Linda Rhea, *Hugh Swinton Legaré: A Charleston Intellectual* (Chapel Hill: University of North Carolina Press, 1934), 53–54. Michael O'Brien has pointed to Legaré's suspicion of the excesses of rationalism and enthusiasm by emphasizing Legaré's "mixed feelings" toward the common law. See Michael O'Brien, *A Character of Hugh Legaré* (Knoxville: University of Tennessee Press, 1985), 145–49.

48. See, for example, Smyth, "Presbyterianism, the Revolution, the Declaration, and the Constitution," in *Works,* 3:437–75.

49. Smyth, "The Sin and the Curse," in ibid., 7:540.

50. Commanger, 210.

11. Slavery: "That Course Indicated by Stern Necessity"

1. Theodore D. Jervey, *Robert Y. Hayne and His Times* (New York: Macmillan, 1909), 135.

2. Karl Mannheim has noted that representatives of a ruling social order label an idea utopian because it is not realizable according to *their* order. "Whenever an idea is labelled utopian," Mannheim insisted, "it is usually by a representative of an epoch that has already passed. On the other hand, the exposure of ideologies as illusory ideas, adapted to the present order, is the work generally of representatives of an order of existence which is still in process of emergence. It is always the dominant group which is in full accord with the existing order that determines what is to be regarded as utopian, while the ascendant group which is in conflict with things as they are is the one that determines what is regarded as ideological." Karl Mannheim, *Ideology and Utopia,* trans. Louis Wirth and Edward Shils (New York: Harcourt, Brace and World, 1936), 203.

3. For a masterful treatment of antislavery, see David Brion Davis, *Slavery and Human Progress* (New York: Oxford University Press, 1984). Drew Gilpin Faust, ed., *The Ideology of Slavery: Proslavery Thought in the Antebellum South, 1830–1860* (Baton Rouge: Louisiana State University Press, 1981), is a good starting point for contemporary interpretations of proslavery thought. Also see Bertram Wyatt-Brown, "Modernizing Southern Slavery: The Proslavery Argument Reinterpreted," in J. Morgan Kousser and James M. McPherson, eds., *Region, Race, and Reconstruction: Essays in Honor of C. Vann Woodward* (New York: Oxford University Press, 1982).

4. See Elizabeth Fox-Genovese and Eugene D. Genovese, "The Divine Sanction of Social Order: Religious Foundations of the Southern Slaveholders' World View," *Journal of the American Academy of Religion* 55 (Summer 1987): 211–33, esp. 222.

5. Jervey, 393–94.

6. Louisa Cheves Stoney, ed., *Autobiographical Notes, Letters and Reflections by Thomas Smyth, D.D.* (Charleston: Walker, Evans and Cogswell, 1914), 79.

7. Ibid., 55–56.

8. See J. H. S. Burleigh, *A Church History of Scotland* (London: Oxford University Press, 1960), 334–69.

9. Thomas Smyth, "The Claims of the Free Church of Scotland," in *The Collected Works of the Rev. Thomas Smyth, D. D.,* ed. J. W. Flinn, 10 vols. (Columbia: R. L. Bryan, 1908), 3:505–06.

10. The strange paradox of Southern whites being fiercely devoted to the idea of liberty while at the same time being defenders of slavery has been explored by a number of historians. See Edmund S. Morgan, *American Slavery, American Freedom* (New York: W. W. Norton, 1975); William J. Cooper, *Liberty and Slavery* (New York: Knopf, 1983); and Kenneth S. Greenberg, *Masters and Statesmen: The Political Culture of American Slavery* (Baltimore: Johns Hopkins University Press, 1985).

11. W. P. Garrison and F. J. Garrison, *William Lloyd Garrison, 1805–1879: The Story of His Life as Told by His Children,* 4 vols. (New York: Century, 1885–89), 3:150–51.

12. *Liberator,* April 12, 1844.

13. Frederick Douglass, *Life and Times of Frederick Douglass* (New York: Collier, 1962), 252. See also William Hanna, *Memoirs of the Life and Writings of Thomas Chalmers* (New York: Harpers, 1852), 444.

14. *Liberator,* April 26, 1844.

15. Ibid., February 2, 1846. See also April 3, 1846.

16. Hanna, 567.

17. Ibid., 567–75.

18. L. Stoney, 367–68.

19. Ibid., 369–70.

20. See Evangelical Alliance, *Report of the Proceedings of the Conference, Held at Freemason's Hall, London, August 19th to September 2nd Inclusive* (London: Partridge and Oakey, 1847), xcviii.

21. Ibid., 286, 290–95.

22. Ibid., 304–09.

23. Ibid., 460–75; *Liberator,* February 27, 1846; Philip Foner, *The Life and Writings of Frederick Douglass,* 5 vols. (New York: International Publishers, 1950), 4:184.

24. The increasing isolation of Southerners can be traced through the *MGAP-CUSA(OS),* 1844–50 (in PHSM), as churches of Britain withdrew their relations with the Presbyterian Church in the U.S.A. because it allowed slaveholders to be communicant members.

25. Second Presbyterian Church, Minutes of the Session, May 1847, January 1848, PHSM. John B. Adger, *My Life and Times* (Richmond: Presbyterian Committee of Publication, 1899), 164–65. See also Adger's letter to the Charleston *Mercury,* July 28, 1847.

26. Second Presbyterian, Minutes of the Session, December 1848.

27. Adger, *My Life,* 166–67.

28. Charleston *Mercury,* July 23 and 26, 1847; Adger, *My Life,* 172. For Thornwell's scornful dismissal of Magrath's arguments, see "Religious Instruction of the Black Population," *SPR* 1 (December 1847): 108.

29. Paul Trapier, *The Religious Instruction of the Black Population. The Gospel to be Given to Our Servants. A Sermon Preached in Several Protestant Episcopal Churches in Charleston on Sundays in July, 1847* (Charleston, 1847); "Autobiography of the Rev. Paul Trapier," *Publication of the Dalcho Historical Society of the Diocese of South Carolina* 17: 27–28; Robert F. Durden, "The Establishment of Calvary Church, Charleston, S.C.," *Publication of the Dalcho Historical Society of the Diocese of South Carolina* (1965): 64–71.

30. *Public Proceedings Relating to Calvary Church, And the Religious Instruction of Slaves* (Charleston: Miller and Browne, 1850), 23.

31. Calvary Episcopal Church flourished for a few years but began to decline after Tra-

pier's resignation in 1857 because of ill health. In 1856 it reached its peak with 55 black members, with up to 600 attending Sunday school classes.

32. James Henley Thornwell, "Slavery and the Religious Instruction of the Colored Population," *SPR* 4 (July 1850): 105–41, esp. 136–41. See also James O. Farmer, *The Metaphysical Confederacy: James Henley Thornwell and the Synthesis of Southern Values* (Macon: Mercer University Press, 1986), 195–233, esp. 220–27. Farmer's analysis of the sermon is particularly helpful in placing it within the larger context of Thornwell's thought.

33. Thornwell developed the idea of the crisis in industrializing societies most fully in his "Sermons on National Sins," in John B. Adger and John L. Girardeau, eds., *The Collected Writings of James Henley Thornwell*, vols. 3 and 4 (Richmond: Presbyterian Committee of Publication, 1873), 4:510–48.

34. Ibid., 404–05.

35. See Fox-Genovese and Genovese, 217–19; and D. Davis, passim. On the Southern debate—largely set within the proslavery argument—on the nature of society, see also Eugene D. Genovese, *The World the Slaveholders Made* (New York: Pantheon Books, 1969), esp. 118–224; and Faust, *Ideology of Slavery*, esp. the introduction.

36. Adger and Girardeau, 4:404, 419. Thornwell's address at Anson Street shows, perhaps more clearly than any other single work by the low country clergy, the degree to which they were dominated by the metaphor of the middle way. Over and over again he speaks of the dangers of extremes, of "Scylla on the one side and Charybdis on the other" (402). See also 107–08.

37. Ibid., 419–20.

38. Ibid., 418.

39. Ibid., 432. Thornwell develops more fully the idea of family as fundamental to social order in "The Baptism of Servants," *SPR* 1 (June 1847): 63–102, and in "Duties of Masters," *SPR* 8 (October 1854): 266–83. In "Duties of Masters," Thornwell wrote that the master-servant relationship is "to be regarded as belonging to the family, coming under the same policy and benevolent discipline, regulating other family relationships." Such a perspective was found in the catechism of Charles C. Jones, widely used throughout the low country, for the religious instruction of slaves.

40. See Mannheim, 229–39, esp. 229–30; Paul Ricoeur, *Lectures on Ideology and Utopia*, ed. George H. Taylor (New York: Columbia University Press, 1986), 278–79.

41. Adger and Girardeau, 4:399–400.

42. For the role of counterutopias, see Mannheim, 208, 213, 234–35, 239–42, 249–50; for conservative utopias as counterutopias, see esp. 234–35. See also Ricoeur, *Lectures*, 274, 289.

43. Liberal utopianism is described by Mannheim as being associated with "bourgeois liberalism" with its confidence in education and the possibility of changing reality through better knowledge. Liberal utopianism is governed by a sense of unilinear progress—history is like an individual with childhood and maturity—with change coming as the result of historical evolution. See Mannheim, 219–29, and Ricoeur, *Lectures*, 277–78. For the low country Reformed community's participation in such perspectives, which were so widespread in nineteenth-century America, see chap. 12. Even in his Anson Street address, Thornwell was concerned with the whole notion of progress; see Adger and Girardeau, 4:427–28. See also Farmer, *Metaphysical Confederacy*, 248–50. And see Jack P. Maddox, Jr., "Proslavery Millennialism: Social Eschatology in Antebellum Southern Calvinism," *American Quarterly* 31 (1979): 48–52.

44. "To maintain," Thornwell told his Charleston audience, "that the same things are universally obligatory, without regard to circumstances or relations, that what is exacted of one must necessarily be exacted from another, however different or even incongruous their

outward states, is to confound the obligations of rulers and subjects, of parents and children, of guardians and wards, and to plunge the community into irretrievable confusion" (Adger and Girardeau, 4:424). To assume that "the duties of all men are specifically the same," without taking into account their place in society, would lead to anarchy and confusion. Such an emphasis on the concrete, on the particular place of people in the social order, was a way of answering the abolitionists who said slaveholders ought to follow the Golden Rule. If slave-holders did to their slaves what the slaveholders would have done to themselves if they were slaves, the abolitionist argument went, then slaves would be freed. The response from Thorn-well was that the Golden Rule requires that I do to my slave what I would want done to me in that particular place *as a slave*. The Golden Rule, it was said, does not call for a change in a person's social position. See ibid., 457–59.

45. See Adger, *My Life*, 164–78.

46. For a description of Girardeau's preaching style and techniques, see George A. Blackburn, ed., *The Life Work of John L. Girardeau, D. D., LL.D., Late Professor in the Presbyterian Theological Seminary, Columbia, S.C.* (Columbia: State Co., 1916), 70–72.

47. L. Stoney, 194–201; Blackburn, 101–02.

48. See Zion Presbyterian Church, Communicants Roll Book (white membership), 1855–61, and Minutes of the Session, 1856–66, PHSM. For the continuing suspicion of Zion by many in the white community, see Blackburn, 65–66, 101–02; Zion Presbyterian, Minutes of the Session, 1859; L. Stoney, 200.

49. Zion Presbyterian, Minutes of the Session, 1856.

50. See First Baptist Church, Minutes of the Board of Deacons, First Baptist Church, Charleston, S.C., 1840–61, First Baptist Church archives, Charleston; Saint Mary's Roman Catholic Church, Saint Mary's Vestry, 1832–55, Saint Mary's Roman Catholic Church archives, Charleston; Trinity Methodist Church, Record of the Colored Members in the Methodist Church, Charleston, S.C., 1821–61, Trinity Methodist Church archives, Charleston; Saint John's Lutheran Church, Church Register, 1852–61, and Minutes, St. John's Lutheran Church, 1837–45, Saint John's Lutheran Church archives, Charleston; "The Private Register of the Rev. Paul Trapier" [Saint Michael's Episcopal Church, Charleston], *Publication of the Dalcho Historical Society of the Diocese of South Carolina*, no. 7. For the use of family names by African Americans and the denial of those names by whites throughout the South, see Herbert G. Gutman, *The Black Family in Slavery and Freedom, 1750–1925* (New York: Pantheon Books, 1976), 230–56.

51. See Zion Presbyterian Church, Communicants Roll Book (black membership), 1855–61, PHSM, and Minutes of the Session, 1856–66.

52. Zion Presbyterian, Minutes of the Session, 1859.

53. Ibid., 1858–59.

54. For the incongruence between a mode of thought and a given social reality, see Ricoeur, *Lectures*, 3, 169–71, and for utopias in particular, 272–76; and Mannheim, 95–108.

55. See Adger and Girardeau, 4:435, and Adger, *My Life*, 166–67.

56. The emphasis of the low country Reformed community on society being linked through a sense of belonging and affection can be analyzed in light of Max Weber's distinction between Gemeinschaft and Gesellschaft. With Gemeinschaft social connection is achieved through a peoples' organic and emotional ties, while Gesellschaft achieves social connection through contractual ties. The dangers of Gemeinschaft, with coercion hiding behind affectional ties, were all too clear in the South and in Nazi Germany. See Max Weber, *Economy and Society*, ed. Guenther Roth and Claus Wittich, 2 vols. (1968; reprint, Berkeley and Los Angeles: University of California Press, 1978), esp. 1:40–42.

57. The utopianism of the low country white Reformed community, with its strong ideological component, reflects a point Mannheim makes in passing about conservative uto-

pias: "The utopias of ascendant classes are often, to a large extent, permeated with ideological elements" (Mannheim, 203).

12. Secession and Civil War: The End of Moderation

1. See also *MGAPCUSA(OS)*, 1852, PHSM; *Minutes of the Synod of South Carolina,* 1852; Ernest Trice Thompson, *Presbyterians in the South,* 3 vols. (Richmond: John Knox Press, 1963, 1973), 1:422–23. See also Benjamin Morgan Palmer [the younger], ed., *The Life and Letters of James Henley Thornwell* (Richmond: Whittet and Shepperson, 1875), 370, 372–73.

2. James Henley Thornwell, "Critical Notice," *SPR* 5 (January 1851): 110–15.

3. For the conservative, Unionist position among Presbyterian clergy in the Southeast generally, see Margaret B. DesChamps, "Union or Division? South Atlantic Presbyterians and Southern Nationalism, 1820–1861," *Journal of Southern History* 20 (November 1954): 484–98.

4. When Rice was installed as the pastor of the Circular Congregational Church in 1860, three Massachusetts ministers joined in the service: George Blagdon of Boston, John Todd of Pittsfield, and Nehemiah Adams of Boston. Adams's *A South-Side View of Slavery* (Boston: T. R. Marvin, 1854) had made him popular in Charleston if notorious in Boston. See Thomas Smyth, *The Collected Works of the Rev. Thomas Smyth, D. D.,* ed. J. W. Flinn, 10 vols. (Columbia: R. L. Bryan, 1908), 6:170–78.

5. See W. C. Dana, *"Fast Day Sermon": A Sermon Delivered in the Central Presbyterian Church, Charleston, South Carolina, November 21, 1860* (Charleston: Miller, 1860).

6. George Howe, "The General Assembly of 1859," *SPR* 12 (October 1859): 276–81. And see William Childs Robinson, *Columbia Theological Seminary and the Southern Presbyterian Church* (Decatur, Ga., 1931), 38–46.

7. For the broader context of this struggle within the national benevolence societies, see John W. Kuykendall, *Southern Enterprise: The Work of National Evangelical Societies in the Antebellum South* (Westport, Conn.: Greenwood Press, 1982), 133–69. For the role of moderates, North and South, in the coming of the war, see Allan Nevins, *Ordeal of Union,* 2 vols. (New York: Scribner, 1947), 1:315, 357, 366, and 375; Philip Foner, *Business and Slavery: The New York Merchants and the Irrepressible Conflict* (Chapel Hill: University of North Carolina Press, 1941); and Barrington Moore, Jr., *Social Origins of Dictatorship and Democracy: Lord and Peasant in the Making of the Modern World* (Boston: Beacon Press, 1966), chap. 3, "The American Civil War: The Last Capitalist Revolution," esp. 137–40.

8. Charleston *Mercury,* August 21, 1847.

9. Smyth, "The True Basis of Charity and United Christian Effort" (1846), in *Works,* 5:589–611.

10. Louisa Cheves Stoney, ed., *Autobiographical Notes, Letters and Reflections by Thomas Smyth, D. D.* (Charleston: Walker, Evans and Cogswell, 1914), 252.

11. See Seth Bliss, *Letters to the Members, Patrons and Friends of the Branch American Tract Society in Boston; And to those of the National Society in New York. By the Secretary of the Boston Society* (Boston: Crocker and Brewster, 1858), 100–102.

12. *Responsibilities of the Publishing Committee under the Constitution* (New York: American Tract Society, 1858), 6.

13. Ibid., 6–9.

14. Ibid., 9, and Smyth, *Works,* 9:466.

15. *Report and Resolutions, Adopted June 1st, 1858, by the South Carolina Branch of the American Tract Society in Reference to the Action Taken on Slavery, by the Parent Society, at the Last Meeting* (Charleston: Miller, 1858), 4–6.

16. L. Stoney, 278–80. Many of Hallock's letters, not printed in Stoney, are in Smyth's mss. at the PHSM.

17. Smyth, *Works,* 9:451–65.

18. Ibid., 478–91.

19. Ibid.

20. L. Stoney, 555–56.

21. See Steven A. Channing, *Crisis of Fear: Secession in South Carolina* (New York: W. W. Norton, 1974). The best one-volume history of the Civil War is James M. McPherson, *The Battle Cry of Freedom: The Civil War Era* (New York: Oxford University Press, 1988).

22. For the disruption of communication, see Jürgen Habermas, *Knowledge and Human Interest,* trans. Jeremy J. Shapiro (Boston: Beacon Press, 1972), esp. 241–42, 288.

23. See James M. McPherson, *Abraham Lincoln and the Second American Revolution* (New York: Oxford University Press, 1990), 135–36.

24. See Allan Nevins, *The Emergence of Lincoln,* 2 vols. (New York: Scribner, 1950), 2:322–26.

25. Quoted in McPherson, *Lincoln,* 43–44.

26. Smyth, "The Sin and the Curse; Or, The Union and the True Source of Disunion" (1860), in *Works,* 7:543.

27. McPherson, *Lincoln,* 52. See also Smyth, "The Sin and the Curse," 545.

28. Palmer, *Life and Letters of Thornwell,* 607.

29. Smyth, "The Sin and the Curse," 539–47; McPherson, *Lincoln,* 43–64. McPherson emphasizes that many in the North shared the understanding of liberty that dominated the South, which helped to make Lincoln's position truly revolutionary. See 51–54.

30. Smyth, "The Sin and the Curse," 543; emphasis added. Palmer echoed the same cry in his New Orleans pulpit: "We defend the cause of God and religion," he declared, because "the abolition spirit is undeniably atheistic." Thompson, *Presbyterians in the South,* 1:556.

31. Thomas Smyth, "The Battle of Fort Sumter: Its Mystery and Miracle—God's Mastery and Mercy," *SPR* 14 (October 1861): 365–66; idem, "The War of the South Vindicated," in *Works,* vol. 7. The image of exodus from the land of bondage and the image of the Jewish remnant returning from captivity in Babylon were both used and intermingled to inform the central image of a Holy Commonwealth. See Benjamin Morgan Palmer [the younger], *National Responsibilities before God . . .* (New Orleans, 1861), 5. Extensive scholarship has explored the role the churches played in the growing sectional crisis and in the war itself. Among the most helpful studies are James W. Silver, *Confederate Morale and Church Propaganda* (Gloucester, Mass.: Peter Smith, 1964); Chester F. Dunham, *The Attitude of the Northern Clergy Toward the South, 1860–1865* (Philadelphia: Porcupine Press, 1974); Bertram Wyatt-Brown, *Yankee Saints and Southern Sinners* (Baton Rouge: Louisiana State University Press, 1985); James H. Moorhead, *American Apocalypse: Yankee Protestants and the Civil War, 1860–1869* (New Haven: Yale University Press, 1978); and C. C. Goen, *Broken Churches, Broken Nation: Denominational Schisms and the Coming of the American Civil War* (Macon: Mercer University Press, 1985).

32. James Henley Thornwell, "Sermon on National Sins," in John B. Adger and John L. Girardeau, eds., *The Collected Writings of James Henley Thornwell,* vols. 3 and 4 (Richmond: Presbyterian Committee of Publication, 1873), 4:539–41.

33. Barrington Moore is helpful in making these distinctions. "The evidence indicates very clearly," Moore has written, "that plantation slavery was an obstacle to democracy, at least any conception of democracy that includes the goals of human equality, even the limited form of equality of opportunity, and human freedom. It does not establish at all clearly that plantation slavery was an obstacle to industrial capitalism as such. And comparative perspec-

tives show clearly that industrial capitalism can establish itself in societies that do not profess these democratic goals or, to be a little more cautious, where these goals are no more than a secondary current." For Moore, "Labor-repressive agricultural systems, and plantation slavery in particular, are political obstacles to a *particular kind* of capitalism, at a specific historical stage: competitive democratic capitalism we must call it for lack of a more precise term" (B. Moore, 152). Given the social location of the Reformed community in the low country and more particularly of the clergy—think especially of the Adgers and Smyths—one could hardly imagine their being somehow "against capitalism" and a market economy except in its unregulated form. The distinction is subtle but fundamental.

34. James Henley Thornwell, "Relation of the State to Christ," in Adger and Girardeau, 4:480, 549–56, 550.

35. Ibid., 552–55.

36. Ibid., 556.

37. Thornwell, Howe, Smyth, Adger, and Girardeau were all members of Charleston Presbytery. Palmer, a child of the low country, had recently left the presbytery for New Orleans. Thornwell, Adger, and Girardeau would be the primary shapers of the Southern Presbyterian Church's polity. See Thompson, *Presbyterians in the South,* 2:414–41.

38. *Minutes of the Synod of South Carolina,* 1860 (Charleston: Evans and Cogswell, 1861), 8, 28. For earlier calls for a separate Southern Presbyterian Church, see Erskine Clarke, "The Strange Case of Charleston Union Presbytery," *Affirmation* (Fall 1993): 41–58.

39. Smyth, "Battle of Fort Sumter," 382.

40. *MGAPCUSA(OS),* 1861, 330; Spring, *Personal Reminiscences,* 2:180.

41. Smyth, "War of the South Vindicated," 587.

42. *MGAPCCSA,* 1861, 51–52, 52–54, PHSM.

43. See, for example, James Henley Thornwell, "The General Assembly of 1847," in Adger and Girardeau, 4:501–02, and Thornwell, "Societies for Moral Reform," in ibid., 469–71. In 1859, speaking before the Presbyterian General Assembly, Thornwell noted that some might suppose that "opposition to Abolitionism has produced these views [on the Spirituality of the Church]." This, he said, "is a great mistake. They have been formed entirely in regard to other matters. I do not exclude Slavery wholly and absolutely from the sphere of the Church. It has religious aspects. What I exclude is the question touching the manner in which society shall be organized. The relation of its classes and races, their respective rights and privileges, the position of woman, the equality or inequality of citizens,—these are questions which belong to the State; and when the State does not violate the law of God, the Church has nothing to do but to accept society as given, and labour to make all its parts work harmoniously" (Thornwell, "Speech on African Colonization," in ibid., 475–76).

44. Thompson, *Presbyterians in the South,* 2:414.

45. In an otherwise helpful article, Jack P. Maddox misses this critical distinction between church (and the activities of its courts) and the cultural role of religion. See Jack P. Maddox, Jr., "From Theocracy to Spirituality: The Southern Presbyterian Reversal on Church and State," *Journal of Presbyterian History* 56 (Winter 1976): 438–57. See also James O. Farmer, *The Metaphysical Confederacy: James Henley Thornwell and the Synthesis of Southern Values* (Macon: Mercer University Press, 1986), 257–60.

46. For the important place of "the Spirituality of the Church" in Southern Presbyterian thinking, see Ernest Trice Thompson, *The Spirituality of the Church: A Distinctive Doctrine of the Presbyterian Church in the United States* (Richmond: John Knox Press, 1961).

47. *MGAPCCSA,* 1861, 54–55.

48. For the question of a distinct Southern identity, see Grady McWhiney, *Southerners and Other Americans* (New York: Basic Books, 1973); Edward Pessen, "How Different from

Each Other Were the Antebellum North and South?" *American Historical Review* 85 (1980): 1119–49; Richard E. Beringer et al., *Why the South Lost the Civil War* (Athens: University of Georgia Press, 1986); and Drew Gilpin Faust, *The Creation of Confederate Nationalism: Ideology and Identity in the Civil War South* (Baton Rouge: Louisiana State University Press, 1988).

49. *MGAPCCSA*, 1861, 55–59.

50. For conservative reaction following Reconstruction, see McPherson, *Lincoln*, esp. 145–52; Eric Foner, *Reconstruction: America's Unfinished Revolution 1863–1877* (New York: Harper and Row, 1988); Forrest G. Wood, *The Racist Response to Emancipation and Reconstruction* (Berkeley and Los Angeles: University of California Press, 1968); C. Vann Woodward, *American Counterpoint: Slavery and Racism in the North-South Dialogue*, 3d ed. (New York: Oxford University Press, 1971); and William Gillette, *Retreat from Reconstruction 1869–1879* (Baton Rouge: Louisiana State University Press, 1979).

13. The Challenge of an Almost New Order: "Hold Your Ground, Sir!"

1. See Peter A. Coclanis, *The Shadow of a Dream: Economic Life and Death in the South Carolina Low Country, 1670–1920* (New York: Oxford University Press, 1989), 111–58.

2. *New York Times*, March 6, 1865; Sidney Andrews, *The South Since the War* (1866; reprint, New York: Arno Press, 1969), 26. The New York paper was full of vivid and generally reproachful descriptions of Charleston in the months after the city's fall. See also *New York Times*, February 22, March 9, April 4, and July 24, 1865.

3. For descriptions of the war in the low country, see Joel Williamson, *After Slavery: The Negro in South Carolina During Reconstruction, 1861–1877* (Chapel Hill: University of North Carolina Press, 1965), 3–31; E. Milby Burton, *The Siege of Charleston 1861–1865* (Columbia: University of South Carolina Press, 1970); and Walter J. Fraser, Jr., *Charleston! Charleston! The History of a Southern City* (Columbia: University of South Carolina Press, 1989), 247–70.

4. A. S. Salley, "The History of the Stoney Creek Presbyterian Congregation," *Charleston News and Courier*, October 29 and November 5, 1933; O. E. Johnson, "The Old White (Congregational) Church at Dorchester, S.C.," in *Services at the Laying of the Corner Stone of the New Presbyterian Church of Summerville, S.C., May 7, 1895* (Charleston: Walker, Evans and Cogswell, 1895), 20; Petrona Royall McIver, "Wappetaw Congregational Church," *SCHM* 58 (1957): 85–93; Statistical Reports of Charleston Presbytery in *MGAPCUS*, 1866–76, PHSM.

5. A good example of a church with strong Congregational roots and sympathies leaving behind its Congregationalism and becoming Presbyterian is Wappetaw. See McIver, and see George N. Edwards, *A History of the Independent or Congregational Church of Charleston South Carolina* (Boston: Pilgrim Press, 1947).

6. G. Edwards, 92–102.

7. See Edward McCrady, *The History of South Carolina under the Royal Government, 1719–1776* (New York: Macmillan, 1899).

8. See Edmund L. Drago, *Initiative, Paternalism, & Race Relations: Charleston's Avery Normal Institute* (Athens: University of Georgia Press, 1990); Willie Lee Rose, *Rehearsal for Reconstruction: The Port Royal Experiment* (Indianapolis: Bobbs-Merrill, 1964); James D. Anderson, *The Education of Blacks in the South, 1860–1935* (Chapel Hill: University of North Carolina Press, 1988); Leon F. Litwack, *Been in the Storm So Long: The Aftermath of Slavery* (New York: Alfred A. Knopf, 1979), 450–501; Robert C. Morris, *Reading, 'Riting, and Reconstruction: the Education of Freedmen in the South, 1861–1870* (Chicago: University of Chicago Press, 1981); Joe Martin Richardson, *Christian Reconstruction: The American Missionary*

Association and Southern Blacks, 1861–1890 (Athens: University of Georgia Press, 1986); and Williamson, 180–239.

9. McIver, 91–92.

10. Litwack, 167.

11. See Augustine Thomas Smythe Letters, December 12, 1865, SCHS. The momentous experience of black slaves becoming free is analyzed with brilliant insights in Litwack, 387– 449.

12. Litwack, 122.

13. *Charleston Daily Courier,* March 22, 1865; *New York Times,* April 4, 1865.

14. *New York Times,* April 11, 1865. See Henry Ward Beecher, *Sermons* (New York: Harper and Brothers, 1868), 24–31; W. P. Garrison and F. J. Garrison, *William Lloyd Garrison, 1805– 1879: The Story of His Live as Told by His Children,* 4 vols. (New York: Century, 1885–89), 4:136; and Williamson, 77.

15. Williamson, 336. See *Proceedings of the Colored People's Convention of the State of South Carolina, held in Zion Church, Charleston, November, 1865* (Charleston, 1865). For the use of Zion as a meeting place, see also Herbert Aptheker, "South Carolina Negro Conventions, 1865," *Journal of Negro History* 31 (January 1946): 91–97.

16. Chester F. Dunham, *The Attitude of the Northern Clergy Toward the South, 1860– 1865* (Philadelphia: Porcupine Press, 1974), 210–11.

17. See Drago, 2–3; Litwack, 450–501.

18. John L. Girardeau, *Confederate Memorial Day at Charleston, S.C.: Re-interment of the Carolina Dead from Gettysburg* (Charleston: William G. Mazyck, 1871), 3, 8.

19. Ibid., 8.

20. Ibid., 9–10.

21. Ibid., 10–15.

22. Ibid., 17.

23. Ibid., 18.

24. See "Ideology as a Cultural System," in Clifford Geertz, *The Interpretation of Cultures: Selected Essays* (New York: Basic Books, 1973), esp. 218–19; and Paul Ricoeur, *Lectures on Ideology and Utopia,* ed. George H. Taylor (New York: Columbia University Press, 1986), 258–61. Eric Erikson also speaks, as does Geertz and Ricoeur, of ideology as a guardian of identity. See Eric Erikson, *Identity: Youth and Crisis* (New York: W. W. Norton, 1968), 133.

25. Girardeau, *Confederate Memorial Day,* 18. In the years before the war, Thornwell had contrasted an "American spirit" with a "Yankee spirit." The "Yankee spirit," with what Southerners regarded as a strange blend of materialism and idealism, was disdained as a deviant from the "American spirit," which, it was claimed, was best seen in the South. Benjamin Morgan Palmer [the younger], ed., *The Life and Letters of James Henley Thornwell* (Richmond: Whittet and Shepperson, 1875), 482–83.

26. For the scholarly debate over Southern nationalism, see Walter J. Fraser, Jr., and Winfred B. Moore, Jr., eds., *From the Old South to the New: Essays on the Transitional South* (Westport, Conn.: Greenwood Press, 1981), 277–78; Richard E. Beringer et al., *Why the South Lost the Civil War* (Athens: University of Georgia Press, 1986); and Emory Thomas, *The Confederate Nation, 1861–1865* (New York: Harper and Row, 1979). See also Erskine Clarke, "Southern Nationalism and Columbia Theological Seminary," *Journal of Presbyterian History* 66 (Summer 1988): 123–33; and James O. Farmer, "Southern Presbyterians and Southern Nationalism: A Study in Ambivalence," *Georgia Historical Quarterly* (Summer 1991): 275–94.

27. See Thomas Smyth, "The War of the South Vindicated," *SPR* 15 (April 1863): 479– 515; and Benjamin Morgan Palmer [the younger], *National Responsibilities before God . . .* (New Orleans, 1861).

28. Girardeau, *Confederate Memorial Day,* 19.

29. For the ritual of Confederate Memorial Day as a profoundly ideological act, see Ricoeur, *Lectures,* 261.

30. Girardeau, *Confederate Memorial Day,* 20.

31. See John Stuart Mill, *On Liberty* (1865; reprint, edited by David Spitz, New York: Norton, 1975); and Bernard Bailyn, *The Ideological Origins of the American Revolution* (Cambridge: Harvard University Press, 1967); John Philip Reid, *The Concept of Liberty in the Age of the American Revolution* (Chicago: University of Chicago Press, 1988).

32. For the counterrevolution that followed Reconstruction, see James M. McPherson, *Abraham Lincoln and the Second American Revolution* (New York: Oxford University Press, 1990), esp. 132–52; and Eric Foner, *Reconstruction: America's Unfinished Revolution 1863–1877* (New York: Harper and Row, 1988).

33. See Erskine Clarke, "The History of Ecumenical Relations in the Southern Presbyterian Church," *MGAPCUS,* 1976, 466–77.

34. For the origin of the phrase "the Calhoun of the Church," see James O. Farmer, *The Metaphysical Confederacy: James Henley Thornwell and the Synthesis of Southern Values* (Macon: Mercer University Press, 1986), 41.

35. It needs to be emphasized that the churches of the South have had a profound interest in social questions despite their attempts—often unsuccessful—to keep official silence on many social issues, to maintain what Thornwell and other Presbyterians called the "Spirituality of the Church." A number of scholars, most recently Sam Hill, have argued that "the Christianity of the North has regularly declared its responsibility for the health and direction of the society at large, while the church in the South has not." Such a distinction obviously ignores the black churches of the South. But it also misses by implication the way in which the "official silence" of the white churches was a powerful, deliberate tool for supporting the status quo, particularly in regard to race. The methods of the Southern churches in trying to influence society were not always the same as those in the North. Often they were less direct, more oblique, cushioned about by the manners and folkways of Southern society itself. But the Southern church, no less than the church in the North, was in a dynamic relationship with its surrounding culture and society and sought consciously to influence its shape and direction. A "transactional" method of social analysis, in contrast to a "structural functional" approach that emphasizes official actions, helps to clarify the ways in which Southern churches and church leaders influenced Southern society. See Sam S. Hill, Jr., *The South and the North in American Religion* (Athens: University of Georgia Press, 1980), 2. See also Charles Reagon Wilson, *Baptized in Blood: The Religion of the Lost Cause, 1865–1920* (Athens: University of Georgia Press, 1980); and Jerald C. Brauer, "Regionalism and Religion in America," *Church History* 54 (September 1985): 374–75.

36. See Williamson, 3–8, and Litwack, 111–17.

37. F. D. Jones and W. H. Mills, *History of the Presbyterian Church in South Carolina Since 1850* (Columbia: R. L. Bryan, 1926), 604–07. For the identification of Hedges as the black pastor, see *Second Annual Report,* 1866–67, COF, 27, PHSP.

38. Andrew E. Murray, *Presbyterians and the Negro—A History* (Philadelphia: Presbyterian Historical Society, 1966), 141–42; [John B. Adger?], "The Northern General Assembly (O.S.) of 1866," *SPR* 17 (September 1866): 279–84. For the important role of the Freedmen's Bureau, see Martin Abbott, *The Freedmen's Bureau in South Carolina, 1865–1872* (Chapel Hill: University of North Carolina Press, 1967).

39. Zion Presbyterian Church, Minutes of the Session, 1866–74, PHSM.

40. Other influential white leaders included F. M. Robertson, Archibald Campbell, and Frederick Fanning. Robertson, a prominent physician, was a member of a wealthy family that gave much support to Zion. Campbell served as steward of the orphan house and treasurer of the city of Charleston and was known for his "kindly consideration of the poor." Fanning

had been an elder at Second Presbyterian before joining Zion and being elected its first elder. He was the white primarily responsible for the instruction of black candidates for admission into the church. He met one night a week with them, "praying with them and affording them catechetical teaching." He was reported to have a "deep and unfeigned interest in their spiritual welfare" (ibid., February 1867 and April 1, 1869).

41. John L. Girardeau, "Our Ecclesiastical Relations to Freedmen," *SPR* 21 (July 1867): 7.

42. See Murray, 140–52; Ernest Trice Thompson, *Presbyterians in the South*, 3 vols. (Richmond: John Knox Press, 1963, 1973), 2:195–202.

43. John B. Adger, *My Life and Times* (Richmond: Presbyterian Committee of Publication, 1899), 177.

44. See C. Vann Woodward, *The Strange Career of Jim Crow*, 3d ed. (New York: Oxford University Press, 1974). See also Williamson, chap. 10, "The Separation of the Races," 274–99.

45. The old paternalism struggled to maintain its vision. "The ground of color," declared the South Carolina Presbytery with John Adger's urging in 1866, "is a schismatical foundation on which a church may not be built. The same principle . . . would admit the organization of a white man's church into the membership of which no colored person could be received. . . . We greatly desire . . . that our churches . . . should be composed as hitherto of men of both colors" (Jones and Mills, 131).

46. For the difficulties of working out a new relationship between blacks and whites in the churches, see Louisa Cheves Stoney, ed., *Autobiographical Notes, Letters and Reflections by Thomas Smyth, D. D.* (Charleston: Walker, Evans and Cogswell, 1914), 694–96; Bernard Edward Powers, Jr., "Black Charleston: A Social History 1822–1885" (Ph.D. diss., Northwestern University, 1982), 211–12; and G. Edwards, 86, 94.

14. The African American Reformed Community: Between Two Worlds

1. See Theodore H. Von Laue, *The World Revolution of Westernization: The Twentieth Century in Global Perspective* (New York: Oxford University Press, 1987). Von Laue's study, while not addressing directly the situation of African Americans following the Civil War, provides an important contextual framework for understanding the challenges they faced.

2. For the predicament faced by non-Westerners, for the "Westernized non-Western intelligentsia," see ibid., 29, 31, 241, 271, and 308. The predicament for African American scholars has been poignantly expressed by theologian James Cone, who discovered his "captivation to white concepts" even in the midst of his critique of white systems of thought. See James H. Cone, *My Soul Looks Back* (Maryknoll, N.Y.: Orbis Books, 1986), 61, 77.

3. The issue of the freed peoples' adopting the "Yankee ethic" is handled most fully in Leon F. Litwack, *Been in the Storm So Long: The Aftermath of Slavery* (New York: Alfred A. Knopf, 1979); see esp. 450–556. For these issues more narrowly focused on South Carolina, see Joel Williamson, *After Slavery: The Negro in South Carolina During Reconstruction, 1861–1877* (Chapel Hill: University of North Carolina Press, 1965), esp. 189–239; and George Brown Tindall, *South Carolina Negroes, 1877–1900* (Columbia: University of South Carolina Press, 1952). The issue provides a primary focus for Edmund L. Drago's *Initiative, Paternalism, & Race Relations: Charleston's Avery Normal Institute* (Athens: University of Georgia Press, 1990).

4. The term *reculturation* is Von Laue's. See Von Laue, 5.

5. Among the most prominent members of the low country African American community who were well on the road to reculturation were those who had been a part of Charleston's free black community.

6. Du Bois quoted in Eugene D. Genovese, *Roll, Jordan, Roll: The World the Slaves Made* (New York: Pantheon Books, 1974), 238.

7. Drago gives numerous examples from Avery of such a belief under the heading "social uplift philosophy." For a similar expression of the need for accommodation by a rural Presbyterian pastor on Edisto Island, see *MGAPCUSA*, 1929, 139, and 1931, 128–29, PHSM. See also William H. Myers, "The Hermeneutical Dilemma of the African American Biblical Student," in Cain Hope Felder, ed., *Stony the Road We Trod: African American Biblical Interpretation* (Minneapolis: Fortress Press, 1991).

8. Von Laue argues that a culture resembles an iceberg: "only a very minor part of its substance is visible to the conscious mind; the bulk lurks below the surface of awareness, although an intrinsic part of it. The collective subconscious is the reservoir of social discipline, the repository of all past actions that have become part of the skills of survival under a given set of unique circumstances." As "self-contained universes built up in response to unique circumstances," cultures are, he argues, "mutually incompatible." See Von Laue, 375–76. It is not necessary to agree with his conclusion to appreciate the sharpness with which he has drawn the issues. The question of compatibility or incompatibility of cultures provides a central question to this chapter.

9. Bureau of the Census, *Twelfth Census of the United States, 1900: Population, Part I* (Washington, D.C.: U.S. Government Printing Office, 1903), 555, 569, 572; *Handbook of South Carolina: Resources, Institutions and Industries of the State* (Columbia: State Co., 1907), 524–28.

10. I. A. Newby, *Black Carolinians: A History of Blacks in South Carolina from 1895 to 1968* (Columbia: University of South Carolina Press, 1973), 193. See also George A. Devlin, "South Carolina and Black Migration 1865–1940: In Search of the Promised Land" (Ph.D. diss., University of South Carolina, 1984).

11. For white Carolinians also leaving the state in great numbers, see *Handbook of South Carolina*, 9–10, 531. For the poverty of the region, see Peter A. Coclanis, *The Shadow of a Dream: Economic Life and Death in the South Carolina Low Country, 1670–1920* (New York: Oxford University Press, 1989), 111–60.

12. *Fifth Annual Report*, COF, 1869–70, 17, PHSP; *Third Annual Report*, COF, 1867–68, 34, PHSP; *MGAPCUSA*, 1873, 666.

13. *MGAPCUSA*, 1867 and 1873–90; *MGAPCUS*, 1873–90, PHSM.

14. "A Brief History" (of the Edisto Island Presbyterian Church), 1, typescript, PHSM; *Fourth Annual Report*, COF, 1868–69.

15. *MGAPCUSA(OS)*, 1860, 1870, 1879; *Proceedings of the Meeting in Charleston, S.C., May 13–15, on the Religious Instruction of the Negroes, Together with the Report of the Committee, and the Address to the Public* (Charleston: B. Jenkins, 1845), 47; E. T. H. Shaffer, *History of Bethel Presbyterian Church: From the Founding in 1728 Down to the Present Time—1928* (Walterboro, S.C.: Press and Standard, [1928]); *MGAPCUS*, 1870–79. For the little Summerville church see, *MGAPCUSA*, 1870–90; *MGAPCUS*, 1870–90.

16. William Heyward, who worshiped at Stoney Creek, was providing the use of a house for the pastor of the "Negro Mission" in 1868. In 1879 the Salem congregation left Charleston Presbytery and became a part of the African American Atlantic Presbytery of the Northern Assembly. With this move it adopted the name Beaufort Salem Presbyterian Church. *MGAPCUSA*, 1879; *MGAPCUS*, 1866–79; Beaufort County Courthouse, *Deed Book 152*, 43; Gregory-Elliott papers, no. 870, Southern Historical Collection, University of North Carolina at Chapel Hill.

17. Bernard Edward Powers, Jr., "Black Charleston: A Social History 1822–85" (Ph.D. diss., Northwestern University, 1982), 211–12; Larry Koger, *Black Slaveowners: Free Black Slave*

Masters in South Carolina, 1790–1860 (Jefferson, N.C.: McFarland, 1985), 157, 197; *First Annual Report,* COMFF, 1870–71, 12, PHSP.

18. *MGAPCUSA,* 1880.

19. Ibid., 1866–80; *MGAPCUS,* 1867–79; *Annual Report*(s), COF, 1865–69; *Annual Report*(s), COMFF, 1870–80.

20. Powers, 218 and 230. Plymouth Congregational's membership was, however, close to 200 by 1876, approximately the same size as the antebellum black membership of Circular Congregational Church. For the failure of Congregationalism to establish itself firmly in the African American community of the South, see Joe Martin Richardson, *Christian Reconstruction: The American Missionary Association and Southern Blacks, 1861–1890* (Athens: University of Georgia Press, 1986), 98–102, 147–59.

21. *MGAPCUSA,* 1867–80; *MGAPCUS,* 1867–80.

22. See letter in *Fourth Annual Report,* COF, 1868–69, 43.

23. The presbytery included the mission work that had been undertaken in the low country. *Second Annual Report,* COF, 1866–67, 8.

24. The strength of Atlantic Presbytery was centered in two areas: first, in Charleston and in the coastal region immediately south of the city and second, in an area around Sumter and in particular around the old Salem Black River Church. While these churches in the Sumter area would play an important role in the history of Atlantic Presbytery for more than a hundred years, they are not directly included here because they lie outside the geographical bounds of this study. *MGAPCUSA,* 1865–76. The bounds of the present study are described in the introduction. The New School General Assembly was also active in South Carolina, sending missionaries to work among the freed people. In 1868 the New School organized the Presbytery of South Carolina, which included eight up-country black churches, the large mission of Ennals Adams in Charleston, the black Summerville Presbyterian Church, and a school and church at Bluffton. This presbytery continued in existence for one year after the reunion of the Old and New Schools in the North in 1869. In 1870 it became a part of Atlantic Presbytery. *MGAPCUSA*(NS), 1865–69, PHSM.

25. See app. D.

26. The work of Northern missionaries and teachers has been carefully addressed by many scholars. Among the most important studies are James D. Anderson, *The Education of Blacks in the South, 1860–1935* (Chapel Hill: University of North Carolina Press, 1988); Henry Allen Bullock, *A History of Negro Education in the South from 1619 to the Present* (Cambridge: Harvard University Press, 1967); Paul H. Douglass, *Christian Reconstruction in the South* (Boston: Pilgrim Press, 1909); Elizabeth Jacoway, *Yankee Missionaries in the South: The Penn School Experiment* (Baton Rouge: Louisiana State University Press, 1980); Jacqueline Jones, *Soldiers of Light and Love: Northern Teachers and Georgia Blacks* (Chapel Hill: University of North Carolina Press, 1980); Robert C. Morris, *Reading, 'Riting, and Reconstruction: the Education of Freedmen in the South, 1861–1870* (Chicago: University of Chicago Press, 1981); Richardson, 163–64; Willie Lee Rose, *Rehearsal for Reconstruction: The Port Royal Experiment* (Indianapolis: Bobbs-Merrill, 1964); Litwack, 450–501; and Drago, passim.

27. Louisa Cheves Stoney, *Autobiographical Notes, Letters and Reflections by Thomas Smyth, D. D.* (Charleston: Walker, Evans and Cogswell, 1914), 206; Thomas Holt, *Black over White: Negro Political Leadership in South Carolina during Reconstruction* (Urbana: University of Illinois Press, 1977), 53–54, 83; Williamson, 180–239; Powers, 257–58. For Cardozo's reputed father, see Melvin M. Leiman, *Jacob N. Cardozo: Economic Thought in the Antebellum South* (New York: Columbia University Press, 1966). The American Missionary Association's extensive work in the South is explored in Richardson. See also Alfred Knighton Stanley, *The Children is Crying: Congregationalism among Black People* (New York: Pilgrim Press, 1979).

28. Quoted in Litwack, 477.

29. Holt, 53–54, 83; Powers, 257–58.

30. Powers, 255; Litwack, 471.

31. *MGAPCUSA*(NS), 1855–60, 1866–68; *MGAPCUSA*, 1871–76; Powers, 212, 224, 231, 258; Holt, 89.

32. Holt, 83, 85–86.

33. See app. D; *Second Annual Report*, COMFF, 1871–72, 5; *Annual Reports*, COMFF, 1872–79; *MGAPCUSA*, 1871–80.

34. Holt, 85, 87, 139; Powers, 221. Anna M. Nichols, of Toledo, Ohio, an instructor at Avery, noted in 1885 that before the war Charleston was "the Athens of the South," and its African American inhabitants, "breathing the same air as the more favored race, they naturally imbibed some of its cultured modes of thought" (Drago, 107–08).

35. Holt, 53–54, 83; Powers, 257–58; Williamson, 383–84, 390–91.

36. Powers, 255; Litwack, 471.

37. Powers, 212, 224, 231, 258; Holt, 89.

38. Holt, 83, 85–86.

39. Ibid., 85, 87, 139; Powers, 221.

40. See Von Laue, 3–9, 302–03.

41. Memory could thus function, as could a utopian vision, to shatter the ideological claims of a dominant power or class. By giving a different reading to the past, an alternative memory could give a different reading of the present. See Michael Walzer, *Interpretation and Social Criticism* (Cambridge: Harvard University Press, 1987). See also Hans-Georg Gadamer, *Truth and Method* (New York: Crossroads, 1984), esp. "Hermeneutics and Historicism," 460–91; and Paul Ricoeur, *The Conflict of Interpretations* (Evanston: Northwestern University Press, 1974).

42. The development of such perspectives could be seen most clearly at Avery Normal Institute. In 1916, for example, the Avery salutatorian declared: "The Negro Folk song stand today not simply as the sole American Music, but as the most beautiful expression of human experience born this side of the seas altho it has been neglected and even now is half [despised], and is continually mistaken and misunderstood, still it remains as the singular spiritual heritage of the nation and the greatest gift of the Negro people" (Drago, 169).

43. My interviews with pastors in 1989 indicated that spirituals, which in earlier years had not been a part of many worship services, were being sung with increased frequency in African American Presbyterian congregations.

44. See above, chap. 14, and Von Laue, 38–39. Third-generation immigrants reflected a similar experience. Thoroughly acculturated, having forgotten the language of their grandparents, they became more interested than their parents in discovering their roots. See Randall M. Miller and Thomas D. Marzik, eds., *Immigrants and Religion in Urban America* (Philadelphia: Temple University Press, 1977).

45. The poverty and racial oppression that low country African Americans continued to face can best be seen in Coclanis, 111–60; Williamson, 363–417; and Tindall, passim.

46. *Second Annual Report*, COF, 1866–67, 8, 14, 66–67; *Third Annual Report*, COF, 1867–68, 14–15.

47. Another early pastor from among the ranks of the recently freed was Smart Campbell. See Inez Moore Parker, *The Rise and Decline of the Program of Education for Black Presbyterians of the United Presbyterian Church U.S.A., 1865–1970* (San Antonio: Trinity University Press, 1977), 40–41; *MGAPCUSA*, 1867–76. Parker refers to Campbell as "Paul Campbell," but the official records give his name as "Smart Campbell." See also *Annual Reports* of COF, 1866–69, and of COMFF, 1870–76.

48. I. Parker, 41.

49. Using the waterways as his circuit, Moultrie made his preaching rounds from Edisto to Wadmalaw to Yonges Island and Saint Andrews. See *MGAPCUSA*, 1869–90.

50. I. Parker, 41; *MGAPCUSA*, 1867–76.

51. For a dialectical model of interpreting the African American religious experience in general, see C. Eric Lincoln and Lawrence H. Mamiya, *The Black Church in the African American Experience* (Durham: Duke University Press, 1990), esp. 12–20.

15. The African American Reformed Community: "Two Warring Ideals in One Dark Body"

1. *MGAPCUSA*, 1917, 418–19, PHSM; Inez Moore Parker, *The Rise and Decline of the Program of Education for Black Presbyterians of the United Presbyterian Church U.S.A., 1865–1970* (San Antonio: Trinity University Press, 1977), 139–86.

2. *Teacher's Monthly School Report,* Saxton School, March 1868, FBR.

3. Edmund L. Drago, *Initiative, Paternalism, & Race Relations: Charleston's Avery Normal Institute* (Athens: University of Georgia Press, 1990), 57–58, 90–93, 196–247.

4. *Teacher's Monthly School Report,* Zion, January 1868, FBR; *Teacher's Monthly School Report,* Wallingford, January 1869 and January 1870, FBR; Bernard Edward Powers, Jr., "Black Charleston: A Social History 1822–1855" (Ph.D. diss., Northwestern University, 1982), 260; *Tenth Annual Report,* COMFF, 1879–80, 15, PHSP; *Fourth Annual Report,* COF, 1868–69, 10, 13, 57–58, PHSP; *Twelfth Annual Report,* COMFF, 1880–81, 28.

5. *Teacher's Monthly School Report,* Presbyterian Home Mission, March 1870, FBR; *Monthly Report of Freedmen's School at Charleston, S.C.,* January 1870, Presbyterian Committee of Home Missions, PHSP.

6. *Teacher's Monthly School Report,* Shaw, October 1867, January 1868, January 1869, and January 1871, FBR; Powers, 224, 258.

7. *Teacher's Monthly School Report,* James Island, January 1869, FBR; *Third Annual Report,* COF, 1867–68, 68.

8. *MGAPCUSA*, 1927, 88; I. Parker, 180–82.

9. *Annual Reports,* COF, COMFF, 1868–71. *Teacher's Monthly Report,* Johns Island, May 1867, FBR. Jacob Charles Moultrie held classes at the Saint Andrews church. *MGAPCUSA*, 1917, 420 and 1929, 196; I. Parker, 182.

10. *MGAPCUSA*, 1928, 89–90, and 1929, 196; I. Parker, 142–44; *Annual Reports,* COF, COMFF, 1866–82; *Teacher's Monthly Report,* Hope School, January 1870, FBR; I. Parker, 144.

11. *Eighth Annual Report,* COMFF, 1877–78, 22–23; *MGAPCUSA*, 1893, 51, 341; Joe Martin Richardson, *Christian Reconstruction: The American Missionary Association and Southern Blacks, 1861–1890* (Athens: University of Georgia Press, 1986), 178 and picture opposite 183.

12. For Harden Academy, see *MGAPCUSA*, 1929, 145, 198. For Bamberg, see *MGAPCUSA*, 1921, 344. For Blackville and the Emmerson Industrial Institute, see *MGAPCUSA*, 1904, 54, and 1929, 196; I. Parker, 179–80, 159–61.

13. *MGAPCUSA*, 1901, 321; 1914, 429–30; 1917, 418–19; *Teacher's Monthly Report,* Johns Island, May 1867; I. Parker, 161 f.

14. Drago, passim; I. Parker, 180.

15. I. Parker, passim; Drago, 248–66.

16. For the disciplined curriculum at Avery, with its intentional program of recultura- tion, see Powers, 261, 393–94 n. 28; Drago, passim. Of 334 students at Avery in 1869, 170

were free before the war. See *Teachers' Monthly School Report*, Avery, February 1869, FBR. See also Richardson, 208–09.

17. Powers, 244. Cardozo's fellow Charlestonian, African Methodist Episcopal Bishop Daniel Payne, had a similar perspective: "New England ideas, sentiments, and principles," he declared, "will ultimately rule the entire South." Daniel A. Payne, *Recollections of Seventy Years* (1888; reprint, New York, 1969), 163n. See also Leon F. Litwack, *Been in the Storm So Long: The Aftermath of Slavery* (New York: Alfred A. Knopf, 1979), 450–501.

18. For the role of female teachers and the assumptions about the place of women, see *Second Annual Report*, COF, 1866–67, 10–11; see also Litwack, 476–501; Richardson, 163–64, 171; and Henry L. Swint, *The Northern Teacher in the South 1862–1870* (New York: Octagon Books, 1967). On the difficulties schoolmarms faced, see Richardson, 171. For the debate about Northern teachers versus Southern black teachers, see Powers, 254, 257–58; and Thomas Holt, *Black over White: Negro Political Leadership in South Carolina during Reconstruction* (Urbana: University of Illinois Press, 1977), 70.

19. Telephone interview with Dorothy Smith, Edisto Island, 1989. See also Margaret Washington Creel, *"A Peculiar People": Slave Religion and Community-Culture among the Gullahs* (New York: New York University Press, 1988). For the relationship of language to a world view and ethos, see "Thick Description: Toward an Interpretive Theory of Culture," and more fully, "Ideology as a Cultural System," in Clifford Geertz, *The Interpretation of Cultures: Selected Essays* (New York: Basic Books, 1973).

20. In 1867 the Presbyterian Committee on Freedmen emphasized the need for self-discipline and a new sense of propriety by focusing on the role of the newly freed African American woman, who was critical for the community's internalization of such values. *Second Annual Report*, COF, 1866–67, 10–11. More than sixty years later, the Reverend William Lee Metz of Edisto praised the cultural transformation that had taken place in the students at Larimer under the tutelage of his wife Eola. *MGAPCUSA*, 1931, 128–29.

21. See Paul Ricoeur, *Lectures on Ideology and Utopia*, ed. George H. Taylor (New York: Columbia University Press, 1986), xxxiii, 300–14. The utopian vision consequently helps to shape the community's identity, its understanding of who and what it is.

22. George C. Rowe, pastor of Plymouth and intimately involved in the life of Avery, published in 1890, for example, a collection of poems on African American heroes: *Our Heroes: Patriotic Poems on Men, Women and Sayings of the Negro Race* (Charleston: Walker, Evans and Cogswell, 1890). Recalling her days as a Larimer student in the 1930s, an Edisto Island resident noted: "Long before it was popular, we had regular classes in African American history. We were taught to respect our past." Telephone interview with Dorothy Smith.

23. For tensions between AMA and local leaders of Avery, see Drago, passim, but esp. 90–94, 196–247. Even with the tighter control by the AMA, in contrast to the Presbyterian board, local supporters of Avery exerted significant influence over its management.

24. "Our church," declared the Presbyterian Board of National Missions in 1929, "early accepted the responsibility of lifting the [freed] people out of the depths. It realized that its first duty was to train Negroes, who in turn became leaders among their own people" (*MGAPCUSA*, 1929, 139).

25. For the solidarity of the larger African American community in South Carolina, despite its diversity, see Joel Williamson, *After Slavery: The Negro in South Carolina During Reconstruction, 1861–1877* (Chapel Hill: University of North Carolina Press, 1965), 305–06.

26. George Brown Tindall, *South Carolina Negroes, 1877–1900* (Columbia: University of South Carolina Press, 1952), 44, 81, 151, 78.

27. Ibid., 56; *90th Anniversary: St. Luke Presbyterian Church (USA), Orangeburg, South Carolina*, 1–2, CAPO.

28. Tindall, 48, 69–70, 83, 90–91, 100, 112, 121. I. A. Newby, *Black Carolinians: A History of Blacks in South Carolina from 1895 to 1968* (Columbia: University of South Carolina Press, 1973), 109–11.

29. Newby, 110–11.

30. See Carter G. Woodson, ed., *The Works of Francis James Grimké*, 2 vols. (Washington, D.C.: Associated Publishers, 1942), 1:Introduction.

31. *MGAPCUSA*, 1927, 87–88; 1928, 89–90; 1931, 128–29; and telephone interview with Dorothy Smith.

32. Such transformist perspectives had been present in the community since the end of the Civil War. See the report of Jonathan C. Gibbs in the *Christian Recorder*, February 3, 1866.

33. See app. D.

34. Edgar Sutton Robinson, *The Ministerial Directory of the Ministers in [the Presbyterian Church]* (Oxford, Ohio: Ministerial Directory Co., 1898), 393; *MGAPCUSA*, 1890–1943.

35. *MGAPCUSA*, 1893.

36. Atlantic Presbytery, Minutes, 1886–1908, PHSM, see esp. March 6, 1888, 37–43; November 25, 1903, 200–203; April 12, 1905, 267; September 27, 1905, 297–98; September 28, 1906, 325–26; April 12, 1907, 345. For earlier discipline of a white minister, see Charleston Union Presbytery, Minutes, November 9, 1830, PHSM.

37. *MGAPCUSA*, "Atlantic Presbytery," 1900–1940. For Congregational statistics, see Alfred Knighton Stanley, *The Children is Crying: Congregationalism among Black People* (New York: Pilgrim Press, 1979), 138.

38. *MGAPCUSA*, 1940, 410; Stanley, 138.

39. One way to understand the success of the Methodist and Baptist traditions among African Americans is to see a greater cultural congruence of these religious traditions with African American traditions. Methodists and Baptists consequently had a greater ability to move more successfully over the distance that separated them from traditional African American culture. See Powers, 182, 188, 204.

40. W. E. B. Du Bois, *The Soul of Black Folk* (1903; reprint, Greenwich, Conn.: Fawcett, 1961), 3–4.

16. The White Reformed Community, 1876–1941: A "Little World" in Travail and Transition

1. Peter A. Coclanis, *The Shadow of a Dream: Economic Life and Death in the South Carolina Low Country, 1670–1920* (New York: Oxford University Press, 1989), 121. See also Alice Hanson Jones, *Wealth of a Nation To Be: The American Colonies on the Eve of the Revolution* (New York: Columbia University Press, 1980), 50–85, 294–380.

2. Coclanis, 63, 90–91, 121.

3. Ibid., 128–29, 155. For comparisons of the low country's mean per capita income with that of the United States, 1929–69, see ibid., 199. Historians have vigorously debated the causes of this great reversal. Some, in a continuation of the image of the low country as the land of the Cavalier, have described the work habits of Charleston business leaders as "lethargic" and "decadent." See Don Harrison Doyle, "Urbanization and Southern Culture: Economic Elites in Four New South Cities (Atlanta, Nashville, Charleston, Mobile): c. 1865–1910," in Orville V. Burton and Robert C. McMath, Jr., eds., *Toward a New South? Studies in Post–Civil War Southern Communities* (Westport, Conn.: Greenwood Press, 1982), 31, 23. Similar arguments are made by Frederic C. Jaher, "Antebellum Charleston: Anatomy of an Economic Failure," in Orville V. Burton and Robert C. McMath, Jr., eds., *Class, Conflict,*

and *Consensus: Antebellum Southern Community Studies* (Westport, Conn.: Greenwood Press, 1982), 207–31; Frederic C. Jaher, *The Urban Establishment: Upper Strata in Boston, New York, Charleston, Chicago, and Los Angeles* (Urbana: University of Illinois Press, 1982); John P. Radford, "Social Structure and Urban Form: Charleston, 1860–1880," in Walter J. Fraser, Jr., and Winfred B. Moore, Jr., eds., *From the Old South to the New: Essays on the Transitional South* (Westport, Conn.: Greenwood Press, 1981), 81–91; and Don Harrison Doyle, "Leadership and Decline in Postwar Charleston, 1865–1910," in Fraser and Moore.

Other economic historians have pointed in a different direction, insisting the economic demise of the low country had roots deep in the region's history and the laws of supply and demand. They insist that low country planters and merchants responded "to the area's economic problems with considerable vigor, albeit within the limits imposed by the environment, the low country's economic structure, and by the area's position in the international economic hierarchy." Indeed, their "efforts to increase productivity, redirect the western trade, and to diversify the low-country economy to a degree are indicative of considerable enterprise rather than entrepreneurial lethargy." See Coclanis, 111–58 and, for above quotes, 137–39. See also Eugene D. Genovese, *The Political Economy of Slavery: Studies in the Economy and Society of the Slave South* (New York: Pantheon Books, 1965); James Oakes, *The Ruling Race: A History of American Slaveholders* (New York: Knopf, 1982); and Alfred Glaze Smith, *Economic Readjustment of an Old Cotton State: South Carolina, 1820–1860* (Columbia: University of South Carolina Press, 1958). For a succinct statement of the opposing views on the Southern economy, see Stanley L. Engerman, "Some Economic Factors in Southern Backwardness in the Nineteenth Century," in John F. Kain and John R. Meyer, eds., *Essays in Regional Economics* (Cambridge: Harvard University Press, 1971), 279–306.

4. See Francis Butler Simkins, *Pitchfork Ben Tillman: South Carolinian* (1944; reprint, Baton Rouge: Louisiana State University Press, 1967), 72–74; Francis Butler Simkins and Robert H. Woody, *South Carolina During Reconstruction* (Chapel Hill: University of North Carolina Press, 1932), 37–43, 95–103; and Don Harrison Doyle, *New Men, New Cities, New South: Atlanta, Nashville, Charleston, Mobile, 1860–1910* (Chapel Hill: University of North Carolina Press, 1990), 92.

5. *Handbook of South Carolina: Resources, Institutions and Industries of the State* (Columbia: State Co., 1907), 531; Doyle, *New Men*, 171–73.

6. First (Scots) Presbyterian Church, Membership List, First (Scots) Presbyterian Church archives, Charleston; *Manual for the Use of the Members of the Second Presbyterian Church, Charleston, S.C.* (Charleston: Walker, Evans and Cogswell, 1894), 81–121; Edisto Island Presbyterian Church, Session Records, 1890–1941, PHSM; Johns Island Presbyterian Church, Minutes of the Session, 1867–1904, 1911–46, PHSM; New Wappetaw Presbyterian Church, Minutes of the Session, 1870–1940, PHSM.

7. These families can be most easily traced in the congregational histories compiled and printed in F. D. Jones and W. H. Mills, *History of the Presbyterian Church in South Carolina Since 1850* (Columbia: R. L. Bryan, 1926), and in Margaret A. Gist, ed., *Presbyterian Women of South Carolina* (Woman's Auxiliary of the Synod of South Carolina, 1929).

8. Between 1876 and 1893, for example, of the new members who joined the Second Presbyterian Church, 61 percent (304 of 498) were women, a percentage that reflected statewide statistics in the 1920s when 63 percent of the white Presbyterians in South Carolina were estimated to be women. *Manual for the Use of the Members*, 81–121; Gist, xviii.

9. See Gist, 437.

10. For the role of pious women in late nineteenth-century American culture, see Kathryn Kish Sklar, *Catherine Beecher: A Study in American Domesticity* (New Haven: Yale University Press, 1973); Ann Douglas, *The Feminization of American Culture* (New York:

Alfred A. Knopf, 1977); and Barbara Leslie Epstein, *The Politics of Domesticity: Women, Evangelism, and Temperance in Nineteenth-Century America* (Middletown, Conn.: Wesleyan University Press, 1981). In the 1920s Francis B. Mayes told a meeting of Presbyterian women in Charleston that "By Divine right women are the makers of the home—men are the builders—but in a far finer sense, the making has been given into our hands" (Gist, xviii).

11. Women, said Francis B. Mayes, have "the most difficult, most delicate, most constructive duties entrusted to any created being. Oh, the glory or tragedy of motherhood!" (Gist, xviii). For the economic sources of these changes, see Douglas, passim; Epstein, passim.

12. Gist, 766.

13. See app. E.

14. Starting points for tracing these networks of family relationships are E. C. Scott, *Ministerial Directory of the Presbyterian Church, U.S. 1861–1941* (Austin: Von Boeckmann-Jones, 1942), and Louis C. LaMotte, *Colored Light: The Story of the Influence of Columbia Theological Seminary, 1828–1936* (Richmond: Presbyterian Committee of Publication, 1937).

15. See app. E.

16. John L. Girardeau, *Confederate Memorial Day at Charleston, S.C.: Re-interment of the Carolina Dead from Gettysburg* (Charleston: William G. Mazyck, 1871), 18.

17. Sixty-three percent of those who served five years in the low country went to Columbia Theological Seminary. See app. E.

18. To a considerable degree, the same was true for Union in Virginia and for Princeton. For Princeton, see Lefferts A. Loetscher, *The Broadening Church: A Study of Theological Issues in the Presbyterian Church Since 1869* (Philadelphia: University of Pennsylvania Press, 1954), 54, 64, 77.

19. Doyle, *New Men,* 253–303.

20. Ibid., 194–95; Tom W. Shick and Don Harrison Doyle, "The South Carolina Phosphate Boom and the Stillbirth of the New South, 1867–1920," *SCHM* 86 (1985): 18, 25.

21. Louisa Cheves Stoney, ed., *Autobiographical Notes, Letters and Reflections by Thomas Smyth, D. D.* (Charleston: Walker, Evans and Cogswell, 1914), 657, 745. Smyth was also president of the Belton mill, fifth in the state (of 111 mills in 1907) in the value of its yearly product. *Handbook of South Carolina,* 457–60. David L. Carlton, " 'Builders of a New State,' " in Fraser and Moore, 52.

22. Doyle, *New Men;* David L. Carlton, *Mill and Town in South Carolina 1890–1920* (Baton Rouge: Louisiana State University Press, 1982); John A. Hamilton, *History of the Orangeburg Presbyterian Church, Orangeburg, South Carolina* (Orangeburg: R. Lewis Berry, 1896).

23. Prominent among those who were vigorous advocates of a revived low country economy were Augustine Smythe, Judge Charles H. Simonton, longtime president of the corporation of Second Presbyterian, and U.S. Congressman George Swinton Legaré, a fellow Sunday school teacher with J. Adger Smyth at Second Church. See William J. Cooper, Jr., *The Conservative Regime: South Carolina, 1877–1890* (Baltimore: Johns Hopkins University Press, 1968), 128–31; Simkins, 182–83, 220–22, 375 f.

24. Doyle, *New Men,* 291–300.

25. For the scholarly debate around the question of continuity or discontinuity between the Old South and the New, see C. Vann Woodward, *A History of the South,* vol. 9, *Origins of the New South, 1877–1913* (Baton Rouge: Louisiana State University Press, 1951), and Doyle, *New Men.* Coclanis argues for structural continuity but sees in that continuity considerable entrepreneurial enterprise (137–39). With the white Reformed community in the low country, there was clear continuity both in leadership and in a spirit of vigorous business activity. The Adgers represent perhaps the clearest example.

26. See E. Merton Coulter, *George Walton Williams: The Life of a Southern Merchant and Banker, 1820–1903* (Athens, Ga.: Hibriten Press, 1976).

27. See Samuel N. Eisenstadt, *The Protestant Ethic and Modernization: A Comparative View* (New York: Basic Books, 1968); and Richard Weiss, *The American Myth of Success: From Horatio Alger to Norman Vincent Peale* (New York: Basic Books, 1969).

28. See Carlton, *Mill and Town*, 90–91.

29. See Daniel Walker Howe, ed., *Victorian America* (Philadelphia: University of Pennsylvania Press, 1976), 3–28; and Eisenstadt, passim.

30. The now classic study of these changes is Robert H. Wiebe, *The Search for Order: 1877–1920* (New York: Hill and Wang, 1967).

31. For the traditional understanding of discipline in Reformed churches, see John T. McNeill, *The History and Character of Calvinism* (1954; reprint, London: Oxford University Press, 1967), 139. The last significant case of discipline by a church session in the low country (that I have been able to uncover) occurred in the 1880s. On church discipline generally in the Southern Presbyterian Church, see Ernest Trice Thompson, *Presbyterians in the South*, 3 vols. (Richmond: John Knox Press, 1963, 1973), 2:399–403. For developments in pastoral counseling during this period, see E. Brooks Holifield, *A History of Pastoral Care in America: From Salvation to Self-Realization* (Nashville: Abingdon Press, 1983), 159–209. For the broader cultural shifts associated with these changes, see Robert C. Fuller, *Americans and the Unconscious* (New York: Oxford University Press, 1986), 51–95; and Philip Rieff, *The Triumph of the Therapeutic: Uses of Faith after Freud* (Chicago: University of Chicago Press, 1966).

32. See, for example, Westminster Presbyterian Church, Session Minutes, 1890–1900, PHSM; and John B. Adger, "Plans of Church Finance," *SPR* 33 (January 1879): 92–111.

33. Charleston Presbytery, Minutes, 1900–1915, PHSM.

34. Augustine Smythe was a heavy investor in his brother Ellison Smyth's textile enterprise. L. Stoney, 675. *Manual for the Use of the Members*, 20–21. See also Gist, 169.

35. George A. Blackburn, ed., *The Life Work of John L. Girardeau, D. D., LL.D., Late Professor in the Presbyterian Theological Seminary, Columbia, S.C.* (Columbia: State Co., 1916), 141–42.

36. John L. Girardeau, *Instrumental Music in the Public Worship of the Church* (Richmond: Whittet and Shepperson, 1888). By the first decade of the twentieth century, organs were being used in country and small-town churches such as Rockville and McClellanville. See Annie Jenkins Batson, *Rockville Presbyterian Church, Wadmalaw Island, South Carolina* (Charleston: Walker, Evans and Cogswell, 1976), 25. Interview with Elizabeth Duke Warren, Summerville, S.C., April 1988.

37. Jones and Mills, 438, 440, 454. For denomination-wide developments, see Thompson, *Presbyterians in the South*, 3:384–402; and Hallie Paxon Winnsborough, *The Women's Auxiliary* (Richmond: Presbyterian Committee of Publication, 1927).

38. Gist, 202, 157.

39. James Woodrow, "Female College Commencement," *Southern Presbyterian*, August 5, 1880, 2; Winnsborough, 26–27.

40. See William Plummer Jacobs, *The Pioneer* (Clinton, S.C.: Jacobs Press, 1935), 93–94; and Carlton, *Mill and Town*, 181–82.

41. See Jürgen Habermas's note on Marx: "Thus, according to Marx, the distinguishing feature of capitalism is that it has brought ideologies from the heights of mythological or religious legitimations of tangible domination and power down into the system of social labor. In liberal bourgeois society the legitimation of power is derived from the legitimation of the market, that is from the 'justice' of the exchange of equivalents inherent in exchange relations." Jürgen Habermas, *Knowledge and Human Interest*, trans. Jeremy J. Shapiro (Bos-

ton: Beacon Press, 1972), 60. Paul Ricoeur has also concluded that "in the capitalistic era the major ideology is no longer a religious ideology but precisely a market ideology." Paul Ricoeur, *Lectures on Ideology and Utopia,* ed. George H. Taylor (New York: Columbia University Press, 1986), 230.

42. The growth of individualism in the churches found expression in the ritual of the Lord's Supper. By 1900, most of the churches had given up the practice of participants coming to the front, sitting together around one table, and drinking of one cup and eating one loaf. In the place of this enactment of the Last Supper, the churches began to pass trays of individual small cups and individually chopped pieces of bread to participants who remained in their seats.

43. For the cultural transformations taking place during the 1920s, see Daniel Bell, *The Cultural Contradictions of Capitalism* (New York: Basic Books, 1976), 33–84. For the movement in American culture toward an "expressive individualism" with its quest for self-fulfillment and its affinities with psychotherapy, see Robert Bellah, et al. *Habits of the Heart: Individualism and Commitment in American Life* (Berkeley and Los Angeles: University of California Press, 1985).

44. Alasdair MacIntyre has persuasively described what he calls a "bureaucratic individualism," a culture exemplified by the manager and the therapist. This culture is increasingly reflected in the churches of the low country. See Alasdair MacIntyre, *After Virtue: A Study in Moral Theory* (Notre Dame, Ind.: University of Notre Dame Press, 1981), 33.

45. See Harold Prince, *A Presbyterian Bibliography: The Published Writings of Ministers Who Served in the Presbyterian Church in the United States During Its First Hundred Years, 1861–1961* (Metuchen, N.J.: Scarecrow Press, 1983).

46. John Newton Thomas, for example, received a Ph.D. from the University of Edinburgh and spent a year at the University of Berlin, but he published very little.

47. See Thompson, *Presbyterians in the South,* 3:486–88. For the theological positions and social context of Fundamentalism and modernism, see George M. Marsden, *Fundamentalism and American Culture* (New York: Oxford University Press, 1980); and William R. Hutchison, *The Modernist Impulse in American Protestantism* (1976; reprint, Oxford: Oxford University Press, 1982).

17. From "Our Little World" to the Sun Belt

1. For the development of "modern Charleston," see Walter J. Fraser, Jr., *Charleston! Charleston! The History of a Southern City* (Columbia: University of South Carolina Press, 1989), 394–442.

2. For the characteristics of the Sun Belt, see Richard M. Bernard and Bradley R. Rice, eds., *Sunbelt Cities: Politics and Growth Since World War II* (Austin: University of Texas Press, 1983), 1–30; Randall M. Miller and George E. Pozzetta, eds., *Shades of the Sunbelt: Essays on Ethnicity, Race, and the Urban South* (New York: Greenwood Press, 1988); and Carl Abbott, *The New Urban America: Growth and Politics in Sunbelt Cities* (Chapel Hill: University of North Carolina Press, 1987).

3. The term *Black Belt* refers here to a predominantly African American region in a city or state. In this study it refers to Colleton, Hampton, Allendale, Barnwell, Bamberg, and Orangeburg Counties.

4. Bureau of the Census, *U.S. Census of Population, 1980,* "South Carolina Counties," vol. 1, sec. A, table 2; *South Carolina Estimated Population By Age, Race, and Sex As Of July 1, 1988,* South Carolina Division of Research and Statistical Services, State Data Center, Columbia.

5. *South Carolina Estimated Population.* For nineteenth-century figures, see *Handbook of South Carolina: Resources, Institutions and Industries of the State* (Columbia: State Co., 1907), 524–28.

6. Charleston Trident Chamber of Commerce, *Charleston Trident Area, South Carolina, Executive Summary,* 1989, Charleston.

7. See Greater Beaufort Chamber of Commerce, *Area Demographics, 1989,* Beaufort, S.C.; and Fraser, 323–438.

8. *Charleston Trident Area,* 4–7. See also Greater Beaufort, *Area Demographics,* 14.

9. *U.S. Census,* "South Carolina Counties." *MGAPCUS,* 1940, 1950, 1960, 1970, 1980, PHSM.

10. *MGAPCUS,* 1940–82; *MGAPC(USA),* 1983–88.

11. Ibid., 1940–80.

12. See James A. Davis, *General Social Surveys, 1972–1984* (Chicago: National Opinion Research Center, 1984). For an analysis of the Presbyterian data collected in the General Social Surveys, see Wade Clark Roof and William McKinney, *American Mainline Religion: Its Changing Shape and Future* (New Brunswick: Rutgers University Press, 1988), 85–87, 119–22, 233–34.

13. See Roof and McKinney, 130.

14. See, for example, First (Scots) Presbyterian Church, *Church Directory,* 1988, Charleston.

15. The eight congregations, selected to reflect both the major areas of membership and some geographical variety, included six congregations established before 1945, one established in 1957, and one established in 1976: First (Scots) and Westminster in Charleston; Mount Pleasant; First Presbyterian, Orangeburg; Bethel, Walterboro; Summerville; Dorchester; and First Presbyterian, Hilton Head. The records of Summerville were reviewed from 1963 to 1988.

16. These figures do not include children of the congregations and those adults who joined by a first-time "profession of faith." The studies that yielded these statistics have been deposited at the PHSM.

17. See Roof and McKinney, 85–87, 119–22, 233–34.

18. See *MGAPCUS,* 1980.

19. The "changes in the social norms" for women in the United States are summarized in Daniel Yankelovich, *New Rules: Searching for Self-Fulfillment in a World Turned Upside Down* (New York: Random House, 1981), xiv–xvi, 93.

20. See Lois A. Boyd and R. Douglas Brackenridge, *Presbyterian Women in America: Two Centuries of a Quest for Status* (Westport, Conn.: Greenwood Press, 1983), 207–24.

21. List of members and their occupations in 1945 provided by trustee Jervey Royall. Occupation of members in 1985 compiled by Jervey Royall and church secretary Patricia S. Ayers. Church officers are taken from "Bulletin, Mount Pleasant Presbyterian Church," November 13, 1988. For size of congregation and number of women in 1988, see *MGAPC(USA),* 1988, PHSM.

22. Margaret W. Creel, *"A Peculiar People": Slave Religion and Community-Culture among the Gullahs* (New York: New York University Press, 1988); and Patricia Jackson-Jones, *When Roots Die: Endangered Traditions on the Sea Islands* (Athens: University of Georgia Press, 1987).

23. The Frasers, who were the primary developers of Hilton Head, are descended from Puritan families who settled Dorchester in 1696. See "The Ultimate Resort Playground," *Tennis* 25, no. 12 (April 1990): 85–88.

24. The analysis of the Hilton Head congregation is drawn from the report of par-

ish consultant Lyle E. Schaller of the Yokefellow Institute, Naperville, Ill., *First Presbyterian Church, Hilton Head, South Carolina,* First Presbyterian Church, Hilton Head.

25. Ibid., "The Context for Planning," 1–5.

26. *MGAPCUS,* 1945–82; *MGAPC(USA),* 1983–90; E. D. Witherspoon, Jr., *Ministerial Directory of the Presbyterian Church, U.S., 1861–1983* (Atlanta: Darby, 1986).

27. There is a vast literature on the rise of the manager and a bureaucratic ethos, beginning with the seminal work of Max Weber; see especially his *The Theory of Social and Economic Organization,* trans. A. M. Henderson and Talcott Parsons (New York: Free Press, 1947). For more recent treatments, see Alasdair MacIntyre, *After Virtue: A Study in Moral Theory* (Notre Dame, Ind.: University of Notre Dame Press, 1981); Robert Bellah, et al., *Habits of the Heart: Individualism and Commitment in American Life* (Berkeley and Los Angeles: University of California Press, 1985); Alfred D. Chandler, *The Visible Hand: The Managerial Revolution in American Business* (Cambridge: Harvard University Press, 1977); and Michael Maccoby, *The Gamesman* (New York: Simon and Schuster, 1976).

28. *Charleston-Atlantic Presbytery 1990 Directory,* CAPO. Thomas W. Horton was the first executive of Charleston Presbytery. At the time of reunion, Barry Van Deventer, executive presbyter of Charleston Presbytery, became executive presbyter of Charleston-Atlantic. Ferdinand Pharr, executive presbyter of Atlantic Presbytery, became the associate executive presbyter and stated clerk of Charleston-Atlantic Presbytery.

29. On the therapeutic culture, see Philip Rieff, *The Triumph of the Therapeutic: Uses of Faith after Freud* (Chicago: University of Chicago Press, 1966); Christopher Lasch, *The Culture of Narcissism: American Life in an Age of Diminishing Expectations* (New York: W. W. Norton, 1978); Richard Sennett, *The Fall of Public Man* (New York: Knopf, 1977); MacIntyre; and Bellah et al.

30. See Bellah et al., 47. Not only a review of church records but the author's interviews (1988–89) with pastors emphasized this point.

31. Author's interviews with pastors, 1988–89. For the larger context of these developments in the churches, see Robert C. Fuller, *Americans and the Unconscious* (New York: Oxford University Press, 1986), 151–200. For important steps toward a return of discipline in sexual matters, see *MGAPC(USA),* 1991.

32. See Edward LeRoy Long, Jr., "Ministry and Scholarship in the Reformed Tradition," in Daniel B. Clendenin et al., eds., *Scholarship, Sacrament, Service: Historical Studies in Protestant Tradition* (Lewiston, N.Y.: E. Mellen Press, 1990), 1–28, esp. 11–12. H. Richard Niebuhr noted in the 1950s the rise of what he called "the pastor-director" whose primary function was directing the organization of the congregation. See his *The Purpose of the Church and Its Ministry* (New York: Harper and Brothers, 1956), 48. The development of the Doctor of Ministry degree (D.Min.) in U.S. theological education in the early 1970s was both a reaction to and a significant stimulant for the transformation of the minister into a church manager. Providing a professional degree in ministry, D.Min. programs generally had as a major component a strong emphasis on such techniques as "organizational management" or "conflict management." This emphasis was particularly true of McCormick Theological Seminary in Chicago, which offered extension courses in South Carolina in which a number of Charleston Presbytery pastors participated. See *Catalog,* McCormick Theological Seminary, 1973–83, Chicago. The D.Min. degree, Edward Long has written, "typically enhances the leadership qualifications of those who undertake the course of study needed to obtain it, but generally speaking, its consequences are to make them more professional, not more scholarly" (Long, 19). The differences between the term *scholar* and the term *professional,* as applied to professions in general, are discussed in chap. 4 of Jaroslav Pelikan, *Scholarship and Survival: Questions on the Idea of Graduate Education* (Princeton: Carnegie Foundation for the Advancement of Teaching, 1983).

33. For these developments in theological education, see E. Brooks Holifield, *A History of Pastoral Care in America: From Salvation to Self-Realization* (Nashville: Abingdon Press, 1983), 259–348. The great majority of Charleston Presbytery ministers who graduated from seminary after 1945 received at Columbia or Union seminary instruction in pastoral care heavily influenced by the work of Gordon Allport, Abraham Maslow, and especially Carl Rogers. These "humanistic psychologists" thought of themselves as constituting a "third force" in psychology—between behaviorism and psychoanalysis—and emphasized the human potential for growth, fulfillment, self-realization, and creativity. Much of their influence in the seminaries was mediated through the Princeton Theological Seminary professor, Seward Hiltner. See *Catalogs* of Columbia Theological Seminary, Decatur, Ga., and Union Theological Seminary, Richmond, 1960–90, and Columbia's *Professional Assessment Procedure: Columbia Theological Seminary, 1980–1981,* Decatur, Ga.

34. The emphasis on neutrality was encouraged by the "nondirective" and "client-centered" approaches to pastoral care taught in the seminaries.

35. See Bellah et al., 50–51.

36. Courses in Bible, for example, were offered by such internationally known scholars as James L. Mays, Walter Brueggemann, and David Gunn. Mays was longtime editor of the journal *Interpretation;* Brueggemann, who delivered the Beecher Lectures at Yale in 1989, was president in 1990 of the prestigious Society for Biblical Literature; and Gunn was editor of the *Journal for the Study of the Old Testament.*

37. Interviews with pastor James Lowry, Christian educator Jessie Mikell, members of the session and diaconate, 1988–89.

38. Robert Dunham, "The Self and Its Potential: Theological Considerations" (S.T.M. thesis, Yale Divinity School, 1979).

39. *MGAPC(USA),* 1984–89. These evaluations are based on extensive interviews with pastors and lay leaders during 1988–89.

40. *U.S. Census,* "South Carolina Counties."

41. *MGAPCUSA,* 1957, and *MGAUPCUSA,* 1958–80, both in PHSM.

42. Alleen S. Wood, "History of Edisto United Presbyterian Church," 1981, 2 (typescript, CAPO); "The Dedication: The Edisto United Presbyterian Church of the United Presbyterian Church, U.S.A., February 8, 1970," CAPO.

43. List of marriages provided by Janie W. Chisolm of Saint James Presbyterian Church.

44. *MGAPC(USA),* 1988. See Boyd and Brackenridge, 107–38. See also Renita J. Weems, "Reading Her Way through the Struggle: African American Women and the Bible," in Cain Hope Felder, ed., *Stony the Road We Trod: African American Biblical Interpretation* (Minneapolis: Fortress Press, 1991), 57–77.

45. These issues are forcefully addressed by J. Deotis Roberts in *Roots of a Black Future: Family and Church* (Philadelphia: Westminster Press, 1980), esp. 74–79.

46. Zion-Olivet figures compiled by Lois Simms. The congregation's roll, with Simms's notes on "vocation" and "education" and her "Summary Findings," have been placed on file at the PHSM. The denominational percentages of college graduates are taken from the General Social Survey. See Roof and McKinney, 112–13, table 4.2.

47. Simms, "Summary Findings."

48. See Edmund L. Drago, *Initiative, Paternalism, & Race Relations: Charleston's Avery Normal Institute* (Athens: University of Georgia Press, 1990), 246–49. Lois Simms, longtime teacher at Avery, provided information on the relationship between Plymouth and Avery.

49. Interview with Larry B. McCutcheon, African American Methodist minister and college chaplain at South Carolina State College, 1990.

50. Church directory with listing of employment of members prepared by William Holmes, clerk of session, Saint Paul Presbyterian Church, placed on file at the PHSM.

51. For length of service and family connections of pastors, see Atlantic Presbytery, Minutes, 1940–80, PHSM.

52. Ibid.

53. Fraser, 414–16.

54. Interviews with Ferdinand Pharr and McKinley Washington, Charleston, S.C., 1988, 1989. See also Drago, 284.

55. Statistical reports on Atlantic Presbytery, *MGAPCUSA,* 1945–82.

56. Fraser, 394–438.

57. *Brown* v. *Board of Education of Topeka;* Ernest Trice Thompson, *Presbyterians in the South,* 3 vols. (Richmond: John Knox Press, 1963, 1973), 3:539.

58. Johns Island Presbyterian Church, Minutes of the Session, June 6, 1954, PHSM.

59. Westminster Presbyterian Church, Session Minutes, June 23, 1954, PHSM.

60. Ibid.; Thompson, *Presbyterians in the South,* 3:574–75; *MGAPCUS,* 1955, 1982.

61. See Rick Nutt, "The Tie That No Longer Binds: The Origins of the Presbyterian Church in America," in Milton J. Coalter et al., eds., *The Confessional Mosaic: Presbyterian and Twentieth-Century Theology* (Louisville: Westminster/John Knox Press, 1990), 236–56.

62. Interview with Ferdinand Pharr, Charleston, S.C., 1989.

63. The Dorchester congregation, with Richard Cushman as pastor, moved toward a racially pluralistic membership. Naval and air force officers were an important part of this development. Dorchester Presbyterian Church Directory, 1989, Dorchester Presbyterian Church, Summerville, S.C.

Bibliography

Books, Dissertations, and Pamphlets

Abbott, Carl. *The New Urban America: Growth and Politics in Sunbelt Cities.* Chapel Hill: University of North Carolina Press, 1987.

Abbott, Martin. *The Freedmen's Bureau in South Carolina, 1865–1872.* Chapel Hill: University of North Carolina Press, 1967.

Adger, John B. *My Life and Times.* Richmond: Presbyterian Committee of Publication, 1899.

———, ed. *The Collected Writings of James Henley Thornwell.* Vols. 1 and 2. Richmond: Presbyterian Committee of Publication, 1871.

Adger, John B., and John L. Girardeau. *The Collected Writings of James Henley Thornwell.* Vols. 3 and 4. Richmond: Presbyterian Committee of Publication, 1873.

Ahlstrom, Sydney E. *A Religious History of the American People.* New Haven: Yale University Press, 1972.

Alden, Richard. *The South in the Revolution, 1763–1789.* Vol. 3 of *A History of the South.* Edited by Wendell H. Stephenson and E. Merton Coulter. 10 vols. Baton Rouge: Louisiana State University Press, 1957.

Alexander, James W. *The Life of Archibald Alexander.* New York: Charles Scribner, 1854.

Althusser, Louis. *For Marx.* Translated by Ben Brewster. New York: Vintage Books, 1970.

American Church History Series. New York: Christian Literature Co., 1894.

Anderson, James D. *The Education of Blacks in the South, 1860–1935.* Chapel Hill: University of North Carolina Press, 1988.

Andrews, Sidney. *The South Since the War.* 1866. Reprint. New York: Arno Press, 1969.

Archdale, John. *New Description of That Fertile and Pleasant Province of Carolina,* 1707.

Armstrong, Brian. *Calvinism and the Amyraut Heresy: Protestant Scholasticism and Humanism in Seventeenth-Century France.* Madison: University of Wisconsin Press, 1969.

Asbury, Francis. *The Journal and Letters of Francis Asbury.* Edited by Elmer T. Clark. 3 vols. Nashville: Abingdon Press, 1958.

Awolalu, Omosade, and P. Adelumo Dopamu. *West African Traditional Religion.* Ibadan, Nigeria: Onibonoje Press, 1979.

Bailyn, Bernard. *The Ideological Origins of the American Revolution.* Cambridge: Harvard University Press, 1967.

———. *Voyagers to the West: A Passage in the Peopling of America on the Eve of the Revolution.* New York: Vintage Books, 1988.

Barkley, John M. *A Short History of the Presbyterian Church in Ireland.* Belfast: Publications Board, Presbyterian Church in Ireland, 1959.

Barraclough, Geoffrey, ed. *The Times Atlas of World History.* London: Times Books, 1979.

Barry, John M. *Natural Vegetation of South Carolina*. Columbia: University of South Carolina Press, 1980.

Bastide, Roger. *African Civilization in the New World*. New York: Harper and Row, 1971.

Batson, Annie Jenkins. *Rockville Presbyterian Church, Wadmalaw Island, South Carolina*. Charleston: Walker, Evans and Cogswell, 1976.

Battaglia, Anthony. *Toward a Reformulation of Natural Law*. New York: Seabury Press, 1981.

Becker, Carl. *The Heavenly City of the Eighteenth-Century Philosophers*. New Haven: Yale University Press, 1932.

Beecher, Henry Ward. *Sermons*. New York: Harper and Brothers, 1868.

Bell, Daniel. *The Cultural Contradictions of Capitalism*. New York: Basic Books, 1976.

Bellah, Robert, et al. *Habits of the Heart: Individualism and Commitment in American Life*. Berkeley and Los Angeles: University of California Press, 1985.

Belo, Fernando. *A Materialist Reading of the Gospel of Mark*. Maryknoll, N.Y.: Orbis Books, 1981.

Bendix, Reinhard. *Max Weber: An Intellectual Portrait*. London: Methuen, 1959.

Berger, Peter L., and Thomas Luckmann. *The Social Construction of Reality*. Garden City, N.Y.: Doubleday, 1966.

Beringer, Richard E., et al. *Why the South Lost the Civil War*. Athens: University of Georgia Press, 1986.

Berlin, Ira. *Slaves Without Masters: The Free Negro in the Antebellum South*. New York: Random House, Pantheon Books, 1974.

Berlin, Ira, and Ronald Hoffman, eds. *Slavery and Freedom in the Age of the American Revolution*. Charlottesville: University of Virginia Press, 1983.

Bernard, Richard M., and Bradley R. Rice, eds. *Sunbelt Cities: Politics and Growth Since World War II*. Austin: University of Texas Press, 1983.

Bernheim, G. D. *History of the German Settlements and of the Lutheran Church in North and South Carolina*. Philadelphia: Lutheran Bookstore, 1872.

Bertram, Michael. *The Changing Profile of the Natural Law*. The Hague: Nijhoff, 1977.

Biéler, André. *The Social Humanism of Calvin*. Richmond: John Knox Press, 1964.

Birney, Catherine H. *The Grimké Sisters: Sarah and Angelina Grimké*. Westport, Conn.: Greenwood Press, 1964.

Blackburn, George A., ed. *The Life Work of John L. Girardeau, D. D., LL.D., Late Professor in the Presbyterian Theological Seminary, Columbia, S.C.* Columbia: State Co., 1916.

Blassingame, John. *The Slave Community: Plantation Life in the Antebellum South*. Rev. ed. New York: Oxford University Press, 1979.

Bliss, Seth. *Letters to the Members, Patrons and Friends of the Branch American Tract Society in Boston; And to those of the National Society in New York. By the Secretary of the Boston Society*. Boston: Crocker and Brewster, 1858.

Bloch, Maurice. *Marxism and Anthropology*. Oxford: Oxford University Press, 1983.

Boles, John. *Black Southerners: 1619–1869*. Lexington: University Press of Kentucky, 1983.

———. *The Great Revival, 1787–1805: The Origins of the Southern Evangelical Mind*. Lexington: University Press of Kentucky, 1972.

———, ed. *Masters and Slaves in the House of the Lord: Race and Religion in the American South, 1740–1870*. Lexington: University Press of Kentucky, 1988.

Bolton, S. Charles. *Southern Anglicanism: The Church of England in Colonial South Carolina.* Westport, Conn.: Greenwood Press, 1982.

Bonomi, Patricia U. *Under the Cope of Heaven: Religion, Society and Politics in Colonial America.* New York: Oxford University Press, 1986.

Bost, Raymond Morris. *The Reverend John Bachman and the Development of Southern Lutheranism.* Ph.D. diss., Yale University, 1963. Ann Arbor, Mich.: University Microfilms, 1963.

Bouwsma, William J. *John Calvin: A Sixteenth Century Portrait.* New York: Oxford University Press, 1988.

Bowden, David K. *The Execution of Isaac Hayne.* Lexington, S.C.: Sandlapper Press, 1977.

Boyd, Lois A., and R. Douglas Brackenridge. *Presbyterian Women in America: Two Centuries of a Quest for Status.* Westport, Conn.: Greenwood Press, 1983.

Bozeman, Theodore Dwight. *Protestants in an Age of Science: The Baconian Ideal and Antebellum Religious Thought.* Chapel Hill: University of North Carolina Press, 1977.

Breen, Quirinus. *John Calvin: A Study in French Humanism.* Chicago: University of Chicago Press, 1931.

Bridenbaugh, Carl. *Mitre and Scepter: Transatlantic Faiths, Ideas, Personalities, and Politics, 1689–1775.* New York: Oxford University Press, 1962.

———. *Myths and Realities: Societies of the Colonial South.* Baton Rouge: Louisiana State University Press, 1952.

Bromiley, G. W., ed. *Zwingli and Bullenger.* Vol. 24 of *Library of Christian Classics.* Philadelphia: Westminster Press, 1953.

Brueggemann, Walter. *Interpretation and Obedience: From Faithful Reading to Faithful Living.* Minneapolis: Fortress Press, 1991.

Brunhouse, Robert L., ed. *David Ramsay, 1749–1815: Selections From His Writings.* Philadelphia: American Philosophical Society, 1965.

Bullock, Henry Allen. *A History of Negro Education in the South from 1619 to the Present.* Cambridge: Harvard University Press, 1967.

Bureau of the Census. *Historical Statistics of the United States: Colonial Times to 1970.* 2 vols. Washington, D.C.: U.S. Government Printing Office, 1975. 2:1155, 1174.

———. *Statistical View of the United States . . . A Compendium of the Seventh Census.* Washington, D.C.: A. O. P. Nicholson, 1854.

———. *Twelfth Census of the United States, 1900: Population, Part I.* Washington, D.C.: U.S. Government Printing Office, 1903.

———. *U.S. Census of Population, 1980.* "South Carolina Counties." Vol. 1, sec. A, table 2.

Burleigh, J. H. S. *A Church History of Scotland.* London: Oxford University Press, 1960.

Burton, E. Milby. *The Siege of Charleston 1861–1865.* Columbia: University of South Carolina Press, 1970.

Burton, Orville V., and Robert C. McMath, Jr., eds. *Class, Conflict, and Consensus: Antebellum Southern Community Studies.* Westport, Conn.: Greenwood Press, 1982.

———. *Toward a New South? Studies in Post–Civil War Southern Communities.* Westport, Conn.: Greenwood Press, 1982.

Butler, Jon. *Awash in a Sea of Faith: Christianizing the American People.* Cambridge: Harvard University Press, 1990.

———. *The Huguenots in America: A Refugee People in New World Society.* Cambridge: Harvard University Press, 1983.

Caldwell, S. C., et al. *The Presbyterian Church of Edisto Island.* 1933. Reprint. 1963.

Calhoon, Robert M. *Evangelicals and Conservatives in the Early South, 1740–1861.* Columbia: University of South Carolina Press, 1988.

Calhoun, John C. *Works of John C. Calhoun.* Edited by Richard K. Cralle. 4 vols. New York: D. Appleton, 1854.

Calvin, John. *Institutes of the Christian Religion.* Edited by John T. McNeill. Vols. XX and XXI of *Library of Christian Classics.* Philadelphia: Westminster Press, 1960.

Cameron, James K., ed. *First Book of Discipline: With Introduction and Commentary.* Edinburgh: Saint Andrew's Press, 1972.

Cappon, Lester J., et al. *Atlas of Early American History: The Revolutionary Era, 1760–1790.* Princeton: Princeton University Press, 1976.

Carlton, David L. *Mill and Town in South Carolina 1890–1920.* Baton Rouge: Louisiana State University Press, 1982.

Carwardine, Richard. *Trans-Atlantic Revivalism: Popular Evangelicalism in Britain and America, 1790–1865.* Westport, Conn.: Greenwood Press, 1978.

Cassirer, Ernst. *The Philosophy of the Enlightenment.* Princeton: Princeton University Press, 1951.

Cauthen, Henry F., Jr. *Charleston Interiors.* Charleston: Preservation Society of Charleston, 1979.

Chandler, Alfred D. *The Visible Hand: The Managerial Revolution in American Business.* Cambridge: Harvard University Press, 1977.

Channing, Steven A. *Crisis of Fear: Secession in South Carolina.* New York: W. W. Norton, 1974.

Clark, Kenneth. *Civilization: A Personal View.* New York: Harper and Row, 1969.

Clarke, Erskine. *Wrestlin' Jacob: A Portrait of Religion in the Old South.* Atlanta: John Knox Press, 1979.

Clendenin, Daniel B., et al., eds. *Scholarship, Sacrament, Service: Historical Studies in Protestant Tradition.* Lewiston, N.Y.: E. Mellen Press, 1990.

Clowse, Converse D. *Economic Beginnings in Colonial South Carolina, 1670–1730.* Columbia: University of South Carolina Press, 1971.

Coalter, Milton J., et al., eds. *The Confessional Mosaic: Presbyterian and Twentieth-Century Theology.* Louisville: Westminster/John Knox Press, 1990.

Coclanis, Peter A. *The Shadow of a Dream: Economic Life and Death in the South Carolina Low Country, 1670–1920.* New York: Oxford University Press, 1989.

A Collection of Hymns for Public and Private Worship, Approved of by the Presbytery of Charleston. Charleston: J. MacIver, 1796.

A Colored American. *The Late Contemplated Insurrection in Charleston, S.C. . . .* New York: Printed for the Author, 1850.

Commanger, Henry Steele. *Theodore Parker.* Boston: Little, Brown, 1936.

Cone, James H. *My Soul Looks Back.* Maryknoll, N.Y.: Orbis Books, 1986.

The Confession of Faith, the Larger Catechism, the Directory for Public Worship, the Form of Presbyterial Church Government. Edinburgh: William Blackwood and Sons, 1959.

Cooper, William J. *The Conservative Regime: South Carolina, 1877–1890.* Baltimore: Johns Hopkins University Press, 1968.

———. *Liberty and Slavery.* New York: Knopf, 1983.

Copleston, Frederick. *A History of Philosophy.* 10 vols. Garden City, N.Y.: Image Books, 1965.

Correspondence Between the Rev. Messr. Dana and Smyth, through the Hon. R. B. Gilchrist and the Rev. Dr. Bachman. Charleston: W. Haynes, 1847.

Coulter, E. Merton. *George Walton Williams: The Life of a Southern Merchant and Banker, 1820–1903.* Athens, Ga.: Hibriten Press, 1976.

Craig, Gordon A. *The Germans.* New York: Meridian, 1983.

Crane, Verner W. *The Southern Frontier, 1670–1732.* Ann Arbor: University of Michigan Press, 1929.

Creel, Margaret W. *"A Peculiar People": Slave Religion and Community-Culture among the Gullahs.* New York: New York University Press, 1988.

Crosby, Alfred W. *The Columbia Exchange: Biological and Cultural Consequences of 1492.* New York: Cambridge University Press, 1986.

Cross, Whitney R. *The Burned-Over District: The Social and Intellectual History of Enthusiastic Religion in Western New York, 1800–1850.* Ithaca: Cornell University Press, 1950.

Crow, Jeffrey J., and Larry E. Tise, eds. *The Southern Experience in the American Revolution.* Chapel Hill: University of North Carolina Press, 1978.

Curtin, Philip D. *The Atlantic Slave Trade: A Census.* Madison: University of Wisconsin Press, 1969.

Dalcho, Frederick. *An Historical Account of the Protestant Episcopal Church in South Carolina.* Charleston: E. Thayer, 1820.

Dana, W. C. *"Fast Day Sermon": A Sermon Delivered in the Central Presbyterian Church, Charleston, South Carolina, November 21, 1860.* Charleston: Miller, 1860.

————. *Statement of the Difficulties in the General Assembly of the Presbyterian Church, in their Bearing on the Southern Churches: with an Appendix Relating to the Charleston Union Presbytery.* Charleston: B. B. Hussey, 1839.

David, Paul A., et al. *Reckoning with Slavery: A Critical Study in the Quantitative History of American Negro Slavery.* New York: Oxford University Press, 1976.

Davis, David Brion. *Slavery and Human Progress.* New York: Oxford University Press, 1984.

Davis, James A. *General Social Surveys, 1972–1984.* Chicago: National Opinion Research Center, 1984.

Davis, Richard Beale. *Intellectual Life in the Colonial South, 1585–1763.* Knoxville: University of Tennessee Press, 1978.

DeBow, J. D. B. *Statistical View of the United States.* Washington, D.C.: A. O. P. Nicholson, 1854.

Devlin, George A. "South Carolina and Black Migration 1865–1940: In Search of the Promised Land." Ph.D. diss. University of South Carolina, 1984.

Dobyns, Henry F. *Their Number Become Thinned: Native American Population Dynamics in Eastern North America.* Knoxville: University of Tennessee Press, 1983.

Douglas, Ann. *The Feminization of American Culture.* New York: Alfred A. Knopf, 1977.

Douglass, Frederick. *Life and Times of Frederick Douglass.* New York: Collier, 1962.

Douglass, Paul H. *Christian Reconstruction in the South.* Boston: Pilgrim Press, 1909.

Doyle, Don Harrison. *New Men, New Cities, New South: Atlanta, Nashville, Charleston, Mobile, 1860–1910.* Chapel Hill: University of North Carolina Press, 1990.

Drago, Edmund L. *Initiative, Paternalism, & Race Relations: Charleston's Avery Normal Institute.* Athens: University of Georgia Press, 1990.

Du Bois, W. E. B. *The Soul of Black Folk.* 1903. Reprint. Greenwich, Conn.: Fawcett, 1961.

Dunham, Chester F. *The Attitude of the Northern Clergy Toward the South, 1860–1865.* Philadelphia: Porcupine Press, 1974.

Dunham, Robert. "The Self and Its Potential: Theological Considerations." S.T.M. thesis, Yale Divinity School, 1979.

Durkheim, Emile. *The Elementary Forms of the Religious Life.* 1915. Reprint. London: Allen and Unwin, 1964.

Eaton, Clement. *The Mind of the Old South.* Rev. ed. Baton Rouge: Louisiana State University Press, 1967.

Edwards, George N. *A History of the Independent or Congregational Church of Charleston South Carolina.* Boston: Pilgrim Press, 1947.

Edwards, Jonathan. *The Works of President Edwards.* Edited by Sereno E. Dwight. 10 vols. New York: S. Converse, 1829–30.

Eisenstadt, Samuel N. *The Protestant Ethic and Modernization: A Comparative View.* New York: Basic Books, 1968.

Elkins, Stanley M. *Slavery: A Problem in American Institutional and Intellectual Life.* Chicago: University of Chicago Press, 1959.

Epstein, Barbara Leslie. *The Politics of Domesticity: Women, Evangelism, and Temperance in Nineteenth-Century America.* Middletown, Conn.: Wesleyan University Press, 1981.

Erikson, Eric. *Identity: Youth and Crisis.* New York: W. W. Norton, 1968.

Evangelical Alliance. *Report of the Proceedings of the Conference, Held at Freemason's Hall, London, August 19th to September 2nd Inclusive.* London: Partridge and Oakey, 1847.

Farmer, James O. *The Metaphysical Confederacy: James Henley Thornwell and the Synthesis of Southern Values.* Macon: Mercer University Press, 1986.

Faust, Drew Gilpin. *The Creation of Confederate Nationalism: Ideology and Identity in the Civil War South.* Baton Rouge: Louisiana State University Press, 1988.

———. *A Sacred Circle: The Dilemma of the Intellectual in the Old South, 1840–1860.* Baltimore: Johns Hopkins University Press, 1977.

———, ed. *The Ideology of Slavery: Proslavery Thought in the Antebellum South, 1830–1860.* Baton Rouge: Louisiana State University Press, 1981.

Felder, Cain Hope, ed. *Stony the Road We Trod: African American Biblical Interpretation.* Minneapolis: Fortress Press, 1991.

Feuerbach, Ludwig. *The Essence of Christianity.* Translated by George Eliot. 1841. Reprint. New York: Harper, 1957.

Finney, Charles G. *Lectures on Revivals of Religion.* Edited by W. G. McLaughlin. Cambridge: Harvard University Press, 1960.

Finnis, J. M. *Natural Law and Natural Rights.* Oxford: Clarendon Press, 1980.

Fogel, Robert W., and Stanley L. Engerman. *Time on the Cross: The Economics of American Negro Slavery.* Boston: Little, Brown, 1974.

Foner, Eric. *Reconstruction: America's Unfinished Revolution 1863–1877.* New York: Harper and Row, 1988.

Foner, Philip. *Business and Slavery: The New York Merchants and the Irrepressible Conflict.* Chapel Hill: University of North Carolina Press, 1941.

———. *The Life and Writings of Frederick Douglass.* 5 vols. New York: International Publishers, 1950.

Fraser, Walter J., Jr. *Charleston! Charleston! The History of a Southern City.* Columbia: University of South Carolina Press, 1989.

Fraser, Walter J., Jr., and Winfred B. Moore, Jr., eds. *From the Old South to the New: Essays on the Transitional South.* Westport, Conn.: Greenwood Press, 1981.

Frazer, Antonia. *Cromwell: Our Chief of Men.* London: Weidenfeld and Nicolson, 1973.

Frazier, E. Franklin. *The Negro Family in the United States.* Chicago: University of Chicago Press, 1968.

———. *The Negro in the United States.* Chicago: University of Chicago Press, 1940.

Freire, Paulo. *Pedagogy of the Oppressed.* Translated by Myrna Bergman Ramos. New York: Herder and Herder, 1970.

Fuller, Robert C. *Americans and the Unconscious.* New York: Oxford University Press, 1986.

Gabriel, Ralph. *The Course of American Democratic Thought.* New York: Ronald Press, 1940.

Gadamer, Hans-Georg. *Truth and Method.* New York: Crossroads, 1984.

Gallay, Alan. *The Formation of a Planter Elite: Jonathan Bryan and the Southern Colonial Frontier.* Athens: University of Georgia Press, 1989.

Garrison, W. P., and F. J. Garrison. *William Lloyd Garrison, 1805–1879: The Story of His Life as Told by His Children.* 4 vols. New York: Century, 1885–89.

Gaustad, Edwin S. *The Great Awakening in New England.* New York: Harper and Row, 1957.

Geertz, Clifford. *The Interpretation of Cultures: Selected Essays.* New York: Basic Books, 1973.

Genovese, Eugene D. *The Political Economy of Slavery: Studies in the Economy and Society of the Slave South.* New York: Pantheon Books, 1965.

———. *Roll, Jordan, Roll: The World the Slaves Made.* New York: Pantheon Books, 1974.

———. *The World the Slaveholders Made.* New York: Pantheon Books, 1969.

George, Timothy, ed. *John Calvin & the Church.* Louisville: Westminster/John Knox Press, 1990.

Gillette, William. *Retreat from Reconstruction 1869–1879.* Baton Rouge: Louisiana State University Press, 1979.

Girardeau, John L. *Confederate Memorial Day at Charleston, S.C.: Re-interment of the Carolina Dead from Gettysburg.* Charleston: William G. Mazyck, 1871.

———. *Instrumental Music in the Public Worship of the Church.* Richmond: Whittet and Shepperson, 1888.

Gist, Margaret A., ed. *Presbyterian Women of South Carolina.* Woman's Auxiliary of the Synod of South Carolina, 1929.

Glen, James. *Description of South Carolina,* 1761.

Glock, C. Y., and P. E. Hammond, eds. *Beyond the Classics? Essays in the Scientific Study of Religion.* New York: Harper and Row, 1973.

Goen, C. C. *Broken Churches, Broken Nation: Denominational Schisms and the Coming of the American Civil War.* Macon: Mercer University Press, 1985.

———. *Revivalism and Separatism in New England.* New Haven: Yale University Press, 1962.

Green, Robert W., ed. *Protestantism and Capitalism: The Weber Thesis and Critics.* Boston: D. C. Heath, 1959.

Greenberg, Kenneth S. *Masters and Statesmen: The Political Culture of American Slavery.* Baltimore: Johns Hopkins University Press, 1985.

Griffin, Clifford S. *Their Brothers' Keepers: Moral Stewardship in the United States, 1800–1965.* New Brunswick: Rutgers University Press, 1960.

Grimké, Thomas. *Address at the celebration of the Sunday School Jubilee, or, the fiftieth year from the institution, in the hall of the Sunday School Depository, on Wednesday evening, 14th of September, 1831.* Philadelphia: American Sunday School Union, 1832.

Gutman, Herbert G. *The Black Family in Slavery and Freedom, 1750–1925.* New York: Pantheon Books, 1976.

———. *Slavery and the Numbers Game: A Critique of "Time on the Cross."* Urbana: University of Illinois Press, 1975.

Habermas, Jürgen. *Knowledge and Human Interest.* Translated by Jeremy J. Shapiro. Boston: Beacon Press, 1972.

Hamilton, John A. *History of the Orangeburg Presbyterian Church, Orangeburg, South Carolina.* Orangeburg: R. Lewis Berry, 1896.

Handbook of South Carolina: Resources, Institutions and Industries of the State. Columbia: State Co., 1907.

Hanna, William. *Memoirs of the Life and Writings of Thomas Chalmers.* New York: Harpers, 1852.

Hanson, Paul. *The Dawn of Apocalyptic.* Philadelphia: Fortress Press, 1975.

Hardman, Keith J. *Charles Grandison Finney, 1792–1875: Revivalist and Reformer.* Syracuse: Syracuse University Press, 1987.

Hatch, Nathan O. *The Democratization of American Christianity.* New Haven: Yale University Press, 1989.

Heimert, Alan E. *Religion and the American Mind from the Great Awakening to the Revolution.* Cambridge: Harvard University Press, 1966.

Heimert, Alan E., and Perry Miller. *The Great Awakening: Documents Illustrating the Crisis and Its Consequences.* Indianapolis: Bobbs-Merrill, 1967.

Hennesey, James. *American Catholics: A History of the Roman Catholic Community in the United States.* New York: Oxford University Press, 1981.

Henry, Stuart C. *George Whitefield: Wayfaring Witness.* New York: Abingdon Press, 1957.

Herskovits, Melville J. *The Myth of the Negro Past.* Gloucester, Mass.: P. Smith, 1924.

Hewat, Alexander. *An Historical Account of the Rise and Progress of the Colonies of South Carolina and Georgia.* 2 vols. in 1. London, 1779. Reprinted in R. B. Carroll, comp. *Historical Collections of South Carolina.* 2 vols. New York: Harper and Brothers, 1836.

Hill, Christopher. *God's Englishman: Oliver Cromwell and the English Revolution.* New York: Dial Press, 1970.

Hill, Sam S., Jr. *The South and the North in American Religion.* Athens: University of Georgia Press, 1980.

Hirsch, Arthur Henry. *The Huguenots of Colonial South Carolina.* London: Archon Books, 1962.

History of Bethel Church (Walterboro) 1728–1928. Walterboro, S.C.: Press and Standard, 1928.

Hodge, Charles. *Systematic Theology.* 3 vols. New York: Charles Scribner's Sons, 1893.

Holifield, E. Brooks. *The Gentlemen Theologians: American Theology in Southern Culture, 1795–1860.* Durham: Duke University Press, 1978.

———. *A History of Pastoral Care in America: From Salvation to Self-Realization.* Nashville: Abingdon Press, 1983.

Hollis, Daniel W. *The University of South Carolina.* 2 vols. Columbia: University of South Carolina Press, 1951.

Holt, Thomas. *Black over White: Negro Political Leadership in South Carolina during Reconstruction.* Urbana: University of Illinois Press, 1977.

Honigmann, John J. *Handbook of Social and Cultural Anthropology.* Chicago: Rand McNally, 1973.

Hooykaas, Reijer. *Religion and the Rise of Modern Science.* Edinburgh: Scottish Academic Press, 1972.

Hovenkamp, Herbert. *Science and Religion in America, 1800–1860.* Philadelphia: University of Pennsylvania Press, 1978.

Howe, Daniel Walker, ed. *Victorian America.* Philadelphia: University of Pennsylvania Press, 1976.

Howe, George. *History of the Presbyterian Church in South Carolina.* Vol. 1. Columbia: Duffie and Chapman, 1870. Vol. 2. Columbia: W. J. Duffie, 1883.

Hutchison, William R. *The Modernist Impulse in American Protestantism.* 1976. Reprint. Oxford: Oxford University Press, 1982.

Isaac, Rhys. *The Transformation of Virginia, 1740–1790.* Chapel Hill: University of North Carolina Press, 1982.

Jackson-Jones, Patricia. *When Roots Die: Endangered Traditions on the Sea Islands.* Athens: University of Georgia Press, 1987.

Jacobs, William Plummer. *The Pioneer.* Clinton, S.C.: Jacobs Press, 1935.

Jacoway, Elizabeth. *Yankee Missionaries in the South: The Penn School Experiment.* Baton Rouge: Louisiana State University Press, 1980.

Jaher, Frederic C. *The Urban Establishment: Upper Strata in Boston, New York, Charleston, Chicago, and Los Angeles.* Urbana: University of Illinois Press, 1982.

Jervey, Theodore D. *Robert Y. Hayne and His Times.* New York: Macmillan, 1909.

Johnson, Michael P., and James L. Roark. *No Chariot Let Down: Charleston's Free People of Color on the Eve of the Civil War.* Chapel Hill: University of North Carolina Press, 1984.

Johnson, Thomas Cary. *The Life and Letters of Benjamin Morgan Palmer.* Richmond: Presbyterian Committee of Publication, 1906.

Jones, Alice Hanson. *Wealth of a Nation To Be: The American Colonies on the Eve of the Revolution.* New York: Columbia University Press, 1980.

Jones, Charles C. *Annual Report of the Missionary to the Negroes, in Liberty County, (Ga.) Presented to the Association, November 1833.* Charleston: Observer Office Press, 1934.

———. *A Catechism of Scripture, Doctrine and Practice: for Families and Sabbath Schools, Designed also for the Oral Instruction of Colored Persons.* 3d ed. Savannah: T. Purse, and New York: Leavitt, Trow, 1845.

Jones, F. D., and W. H. Mills. *History of the Presbyterian Church in South Carolina Since 1850.* Columbia: R. L. Bryan, 1926.

Jones, Jacqueline. *Soldiers of Light and Love: Northern Teachers and Georgia Blacks.* Chapel Hill: University of North Carolina Press, 1980.

Joyner, Charles. *Down by the Riverside: A South Carolina Slave Community.* Urban: University of Illinois Press, 1984.

Kain, John F., and John R. Meyer, eds. *Essays in Regional Economics.* Cambridge: Harvard University Press, 1971.

Kaplan, Bert. *Studying Personality Cross-Culturally.* Evanston: Row, Peterson, 1961.

Kaplan, Sidney. *The Black Presence in the Era of the American Revolution.* 1973. Reprint. Amherst: University of Massachusetts Press, 1988.

Kardiner, Abraham. *The Psychological Frontiers of Society.* New York: Columbia University Press, 1945.

Kendal, R. T. *Calvin and English Calvinism to 1649.* Oxford: Oxford University Press, 1980.

Kennedy, Lionel H., and Thomas Parker. *An Official Report of the Trials of Sundry Negroes, Charged with an Attempt to Raise an Insurrection in the State of South Carolina.* Charleston: James R. Schenck, 1822.

Kingdon, Robert M. *Geneva and the Consolidation of the French Protestant Movement, 1564–1572.* Madison: University of Wisconsin Press, 1967.

Klingberg, Frank J. *An Appraisal of the Negro in Colonial South Carolina: A Study in Americanization.* Philadelphia: Porcupine Press, 1975.

Koger, Larry. *Black Slaveowners: Free Black Slave Masters in South Carolina, 1790–1860.* Jefferson, N.C.: McFarland, 1985.

Kousser, J. Morgan, and James M. McPherson, eds. *Region, Race, and Reconstruction: Essays in Honor of C. Vann Woodward.* New York: Oxford University Press, 1982.

Kuykendall, John W. *Southern Enterprise: The Work of National Evangelical Societies in the Antebellum South.* Westport, Conn.: Greenwood Press, 1982.

Lambert, Robert Stansbury. *South Carolina Loyalists in the American Revolution.* Columbia: University of South Carolina Press, 1987.

LaMotte, Louis C. *Colored Light: The Story of the Influence of Columbia Theological Seminary, 1828–1936.* Richmond: Presbyterian Committee of Publication, 1937.

Lasch, Christopher. *The Culture of Narcissism: American Life in an Age of Diminishing Expectations.* New York: W. W. Norton, 1978.

Leach, Edmund. *Culture and Communication: The Logic by Which Symbols Are Connected.* Cambridge: Cambridge University Press, 1976.

Leder, Lawrence H., ed. *The Colonial Legacy.* 3 vols. New York: Harper and Row, 1971.

Leiman, Melvin M. *Jacob N. Carodozo: Economic Thought in the Antebellum South.* New York: Columbia University Press, 1966.

Leith, John. *Introduction to the Reformed Tradition: A Way of Being the Christian Community.* Atlanta: John Knox Press, 1977.

———. *John Calvin's Doctrine of the Christian Life.* Louisville: Westminster/John Knox Press, 1989.

Leonard, Emile. *A History of Protestantism.* London: Nelson, 1967.

Lerner, Gerda. *The Grimké Sisters from South Carolina: Rebels against Slavery.* Boston: Houghton Mifflin, 1967.

Leyburn, James G. *The Scotch-Irish: A Social History.* Chapel Hill: University of North Carolina Press, 1962.

Lilly, Edward G. *Beyond the Burning Bush: First (Scots) Presbyterian Church, Charleston, S.C.* Charleston: Garnier, 1971.

———. *Historic Churches of Charleston.* Charleston: John Huguley, 1966.

Lincoln, C. Eric, and Lawrence H. Mamiya. *The Black Church in the African American Experience.* Durham: Duke University Press, 1990.

Linton, Ralph. *The Cultural Background of Personality.* New York: Appleton-Century-Croft, 1945.

Liscombe, Rhodri W. *The Church Architecture of Robert Mills*. Easley, S.C.: South Historical Press, 1985.

Littlefield, Daniel C. *Rice and Slaves: Ethnicity and the Slave Trade in Colonial South Carolina*. Baton Rouge: Louisiana State University Press, 1981.

Litwack, Leon F. *Been in the Storm So Long: The Aftermath of Slavery*. New York: Alfred A. Knopf, 1979.

Loetscher, Lefferts A. *The Broadening Church: A Study of Theological Issues in the Presbyterian Church Since 1869*. Philadelphia: University of Pennsylvania Press, 1954.

Lofton, John. *Insurrection in South Carolina: The Turbulent World of Denmark Vesey*. Yellow Springs, Ohio: Antioch Press, 1964.

Loveland, Anne C. *Southern Evangelicals and the Social Order, 1800–1860*. Baton Rouge: Louisiana State University Press, 1980.

Lumpkin, Katherine Du Pre. *The Emancipation of Angelina Grimké*. Chapel Hill: University of North Carolina Press, 1974.

Luzbetak, Louis J. *The Church and Cultures: New Perspectives in Missiological Anthropology*. Maryknoll, N.Y.: Orbis Books, 1988.

Maccoby, Michael. *The Gamesman*. New York: Simon and Schuster, 1976.

McCrady, Edward. *The History of South Carolina in the Revolution, 1775–1780*. New York: Macmillan, 1901.

———. *The History of South Carolina in the Revolution, 1780–1783*. New York: Macmillan, 1902.

———. *The History of South Carolina under the Royal Government, 1719–1776*. New York: Macmillan, 1899.

MacIntyre, Alasdair. *After Virtue: A Study in Moral Theory*. Notre Dame: University of Notre Dame Press, 1981.

MacLeod, Duncan J. *Slavery, Race and the American Revolution*. London: Cambridge University Press, 1974.

McLoughlin, William O. *Revivals, Awakenings, and Reform: An Essay on Religion and Social Change in America*. Chicago: University of Chicago Press, 1978.

McNeill, John T. *The History and Character of Calvinism*. 1954. Reprint. London: Oxford University Press, 1967.

McPherson, James M. *Abraham Lincoln and the Second American Revolution*. New York: Oxford University Press, 1990.

———. *The Battle Cry of Freedom: The Civil War Era*. New York: Oxford University Press, 1988.

McWhiney, Grady. *Southerners and Other Americans*. New York: Basic Books, 1973.

Malinowski, Bronislaw. *Magic, Science and Religion, and Other Essays*. 1925. Reprint. London: Souvenir Press, 1974.

Mannheim, Karl. *Ideology and Utopia*. Translated by Louis Wirth and Edward Shils. New York: Harcourt, Brace, and World, 1936.

Manual for the Use of the Members of the Second Presbyterian Church, Charleston, S.C. Charleston: Walker, Evans and Cogswell, 1894.

Marsden, George M. *The Evangelical Mind and the New School Presbyterian Experience*. New Haven: Yale University Press, 1970.

———. *Fundamentalism and American Culture*. New York: Oxford University Press, 1980.

Marshall, Gordon. *In Search for the Spirit of Capitalism*. London: Hutchinson, 1982.

————. *Presbyteries and Profits: Calvinism and the Development of Capitalism in Scotland.* Oxford: Oxford University Press, 1980.

Marx, Karl. *Critique of Hegel's "Philosophy of Right."* Edited by Joseph O'Malley. Cambridge: Cambridge University Press, 1970.

Marx, Karl, and Friedrich Engels. *Basic Writing on Politics and Philosophy.* Edited by Lewis S. Feuer. Garden City, N.Y.: Doubleday, 1959.

————. *On Religion.* Moscow: Progress, 1957.

Mathews, Donald G. *Religion in the Old South.* Chicago: University of Chicago Press, 1977.

May, Henry F. *The Enlightenment in America.* New York: Oxford University Press, 1976.

Mbiti, John S. *African Religions and Philosophy.* Garden City, N.Y.: Anchor Books, 1970.

Memorial Volume of the Semi-Centennial of the Theological Seminary at Columbia, South Carolina. Columbia: Presbyterian Publishing House, 1884.

Meriwether, Colyer. *History of Higher Education in South Carolina.* Reprint. Spartanburg, S.C.: Reprint Co., 1972.

Meriwether, James B., ed. *South Carolina Women Writers.* Spartanburg, S.C.: Reprint Co., 1979.

Merton, Robert K. *Social Theology and Social Structure.* Glencoe, Ill.: Free Press, 1957.

Meyer, Donald H. *The Instructed Conscience.* Philadelphia: University of Pennsylvania Press, 1972.

Mill, John Stuart. *On Liberty.* 1865. Reprint. Edited by David Spitz. New York: W. W. Norton, 1975.

Miller, Perry. *The Life of the Mind in America from the Revolution to the Civil War.* New York: Harcourt, Brace and World, 1965.

————. *The New England Mind: The Seventeenth Century.* New York: Macmillan, 1939.

Miller, Perry, and Thomas H. Johnson, eds. *The Puritans: A Source Book of Their Writings.* Rev. ed. 2 vols. New York: Harper Torchbooks, 1963.

Miller, Randall M., ed. *The Afro-American Slaves: Community or Chaos.* Malabar, Fla.: R. E. Krieger, 1981.

Miller, Randall M., and Thomas D. Marzik, eds. *Immigrants and Religion in Urban America.* Philadelphia: Temple University Press, 1977.

Miller, Randall M., and George E. Pozzetta, eds. *Shades of the Sunbelt: Essays on Ethnicity, Race, and the Urban South.* New York: Greenwood Press, 1988.

Miller, Samuel. *Letters on Clerical Manners and Habits.* New York: G. and C. Carvill, 1827.

Mitchell, Henry H. *Black Preaching.* Philadelphia: Westminster Press, 1970.

Monter, William. *Calvin's Geneva.* New York: Wiley, 1967.

Mood, F. A. *Methodism in Charleston: A Narrative.* Nashville: E. Stevenson and J. E. Evans, 1856.

Moore, Barrington, Jr. *Social Origins of Dictatorship and Democracy: Lord and Peasant in the Making of the Modern World.* Boston: Beacon Press, 1966.

Moorhead, James H. *American Apocalypse: Yankee Protestants and the Civil War, 1860–1869.* New Haven: Yale University Press, 1978.

Morgan, Edmund S. *American Slavery, American Freedom.* New York: W. W. Norton, 1975.

Morris, Brian. *Anthropological Studies of Religion: An Introductory Text.* Cambridge: Cambridge University Press, 1987.

Morris, Robert C. *Reading, 'Riting, and Reconstruction: The Education of Freedmen in the South, 1861–1870.* Chicago: University of Chicago Press, 1981.

Mullett, Michael. *Radical Religious Movements in Early Modern Europe.* London: Allen and Unwin, 1980.

Murray, Andrew E. *Presbyterians and the Negro—A History.* Philadelphia: Presbyterian Historical Society, 1966.

Myers, Robert Manson, ed. *The Children of Pride: A True Story of Georgia and the Civil War.* New Haven: Yale University Press, 1972.

Nevins, Allan. *The Emergence of Lincoln.* 2 vols. New York: Scribner, 1950.

———. *Ordeal of Union.* 2 vols. New York: Scribner, 1947.

Newby, I. A. *Black Carolinians: A History of Blacks in South Carolina from 1895 to 1968.* Columbia: University of South Carolina Press, 1973.

Nichols, James Hastings. *Corporate Worship in the Reformed Tradition.* Philadelphia: Westminster Press, 1968.

Niebuhr, H. Richard. *The Purpose of the Church and Its Ministry.* New York: Harper and Brothers, 1956.

Oakes, James. *The Ruling Race: A History of American Slaveholders.* New York: Knopf, 1982.

O'Brien, Michael. *A Character of Hugh Legaré.* Knoxville: University of Tennessee Press, 1985.

O'Brien, Michael, and David Moltke-Hansen, eds. *Intellectual Life in Antebellum Charleston.* Knoxville: University of Tennessee Press, 1986.

Olson, Jeannine E. *Calvin and Social Welfare: Deacons and the Bourse Française.* Selinsgrove, Pa.: Susquehanna University Press, 1989.

Owens, Harry P., and Carl N. Degler, eds. *Perspectives and Irony in American Slavery.* Jackson: University Press of Mississippi, 1976.

Palmer, Benjamin Morgan [the younger]. *National Responsibilities before God. . . .* New Orleans, 1861.

———. *The Life and Letters of James Henley Thornwell.* Richmond: Whittet and Shepperson, 1875.

Parker, Inez Moore. *The Rise and Decline of the Program of Education for Black Presbyterians of the United Presbyterian Church U.S.A., 1865–1970.* San Antonio: Trinity University Press, 1977.

Parkin, Frank. *Max Weber.* London: Tavistock, 1981.

Parrington, Vernon Louis. *Main Currents in American Thought.* Vol. 2, *The Romantic Revolution in America, 1800–1860.* New York: Harcourt, Brace, 1927.

Parsons, Talcott. *The Social System.* Glencoe, Ill.: Free Press, 1951.

Payne, Daniel A. *History of the African Methodist Episcopal Church.* New York: Arno Press, 1969.

———. *Recollections of Seventy Years.* 1888. Reprint. New York, 1969.

Pease, William H., and Jane H. Pease. *The Web of Progress: Private Values and Public Styles in Boston and Charleston, 1824–1843.* New York: Oxford University Press, 1985.

Pelikan, Jaroslav. *Scholarship and Survival: Questions on the Idea of Graduate Education.* Princeton: Carnegie Foundation for the Advancement of Teaching, 1983.

Pinckney, H. L. *An address delivered before the Methodist Benevolent Society, at their anniversary meeting, in the Methodist Protestant Church, in Wentworth Street, on the 1st Monday in July 1835.* Charleston: E. J. Van Brunt, 1835.

Poggi, Gianfranco. *Calvinism and the Capitalist Spirit.* London: Macmillan, 1983.

Powers, Bernard Edward, Jr. "Black Charleston: A Social History 1822–1885." Ph.D. diss., Northwestern University, 1982.

Prestwich, Menna, ed. *International Calvinism, 1541–1715.* Oxford: Clarendon Press, 1985.

Prince, Harold. *A Presbyterian Bibliography: The Published Writings of Ministers Who Served in the Presbyterian Church in the United States During Its First Hundred Years, 1861–1961.* Metuchen, N.J.: Scarecrow Press, 1983.

Proceedings of the Meeting in Charleston, S.C., May 13–15, 1845, on the Religious Instruction of the Negroes, Together with the Report of the Committee, and the Address to the Public. Charleston: B. Jenkins, 1845.

Public Proceedings Relating to Calvary Church, And the Religious Instruction of Slaves. Charleston: Miller and Browne, 1850.

Quarles, Benjamin. *The Negro in the American Revolution.* Chapel Hill: University of North Carolina Press, 1961.

Quattlebaum, Paul. *The Land Called Chicora: The Carolinas under Spanish Rule with French Intrusions 1520–1670.* Gainesville: University of Florida Press, 1956.

Raboteau, Albert J. *Slave Religion: The "Invisible Institution" in the Antebellum South.* New York: Oxford University Press, 1978.

Radcliffe-Brown, A. R. *Structure and Function in Primitive Society.* London: Cohen and West, 1952.

Ramsay, David. *The History of South Carolina, From its First Settlement in 1670 to the Year 1808.* 2 vols. in 1. Charleston: David Longworth, 1809.

Records of the Presbyterian Church in the United States of America. Philadelphia: Presbyterian Board of Publication, 1841.

Reid, John Philip. *The Concept of Liberty in the Age of the American Revolution.* Chicago: University of Chicago Press, 1988.

Report and Resolutions, Adopted June 1st, 1858, by the South Carolina Branch of the American Tract Society in Reference to the Action Taken on Slavery, by the Parent Society, at the Last Meeting. Charleston: Miller, 1858.

Report of the Special Committee Appointed by the Protestant Episcopal Convention, at its Session in 1858, to Report on the Duty of Clergymen in Relation to the Marriage of Slaves. Charleston: Walker, Evans, 1859.

Responsibilities of the Publishing Committee under the Constitution. New York: American Tract Society, 1858.

Rhea, Linda. *Hugh Swinton Legaré: A Charleston Intellectual.* Chapel Hill: University of North Carolina Press, 1934.

Ribault, Jean. *The Whole and True Discoverye of Terra Florida: A Facsimile Reprint of the London Edition of 1563 together with a Transcript of the English Version in the British Museum.* Deland: Florida State Historical Society, 1927.

Richardson, Joe Martin. *Christian Reconstruction: The American Missionary Association and Southern Blacks, 1861–1890.* Athens: University of Georgia Press, 1986.

Ricoeur, Paul. *The Conflict of Interpretations.* Evanston: Northwestern University Press, 1974.

———. *Lectures on Ideology and Utopia.* Edited by George H. Taylor. New York: Columbia University Press, 1986.

Rieff, Philip. *The Triumph of the Therapeutic: Uses of Faith after Freud.* Chicago: University of Chicago Press, 1966.

Rischin, Moses, ed. *The American Gospel of Success.* Chicago: Quadrangle Books, 1965.

Roberts, J. Deotis. *Roots of a Black Future: Family and Church.* Philadelphia: Westminster Press, 1980.

Robinson, Donald L. *Slavery in the Structure of American Politics, 1765–1820.* New York: Harcourt Brace Jovanovich, 1971.

Robinson, Edgar Sutton. *The Ministerial Directory of the Ministers in [the Presbyterian Church].* Oxford, Ohio: Ministerial Directory Co., 1898.

Robinson, William Childs. *Columbia Theological Seminary and the Southern Presbyterian Church.* Decatur, Ga., 1931.

Rogers, George C., Jr. *Charleston in the Age of the Pinckneys.* Norman: University of Oklahoma Press, 1969.

Roof, Wade Clark, and William McKinney. *American Mainline Religion: Its Changing Shape and Future.* New Brunswick: Rutgers University Press, 1988.

Rose, Willie Lee. *Rehearsal for Reconstruction: The Port Royal Experiment.* Indianapolis: Bobbs-Merrill, 1964.

Rossi, Ino. *People in Culture: A Survey of Cultural Anthropology.* New York: Praeger, 1980.

Rowe, George C. *Our Heroes: Patriotic Poems on Men, Women and Sayings of the Negro Race.* Charleston: Walker, Evans and Cogswell, 1890.

Sabine, Lorenzo. *Loyalists of the American Revolution.* 2 vols. Boston, 1864.

Schaff, Philip. *The Creeds of Christendom, with a History and Critical Notes.* 6th ed. 3 vols. Grand Rapids: Baker House, 1967.

Scott, E. C. *Ministerial Directory of the Presbyterian Church, U.S. 1861–1941.* Austin: Von Boeckmann-Jones, 1942.

Segall, Marshall H., et al. *Human Behavior in Global Perspective.* New York: Pergamon Press, 1990.

Sennett, Richard. *The Fall of Public Man.* New York: Knopf, 1977.

Services at the Laying of the Corner Stone of the New Presbyterian Church of Summerville, S.C., May 7, 1895. Charleston: Walker, Evans and Cogswell, 1895.

Shaffer, E. T. H. *History of Bethel Presbyterian Church: From the Founding in 1728 Down to the Present Time—1928.* Walterboro, S.C.: Press and Standard, [1928].

Silver, James W. *Confederate Morale and Church Propaganda.* Gloucester, Mass.: Peter Smith, 1964.

Simkins, Francis Butler. *Pitchfork Ben Tillman: South Carolinian.* 1944. Reprint. Baton Rouge: Louisiana State University Press, 1967.

Simkins, Francis Butler, and Robert H. Woody. *South Carolina During Reconstruction.* Chapel Hill: University of North Carolina Press, 1932.

Sinnott, Edmund W. *Meeting House and Church in Early New England.* New York: McGraw-Hill, 1963.

Sirmans, M. Eugene. *Colonial South Carolina: A Political History, 1663–1763.* Chapel Hill: University of North Carolina Press, 1966.

Skinner, Quentin. *The Foundations of Modern Political Thought.* 2 vols. Cambridge: Cambridge University Press, 1978.

Sklar, Kathryn Kish. *Catherine Beecher: A Study in American Domesticity.* New Haven: Yale University Press, 1973.

Smith, Alfred Glaze, Jr. *Economic Readjustment of an Old Cotton State: South Carolina, 1820–1860.* Columbia: University of South Carolina Press, 1958.

Smith, H. Shelton, Robert T. Handy, and Lefferts A. Leotscher. *American Christianity: An Historical Interpretation with Representative Documents.* 2 vols. New York: Charles Scribner's Sons, 1960.

Smith, Josiah. *Solomon's Caution against the Cup . . . Delivered at Cainhoy* (Boston, 1730).

Smith, Timothy L. *Revivalism and Social Reform: American Protestantism on the Eve of the Civil War.* New York: Abingdon Press, 1965.

———. *Revivalism and Social Reform in Mid-Nineteenth-Century America.* New York: Abingdon Press, 1957.

Smyth, Thomas. *The Collected Works of the Rev. Thomas Smyth, D. D.* Edited by J. W. Flinn. 10 vols. Columbia: R. L. Bryan, 1908.

———. *The Late Charleston Union Presbytery: the Occasion of its Division Fairly Stated: and the Action of Presbytery Fully Justified.* Charleston: Observer Office Press, 1840.

———. *An Order for Funeral Services.* Boston: S. N. Dickinson, 1843.

Sobel, Mehal. *Trabelin' On: The Slave Journey to an Afro-Baptist Faith.* Westport, Conn.: Greenwood Press, 1979.

———. *The World They Made Together.* Princeton: Princeton University Press, 1987.

South Carolina Synod of the Lutheran Church in America. *A History of the Lutheran Church in South Carolina.* Columbia: R. L. Bryan, 1971.

Spring, Gardiner. *Personal Reminiscences.* 2 vols. New York: Scribner, 1886.

Stacy, James. *History of the Midway Congregational Church, Liberty County, Georgia.* Rev. ed. Newnan, Ga.: S. W. Murray, 1903.

———. *Published Records of Midway Church.* Newnan, Ga.: S. W. Murray, 1894.

Stammp, Kenneth. *The Peculiar Institution: Slavery in the Ante-Bellum South.* New York: Knopf, 1956.

Stanley, Alfred Knighton. *The Children is Crying: Congregationalism among Black People.* New York: Pilgrim Press, 1979.

Starobin, Robert S., ed. *Denmark Vesey: The Slave Conspiracy of 1822.* Englewood Cliffs, N.J.: Prentice-Hall, 1970.

Stoeffler, F. Ernest. *Continental Pietism and Early American Christianity.* Grand Rapids: Eerdmans, 1976.

Stoney, Louisa Cheves, ed. *Autobiographical Notes, Letters and Reflections by Thomas Smyth, D. D.* Charleston: Walker, Evans and Cogswell, 1914.

Stoney, Samuel Gaillard. *This Is Charleston: A Survey of the Architectural Heritage of a Unique American City.* Charleston: Carolina Art Association, 1944.

Stuckey, Sterling. *Slave Culture in America: Nationalist Theory and the Foundations of Black America.* New York: Oxford University Press, 1987.

Swint, Henry L. *The Northern Teacher in the South 1862–1870.* New York: Octagon Books, 1967.

Tawney, R. H. *Religion and the Rise of Capitalism.* 1926. Reprint. New York: New American Library, 1947.

Tennent, Mary A. *Light in Darkness: The Story of William Tennent, Sr. and The Log College.* Greensboro, N.C.: Greensboro Printing Co., 1971.

Tewksbury, Donald G. *The Founding of American Colleges and Universities Before the Civil War.* New York: Bureau of Publications, Columbia University, 1932.

Thomas, Emory. *The Confederate Nation, 1861–1865.* New York: Harper and Row, 1979.

Thompson, Ernest Trice. *Presbyterians in the South.* 3 vols. Richmond: John Knox Press, 1963, 1973.

———. *The Spirituality of the Church: A Distinctive Doctrine of the Presbyterian Church in the United States.* Richmond: John Knox Press, 1961.

Thornwell, James Henley. *Thoughts Suited to the Present Crisis; A Sermon on the Occasion of the Death of the Hon. John C. Calhoun . . . April 21, 1850.* Columbia, 1850.

Thorp, Margaret F. *Female Persuasion: Six Strong-Minded Women.* New Haven: Yale University Press, 1949.

Tindall, George Brown. *South Carolina Negroes, 1877–1900.* Columbia: University of South Carolina Press, 1952.

Townsend, Leah. *South Carolina Baptists, 1670–1805.* Florence, S.C., 1935.

Trapier, Paul. *The Religious Instruction of the Black Population. The Gospel to be Given to Our Servants. A Sermon Preached in Several Protestant Episcopal Churches in Charleston on Sundays in July, 1847.* Charleston, 1847.

Trevor-Roper, Hugh R. *Religion, the Reformation, and Social Change.* 3d ed. London: Secker and Warburg, 1984.

Trinterud, Leonard J. *The Forming of an American Tradition: A Re-Examination of Colonial Presbyterianism.* Philadelphia: Westminster Press, 1949.

Troeltsch, Ernst. *The Social Teaching of the Christian Churches.* Translated by Olive Wyon 2 vols. New York: Harper Torchbooks, 1960.

Tuck, Richard. *Natural Rights Theories: Their Origin and Development.* Cambridge: Cambridge University Press, 1979.

Tupper, Henry Allen. *Two Centuries of the First Baptist Church of South Carolina.* Baltimore: R. H. Woodward, 1889.

Turner, Victor. *The Ritual Process.* Chicago: Aldine, 1969.

———. *Schism and Continuity in an African Society.* Manchester: Manchester University Press, 1957.

Tylor, Edward B. *Primitive Culture.* London: Murray, 1913.

Vischer, Lukas. *Reformed Witness Today: A Collection of Confessions and Statements of Faith Issued by Reformed Churches.* Bern: Evangelische Arbeitsstelle Oekumene Schweiz, 1982.

Von Laue, Theodore H. *The World Revolution of Westernization: The Twentieth Century in Global Perspective.* New York: Oxford University Press, 1987.

Waddell, Gene. *Indians of the South Carolina Lowcountry: 1562–1751.* Spartanburg, S.C.: Reprint Co., 1980.

Wade, Richard C. *Slavery in the Cities: the South 1820–1860.* New York: Oxford University Press, 1964.

Walker, Williston. *The Creeds and Platforms of Congregationalism.* Boston: Pilgrim Press, 1960.

Wallace, A. F. C. *Culture and Personality.* New York: Random House, 1961.

Wallace, David Duncan. *The History of South Carolina.* 3 vols. New York: American Historical Society, 1934.

———. *South Carolina: A Short History.* Columbia: University of South Carolina Press, 1961.

Wallace, Ronald S. *Calvin's Doctrine of the Christian Life.* Edinburgh: Oliver and Boyd, 1959.

Walzer, Michael. *Interpretation and Social Criticism.* Cambridge: Harvard University Press, 1987.

———. *The Revolution of the Saints: A Study in the Origins of Radical Politics.* Cambridge: Harvard University Press, 1965.

Waring, Joseph I. *History of Medicine in South Carolina, 1670–1825.* Columbia: South Carolina Medical Association, 1964.

Weber, Max. *Economy and Society.* Edited by Guenther Roth and Claus Wittich. 2 vols. 1968. Reprint. Berkeley and Los Angeles: University of California Press, 1978.

———. *The Protestant Ethic and the Spirit of Capitalism.* Translated by Talcott Parsons. 1930. Reprint. New York: Scribner, 1958.

———. *The Sociology of Religion.* Translated by E. Fishoff. Edited by Talcott Parsons. London: Methuen, 1965.

———. *The Theory of Social and Economic Organization.* Translated by A. M. Henderson and Talcott Parsons. New York: Free Press, 1947.

Weir, Robert M. *Colonial South Carolina: A History.* Millwood, N.Y.: KTO Press, 1983.

White, Henry Alexander. *Southern Presbyterian Leaders.* New York: Neale, 1911.

Whitefield, George. *Journals.* London: Banner of Truth Trust, 1965.

———. *The Works of the Reverend George Whitefield.* 6 vols. London: Edward and Charles Dilly, 1772.

Wiebe, Robert H. *The Search for Order: 1877–1920.* New York: Hill and Wang, 1967.

Wilkramanayake, Marina. *A World in Shadow: The Free Black in Antebellum South Carolina.* Columbia: University of South Carolina Press, 1973.

Williams, Thomas Leonard. "The Methodist Mission to the Slaves." Ph.D. diss., Yale University, 1943.

Williamson, Joel. *After Slavery: The Negro in South Carolina During Reconstruction, 1861–1877.* Chapel Hill: University of North Carolina Press, 1965.

Wilson, Charles Reagon. *Baptized in Blood: The Religion of the Lost Cause, 1865–1920.* Athens: University of Georgia Press, 1980.

Winnsborough, Hallie Paxon. *The Women's Auxiliary.* Richmond: Presbyterian Committee of Publication, 1927.

Witherspoon, E. D., Jr. *Ministerial Directory of the Presbyterian Church, U.S., 1861–1983.* Atlanta: Darby, 1986.

Wood, Forrest G. *The Racist Response to Emancipation and Reconstruction.* Berkeley and Los Angeles: University of California Press, 1968.

Wood, Peter H. *Black Majority: Negroes in Colonial South Carolina from 1670 through the Stono Rebellion.* New York: W. W. Norton, 1974.

Woodmason, Charles. *The Carolina Backcountry on the Eve of the Revolution: The Journal and Other Writings of Charles Woodmason, Anglican Itinerant.* Edited by Richard J. Hooker. Chapel Hill: University of North Carolina Press, 1953.

Woodson, Carter G., ed. *The Works of Francis James Grimké.* 2 vols. Washington, D.C.: Associated Publishers, 1942.

Woodward, C. Vann. *American Counterpoint: Slavery and Racism in the North-South Dialogue.* 3d ed. New York: Oxford University Press, 1971.

———. *A History of the South.* Vol. 9, *Origins of the New South, 1877–1913.* Baton Rouge: Louisiana State University Press, 1951.

———. *The Strange Career of Jim Crow.* 3d ed. New York: Oxford University Press, 1974.

Wright, Benjamin Flecher. *American Interpretations of Natural Law.* 1931. Reprint. Russell and Russell, 1962.

Wyatt-Brown, Bertram. *Yankee Saints and Southern Sinners.* Baton Rouge: Louisiana State University Press, 1985.

Yankelovich, Daniel. *New Rules: Searching for Self-Fulfillment in a World Turned Upside Down.* New York: Random House, 1981.

Articles

Adger, John B. "Christian Doctrine of Human Rights and Slavery." *SPR* 2 (March 1849): 569–87.

[————?]."The Northern General Assembly (O.S.) of 1866." *SPR* 17 (September 1866): 279–84.

————."Plans of Church Finance." *SPR* 33 (January 1879): 92–111.

Ahlstrom, Sydney E. "The Scottish Philosophy and American Theology." *Church History* 24 (September 1955): 257–72.

Aptheker, Herbert. "South Carolina Negro Conventions, 1865." *Journal of Negro History* 31 (January 1946): 91–97.

"Autobiography of the Rev. Paul Trapier." *Publication of the Dalcho Historical Society of the Diocese of South Carolina* 17:27–28.

Banner, Lois W. "Religious Benevolence as Social Control: A Critique of an Interpretation." *Journal of American History* 60 (1973): 23–41.

Brauer, Jerald C. "Regionalism and Religion in America." *Church History* 54 (September 1985): 374–75.

Butler, Jon. "Enthusiasm Described and Decried: The Great Awakening as Interpretive Fiction." *Journal of American History* 69 (1982): 305–25.

Calhoun, Jeanne A., Martha A. Zierden, and Elizabeth A. Paysinger. "The Geographic Spread of Charleston's Mercantile Community, 1732–1767." *SCHM* 86 (1985): 182–220.

Canny, Nicholas P. "The Ideology of English Colonization: From Ireland to America." *William and Mary Quarterly* 30 (October 1973): 575–98.

Clarke, Erskine. "The History of Ecumenical Relations in the Southern Presbyterian Church." *MGAPCUS,* 1976, 466–77.

————. "Southern Nationalism and Columbia Theological Seminary." *Journal of Presbyterian History* 66 (Summer 1988): 123–33.

————. "The Strange Case of Charleston Union Presbytery." *Affirmation* (Fall 1993): 41–58.

DesChamps, Margaret B. "Union or Division? South Atlantic Presbyterians and Southern Nationalism, 1820–1861." *Journal of Southern History* 20 (November 1954): 484–98.

Dunn, Richard S. "The English Sugar Islands and the Founding of South Carolina." *SCHM* 72 (1971): 81–93.

Durden, Robert F. "The Establishment of Calvary Church, Charleston, S.C." *Publication of the Dalcho Historical Society of the Diocese of South Carolina* (1965): 64–71.

Edgar, Walter B. "Notable Libraries of Colonial South Carolina." *SCHM* 72 (1971): 105–10.

Farley, M. Foster. "The South Carolina Negro in the American Revolution, 1775–1783." *SCHM* 79 (1978): 75–86.

Farmer, James O. "Southern Presbyterians and Southern Nationalism: A Study in Ambivalence." *Georgia Historical Quarterly* (Summer 1991): 275–94.

Fox-Genovese, Elizabeth, and Eugene D. Genovese. "The Divine Sanction of Social Order: Religious Foundations of the Southern Slaveholders' World View." *Journal of the American Academy of Religion* 55 (Summer 1987): 211–33.

Friedlander, Amy, ed. "Commissary Johnston's Report, 1713." *SCHM* 83 (1982): 259–71.

Gallay, Alan. "The Origins of Slaveholders' Paternalism: George Whitefield, the Bryan Family, and the Great Awakening." *Journal of Southern History* 53 (August 1987): 369–94.

Geiger, Florence Gambill. "St. Bartholomew's Parish As Seen By Its Rectors, 1713–1761." *SCHGM* 50 (1949): 175 f.

Girardeau, John L. "Our Ecclesiastical Relations to Freedmen." *SPR* 21 (July 1867): 7.

Goldbatt, Gloria. "The Queen of Bohemia Grew Up in Charleston." In the South Carolina Historical Society's *Carologue* (Autumn 1988): 10–11.

Harris, Robert L. "Charleston's Free Afro-American Elite: The Brown Fellowship Society and the Humane Brotherhood." *SCHM* 82 (1981): 289–310.

Higgins, W. Robert. "Charles Town Merchants and Factors Dealing in the External Negro Trade: 1735–1775." *SCHGM* 65 (1964): 205–17.

———. "The Geographical Origins of Negro Slaves in Colonial South Carolina." *South Atlantic Quarterly* 70 (Winter 1971): 34–47.

———. "The South Carolina Revolutionary Debt and Its Holders, 1776–1780." *SCHM* 72 (1971): 15–29.

Hodge, Charles. "Inspiration." *Princeton Review* 29 (October 1857): 660–98.

Hoffman, Paul E. "Legend, Religious Idealism, and Colonies: The Point of Santa Elena in History, 1552–1566." *SCHM* 84 (1983): 59–71.

Hollis, Daniel W. "James Henley Thornwell and the South Carolina College." *Proceedings of the South Carolina Historical Association* (1953): 17–36.

Howe, George. "The General Assembly of 1859." *SPR* 2 (October 1859): 513–604.

———. "The Genuineness of the Pentateuch." *SPR* 4 (October 1850): 256–94.

———. "Unity of the Race." *SPR* 3 (July 1849): 124–66.

Isaac, Rhys. "Evangelical Revolt: The Nature of the Baptists' Challenge to the Traditional Order in Virginia, 1765–1775." *William and Mary Quarterly* 31 (July 1974): 345–68.

Jackson, Harvey H. "Hugh Bryan and the Evangelical Movement in Colonial South Carolina." *William and Mary Quarterly* 43 (1986): 594–614.

Jones, Newton B., ed. "Writings of the Reverend William Tennent, 1740–1777." *SCHM* 61 (1960): 129–45, 196–209.

Kelsey, R. W. "Swiss Settlers in South Carolina." *SCHGM* 23 (1922): 85–92.

Kenny, William Howland, III. "Alexander Garden and George Whitefield: The Significance of Revivalism in South Carolina, 1738–1741." *SCHM* 71 (1970): 1–16.

Kovacik, Charles F., and Lawrence S. Rowland. "Images of Colonial Port Royal, South Carolina." *Annals of the Association of American Geographers* 63 (September 1973): 331–40.

McCord, Louisa. "Woman and Her Needs." *DeBow's Review* (1852): 289–90.

McIver, Petrona Royall. "Wappetaw Congregational Church." *SCHM* 58 (1957): 34–41, 84–93.

Maddox, Jack P., Jr. "From Theocracy to Spirituality: The Southern Presbyterian Reversal on Church and State." *Journal of Presbyterian History* 56 (Winter 1976): 438–57.

———. "Proslavery Millennialism: Social Eschatology in Antebellum Southern Calvinism." *American Quarterly* 31 (1979): 48–52.

Merrens, Harry Roy, and George D. Terry. "Dying in Paradise: Malaria, Mortality, and the Perceptual Environment in Colonial South Carolina." *Journal of Southern History* 50 (November 1984): 533–50.

Moore, Alexander, ed. " 'A Narrative . . . Of An Assembly . . . January the 2d, 1705/6': New Light on Early South Carolina Politics." *SCHM* 85 (1984): 181–86.

Morgan, Edmund S. "The Puritan Ethic and the American Revolution." *William and Mary Quarterly* 24 (1967): 3–43.

O'Brien, Susan. "A Transatlantic Community of Saints: The Great Awakening and the First Evangelical Network, 1735–1755." *American Historical Review* 91 (1986): 811–32.

Palmer, Benjamin Morgan [the younger]. "Baconianism and the Bible." *SPR* 6 (October 1852): 226–53.

Parker, Harold M., Jr. "The Cassville Convention: Aborted Birth of a Southern Presbyterian Church." *Historian* 42 (1980): 612–30.

Pennington, Edgar L. "Original Rules and Members of the Charlestown Library Society." *SCHGM* 23 (1922): 169–70.

Pessen, Edward. "How Different from Each Other Were the Antebellum North and South?" *American Historical Review* 85 (1980): 1119–49.

Pratt, George, and J. G. Gunlop. "Arrival of the Cardross Settlers: *The Carolina Merchant;* Advice of Arrival." *SCHGM* 30 (1929): 69–79.

"The Private Register of the Rev. Paul Trapier" [Saint Michael's Episcopal Church, Charleston]. *Publication of the Delcho Historical Society of the Diocese of South Carolina,* no. 7.

"Religious Instruction of the Black Population." *SPR* 1 (December 1847): 89–120.

"Renan's Origins of Christianity." *SPR* 17 (January 1866): 301–30.

Ricoeur, Paul. "Ideology, Utopia, and Faith." *Center for Hermeneutical Studies* 17 (1976): 9–28.

Salley, A. S. "The History of the Stoney Creek Presbyterian Congregation." *Charleston News and Courier,* October 29 and November 5, 1933.

Schmidt, Leigh Eric. " 'The Grand Prophet,' Hugh Bryan: Early Evangelicalism's Challenge to the Establishment and Slavery in the Colonial South." *SCHM* 87 (1986): 238–50.

Shaffer, Arthur H. "Between Two Worlds: David Ramsay and the Politics of Slavery." *Journal of Southern History* 50 (April 1984): 175–96.

Shick, Tom W., and Don Harrison Doyle. "The South Carolina Phosphate Boom and the Stillbirth of the New South, 1867–1920." *SCHM* 86 (1985): 18–25.

Shiels, Richard D. "The Feminization of American Congregationalism, 1730–1835." *American Quarterly* 33 (1981): 46–62.

Simmons, Slann L. C., ed. "Records of the Willtown Presbyterian Church 1738–1841." *SCHM* 62 (1961): 33–50, 107–63, 172–81, 219–24.

Smyth, Thomas. "The Battle of Fort Sumter: Its Mystery and Miracle—God's Mastery and Mercy." *SPR* 14 (October 1861): 365–99.

———."The War of the South Vindicated." *SPR* 15 (April 1863): 479–515.

"The Southern Presbyterian Church and Slavery." *Western Presbyterian Herald,* 1837, 118.

Thornwell, James Henley. "The Baptism of Servants." *SPR* 1 (June 1847): 63–102.

———. "Critical Notice." *SPR* 5 (January 1851): 110–15.

———. "Duties of Masters." *SPR* 8 (October 1854): 266–83.

———. "Public Instruction in South Carolina." *SPR* 8 (January 1854): 435–40.

———. "Slavery and the Religious Instruction of the Colored Population." *SPR* 4 (July 1850): 105–41.

"The Unity of the Human Race." *SPR* 5 (April 1852): 572–601.

Webber, Mabel L. "Register of the Independent or Congregational (Circular) Church." *SCHGM* 18 (1917): 27–37, 53–59, 135–40.

———, ed. "Josiah Smith's Diary, 1780–1781." *SCHGM* 33 (1932): 1–7, 79–84, 197–204, 281–88, and *SCHGM* 34 (1933): 31–39, 67–84, 138–48, 194–210.

———. "Spanish Depredations, 1686." *SCHGM* 30 (1929): 81–89.

Woodrow, James. "Female College Commencements." *Southern Presbyterian*, August 5, 1880, 2.

Woodward, C. Vann. "The Southern Ethic in a Puritan World." *William and Mary Quarterly* 25 (1968): 343–70.

Manuscripts

CAPO

Wood, Alleen S. "History of the Edisto United Presbyterian Church" (typed manuscript, 1981), 2.

Charleston Library Society, Charleston, S.C.

Archibald Simpson Journal, 1768–83.

Furman University Archives, Greenville, S.C.

Reports of State Conventions of Baptist Churches in South Carolina, 1821–60.

Individual Church Archives, Charleston, S.C.

Circular Congregational Church
    Book of Church Records, 1825–50.
    Independent [Congregational] Church Register, 1796–1824.
    Record Book, 1844–60.
    Statement of Faith and Constitution with list of signatures.
First Baptist Church
    Minutes of the Board of Deacons, First Baptist Church, Charleston, S.C., 1847–70.
First (Scots) Presbyterian Church
    Antebellum membership list.
    Membership List.
Saint John's Lutheran Church
    Church Register, 1852–61.
    Minutes, Saint John's Lutheran Church, 1837–45.
Saint Mary's Roman Catholic Church
    Saint Mary's Vestry, 1832–55.
Trinity Methodist Church
    Minutes of Quarterly Conference Meetings of Cumberland Church and Trinity Church, 1845–91.
    Record of the Colored Members in the Methodist Church, Charleston, S.C., 1821–80.

Presbyterian Historical Society, Montreat, N.C.

Atlantic Presbytery
    Minutes, 1886–1908, 1940–80.

Bethel Pon Pon Presbyterian Church
  Session Minutes, 1736–76, 1783–1861.
  Trustee Minutes, 1783–1861.
"A Brief History" (of the Edisto Island Presbyterian Church), typescript.
Charleston Presbytery
  Minutes, 1850–60, 1870–1915.
Charleston Union Presbytery
  Minutes, 1822–40.
Dorchester Independent Church
  Records, 1794–1854.
Edisto Island Presbyterian Church
  Session Records, 1890–1941.
Hills, Isabel H. "Historical Sketch of the Johns Island Presbyterian Church, 1710–
    1937" (1937).
Hutson, William. "Account of Marriages, Baptisms, and Burials &c."
James Island Presbyterian Church
  Records, 1833–61.
Johns Island Presbyterian Church
  Minutes of the Session, 1850–1904, 1911–46, 1954.
Midway Congregational Church
  Minutes of the Session, 1837–60.
New Wappetaw Presbyterian Church
  Minutes of the Session, 1870–1940.
Second Presbyterian Church
  Manual of the Roll of The Colored Communicants of the Second Presbyterian
    Church.
  Minutes of the Session, 1817–60.
Stoney Creek Independent Presbyterian Church
  Book of the Congregation, 1823–61.
  Covenant and Register, 1743–60.
  Financial Records, 1823–61.
  Minutes and Accounts, 1773–1860.
  Register, 1832–33.
  Session Minutes, 1855–61.
Summerville Presbyterian Church
  Minutes of the Session, 1859–1905.
  Miscellaneous Records, 1859–61.
Third Presbyterian Church
  Letters of Transfer and Materials Relating to "Colored People," 1822–78.
  Register, 1827–81.
  Register of the Coloured Members of the 3rd. Presbyterian Church, 1826–60.
  Roll Book and Letters of Transfer.
  Rules for the Burial Ground Held by the Third Presbyterian or Central Church,
    Charleston, for the Use of its Colored Members.
  Session Minutes, 1824–81.
Wappetaw Independent Presbyterian Church
  Congregational Record Book.
  Treasurer's Record Book.

Westminster Presbyterian Church
    Session Minutes, 1875–1975.
Wilton Presbyterian Church
    Records, 1850–61.
    Register of Communicants, 1860.
Zion Presbyterian Church
    Communicants Roll Book (black membership), 1855–76.
    Communicants Roll Book (white membership), 1855–76.
    Minutes of the Session, 1856–74.

South Carolina Historical Society, Charleston, S.C.

Adger-Smyth Papers.
Augustine Thomas Smythe Letters.
Edisto Island Presbyterian Church
    Membership List, 1821–61.
    Register, 1816–1901.
    Session Minutes, 1837–61, 1866–1900.
Fielden-Smythe Papers.
Minutes of the Charleston Baptist Association, 1840–61.
Smythe Family Papers.

South Caroliniana Library, University of South Carolina, Columbia, S.C.

Adger-Smyth[e]-Flynn Papers.
John LaFayette Girardeau Papers.
James Henley Thornwell Papers.

Wofford College Archives, Spartanburg, S.C.

Minutes of the Annual Conference of the Methodist Episcopal Church in South
    Carolina, 1831–60.

Printed Reports and Newspapers

Annual Report(s), COF, 1865–82. PHSP.
Annual Report(s), COMFF, 1866–82. PHSP.
Catalog. Columbia Theological Seminary, 1960–90. Decatur, Ga.
Catalog. McCormick Theological Seminary, 1973–83. Chicago.
Catalog. Union Theological Seminary, 1960–90. Richmond, Va.
Charleston-Atlantic Presbytery 1990 Directory. CAPO.
Charleston Daily Courier, 1865. SCHS.
Charleston Mercury, 1838–61. SCHS.
Charleston Observer, 1835–45. SCHS.
Charleston Trident Chamber of Commerce. *Charleston Trident Area, South Carolina,*
    Executive Summary, 1989. Charleston.
Christian Recorder, 1866. PHSP.
First (Scots) Presbyterian Church. *Church Directory,* 1988. Charleston.
Greater Beaufort Chamber of Commerce. *Area Demographics, 1989.* Beaufort, S.C.
Journal of the Proceedings of the Protestant Episcopal Church in the Diocese of South Caro-
    lina, 1825–1860. SCHS.

Liberator, 1844–46.

MGAPCUS, 1866-1982. PHSM.

MGAPCUSA, 1810–37, 1866–1982. PHSM.

MGAPCUSA(NS), 1840–65. PHSM.

MGAPCUSA(OS), 1839–61. PHSM.

Minutes of the Annual Conference of the Methodist Episcopal Church in South Carolina, 1831–60. SCHS.

Minutes of the Synod of South Carolina, 1852 and 1855. PHSM.

Minutes of the Synod of South Carolina. Charleston: Evans and Cogswell, 1861.

New York Times, 1865.

90th Anniversary: St. Luke Presbyterian Church (USA), Orangeburg, South Carolina, 1–2. CAPO.

Presbyterian Committee of Home Missions. *Monthly Report of Freedmen's School at Charleston, S.C.* January 1870. PHSP.

Presbyterian Outlook, 1979.

Proceedings of the Colored People's Convention of the State of South Carolina, held in Zion Church, Charleston, November, 1865 (Charleston, 1865).

Professional Assessment Procedure: Columbia Theological Seminary, 1980–1981. Decatur, Ga.

Schaller, Lyle E., of the Yokefellow Institute, Naperville, Ill. *First Presbyterian Church, Hilton Head, South Carolina.* First Presbyterian Church, Hilton Head.

South Carolina Division of Research and Statistical Services. *South Carolina Estimated Population by Age, Race, and Sex As Of July 1, 1988.* State Data Center, Columbia.

Southern Christian Sentinel, 1839–40.

Teacher's Monthly Report, Hope School. January 1870. FBR.

Teacher's Monthly Report, Johns Island. May 1867. FBR.

Teacher's Monthly School Report, Avery. February 1869. FBR.

Teacher's Monthly School Report, James Island. January 1869. FBR.

Teacher's Monthly School Report, Presbyterian Home Mission. March 1870. FBR.

Teacher's Monthly School Report, Saxton School. March 1868. FBR.

Teacher's Monthly School Report, Shaw. October 1867, January 1868, January 1869, January 1871. FBR.

Teacher's Monthly School Report, Wallingford. January 1869, January 1870. FBR.

Teacher's Monthly School Report, Zion. January 1868. FBR.

Index

abolitionists, 180, 183–89

Adam, Smith, 265

Adams, Ennals, 234, 237, 244, 305, 366 (n. 24)

Adams, Hugh, 52, 303

Adams, Nehemiah, 358 (n. 4)

Adams, Robert M., 305

Adams, William H., 309

Address, Occasioned by the Late Invasion of the Liberties of the American Colonies by the British Parliament, 93

Adger, James, 144, 151, 156, 263, 346 (n. 10)

Adger, James, and Company, 263

Adger, John B., 120, 156, 158, 165, 226, 262, 269, 281, 305, 309;
  and Denmark Vesey revolt, 122;
  at Evangelical Alliance, 187–89;
  as minister of Anson Street Presbyterian Church, 195;
  and paternalistic vision, 364 (n. 43);
  photo of, *167;*
  proposes new work among African Americans, 189–91;
  and secession, 211;
  as Unionist, 201, 211

Adger, Robert: as leader of Zion Presbyterian Church, 195–96, 226

Adger family, 198, 263–64, 265

Adopting Act, 48, 49

Africa, 33–34

African Americans:
  and American Revolution, 102–4, 334 (n. 50);
  begin to join churches, 64, 86–88, 326 (n. 7);
  and colonial society, 33;
  as domestics, 160, 349 (n. 60);
  and the Great Awakening, 86–88;
  images of, 1;
  influence on low country culture, 105, 273–74;
  join churches different from those of white owners, 159–60;
  membership in white-dominated churches, 125–31;
  and modernity, 229–31, 240;
  re-order lives after Civil War, 218–20.
  See also spirituals

African American community:
  early history of, 34;
  and Northern migration, 231–32;
  schools of, 217, 237, 242

African American Reformed community:
  and baptism, 86, 135–37;
  character of during slavery, 130–35;
  "character type" of members, 135;
  class leaders of, 129, 234;
  coherence of, 243–56, 283, 285–86;
  and Congregational churches, 217–18, 243, 255;
  continuity of, 235–36, 247–48, 249, 283–84;
  discipline in, 129, 196, 254;
  as distinctly Reformed, 230, 284;
  on Edisto Island, 225–26, 252, 285;
  emergence of, 125;
  and emphasis on education, 162, 282, 284–85;
  establishment of independent congregations within, 232–36;
  free blacks in, 160–61, 234;
  following emancipation, 229–42;
  ideological needs of, 248, 252;
  ignored by historians of region, 315 (n. 22);
  and joining the community, 131–35;
  limited expansion of, beyond antebellum roots, 255–56, 283, 286;
  loss of membership, 234;
  and modernity, 230–31;
  as part of two worlds, 140–41, 229–42, 249, 252–53, 255–56;
  poor funds of, 129;
  in post-World War II period, 283–86;
  and reculturation, 230–31, 236, 238, 239, 240, 247–48;
  relationship to white society, 130, 248;
  remembers its past, 239–42, 248;
  role of, 247;
  and rural congregations, 162, 233–34, 235–36;
  school system of, 243–49;
  slaves and Lord's Supper, 65–69;
  social profiles of, 7, 142, 159–62, 249–52, 255–56, 284–86;
  as a subgroup, 6–7, 129–30, 252–53, 255–66, 275, 345 (n. 1);

About the Author

Erskine Clarke is Professor of American Religious History, Columbia Theological Seminary. He received his bachelor's degree from the University of South Carolina and his master's degree and doctorate from Union Theological Seminary, Virginia. Among his publications is *Wrestlin' Jacob: A Portrait of Religion in the Old South* (1979), which was selected by *Choice* as one of the Outstanding Academic Books of the Year. For this book, the author was named Author of the Year by the (Georgia) Council of Writers and Journalists.